The Congress of Vienna

The Congress of Vienna

 POWER AND POLITICS
AFTER NAPOLEON

BRIAN E. VICK

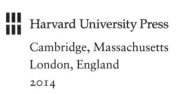 Harvard University Press

Cambridge, Massachusetts
London, England
2014

First printing

Library of Congress Cataloging-in-Publication Data

Vick, Brian E., 1970–
  The Congress of Vienna : power and politics after Napoleon / Brian E. Vick.
    pages   cm.
  Includes bibliographical references and index.
  ISBN 978-0-674-72971-1 (alkaline paper)
    1. Congress of Vienna (1814–1815) 2. Napoleonic Wars, 1800–1815—Peace.
3. Napoleonic Wars, 1800–1815—Treaties. 4. Napoleonic Wars, 1800–1815—
Diplomatic history. 5. Europe—Politics and government—1789–1815.
  I. Title.
  DC249.V45 2014
  940.2'744—dc23   2014004758

Contents

The Congress of Vienna

Introduction

In popular memory, and popular history, the Congress of Vienna lives as much as a grand spectacle of parties, dancing, and festivities as it does as a diplomatic summit convened to settle the future of Europe in the wake of Napoleon's defeat. Images of waltzes, pseudo-medieval knightly tournaments, and sexual intrigues dance alongside those of the diplomatic intrigues, and the illustrious figures of the statesmen Prince Talleyrand, Prince Metternich, and Lord Castlereagh alongside the rulers Tsar Alexander, King Friedrich Wilhelm III of Prussia, and Emperor Franz I of Austria. Scholarly accounts of the Congress on the other hand have mostly screened out the festive dimension in order to center on the diplomatic maneuverings as the essence of the event. Offer and counteroffer, the play of power politics, and the rules both intricate and unsubtle of raison d'état and Realpolitik stand at the core of such analyses. Yet the diplomacy, like the diplomats themselves, did not remain in a hermetically sealed room or black box, somehow set apart from broader society, culture, and ideas. The days of diplomatic relations as solely sovereign arcana, secret and out of the public eye, were long gone by 1800, even if the day of a completely transparent system of international relations operating in the full light of public scrutiny had not yet arrived (has, for that matter, still not arrived). Nor do the festivities, socializing, and cultural exchanges simply represent local color, or titillating details to spice up the historical narrative. Knowledge of the wider culture and political culture is essential to understanding both the Congress of Vienna and European international relations, while at the same time, renewed attention to the

Congress reveals much about that surrounding culture and political culture, in Europe's transition from the revolutionary and Napoleonic periods into the Restoration and nineteenth century.[1]

Through the lens of the Vienna Congress, this book explores and reinterprets the institutions and social networks, media and markets, and political and symbolic languages that constituted post-Napoleonic political culture. Its investigations into the making and celebrating of peace in Vienna offer insights into the composition and functioning of a European political and cultural elite, the ramifications of commemorative print and material culture, the influence of religion, and the balance of liberal, conservative, and nationalist ideologies in this era. Elite women, transconfessional currents of religious revival, the press and public opinion, and liberal and nationalist ideas all played greater roles than usually depicted in the literature on diplomacy or political culture. The change of approach also brings into focus such important yet less studied aspects of Congress politics as the efforts to abolish the African slave trade, to extend Jewish civil rights and defend against a threatened anti-Jewish backlash, and to reshape relations with the Islamic Ottoman Empire and the Barbary corsairs. While the majority of the diplomatic action did concern the area of Europe from the Low Countries to Poland, and from Scandinavia to Italy, most histories of the Congress overlook the extent to which the Mediterranean and the Islamic world also drew attention, from statesmen and publics alike.

In pursuit of such wider and deeper perspectives on the Congress and international relations, this study examines documents both private and official from a broad range of diplomats, in German, French, Italian, and English—but also goes beyond them. It pays equal attention to similar sources from outside the magic circle of high politics, including those relating to the *salonnières* and other figures of Viennese, German, and European social and cultural life who found their way to the Congress, some never before used for this purpose. The reports of the infamous Habsburg police spies feature, as do newspapers, cultural periodicals, and works of music from the scene. Marketed images and objects of material culture, from prints and medallions to painted porcelain and glass, round out the array of primary sources. Connecting these disparate kinds of "documents" enables a fuller understanding of both the diplomacy of the Vienna Congress and the political culture of nineteenth-century Europe as they emerged from the storms and stresses of the Napoleonic era.

The book divides into two parts: an analysis of political sociability, communication, and religiosity, followed by accounts of several diplomatic battles in 1814–1815 as they unfolded within this wider, multilayered political culture. The book generally follows thematic lines, yet preserves the historical narrative when discussing specific negotiations. The first three chapters explore the various layers of post-Napoleonic political culture as exhibited at the Congress in festivities and display, the press and the market for political and patriotic memorabilia and entertainment, and the mixed-gender world of salon culture and elite networks, in each case considering the roles of both governmental and nongovernmental actors. Taken together, these dimensions provided the milieu and venues for political interaction, and the interface between the central core of decision-makers and the broader publics that had become so crucial in preceding decades. The first section of the book presents important revisions to the central prevailing paradigm for the study of eighteenth- and nineteenth-century political culture, which is still the model of the public spheres derived from Jürgen Habermas.[2] The active role of women; the mingled participation of aristocratic and educated middle-class elements; the transnational links from France and Italy through central and eastern Europe and on into Russia; the recourse to new types of network analysis; and the emphasis on the use of new political and cultural languages and practices to bind groups together and to appeal to broader publics through image, object, word, and spectacle: each element represents a significant departure from the standard picture. Reframing secular histories of political culture to recover their partly religious contexts also marks a sharp intervention in the field. Together, these shifts of perspective undercut prevalent interpretations of the era as a simple transition from a courtly-aristocratic to a bourgeois public sphere, or as an attempt at "restoration" of the Old Regime after Napoleon's defeat.

The four subsequent chapters recount the Vienna negotiations as the efforts to reconstruct Europe's political boundaries, institutions, and security arrangements intersected with this multiplex political culture, at a moment of intense uncertainty when a majority of Europeans faced yet another change of regime. Even as a diplomatic conference, the Congress of Vienna did not form a single event, but rather a not always tightly connected series of parallel and sequential talks, committees, and conversations, both formal and informal, taking place in recognized diplomatic venues and in broader court and salon society. The discussion culminates by showing how the diplomatic showdown over the dispensation of Saxony and the Polish lands—always the focus of Congress histories, and always retold in power-political terms—discloses new facets within the framework of this broader political culture. Leading up to that treatment, the book examines several struggles that, while often receiving less attention, prove equally compelling and equally vital for understanding diplomacy and international relations in the early nineteenth century, from the politics of religious reconstruction and religious freedom, to abolition of the African slave trade and confrontations with Islamic states, to concerns about nationhood and constitutions in numerous European contexts. Here too the Vienna Congress represented more than a conservative reaction, or "a World Restored." Across a wide range of issues, intervention to secure certain human rights—for minority groups or for whole bodies of subject-citizens—figured prominently on the Congress agenda.[3]

Throughout the book, the role of national identity and ideas of nationhood forms an important theme. This may surprise many readers. After all, the Vienna Congress has long borne the reputation of having ignored the desires for nationhood of peoples at the time, and of short-sightedness in missing the signs pointing toward the future growth of nationalism and nation-states. At the same time, recent scholarship on the period as a whole has strongly argued that the prevalence of nationalism in the Napoleonic Wars—the underlying assumption behind such critiques—was itself largely a myth created by later nationalists, and that such sentiments did not yet extend to the masses at that time and even found fewer adherents among the middle classes and elites than has often been claimed.[4] This notion of weak national sentiment would at least explain any lack of attention to the issue at the Congress, as there would have been little to which the delegates could have responded.[5]

If one takes as the measure of nationalism the drive for fully independent ethnically defined nation-states of the sort that shaped the Versailles Treaties of 1919, or more narrowly, the Prussian-led German nation-state of 1871, then these clearly represented minority views in 1814. But if one reexamines the Congress and its surrounding political culture with a looser definition of national identity and national politics in mind, the evidence becomes much more plentiful. Whether in the press or in festive display, in salon conversations or in highest-level negotiations, nationality and nationalism emerge as significant themes, and were thought to be so by most observers at the time, whether they welcomed the trend or opposed it. These currents existed, and statesmen and rulers responded to them more than has been thought.

The difference was that the most prevalent version of nationalism in the early nineteenth century still proved quite compatible with smaller-scale state and regional identities, and with dynastic patriotism, whether of smaller states or supranational empires. Among the visitors in Vienna in these years featured several of the seminal figures in the development of the theory and cultural and political practice of early nationalism, and precisely of this federalist approach, from the Germans Wilhelm von Humboldt and Jacob Grimm to the Austro-Slav Slovene Jerneij Kopitar and the Polish prince Adam-Jerzy Czartoryski. That nations and national identities represent social constructions has become a matter of scholarly orthodoxy, but it has proven harder to grasp the fact that early nineteenth-century definitions of nationhood were for precisely this reason quite disparate, mixing civic, ethnolinguistic, and historical criteria and applying to multiple levels of the hierarchy of community and state structures. Calls for "national" political mobilization and patriotic loyalty could appeal to common language, history, or political institutions as well as to national character, and could center on provincial, regional, state, dynastic, and imperial identities as well as ethnic, or on what would later come to be called the nation-state. Being so malleable, the concepts and practices of nationhood were widely available and widely employed.

Religion is another subject that does not usually leap to mind in connection with the Vienna Congress. Modern diplomatic history has tended to be analyzed in mostly secular terms, and in comparison to the age of religious warfare in early modern Europe, that is on balance true. But when one looks more carefully, both religious belief and religious politics occupied participants' attention to a considerable degree. Religious revival and sociability featured prominently on the Congress social scene and influenced its politics as well. The second part of the book examines the problems of reconstructing the Catholic Church after the revolutionary and Napoleonic caesuras and above all highlights the contested efforts to expand regimes of religious toleration, religious liberty, and even religious equality in many European states during this period of redrawing the map of Europe and the political rules of the game. This applies both to relations among Christian denominations and to the even more contentious question of relations with European Jewry, primarily but not only in the German lands.

Studies of the Congress of Vienna tend to follow one of two tracks, with diplomacy at the center of each. In the effort to trace the diplomatic narrative and to explain why the Congress turned out as it did, most historians have looked to the level of personalities and power politics. Political science and international relations approaches have concentrated on models of international relations and state systems, to decide which might best describe the Vienna settlement: bipolar hegemony between Britain and Russia, or multipolar balance of power including Austria, France, and perhaps Prussia.[6] Military and diplomatic history have always emphasized great individuals as the driving forces of history (usually though not always meaning great men), and the end of the Napoleonic era has been no different. Debate has centered on the question of which of the Congress's great men did most to shape its course and outcome. Many historians highlight either the Austrian foreign minister, Prince Metternich, or his French counterpart, the wily Prince Talleyrand; others stress the activity of Britain's foreign secretary, Lord Castlereagh. Most historians also underscore Tsar Alexander's role in the diplomacy surrounding Napoleon's fall and the reconstruction of Europe, but primarily as misguided idealist or aggrandizing, vainglorious villain. Whether he is given credit for tempering his position as Russian autocrat with the heritage of Enlightenment liberalism taught him by his Swiss tutor General Frédéric de la Harpe, or whether the messianic or Russian imperialist dimensions of his character take precedence, he serves as foil for the hero of the hour, doing most to oppose the farsighted plans of Castlereagh, Talleyrand, or Metternich for restoring European equilibrium, if ultimately not enough to prevent those plans from coming to fruition. In all this, of course, the other rulers of Great Powers, Austria's Kaiser Franz and Prussia's King Friedrich Wilhelm, become secondary players, as do the smaller states' rulers, and the second-tier diplomatic figures, whether the primary statesmen of lesser states or the subordinate diplomats of major ones.

Brendan Simms has challenged the concentration on statesmen in favor of focusing on the more exclusive circles of rulers and their immediate favorites, advisors, and officials in "the antechamber of power" as the real locus of decision-making. At the same time, Simms rather made a virtue of bracketing out social, cultural, and ideological frameworks from foreign policy.[7] A fuller understanding even of high politics and diplomacy, however, requires a combination of all three levels of analysis: the rulers, the statesmen, and the realm of sociability and culture, of what I think should still be conceived of as "political culture." The term involves more than just applying the methods of cultural history and social theory, or analysis of political ritual, but also invites engagement with the history of ideas, including the newer "Ideas in Context" approaches pioneered by Quentin Skinner and J. G. A. Pocock. Ideas in Context has the particular merit of extending coverage of political discourse beyond the usual canon of big names, and of doing so in a way that acknowledges the dimension of authorial subjectivity and intent. At the same time, with its notion of "political languages" it captures through its Anglo-American version of the linguistic turn the sense in which individuals are constrained by prevailing discourses as much as they are empowered by them. Language is not a "prison-house," yet it presents boxes outside which it is difficult to think. These languages were shaped not solely by the great political theorists but also by the lesser figures with whom they stood in conversation and confrontation. And these encounters were rarely conducted only at the level of theory but equally involved pragmatic politics, that is, the desire to manipulate political languages so as to influence and persuade publics and decision-makers in pursuit of immediate political aims.[8]

Partly for this reason, I argue that much the same is true for diplomacy, in the practice of what I call "influence politics." In order to understand the languages, the ideas, and the diplomatic wrangling, one must scrutinize the interventions of second-tier officials and writers alongside the primary statesmen, and of both alongside the rulers and court cliques. The study of politics and political languages can also gain from notions from the study of networks, sociability, and media. In this respect, going beyond the usual canon implies not just exploring the writings of second-tier thinkers and pamphleteers to uncover the broader political languages, but also opening up the analysis to the second rank of political actors more generally: diplomats and statesmen, plus the wider society of politically engaged individuals with potential influence on political discourse or political decisions, be they middle-class or noble, women or men. Alongside the relationships between individuals, such an approach shines a spotlight on the images and objects that they exchanged, as well as the words and texts.[9] Hence the concept of political languages, like that of discourse more generally, can be further extended into the realm of display and symbolism. This bears implications for the study of both politics and culture, insofar as actors at each level draw on the other for their vocabulary and grammar. Cultural figures are influenced by political discourse and sometimes attempt to influence it, while politicians are influenced by cultural discourse, and often try to influence it as well.[10]

Politics—this broader influence politics—encompassed all these levels of political culture, in the actors' conscious intentions and planning, but also in ways of which they were not aware. Statesmen took public opinion very directly into account, sometimes hoping to manipulate it,

Even in this phase, however, the wider world of European political culture was not so far removed from the action. At several points, the headquarters came within reach of cosmopolitan spa towns, or larger cities with cultural resources that allowed brief but blessed interludes of cultivated theater and salon entertainment. Sometimes they made do with the men available but more often turned to the women in the area to invigorate such exchanges. Nesselrode, for example, wrote to his wife (still following behind the lines) of an evening in the Polish town of Płock during which he had played a Spontini march on his lodging's piano and accompanied a British diplomat who sang another popular number from the Italian-language Parisian opera, all for the entertainment of a small dinner party. The town also offered at least passable theater and opera.[14] More indicative of preferred social and political normalcy, at a crucial phase in the negotiations over Austria's entry into the coalition in the summer of 1813, the Duchess of Sagan played an important mediating role as hostess for sensitive meetings among the main actors at her country estate. A Russian subject, adoptive Austrian, and lioness of Viennese society, with a lovely palais in the rolling countryside of Bohemia, she provided a perfect location for such exchanges and could help keep them from boiling over in the contentious passions of coalition-making.[15] Moreover, the cities, and the ladies and salons, never lay too far away for correspondence, and rulers and diplomats kept in touch with the state of public opinion at this level. Nor did they ignore the newspapers and pamphlet wars lighting up the European public sphere in this period, to monitor, and to influence and be influenced by public opinion on the larger scale as well. Even on such questions as that of whether people would accept peace with Napoleon or instead insist on his removal as a precondition to signing a peace, Metternich, Castlereagh, Nesselrode, Tsar Alexander, and Austrian Kaiser Franz all lent an ear to those hoping to influence them, or at least reporting on the state of political discussion at various levels and locations around Europe.

Histories of the Vienna Congress sometimes start with the negotiations leading to the Treaty of Paris in the spring of 1814, and the talks in London that summer.[16] The decisions made and deferred there did much to set the agenda for the parleys in Vienna. The Bourbon dynasty was restored in France, but as a constitutional regime, and largely limited to the borders of 1792 (but not those of 1790 as some hardliners had desired). Britain arranged for all colonial issues to be settled in Paris, lest questions of its maritime rights and imperial power be raised in Vienna in the ticklish context of a possible new system of international law. Or at least, it had almost done so, with the crucial matter of international abolition of the slave trade still to be dealt with, crucial insofar as it had become such an object of public concern in Britain following British abolition in 1807. But the territorial settlements in Germany, Italy, and Switzerland, the constitution for the new German federation called for in the Paris treaty, and above all the question of the dispensation of Russian-occupied Poland all remained for the Allies to settle in Vienna, or if they possibly could, before they arrived: during the summer's celebratory stay in London, or immediately on arrival in Vienna a few weeks before the Congress itself was scheduled to open. Already in both the Paris and London phases of negotiation, the diplomacy was fully enmeshed in the social whirl of a reunited Europe celebrating the peace, and in the press and salon campaigns swirling around various issues as well.

The decision to hold a congress in Vienna was made already in late 1813, at about the time the Allied armies forced the crossing of the Rhine. The idea had been born even before, allegedly on the battlefield of Leipzig, while some of the first planning documents mulling over possibilities for entertaining foreign guests during the Congress appeared in January 1814. Preparations for Kaiser Franz's return took precedence (it would after all occur first, and was in some ways meant to be an even more impressive show), but after that had taken place in June, the detailed planning and the actual preparatory work for the Congress shifted into high gear.[17]

It is important to recognize that the Congress of Vienna was never meant to be a solely diplomatic event. Instead, its organizers planned it just as much as a celebration of the peace following Napoleon's defeat: a celebration of peace most specifically after the last victorious campaign, but also a celebration of the end (they thought) to a quarter century of war and revolution. As the Abbé de Pradt put it in his 1815 history of the Congress, it had the "character of a great solemnity celebrated in honor of the pacification of Europe" and was "the festival of its repose."[18] Even in diplomatic terms, this already represented a different kind of congress. It met not so much to make peace—that had already been sealed in Paris—as to cement and extend an existing one. Previous congresses, such as those in Utrecht or Westphalia, had had to wait until their conclusions for festivities commemorating the peace; the Vienna Congress on the contrary could begin with them.[19] Large-scale ceremonies involving various multiple rulers had already occurred in 1814 in Paris and London. But the Austrians did not want Prince Regent George and the English to have all the credit, hence in part the invitation to Vienna. Complaints about mixing business and pleasure, then and since, miss the nature of the enterprise. No one, after all, even knew that there would need to be a *diplomatic* Congress of Vienna of any real significance or duration until well after the invitations had been sent and the planning begun for the sovereigns' visit.

Under these circumstances, while certain statesmen arrived early for preparatory talks, the Vienna Congress really began with the festivals. First came those marking the arrivals of the various crowned heads, climaxing with the meeting of Tsar Alexander, King Friedrich Wilhelm of Prussia, and their host, Kaiser Franz, just outside Vienna on 25 September. Then began the round of ceremonies and entertainments to welcome—and to wow—the majestic guests and their large military and diplomatic entourages. Nor should it be forgotten that the pomp and display was also meant to impress the other wealthy, powerful, and famous visitors, the loyal but expectant population of Vienna, and the reading public in Europe at large. All anticipated something spectacular, something suited to this unparalleled gathering of rulers at such a historic moment, and for the most part they were not disappointed. From parades, mass festivals, and religious observances to parties, dancing, and theater, and to a reenacted chivalric tournament and a Handel oratorio performed by seven hundred volunteer singers and musicians, the court and city cooperated to stage a memorable show.

David Cannadine has suggested that in order to understand royal spectacle no fewer than ten distinct elements need to be brought into play, from the political power and personal character of the monarch to economic and social structures, the nature of the media, the state of technology, fashion, and commercialization, the self-image of the nation, the circumstances of the capital in which festivities are to be staged, and the attitudes of those responsible for liturgy, music, choreography, and ceremonial.[20] To these one should add at least two more: the nature and role of war and the military, and that of piety and religiosity. Unlike Cannadine's depiction of British spectacle as rather inept, on the Continent the state of technology, the media, and the market combined with the self-image of the rulers, nations, and functional elites to facilitate a quite colorful and widely disseminated display in this period between the early modern Old Regime and the late nineteenth-century "invention of tradition." Military, dynastic, and religious themes predominated in these festivities, yet newer forms of patriotic, populist, and national imagery manifested a significant presence as well. All of this display, in its various guises and levels of public involvement, provided venues not simply for the courtly representational display of power but also for exchange or a kind of dialog between the orchestrators of the festivities and the publics. In several respects, therefore, display also partook of the functions of the bourgeois-critical public sphere, or public sphere as such, including in the context of public opinion. Studying the planning, execution, and reception of these events reveals much about European political culture and about their role in shaping political outcomes.

Festivals did not constitute the only connection between political figures and publics. The press and press policy, and print culture in general, played central if understudied parts in the Congress and in European political culture of the post-Napoleonic era. As with Congress festive culture, the press assumed importance precisely because governments at the time were so concerned with public opinion as a factor in politics and diplomacy. They could not ignore it, and neither can historians. The Congress was also publicized and commemorated in the welter of other media that marked the period, ranging in the realm of print culture from celebratory or satiric prints to showpiece sheet music composed for the occasion, and in that of material culture from specially minted medallions to patriotic and portrait-bearing glasses and porcelain. The genre of what has come to be called "spectacular realities" already occupied a noteworthy niche in Congress Europe through various panoramas, dioramas, and wax displays, as did that of games, from playing cards to parlor and board games. The connections between this dimension of European culture and political culture and the realm of politics and diplomacy merit more scrutiny than they have heretofore received.

In thinking of media and display, it is on balance true that as one might expect, festivities tended to emerge from the courtly-aristocratic sphere and the political writings, prints, and memorabilia from the market-driven middle-class public sphere of the Habermasian sort. As we shall see, however, the domains of courts and governments on the one hand and markets and entrepreneurs on the other were inextricably intertwined at this time, in the transition between early modern and modern. Like the realm of display, that of the press and even to some extent of memorabilia showed significant activity by both governmental and private figures, operating at times independently, at times in cooperation, and with state and private roles sometimes coinciding in the same individual. At the same time, governments proved unable to control the process of publicity in part because it formed both a sub- and transnational rather than a state-level phenomenon, composed of networks acting on the European plane.

The social networks of the European elite were also European in scope. European salon culture had never really stood isolated from the diplomacy of the Allied headquarters as they marched across Europe in 1813–1814 and had already featured in the festivities and negotiations in Paris and London following the victory, but it reached its pinnacle in Vienna during the Congress. With much of Europe's social, cultural, and political elite present in the city, the European salon scene found itself recreated in the Austrian capital, not so much in miniature as simply concentrated on a smaller geographic scale. The statesmen themselves did not neglect to keep open house and lure the influential or knowledgeable into their orbits in this fashion, but it was the ladies as mavens of society who took the lead and set the tone for sociability in general and political sociability in particular. Salons and entertainments functioned in part as diversions and distractions as most historians have claimed, but at the same time they provided settings for informal political contacts and exchanges as well as an alternate space for the formation of public opinion, perhaps just as important for diplomatic outcomes as that of the press. Congress sociability also encompassed a significant religious dimension that helped shape Congress religious politics. As with political culture in this period more broadly, salons should not be thought of as purely secular in nature.

Current scholarly orthodoxy suggests that a rapid shift to all-male forms of sociability and politics occurred in the late eighteenth and early nineteenth centuries through the growth of the bourgeois-nationalist public sphere and the demise of salon culture. The material on salons and women in politics here, however, shows that the change was not as swift, smooth, or total as typically thought. Salons, like festivities, functioned right alongside the worlds of print and market as arenas for the contested formation of public opinion, by actors both governmental and private, aristocratic and bourgeois, male and female.

After depicting the varied layers of political culture and political communication in Europe as they operated at the Congress, I recount several central political struggles of the Congress as they were contested at these multiple levels. For most of the issues under consideration, the negotiations and public debate stretched intermittently over several months, indeed often beginning before and ending after the Congress. That is, they occurred in parallel, and it is important to keep in mind the temporal overlap among the talks when dealing with any single issue. For this reason a brief narrative overview of the Congress becomes all the more necessary here.

One can roughly divide the history of the Vienna Congress into three blocks. One break occurred around the middle of December 1814, in the sharpening of the crisis among the Allies over the Polish and Saxon lands, and another around the middle of February and early March 1815, with the resolution of that crisis quickly followed by Napoleon's return to Paris from his exile on Elba and the subsequent preparations for renewed war and speedy winding-up of the remaining negotiations. Despite the critical comments of many contemporaries and historians, alongside all the celebration and revelry of the Congress's early weeks, the rulers and statesmen still proved perfectly able to get down to work. And it turned out that there was much work to do, as so much unfinished business remained from the Peace of Paris. In moving forward, the signatory powers of the Treaty of Paris established two main commissions, one, consisting of all eight of those states, to handle matters of general European concern, and a second, comprising the five strongest German powers (Austria, Prussia, Hanover, Bavaria, and Württemberg), to draft a German constitution. Behind the scenes, however, and officially-unofficially, the Quadruple Alliance of Austria, Britain, Prussia, and Russia still held sway, as the ministers of those powers continued to try to settle the various questions, in part among themselves and in part in consultation with whichever other states and interest groups might be concerned in any given matter.

At the European level, the thorniest problem proved the partly related questions of what to do with the lands of the Kingdom of Saxony and of the Napoleonic Duchy of Warsaw (partial successor state to the former Kingdom of Poland, partitioned out of existence in the 1790s). Tsar Alexander claimed the Polish territories to create a new Kingdom of Poland with national institutions and a Polish constitution, but under Russian suzerainty. His ally Prussia, only partly to compensate for its lost Polish possessions, wanted permanent title to the whole of Saxony, whose king, Friedrich August, had (unfortunately for him) not abandoned Napoleon for the Allies before his capture at the decisive Battle of Leipzig in October 1813. Some leading Poles such as Prince Adam Czartoryski and some segments of European public opinion sympathetic to the Poles supported Alexander's idea, but the other powers almost unanimously decried it as a menacing lurch westward by the already colossal Russian Empire, one that left Berlin and Vienna dangerously exposed.

October and November were taken up above all with the unavailing efforts of Metternich, Castlereagh, and Prussian chancellor Prince Hardenberg (with some added pressure from Talleyrand) to convince Alexander to retreat from his plans. Metternich even persuaded his master, Kaiser Franz, to agree to Prussia's acquisition of Saxony if Hardenberg could deliver an acceptable deal on Poland, however unpopular the disappearance of an independent Saxony would be in the German states and Austria. When it became clear that Hardenberg had failed, not least because King Friedrich Wilhelm of Prussia stood by his staunch ally the tsar even against his ministers' advice, the British, Austrians, and French began to focus on the other problem of preventing Prussia's annexation of Saxony. The shift of alliances involved provoked a diplomatic explosion and subsequent stalemate in mid-December. Hardenberg turned over confidential correspondence with Metternich to the tsar in order to expose what he perceived to be Austria's duplicity in first agreeing to Saxon annexation and then reneging, a favor Metternich promptly returned. Relations among the main figures proved understandably rocky and communication difficult for several weeks thereafter. Alexander's dislike of Metternich had been building for almost a year and now reached its peak.[21] In the standoff over Poland and Saxony, Europe risked a renewed outbreak of war in late 1814 and early 1815, an event feared by many onlookers and statesmen alike, even as others remained confident that such a war would simply be too unpopular and too expensive for anyone to allow it to occur.

Historians, like many concerned contemporaries, have generally claimed that along with the distracting festivities, the diplomatic logjam of the Poland-Saxony crisis prevented the Congress from ever really getting going in the autumn of 1814. Actually, multitasking and working in parallel allowed discussions to begin on most fronts. Lagging progress typically owed more to the disparity of views in these various negotiations and the tenacity with which they were held than to the lack of unity occasioned by the disagreements over Poland and Saxony. October saw the first meetings of the German Committee to draft a constitution for the new German Confederation, and talks commenced on the first element of the territorial settlement in Italy, the cession of the former city-state of Genoa to the restored Kingdom of Piedmont-Sardinia, as called for in a secret clause of the Treaty of Paris. In December, the Genoese handover became the first item of business to be successfully concluded. The powers additionally appointed a Swiss Committee to start work on the territorial and constitutional settlements in the Swiss cantons, which also involved possible border adjustments with France, Piedmont, and Habsburg Italy as well as substantial input from British and Russian diplomats. Delegates from smaller states and nongovernmental constituencies simultaneously began the laborious process of canvassing support for their various aims. The representatives of the German Hanseatic city-states of Bremen and Lübeck, for instance, promoted measures against the taking of European ships and captives by the Barbary corsairs and sought backing for the expulsion of recent Jewish immigrants, while the representatives of the Jewish communities of those cities strove to thwart the latter plans through their own diplomatic initiatives. In line with the argument here about European political culture and its role in international relations, all of these diplomatic encounters took place not solely in chancellery conference rooms but through related op-ed campaigns in the press, and amid the festivities and salon conversations rather than separately from them.

Nor did the diplomatic stalemate and threat of renewed war at the height of the crisis in December and January spell the end of diplomacy in other areas. Even as Austria, Britain, and France signed a secret defensive alliance against Russia and Prussia in early January, Prussia and Austria fired the opening salvos of their joint humanitarian campaign to bring diplomatic pressure to bear on the Hanseatic towns in favor of Jewish rights. Not long after, the Committee of Eight began deliberations on abolition of the African slave trade (but not on the Barbary corsairs), resulting in an international declaration against the "infamous trade" in February, just prior to the final resolution of the Polish-Saxon crisis and Castlereagh's departure from Vienna. January also saw continued progress regarding Switzerland, with the outlines of the final settlement appearing in a committee report on 16 January. The German Committee had ground to a halt, but more from the refusal of Württemberg and Bavaria to accept Austrian and Prussian constitutional models than from discord between the two main powers over Saxony. While not essential, the resolution of the crisis certainly acted as a spur to progress, partly through the restoration of relative goodwill and a more cooperative spirit, partly in that once two of the main outstanding pieces of the puzzle that was the map of Europe were fixed, the other pieces started to fall into place as well.

The restored harmony did not last. War did finally come, and from a different, though hardly unpredictable or unpredicted direction, with the

escape of the Allies' nemesis Napoleon from Elba. Napoleon was certainly wrong to boast that his escape from his island empire and resumption of power in Paris spelled the Congress's end. Nor did his
return suddenly dispel the clouds of conflict surrounding the Allies; the
resumption of relatively amicable negotiations, as we have seen, had
already occurred several weeks prior. To that extent Napoleon's return
was as ill-timed as it was ill-starred. The Allies rallied immediately, with
even Bavaria eager to contribute troops; there was never any question of
peace with Bonaparte, or that the war would not recommence quickly.
(Whether Louis XVIII would again be lifted back onto the throne was
another matter, about which there was considerably more debate.)

The effects of Napoleon's return on the Congress were, however,
more mixed than usually recognized. On the one hand the war provided a powerful impetus to speed negotiations and to present Europe
with a concluded Vienna settlement before the armies actually clashed.
Details remained to be ironed out in the Polish treaties, and a constitution drafted for the new Republic of Cracow. The powers also still had
to secure King Friedrich August's agreement to the deal ceding part
of Saxony to Prussia. Much remained undecided about the settlement
in Italy, a particularly sensitive area given Napoleon's history in the
peninsula and the continued presence of his former marshal Joachim
Murat as king of Naples. To the extent that Talleyrand and the French
delegation—now representing a king in exile—had lost so much bargaining power, hopes for a rapid settlement in both Italy and Switzerland
improved. This did not, however, prevent Talleyrand from continuing to
haggle, and the final deals were still not easy to conclude.

Despite the universal agreement on the necessity of combating
Bonaparte, Allied amity and unity did not immediately win the day. Disagreements about subsidies, troop contributions, and command structures
quickly became acrimonious, both between the main Allied powers and
the smaller states being brought into the coalition, and among the powers themselves. Bremen was somewhat unusual in being so forthcoming
about the war effort, with its Congress representative, Johann Smidt,
still believing that the Hanseatic cities needed to prove their patriotism
and utility as a way of cementing their independence and bolstering
their status in Germany, but even this did not prevent conflicts between
him and Prussian chancellor Hardenberg about provisioning Prussian
troops.

Nor did Napoleon's return automatically smooth the path toward the
other main outstanding goal of the Congress, the creation of a German
constitution for a new German Confederation. Metternich and Harden-

berg certainly desired a swift solution, in order that the German constitution could form part of the overall Vienna settlement and accrue the associated benefits of international guarantee and moral capital. And they
did convene with their constitutional experts Wilhelm von Humboldt
and Johann von Wessenberg and with Count Münster of Hanover in order to begin where they had left off in November and hammer out a new
draft to present to the now enlarged German Committee. Precisely because of the urgency, however, smaller states now had much-increased
bargaining power and almost a veto over measures they disliked; they
could always threaten not to join the Confederation under those terms.
At a time when Metternich in particular wanted to present a fully united
front against Napoleon, this represented a potent threat, and as we shall
see, affected the final form of the constitution, not least regarding Jewish
rights and the reconstruction of the Catholic Church. Above all to secure
Bavarian participation, items like the Federal Supreme Court had to be
cut, and the degree of equality and residual sovereign power of the member states emerged much greater than in earlier drafts, certainly against
the wishes of Prussia, if not—perhaps—of Metternich.[22]

Just as many histories of the Congress do not begin with the gathering
in Vienna in the autumn of 1814, many extend beyond the signing of the
Final Act in June 1815, at least to the signing of the Holy Alliance of Tsar
Alexander in September and of the Second Peace of Paris in November
1815. While this book will not carry the narrative through the summer in
the same way, it will occasionally draw on those later discussions. Even
more significantly, many of the individual strands of negotiation covered
here involve a coda that points to one of the book's principal conclusions.
Namely, even the hardest-won settlements and compromises often only
represented a temporary resting point before the resumption of the struggle thereafter. This held true above all regarding Barbary, abolition, and
Jewish rights, but the same occurred with the Genevan settlement, the
borders between Prussian and Russian Poland, and the final dispensa-
tions of several of the constitutions initially drafted in the context of the
Congress. The Final Act was meant to and ultimately did carry great legal
weight and moral force, helping to establish the Vienna system and the
relative peace in Europe over the coming thirty-eight or even ninety-nine
years. But it also remained partly provisional. Even when the letter of the
treaty-bound law remained unchanged, contestation over its interpretation and ultimate implementation often continued with little letup.

One could write a whole book about many of the topics treated here:
festive and consumer culture; salons; religious revival and sociability;

abolition of the slave trade and the Barbary corsairs; the development of political ideologies in the 1810s. And of course entire books have been written about Congress diplomacy itself. But it is precisely the interplay and interlocking of these various dimensions that most urgently need capturing. The worlds of culture and society were suffused with politicized messages, and those of political culture and diplomacy played out on these cultural and social fields. Describing this complex political universe forms the mission of this book. Tracing its fascinating interlaced pathways through the Congress of Vienna bears implications for the study of political culture deep into the nineteenth century, and for the analysis and practice of politics and diplomacy to this day.[23]

CHAPTER ONE

Peace and Power in Display

In the autumn of 1814, most eyes in Europe turned to Vienna. On Sunday, 25 September, many were fixed—directly or vicariously—on the parade route by which Tsar Alexander and King Friedrich Wilhelm of Prussia would enter the city. The Tabor Bridges formed the cynosure of attention, where the pair was greeted by Emperor Franz of Austria. That liminal moment on the far side of the bridge, within the suburbs but just outside the city proper, gave rise to numerous verbal and visual depictions of "the three monarchs" or "the three allies" and still provides some of the most-reproduced images associated with the Congress of Vienna (Figure 1.1). Prince Trauttmansdorff and the court officials in charge of etiquette and festivities had of course carefully choreographed the ceremonial details beforehand (out of deference to the tsar's hearing-impaired left ear, the tsar rode on Franz's left rather than his right).[1] Yet the entry represented a celebration not just of the court but also of the city and its citizenry. The military escort and associated parade constituted a major part of the event, beginning with the early-morning cannon salvos that announced the approach of the foreign sovereigns several hours in advance (needlessly early, complained a rudely awakened Prince Metternich). Leading and concluding the procession, however, came units not just of the regular army and its marching bands but also of the civilian militia. The citizen military units and their role in ceremonial can be traced back to early modern and medieval times, but in this case they also reflected the brand new institutions of the Wars of Liberation and the dawning age of mass armies, patriotic participation, and total

FIGURE 1.1 *Reception of Tsar Alexander I of Russia and King Friedrich Wilhelm III of Prussia near Vienna on 25 September 1814.* Colored lithograph by Franz Wolf after Johann Nepomuk Hoechle, Vienna, 1835. (ÖNB/Vienna, Pk 187,12)

war during the revolutionary and Napoleonic eras. The parade continued to the great star of the Prater park and then wound through the narrow streets of the old city center to the Imperial Palace, waiting ready to house the imperial and royal guests. Gathered to greet them stood thirty white-clad young maidens, who presented the tsar and the Prussian king with wreaths and a poem. Classic symbols of innocence and futurity, reminders of what one had been fighting to defend, the girls were led by their French instructor, suggesting reconciliation within the European family after decades of war.[2]

This sort of monarchical meeting and associated pomp might seem perfectly normal from a twenty-first-century perspective, with its frequent photo-op encounters and summit meetings between heads of state, and with two centuries of such intersovereign moments to draw on in the collective memory, be it monarchical or republican. In the eighteenth century, however, such a coming together of sovereigns was extremely rare, and almost unthinkable. Instead, eighteenth-century rulers typically remained in their territories and left it to their mostly not-yet professional ambassadors and envoys to communicate with other rulers and to represent them at their courts—not just presenting their views, but serving as a representation of their sovereign persons in the more richly symbolic sense. If rulers had met, it would simply have heightened the dangers of tension, insult, and resultant war. Status, reputation, and ceremonial protocol remained all-important points of conflict. Attitudes began to change during the Napoleonic period, in gatherings such as the Congress of Erfurt or the famous encounter between Napoleon and Tsar Alexander at Tilsit. But it was the Congress of Vienna that first fully explored the possibilities of such meetings, in conditions more or less freely chosen rather than coerced, and with the expectation that it might promote lasting peace rather than imminent war.[3]

The choreographers of Congress events like Prince Trauttmansdorff of course drew heavily on the fund of traditional display and representational culture from the old courtly-aristocratic public sphere, even as the novel presence of so many royals offered opportunities for creative experimentation and potentially headache-inspiring conundrums of etiquette. At the same time, however, the sovereigns' presence in Vienna during the Congress shone a spotlight on a preexisting web of institutions, mechanisms, and languages of political culture involving voluntarist civic elements of representation and display and driven in part by grassroots patriotism and market forces in entertainment culture of the sort associated with the new, socially and communicatively broader public sphere, sometimes called the bourgeois public sphere, though more recent literature has shown the extent to which it was constituted by middle-class and aristocratic elements in combination.[4] This public web was comprised to a significant degree of actors positioned in both systems, the state or courtly and the voluntary or market-driven.

In taking the culture of display as the subject of investigation, this chapter adopts a somewhat different approach from much of the existing literature on the "new political history" or court culture. Such studies tend toward analyses of symbolism and ritual grounded in anthropological theory. They focus on long-term continuities and gradual transitions in the symbolism of power, and often emphasize the differences between the representational public sphere on the one hand and the realm of print culture and political debate on the other (with its own manner of legitimating or contesting power). Here, the aim is rather to illuminate the similarities and interconnections between the two arenas of representation, as both emerged from a common overarching political culture made up of elements of display, print media, and visual, musical, and material culture in the new world of broader publics and efficient markets. In that realm, elements of tradition and references to the newest cultural trends and political events coexisted and coalesced in crucial ways that were stimulating for contemporaries and are revealing to historians. The mixture of religious and military display in particular stands out in this regard, each reflecting newer meanings in contemporary contexts as well as those inherited from tradition. In a social sense too, festive culture in Vienna tended to bring the classes closer together and to shrink rather than exaggerate the distances within social hierarchies and between rulers and subjects. This chapter also contributes to debates about the significance of gender and the role of women in public and politics during this period. As we shall see, while the militarization and democratization that helped blur class distinctions did promote a partial masculinization of the public sphere, opportunities for women's presence increased as well.

If this chapter's recognition of the extent of mixing of court, state, and private initiatives in the production of festive culture and display marks relatively new ground, it also intervenes in an older but ongoing debate about the level of public participation in representational culture and its political effects. Jürgen Habermas's relative praise for the bourgeois public sphere of print culture, civil society, and parliamentary politics formed only a small part of a larger critique of post–Second World War society and politics as being simply acclamatory and focused on the admiration of celebrity in ways not unlike the court-based aristocratic representational culture of the medieval and early modern public sphere. Slogans rather than reasoned arguments shaped political debate, and glitzy campaigns and advertising swayed potential voters emotionally and viscerally more than intellectually, analogous to the legitimation of power in older ceremonies and festivals. In France during the radical 1960s, Guy Debord and the Situationists similarly critiqued the modern "society of the spectacle" and the mass culture of entertainment and consumption that fed it. In their analysis, atomized individuals cling to the illusion of agency in choosing what they have been led to desire, isolated from collective experience, and distracted from pushing for social and political change. Both points of view remain influential among historians and contemporary social and cultural critics. Other scholars, however, have begun to rehabilitate the realm of spectacle and entertainment culture as potentially more empowering and liberating than merely mind-numbing, both for its classic phase in the late nineteenth and early twentieth centuries and for Napoleonic pageantry and festivities. For some, the public's role in early modern and nineteenth-century parades and display was to line the streets, behave, and make plenty of cheerful noise when the great and the good passed by. But considerable room for popular input and participation remained as well, in ways that bore implications for the liberalization or democratization of politics in the revolutionary and Napoleonic eras. Monarchical representation could itself function as a form of political communication that involved spectators' active interpretation.[5] The present discussion too highlights the participatory rather than simply acclamatory side of the culture of display after Napoleon.

Even contemporaries sometimes proved keen to contest the idea that spectatorship implied mere gawking, or slavish fawning. Referencing the array of accounts and images of the three allied rulers that had preceded their entry to Vienna on 25 September, the coverage in the new Viennese cultural periodical the *Rigas of Peace* claimed:

> It was not three monarchs, surrounded by the trappings [Prunk] of majesty, stared at with senseless curiosity: it was the sight of these three, blessed by all the peoples of Europe, worshipped in particular by their own peoples, honored by all men of heart and spirit for their own sake; it was *these* three, friends bound through fate, through sufferings and joys, through their own hearts, which captivated all gazes and made their appearance an angel's apparition for every joy-drunk eye and for every delighted heart.

By this account, the acclamation represented not obedient noise to play a part but instead something deeply felt, involving close identification with the rulers as human beings, and broader sentimental and patriotic discourses by "men of heart and spirit" in this era of war and peace.[6]

Military and Religious Display

Although the image of the dancing Congress often comes first to mind when one thinks of its festive culture, the Congress offered almost as many opportunities for military as for terpsichorean display. Troops on parade, as we have seen, already marked the arrival of Tsar Alexander and the king of Prussia on 25 September, and further military displays occurred on 30 September and 1, 2, 6, 8, 9, 10, and 18 October, just to take examples from the Congress's first weeks. The pace slackened thereafter but never halted. If anything, the Viennese and their visitors experienced an even greater density of display after Napoleon's return, as from late March to early May an almost unending succession of reviews and parades took place for the troops marching through Vienna on their way to the Rhine.[7]

It is important to note in this context that such militarized political spectacle, ancient though it might seem, for the most part falls under the heading of "invented traditions" and has more recent origins than one might think. This is not to say that kings had not paraded their troops before, or that crowds had not watched them do so—the spring troop revue in the Berlin Tiergarten by Prussia's "Soldier King," Friedrich Wilhelm I, already represented a "spectacle for the entire city" in the early eighteenth century, and Prussian style sparked imitations later in the century elsewhere in the Holy Roman Empire, in parades and in the increasingly standard wearing of uniforms by rulers, courts, and even civilian officials.[8] Yet such exercises began to assume more modern forms and meanings at about the same time as the changes in the public sphere of the later eighteenth century, and did not get into full swing until the Napoleonic wars, in part through imitation of Napoleonic rule and display itself, where reviewing troops in choreographed spectacle constituted a crucial aspect of his appeal to legitimacy. Such militarized display also drew on the seminal role of the French National Guard and other military units in stagings or representations of the nation during the French Revolution.[9] It was significant in this regard that along with planning the Congress and negotiating peace, one of the preoccupations of Prince Metternich and Emperor Franz in the year 1814 was to introduce a new set of uniforms for government officials, making sure that everything looked just right and in the best of taste. Such a move would both boost morale and self-image among the bureaucrats and make the desired impression on state occasions.[10]

It is worth emphasizing that such festive and patriotic use of soldiers, uniforms, and martial music did not have to wait until the classic age of "invented traditions" in the late nineteenth century to find eager promoters or enthusiastic publics. If anything, the main difference in 1814 was that the spectacle did not need to come bearing the blatant trappings of the traditional but proved all the more effective when making the regime seem to be working in the spirit of the times and at the cutting edge of postrevolutionary political culture. The Prussian diplomat and litterateur Karl Varnhagen von Ense underscored these trends, observing that "the modern festival is essentially military; the earlier religious, the later courtly character of public opulence is entirely merged in the military, which speaks most clearly to the crowd and still commands from it the most respect, through earnestness and efficiency."[11]

Military spectacle also made up the lion's share of public display at the Napoleonic precursor to the Vienna Congress, the Congress of Erfurt of 1808. If the Austrians were to put on a better, and more legitimate, show in Vienna in 1814, then they needed to surpass the revolutionary Corsican on the same field—the parade ground—even as they emphasized the courtly and religious dimensions of display as well. In this way, too, restoration governments could combine reinvention of tradition with assertion of their fully modern and up-to-date status. Since Tsar Alexander cherished a well-known love of troop reviews and parades, the planners also served the parallel goal of playing to the preferences of their most important guest.[12]

Military display performed a variety of functions and was more than just a vehicle for eliciting acclamation. Most important here, military display served immediate political purposes. It too represents a "speech act" with an illocutionary force, or intended effect among its observers, and indeed among those performing. A good review or maneuver could showcase the military capacity, skill, and efficiency of the army in question, as well as allow it to demonstrate its esprit de corps and its patriotic commitment to both ruler and country (pater and patria, father-figure and fatherland). Done right, such display could even help build those very qualities, in practicing for the events and in receiving praise from commanders, rulers, and cheering crowds.[13]

Even the acclamation of subjects or citizens could serve a useful purpose, as a reminder for watching foreigners of the populace's patriotic sentiment, itself not just a mark of the power of the throne but a source of that power, at least in the new era of nations and states. When the veterans being honored at a festival on 6 October toasted the visiting rulers, they included a pointed reminder: "To the friends and allies of our monarch. They are witnesses of our veneration of him."[14] The role of the public was in any case different in the age of large citizen armies than it had been in that of mercenary or small standing armies, with its sharper differentiation between the "military estate" and civilians. Now a much closer identity between populace and soldiers played out, and the cheers became in part a recognition of self and an acclamation of dynasty and of nation alike. As a German ladies magazine observed of the festival commemorating the one-year anniversary of the Battle of Leipzig, "innumerable spectators surrounded this happy scene, and formed with the soldiers a true people's festival [Volksfest]."[15] Popular sovereignty in the strict constitutional sense remained an object of post-revolutionary distaste to most European rulers, but they knew that their power rested in part on the goodwill and even at times on the more or less enthusiastic support of the populace. The latter in turn primarily acclaimed and legitimated the monarchs' sovereignty through their participation in festive culture, but in part they celebrated their own role in sovereignty as well.[16]

The fact that civic militia units enjoyed a prominent part in the military display served to reinforce this tendency. Now that the breadth of popular mobilization and the degree of patriotic commitment had become measures of state power and military strength, it was all to the good to gesture to the enthusiasm of and for the militia when putting on a show to impress foreign observers. Many remarked on the impressive appearance made by the Viennese civic guard on parade duty, from the minor Viennese official Matthias Perth to the Prussian official and writer Carl Heun and the imperial aristocrat Count Henrich Stolberg.[17] Patriotic painters like Peter Krafft took up such subjects, as in his acclaimed *Departure of the Militiaman,* shown to adoring crowds in the gallery of Duke Albert of Saxe-Teschen (the Albertina), and reaching an even wider audience in the pages of the *Friedensblätter,* which featured the work as the first of its special edition copperplate engravings for subscribers (still a relatively new gimmick at the time, particularly in Austria). An article lauding the militia accompanied the plate.[18] Even Tsar Alexander had a soft spot for volunteers and militias, particularly if they came with pretty uniforms. The tsar had the Saxon Volunteers—with uniforms and insignia designed by the Romantic painter and sometime official Friedrich August von Klinkowström—declared part of his corps of body guards.[19]

It is important to keep in mind that the public or audience for such displays comprised different layers. Such events were staged not just for the watching crowds and dignitaries but also for more remote audiences. The diplomatic corps always attended and often reported back on the state of the army, and the state of public opinion. During the campaign against Napoleon in 1813, for example, Metternich's deputy in Vienna, Joseph von Hudelist, thought that the sight of Austrian units parading through town on their way to the front had a salutary effect on observers, cheering crowds and diplomats alike. During the Congress this effect worked still more directly, in that not just the ambassadors but the rulers and generals were right there, able to take in the scene and its significance for themselves. Such concerns occupied the minds of Emperor Franz, Field Marshal Prince Schwarzenberg, and even Metternich, since the uniforms, equipment, and performance of Austrian troops had not been as inspiring as they might have wished during the recent campaign. Congress display and ceremonial offered opportunities to correct that impression among the assembled rulers and watching publics. Metternich received similar advice from his ambassador in London, who thought it "most essential to remedy this opinion in Europe generally," and the Congress a good occasion for it. Hence the Vienna garrison was strengthened and received new equipment and uniforms, plus extra duty pay for the duration of the Congress. More tickets for officers to court festivities were requested too. Schwarzenberg hoped the measures would also bolster the army's "spirit."[20] There is even some evidence that the military and patriotic displays achieved the desired effect. The tsar's advisor Baron Stein recorded in his diary that according to the nearby observer Crown Prince Wilhelm of Württemberg, Alexander was "unpleasantly moved" by the grand festival of 18 October. "In the carriage of the troops, in the lively participation of the spectators, in the opulence that showed itself in the whole, he found something that contradicted his opinion of Austria's weakness, and that disturbed him in his high ideas of invincibility."[21]

Newspaper reports played their part in spreading the word, too, for a socially as well as geographically wider audience. Even the *Diario di Roma*—likely with a little assistance from Austria's Vatican representative—included a laudatory account of the artillery maneuvers in Bruck an der Leitha on 7 October. The article praised the power and precision of the destruction wreaked on the specially constructed target fortifications, evidence, it claimed, of the continued fame and skill of the Austrian artillery and pioneer corps. Such acclamation could only reach so far, however, particularly when lacking the helping hand of the state in question. The *Vossische Zeitung* in Berlin proved less impressed with the artillery maneuvers of 3 October near Vienna. The once and potentially future Austro-Prussian rivalry shone through.[22]

For all that the more purely military maneuvers and parades performed a number of functions, probably the most striking thing about the public displays of the Vienna Congress was the mixture of the military and the religious. This combination could be seen in the special hybrid category of the *Kirchenparade,* or parade joined with mass, but also characterized the various Te Deum services and above all the grand celebration of the first anniversary of the victory over Napoleon at Leipzig on 18 October. Impressive "solemn Kirchenparaden" took place on the first two Sundays following the entry of Alexander and Friedrich Wilhelm and helped set the tone for the Congress. Several battalions of infantry and cavalry marched out to the exercise grounds beyond the city gates and formed massed squares around the marquee erected to serve as chapel. They were reviewed there by four rulers on horseback, who then dismounted and celebrated mass in the tent. The troops for their part sang in German during the service, accompanied by military band.[23] According to a newspaper account, the "sublime moment" when the sovereigns knelt together as they had at Leipzig the year before made a "deep impression" on the thousands of spectators.[24]

Religious display of course frequently came unconnected to military, just as military display most often came without religious trappings. Since the Congress lasted so long, visitors were able to witness the full pageantry surrounding the cycles of the Roman Catholic religious calendar in the Habsburg capital. Advent and Christmas, Lent and Easter, even Ascension and Corpus Christi: church services and communal processions put both the Habsburg dynasty and the old corporate world of church, town, and court on colorful display throughout the Congress.

These ceremonies highlighted the Habsburg dynasty's noted Baroque piety or *Pietas Austriaca.* The Christian religious calendar helped frame the rhythms and symbolism of display and court life at most European courts in the early modern period, but it proved particularly central among the Habsburgs. Austrian culture as a whole has been analyzed in part as an outgrowth of the peculiarly sensuous version of Baroque piety, symbolism, and religious art of the Catholic Reformation, with ramifications through the period of fin-de-siècle Viennese modernism and beyond.[25] In this sense religious ceremonial and display emerged as the most traditional component of Congress festive culture. Even here, though, it is important to realize that the pageantry in part represented a reinvented tradition or at least a tradition with discontinuities. During the Enlightenment, Joseph II had begun to curtail the number of festive occasions and the dynasty's involvement in them. Only during Leopold's and Franz's reigns in the postrevolutionary 1790s did the court reemphasize religious ceremonial and the ruling family's role within it, as with the revival of the Maundy Thursday foot-washing ritual that made such an impression at the Congress.[26] The sight of the emperor and empress serving food and drink in "Christian humility" to a collection of the oldest men and women of the city, septuagenarians and octogenarians to a man and woman, and then bathing their aged feet was found moving and religiously sublime by Catholic and Protestant alike.[27]

The juxtaposition of religious and military elements came together particularly strongly in the celebration on 18 October in the Prater of the first anniversary of the victory over Napoleon at the great Battle of the Nations near Leipzig. At once a religious ceremony and a mixed imperial and populist national military festival, this event was in the words of a Berlin newspaper "a religious and military festival of joy."[28] As with much other nationalist symbolism throughout the nineteenth century, the conjunction of religious ritual and nationhood helped undergird the idea of the sacrality of the nation, without meaning that nationalism somehow replaced Christianity as a substitute religion. Both the religious and the national dimensions promoted the blending of hierarchical and democratic elements in the festival, as the shrinking distance between rulers and populace characteristic of Congress festivities was much on display.

Surprisingly, this grandest of all Congress festivals boasted the least prior preparation. It was actually conceived and approved quite late on, less than two weeks before the event. The "Grosses Militärisches Praterfest" was staged for the most part not by officials of court and state but by the army. They enjoyed access to the relevant experts in the court service, caterers and interior designers and so on, but they carried out the work of organizing, constructing, and decorating themselves, under the command of General Langenau. The Leipzig festival represented the wishes of the Austrian commander, Prince Schwarzenberg, who even at the time of the battle had felt a deep desire to commemorate the occasion, and charged his wife to begin making arrangements on his estate to do so. In October 1815, after the final victory over Napoleon, Schwarzenberg indeed celebrated the second anniversary on his estate (notably, again in the company of Tsar Alexander), but for the first he wanted to honor the soldiers, the real heroes of the day, in a fitting manner before the Congress and the eyes of Europe. On 15 October he could finally report to his wife Franz's approval of the festivities, and only on 12 October does the first documentary evidence show the organizers swinging into action.[29]

FIGURE 1.2 *It Was the Eighteenth of October.* Gouache and chronogram by Balthasar Wigand of the celebration of the first anniversary of the Battle of Leipzig, 1814. (Image © Wien Museum)

Why the emperor had a late change of heart or mind is unknown. Perhaps Schwarzenberg's entreaty proved decisive, or his own desire to do something for the soldiers; perhaps the notion of putting on an imposing if expensive show that could at once appeal to Tsar Alexander and give him pause for thought about Austrian strength and patriotic fervor became increasingly attractive as the standoff over Poland and Saxony hardened. Perhaps the emperor even in part wanted to do something to overshadow the planned celebrations of the day in so many parts of Germany by German nationalists inspired by the anti-Napoleonic propagandist and would-be national awakener Ernst Moritz Arndt. Any or all of these are possible; for lack of evidence we cannot know. In the event, the festival served all these purposes. The Praterfest ended up being the only Austrian entry in the subsequent patriotic book compilation of all the Leipzig celebrations across Germany, but that single item was made to count, its five-page description the longest and most impressive in the whole work.[30]

The festival involved a religious service as well as a massive review and banquet for the fourteen thousand regulars of the newly strengthened Vienna garrison (relieved of duty by city militia units for the occasion). Pontoon bridges were flung across the Danube arm to connect the Prater proper with the Simmering Heath and contain all the tables and troops. Captured French arms adorned the bridges, and dotting the park stood numerous smaller pyramids and columns of French cannons, rifles, and banners; the troops also constructed a seven-story tower from the same materiel. The organizers likewise decorated the *Lusthaus,* or pleasure house, at the center of the Prater with the detritus of the Napoleonic war machine, along with medieval weapons and knights in armor from the Vienna arsenal, as well as readying it for an opulent repast for the rulers and entourages. The Lusthaus sported imperial and Habsburg banners and eagles, as did the barges and pontoon bridges on the Danube (yellow and gold, and red and white). A festival atmosphere reigned among the thousands of soldiers and the even larger number of spectators (Figure 1.2).[31]

The mass for the dead and victory Te Deum took place right by the Bach equestrian circus and the Panorama, but this reminder of entertainment culture did nothing to impair the occasion's religious solemnity. The myriad troops defiled into squares surrounding the chapel tent, in which the service was celebrated and in which the rulers, generals, and ladies participated in the mass. As in the parade masses of preceding weeks, the sight of so many soldiers kneeling and baring their heads for the service, and the sound of them singing the German responses and hymns, produced a profound impression. Young Anna Eynard of Geneva recorded in her diary that the effect of the army on its knees, and of the crowds, was "impossible to express." The writer, official, and Goethe relation Carl Heun reported that at that "truly heavenly moment" there was a silence as if no one else were present in the Prater. When during the Te Deum massive cannon salvos resounded, on the contrary, "the earth moved beneath one's feet, the heart in the breast, the tear of joy in the eye." All of this made it for him "one of the most blessed moments of my life."[32]

The festivity's religious emphasis proved equally pronounced in the published representations that followed, whether in the newspapers or in music. Anton Diabelli, in a section marked "Andante religioso" in his "Tone Portrait" written for the occasion, also captured the contrasting silence of the crowds and crashing of the cannons, along with the moment when the monarchs and entourages "kneel before the altar in humility, to bring their thanks to the Highest." The rival composition by Adalbert Gyrowetz similarly portrayed in a stately andante how the "most heartfelt emotion gripped all souls at the conclusion of the solemn thanksgiving offering."[33]

Though most on balance experienced and remembered the day as a joyous celebration of returning peace and victory, for many there were also moments of remembered pain and suffering, above all during the initial solemn mass for the souls of the dead, which preceded the Te Deum and subsequent festivities. The festival was after all first and foremost to honor the survivors, and the fallen. Numerous families and friends that day mourned loved ones lost in the wars, even in the Battle of Leipzig itself. Dorothea Schlegel shed "many tears of thankfulness" as well as of "sympathy" during the ceremony. Happily, she was not among those who had lost a child; her son Philipp, a volunteer in the famous Lützow rifle corps, had seen action at Leipzig and elsewhere but came through safely. Yet she remained acutely sensitive to the many present who were less fortunate.[34]

The festival in the Prater was obviously an Austrian production, designed to showcase Austrian prowess and patriotism and to serve its political goals. This did not, however, prevent Tsar Alexander from intervening in the event to score political points of his own. First, both he and his brother Grand Duke Constantine elected not to remain among the guests but rather to don the appropriate uniforms of the regiments of which they had been presented honorary command and lead them personally during the review. When the regimental columns drew even with the Austrian emperor, the Russian ruler saluted, just as would a general in Austrian service. In a dramatic moment, the tsar also came forward for a public embrace with Franz. All of this served to emphasize the solidity of the alliance between the rulers and the depth of feeling between them, at the same time as it was offered in a spirit of (for the most part falsely modest) deference of the younger tsar to Europe's elder sovereign, and of guest to host. Each move garnered suitable cheers from the closely watching public. Such an effort to create good feeling may simply have been one of the tsar's typical public gestures, but neither was it impolitic at a moment of increasing crisis between the Great Powers over his Polish plans, when he may have felt his initial popularity in Vienna beginning to wane. Alexander continued to curry favor with the Viennese public and veterans later in the afternoon, when at another dramatic moment he toasted the health of both from the balcony of the Lusthaus where the high dignitaries were being fêted, again to loud acclaim. The watching Austrian official Matthias Perth thought this "beautiful moment . . . forever unforgettable for me." The tsar's act was even immortalized in one of the copperplate prints celebrating and capitalizing on the occasion and hence extended its communicative effects in time, space, and society.[35]

In reaching out to the public the tsar in some ways simply followed the symbolic lead of the Austrian authorities, who to an even greater extent than in other festivities encouraged a lessening of the distance—symbolic and real—between citizens and crowned heads. Citizenry, soldiers, and exalted guests literally at times rubbed elbows. Here, the rulers and generals mingled with the soldiers after dining, including exchanging toasts. Nor was this solely a matter of military courtesy, as civilians among the crowd—men, women, and children—themselves intermingled amid the ranks of soldiers. Visual representations of the festival reinforce this picture, confirming the fact of such mixing in the event itself, and showing that social mixing featured in the way the festivity was remembered, and was meant to be remembered. The proximity of sovereigns, soldiers, and crowds at the Leipzig anniversary also received due praise in the poem by Friedrich Kanne that provided the text for Anton Diabelli's tone portrait: "The sublime ones near the joyous tables and drink to their brothers' well-being"; "Look yonder, the emperors and the kings, they pass through the warriors' ranks."[36]

"Sublime" the rulers remained, but they were also now the soldiers' "brothers."

Along with lines of class, those of gender also blurred in the Congress festivities. That a militarized public realm would also be correspondingly masculinized is not a false impression, but neither will it do to overstate the exclusion of women or their restriction to purely domestic roles (even when in public). At some ceremonies women, or sometimes girls, played important symbolic or even active roles. White-clad maidens, already noted at the arrival ceremony for Alexander and Friedrich Wilhelm, were rarely missing from any festival or display. They could always function as symbols of purity to reflect on whatever was being celebrated, and in the military context they also served as reminders of what the soldiers were to defend, or had defended. Socially, the girls could come from orphanages, the families of the high aristocracy, or the middle classes in between.[37] Even at purely military events, women could step forth. Grand Duchess Catherine and Tsarina Elisabeth of Russia, for example, "honored" the military maneuver on the Simmering fields in early October, and in April 1815 during the new campaign against Napoleon, Empress Maria Ludovica of Austria and Grand Duchesses Catherine and Marie similarly observed a troop review.[38]

Royal consorts also played more active public roles. Maria Ludovica supplied a gold-embroidered silver ribbon for the standard of the Austrian infantry regiment of which Tsar Alexander had been given honorary command. In addition to her name and "the 18th of October," the empress had with her own hands (at least allegedly) embroidered the inscription: "Alexander and Franz this very day formed an inseparable bond."[39] Tsarina Elisabeth had for her part done the needlework for the banner itself—the word "Eintracht," or "concord"—which was presented to the regiment on 12 December. She had participated in similar ceremonies in Russia at the beginning of the 1812 campaign. In this instance, Elisabeth handed over the banner to a detachment of officers who rode to the Hofburg to retrieve it for the occasion. At the benediction ceremony, Maria Ludovica affixed banner to pole, and "with a loud and firm voice" (if allegedly also with a blush) she addressed the men with the appropriate words, "what a great honor it was for them, that the autocrat of Russia had recognized the regiment by being its commander, and that this consideration would bind the already existing friendship between the two empires even more tightly."[40] In this the empresses imitated the seamstresses of the women's patriotic associations of the Wars of Liberation in many parts of Germany, as indeed in Britain. Not only did these Betsy Rosses sew and/or embroider military banners themselves, but they often assumed significant parts in the ceremonial display surrounding their benediction.[41]

The representations of the festivities in words, image, and music did not hide the active presence of women, and in some ways emphasized it. By Caroline Pichler's account, she and her family featured among the civilians who sat down to dine with the soldiers being fêted at the Leipzig anniversary festival, and the memoirs of Roxandra Stourdza also noted the mixture of soldiers, citizens, and foreigners.[42] This experience, too, found an echo in the recounting of the climactic postprandial toasts in the poetic accompaniment to Anton Diabelli's piano portrayal of the festivity: "The beauties of Vienna glorify this festival, and array themselves amid the rejoicing gathering. They too swing the glass high, with sweet modesty and joyous blushing."[43] The visual depictions of the event do not show women actually sitting at the tables in the way described by Pichler, but most do clearly depict women (and children) in close proximity, sauntering with other male spectators, and even placed amid the serried rows of soldiers' tables. This holds true of the title-page copperplate of the Diabelli piece, with ladies prominently displayed in the crowd, some with male companions, others without, but one can also see them in the title plate of the competitor to Diabelli's work by Gyrowetz. The more sumptuous color print from Artaria also depicted a mixed crowd. Tensions surrounding gender relations register, as with the emphasis on blushing, but without obscuring women's participation in public display.

Court, City, and Nation on Display

The grand performance of Handel's oratorio *Samson* on 16 October offers a classic instance of the joining of court and city, middle class, gentry, and high aristocracy in a blend of older representational culture and newer civic associational life and concert culture. The concert was staged by the recently founded Society of Friends of Music, itself an outgrowth of another charitable association founded during the wars, the Society of Noble Ladies for the Promotion of the Good and the Useful. The Musikfreunde formed a mixed group of male and female, aristocratic and bourgeois dilettantes and assembled a massed chorus and orchestra of over seven hundred performers for the occasion. The performance surpassed even the London Handel concerts mustering around six hundred, and thus presented the opportunity to demonstrate the robustness of Austrian associational life and civil society as well as of its aristocratic culture, through a "musical festivity that no other capital is capable of giving on such a scale." The choice of oratorio disappointed some, but did show Viennese connoisseurship at the forefront of taste, as *Samson* had been the only Handel oratorio not yet performed outside England. The Old Testament context and the themes of overthrowing false gods and mourning a patriot hero also made the selection particularly appropriate for the Vienna Congress.[44]

The so-called Volksfest, or People's Festival, provides perhaps the best example of the blending of elements of the older court-based representational and newer bourgeois public spheres, in the persons and institutions involved as in the political and cultural languages being communicated. Held in the Augarten, another of Vienna's main parks, opened to the public by Joseph II in 1775, the Volksfest featured among the most important and spectacular of the official festivities. The court and government under Prince Trauttmansdorff, however, did not directly plan and stage it. Rather, it showcased the patriotic and entrepreneurial initiative of one Franz Jan, who had been putting on similar large-scale popular entertainments for several years. At the same time, though, neither was the Volksfest a pure outgrowth of the new market-driven public sphere. Jan himself additionally held the position of court caterer, and as it turns out, he also accepted a partial subsidy from the emperor to help finance the extravaganza. When the Congress was postponed from July to the autumn, officials presented Jan with the option of either staging the festival as planned in July or waiting for the august foreign visitors and promoting the event on his own tab come fall, with no further subsidies. Jan, not an entrepreneur to let slip a historic opportunity, chose the latter course.

In the event, he claimed to have lost so much money that he repeatedly petitioned for another subvention to cover the difference. Despite Prince Trauttmansdorff's support, the emperor and his primary advisor, Count Wallis, remained unmoved by Jan's pleas, relenting neither when he piteously pointed to his potential financial ruin nor when he invoked the language of patriotism. The Volksfest, he claimed, truly constituted a national festival, and it had been a matter of "national honor" to put on an impressive (read sumptuously expensive) show. The emperor, already angry at the overcrowding and consequent public order problems, simply responded that he shouldn't have overspent.[45]

At the center of the Volksfest stood the celebration and feasting of four hundred injured Austrian veterans. For their and the other spectators' entertainment, Jan arranged a variety of displays, from equestrian trick-riding and circus acrobatics to ballroom dancing and demonstrations of folk dances, plus a large series of fireworks and figurative illuminations. The kaiser and his illustrious foreign guests also graced the event, partly to honor the soldiers, partly to enjoy it, and partly to enhance its entertainment value. The veterans, as well as the rulers and their entourages, were admitted without charge; the rest paid admission. In the spirit of market economics, ticket prices varied with quality: least for standing room, most for seats on the specially erected tribune, and standing room on the tribune for those in between. The banquet followed the entertainment, and after the meal an exchange of toasts, wherein the monarchs mingled with the crowds and soldiers, receiving toasts from the wounded veterans, including from one Sergeant Platzer, who had lost an arm in the recent wars but raised the remaining one to honor the rulers and generals, as well as the troops. "Long live the allied soldiers, our brothers! May their mutual respect, love, and unity endure forever!" Platzer exclaimed in his final pledge. The sovereigns then toasted the veterans in turn, with Tsar Alexander seizing a glass and leading the way.[46]

Perhaps in part because it represented more a private than an official initiative, the Volksfest proved more controversial in its reception. The government and some spectators felt aggrieved chiefly through the breakdown in crowd control; Jan sold too many tickets for the space and arrangements. Stories circulated of noble ladies with dresses torn or jewels gone missing in the crush. Other critical voices pointed to the sluggishness of the fireworks displays (much slower, some thought, than those in Paris). The folksy and popular *Eipeldauer Letters* also chronicled the difficulties faced by Jan and his crew, as wind and weather wreaked havoc with the preparations for the fireworks, and as the delayed start occasioned by the sovereigns' late arrival meant that encroaching darkness brought an early end to the sporting entertainments. On the whole, though, the fictitious provincial from Eipeldau defended Jan, pointing out that if a foreigner had organized the same event, everyone would have said it was "superb," but since he was a mere Austrian, everyone complained instead.[47] It was, after all, not just in the privately sponsored festivals that things occasionally went wrong. The court-staged fireworks display a few days prior on 29 September certainly impressed, but a few glitches gave rise to some acerbic humor. In the representation of the temple of liberation there appeared, instead of an allegorical figure of Germania as companion to that of Gallia, a second Gallia. And an extinguished lantern in the belt of the illuminated allegorical figure of "Concord" (gendered female of course, as allegorical figures generally were) led to what the editor of the Prague periodical *Hesperus* termed "an ominous void." Whether it was ominous with respect to sexual modesty or to international politics he left unclear.[48]

The range of activities and symbolism in the Volksfest shows its mixed origins in the realm of courtly representation and modern entertainment culture and populist politics. The centerpiece and ostensible occasion for the event, the celebration and feeding of the disabled veterans of Vienna's Invaliden hospital, involved one of those patriotic and charitable gestures that abounded in the years 1813 and 1814. Many were the charitable associations founded, collections taken up, benefit concerts staged, and patriotic and celebratory texts printed whose proceeds went to support wounded soldiers or the widows and orphans of the fallen. Both entertainment culture and political culture were shaped in these years to a large degree by just such public demonstrations emerging from within civil society.[49] The concert in which Beethoven conducted his Seventh Symphony and *Wellington's Victory* and premiered his cantata honoring the Congress, *The Glorious Moment,* undoubtedly proved the most famous such occasion, but it was one among many. Aloys Weissenbach, the cantata's librettist, was himself a former military surgeon and had offered one of his previous patriotic productions, a poem celebrating the return and ceremonial entry of Emperor Franz to Vienna back in June, for a similar charitable purpose. For that matter, the grand concert performance of Handel's oratorio *Samson* by the Society of Friends of Music in the Hofburg's Winter Riding School on 16 October represented an extension of previous benefit concerts in the same format by that new-style association within civil society and its parent institution the Society of Noble Ladies for the Promotion of the Good and the Useful. At the same time, like Jan's festival, it belonged just as much to the official cycle of court festivities that opened the Congress, accounted for in the court's planning by figures such as Count Moritz von Dietrichstein, who was also a Society board member.[50]

The patriotic symbolism at the Volksfest referenced several levels of identity and helps make a broader point about the potential for coexistence of local-civic, regional, ethnically or historically national, and state-based and dynastic varieties of patriotism. Excepting the municipal level, any of the other scales can merit the appellation "national" and "nationalist"—it is anachronistic to employ late nineteenth-century definitions of nationhood alone. Moreover, these do not have to be competing identities but can rather be multiple, even at times mutually reinforcing. The symbols chosen for the illuminations paid homage to the notion of Europe as a collection of dynasties, with the initials of the three main allied sovereigns and the august spouses of the emperor and tsar. But they also paid tribute to the notion of a Europe of nations, adding certain images associated with these states, either existing or emerging sites of memory. Hence the monarchs walked through a glowing representation of Berlin's Brandenburg Gate with its newly restored Victory Quadriga (recovered from Napoleon's Paris) on the way to view an illumination of the Cannon Monument of Moscow, constructed from captured French arms after the French defeats and turning of the tide in 1812, and here surrounded by "groups in Russian costume." The Metternich-controlled daily the *Oesterreichische Beobachter* duly publicized all of these alliance-building details, which were then reprinted in other European papers.[51] The third image or symbol represented the spire of Saint Stephen's Cathedral in Vienna. It served as much as an icon of Viennese civic identity as of Austrian—and/or German—national identity, but in the present context it stood for all. The Catholic priest and Romantic playwright Zacharias Werner found the less-than-life-size illuminated transparency of the tower considerably less inspiring than its real-life counterpart by moonlight (as he noted in one of his Congress sermons), but the choice of symbol for mixed civic and national identities was still a felicitous one.[52]

The juxtaposition of various levels of identity, German, Austrian, and even local, is significant. Scholars often cite the existence of state-based or dynastic identities and patriotism in this period as evidence against the possible existence of an overarching German nationalism at this early date, in opposition to old nationalist myths of a national awakening during the Wars of Liberation. But the various levels of patriotism were not mutually exclusive, and as recent scholarship from the German case suggests, could coexist or even reinforce one another in federative conceptions of nationhood: German, Saxon, Lusatian; Brandenburger, Prussian, and German. Elements of such synchronicity emerge at the level of display in this chapter and become even more central in the discussion of the role of nationalism, in Germany and generally, in Chapter 6.[53]

The Volksfest imagery bears similar implications for the problem of Austrian identity. There historians typically stress the dilemma that Austrian identity could really only be supranational, equivalent to Habsburg dynastic patriotism. Both were threatened by the competing presence of ethnic or national identities in the multilingual Habsburg Empire. And yet, just as various local, regional, provincial, state, and dynastic identities (including Austrian) coexisted with an overarching German national identity, the same held true within the Habsburg lands. Federative conceptions of nationality proved paramount there too. One could be Styrian or Carinthian or Hungarian and at the same time Austrian (and German, Slovene, or Magyar).

In fact, according to prevalent ideas at the time, one came to be a Habsburg or Austrian patriot in part through experiencing provincial or "national" patriotism. During the campaign of 1809, when the government and its publicists deliberately invoked nationalist rhetoric and identity as a means of mobilizing resources for war against Napoleonic France, the official policy had partly relied on that scheme (they did not appeal to German nationalism alone). Officials and publicists attempted to inspire regional and ethnic patriotism as stepping-stones to the higher level—call it national, or supranational as one will, so long as one recognizes that the two levels did not only stand in competition, and that the term "national" remains a proper one for this kind of mixed civic and ethnic, as opposed to exclusively ethnic-based version of large-scale state and popular identity. The goal of broad patriotic mobilization and participation remained the same as in "normal" nationalism, and appeals to symbols of historical memory, language, and folklore worked similarly, too, whether the subject of the patriotic sentiment was a province (Land), or a people within a province. References to the "Tyrolean nation" or the "nation of Vorarlberg" had appeared already in the late eighteenth century, even as overlain and partly competing German, Catholic, and Habsburg identities kept these provincial "nations" internally disparate.[54]

The program of the *Vaterländische Blätter für den österreichischen Kaiserstaat* of 1809, for example, associated with Count Stadion's foreign policy, aimed to create "love of the fatherland" (a dynastic Austrian patriotism) through "knowledge of the fatherland," which could only mean through knowledge of the various provinces and peoples of the monarchy. From the many provincial and ethnic patriotisms would come the overarching national one: Austrian. As Stadion informed the Russian chargé Baron Anstett in 1808, "We have constituted ourselves

as a nation." The group around Archduke Johann and Baron Joseph Hormayr, with the latter's ideal of a "federation of peoples with equal rights
and autonomous provinces," likewise worked to instill knowledge
and love of the various fatherlands in pursuit of an ultimate Austrian
identity. Landscape, history, natural history, and—significantly in the
present context—national costumes all provided imagery suitable to the
task. Hence publications like the *Vaterländische Blätter* included pieces
on the various portions of the realm, from Hungary and Bohemia to
Tyrol.[55]

The process and the policy worked most clearly in the realm of music. Heinrich von Collin's *Songs of Austrian Militiamen* specifically
avoided German nationalist rhetoric, and these songs were translated
into other languages of the empire; Collin's preface reinforced the idea
that Austria itself formed a worthy object of patriotism, in part because
"under no other government would the constitution, language, customs, and distinctive qualities [Eigenthümlichkeiten] of each particular
people be so nurturingly honored." The famous final concert of Haydn's
Creation with the elderly composer in attendance analogously featured
an Italian translation and united Italian and German performers, with
an eye or ear to Austria's lost Italian possessions. In 1814, Joseph Sonnleithner and the high official Count Saurau similarly called for the new
Society of Friends of Music to begin collecting folk songs from the various peoples of the empire.[56]

These relationships looked and played distinctly in a Habsburg monarchy and a Europe of rising national discourses and practices, but at
the same time, they still fit partly within a context of "composite states"
or "composite monarchies," that is, states compounded of various historic provinces or principalities, which individually enjoyed considerable privileges of autonomy, separate laws, and estates-based representative bodies. As J. H. Elliott suggestively remarked at the conclusion
of his seminal essay on composite monarchies, the development of Romanticism and nationalism in the late eighteenth and early nineteenth
centuries gave impetus to the drive to centralize nation-states, but it
also spurred a strengthening of attachments to their component parts,
the regions, provinces, and ethnic groups; the countervailing tendencies
toward unity and diversity led to "complex and constantly changing
shifts in the balance of loyalties."[57] The tense relationship between provincial elites and central governments, hovering between mutual support
and mutual contestation, had also marked the early modern phase of
state-building, in that Europe of composite monarchies. The difference

FIGURE 1.3 *Peace Festival of the Peoples of Austria*, by Johann Josef Schindler, oil on canvas,
c. 1815. (Image © Wien Museum)

in the Congress period of Romanticism and a gradualist, historicist liberalism (or reform conservatism) was that one might think of such diversity as a strength, as something to be cultivated rather than simply tolerated. The German lands stood out in this context, with their stronger tradition of federative national identity, but similar practices and patterns of thought held elsewhere in Europe as well. As Archduke Johann wrote to the curator of the Johanneum museum in Graz devoted to Steyermark's history, peoples, and land, "Austria's strength consists in the provinces' difference . . . which should be carefully preserved," since the provinces still "saw themselves as independent from the rest, but worked loyally toward the common goal."[58]

Against this backdrop, it is telling that Jan arranged for a display of "national dances" as part of the Folk or People's Festival, and that the newspapers, including Metternich's semiofficial *Austrian Observer*, publicized these details. Tents like columned temples were erected in which men and women in appropriate costumes of the component national, regional, or ethnic groups of the Habsburg Empire performed their traditional dances for the spectators' entertainment, but also edification. In this instance, the tents offered a taste of Tyrolean, Hungarian, Bohemian, and Lower Austrian folk dance, to give a sense of the realm's geographic and ethnic reach. Such a gesture had a whiff of older styles of representation, in which displays of subject peoples in traditional peasant garb helped demonstrate the extent of power and dominion. But in 1814, as portrayed in the Augarten, the display of national dancing projected much more the tone and language of the new public sphere and its attendant patriotic, or nationalist, political culture. The new interest in folklore and folkways associated with Romantic nationalism certainly played a role, as did the assertion of a populist, specifically national identity. The display's cross-class and mixed-gender dimensions also stand out, for performers and public.[59]

The Volksfest dancing was not an isolated instance of such juxtaposed regional-ethnic and broader national or dynastic identities and patriotism. From the realm of visual culture, Johann Josef Schindler's painting *Peace Festival of the Peoples of Austria* featured a cornucopia and an altar with burning hearts celebrating Emperor Franz, all ringed by a semicircle of masculine figures representing twelve national or regional groups in appropriate native costumes and coiffures (Figure 1.3). Saint Stephen's Cathedral of Vienna rises iconically on the horizon. A board or "society game" sought the patriotic market, for three to fifteen players, with fifteen copperplate images of "inhabitants of the Austrian empire" (all couples) in their "national costumes," from Viennese, Upper Austrian, and Tyrolean to Polish, Hungarian, Bohemian, Transylvanian, Slavonian, and Croatian.[60] From the home of spectacle on the stage, the acclamatory musical play *The Consecration of the Future* by the previously noted Joseph Sonnleithner, with which Emperor Franz had been welcomed back to his capital in June 1814, paraded across the boards both allegorical female figures of "Austria" and the empire's component provinces, plus fifty pairs of men and women in even more precisely located regional and ethnic garb. The couples in "national costume" allegedly drew "the greatest attention" of the whole show. Many even boasted speaking parts and hence did not appear completely passive before the public. The public itself, that is, the audience, proved similarly active, collective, and vocal, when on this occasion, as so often in these years and months, they joined the fifty couples in Austrian *Tracht* in a rendition of the Austrian national anthem "God Save Franz the Kaiser," with lyrics by Viennese poet Lorenz Leopold Haschka and music by none other than Joseph Haydn. The anthem was of course partly modeled on the English "God Save the King," and its music was later borrowed for the German national anthem. The Austrian version was no less national than the British for being, like it, simultaneously a demonstration of monarchical and dynastic sentiment. Commissioned by the above-mentioned Count Saurau, it was translated into all the main languages of the Habsburg monarchy.[61]

Perhaps surprisingly, given his reputation as an antinationalist, but in line with his newspaper's coverage of the Volksfest folk dancing, Metternich adopted a similar measure at one of the most impressive balls he gave for Congress high society. For a costume theme, Metternich requested guests to attend in the traditional dress of one of the peoples of the Habsburg Empire. If possible, they were to coordinate their efforts so as to offer visually compelling full quadrille sets in the same attire. Even, or perhaps especially the foreign guests were expected to play along and contribute to this display of Habsburg dynastic power and supranational national identity. Countess Elise Bernstorff, for example, wife of the Danish ambassador, joined with others to make up a set representing Transylvanian folk dress; Hanne Smidt, teenaged daughter of the delegate from Bremen, received help from Sophie Schlosser of Frankfurt and an Italian painter to attend as an Italian peasant. All of this gave Metternich's press organ the opportunity to observe of the fifteen hundred guests that "one was tempted to believe that all the provinces of the Austrian Empire, particularly those that an envious fate had for a short time separated from the beloved motherland, had sent the flower of their youths and ladies in their richest and most splendid festive adornment in order to express worthily their joy and premonitions of a happy future."[62]

The patriotic Genevan republican Anna Eynard chose not to play along, or at least not quite. In keeping with the rustic and patriotic peasant garb concept, but breaking with the request that it be Austrian, she instead donned the dress of the mountain Swiss from her own region. Her costume did not, therefore, obtrude or detract in a general way, but on the finer scale her expression of Swiss-Genevan patriotism stood out clearly enough. She received many compliments, not least from Tsar Alexander, and as the Swiss were expected to be patriotic and independent, no one took offense, with any remarks confined to good-natured teasing.[63] The mixture of Genevan-local and Swiss-national patriotism points to the coexistence of such layers of identity in wider European contexts as well. The fact that this was at heart a European elite, with all the implications for culture transfer that that entails, made such a spread of ideas all the more likely (something that will be seen again in the chapter on salon sociability and subsequently).

Along with the pointed inclusion of Tyroleans in the Volksfest dancing and the other occasions for displaying the component parts of the Habsburg Empire, the Volksfest also featured the popular Tyrolean singers of the Kaerntnertor Theater.[64] Display usually tends not to point quite so directly to diplomatic disputes, but in this instance one has to imagine that both the Austrians and the Bavarians saw the point in their continuing wrangling over the return of the Tyrol and Inn region to the Habsburgs (the area having been given to the newly minted Kingdom of Bavaria in 1806 by Napoleon). It has even been claimed that the Volkfest boasted an archery contest among Tyrolean bowmen, won by none other than the son of Andreas Hofer, martyred leader of the insurrection of 1809 against their new Bavarian overlords and the latter's Napoleonic allies. This would make the point about the political implications of the Tyrolean symbolism still more fully, but for lack of a reliable confirming source, this seems to be one of those historical facts that truly is too good to be true.[65]

While the festivity in honor of the Battle of Leipzig put on by Metternich on the evening of 18 October in the garden of his suburban villa on the Rennweg is often seen as an afterthought following the stirring events of the morning and afternoon, it had in fact been in preparation for months, even before Metternich's return to Vienna that summer. The festival in the Prater, as we have seen, was actually the afterthought. It has also often been presented as the festival of peace, Metternich's counterpoint to the militarist atmosphere in the Prater earlier that day, but this does not really hold either.[66] Partly with respect to the occasion, and partly to the tsar's preferences, Metternich always intended to incorporate a pronounced military component in its décor, with wreaths of laurel and oak rather than olive branches or rainbows to bracket its blazing illuminations of the Allies' initials and the massive word "Leipzig." At the entrance even stood a large field tent bedizened with "weapons and trophies."[67]

Metternich's festival, though heavily subsidized by the court, was a private event, not a public one in the same way as that in the Prater, or at least, it was aimed primarily at that "courtly-diplomatic partial-public" representing the important European opinion- and decision-makers, and only secondarily at the milling crowds outside the gardens or the reading publics further afield. Female guests contributed to the atmosphere, too, by wearing white or blue gowns and laurel, oak, or olive leaves, in the spirit of both victory and peace.[68] A grand ball provided the occasion's centerpiece, in the eyes of some observers approaching or even surpassing the beauty and glitz of the splendid court balls. Tsar Alexander, pursuing his vendetta against Metternich, stood almost alone in having dismissive words for the display, telling Princess Esterhazy that the commemorative day would have been better served without the evening encore after the moving events of the morning and afternoon.[69] Given the effort and expense to flatter him and his tastes, this was rather uncharitable of the tsar, but not unexpected.

Metternich's ball constituted a sort of hybrid between official and unofficial, an outgrowth of court life, ministerial duties, and salon sociability among the high aristocracy. The Vienna Congress lives in popular memory today as much as anything for the glittering parties and dancing, these too located somewhere in that middle area between the two types of representation and sociability. The court offered many memorably lavish balls and receptions during the Congress. Court functions, these were closed to the wider public if recounted in the newspapers, and organized by the officials in charge of ceremony, though still dependent in part on the magnates of the realm playing their part, above all in the display of their wealth (in the Habsburg case typically in jewels more than in fashionable attire; the traditional garb of the Hungarian nobility in their national dress, was however by all accounts as or more impressive). Similarly, since the court could not afford to keep the illustrious guests sufficiently entertained on its own account, it relied on the high aristocrats to step in with their own occasions for diversion and display.[70] Hence the Zichys and the Trauttmansdorffs in particular joined the Metternichs in throwing luxurious parties and fêting the foreign notables.

The court also, however, maintained its distinctive tradition during the Congress of staging opulent balls for a mixed public of nobles and Viennese citizenry. These ridottos or *Redouten* took place in the smaller or larger Redoute Halls (or both at once plus the Riding School for the largest occasions). Of the first two ridottos early on, the smaller on 9 October was planned for four thousand guests; the larger on 2 October boasted tickets for ten thousand. On each occasion, extra attendees may have found their way in too, but unlike Jan's Volksfest in the Augarten, crowd control never became a problem (unless one counts the rather large quantity of imperial silverware that went missing, whether as souvenirs or as items for pawnshops during difficult financial times is unclear).[71] Finally, the court could count on the resources of various public, admission-charging establishments such as the luxurious suburban Apollo Rooms in the Zieglergasse to stage large parties of their own, which the noble and even crowned guests could also attend alongside the wider public, including the shopkeeper class.[72]

In such teeming mixed venues, and in the larger high-society balls and soirees themselves, it naturally occurred that the crowned heads and their families often came into close contact with the wider public, wealthy and less wealthy alike. That the same occurred in some of the larger outdoor festivities, as at the Prater and the Augarten parks, has already been noted, with the crowds and press coverage wildly enthusiastic about such proximity. For the indoor entertainments, however, the propinquity provoked considerable negative opinion. The critical comments came from varied geographic and social locations. Talleyrand, that powdered product of Old Regime etiquette, wrote his royal master that he did not like to see royals at teas and balls among "simple private individuals," as they lost "grandeur" in the process, and went on to flatter Louis with the remark that in order to see proper royalty one had to go to France. But this was not solely flattery, as he expressed much the same sentiment to Jean-Gabriel Eynard.[73] The republican Eynards of Geneva came down almost equally sharply against this kind of royal condescension. Jean-Gabriel thought "the masters of the world" should show "more dignity" rather than mingle. His wife, Anna, had the same reaction. "How wrong they are, these potentates, to show themselves like this without dignity, without anything that distinguishes them." She went on to explain, "monarchs should not be seen up close, there always needs to be a distance between them and us that we could suppose to be the result of their superiority."[74] This was perhaps somewhat ungrateful of the pair since they benefited from the trend, becoming sought-after companions of the tsar and his sister Grand Duchess Catherine; by January Anna was even dancing with Alexander and King Friedrich Wilhelm. Eynard maintained his opinion, however, even debating the matter with Alexander and Prince Eugène Beauharnais. They thought it "convenient" to be able to escape being continually on regal display, but Eynard claimed they were "almost obliged to admit I was right," with Napoleon's protégé Eugène at least conceding that "royal dignity had received a very large check" and that "the people need prestige."[75]

Among the voices supportive of monarchical promiscuity, the Viennese *Friedensblätter* noted that the sovereigns appeared in civilian clothes at the benefit ridotto for the university medical faculty's widows' fund and "mingled with the crowd of happy people of all estates." The royals thus had the "rare pleasure" to escape "the restriction of representation" and to move according to their "free personalities." At the splendid ridotto of 2 October, the crowds were said to be "in transports" at seeing the rulers in civilian clothes and in "friendly proximity."[76] The Russian officer and memoirist Alexander Ivanovich Mikhailovsky-Danilevsky, adjutant to Tsar Alexander, also wrote approvingly of the monarchs "getting to know their subjects and socializing with them on a friendly footing."[77] Johann Smidt and his family, from the city-state of Bremen and just as republican as the Genevan Eynards, also praised the opportunity to see the sovereigns up close; Smidt's daughter, like Anna Eynard, even participated in dance sets with the tsar and the Prussian king. "One could hardly distinguish them from private persons," Smidt wrote, with approval rather than consternation.[78]

Scholars have recently emphasized that European rulers did not often set out to craft a simpler image or to use royal display or royal memorabilia in order to appeal to broader bourgeois or plebeian publics; the "humanization" of European monarchy just happened, an unintended consequence, without their effort or even despite them.[79] In this instance, it may simply be that the rulers were pleased to feel on vacation during the festivities and to shed the constraints of normal court etiquette. Insiders such as Roxandra Stourdza and Baron Nostitz certainly thought so, and perhaps just as significantly were echoed in press coverage as in the example quoted above from the *Friedensblätter*. The decreased distance did, however, have the effect of increasing popularity and goodwill, whether rulers behaved that way calculatedly or from their own desires.[80] The proximity of rulers and publics also fits with the moves toward making diplomatic etiquette and precedence rules simpler and less formal that marked the Vienna Congress and proved one of its more lasting diplomatic legacies.[81]

The extent and limits of cross-class sociability also show through in examining the dancing. Of the Prince de Ligne's lifetime of noted bon mots, perhaps the most remembered these days remains his pointed critique of Congress diplomacy, or rather of its lack of progress: "The Congress dances, but does not advance." As with the festive life generally, dancing abounded there. When authors mention dance at the Congress, they often reference the waltz, that hallmark of Viennese culture, later immortalized in the melodic strains of the Strausses and traditionally associated with the middle classes and the growth of bourgeois cultural influence.[82] Waltzing did go on, and one could say quite a bit about it in connection with the Congress, but its distinguishing dance was actually the polonaise, considered at the time the epitome of aristocratic elegance. The polonaise craze swept through the city's ballrooms and into the market for sheet music discussed in the next chapter. A stately line dance on a grand scale, the polonaise offered ample opportunity for conversation, and even at times for a certain amount of hilarity—on one occasion, the line through the rooms of Russian representative Count Rasumovsky strung out so far that the head and the tail suddenly found themselves face-to-face and didn't know which way to go. With considerable laughter, the tsar and the other guests managed to extricate themselves from this almost unprecedented difficulty.[83] For the most part, however, the polonaise connoted order and hierarchy, as participants' social ranks were clearly legible in the order of the promenading pairs. The visibility of the famed rulers and heroes contributed for a time to the polonaise's popularity, as spectators could gaze their fill upon the celebrities. Before long, however, monotony and boredom dominated the public response to the seemingly never-ending traipse through the rooms of various venues. Having exercised their eyes sufficiently, most instead grew eager to exercise their feet on some other dance, livelier and with wider participation. Already at the Grand Redoute of 9 October, Anna Eynard professed herself "bored by the monotony of the dance of the sovereigns." Her husband Gabriel also found the incessant polonaising "insipid" and "monotonous," and by November he declared the dance the "mortal enemy of the spectator."[84] Baron Nostitz likewise bemoaned the "boring" change in Viennese dance culture, previously all waltzes, with the occasional quadrille and Scottish reel, "now almost nothing but polonaises."[85]

Courts, Europe, and Encounters with History

Even beyond the dancing and the marching, the concerts and the grand festivals, the court- and state-based festive culture showed great splendor and variety. This culture was filled with references to history, sometimes to recent history, in either case with political implications. And even amid the meticulous planning for such events, external political actors could nudge the political messages and symbolism in alternative directions.

Through the glittering and opulent court balls, ridottos, court theatricals, tableaux vivants, and other events staged for restricted or broader publics, the Viennese planners were in part making a declaration of the capacity of the court, state, and dynasty to put on such affairs, ideally, in a way that would surpass other capitals. They staked Habsburg Vienna's claim to be the arbiter of taste—hence on the cutting edge of the modern—and to be the bearer of tradition, with all that that implied for its historical legitimation at a moment of political restoration. Balancing the notably novel with the patina and aura of the time-honored was the goal, much as with the military exercises and parades. The closest the Congress and Prince Trauttmansdorff came to the invention or at least revival of tradition probably involved the banquet, opera, and illumination in the Orangerie of Schönbrunn Palace on 11 October, and the grandly staged Carousel or medieval tournament that remains perhaps the best remembered Congress festivity. The prince *Obersthofmeister* wanted the fest in Schönbrunn to recapture the glory days of Joseph II for its illustrious participants, and its exquisite decoration and day-bright lighting may have succeeded. The event was exclusively for the court, but at the end, after the great ones had headed back to Vienna and the Hofburg for the night, the doors were opened to the curious crowds who had gathered to witness the event.[86]

The greatest and most eagerly anticipated of the court spectaculars was the medievalizing Carousel, with members of the resident and visiting aristocracy appearing as knights and ladies in a grand evocation of the age of chivalry. The excuse to show off wealth, above all glittering jewels, also constituted a noted feature of the occasion. The event was originally to have been staged outdoors at the perfectly appropriate setting of the recently renovated neo-Gothic castle in Laxenburg park a few kilometers outside the city. But with the delay to the Congress pushing the date back into November, it had to be put on indoors instead in Fischer von Erlach's great Winter Riding School, attached to Vienna's Hofburg palace, where the Lippizaner stallions still perform their "airs above the ground" today.[87] Such was the pent-up demand to see the spectacle that when illness forced Tsar Alexander to miss the performance, it was repeated not just once, for him, but twice.

The Carousel certainly entailed an element of invented tradition, but at the same time it was presented with a rather self-conscious historicism and at times a slightly postmodern staginess as if everyone was in on the joke, that however grand and entertaining, this was not the real thing or the past brought back to life. The skeptical Prussian official and poet Friedrich August Staegemann thought the knights looked like "heroes from a stage comedy," but even he had to admit that the spectacle exceeded his expectations.[88] One element of tradition, or historicism, that did not always come across as playful involved the continued use of Turks' heads as targets for the demonstrations of the horsemen's skill with the lance (Figure 1.4). At least according to the commentator in the periodical *Hesperus,* an Armenian sitting next to him became angry at the circumstance, observing that since Europe had arrived at a higher level of "culture" since the days of the Renaissance carousels, they could have done without such an exhibition.[89] Here, progress and historicism may have come into conflict.

Room for interpretation also remained in the representation's meaning, both in the reception of the symbols provided by the choreographers and in a certain jockeying for symbolic position on the part of participants and spectators. On the latter score, Dorothea de Talleyrand-Périgord decided to embellish her costume as one of the tourney's ladies of honor by adding the golden lilies of the House of Bourbon to the scarf that she would grant as a favor to her knight-escort. Already significant as a declaration of loyalty to the restored Louis XVIII and Bourbon dynasty in France, the move was all the cleverer in linking the dynasty to the tournament, and to the aura of dynastic legitimacy attached to the medieval history that was to be performed and reimagined that night. Moreover, the gesture pointed not only to the position of France itself, still struggling to reclaim its place among the Great Powers and the nations of Europe, but also to the fortunes of the

FIGURE 1.4 *Carousel Given in the K. K. Winter Riding School in the Presence of the High Allies in the Year 1814*. Copperplate by Artaria and Co., Vienna, 1815. (ÖNB/Vienna, LW 72588-C)

dynasty in Naples (still controlled by Napoleon's marshal, King Joachim), and perhaps even of Louis's relation the king of Saxony, still held prisoner by Prussia at the height of the contestation over Poland and Saxony. In all of this Dorothea acted with the full and admiring approval of her uncle-in-law, who reported back on this symbolic act to her mother (and his mistress) the Duchess of Courland. At least in Talleyrand's account, Dorothea's lilies made a "great impression."[90]

The bourgeois literary star and official's wife Caroline Pichler did not feature among the ladies and knights, but she too thought to exploit the occasion for a public symbolic gesture. Inspired in part by the Carousel, she entered the lists in the ongoing and vibrant debate over the adoption of "German national dress" as a leading proponent of such a move, arguing that German women should wear "old-German" costume, reflecting the modes of Germany's glory days during the "romantic Middle Ages." The designs suggested actually followed more closely those of the fifteenth century and Renaissance, but then, most Romantic medievalizing tended to conflate early modern and medieval, from Wackenroder and Tieck's pathbreaking celebration of the art of Albrecht Dürer and Raphael to the very tournament everyone was about to watch. Pichler specially composed a poem for the event, "Viennese Women of the Sixteenth Century," and she and her daughter intended to seize the occasion of a subsequent court sponsored ball to advertise their campaign further by appearing in appropriate garments and distributing copies of the poem. With suitable medieval allusions, the verses depicted the wonder of these honored ancestors as they awoke from the crypt to witness the pageantry of the Carousel and to adjure nineteenth-century German women to turn from foreign fashions and return to "German dress."

Unlike Dorothea's, the scheme did not ultimately come off, since on the night of the *Redoute* Caroline fell victim to one of her debilitating migraines and could not attend. She had to content herself instead with publishing the poem in the Viennese literary-political journal the *Sammler* and as part of the coverage of the Carousel in the popular German *Journal des Luxus und der Moden* of Justin Bertuch, whose son figured among the spectators that night (Bertuch's journal also published Pichler's essay on German national costume).[91] Just as Anna Eynard had elected to wear Swiss costume to Metternich's Habsburg-themed ball to mark her patriotic loyalties, Pichler and Dorothea could even co-opt major court festivities for their political purposes.

That private figures should think to use such occasions for political self-expression is not so far-fetched as it might seem for the early nineteenth century. For certain types of representational display it constituted almost normal practice, particularly with urban celebratory illuminations. Though ordered by the court, the design of the lighting displays on individual houses was left to the proprietors or inhabitants. The displays by a Prince Trauttmansdorff or Field Marshal Prince Schwarzenberg of course did double duty in setting a tone as officials and private individuals. All drew on an established cultural-political repertoire of symbols and language, but with space for significant variations on the themes. At least a few bold Viennese, for example, found ways to work expressions of dissent into the illumination in honor of Napoleon's birthday during the French occupation of 1809. One resident placed in his window the words "O, Napoleon, how great is thy fame! / But we prefer Franz just the same." Through an acrostic display, another homeowner wrote, "Zur Weihe An Napoleons Geburtstag" ("For dedication on Napoleon's birthday," the initial letters reading "ZWANG," or compulsion). The initials (and the message) stood out even more as they were unsubtly painted blood red.[92]

In 1814 illuminations of the city took place in honor of Emperor Franz's return in June and of Alexander's arrival in September. While as a rule little is known of the details of such displays, for Franz's homecoming an extraordinary patriotic book publication preserved precisely that. The expressions of patriotism could employ suitably paternalist language, with reference to "subjects' love" and "the happiness, O Franz, to be ruled by you!" But they could also be cast in the language of German nationhood, from which the government was attempting to retreat in these years: "Rejoice, ye Germans!" or Franz denominated "Germany's savior."[93] The illuminations additionally offered a public space in which women could make themselves heard. The professor's widow Julie Sebald, for example, offered her own acrostic: "Friede Ruhm Anfang Neuer Zeiten" (FRANZ—"peace, glory, the beginning of a new age"). Frau Sebald's was just as patriotic, if considerably less subversive, than that above, though it too indicated a desire for change with its final phrase. The widow Burkhard was another who expressed her preference for German over dynastic patriotism with her invocation of "our German Reich."[94]

Despite all the similarly independent symbolic action taking place alongside the Carousel, most eyes focused on the spectacle itself. Prince Trauttmansdorff and his staff divided the participants, ladies and knights, into four quadrilles, the ladies decked in pearls and diamonds and appearing in costumes of a particular color: black, white, blue, and red. The "old-German knights" rode forth in Renaissance finery of embroidered black velvet and bright plumage to demonstrate their prowess with lance and sword and to put the gleaming white horses through their military and dancing paces, from contredanse and quadrille to (it had to be) a polonaise. The color, the pageantry, and the quasi-medieval costumes were much admired—"Quelle fête, quelle magnificence!" enthused young Anna Eynard to her diary. The Russian officer Mikhailovsky-Danilevsky, almost blinded by the ladies' jewels, thought it a festivity "whose like I had never seen," showing the glory of the Habsburg Empire, whose "nobility has no match in Europe, brilliantly clad and on the most marvelous horses."[95] The panegyric author Christoph von Felsenthal celebrated the Carousel as a high point of Congress display with appropriate references to imperial traditions dating back to the great medieval and Renaissance Habsburgs Rudolph and Maximilian, to courtly troubadour or "Minnesänger" chivalry, and to "German virtues" and "loyalty." Or as Cotta's popular German cultural periodical the *Morning Journal for the Educated Classes* put it, "the old knightly world, the cradle of the splendid families whom we now see on the thrones and in their vicinities, was to be called forth from the mouldering parchment, from the history books, and to be paraded, not unworthily, before the heroes of the day."[96] Government officials could not have affirmed the link between the Romantic glorification of the Middle Ages and that of the present rulers and nobles any more effectively, or probably even as effectively.

Here, too, reception allowed room for interpretation of the symbols, as with Felsenthal's Germanic emphasis to accompany the Habsburg dynastic language. One contemporary illustrator and a subsequent strand of historical interpretation on the other hand built on the Carousel's colorful base to imagine a pageant of a Europe of Nations, with each quadrille signaling the medieval (or Renaissance) past of a major European state or people. The first quadrille offered "old-German knights" in yellow fifteenth-century garb with lances and ostrich plumes, and the second presented riders in "Polish costume," of later date, with ulan lances and shako-like hats (Figure 1.5). Hungarians appeared in their leopard-skin capes, while the French quadrille in the oldest-looking "knightly costume" with broadswords (and more ostrich feathers) completed the cycle. In this guise, the legitimating medieval imagery not only looked back to the Middle Ages as a time of chivalry, social hierarchy,

II.ABTEILUNG | II . QUADRILLE

POHLNISCHES COSTUME | COSTUMES POLONOISES

à Vienne chez T.Mollo et Comp.

FIGURE 1.5 "Polish Costume." Second quadrille from *Four Groups from the Carousel*. Colored stipple engraving by Tranquillo Mollo after Matthäus Loder, Vienna, c. 1815. (Image © Wien Museum)

and a vivid court life of anointed kings and vassal lords but also represented the pan-European dimension of this aristocratic and royal culture and society. The more famous Artaria prints of the Carousel focused instead, more traditionally, on simply giving the names of the
noble knights who formed each group (Figure 1.4).[97] Perhaps of some
solace to Caroline Pichler as she recovered from her migraine and her
disappointment, the Viennese *Friedensblätter* and a premier German
cultural periodical both reported on the Carousel with the observation
that the knights and ladies all appeared in "old-German costume," thus
claiming the Middle Ages as part of the German national past.[98]

When placed alongside the troubadour revival in the court theatricals,
the knightly decorations at the main pavilion during the Leipzig anniversary fest in the Prater, and the tours and displays at the imperial neo-
Gothic Franzensburg in Laxenburg park, medievalism certainly emerges
as a leitmotif of Congress political culture. If one also adds the religious
ceremonies celebrated during the Congress, particularly those in the
Gothic-spired Saint Stephen's Cathedral, the theme becomes still more
prevalent. It represents an important respect in which Romantic cultural currents shaped European political culture in these years.

Yet encounters with the past in ceremonial did not always mean
looking to tradition; they could also involve working through contemporary history. One of the most noted fests or ceremonies of the Vienna
Congress was the memorial put on for Louis XVI by Prince Talleyrand
on 21 January 1815, the twenty-second anniversary of his execution by
guillotine during the French Revolution. It did not really form part of
the Congress program but was accepted as such even by the authorities,
and certainly by most of the public. The Austrian government did not
stage it, but Talleyrand acted not as a private individual but rather in
his capacity as representative of the French king (with considerable cooperation from local church, municipal, and court officials, also in their
official capacities). Talleyrand pulled out all the stops for the occasion,
bringing in the leading architect and designer Charles Moreau and the
noted painter Jean-Baptiste Isabey to decorate the church and catafalque,
and putting his house pianist and composer Sigismund Neukomm to
work composing a funeral mass for large choir. Codirecting the chorus
stood none other than Habsburg Court Kapellmeister Antonio Salieri,
while the Archbishop of Vienna, Prince Hohenwart, performed the service of the dead. All the clerics of Saint Stephen's were to join in the
singing of the service, and all the church bells in the city were to ring.

City officials also helped coordinate tickets and crowd control, with three separate doors: for the high guests; for those with tickets; and for the general "public," admitted without charge.[99]

Most of the sovereigns and illustrious guests attended the event, many likely with some skepticism, given Talleyrand's revolutionary and Napoleonic associations. As Henrich zu Stolberg-Wernigerode, a pointed nonattendee, noted with pithy acerbity in his diary, "very touching, the murderer for the murdered."[100] That Moreau had a revolutionary chapter in his biography and Isabey a Napoleonic one may have rein- forced that impression, but then, more than Talleyrand himself, the two had been rehabilitated and warmly embraced at the Congress. Moreau had renovated palaces and designed fests in the Habsburg monarchy for over a decade (most recently doing sets for the court theatricals and preparing Metternich's garden festivity honoring the Leipzig anniver- sary on 18 October); Isabey for his part became more or less the official Congress portraitist and commemorative painter, his well-attended ate- lier itself almost a salon. As such, and as with Talleyrand's royal service, their activities spoke to the *ralliement,* or conjunction of republican, Napoleonic, and royalist elites, that had begun under Napoleon and continued under the first restoration in what amounted to a far-reaching amnesty.[101] Neukomm hailed from Salzburg and had studied with both Michael and Joseph Haydn in Vienna, hence Talleyrand could hope for some hometown favoritism in his case.[102]

The ceremony was essentially a service for the dead, and as such a re- ligious event, but as much or more than many of the other festivals, it also carried a self-consciously political edge. Talleyrand intended it to offer "a great lesson," to "an end moral and political." Talleyrand's deputy in Paris Count Jaucourt deemed the occasion "entirely political" and a "true Congress affair"; with flattering hyperbole, Jaucourt thought it would do more against Joachim Murat's regime in Naples than would the Austrian army.[103] It did, after all, put the spotlight on the principle of monarchical legitimacy, and provide a poignant reminder—likely superfluous for most attendees—of the dangers of revolution. The ser- mon, ghostwritten by Talleyrand and the royalist member of the French delegation the Comte de Noailles for the Abbé Zaignelins, who presided on the occasion, formed the most clearly political element of the cere- mony, underscoring the principle of legitimacy and the legitimacy of the Bourbon dynasty in particular, in France and beyond (including Naples, but also with implications for Saxony). Most accounts agree that the abbé's sermon—or as the Sardinian representative Saint-Marsan called it, "discours semi-politique"—did not come off well, being nearly inaudible and in any case pronounced in a strong Alsatian accent.[104] Those who could not follow the discourse on the day, however, were able to catch up a few weeks later when on Talleyrand's instructions the text appeared with the account of the service in the Parisian daily the *Moniteur*. While the sermon may have struck some as overly political, it need not have seemed out of place in an ecclesiastical context, as loyalist sermons remained a staple of polities with established churches across Europe. In a manner that would likely have pleased counterrevolutionary religious conservatives such as Joseph de Maistre and Louis Bonald, the sermon decreed religion conjoined with royalty to be the necessary and essential condition for the foundation of states and blamed the Revolution above all on the influence of irreligious Enlightenment philosophes. The abbé also strongly asserted Louis XVI's status as martyr, indeed a Christ-like figure: "Louis was the victim of his love for his people, according to the example of his divine master, who offered himself in sacrifice for humanity, however unworthy." That the sermon was not wholly reactionary, and therefore in line with Talleyrand's own approach to the Bourbon restoration, emerged in the stress on the previous king's willingness to compromise, to listen to his people, and to insist on ruling according to the law, as reinforced through quotations from his political testament penned at the time of his execution. But on balance the emphasis clearly lay on the role of Louis and the Bourbons in monarchic revival, whereby Louis "had to show to Europe a Christian and a martyred king, to sanctify royal power by his sacrifice, to consecrate the principles of authority and legitimacy by his torment, and by the holiness of his death, to give to the blood of the Bourbons a new luster."[105]

The more purely symbolic or traditional dimensions in Moreau's décor received frequent but by no means universal acclaim; the music and its performance as conducted by Salieri and Neukomm on the other hand seemed to win over even the skeptical. Senator Hach of Lübeck found the cathedral "excellently decorated" and the catafalque "beautiful." Baron Nostitz on the contrary deemed it "bad theater decoration," and Saint-Marsan "petty grandeur." In his diary, as in his published account a couple of months later, the editor Carl Bertuch critiqued the décor but lauded Neukomm's Requiem. The Congress *Chronicle* found the decoration "wholly in the spirit of simple majesty and a sublime taste" and the music "splendid."[106] Around the corners of the funeral catafalque, Moreau had placed four allegorical figures: mourning France;

Europe weeping; Hope, with an anchor; and finally Religion, with the testament of Louis XVI, and her eyes upon heaven.[107] The inclusion of Europe alongside France allows various readings: that Europe shared France's feelings on this occasion, or that France was now reintegrated as a part of postrevolutionary Europe. The cruciform anchor's hopeful desire for stability after the stormy seas of the revolutionary era, and the role of religion in buttressing that stability and in upholding the legitimacy of the Bourbon kings in France (and elsewhere), were neither subtle nor ambiguous.

Neukomm's Requiem setting stands out in part through its lingering and deeply felt *Dies irae* section. Whether listeners identified the terrors of the Day of Judgment with the harrowing experiences of the revolutionary and Napoleonic years is hard to say, but it would not have represented such a stretch for Tsar Alexander or other evangelicals, who often sought and found the signs of the times in that turbulent recent history. Such an interpretation would also have dovetailed with the theodicy of the ghostwritten sermon—on the text 1 Kings 8:43, "That all the peoples of the earth may learn to fear the name of the Lord"— according to which the Revolution and its tribulations formed part of the providential plan.[108] The *Moniteur* account at least claimed that the *Dies irae* and immediately following offertory proved the section of the mass that most struck the audience, a comment that gives some hint as to how those who staged the event hoped it would be interpreted and remembered. The minor Austrian official Matthias Perth also singled out the *Dies irae* and Neukomm's sister's solo for praise, and felt all the music demonstrated "simple dignity with emphasis and effect."[109]

Similarly, one cannot know whether any of the attendees heard in the pleas for eternal rest an echo of desires for earthly peace and repose in Europe. The "crescendo of jubilation" in the "Pleni sunt coeli et terra" reference to the glory of God in the Sanctus would not have been out of place in the various Te Deum settings that had celebrated the victory and peace in recent months.[110] What does seem clear is that many were moved to contemplate not simply the service's religious dimension but also the experience of Louis XVI and its political and historical implications for their generation. Perth in his diary thought back on how much blood and upheaval had flowed from this source over the past twenty-two years, and believed a new age was beginning. In the press, the Congress *Chronicle* found that the service stimulated reflections on the Revolution and on "the royal martyr Louis."[111]

If on the whole more welcoming than the reception in Congress diaries, the ceremony's reception in print was not completely unproblematic from the French perspective. The emphasis on legitimacy and anti-revolutionary sentiment came through well enough, but in at least one instance, with a more anti-French echo than was probably desired. The commemoration was taken up into a series of prints of Congress festivities published in Nuremberg, which was certainly a mark of success, and the catafalque and Bourbon lilies received their imposing symbolic due, but the accompanying text still did less to rehabilitate France than Talleyrand might have hoped. The caption interpreted the service as an "expiatory offering" that finally "cast the veil" over twenty years of French "errancy" (Figure 1.6).[112] The author of the coverage in Metternich's *Oesterreichischer Beobachter,* Congress secretary and Metternich's trusted collaborator Friedrich Gentz, could not have been more flatteringly chosen but had to defend himself against the complaints of the French number two, Dalberg, about the account's religious rather than political emphasis. The French delegation could at least take heart in the fact that while Gentz highlighted the event as a moment to contemplate the tumult and sufferings unleashed by the Revolution, he went out of his way to stress that these were the result of failings not in the French alone but in a whole European generation. And whatever Dalberg's criticisms, Gentz's essay pleased Talleyrand and King Louis sufficiently that they ordered a translation in the *Moniteur.*[113]

Talleyrand and the two churches involved all ultimately had reason for satisfaction. The Cathedral of Saint Stephen got to keep over a hundred kilos of wax remaining from the ceremony's lighting, and Talleyrand had all the other decorations sent to Abbé Zaignelins's Church of Saint Anne, the French national church in Vienna. The French government rewarded old Archbishop Hohenwart with a special jeweled crucifix and ring, while Talleyrand received the congratulations not only of his deputy Count Jaucourt, but more importantly of his king, Louis XVIII, brother of the departed.[114] In order to enhance the festivity's resonance even beyond the press, Jaucourt sent a circular note to French diplomats abroad celebrating the occasion as a tribute to "the sacred principles" on which rests "the happiness of nations," and as a "touching homage" to the French royal house. He instructed France's diplomatic agents to talk up the festivity in this sense, in order to "render durable . . . the salutary impression that this event could not have failed to produce upon peoples and governments."[115]

With the Carousel, the requiem for Louis XVI, and the opulent court sleigh ride of 22 January, the most famous Congress festivities had come

FIGURE 1.6 *Solemn Service of the Dead for His Former Majesty Louis XVI on 21 January, 1815.* Colored engraving by Friedrich Campe, Nuremberg, 1815. (Anne S. K. Brown Military Collection, Brown University Library)

and gone, but the display and entertainments continued. The sleigh ride became a court coach ride with approaching spring, and religious ceremonies displaying Habsburg piety came to the fore during Lent and Easter. The parades and military panoply also returned in force following Napoleon's escape from Elba, as troop units destined for the Army of the Rhine were routed through Vienna. What kind of impressive festivity and display would have closed the Congress of Vienna with the signing of the Final Act had Napoleon not reappeared will never now be known. That it would have been created and contested on various social levels, and been instructive as to the way that Congress politics was meant to be interpreted and remembered, should however be clear.

CHAPTER TWO

Selling the Congress

The Vienna Congress was never just about Vienna. Just as its political implications stretched through Europe and beyond, so too did the public before whom words, gestures, and display were performed, and with whom the statesmen and rulers in Vienna stood in partial dialog. Commemorative and patriotic participation involving broad publics occurred not just in the display and festivities but also in the even wider print, visual, musical, and material culture surrounding the Congress. This dynamic and diverse commodity culture in turn blended with a vibrant and growing assortment of visual entertainments, all intertwined with political culture at both the local and transnational levels. Together, these cultural and political trends constituted a surprisingly modern, market-driven, market-savvy, and multimedia culture of what can be called political consumption.

This diverse array of patriotic consumer goods preceded as well as followed the Congress, shaping as well as transmitting the experience of it. As the coverage of the arrival ceremonies for Tsar Alexander and King Friedrich Wilhelm of Prussia in a Viennese cultural periodical explained, "for a year how often have we seen *images* of the three monarchs in all forms, painted on paper, canvas, wood, and all sizes; how often have their united names been invoked in patriotic songs, celebrated in theaters, and greeted with loud rejoicing. Now, what was otherwise only an inspiring idea, was realized before our eyes."[1] Although the author of these lines stressed the gulf between prior representation and reality, and to the advantage of the latter, in the present context the words show clearly the extent to which all the previous images and evocations of monarchical meetings helped to frame the experience itself for spectators.

Governmental and court actors played important roles in this political marketplace, above all in the press, but to a greater extent than in the festive display private entrepreneurs took the initiative. These individuals (usually but not always men) were motivated in part by patriotism but just as much or more by the desire to profit from the patriotic sentiments and buying habits of the wider public, including the middle classes, who were also hungry to feel a connection with the celebrities of the day and the stirring current events surrounding them. To a significant degree this fact meant that regimes could take monarchist sentiment almost for granted and could rely on the cooperation of (partly) independent actors to publicize the displays of power and legitimation to the now-wider groups of the politically aware and participating. It also meant, however, that governments forfeited some of the control over expressions of patriotic and dynastic sentiment that they might otherwise have wished, with the result that more populist notes were sounded as well.

Spectacle and Display in the Market

Festivities such as the October Leipzig anniversary celebration in the Prater did much to commemorate the recent wars and to promote a new pacific order, but memory was shaped and contemporary history brought alive for the wider public not only in the realm of display but also in special market-driven extravaganzas already pointing toward the "spectacular realities" of the later nineteenth century. The late eighteenth and early nineteenth centuries witnessed the dramatic development of several new forms of visual entertainment for broader paying publics. Related both to the broad cultural shift toward historicism and to the growth of a politically aware reading public, these displays all aimed to use new techniques to create the illusion of reality, a "spectacular" reality. The wax museums of Philippe Curtius and his collaborator Marie Grosholtz, the future Madame Tussaud, remain the most famous example, beginning already before the Revolution in the 1770s.[2] Just before 1789, the Briton Robert Barker patented the even more spectacular "panorama" as a massive curved mural painting specially lit in a darkened room to convey the illusion of actually being on the scene with a commanding view of interesting or inspiring locales, ideally with a full 360-degree view. Panoramas often featured cityscapes of notable places, battle scenes, or sometimes beautiful or sublime landscapes.[3] In the same period, entrepreneurs spectacularized smaller-scale vistas by adding motion and action through both mechanical means and optical tricks, to yield the format known as the diorama.[4] Partly born out of the spirit of monumental stage sets for plays and above all opera—which had increasingly become as dependent on visual splash and dash as on musical bravura for its popular success—panoramas also sparked competition from theaters in return. Theater directors and stage managers at various times staged impressive displays of their own, independently of any play or opera, simply to cash in on the demand for visual spectacle as such. Like the smaller dioramas, theaters could use cleverly illuminated moving scenery and multiple translucent layers to create the dramatic illusion of motion and change over time.[5]

While there has been a tendency at the time among critical contemporaries and since among cultural historians to consider these displays pure visual pleasure and escapism, that is, as entertainment alone, political resonances were also not far to seek. It is significant that the choice of scenes often followed the siren call of current events and a desire for learning as well as pleasure, not so different from the world of print and newspapers as might at first appear. One historian has referred to panoramas as the "newsreels of the Napoleonic era."[6] The scholars of the French Institute had in 1800 already upheld the value of satisfying "curiosity" about distant places as one of the prime advantages of the new form of display, "as an object at the same time of instruction and utility."[7]

If the first successful panoramas showed the near and familiar—the cityscape of London to Londoners, and of Paris to Parisians—very soon taste turned to the excitingly distant and newsworthy. Barker had already presented British naval battles against revolutionary France to Londoners in the 1790s, and in 1800 Robert Ker Porter celebrated imperial Britain's defeat of Tipu Sultan in India the previous year with "The Great Historical Picture of the Storming of Seringapatam," printed key included. Paris twice received panorama treatment in London at the end of the Napoleonic wars, in 1814 as depicted from Montmartre, and in 1815 from the perspective of the Tuileries; the victory spirit also supported a panorama of Berlin featuring a military parade.[8] In Berlin in 1808, the artist and future architect of Berlin Karl Friedrich Schinkel exhibited the grand Panorama of Palermo, from drawings made himself on location, to give the display that added touch of verisimilitude. Schinkel and his collaborator Wilhelm Gropius, entrepreneur and owner of a small mechanical theater, also at various times offered smaller-scale illuminated scenes with moving figures, sound effects, and music, spanning locales from Cape Town to Constantinople, and from Mount Aetna to a Romantic medievalizing patriotic fantasy of a Gothic cathedral by the sea.[9]

All of these forms of spectacular representation came into play during the Vienna Congress as well, profiting from the suddenly expanded European market that had moved into town. Like London and Paris, Vienna too had its panorama. Barker's view of London stopped in Vienna on its European tour of 1799–1801, and one of its custodians, William Barton, married a local woman and stayed on in the Habsburg capital. Before long he created his own Panorama of Vienna in the Prater park—roughly six meters high and seventy-five in circumference—and sent the painting on tour in its turn, through Germany and Denmark to Amsterdam and St. Petersburg. Further successful panorama displays of Prague and Gibraltar followed, though the rotunda in the Prater had to be rebuilt after its destruction by the invading French in 1809. In April 1814, the now-widowed Therese Barton, a "pleasant, well-educated woman," launched a new enterprise, the last work of her husband, namely, a Panorama of Paris. This came mere weeks after the Allied armies and leaders entered the captured French capital, and coincidentally on the same day as news of the Allied victory made its own ceremonial entry into the Austrian capital.[10] The conjunction of entertainment, politics, and current events in such cashing in was clear enough. The proprietor chose Paris to represent in part because no other city "under the present circumstances arouses general interest in a political respect too so much as Paris," a conclusion echoed by the patriotic cultural periodical *Hesperus* in its review of the Panorama. By June, the Panorama had been made even more current, and with a stronger connection to the realm of dynastic display, as Madame Barton augmented the exhibit with the ceremonial entry of the restored Bourbon monarch Louis XVIII. Admission to the Panorama cost 2 gulden, and each visitor also received a souvenir guide, "free" of course, in the form of a colorful aquatint "topographical explanation," with the main sites listed in German and French (Figure 2.1). The price of admission would purchase about ten kilos of bread, five kilos of beef, or a meal in a restaurant, hence the Panorama represented an item of primarily middle- to upper-class consumption.[11]

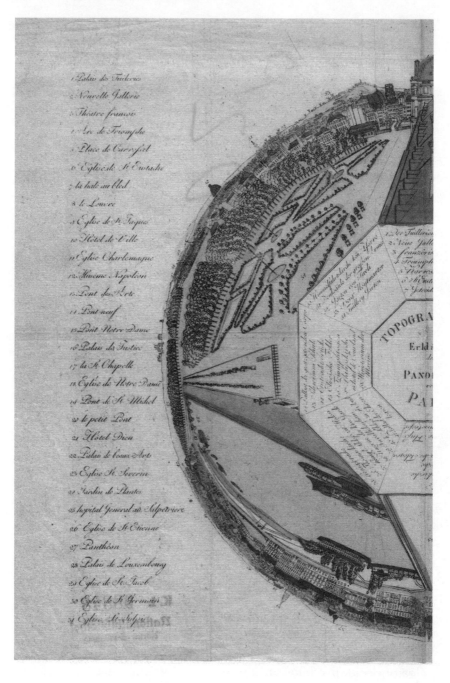

1. Palais des Tuileries
2. Nouvelle Gallerie
3. Théâtre françois
4. Arc de Triomphe
5. Place de Carrousel
6. Eglise de St. Eustache
7. la halle au bled
8. le Louvre
9. Eglise de St. Jaques
10. Hôtel de Ville
11. Eglise Charlemagne
12. Musæe Napoléon
13. Pont des Arts
14. Pont neuf
15. Pont Notre Dame
16. Palais de Justice
17. la St. Chapelle
18. Eglise de Notre Dame
19. Pont de St. Michel
20. le petit Pont
21. Hôtel Dieu
22. Palais de beaux Arts
23. Eglise St. Severin
24. Jardin de Plantes
25. hopital general dit Salpetriere
26. Eglise de St. Etienne
27. Panthéon
28. Palais de Louxembourg
29. Eglise de St. Jacob
30. Eglise de St. Germain
31. Eglise St. Sulpice

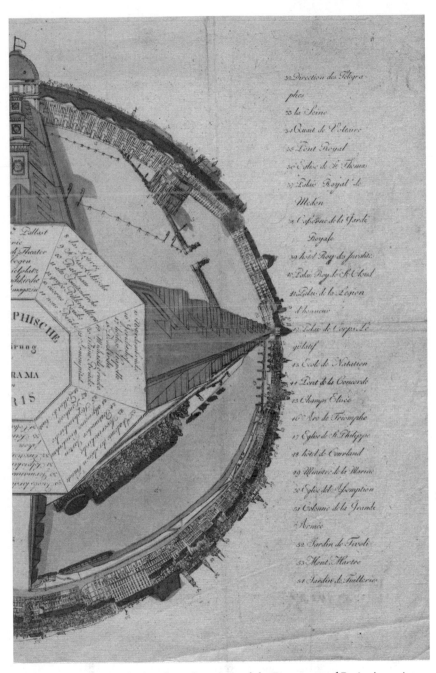

FIGURE 2.1 *Topographical Explanation of the Panorama of Paris.* Aquatint, 1814. (ÖNB/Vienna, K I 98848)

As the correspondent of the Austrian provincial paper the *Bregenz Weekly* asserted in his coverage of the Panorama, it "offers the foreigner beautiful memories, particularly through the presentation of the entry of Louis XVIII." He went on to observe with a certain dry patriotic glee: "in Paris a few years ago it was only Vienna that was on exhibit [after its capture by Napoleon]. Now the matter is reversed. One can see Paris in miniature and Vienna lifesize at just that spot."[12] The Viennese and their visitors were thus able to participate vicariously in the occupation of the French capital and to an extent reempower themselves after the double experience of French occupations of Vienna in 1805 and 1809. The North German official and writer Carl Heun also felt patriotically and historically moved by seeing the Panorama. The "illusion" proved so powerful that he found it difficult to grasp that he was seeing Paris from the Prater, and he was seized by "the great thought that Napoleon no longer has this wonderfully beautiful viewpoint [from the palace], which for the quiet, delighted viewer swells the breast with thanks and joy, such that it, in itself small, grows large and larger like the Panorama itself."[13]

In Berlin, the patriotic Christmastime dioramas of Gropius and Schinkel in their new "Mechanical Theater" likely promoted a similar reempowerment, starting with the madly successful Burning of Moscow in December 1812 and followed the next year by a depiction of the Battle of the Nations at Leipzig. In 1814 came Bonaparte on Elba; not to miss the opportunity for a sequel, Christmas 1815 saw the pair celebrate Bonaparte's second defeat with Napoleon on St. Helena.[14] An Elba display also appeared at the Cosmorama in the Parisian Palais-Royal, followed by a diorama on the same subject at Monsieur Pierre's Théâtre pittoresque et mécanique, both likely of interest to quite divergent constituencies, some harboring feelings about the isle and its new ruler very different from those in Berlin. It should be noted that a new Panorama of Vienna also featured in Paris in the autumn of 1814, but the correspondent of the *Bregenz Weekly* could have taken comfort in the thought that the selection of Vienna had a very different connotation in 1814 than in 1809. Now Congress Vienna compelled news-watchers' attention.[15]

While the Panorama of Paris invited viewers to participate in the conquest of the French capital, it is still significant that after the first two months its political tone or implications changed. Rather than depicting the Allied entry, Mrs. Barton chose to enhance the display with the return of Louis XVIII. Coming full circle on the Revolution, and to an extent showing that this was a new France that could be welcomed back into the European family of nations, this decision could only have been a hopeful sign for Talleyrand. Unlike the commemoration of Louis XVI staged by Talleyrand in January 1815, however, he had no input this time. The display's shift in political tenor must also have appealed to Metternich, as he sought to overcome the spirit of rancor and reintegrate a post-Napoleonic France into the European system. So far as one can infer from the silence in the archives, the choice was entirely the proprietor's, with an eye to the market rather than the political preferences of the government. But as in the case of Talleyrand's celebration of Louis XVI and its depiction in visual culture, one could not be sure that the intended message would be the one received. Hence in this instance, the editor of *Hesperus* approved the choice of Paris and the work's general execution, but also drew attention to the role of "this capital city of Gaul" in the "twenty-five years of suffering brought upon Europe by its unsteady inhabitants." The reconciliationist policies of Metternich and Talleyrand may ultimately have been well served by the display, but it was still an uphill struggle.[16] For those who could not catch the panorama, or who simply could not get enough of seeing representations of the French capital, a competing bas-relief model of Paris also opened in time for the Congress at the White Ox inn. It too was said "to put one right on the scene" and to "give occasion to reflections on the place where they are, and that which they see."[17]

Paris by no means proved the only attraction. Another, still more spectacular show drawing on recent historical events garnered glowing reviews, the subject in this instance nothing less than the Burning of Moscow. On display at the Kaerntner Gate Theater, the large illuminated transparency of the Russian capital's destruction in the face of Napoleon's invasion took up the entire back wall behind the stage and showed the dramatic unfolding of the scene with life-size images of the fleeing, doubtless employing all the tricks of composition, gesture, and expression from the genre of history painting to pluck the strings of viewers' emotions and shape the responses of terror and pity. The city in the background reportedly appeared "like a living, storm-tossed sea of flame" and seemed to deliver the desired dramatic effect.[18]

Like much else in this period's representational display and culture, the Moscow exhibition involved a mix of court and city or market, and marked a truly European endeavor. Its painter, Matthias Klotz, was at once a court stage painter from Munich and an entrepreneur, and the exhibit was to move on to Prague and Budapest after its timely stay in

Vienna. The Panorama of Paris, though lacking court connections, was itself a European phenomenon, as its creator, William Barton, was an Englishman, possibly working in conjunction with the Parisian panoramist Pierre Prévost, the whole being carried on by his widow and an Austrian collaborator after its first exhibition in Prague. And it too would go on tour, to St. Petersburg, with a new printed key in Russian.[19]

For those who could not tear themselves away from the idea or image of the destruction of the Russian capital and all it represented, one could get a second perspective on the event in the Optical-Mechanical Theater in the Jägerzeile. This institution featured its own version of the burning of Moscow, and in a medium that, though smaller in scale, allowed it to bowl over viewers with hundreds of colorful moving mechanical figures and scenic special effects. On a small stage like a glorified marionette theater, the audience could see and hear historic scenes unfold. The Optical-Mechanical Theater possessed the added virtue of versatility. Along with the destruction of Moscow in 1812, which sparked the German Wars of Liberation, viewers could also see representations of the Battle of the Nations at Leipzig in 1813, the Allied crossing of the Rhine at Schaffhausen, and the Allied entry into Paris at the end of March 1814. In this way they were able to march along with more or less the entire progress of recent history just as they could if they purchased a volume of prints of the dramatic moments of the Wars of Liberation. Another small "optical-mechanical theater" operated in the art gallery of Count Deym, in which for 1 gulden—half the price of the Panorama—one could witness the demolition of the bridge across the Elbe at Dresden by the retreating French, the storming of Leipzig with the three Allied monarchs at the head of their armies, and finally once again the Allied entry into Paris. Striving for what the commentator in *Hesperus* termed a "total impression" (what today might be termed virtual reality), the designers included military music and pistol fire to enhance the exhibition's multimedia and sensory effect. A reviewer, however, thought the latter simply too loud (particularly for ladies) and too smoky.[20]

Adding to the series of early "spectacular realities" surrounding the Congress, Vienna in 1814 even boasted a wax museum. Among numerous genre and mythological subjects, several portraits illustrative of current events also appeared. Emperor Franz and Empress Maria Ludovica of course headed the list, alongside Franz's daughter Marie Louise, the empress of France, her husband Napoleon, and their small

son, the ill-starred Duke of Reichstadt. A representation of the hero of
the 1809 Tyrolean uprising Andreas Hofer also featured (perhaps less
welcome to a government that had recently punished the plotters of a
new Tyrolean rebellion against the French in 1813, unless the reminder
of Austrian claims on the temporarily Bavarian territory now seemed
timely). There was also to have been one of Austria's ally the king of
Prussia, but the eyes had been ordered elsewhere and had yet to arrive,
hence the prudent decision to delay its unveiling. In July, images of
Franz, Napoleon, and an intended Alexander all fell victim to a bold
burglary, seemingly with criminal more than political motivations, wax
being a valuable commodity then.[21] Royal portraits could also enter the
realm of spectacle on the stage, in the theater, and not only in court
theaters in honor of sovereign guests on state occasions. The first act of
the oft-performed comic play *The Citizens of Vienna,* by the popular
writer and actor Adolf Bäuerle, for example, closed with a rousing "patriotic festival" featuring portraits of the three allied monarchs atop
pyramids while a "song of praise" was caroled by all. So much did the
scene and song please "the entire public" that they always demanded an
encore.[22]

As with the case of the culture of display and parades, there is considerable debate about the implications of effects-driven "spectacular realities" for society and political culture. Some scholars follow the lead of
critical theorists and Situationist Guy Debord in arguing for the mind-
numbing role of spectacle—like other forms of emerging consumer society and entertainment culture—in defusing the revolutionary potential of the crowd and deflecting it from interest or participation in
politics. Others have instead emphasized the democratizing and emancipatory potential of such forms of entertainment, particularly insofar
as they empowered spectators by allowing them individual agency in
how they interacted with the exhibits or encouraged their more active
participation as part of a collective experience.[23] As in the discussion of
festivities, the material here tends to support the latter position, a pattern visible again in surveying the wider field of political consumption.

　But the answer also depends in part on the medium and exhibit in
question. The transparency of the burning of Moscow in the Kaerntnertor Theater or the various dioramas probably did partake more of the
realm of pure passive visual spectacle, with their focus on stage effects
and stationary audiences (film might be the comparable medium
today). Yet as in the case of film, viewers could still engage in critical

commentary on the representations put before them. And such exhibits, like the other spectacles available, did at least offer the sense of witnessing and participating in the military and political events that were shaping the new century, something that set them apart from, say, the pure circus of Bach's equestrian shows in the Prater. (And to do the latter justice, even they kept somewhat current as well, with Cossack trick-riders on small Asian ponies playing to the ongoing craze for things Russian.) The artist behind the large Burning of Moscow display also allegedly used the recent luxury edition by the traveler Count Carl von Rechberg (brother of the Bavarian diplomat Count Aloys von Rechberg), with its sumptuous hand-colored illustrations of the peoples of the Russian Empire, as a guide to the depictions of figures and costumes, which may have heightened its sense of educational value as exotic ethnography and geography.[24]

Full-circle panoramas like that of Paris on the other hand increased the viewer's ability to choose his or her perspective in turning from one point to another and surveying the scene from on high. Panoramas also called on viewers' active engagement in something that could feel like good middle-class education through seeking out various points of interest using the accompanying topographic diagrams. The diagram of the Panorama of Paris in Vienna was still of the circular type, originally developed for panorama views: it showed a running silhouette of the buildings mapped onto the circumference of the page and bore numbers relating to the key of named sites (Figure 2.1). This radial style of representation emphasized the panorama's emancipatory potential precisely by highlighting the medium's novelty and the multiple perspectives to choose from as one rotated the page to reflect the changing orientation of one's body (as opposed to locking the spectator into one position outside the picture surface in the manner of classic rectilinear perspective).[25] The sense of mastery over the French capital in such a view must also, as suggested above, have proven empowering in its own way to a populace that had too often been on the receiving end of French power.

All in all, attendance at such exhibits probably expressed a level of political awareness and engagement not far short of newspaper readership. And as with comparisons between cinema and television in modern media studies, there is something to be said for the idea that in all of these spectacles people came together for a social experience of witnessing that was in its own way more political than the often private experience of reading. In an age in which alienation and the decline of civil society among those who are "bowling alone"—in Robert Putnam's phrase—have come to seem the problem, and in which debates rage about whether internet-based social media expand or reduce the range and experience of human contact, it is wise not to underestimate the social and political implications of spectacles that were still public and shared experiences.[26] Finally, all of these types of informative spectacle also promoted women's participation and helped transcend the public-private divide, as women acquired increased access to places, events, and knowledge from which they were otherwise often excluded.[27] The figures in the scenes and reviewers' commentary about the effects of noise and smoke could reinforce gender stereotypes, but on balance attendance at such spectacles offered women as well as men both educational opportunities and a measure of political engagement.

Congress Memorabilia and Markets: Prints, Music, and Material Culture

Disseminating the panoply of court and festive culture to still wider publics, beyond the thousands of spectators present to the politically aware reading publics farther afield, was always a desideratum for governments. Publications, often illustrated, of royal ceremony had been aimed at foreign rulers, courts, and elite publics for much of the early modern era as a way of impressing them with the glory and wealth of the dynasty and state in question.[28] Yet just as some recent research has questioned whether rulers and officials were truly interested in using the culture of display as a mechanism of rule, scholars have also suggested that regimes showed little inclination, and at times considerable disinclination, to draw on the new consumer culture of images and objects in order to appeal to broader publics.[29] This is on balance true, but to some extent the question did not really arise. Officials did not have to worry very much about accomplishing this goal. Even more than in the staging of festivities such as the Volksfest, entrepreneurs and other nonstate actors were only too eager to step in. A culture of what may be called political consumption was already very much in the making, and had been so since at least the period of the Seven Years War. This culture was less critical and satirical than in the print shops and window displays of London, in the tug-of-war there between government and opposition and in the conditions of a freer press, but it existed nonetheless and helped shape the landscape of political culture on the

Continent as well. And as in Britain, public opinion was its leitmotif and guiding star.

Congress celebrities and festivities received coverage first of all in the newspaper and periodical press, but just as importantly and effectively in other media as well, including prints, adulatory poems, music compositions, and commemorative objects.[30] One could see, read about, or hear echoes of the royal guests and their activities, just as one had been able to take in the events of the wars in the years preceding, through numerous newspaper accounts and books, battle prints, and battle symphonies. Each represented its own genre, with its genre-specific rules, expectations, and formulae, even for variations. Yet quite frequently the various media were combined to give a fuller and more exciting, or perhaps merely more marketable, experience. As with the spectacular realities just examined, working in multiple media and on several senses simultaneously made up part of the attraction. All the volunteerism and activity of civil society was useful and contributed to a diverse political culture, but at the same time it created potential difficulties for governments wanting to keep strict control of politics, just as similar patriotic developments had both aided and worried the British government in its efforts to mobilize the public for the fight against Napoleon.[31]

Much of the Congress-related commemorative consumption remained keyed to the presence of the various famous personalities in Vienna rather than to any specific event. This applied above all to the crowned heads, with Tsar Alexander primus inter pares. His rather rosy-cheeked face and green-uniformed bust appeared wreathed in laurel or oak on drinking glasses painted in color by Anton Kothgasser and associates in the new technique pioneered by the Mohn family of Dresden. (Previously such painting had been restricted to porcelain.) One series of glasses carried the inscription "Who here would not gladly crown Alexander with laurel? Did he not also actively help establish the peace for us? Long may he live [vivat!]" The portrait on the tumbler drew on a print from French engraver Louis de St. Aubin; another, slightly later series of glasses featured the tsar as depicted in a print of 1815 by the young Viennese Blasius Höfel, published by the Viennese house Artaria and based on a painting by the Congress portraitist Jean Isabey.[32] Alexander's purportedly well-captured visage even appeared in fine embroidery, after Madame d'Eckmann, a Swedish-born lady of Weimar, came to Vienna to ply her needle for the glorious occasion.[33] The overlapping and interchangeability of images and media—a kind of intertextuality—is already evident in the portraits of Alexander alone.

Alongside Alexander, the use of royal images on porcelain and glass extended to laurel- or oak-framed portraits of Emperor Franz of Austria and King Friedrich Wilhelm of Prussia, who appeared on various tumblers and teacups from Vienna and Berlin. Images of the three allied monarchs also graced snuffboxes and boxes in silver and iron. For the most part such images remained restricted to royal portraits, but the Austrian commander, Prince Schwarzenberg, also adorned at least one series of glasses and saucers, just as he joined the ranks among prints and medallions; the Prussians Marshal Blücher and General Bülow were also so honored.[34]

In addition to portraits, current events sometimes found representation in material culture, as in the series of painted glasses of Napoleon's final home on the island of St. Helena, produced by both Gottlob Mohn and Kothgasser after Waterloo. Kothgasser also celebrated the peace with a French-titled image in green *camaïeu* of a horse grazing and peasants plowing, and another, more dynastically patriotic, of the palm of peace of Franz I, with an eagle perched atop the globe amid other symbols of victory, Habsburg dynasticism, and divine approbation. Using a new technique of transferring prints to other surfaces, images of the battlefield map of the Battle of the Nations at Leipzig came in several series, on both glasses and porcelain teacups and saucers. Russian Cossack cavalrymen also proved a popular subject.[35]

Several series of portraits were to be had as prints, not just of the primary monarchs but of famous generals and minor rulers too. Individual portraits could be purchased for a few florins each, and developing capitalist retail techniques had already discovered the power of volume discounts to entice consumers to buy whole series. In one case, a single portrait of one of the three allied sovereigns cost 4 florins, while one could have all three for 9. In another, if one wanted a print of, say, Tsar Alexander, Empress Maria Ludovica of Austria, or Prince Metternich, then it would set one back 3 florins each (half again the price of admission to the Panorama of Paris); those willing to purchase the entire set would receive a "substantial reduction." In this series, one could even purchase the portrait of Andreas Hofer, hero of the Tyrolean uprising of 1809. Hofer, like the Prussian and Russian generals, but also like the pope, cost only 2 florins.[36] From the Saxon town of Zwickau, the publisher August Schumann (father of young Robert Schumann) linked his weekly to his portrait series the "Gallery of the most renowned princes, commanders, and statesmen of our age" in order to boost sales of both; magazine subscribers received half-price discounts on the portraits as they came out. September, for example, offered Kaiser Franz of Austria and Napoleon's Marshal Massena, at 2 groschen each for subscribers, regularly 4 (less than half a florin).[37]

In a trick dating back to the earliest days of political memorabilia in Stuart England, political portraits and scenes also appeared on brightly colored decks of playing cards. One thirty-six-card game from 1815 offered portraits of the Allied sovereigns and generals plus allegorical and battle scenes. A fifty-four-card tarot or *Tarock* deck from the following year similarly included sovereigns' portraits on the face cards as well as images from the Wars of Liberation. Sovereigns' portraits for the Congress even reached the genre of New Year's greeting cards boasting moving parts, with an entry called "The Three Monarchs."[38] The language of playing cards in turn found an echo in painted glass, with the alliance of the three eastern rulers being celebrated in coded fashion on numerous glasses as the trump of the three highest cards in the tarot deck, the sovereigns not actually appearing in portraits in this case, though an image of Austrian hero Archduke Charles leading a charge featured on card XXI, the "moon."[39]

If paper and cardboard did not satisfy the craving for celebrity souvenir likenesses and mementoes, commemorative medallions could be collected. Ludwig Heuberger did a whole series of portraits of the rulers and statesmen in Vienna, as well as of famous generals from the wars.[40] Johann Baptist Harnisch of Vienna produced a similarly impressive series in honor of the visiting royal rulers and their consorts: "Vindobonum Praesentia Ornat / Mense Octobri MDCLCXIV."[41] The engraver Joseph Lang of the imperial mint issued his own commemorative medallion for the "liberation of Germany," which featured likenesses of the three principal sovereigns.[42] Other medals were more strictly allegorical, in celebration of the peace or victory. Most appeared in the major vernacular languages—German, French, or English—appropriate to the figure and intended market, but a few were also issued in other languages, including Czech for Field Marshal Prince Schwarzenberg of the Bohemian nobility. Many medallions were still minted in Latin, harking back to the genre's classical roots and to the previous language of European diplomacy, and still able to address the classically educated elite across Europe.[43]

As was the case with festivities, court and market, older representational and newer public spheres came together in this context. Medalists typically held court appointments, but they produced sometimes for the government, sometimes on their own behalf or on commission. Similarly, the scholar and Habsburg official Josef von Sonnenfels offered his idea for a peace medallion to Kaiser Franz, but at the same time requested permission to issue it on his own behalf if the emperor declined. After a few minor alterations discussed with Metternich's Chancellery, Sonnenfels's plan was approved for official release.[44]

Like the printed portraits, medallions could usually be purchased singly or in series, to capture one's favorite, or the whole array of rulers and even statesmen on display in Vienna and definitive of European politics in the period. The kings of Denmark, Bavaria—and, notably, Saxony—could join King Friedrich Wilhelm and Emperors Franz and Alexander alongside Metternich, Castlereagh, and Wellington. As with printed portraits, the medallions too were sold in ways that reveal the developed nature of the market and capitalist practices. Medallions cost less per item when purchased in a set, more when acquired singly. One could also often purchase them in either of two or three materials from among gilt or silver-plated brass, silver, bronze, copper, tin, lead, or cast iron, with the cost calibrated to the material. The Heuberger portrait series, for example, was available in either a gilt version or painted in cold enamel on lead (Figures 2.2 and 2.3). Such material and price differentials, with the presumed intent to target different economic strata within the overall market, are hallmarks of a market-driven economy and of the creativity with which entrepreneurs attempt to exploit its possibilities.[45]

Medalists also showed entrepreneurial spirit in branching out beyond the classic commemorative medal. Some patriotic medals were made to serve as pendants for ladies' necklaces. Perhaps the most intriguing and impressive such extensions were the so-called screw medallions. Like other medallions, these objects had images and inscriptions on the obverse and reverse. "The new thing" about them, as the magazine ad for the entry into the market by Johann Endletzberger put it, was that they could also be opened to disclose a further surprise inside, in this case, engraved print portraits of the sovereigns present in Vienna. With an explanatory leaflet and carrying case, the commemorative item sold for 26 florins. They were not actually as new as claimed—"Schraubtaler" or "screw talers" had been around since the late sixteenth century (with, say, an enamel portrait inside like a locket), and some from the Seven Years War already included high-quality print inserts.[46] Johann Thomas Stettner of Nuremberg marketed a screw medallion in tin offering

FIGURE 2.2 Emperor Franz I. Medallion by Ludwig Heuberger, painted in cold enamel on brass, 55mm, 1814. (Kunsthistorisches Museum Vienna)

FIGURE 2.3 Lord Castlereagh. Medallion by Ludwig Heuberger, gilt brass, 55 mm, 1814. (Kunsthistorisches Museum Vienna)

portraits of the three allied sovereigns on the face, and on the reverse a mixed allegorical image of Germania, bearing the helm of Minerva and a spear wrapped in Germanic oak leaves. The patriotic inscription read: "Beautiful like the German oak / Green My People's Happiness." Inside the lucky buyer could reveal twelve miniature engravings of the major battles of the 1814 campaign against Napoleon, complete with descriptions and celebratory patriotic verses.[47]

Heuberger for his part offered a superficially fancier screw medallion in silver celebrating the peace and the rulers who brought it, with appropriate wreaths of laurel, oak, olive, and palm. Inside viewers found twelve cards, six with portraits of the rulers present in Vienna, six with their names, framing laurel leaves, and a star. The cardboard images in this instance come as a bit of a disappointment after the exterior, but the entry in an early collector's catalogue still described the likenesses as "beautifully illuminated and well-captured." The cards also lured clever consumers with an acrostic puzzle spelling out "UNION OF PRINCES" at one letter per card (or almost, thirteen letters on twelve cards): "F-Ü-R-St-E-N-V-E-R-E-I-N". The example of Heuberger's screw medallion in the Vienna Museum of Art History's numismatic collection adds an extra wrinkle to the marketing campaign. The original medallion contained nothing to tie it to the Vienna Congress specifically, as opposed to the peace generally. This example, however, included an extra card announcing: "Vienna glorified by their presence. 1814." Just the added inducement to purchase the medallion for those at the Congress if they had not already done so before (or perhaps even if they had).[48]

Images often involved more than simple portraits or miniature inserts designed to fit inside medallions. One of the more noted was of the "Holy Alliance," that is, the term applied to the alliance against Napoleon as such, as a sort of crusade or holy war, rather than the Holy Alliance that has gone down in history as signed by treaty in September 1815. In this watercolor representation, the three uniformed monarchs stand posed between two Doric columns, with Kaiser Franz laying his right hand upon the clasped right hands of Friedrich Wilhelm and Alexander. The latter pair gaze at one another, their eyes on an earthly plane, while the Habsburg emperor raises his on high, consecrating the bond among the three rulers, and in recognition of the ultimate source of their power, success, and legitimacy. That Franz was accorded the sacral role suggests a certain patriotic prejudice on the part of the artist or audience. Several burning hearts top the columns and make their own emotional appeal, while the flames merge into a realm of heavenly light in which laurel and floral wreaths hover above the sovereigns.[49]

As the weeks and months wore on, other, more satiric or critical images of the rulers and the Congress began to appear, for the most part from other, less strictly censored parts of Germany, or from French and British sources. How much they circulated in Vienna is difficult to say. At least a few British satiric prints made it into Metternich's official collection of Congress documents. One of these caricatures lampooned Lord Castlereagh on his return to Britain from Vienna in February 1815, prophesying a difficult reception in Parliament.[50]

A classic and much-copied German caricature of the Congress offered some colorful but rather inexpert portraits of the rulers and statesmen thronged around the negotiating table, all working—seemingly appropriately enough—beneath the scales-bearing figure of justice, except that in this case she wore no blindfold, thus robbing the Congress of any claims to impartiality (Figure 2.4).[51] More than one print satirized the negotiators' tendency to carve up countries on the map of Europe (if without the savagery of a previous caricature by Gillray of Napoleon and Pitt engaged in carving the globe like a ham) or to trade people like commodities in a triumph of interest-driven rather than rights-based politics. A print published by the London businesswoman Hannah Humphrey depicted a rather glum Duke of Wellington doing cake-cutting honors for the continental rulers as all sat on stage, "Now Performing at the Theatre Royal Europe," while the pit orchestra played "Avarice and Ambition, an Old Song to a New Tune" (Figure 2.5).[52] The little matter of Napoleon's continued proximity on the Italian island of Elba also represented a suitable subject of critical commentary in Congress prints, as with an often-reproduced and in the end not unprophetic image of Alexander, Franz, and Friedrich Wilhelm negotiating over a small table by an open window, while a diminutive but mischievous Napoleon looks on through a spyglass from his nearby islet empire.[53]

Contemporary commentary on such satiric prints is hard to find, certainly much less frequent than observations about printed matter in newspapers and pamphlets. On balance, the political caricatures tended to be critical of the Congress and its politics, whether they originated in Britain, France, or Germany, but this may simply reflect the nature of the genre. When one adds other Congress prints into the mix, above all those featuring specific festivities such as the Leipzig anniversary in the Prater, or portraits of the leading figures, then the balance swings back to the commemorative, and ultimately approving, side of the scale. In the market as well as in festivities, rulers and statesmen knew they could draw on considerable public goodwill at this moment of peacemaking, but they knew too that that public could quickly grow critical when they stepped too far outside expectations.

Commemorative culture and appeals to royal and imperial celebrity or charisma were not restricted to the visual realm. The song noted previously at the close of the play by Adolf Bäuerle formed but a minor example of a major phenomenon. In music, one could find a whole series of the tsar's supposed favorite compositions: "Favorite Dances," as played at the various official balls, a "Favorite March" (for his entry into Vienna on 25 September), and a "Favorite-Quadrille." The virtuoso pianist Tobias Haslinger for his part dedicated a fantasie for piano to both Alexander and King Friedrich Wilhelm of Prussia, but featuring a printed portrait of the former alone. The industrious poet and composer Friedrich August Kanne similarly launched a piano piece titled "The Union of Princes," dedicated to Alexander.[54] Advertisements for the favorite march appeared already on the day following the tsar's arrival, and like many of the other pieces in question, it came in several arrangements, in this instance three: one for piano, a second for flute (with optional guitar accompaniment), and a third for "Harmonie and Turkish Music," (essentially military band, for winds and brass with added percussion). Each arrangement carried a different price, piano being the most expensive. The piece, or pieces, was advertised as available in no fewer than seven of Vienna's music shops. The tune of the "Favorite March" proved so popular that it circulated through several other compositions from multiple publishers during the following months.[55] In February of the new year, a "new Alexander march" came out, again in three arrangements, this time, appropriately enough, including one for winds "and Russian music." The craze for Alexandrine marches naturally extended to the Austrian army's newly loaned and named Kaiser Alexander infantry regiment, for which Beethoven's former student Ignaz Moscheles published two marches that were performed at court festivities (plus a set of variations on the Alexander March theme). Nor did one have to be royal to receive a tribute in martial music—in honor of the Duke of Wellington's arrival in Vienna as the British representative replacing Lord Castlereagh, the tireless Kanne churned out *Wellington in Vienna, Six Triumphal Marches for Pianoforte*.[56] Beethoven had already revived his battle symphony known as

FIGURE 2.4   Caricature of the Vienna Congress. Colored print by Josef Zutz, published by
A. Tessaro, Vienna, 1815. (Anne S. K. Brown Military Collection, Brown University Library)

FIGURE 2.5 English caricature of the Vienna Congress. Colored etching by George Cruikshank, published by Hannah Humphrey, London, January 1815. (Anne S. K. Brown Military Collection, Brown University Library)

Wellington's Victory in a concert for Congress guests during the autumn, alongside his new Congress cantata *The Glorious Moment*.[57]

Notwithstanding the variety of musical forms advertised as the Russian emperor's favorites, Alexander's preferred terpsichorean exercise seems to have been the polonaise. Despite the name, this dance had a dual function in the period almost as Russian national music and official Romanov court music. It was the polonaise, rather than the waltz, that most characterized Congress ballrooms. Not surprisingly, Congress Vienna witnessed a wave of polonaise compositions and publications, with even Beethoven getting in on the act with his Opus 89 Polonaise for Piano dedicated to Tsarina Elisabeth. In this the master was joined by Johann Nepomuk Hummel, court kapellmeister Josef Eybler, Moscheles, the local violin virtuoso Josef Mayseder, Joseph Drechsler, and Johann Peter Pixis (among others).[58]

Besides music with royal associations, there were also publications of the music played at the most spectacular balls, and a selection of Allied marches for piano, two each for Russia, Prussia, and Austria and one each for several others. The British as the other member of the Quadruple Alliance might think their contribution to the cause ill-rewarded with a single entry in the collection, but perhaps this was the penalty paid in loss of popularity, given their preference for supplying the coalitions with subsidies rather than troops. Denmark and Saxony could simply be glad to find themselves counted among the Allies at all, as an advertisement of their adherence to the European cause, however late in the day it had come; on the diplomatic stage that recognition proved harder to come by.[59] With specific reference to the Congress, Joseph Huglmann produced the piano composition "Polymelos or the Musical Congress," in which "various foreign original-national songs" represented the "several different opinions" of the Congress in session. Huglmann presumably followed the Polymelos tradition of the recently deceased Munich court kapellmeister Abbé Vogler. Vogler's first such work in 1806 mixed Bavarian patriotic folk songs with Swedish, Finnish, and Venetian tunes, an "African Romance," and a Swiss herdsman's song perhaps inspired by Schiller's newest drama, *Wilhelm Tell*, which opened with such a piece.[60] Not unlike the collection of marches, in the sense of portraying a Europe of nations through characteristic national tunes, this composition went a step further in presenting the essence of the Congress as a meeting and exchange of national voices at a time of patriotic national experimentation and fervor. It also shifted the emphasis from the military realm of marches—itself newly democratized in the recent wars—to the broader populace, as represented in folk song.

The choice of sovereigns as the main subjects for marketing makes sense in several respects. First, royals still provided the prime focus or symbols of patriotic culture at the time. Artists may also have hoped to obtain payment or patronage directly from the targeted monarch, which at least in Beethoven's case actually worked, since he received some money from the tsarina. To that extent, some musical productions might have looked back to a previous patronage-driven age. By and large, though, it seems clear that the sovereigns' names and images were invoked so frequently as a means of sparking or meeting consumer demand, as part of the new market-driven artistic world. Many of the musical pieces, like adulatory poems and other dedications, were offered in a spirit of humility and "deepest respect" (to quote from the dedicatory title of the Haslinger Fantasie for the tsar and Prussian king). In this sense they came as welcome additions to the panoply of monarchical representations of power, and contributed to the general saturation of dynastic sentiment in most European political culture at the time. The culture of consumption surrounding rulers in the nineteenth century did not, however, differ entirely from celebrity culture of more modern type. The consumption of celebrity can combine a rather slavish admiration for the great, the good, and the beautiful (or at least the famous) with a certain perceived intimacy or assertive claim on them by those who read about them, or who buy the media productions and objects associated with them [61]

There were also moments when the use of monarchical celebrity could undermine or cheapen the sense of charisma. On one occasion, for example, Alexander may have received more marketing publicity than he desired. At least, two Russian officers were heard to express outrage over the fact that a pair of busts of the tsar had been placed outside a wig-maker's shop as a novel means of promoting the wares. Adulation or mockery would be difficult to decide, and perhaps it was in any case left to the individual observer to interpret in his or her own way. So long as passersby stopped, stared, and perhaps even honored the store with their patronage, the shop owner would presumably have been satisfied with the results of his or her clever advertising.[62]

While much of the memorabilia centered on the persons of those present in Vienna, Congress festivities also drew attention. Along with descriptions of festive occasions in the press and celebratory poems, depictions of festivities appeared above all in prints and music. Commemorative medallions, when they went beyond portraits, tended either to depict major victories in the campaign or to commemorate the peace itself, either in general, through pure allegory and classical allusion, or with specific reference to the treaty signed in Paris in May 1814. One of the few that celebrated the Vienna Congress was a simple *jeton* (a cheaper token or coin often used simply for tossing out in numbers on festive occasions like royal weddings), with three not entirely realistic portraits of the main allies Franz, Alexander, and Friedrich Wilhelm leaning against a document-strewn conference table, one of the three with quill poised, and all superimposed against a number of other uniformed figures representing the mixed diplomatic and military elite. The reverse, with the inscription "Foundation of the General Peace," shows a genius of peace floating above a female figure in classical robes kneeling before an allegory of Justice, bearing scales and appropriately blindfolded in this case. In the background appears a cityscape of Vienna, probably more to convey a sense of locale to faraway recipients than of civic pride to the Viennese themselves, insofar as the tower of Saint Stephen's Cathedral remains semirecognizable, but the rest is rather generalized.[63] Somewhat larger and more impressive was a medallion in gilt tin by Friedrich Stammer of Saxe-Hildburghausen.[64]

The Leipzig anniversary festival in the Prater proved the clear winner among Congress festivities in terms of commemorative cultural artifacts. Numerous prints and paintings of the event appeared, depicting the troops at their banquet tables, the sovereigns and generals riding past, the pyramids and towers of captured French weapons and insignia, or the crowds and illustrious guests in and around the Pleasure House, with its festooned banners and decorations of knightly arms and armor. Note has already been made of the emphasis on heterogeneity among the crowds, whether by class or gender. Still compelling two months on, there was even a New Year's greeting card featuring the Pleasure House as it had appeared during the festival.[65] As with many other prints from the period, the images often appeared with bilingual captions in German and French, the better to reach a wider European audience.

The Praterfest also scored at least two fairly notable musical compositions. The prolific and well-established Bohemian composer Adalbert Gyrowetz entered the fray with his *Victory and Peace Festival of the*

Allied Monarchs, a Characteristic Fantasia for Piano, which as an added bonus featured his setting of an alleged new patriotic song by Goethe honoring the day.[66] For his part, Anton Diabelli—prominent enough in his own time but more noted now as providing the inspiration and occasion for Beethoven's *Diabelli Variations* in yet another of the charitable-patriotic ventures of the period—came forth with *The 18th of October,* a "Tongemählde" or "tone painting" of the event set to a celebratory poem by the ubiquitous Kanne.[67] It was noteworthy and characteristic in its blending of monarchist and populist patriotism.

Not only the events themselves in general terms could be thus immortalized, but also specific moments, as with the tsar's jubilantly received toast to the crowds at the Leipzig anniversary banquet, engraved and provided with an accompanying doggerel-poetic recounting of the gesture in a hand-colored print.[68] Emphasizing the drama and energy of the moment, prominent clouds of bright smoke from the accompanying cannons billowed upward perpendicular to the image's main horizontal line of the pontoon bridge—thronged with tiny figures of the crowd—that had been thrown across the arm of the Danube between the two portions of the park. The effect was heightened by the depictions of arms upraised in salutes, cheers, and toasts, of waving banners, and of a rearing horse. At a moment when many rulers' and diplomats' patience with the Russian emperor was wearing thin, the crowd's acclaim and the subsequent publicity in newspapers and prints helped preserve his claims to be backed by public opinion.

Nor was Emperor Franz's role in the festival of 18 October omitted in the commemorative aftermath. His closing toast, drafted beforehand by Metternich, received all the coverage—and potential immortality—either could have desired, not just in the newspapers but also in the poem paired with Diabelli's musical portrait of the event. As the quotation read (marked allegro of course), "the eighteenth of October! May the memory of this glorious day, in a lasting peace, carry over to a distant posterity."[69] The poem even suggested that the glasses used to drink the toasts could be saved to mark the occasion: "Preserve well the consecrated tumblers, for eternal commemoration." At least according to the report of the festival in the *Friedensblätter,* many spectators intended to do so, and to have special inscriptions placed on the glasses in commemoration. It is certainly possible that one or more of the surviving glasses with the image of, say, Tsar Alexander or Kaiser Franz might have been used during the event and specially preserved in remembrance, but I do not know of any clear-cut cases.[70]

If this political and entertainment culture with its commemorative off-shoot was multimedia in the sense that its productions ran the gamut from poems and prints to medallions and tumblers, it is important to note that it was also multimedia in the sense that the individual products themselves often combined elements of different media. This has implications not only for their interpretation now but also for their production context and cultural-political functions then. One of the more remembered images of the Leipzig festival, today usually reproduced alone, actually first appeared as the title copperplate to the Steiner edition of Diabelli's *18th of October* (Figure 2.6). Not to be outdone, the Weigl publication of Gyrowetz's competing composition came "decorated with a magnificent title vignette," as the newspaper advertisement boasted (Figure 2.7). The Steiner version emphasized the massive tower of captured French arms amid the thousands of troops and spectators thronging the scene in minute array. The Weigl offering presented larger portraits of fewer individuals, and at the center of the scene placed the Pleasure House with its Habsburg pennants, decorative knights in armor, and royal spectators on the balcony, with one of the pontoon bridges fading away into the distance across the Danube arm.[71] Even the piano "Fantasie" by Tobias Haslinger in honor of Tsar Alexander and King Friedrich Wilhelm was accompanied by a "magnificent title copperplate" that displayed, according to the newspaper ad, "the well-captured portrait of His Majesty Kaiser Alexander, resting upon an idealized depiction of an altar of thanksgiving worthy of this great monarch, which in the foreground presents in bas-relief the cannon monument, and in the distance the Kremlin of Moscow, and on the side walls is decorated with trophies of victory." The inclusion of the Kremlin added that extra touch of local color, or supposed verisimilitude as to its Russian context. In keeping with good marketing strategy, this visual-aural wonder could be had for 3 florins; the print alone cost 2.[72]

One might think of such productions as the equivalent of coffee-table books for the piano, just the thing to display in the proper middle-class or even aristocratic household with pretensions to culture and to patriotism. Not all sheet music publications sported accompanying plates, not even all of those dedicated to the Congress. But many did, just as had been the case with the publications of battle music celebrating and depicting the victories of the military campaigns. Beethoven's *Battle of*

Vitoria, better known as *Wellington's Victory,* represents simply one of many during this period, and it too appeared with accompanying iconographic plate.[73] If some of this may illustrate early strivings toward the ideal of the "Gesamtkunstwerk," or "total work of art" drawing together the various art forms, most such products only achieved the status of Gesamtkitschwerk, clever perhaps but still kitsch.[74]

Whatever may be the final aesthetic judgment on such pieces (and about the battle music and patriotic music in general, musicologists have been scathing), the multiple media in which they were produced present both problems and opportunities for interpretation. Their mixed appeals to consumers, as listeners and performers, viewers and readers, mean that interpretive methods from the corresponding scholarly disciplines need to be brought to bear in order to sound their meanings fully. From a political point of view, assessing the balance of acclamatory monarchist sentiment and participatory patriotism in representations of the 18 October celebrations, for example, has to take into account the music of Diabelli, the poetry of Kanne, and the frontispiece image of the engraver and publisher. Compared to other images, or to the poetry and music with which it was paired, the print emphasizes the festival as an event of and for the army and the respectable public, with relatively less display of dynastic sentiment. Two Habsburg imperial eagles crown the smaller towers of captured arms, but the mass of the larger victory pyramid, the innumerable throng of tiny soldiers, and the larger depictions of mixed soldiers and citizens (men and women) in the foreground dominate the scene. The print in the Gyrowetz composition for the event proved somewhat more balanced in its mix of dynasty, public, and military, in harmony with the music and words.

The new publication the *Friedensblätter,* or *Pages of Peace,* itself provided an early example of multimedia marketing. As part of the subscription price, readers received periodic special inserts, a song with music and lyrics in copperplate score every month, and quarterly a print of a notable contemporary artwork.[75] The first of the latter appeared on 29 September, just in time for Congress visitors' arrival. It presented the much-talked-about patriotic genre painting of Johann Peter Krafft, *The Departure of the Militiaman,* accompanied by a long review and description of its reception by viewers at the collection of Duke Albert of Saxe-Teschen. One ten-year-old girl was said to be particularly enthralled by the painting when she saw it with her family.[76] The first of the music inserts, in July, was a romantic song-setting by Beethoven,

FIGURE 2.6   Title copperplate of Anton Diabelli, *The 18th of October*, tone portrait for piano, published by Steiner, Vienna, 1814. (ÖNB/Vienna, MS 15.638-qu.4°)

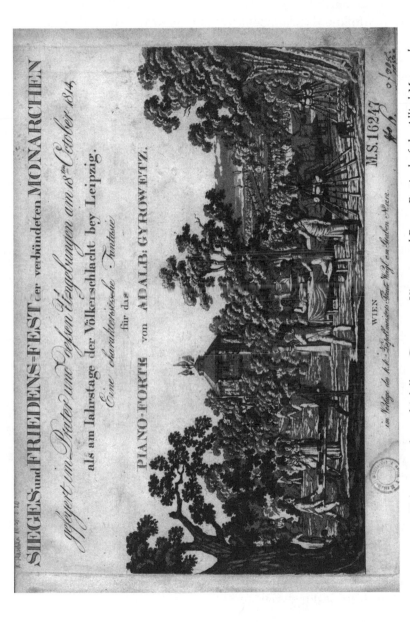

FIGURE 2.7 Title copperplate of Adalbert Gyrowetz, *Victory and Peace Festival of the Allied Monarchs*, fantasie for piano, published by Weigl, Vienna, 1814. (ÖNB Vienna, MS 16.247-qu.4°)

"To the Beloved" (An die Geliebte). The second, even more Romantic, was a poem by the Hessian diplomat, poet, and philosopher Isaac von Sinclair set to music by the indefatigable Kanne.[77] In all of this the *Friedensblätter* followed existing illustrated fashion and cultural magazines such as the *Journal des Luxus und der Moden* in Weimar, the *Journal des Dames et des Modes* in Paris, or the *Belle Assemblée* in London, but perhaps pushed the envelope in the size of the plates and the emphasis on music.

The tendency to combine media likely had something to do with the fact that publishers themselves often operated in multiple areas rather than specializing. Artaria, for example, were about equally noted as publishers of art and music (including at this time Beethoven's revised *Fidelio*); the composer Thaddäus Weigl ran a music publishing business that also issued prints. Steiner, one of the other main music publishing houses, similarly advertised itself as an "Art and Music Publisher."[78] In part, the common underlying printing techniques for prints and sheet music—copperplate engraving and lithography—explain the connection. The links also point to the existence of market incentives to pursue sales in several media, which made it easier to combine the different media in creative ways when the occasion suggested itself. Pairing an engraving with sheet music, or a poem with music, engraving, or both simply made economic sense, even as it added variety and novelty to the offerings.[79] It also, however, foreshadowed the kind of slippage of signs and meanings that characterized the multimedia world of entertainment and political culture of the later nineteenth century (or today). In the end, the multimedia dimension to Congress-era political and entertainment culture points to the nature and significance of the already well-developed market forces and entrepreneurial networks spanning the old and the new public spheres, court and city. This dimension underscores too the continuing need to bring together analyses of early nineteenth-century cultural and political productions from the several points of view of print culture, visual culture, musical culture, and material culture, which are still more often than not carried out separately, even when this entails disaggregating components of what once formed a whole. In this sense the potential value of interdisciplinarity derives not just from present-day professional concerns but also from the nature of the historical material studied.

As has become sufficiently clear, poets and composers, painters and publishers were all jostling to claim a share of the celebratory market.

The cynical would say to profit from it, yet many of the publications and public performances saw proceeds go to charitable causes, hence a certain idealism also has to be conceded. Appearing in such contexts of course provided effective advertising for one's works, and it was good to show that one's heart was in the right patriotic place, but the artists were not so different from the rest of the educated public, and their patriotism no less genuine. Beethoven, it is true, disdainfully if playfully refused the commission to do the equestrian music for the medievalizing Carousel, instead passing it on to his former student Ignaz Moscheles. But between benefit concerts and his Congress cantata, polonaise, and other tasks, Beethoven experienced no shortage of such ventures.[80] Caroline Pichler rather sheepishly confessed in late 1813 that she was overwhelmed with patriotic projects for the coming victory and peace, and that if the day of victory could be slightly delayed without injuring anyone, she would welcome the extra time. She did manage to complete most tasks, including her collaboration with the composer Louis Spohr, the singspiel *Germany Liberated* (Das befreyte Deutschland). The premiere only came over a year later, however, in a performance for the second anniversary of the Battle of Leipzig in 1815 at the "German Victory and Peace Celebration of Music" in the Thuringian town of Frankenhausen.[81]

One of the most imaginative (or desperate) efforts to capture a slice of the patriotic and festive market involved a book of chess games designed to emulate, and to celebrate, the various crucial battles of the Wars of Liberation. "It is not enough," read the notice in the *Friedensblätter*, "that the battles of the late war are described, sung, set to music, and engraved in copper, they can also be played, and to be sure in chess."[82] Games also played a more general role in the marketing of patriotic and festive goods during the Congress period. Patriotic poems, for example, might offer an acrostic puzzle; in one by a likely pseudonymous author, the capitals in the first lines graphically reveal the phrase "GOD BLESS FRANZ AND HIS HIGH ALLIES." One of the most famous visual renderings of the Leipzig anniversary festival of 18 October, for its part, included as caption the chronogram that had graced the Prater on the day, "FVIt DeCIMo oCtaVo oCToBrIs." Adding the larger capital letters as Roman numerals yields for the perspicuous observer the year of the victory, 1813 (Figure 1.2).[83]

The volunteerism, and particularly the gaming aspect of political culture, at times brought out more volunteers than governments really wanted to have, verging on cranks. One hopeful commemorator, for

example, sent a chronosticon to the Austrian emperor at Allied headquarters in late 1813. A composer of sorts, too, he also included a copy
of a song set for winds and military music, a sample from his larger
setting of the German poet Klopstock's *Hermann's Battle*, the epic
poem celebrating the victory of the Teutonic tribes under Arminius
(Hermann) over the Romans in 9 C.E. The piece received a short assessment from Deputy Court Kapellmeister Joseph Eybel, who condemned
it as "highly mediocre" and at the same time "overexcited." The poem
itself formed part of a larger wave of Arminian nationalist mythology
and spawned among others the eponymous play of Heinrich von Kleist,
much more famous than its would-be musical rival; the young Franz
Schubert also composed a bloodily patriotic lied to Klopstock's *Hermann* at this time, but it did not catch on either.[84] Another would-be
celebrant sought civic rather than imperial patronage and submitted his
own "Kronologikon" to the Vienna city magistrates with the suggestion
that it be carved in stone as a "monument" for "posterity." The document actually offered some rather lovely calligraphy, limning the names
of the three royal and imperial allies in gilt and the respective dynastic
colors, but the effect would have been difficult to capture in stone, and
the proposal went nowhere.[85]

In material and visual culture as in public display, more space for the
input of private individuals and more opportunities for customization
remained than one might think. Scholars rightly point to the different,
less nationalist and populist official tone of the Austrian war effort in
1813–1814 compared to that in 1809, when Count Stadion and assis-
tants such as Friedrich Schlegel called the German and Austrian nations to arms. When one takes the broader view of political culture and
includes voluntary patriotic productions, however, the differences become harder to discern. As seen earlier, even the specific strategy of
stimulating both ethnic-provincial and Austrian-Habsburg patriotism
found its echo in the public discourse of mobilization and celebration
in these years.[86] Not all of this nationalist symbolism and rhetoric
would have been wholly welcome to rulers and government officials in
the Habsburg realm or other states. Much of the language was traditional, adulatory, and acclamatory, no problem there, but overtones of
a more democratic or nationalist style of politics and culture also made
themselves heard. "GERMANIA," exclaimed the text to Anton Diabelli's piano tone poem celebrating the Leipzig festival of 18 October,
"soars high on wings of eagles, which, shed of their oppressive chains,
rejoice in their freedom."[87] Invocations of Germania, in the German or

even more in the multinational Habsburg context, were potentially problematic from the government point of view, as was the reference to liberty, however correct skeptical modern scholars are to note that the word in such cases pointed more to freedom from foreign powers than to individual liberties within the polity. But that forms part of the power of the language of liberty (or of other successful political languages): that it is sufficiently ambiguous, and malleable, to support a wealth of meanings in a variety of contexts. Similarly, at a time when Kaiser Franz wanted to focus on his status as emperor of Austria and rejected a return to the German crown of the Holy Roman Empire, the persistent invocations of him as "German Emperor" or "Father of the Germans" were somewhat problematic. Joseph Rossi's patriotic commemorative book itself mixed liberal and paternalist rhetoric, as he claimed: "I lay it hereby as a loyal most obedient subject at the feet of my country's prince, and as an honest citizen in the hands of my dear German countrymen." In his illuminated transparency celebrating the kaiser's return—featured as one of the work's twelve plates— the burgher-confectioner Johann Höflmayr similarly offered a life-size portrait of a stately Franz amid temple columns and laurels, but with the admonition "Rejoice ye Germans!" Even one of the Kothgasser drinking glasses with a portrait of Franz celebrated his bringing of peace with a patriotic verse that, while calling him "Austria's father" as suited his desired paternalist image, also named him "The Father of the Germans."[88]

The Congress and the Press

As readers of the notes will already have observed, the press played an important role in the marketing and commemoration, and in general the consumption and medialization, of the Congress; not for nothing have newspapers and periodicals provided much of the source material for such frequently ephemeral productions. Beyond the art and music publishing discussed above, the standard press and publishing industry constituted an even more central component of European political culture in the first part of the nineteenth century: newspapers and periodicals, pamphlets and books. It is not the purpose here to offer a history of the political press in the early Restoration period, or even of the interrelationships between the government and the press.[89] Sketching the outlines of these relationships, however, remains crucial to understanding the role of governments and public opinion in Congress politics.

The political press was also like the visual, musical, and material culture discussed above in that so much of it was not new. The scale had grown and the political and cultural languages making up its content had changed, but the genres and types of productions for the most part all had precursors. One of the most eye-opening aspects of Andreas Gestrich's account of the formation of the institutions of European public opinion in the eighteenth century was the rapidity with which they could reconstitute themselves on demand—literally on demand, as market forces and the perceived desire for news about Europe's diplomatic destiny could almost instantly produce the desired supply, and as a host of newspapers, correspondents, and pamphlets converged around the early eighteenth-century congresses on which he focuses.[90] Much the same can be seen with the Congress of Vienna. News organs specifically devoted to the event, or at least to the general issue of German and European reorganization after Napoleon, sprang up, while in even greater quantity a pamphlet literature sprouted in German, French, English, and Italian, and by no means always aimed solely at the national public reading in a particular language. The most notable periodical was the *Chronik des allgemeinen Wiener Kongresses* from southwestern Germany; the *Friedensblätter* of Vienna itself was less overtly political but still performed much cultural-political work in the context of post-Napoleonic Austria and Europe. Enhancing the cosmopolitan dimension of Congress press coverage was the continued existence of French-language newspapers outside France, not just in other Francophone lands but for example in Frankfurt, Hamburg, London, and the Netherlands.[91]

The polyglot nature of public media already points to its European dimension, but the transnational connections also extended to the press organs' content. Nothing like AP or Reuters existed in the early nineteenth century, but even without the workings of news agencies, readers still found considerable overlap in the coverage by various outlets, often verbatim. Newspapers all over Europe regularly reprinted material from their counterparts elsewhere, even when this required translation from other languages. Newspapers like the *Morning Chronicle,* the *Times,* and the *Caledonian Mercury* in Britain were filled with reports from the press in Vienna, Frankfurt, Paris, Hamburg, Brussels, and Amsterdam, while the papers in Vienna, Berlin, or Paris also incorporated material from London and from other continental sources. In this way, newspapers duplicated the European networks seen among the educated elites, indeed forming a citation network in their own right. Like other networks, they had their major hubs and minor nodes depending on how much they contributed to the overall flow of information. The *Morning Chronicle* was quoted all over Europe, including in the small Saxon weekly the *Erinnerungsblätter;* the latter was unlikely to be copied even regionally. News organs did sometimes have correspondents, usually meaning quite literally persons who happened already to reside in the city or state in question and send in occasional reports to a newspaper somewhere else (as opposed to professional journalists employed by editors). In a few cases of German newspapers, the Vienna Congress offered an exception to this rule, since two important German editors had come to Vienna in order to lobby for freedom of the press and intellectual property rights, and occasionally supplied their own papers or periodicals with reports (Carl Bertuch for the *Journal des Luxus und der Moden* and Johann Cotta for the *Morgenblatt der gebildeten Stände* and *Allgemeine Zeitung*). For the most part, though, even they operated according to business as usual in enjoying the services of other outlets and correspondents. Even Cotta's *Allgemeine Zeitung,* one of the most respected German newspapers of the period, still regularly included excerpts from other papers' coverage, including that of the *Chronik des allgemeinen Wiener Kongresses.*

Theorists of the public sphere and civil society typically emphasize these as separate from or in opposition to the state as an alternative realm of activity; civil society is in part seen as being defined by the absence of state interference, and the bourgeois public sphere as being constituted by market-driven private individuals rather than by the court officials of the older representational public sphere. But as with festivities and display, old and new public spheres, state and civil society also blended in the realm of the press. A balance prevailed between government direction of the press and the more independent type of public opinion classically associated with the public sphere and its constituent print culture. Reflecting the distinction between censorship and propaganda, governments or their agents at various times tried to win over public opinion by feeding stories to the press, writing pamphlets, supplying positive reviews of said pamphlets, or even running their own newspapers and periodicals, all of this alongside the censors' activities in keeping unwanted news and views out of the public eye.[92]

To that extent the public sphere was less free than it at first appears. At the same time, however, considerable room still remained for press freedom, and freedom of the press still often formed the Enlightenment-era ideal from which governments departed when they felt it necessary. Historians have perhaps overemphasized the restrictive hold of censorship in the period.[93] It is important to take into account the role of voluntarism, as governments could also usually count on a number of writers to defend their goals or policies of their own volition, either from conviction or from the hope of reward. Still, even those writers caught up in the government web in one way or another were often able to express independent views, sometimes to the chagrin of the very regimes for whom they sharpened their quills.[94] Given that newspaper coverage circulated from paper to paper and from country to country, governments or lobbyists could often calculatedly plant a piece in a nearer or more easily accessible newspaper in the hope that it would then be taken up elsewhere, even independently. In the summer of 1815 after the victory over Napoleon, the Hessian and Dutch delegate Hans von Gagern speculated with his superiors and with the Prussian diplomat Humboldt about the possibility of placing some well-written articles in Dutch papers in order to be picked up in England. Having been told by the Earl of Clancarty that English public opinion opposed the idea of giving the French province of Alsace to the German Confederation (a favorite plan of Gagern and other German nationalists), he began to consider ways and means of influencing that opinion.[95]

In part following Napoleonic practice, most of the major powers had their press policies well in place. Metternich had ultimate control over the *Oesterreichische Beobachter,* edited by his longtime secretary Joseph Anton Pilat, and the Austrian government also controlled the court paper the *Wiener Zeitung,* as well as having a quiet hand in supporting the *Vaterländische Blätter* (Patriotic Pages), in part a citizen initiative.[96] No statesman remained more anxious to keep tabs on or influence public opinion than Metternich. In a well-known memorandum of 1808 on the role of public opinion, Metternich had already recognized it as a force that modern, postrevolutionary governments could not ignore. Judicious government activity in the press was the necessary consequence.[97] Metternich and Pilat kept the quality of the news and writing in the *Beobachter* fairly high, partly to attract greater readership directly, but also to increase the chances that newspaper editors elsewhere would elect to reprint material and thus spread it even more widely through a sort of multiplier effect. Metternich also at times tried to influence coverage in foreign organs directly. In December 1814, for instance, upset at allegedly anti-Austrian pieces in the Frankfurt press, Metternich instructed the Habsburg representative there to pressure the mayor to control the newspapers more tightly. Just before the Congress in September, he had his ambassador in London insert an article from the *Beobachter* in one of the main London papers.[98] Metternich's concern for monitoring and if possible shaping public opinion revealed itself not just in his press policy but also in diplomatic personnel decisions—it was precisely for this reason that he persuaded Emperor Franz to appoint the talented and respected Romantic conservatives Friedrich Schlegel (former editor of the *Beobachter*) and Adam Müller to positions respectively in Frankfurt and Leipzig, two nerve centers of German publishing and culture.[99]

The French also planned early for such op-ed style propaganda. Already in October, Talleyrand was coordinating with his deputy in Paris Count Jaucourt about the line to take in foreign policy pieces in ministerial newspapers, and who might be best employed to write them.[100] Talleyrand could already count on the prominent status of Parisian journals in the international news market to ensure that his efforts at spin would find ample reward by being taken into numerous other news organs across the Continent. The renowned (and in Napoleon's day infamous) *Moniteur universel* was one of these often-cited government-influenced papers, alongside the equally well-read *Journal des débats*. Even in states where one might have expected a certain interest-driven caution about reproducing rival French accounts of the Congress, they still appeared in the papers. In December 1814, the Prussian chargé in London gave some testament to the potential influence of French press policy when he reported to Chancellor Hardenberg that French newspaper coverage might have promoted the increasingly cold and tense atmosphere among the diplomats at the Court of St. James, as its "method" was "to isolate the individual parts and gradually set them against one another." On the other hand, he consoled himself and his chief with the thought that given France's current unpopularity among "governments and peoples," French opposition to Prussian expansion might actually convince others of its "necessity for the general good."[101]

Although less well-known, the Russian government also maintained a press presence during this period. Much appeared in Russian and, like the satiric anti-Napoleonic prints, aimed at domestic public opinion. The government also, however, maintained the French-language St. Petersburg *Observateur impartial* with an eye toward the European public, and during the war they had supported a considerable German-language propaganda machine, above all through Baron Stein and his most popular author, Ernst Moritz Arndt (with editions in the tens of thousands). The celebrity playwright and Russian official August von Kotzebue also produced a German newspaper during the conflict, and afterward as Russian consul in Königsberg wrote and edited the *Patriotische Flugblätter* (under Prussian censorship at that point, and at times in feuds with Arndt).[102]

Both in the older literature and more recently, the Prussian and Bavarian governments have been particularly noted for their active propaganda, not least against each other.[103] The Prussian government actually only coordinated a "fraction" of the anti-Bavarian coverage in the German press, but Bavaria's chief minister Count Montgelas believed they lurked behind almost all of it, which in part motivated his shift to a more active press policy in an attempt to combat it.[104]

Hardenberg was an even earlier convert to the idea of press management than Metternich, showing concern for public opinion already as a provincial administrator during the 1790s, and most clearly expressing it in his famous Riga Memorandum of 1807, which helped map out the policies of the Prussian reform era after Prussia's defeat by Napoleon.[105] The Berlin papers themselves remained fairly strictly censored, and received further limitations in autumn 1814 after Hardenberg ordered them to follow the line taken in Metternich's *Oesterreichischer Beobachter* to avoid potential diplomatic upsets.[106] The Berlin *Tagesblatt der Geschichte* was at least a semiofficial organ of Hardenberg's ministry, just as the Berlin *Vossische Zeitung* represented an official court paper, and the Prussians indirectly supported the *Rheinische Merkur* of the Romantic nationalist intellectual Joseph Görres in the Prussian-administered city of Koblenz. Prussia also took an active role in the revival of the moribund Hamburg paper the *Deutsche Beobachter,* as Hardenberg's press adviser Karl Varnhagen von Ense convinced his chief and leading German publisher Johann Cotta to support the venture. The move would give Prussia a more reliable foreign outlet for ministerial views. The deal was sealed in November, with the first issue appearing on 3 January, just in time for the height of the crisis over Saxony.[107] The Prussians also directed pieces to Cotta's principal news outlet, the Augsburg *Allgemeine,* if not as frequently as Austrian police spies claimed. As might be expected from a paper published on Bavarian territory, Cotta also gave much column space to correspondents from or at least favorable to the Bavarian government. At the same time, however, in part by continuing to print Prussian and Austrian material alongside Bavarian, Cotta was able to maintain his paper's reputation as Germany's most impartial and trusted forum for political information, upholding the pluralist ideal of the public sphere.[108]

Governments did not seize every opportunity for press influence, but then, they didn't have to. In September 1814, for example, one of the editors of the new Congress-dedicated journal the *Chronik des allgemeinen Wiener Kongresses* wrote to Chancellor Hardenberg of Prussia to ask if he could supply the paper with diplomatic documents as they became available. At the same time, the editor—an official in the German state of Baden—offered that if Hardenberg would like "a particular account" of them, then all he had to do was signal. Hardenberg, however, responded that while Congress decisions would indeed be made public, he could not send along documents beforehand. Perhaps Hardenberg felt he could rely on coverage sympathetic to Prussia in any case if the journal were written in "a good spirit" as this one promised to be, or perhaps he simply remained content to focus his propaganda efforts on the authors and outlets already in his stable, and under his greater control.[109]

Battles over public opinion, played out in part in the press and in part within civil society, could also occur on smaller political scales. On 22 November, for example, Görres's nationalist *Rheinischer Merkur* ran an article surveying the Leipzig anniversary commemorations across Germany, noting that the city-state of Bremen had failed to observe the occasion and questioning its German-national credentials (it went so far as to accuse them of lingering pro-French sentiments). Bremen's Congress representative, Senator Smidt, was both outraged and worried by this bad press. Not without reason, he thought that Bremen's independent status and that of the other, increasingly anachronistic German city-states depended in part on favorable public opinion, something that could be jeopardized by such an attack in a widely read publication. In response Smidt wrote to his sister in Bremen—a member of the Bremen Women's Association, which had mostly organized the festivities that did take place—to instigate a letter-writing campaign to Görres by the women of Bremen. They were to protest their "injured honor" in the original article and underscore their German as well as Bremen town patriotism.[110] Smidt also saw to it that reports made it into the *Oesterreichische Beobachter* (edited by his friend Pilat) of how the charitable proceeds from Bremen's 18 October celebrations had gone to support German and Austrian war widows and orphans. News of Bremen's generosity toward Austrian veterans' families also appeared in the Viennese *Friedensblätter*. There it figured as proof both that the wave of patriotic sentiment from the wars did not represent a merely passing phenomenon and that "Germans increasingly begin to see one another as one people."[111]

European and particularly German governments of the early nineteenth century have a strong and deserved reputation for exercising negative censorship over the press in their lands, and for that reason I say less about it here. More important instead is to indicate the limits of such efforts. In the Habsburg lands, all sorts of publications received prepublication scrutiny by various officials and specialists for certain areas of literature. The State Chancellery under Metternich employed its censors, Baron Hager's Police Ministry had others, and, for example, the archbishop of Vienna might be requested to assess religious matter, while the Slovene Austro-Slav scholar and Court Library official Jerneij Kopitar was charged with processing Slavic literature. Recommendations for excision or revision could then be communicated to authors, or on rarer occasions an article might be rejected or a work banned entirely (preferably before but sometimes after it was already in circulation).[112] Censorship in the sense of prohibiting a text enjoyed varying success, as it sometimes proved possible for sellers and readers to circumvent official controls. The inflammatory pamphlet *Words of Encouragement before the Vienna Congress,* for example, by Baron Stein's close collaborator the radical nationalist Ernst Moritz Arndt (under the pseudonym "XYZ"), was "strictly forbidden" by the Habsburg police, who were to stop its distribution "in all possible ways" and impound the copies already in Vienna. That same month, it was nonetheless reported to be "read a great deal" there.[113]

It is also important to recognize that for all their reputation for keeping foreign (and allegedly dangerous) ideas out of the hands of potential readers within the Habsburg Empire, Austrian censors did not by any means try to keep all foreign journals and newspapers out of the country. This held even truer during the Vienna Congress, when it would have made a bad impression for visiting diplomats to have seen such obvious evidence of the censors' activity, and fear. In fact, the list of non-Austrian periodicals available from even the official channels of the Post Office was quite impressive. Political and news organs proved as diverse and as readily available as more purely cultural ones, and in fact, given the censors' tendency to focus on moral and religious concerns above political, the latter might have been the more likely targets.

Austrian politicos were reported to be getting their Congress news primarily from foreign papers, at least in part as a result of the negative censorship being practiced in not allowing the official *Wiener Zeitung* to print such stories. (Metternich's *Oesterreichischer Beobachter,* with the monopoly of Austrian coverage, was perhaps deemed too spotty, or too slanted, given that so many Austrians opposed Metternich.) The Post Office offered the conservative *Times,* the ministerial *Courier,* and the opposition *Morning Chronicle* from London, several papers in French and Italian, and nearly twenty-five journals from other German-speaking states, with a similar spread in cultural periodicals. The selection also represented the geographic and linguistic diversity of the Habsburg Empire.[114] Even in the case of the controversial *Rhenish Mercury,* published in the Prussian Rhineland and edited by the radical German nationalist Joseph Görres, the Austrians trod more carefully than one might have thought. They did not act until the Saxon crisis had almost passed in February 1815, and even then they did not place the paper under a full ban but rather took measures to keep it from the broader reading public in inns and coffeehouses. Entirely to have "suppressed individual issues at present during the Congress" would have aroused "much sensation."[115] The Bavarian government's ban on the *Rheinische Merkur* also had limited success, as apparently did those in Württemberg and Baden.[116]

Austrian censors remained to some extent caught in a feedback loop of their own making. Just before the Congress, one of the censors in Metternich's State Chancellery sent a note to the head of police, Baron Hager, complaining of problematic political articles allowed into Austrian periodicals by overly lax censors. He noted that they had already affected the public abroad and pointed to the more general problem: the "sensation" such pieces caused proved all the greater given the Habsburg monarchy's reputation for having a "very strict" censorship, whereby everyone assumed that if an article appeared in an Austrian paper, it must in some measure represent "the secret influence of the government." Since that was often not the case and articles passed through too freely—a recurrent complaint in official correspondence—the situation was potentially embarrassing or even compromising for Austrian foreign policy.[117] The Austrians, censors and diplomats alike, fell victim to their own reputation; they were too strict (thus creating the reputation) but not strict enough to live up to it. Moreover, they did not always agree about what should and should not be printed. Metternich's two main subordinates, Joseph von Hudelist and Friedrich

Gentz, for example, frequently found themselves at loggerheads over press policy, nor did the Police Ministry and the State Chancellery always coordinate smoothly.[118]

The Prussians faced similar problems with the *Rhenish Mercury*. All observers took the paper as a front for Prussian government opinion. The *Merkur* was published in Prussian-administered territory, and its editor Görres did have connections with Arndt, Stein, and to an extent with the Prussian bureaucracy. It did enjoy some protection and did promote some pro-Prussian positions, including support for Prussia's acquisition of Saxony. It was not, however, one of the organs under Hardenberg's control, and it certainly did not always present his views. Stein and Arndt themselves at times proved thorns in official Prussia's side, and some of Görres's other collaborators, such as the Hessian folklorist and legation official Jacob Grimm, were if anything anti-Prussian. But whenever the paper published something objectionable or insultingly polemical (often about Bavaria), it was Hardenberg who heard the complaints.[119] Such contretemps continued over the next year, and in fact worsened, contributing to the paper's ultimate suppression in January 1816.[120] Partly because Hardenberg believed governments were identified more closely with newspapers than with pamphlets, he made a distinction between them in censorship policy. He instructed the Prussian political censor back in Berlin to be stricter than heretofore in his oversight of Prussian newspapers, but more lenient regarding pamphlets.[121]

Talleyrand and the French faced a related difficulty, partly of their own making and partly of Napoleon's. As we have seen, Talleyrand was keen to manipulate the press when needed, hence observers at the time could not be blamed for thinking that organs such as the *Moniteur* and the *Journal des débats* represented ministerial opinion. But at other times Talleyrand was at pains to disavow certain pamphlets and articles that might plausibly have seemed to express governmental views. In February 1815, Talleyrand complained of a potentially damaging pamphlet by the French conservative Louis de Bonald, which he claimed other delegations were buying up for further distribution, rightly judging that the work could strengthen anti-French sentiment. Or, as Count Jaucourt expressed the dilemma in instructing the French ambassador in St. Petersburg to counteract some recent press coverage, now that the French government allowed more material to circulate with its newly liberalized press laws, "it is necessary that one disabuse oneself in Europe about publications of that type and that one lose the habit formed during the previous regime of regarding the language of the French newspapers as the expression of the sovereign's thoughts."[122]

Britain's government, with its well-known long-standing tradition of a freer press, usually avoided the difficulties of being held more responsible for press coverage than they in fact were.[123] Yet at the same time they encountered other problems. Government policies frequently came under more sustained attack from newspapers at home than in those of Britain's competitors abroad. And while British editors allegedly resisted manipulation by foreign powers as they did that by the British government, foreign governments still managed to slip in articles, or at least leveraged their knowledge of British public opinion to good effect in their relations with British diplomacy (as with the aforementioned ploys of Metternich and Gagern, and as occurred in the fraught negotiations over Saxony and Poland).

British diplomats, though in some ways they expressed the most concern about the influence of public opinion and were the most exposed to it, did the least of any of the major powers to try to steer it.[124] This may have been because they were the most comfortable, or at least the most resigned, to working within the framework of a modern public sphere and press. They could remain confident that certain newspapers would support the government, and that the Ministry's voice in Parliament would still be heard, just as they knew that they could not do much to stem the tide of opposition rhetoric in either Parliament or the press. They could also be fairly certain that stories from London papers of both political stripes would continue to be reprinted in newspapers abroad, hence it may have seemed superfluous to expend effort to plant their own pieces in French, Dutch, or German organs. Reliance on voluntarism and individual initiative or entrepreneurial spirit may have seemed sufficient. Hence in the end British diplomats and government figures always remained cognizant of how things would play in the press and public, but did not take such active roles, at least officially, in trying to shape the outcomes of these public debates. The campaign to abolish the African slave trade formed an exception to this rule, as we shall see.

Finally, a brief word is in order about the social breadth of the public behind the public opinion that so concerned governments. The market and audience for the political press was already rather wide by the early nineteenth century. It used to be accepted that the literacy rate in Germany circa 1800 ran perhaps 25 percent, rising to about 40 percent by

1830, and that the real reading public consisted of perhaps only about a percent of the population (on the order of three to five hundred thousand). The latter figure may still catch most of the aristocratic and bourgeois readers whom statesmen had in mind when thinking of the political public, and is itself not a small number. More recent work on readership in Germany, however, suggests that basic literacy may have exceeded 50 percent: higher in some regions, and higher for towns than country, and for men than women. When one also takes into account the practice of reading aloud—for entertainment or information—whether at home or in public places such as taverns and coffeehouses, the circle of the potentially politically aware and engaged "readers" grows still larger. In all of this, German-speaking Europe remained about on par with Britain, and somewhat ahead of French or Italian conditions.[125]

Congress sources also point to at least the perception of a fairly broad and interested reading public, reaching far down the social scale. In recounting his journey to Vienna for the Congress, the Beethoven librettist and dynastic patriotic poet Aloys Weissenbach noted the astute and well-informed political conversations among rural folk he encountered on the way, as well as in Vienna. The star-studded Viennese musical coproduction *Die gute Nachricht* (The Good News, playing on the German term for the Evangel and the good news of Napoleon's defeat) included a comic-patriotic interlude on the theme of newspapers' popularity. Seemingly everyone in town and country was hooked on newspaper reading, and the players even claimed Metternich's *Beobachter* as their "favorite newspaper."[126] For his part, the Romantic painter and sometime official Friedrich August von Klinkowström encountered an innkeeper in Saxe-Gotha who was "such an original" precisely because he had refused to open a newspaper for the last ten years, unwilling to read about Napoleon's empire. His inn formed "the center of Altenburg politics."[127]

The men of the comic play *The Citizens in Vienna* by Adolf Bäuerle kept immersed in current events and exuded patriotism, but then, the review of the play in the folksy Viennese journal the *Eipeldauer Letters* observed with some justice that it was difficult to tell whether their patriotism was being praised or lampooned. The boastfully talkative Staberl, butt of most of the jokes in Bäuerle's plays, certainly read the papers but got everything wrong, reporting at one point that the latest Congress rumor suggested that Constantinople and the Porte were to be united and that Moscow would be ceded to Russia. The wife of the more admirable straight man Redlich too complained that "the political brothers" were at their debating again regarding "the happiness of Europe," but Redlich told her to mind her tongue, "world events" were for everyone, that's why they appeared in newspapers. The above-mentioned "patriotic festival" too, with its portraits of the allied monarchs, patriotic song, and patriotic charitable collection, was apparently played quite seriously, and according to the *Eipeldauer,* to much acclaim. At another point in the play, when one of the wives said something against the war, a male character retorted that only a woman or an idiot could speak so. The women in the audience reportedly protested that equation so effectively that in subsequent performances the line was changed. In various ways publics found a voice amid consumption, including the women among them.[128]

Newspapers, like the images, objects, and entertainments examined earlier, had begun to reach ever larger publics, at least partway down the social scale. This trend gave governments more opportunities for influence, but also opened the door for the influence of broader publics on them in turn, and for the influence of the middlemen entrepreneurs, artists, composers, writers, and editors in both directions. These varied media and associated actors formed an ineluctable component of political culture in post-Napoleonic Europe.

CHAPTER THREE

Salon Networks

Metternich conceived of the Vienna Congress as "Europe without distances," and while he primarily meant the bringing together of Europe's decision-makers in one place to settle the Continent's affairs without undue delays in communication, the term also aptly caught the fact that so much of Europe's social, cultural, and political elite congregated in Vienna for the event.[1] The women, and men, who linked the capitals, spas, and cultural centers of Europe through salons, letters, and publications descended on the city in 1814 from all directions of the compass. And these representatives of European culture and society, like its diplomatic representatives, could now enter into exchanges all together, all at once, and face-to-face, rather than mediated with some lag through correspondence and print. Just as important for present purposes, the two groups, the statesmen and rulers and the *salonnières* and their guests, by no means remained separate, but rather interacted and intertwined, as the politicians participated in broader society and culture, and as the men and women of society and culture found ways and means of political participation. This fact of the salons' presence and political activities shaped the diplomacy, and also reveals much of interest about nineteenth-century Europe beyond the diplomacy.

A particularly striking feature of the Congress is how relatively rare it was that individuals met there for the first time. The Congress of Vienna was more in the nature of a class or family reunion, reacquainting those who already knew one another. Understanding how and why this was the case points toward new scholarship surrounding social networks. The European educated elite was quite literally a "small world." It was also transnational, and cosmopolitan, even as its members simultaneously belonged to different national societies. The salons of the Congress brought even closer together the already-tight linkages of the European social and political elite stretching from Russia and Sweden, through central Europe and Italy, to Paris and London. These networks and their specific hubs, the salons, played important roles in the workings of politics and the formation and perception of public opinion, just as they did in early nineteenth-century European social and cultural life. In addition, although the world of salons is often treated as wholly secular, the exploration here encompasses the dimension of religious sociability and of salons centered on a revival of Christian piety that featured prominently on the European scene during these years. These religious networks too were not only transnational in scope, but transcended confessional boundaries as well.

It may seem surprising to have to defend the notion that salons served political functions in this period, but scholarship of recent decades has tended to deny their political character or influence and instead to classify them as purely literary or cultural in nature. On the one hand salons represent in part a feminine space, and women have been thought to be almost completely confined within the domestic sphere and excluded from any public or political roles. On the other it has been argued that in order for salons to fulfill their function as a venue for the mixing of disparate social and cultural groups and views, they had to avoid talking about anything too controversial (above all politics and religion). As social systems theorist Niklas Luhmann put it, their discourse was restricted to "purpose-free interaction." Even those who highlight the existence of political salons in Germany during and after the 1790s see them coming to an end by the Wars of Liberation in 1813.[2] It is only recently that scholars such as Steven Kale have begun to stress the continued importance of salon sociability for political culture in the Restoration period.[3] As we shall see, women, despite the restrictions on them, did take on political roles, and salons served political functions. Salons provided both a venue for the peaceful if sometimes heated expression of opposing views and a space for the formation of incipient political parties in the absence of more formal institutions such as clubs. A matter of gender history as well as of women's history, the relevant social and political roles in salons were negotiated between men and women and involved contested ideals of masculine and feminine behavior, but the gender dimension also reflects a particularity of the Vienna salon scene: it was not a female preserve but featured men too as salon hosts. The shifting balance of limitations and opportunities for political women emerges clearly in the salon networks.

Networks

European salon culture and patterns of political sociability can fruitfully be analyzed as networks. Ideas about networks come in many forms, but for present purposes a division into two main types will suffice. Classical sociology tended to follow the more common usage of the term, as a chain of connected individuals held together within the broader society by ties of marriage or family, collegiality, friendship, or common belief or purpose. Such an "insider" network could be small or large, readily visible or hidden, as its members pursued their lives in connection with one another and to some extent defined against broader society. Such networks are delineated as much by whom they exclude as whom they include, and exhibit a high degree of "clustering," whereby two individuals with close ties to one another likely also share close ties with others in the group. Since the work of psychologist Stanley Milgram and sociologist Mark Granovetter, however, network analysis has incorporated the notion of "the strength of weak ties" to consider how individuals and small groups of individuals find one another, engage one another's knowledge and services, and generally navigate their social universes in ways that tie together much larger swathes of society than older notions of strongly tied networks recognized. Indeed, these so-called small-world networks have the potential to connect almost all individuals in just a few steps, anywhere in the world, and to make us all "linked," in the phrase of physicist and network theorist Albert-László Barabási. Clustering here can be much less pronounced, as the process still works so long as one group is connected to others by on average slightly more than one member. Small-world networks are consequently more inclusive than exclusive in nature. Networks among Hollywood film actors or scholarly citation networks provide two classic examples, along with the emerging world of social media on the internet. It is this second notion of network, applied to the topology or topography of the social landscape but also to the physical world, that has fueled much of the recent turn to networks and will be most invoked here, without overlooking the continued powerful effects of strong ties.[4]

The early nineteenth-century European social, cultural, and political elite constituted such a small world. For one, the eighteenth-century Republic of Letters lived on. As Marie-Claire Hoock-Demarle has shown, if anything, the web of correspondence among intellectuals grew denser after 1800.[5] I would add that it was not only letters that held the network together, but equally face-to-face encounters in Europe's salons and spas. One might have thought that the sustained disruption of the revolutionary and Napoleonic wars would have shattered the networks of the European social elite, but the opposite held true. The elites and the connections between them were knocked out of shape and displaced by the experience, but the ties often endured, and actually emerged tighter and stronger across a wider elite than before, in part the result of the elite's network structure.[6] Exiles played an important role in the process. Across Europe, from St. Petersburg to London, the well-connected Polish nobility and French émigrés helped link capital to capital, and spa to spa. A further central component of the European network, above all in Vienna, was the now somewhat rootless and wide-ranging former imperial nobility dislocated in the French invasions of the Low Countries and the German states, including the Stadions, the Pergens, and their rivals the Metternichs. And among the exiles, it was the women as much as or more than the men who helped hold the whole construction together during the decades of strain.[7]

The network of connections among Napoleonic and post-Napoleonic Europe's social, cultural, and political elite can be visualized as a web, or a net, with threads running from one person to another representing their social interactions. The strands come together at times to form clusters, or hubs, sometimes indicating the density of social ties in a certain place, or within a certain institution, or simply within a particular insider network. The strands sometimes join in bundles like cables, when multiple links stretch from one cluster to another through the density of communication between certain points. To that extent the image of a spider's web with its delicate silken threads might be replaced by that of a more robust fisherman's net. But as recent small-world network theory has emphasized, the model of a fisherman's net is itself superseded by one more like maps of airline routes or highway systems, to take account of the fact that the clusters, hubs, and links are not of the same or even similar size. Tracking the changes in concentrations does not yield a linear pattern of regular growth distributed along a bell curve but instead tends to follow a scale-free power-law or "rich-get-richer" model of expansion. In such a system, many strands never grow beyond the initial contact, while others grow out of all proportion to their competitors, becoming hubs in the truest sense of the word.[8] Geographically, in terms of the social network of the European elite, this meant that the European capitals, with their inbuilt advantages of the court-based institutions of diplomacy, salons, and the arts, tended to sit atop the social hierarchy as the biggest social hubs, facilitating the densest web of connections. Paris and Vienna occupied the summit of this network even in normal years, and of course all the more so with the massive influx of visitors in 1814. Alongside but farther down the chain of social nexuses came other capital cities such as St. Petersburg, London, and Berlin, and then Dresden, Rome, and Copenhagen, or regional centers such as Milan and Geneva, Prague and Edinburgh.[9]

Incorporating the element of cyclical time and life histories also proves important, as it allows the construction of narratives that capture the movements of individuals from one place to another, and from one social setting to another, at different points in their lives, or different stages in their lives. From such a perspective, university towns, for example, appear more important as connecting points for the life histories of members of elite networks, not just for intellectuals but also for the (usually male in this case) social and political elite generally, so many of whom matriculated at universities such as Oxford or Cambridge, Göttingen or Heidelberg, or famously in the case of diplomats, Strasbourg. These contacts contributed not only to national integration but also to transnational ties and the cosmopolitan, pan-European nature of the European elite. Metternich and his deputy Johann von Wessenberg studied at Strasbourg, as did Johann von Türckheim of Hessen-Darmstadt. Many nobles from the Russian Empire matriculated at Leiden and certain German universities, and almost all the main Russian negotiators at the Congress had attended Strasbourg.[10] With social networks, the significant point is to keep in mind the potential for continued contact and influence later in life through connections made in earlier stages of the life cycle. Nor does cyclical time matter solely in the sense of life cycles. Seasonal patterns contributed on a yearly basis to the mixing of the central European and European elites. Having come in to the capitals from their estates or their friends' estates to enjoy the courtly season, the elites then headed off again for the summer, once again to estates, or for stays in the increasingly popular and more socially mixed spa towns of Europe, Carlsbad or Bad Pyrmont, Bath or Aix-en-Provence. Carlsbad and Teplitz helped to integrate the nobility and cultural noteworthies of Bohemia, Germany, and eastern Europe all the way to Russia, even as they brought together Goethe's Weimar and the Vienna of Beethoven and Prince de Ligne.[11]

It was not simply places and institutions such as princely courts and universities that helped maintain the European network. Above all and more to the point for present purposes, it was people, women and men, connected through correspondence and travel in the world of salons. And they too can be considered in terms of clusters and hubs, insider and small-world networks. Occupying two preeminent nodal points were Madame de Staël, of Paris and Switzerland, and the Duchess of Courland and her daughters, of the Baltic nobility.[12] Through her travels alone, Staël ranged far beyond France and Geneva, encompassing Russia, Sweden, England, Italy, Poland, and German-speaking Europe, the latter most famously including seminal stays in Vienna and Weimar that spread knowledge of German Romanticism and idealist philosophy to France. Staël, however, was probably most famous for her Parisian salon (before her exile by Napoleon) and for her hospitality on her estate at Coppet near Geneva, where many of Europe's social and cultural leaders visited her. Her correspondence network was similarly prodigious. The Courlands for their part had equally peripatetic pasts and were even more regular fixtures of central European society than Staël. From St. Petersburg to Dresden and Teplitz, and from Prague to Paris, as well as on their various estates, the duchess or one or more of her daughters connected aristocrats and rulers and cultural and political figures alike. One usually thinks of Henriette Herz or Rahel Levin as Berlin *salonnières*, but it is important to remember that the Duchess of Courland also featured as a hostess on the Berlin scene when she was in residence. Even more remarkably, her precocious youngest daughter, Dorothea, maintained a separate salon in Berlin, even topping her mother's for intellectual and social diversity. More open to German Romantic currents than her mother, Dorothea also welcomed actors and astronomers as well as literati or the nobility to her establishment. The Jewish identities of Herz and Rahel helped them to translate their social marginality into a central position on the salon scene, operating in a liminal space that made it easier for noble elites to mingle with the educated middle classes, and for men and women of diverse views to come together in some neutrality. In the same way, the outsider position of the Courland ladies, mother and daughters, allowed them to entertain a more diverse, hence interesting and significant group of interlocutors than the Prussian Protestant aristocrats of the Berlin and Potsdam court elite were typically able to do.[13]

Madame de Staël was not in Vienna during the Congress, instead continuing to preside over her salon in Paris after Napoleon's downfall had allowed her to return from exile and entertain the European elite in its negotiating and celebrating there in the spring of 1814. Yet some of her correspondents did appear in Vienna for the Congress, including Talleyrand and the Prussian negotiator Wilhelm von Humboldt. The Duchess of Courland was not in Vienna either until very late in the day; like Germaine, she enjoyed a Napoleon-free Paris until forced to flee on Bonaparte's return in March 1815 during the Hundred Days. Her current lover, Talleyrand, indubitably was in Vienna, though, as were all her four daughters. Her eldest, Wilhelmine Duchess of Sagan, provided one of the most active centers of Congress political and social sociability, particularly among the Austrians. Sagan actually lived in the same building with her bitter rival the Russian Princess Catherine Bagration, a rivalry springing in part from personal considerations, as both had been lovers of Metternich, but significantly here also for political reasons, in that Bagration provided a hub for Russian sociability and supported the Russian cause at the Congress. Bagration had been a racy light of the salon scene in Dresden at the time when Metternich was ambassador to the Saxon court (from which period stemmed their liaison, and their illegitimate daughter, Clementine, somewhat brazenly named for Clemens himself). The Duchess of Courland's youngest daughter, Dorothea de Talleyrand-Périgord, put her experience as *salonnière* to effective use as hostess for her infamous in-law and the French delegation. The two middle daughters, though not noted as hostesses, featured as guests at the entertainments of their sisters and others, before and during the Congress.[14]

One could be a hub and a constitutive supporting member of the European network not just as a host but also as a guest, moving and mediating between one salon and another. The Russian diplomat from Corsica Count Pozzo di Borgo, an archenemy of Napoleon, had been a salon lion in seemingly every capital except (until recently) Paris, from St. Petersburg and London to Vienna itself. The Humboldts too occupied a prominent place in the social network, in their case not only linking the social and political elites but at the same time connecting them to Europe's dynamic intellectual and cultural forces. The Prussian second plenipotentiary, Wilhelm von Humboldt, was a scholar as well as statesman of renown, but was of course still overshadowed by his brother Alexander, famed explorer and scientist. Together and separately, Wilhelm, Alexander, and Wilhelm's intellectually gifted wife,

Caroline, graced Europe's salons from Berlin, Vienna, and Weimar to Paris, Rome, and Madame de Staël's Coppet, and indeed in Alexander's case to Washington, D.C., not to mention Wilhelm's scholarly correspondents in the United States.

To characterize the network of the early nineteenth-century European social, political, and cultural elite, it was at once more highly clustered and represented an even smaller world than one usually encounters with the small-world phenomenon. In many examples, the number of degrees of separation is not the infamous six from the parlor game or play, but more like three or four. Without actually calculating the comparable number for the networks investigated here, it is clear that they are at least as compact and densely connected as these benchmark cases. When one takes into account a hub figure such as Madame de Staël, and all of those whom she knew as correspondents or salon habitués (one degree of separation), the fraction of that elite is already impressive; add the circle of those connected to all of these contacts, and the network is already well on its way to being encompassed.

With the Courlands and Bagration, and the likes of Pozzo and Wilhelm von Humboldt in Vienna, there were plenty of points for the crystallization of social centers during the Congress, as old acquaintances were renewed and new ones formed in this coming together of European diplomatic and court society, as well as much of its cultural elite. At the same time, Vienna itself already offered some important homegrown salons of European import. The most significant was that of Fanny Arnstein, by the time of the Congress Baroness Fanny von Arnstein, after the ennoblement of her husband Nathan. From the 1780s until her death in 1819, Fanny's establishment outshone all others as the hub of Viennese society. During the Congress as well, her salon provided the preeminent venue for sociability—social, cultural, and political— for both the Viennese and the foreign visitors. This is particularly the case when one includes the salon of her sister Baroness Cäcilie Eskeles, as they worked in tandem and were often spoken of in the same breath. The Arnstein and Eskeles families formed a kind of outpost of Berlin Jewish salon society in Vienna and helped to integrate all of central European society and culture. Daughters of the Berlin financier Daniel Itzig, both Fanny and Cäcilie had married into important Jewish banking families in Vienna, and having been raised in the acculturated world of Berlin Jewish salons, set up similar establishments in their adopted home. These soon became even more popular (and glitzily opulent) than their Berlin counterparts. The arrival of Karl Varnhagen von Ense's new wife, Rahel, née Levin, in late October further strengthened the presence of Berlin Jewish salon culture at the Congress, as she soon attracted a conversational circle in Vienna much as she had famously done in Berlin before her marriage.[15]

Also important from a social but even more from a literary and cultural perspective was the salon of Caroline Pichler. More precisely, for the first half of the Congress the salon centered around both Caroline and her mother, Charlotte Greiner. Greiner had been a reader and secretary to Empress Maria Theresa and for decades had led the principal salon for Viennese literary, musical, and Enlightenment figures. Having grown up and been educated in this environment, Caroline stepped seamlessly into the role of *salonnière* herself. In January 1815, however, her mother passed away. This marked the passing of an age to some extent, but also continuity through Caroline.[16]

Like other European salons, which functioned at once to mix and to filter disparate components of society, both Pichler's and Arnstein's establishments brought together the aristocracy and the educated middle classes.[17] To those who could dress, move, and above all speak the part of a man or woman of talent and taste, even when of lower status, salon doors could stand open. Pichler catered more solidly to Viennese "second society," the minor officials and lower aristocracy plus members of the artistic and literary middle classes. This did not stop members of the imperial nobility such as Count Henrich of Stolberg-Wernigerode or Princess Elisabeth of Fürstenberg-Donaueschingen from visiting there as well during the Congress. The Arnstein salon did more to draw the Habsburg high nobility (indeed, European during the Congress) but still functioned as social mixer. As the Prussian diplomat and author Karl Varnhagen von Ense observed, most of the major diplomatic figures found their way there during the Congress "and flowed together with other elements of society in a sort of equality."[18]

Adding to the list of homegrown social venues, Countess Molly Zichy-Ferraris counted as a "power" in Viennese society and her "splendid and elegant salon" as one of the most sought-after in diplomatic circles, in which her pious and by all accounts exceptionally beautiful sister-in-law Countess Julie Zichy provided a prime attraction.[19] Metternich's cousin Flora Countess Wrbna formed another fixture of Viennese society, as did Countess Laure Fuchs. Fuchs still entertained widely across classes, while the Zichys and Wrbnas remained more exclusive in their invitations. All, however, welcomed foreign notables during the Congress, as did Prince and Princess Trauttmansdorff in the former's capacity as master of the court. These examples tend to undercut complaints by some disappointed contemporaries that the Viennese court nobility proved inhospitable to foreigners during the Congress.[20] The salon of the grande dame Countesses Hatzfeld, Pergen, and Cobenzel, however, did seem to cater primarily to the native court elite and former imperial nobility. In this more exclusive and traditional resort of Viennese high society, Countess Pergen had reportedly kept the same formal etiquette—and hours—for decades.[21]

A significant peculiarity of Viennese salons compared to those in Berlin or Paris was that males sometimes featured as the central figures. This was most famously the case with the octogenarian Prince de Ligne, who almost single-handedly connected the salon society of the Napoleonic era with that of Europe's gallant age of Boswell, Casanova, and Catherine the Great. Having fallen on hard times after the revolution, his rooms and hospitality were rather Spartan, but not less coveted for that. Two of Ligne's well-married daughters also figured in the salon (his wife was rather retiring), but even they were overshadowed by his mixed literary and military celebrity.[22] Not unlike Caroline Pichler, Friedrich and Dorothea Schlegel also kept open house evenings for those of literary, scholarly, and religious bent, an institution that drew together Romantics from all over central Europe. Friedrich the literary figure and philosopher was the more famous of the pair, but they shared the stage, and the salon was typically referred to as belonging to the Schlegels plural. Dorothea had her own past in the Berlin Jewish salon world and was a writer and translator of some renown, even if much of her work appeared anonymously or under Friedrich's name.[23]

Some of the most important venues of festive political sociability at the Congress were provided by the leading statesmen. As such they blended into the Viennese pattern of male-centered salons. Among these of course Metternich stood out, as the event's main diplomatic host behind Emperor Franz and Prince Trauttmansdorff. The Metternichs staged several extravagant balls, and held open house at least one night per week as well. Lord and Lady Castlereagh also regularly hosted Congress visitors at their apartments on the Minoritenplatz, just across from the Austrian State Chancellery and the Hofburg. Castlereagh's successor, the Duke of Wellington, on the other hand entertained less regularly than the Castlereaghs, and even when opening the English legation's doors did not always himself appear. Such relative social neglect allegedly caused his popularity to suffer in some quarters and may have hampered the English cause.[24] Count Razumovsky upheld the Russian court's representational duties with great opulence through festivities in his sumptuous suburban palace, until its devastation by fire on New Year's Eve. The Prussians Hardenberg and Humboldt frequently threw dinner parties—often for mixed company, sometimes all-male—but did not typically offer more than food and conversation for their guests' entertainment. These were neither salons nor high-society parties, but still at least served their diplomatic function.

With respect to salon leaders' gender, it is important to note that even the diplomats tended to work in cooperation with their wives or another woman to create the proper atmosphere. Eleonore Princess Metternich was by some accounts less sociable and left some of the representational duties of official life to her husband.[25] Talleyrand, however, chose his niece-in-law to preside over his household precisely because she was already so experienced and well-connected a *salonnière* on the European scene, and if he proved the prime attraction as the chief of the French delegation, Dorothea did not trail far behind as a draw. Talleyrand rightly reckoned that if the French—himself included—would be unpopular at the beginning of the Congress with anti-French sentiment running so high, Dorothea's German and eastern European connections and general popularity would stand the delegation in good stead. The fact that Dorothea's presence guaranteed entrée to her sister Wilhelmine's salon, and thereby to the very top and center of Viennese society, also formed a prime consideration. With the Castlereaghs, too, it was notable that visitors often spoke of spending the evening at Lady Castlereagh's, rather than the noble lord's.[26]

The Castlereagh salon's popularity was by no means a foregone conclusion, or at least, if predictable on grounds of diplomatic importance, its appeal at the purely social level is surprising. In their salon sociability as in many other aspects of manners and social life, the British drew considerable complaint and mockery from their continental counterparts during the Congress. British ways often did not conform to continental standards, particularly after twenty years of relative separation during the wars. London salons and parties were said to aim more at crowds than at conversation, where to achieve a "crush" was the height of social ambition. The Hungarian count Ferenc Széchényi derisively noted in his travel account that since the English speak relatively little, "a quiet gathering is proverbially called English conversation."[27] Continental salons tended to have one or two central figures—usually women, sometimes men—who set the tone and facilitated conversa-

tion, and a certain etiquette as to seating arrangements and propinquity to the *salonnière*. At both the Metternich and Talleyrand salons,
for example, this "French order ruled," and they seemed like "a small
court." Even in the less formal Arnstein salon or the more domestic
Pichler circle (where the women could sometimes be seen at their embroidery), the socializing circulated very much around the ladies of the
house.[28]

At least at first, many observers, such as the Genevan diarists Jean-
Gabriel and Anna Eynard, thought the Castlereaghs frankly impolite,
or at least too casual, concerning themselves very little with their
guests' comfort or entertainment, sometimes not even greeting them,
and not directing them to specific seats or trying to integrate them
into the various conversational groups. And Jean-Gabriel highlighted
that "groups" was in the plural, since the Castlereaghs did not attempt to lead a "general conversation" among the guests. Instead, visitors more or less distributed themselves and made their own conversations. Lady Castlereagh also tended to speak mainly with the men,
while Lord Castlereagh concentrated on the ladies. In all of this the
Castlereagh salon clearly did not follow that older model of sociability centered around a particular figure and drawing in most or all of
the guests.[29]

With time however, the pair warmed to the Castlereaghs' salon and
the manners of its hosts. For one thing, Gabriel decided that the relative
looseness might actually serve a useful function, reminding him rather
of the clubs of his native Geneva, where one might do almost as one
liked of an evening. Moreover, the casualness and simplicity of the gatherings began to appeal, reflecting perhaps the shift of tastes in this era,
from more formal eighteenth-century sociability to one freer and easier,
cozily domestic if still sharp-witted in the nineteenth-century late Enlightenment or Romantic senses.[30] In both respects, the individualist or
decentralized approach to conversation and the matter of changing
tastes, the Castlereagh salon may have pointed toward new functions
for such gatherings in the era's changing public sphere. Salon culture in
this way reflected the connection often posited between the emerging
public sphere and the growing individualism and interiority of the increasingly less status-conscious members of society. (Or, to look at it
another way, the nature of the status, and of the manners and tastes
that marked it out, was itself in flux.) This aspect of salon culture clearly
also had implications for the nature of social and political elites during
the period.

On a lesser scale, some of the other members of the diplomatic community also held open house or entertained regularly. The Princess of Fürstenberg-Donaueschingen provided a gathering point for the high imperial nobility plus the representatives of the smaller German states, the latter of whom above all availed themselves of the hospitality of Baron Gagern, representative of both the German Duchy of Nassau and the new King Willem of the Netherlands. Some of the groups' actual political meetings took place in their residences, but the assemblies were not always political in nature. Having astutely acquired a Parisian chef and a cellar of good Rhenish wine, Gagern further ensured his popularity by hosting regular balls and soirées. During Lent, Baron Gagern raised a few eyebrows by continuing to offer dancing to any Protestants who were so inclined (the pious Viennese, as good Catholics, left off such diversion during that period). The princess also kept a sociable circle, with occasional musical evenings.[31] The Eynards, too, maintained a small-scale salon with regular visitors, including the Russian diplomats Pozzo di Borgo and Capodistrias as well as the future French prime minister the Duke de Richelieu, a friend of Anna's uncle, the Genevan delegate Charles Pictet de Rochemont. It was significantly the junior Eynards rather than the uncle who provided the social center, not just through Gabriel's wealth but also owing to the beauty, musical talents, and precocious intelligence of his wife. The Stourdza family, and above all the daughter of the house, the tsarina's lady-in-waiting Roxandra, for their part kept a salon accommodating the Greeks in town for the Congress.[32]

Two of Metternich's subordinates also kept socially active as hosts (and guests), thus extending his ministry's possibilities for political influence. Most noted, the conservative publicist and secretary to the Congress Friedrich Gentz lived up to his expensive and epicurean (even sybaritic) reputation and hosted numerous select gatherings and dinners in his cramped but luxurious quarters. The conversation and the chance to hear of political developments from one of Europe's best informed provided the main attractions, but Gentz's employment of a noted French chef certainly aided his popularity. The home of Gentz's colleague and friend Anton Pilat, Metternich's secretary and editor of the semiofficial newspaper the *Austrian Observer,* also proved a popular destination. Diplomats liked to drop by his home office to discover the latest news from his collection of European newspapers, but he and his wife additionally maintained a significant salon appealing to Viennese literary and artistic circles as well as to the diplomatic community. Pilat's wife, Elisabeth, née Mengershagen, was sister-in-law of the North German Romantic artist Friedrich von Klinkowström, and it was the joint efforts of the Pilats and the Klinkowströms that ensured the salon's success at these different levels.[33]

Senator Johann Smidt of Bremen, his wife Wilhelmine, and their eldest daughter Hanne maintained another small sociable circle, holding open house frequently if irregularly. Smidt had formed part of the diplomatic community trailing in the wake of the Allied armies all the way to Paris in the spring of 1814, but at that point he had been alone; with his wife accompanying him, the possibilities for hospitality and networking expanded. As one historian characterized the Smidts' activity, "diplomacy for the delegate from Bremen was a political business, which found its backing in the private realm."[34] The pair entertained first and foremost the delegates of the other Hanseatic towns, but other German-speakers from the smaller delegations also found their way there, including the folklorist Jacob Grimm. Senator Hach of Lübeck's attendance may have had as much to do with personal as with political inclinations. The domestic, family atmosphere of the Smidt establishment appealed strongly to him, as he had been forced to leave his wife behind and missed her greatly. Nor did the Smidts' hospitality hinder their ability to take advantage of the rest of the Congress social scene; singly or together they were frequent guests of the Pilats, the Schlegels, and even of Fanny Arnstein and the Metternichs, higher up the social scale.

Salons and Politics in Congress Vienna

According to standard historical accounts, the revolutionary age and nineteenth century were characterized by the exclusion of women from public life, as politics moved into increasingly all-male social spaces like parties and clubs, and (liberal) political ideologies became predicated on the separation of the masculine public sphere of rights and freedoms from the private sphere of feminine domesticity and patriarchal power.[35] As the Congress experience illustrates, women certainly felt the constraints of a patriarchal society, yet the possibilities for public and even political engagement remained considerable, in part because women proved accomplished at circumventing the constraints, and in part because the constraints and male attitudes generally were themselves not as consistently repressive as often thought. Women's political roles required negotiation, but women could and did take up positions in post-Napoleonic political culture.[36]

Perhaps no one captured the nature of the dilemma, and the ambivalence, better than Hedwig Staegemann, the precocious teenage daughter of the Prussian official Friedrich Staegemann and of the *salonnière* Elisabeth Staegemann (née Fischer, but more famous as hostess under her previous married name of Graun). Hedwig felt called to a life more public, something beyond the walls of the domestic circle, and she knew it was not nature but nurture that stood in her way. Yet at the same time she knew that she was in part what her education had made her, and that she therefore also shrank from the calling she felt so strongly. During the period in 1813 when her slightly older brother patriotically reported for the new Prussian militia, she cried out in her diary: "I—O truly, women are not suited to these times! They are suited, but they are made unsuited. Why is everything that ennobles humans stolen from us? The soft education of the female sex makes their spirit as undecided, wavering, and weak as their body." In contrast to the "heroic sphere" open to men, women were only allowed to concern themselves with "monstrosities of fashion" and "the trivialities of life." For Hedwig, "*My* heart rises up against this. It hammers and pounds forcefully and wants to fly boldly out of this petty sphere!" Like many women of the era, she did what she could to overcome those limits. She dove into patriotic German culture, and began to write patriotic poetry in support of the war. The latter was probably not meant to be published, but in the end some was, at first by accident, and then once it became known, at her father's request. (Though most famed as a writer of war poems, in 1815 he was too occupied with diplomatic duties to devote much time to composing new ones for the coming campaign against Napoleon.) Eventually Hedwig became a *salonnière* in her own right.[37]

There were fewer complaints about the involvement of women in politics than one might have expected. There was instead a division of opinion. Heinrich von Treitschke's invective against salon culture at the Congress of Vienna as the "original sin" of diplomacy might have been par for the course in the Victorian era, but it would have stood out in that of the Congress itself, where the political roles of salons, and women, were simply too firmly inscribed in the rules of the game.[38] Acid complaints could certainly be heard about specific instances of women in politics, but this usually had to do with the possible role of amorous relationships, or a position of too great trust reposed by a certain statesman in a certain lady. In that respect the criticism was not so different from that leveled at court favorites or collaborators in the ministerial bureaus, with the sex of the unwelcome interferer less germane. Hardenberg, for instance, had recently been forced to distance himself from his relationship with Amalie Beguelin in Berlin as a result of pressure at court.[39] Similar critique dogged Metternich. Even his subordinate Friedrich Gentz, though he too admired the Duchess of Sagan, complained of how the minister's unhappy love for the *salonnière* led to neglect of business. He had much company in this view, though as so often there were contrasting opinions as well. None other than Emperor Franz had jokingly requested Metternich to make sure that the duchess would be in Vienna, as she was "one of the Congress's most necessary ingredients!"[40]

Back in Berlin, Johann Peter Ancillon, conservative political theorist and former tutor of the Prussian crown prince, was one of the exceptions. Along with the "praetorian spirit of the armies" and the boldness of radical writers, Ancillon included in his list of causes of the spread of unsound political views "the unquiet vanity of ladies, their influence on the opinions of the day, their ever-growing temerity in judging things they do not understand."[41] Closer to Vienna, Baron Karl von Nostitz had little good to say of the Courland ladies' involvement in a masculine world: "now womanly, now manly, now political, now sentimental, now a bit too pious, now frivolous again." And in his critique of the settlement regarding Saxony, he complained of shortsightedness and intrigue, whose "origin lies in our social dealings, in association with women."[42] With Nostitz, at least, the critique might come from the personal realm, the dislike from discomfort; an army officer from a relatively poor noble family, he confessed in his memoirs that he never acquired the "worldly tone" in high society that made one at home in salons. He never felt at ease in the company of women, but rather self-conscious and as if one "loses all freedom of one's own movement" when seemingly under their watchful gaze.[43] Probably the most critical of the major political figures in Vienna was the irascible former Prussian chancellor and current advisor of Tsar Alexander Baron Karl vom Stein, who felt both uncomfortable and irritated at having to circulate in Vienna's high society and political salons and tried when he could to avoid it. Salons may have helped facilitate political communication, but they also promoted "indiscretions," brought together "intriguers," and in general had a "pernicious influence on affairs," at the same time that the politicization undermined the pleasure of salon sociability. Stein was by no means so out of his element as the soldier Nostitz in this milieu, and in fact he relished the atmosphere in the salons of his quasi-patronesses in St. Petersburg, the Russian Princesses Volkonskaia, and regretted it when they left Vienna to return to the motherland.[44]

With more specific political reference, Metternich's chief official, Joseph von Hudelist, denounced the Viennese ladies who during the Wars of Liberation had placed themselves in the vanguard of the anti-Napoleonic war party. Yet even in this case, it was their political views rather than their political involvement that roused his ire, and men who similarly preached the impossibility of peace with Napoleon came off no more lightly.[45] During the Congress itself, Habsburg police spies reported grumblings about some of the political *salonnières*, but here too more against those who seemed to engage in anti-Austrian politics, such as the Russian Princess Bagration (whose sometimes daring behavior and attire also had the distinction of outraging the morality of even that relatively lax time and place). The ladies of the circle around the Countesses Pergen, Hatzfeld, and Cobenzel who nurtured the opposition to the currently unpopular Prince Metternich, on the other hand, even found some sympathy.[46]

Women could also sometimes be critical of political women and of salons' political tone. Baroness Montet complained of hearing too much politics and above all too much military talk in Viennese society during the Wars of Liberation, with women and clergymen the most "bloodthirsty" of the lot. In a letter to her husband Wilhelm, the Prussian second plenipotentiary, Caroline von Humboldt mocked Baroness Lisette von der Reck for alleged political pontification and for her efforts to get Caroline to pass along advice to Wilhelm, writing: "she looks like the whole Congress in corpore."[47] Even young Hedwig Staegemann, though longing for a wider patriotic role in public life, still censured her fellow females at times for what she thought ill-considered political views. At least with Humboldt and Staegemann, though, the subtext was not that women and politics should not mix, but that they sometimes did so in ways that were found misinformed, ineffective, or unpleasant.[48]

From various perspectives then, there were murmurings of discontent about salons and political women, sometimes out of conviction, at others as an argument to be drawn upon in opposition to politics of which one disapproved. On balance, however, salons and women held a recognized place in contemporary political culture. Many important statesmen remained perfectly open to women's involvement in politics, if often with certain limits. These men frequently had political confidantes—sometimes their wives, sometimes lovers or friends—and were very much at home in political salons. Talleyrand was notorious for the bevy of political women around him at any given time, from his niece by marriage Dorothea during the Congress to her mother, Anne, Duchess of Courland (also his lover), and several other friends such as Madame Vaudémont back in Paris. He was even at times willing to share the stage with Madame de Staël. Prince Hardenberg's close relationship with the political *salonnière* Amalie von Beguelin and her husband has already been mentioned, and he also corresponded on political matters with Princess Marianne, wife of Prince Wilhelm of Prussia. As he wrote to her from Vienna in the wake of a temporary disagreement over the treatment of the king of Saxony: "you term it condescension that one converses with you of public affairs. Truly a lovely but groundless modesty. Wise and brilliant ladies such as Your Royal Highness are often better politicians than most men; I wish to speak with you about the most important things!" In addition to explaining further his position on Saxony, he enclosed a pamphlet on the subject from among those composed for public consumption by his delegated authors. Princess Marianne had previously sent Hardenberg a pamphlet on the German constitution, which he felt compelled to counter at some length in defense of estates-based constitutions.[49]

The conservative publicist and statesman Friedrich Gentz claimed to have learned much from some of Vienna's political *salonnières,* including Princess Bagration, Countess Wrbna, and Metternich's flame the Duchess of Sagan.[50] The Austrian second plenipotentiary at the Congress, Baron Johann von Wessenberg, was if not a salon lion then at least quite at home in that milieu. In Napoleonic Paris he had admired Madame de Staël's political salon as well as Talleyrand's confidante Madame Vaudémont; during the Directory he had been a devotee of Madame Tallien's famed establishment. Wessenberg likewise criticized the lack of salons and "the subordinate rank taken by women in society" in Britain, particularly the "barbaric custom" of having the women leave the table before serving the port.[51]

As for the Prussian Humboldt and the Russian head of the Foreign Ministry, Count Nesselrode, it was first and foremost their wives with whom they discussed and corresponded about political matters. Caroline back in Berlin was even more patriotically German—and Prussian—than Wilhelm, which occasionally led to tension between them. Countess Marie Nesselrode (née Princess Guriev) was dissuaded from actually joining her husband at headquarters during the campaign against Napoleon but still followed behind the armies. And like Caroline von Humboldt and Staegemann's wife, Elisabeth, Marie could be depended on to send her husband the latest intelligence regarding public opinion or political and military affairs, and sometimes offered firm advice as well, as for example her adamant warning not to trust Metternich. Nesselrode always listened and sometimes solicited such news, but at least in the latter instance did not heed her; he was notoriously the Russian statesman most under the influence of Metternich and Gentz, with whom he maintained a personal correspondence.[52]

The cases of Humboldt and Metternich prove particularly illustrative of both the acceptance of women as political persons and the limits to this role, in part because they made explicit in their correspondence what elsewhere went unstated. Neither was among the very few male (or female) voices at the time who thought of women as potential fully rights-bearing and participating citizens of the modern state, and neither thought of women as potentially holding office and making political decisions. Humboldt still, however, felt a need to consult his wife Caroline on politics, and in general he believed women had much to contribute to political judgment. As Humboldt explained in a letter to Caroline, "the advice of women is like a guiding star through the desert of life. It shows the direction. How one should accomplish it . . . is left to one's own industry." Humboldt claimed not to like it when women concerned themselves with the details of policy "implementation," but to pronounce on the "meaning and spirit" of affairs was something else. It was only down to the "miserable arrogance and light-mindedness of men," he wrote, that women were not consulted more in politics, something he found "very un-German," since "in Germany's best times it was always different."[53]

Metternich for his part welcomed the Duchess of Sagan's efforts to organize treatment for the wounded during the wars against Napoleon, even where she requested his intervention with the military authorities— charitable work generally and above all nursing was always the most readily available and approved avenue for patriotic public engagement by women during the wars. At the same time, he complained of a political letter from his former lover Princess Bagration, and told Sagan herself, "I would not love you if you did not feel warmly the interests of humanity inseparable from those of empires, and I would love you a little less still if you were political."[54] The duchess thereafter felt the need to soften her political commentary with humorous or apologetic framing, which drew forth a clarification from her correspondent. "I do not love political women," he wrote, "as estate, as profession, but I certainly permit you to do politics as with nursing, as you would write a song, as you love me."[55] Metternich drew the line, in other words, between a woman's making politics her prime vocation, as opposed to one of the avocations appertaining to an aristocratic lifestyle. Wilhelmine expressly did not immediately take Metternich up on his patronizing permission to "talk politics," but after several occasions where Metternich directly sought her opinion she did so, partly reinforcing his peace-first policy but also nudging him in the direction of contemplating continuation of the war if it meant the fall (and preferably death) of Napoleon and a Bourbon restoration.[56]

Something similar seems to have gone on in the relationship between Friedrich and Elisabeth Staegemann. Several years before the Congress, Staegemann had impoliticly commented in a letter to his wife: "of political things I write nothing, since you understand nothing of it." Elisabeth responded that when she had read his letter to some of her circle, "it hurt me all the more that you deny me all participation in politics, whereby I am cast in a bad light among all true patriots." A few months later Elisabeth still gently and humorously prodded her husband to write more to her of current events: "I don't think you suspect me of being gabby, when even with me you have still up to now not entrusted anything to me. A proof that you are not so good a husband as El Cid—or have less trust in me than he in his Ximene."[57] By the time of the Congress, the pair stood on a more confidential footing regarding politics; Elisabeth was kept well-informed by her husband and offered opinions in turn. She still, however, took care to cushion her interventions. Commenting on Prussian policy toward the king of Saxony, she prefaced her remarks with "I don't want to say anything inapt," and concluded, "however, perhaps I'm speaking about this as a blind person about color."[58]

In the Humboldts' case, it seems that in this as in other respects the two considered themselves equals, expressing their opinions, adjusting their views, and agreeing to disagree where fuller agreement proved impossible. This represented the exception in the period's gender relations rather than the rule. For Metternich and Wilhelmine, as for the Staegemanns and likely many others, the balance of political exchange and gender roles itself remained a matter for careful, sometimes ticklish negotiations.

Having established the restricted yet substantial parameters for elite women's participation in politics, we can now examine the role of politics in the salon society that women did so much to shape. For the chief diplomatic salons, it needs little demonstration that they were in part political in character, and that much politics was discussed there. Not unlike with visits to court, guests of the Metternichs and Castlereaghs attended for entertainment and conversation, but also to sift the grist from the rumor mill, to assess the facial expressions and body language of the main diplomatic actors, and to exchange views. Yet politics also percolated in many of the more social or literary salons. That politics constituted an important part of the broader salon scene is quickly shown; the specific ways in which salons functioned within political and diplomatic culture on the other hand merit extra attention.

Salon sociability and networks contributed two main mechanisms to the world of international relations. First, salons provided a relatively informal and neutral space in which diplomats and other politically interested parties could meet and exchange views. And second, salons functioned alongside the press and print culture as a primary vector of public opinion, important both in the formation of public opinion amid the cacophony of voices and as a weathervane of public opinion for those attempting to read it. Government actors proved active at both levels, contributing their voices to influence the direction of opinion and keeping an ear cocked to catch the latest trends. As a historian of the Congress suggested, salons performed some of the functions of what would later become the press conference.[59] In each respect though, salons as an institution of political culture also allowed members of the public beyond government circles opportunities for political participation, whether following or shaping public opinion, or turning its gentle but persistent force to put pressure directly on the decision-makers in their midst.

Concerning the first mechanism, salons worked both to promote exchanges among diplomats and lobbyists of varying descriptions and to serve as clearinghouses of information. Both functions proved particularly important for representatives of the lesser powers, for whom the salons' open spaces and lesser degree of formality and hierarchy might offer their best chance of a stray word with someone important. These representatives also made efforts to meet the power-broker statesmen or rulers in their cabinets during the daytime, but the wait was typically long, and often fruitless, as the door might remain closed to smaller fry. Even the Danish foreign minister and Cardinal Consalvi of the Vatican could not count on being received; still more frequently did the delegates from Geneva or representatives of smaller German states or the former imperial nobility find doors unyielding.[60] Salon sociability at least offered another opportunity for exchange, as when Consalvi cornered Castlereagh in a window embrasure at one of the noble lord's open houses for some intense questioning that prompted Castlereagh to throw up his hands and laughingly exclaim "You're trying to catechize me!" It also offered a cultural space in which women could intervene, if modestly, as at a ball when young Anna Eynard put in a plea with the king of Prussia to look after the interests of her native Geneva. Or in a revealing episode from the height of the crisis over Poland and Saxony, Anna witnessed three of the competing principals, Metternich, Castlereagh, and Nesselrode, singing together in perfect harmony as part of the evening's amusement. With false innocence she asked anxiously whether that harmony was genuine ["juste"] and a good omen. Everyone present got the allusion and laughed, but none dared continue the joke. At that moment there would have been little positive to report.[61]

Salons also offered the best means of intelligence gathering (or rumor collecting). In between the rare meetings with major statesmen, minor representatives could pursue news of the latest developments in multiple locations almost every evening. The process often proved frustrating, as the quality and accuracy of the information was uneven at best, but it at least gave delegates some orientation and something to report back to their rulers. While this clearinghouse function of salon culture perhaps played a greater role for representatives of smaller states, it remained significant for those of the Great Powers as well. This held above all for Talleyrand, insofar as France occupied an anomalous position as a partly acknowledged Great Power that until January 1815 was still excluded from the highest-level negotiations. Whatever contacts or information Talleyrand and the French delegates could draw to or from their own salon weighed heavily, and all of the French diplomats from Talleyrand down plumbed the entertainments at other establishments as well. Talleyrand did not attend the Leipzig anniversary celebration on 18 October, but he did join the evening festivities at Metternich's villa, partly to seek out Emperor Franz (with whom Castlereagh spoke there as well).[62] The other main players also made use of such opportunities at social events, where discussions could be carried on with less formality than at actual conferences. On at least one evening Tsar Alexander found occasion to buttonhole the Prussian Humboldt at Princess Bagration's and drag him off into her boudoir for a more private conference. And Metternich himself used the occasion of an evening at the Duchess of Sagan's to pass Talleyrand a copy of a diplomatic note.[63]

Salons, however, assumed as much or more importance and influence through their role in the formation and evaluation of public opinion. Moreover, it is in this area that the experience of salon culture at the Vienna Congress has most to contribute to broader debates about the nature of salons and the roles of women in political culture, between the domestic and the public spheres. A defining characteristic of a properly functioning public sphere in some models is that it offer a neutral space for the encounter of diverse opinions leading toward areas of agreement, preferably in the spirit of reasoned debate among interlocutors with equality of access. For the eighteenth-century Enlightenment, salons have often been identified as among the most important such open arenas, alongside or even above the press. That women presided in salons helped to moderate the tone of discussion there sufficiently for disputation to take place in relative calm and for reasoned political discussion of a sort to occur that might not have been possible elsewhere. Certainly a more civil or polite form of discourse was practiced there than in the realm of print, which maintained its early modern polemical venom well into the nineteenth century.

An alternative view of salons considers them to be not so unlike the world of newspapers or political clubs, whereby gatherings tended to take on a partisan character in accord with the views of the host or hostess and her selected or self-selecting guests. An Enlightenment salon in Paris or Geneva might still incorporate differences of opinion on many questions, but seen from another perspective, one can still speak of "the party of Enlightenment" and of the groups who tended to support it against opposing government or religious factions. Or in the German context, some salons took up the cudgels for Romantic art and literature as against those who remained true to academic and neoclassical traditions. Even more in Britain, hostesses' assemblies could take on party-political overtones, less so than the all-male clubs like the Tory White's and the Whiggish Brooks's on St. James Street, but noted all the same. During the wars against Napoleon, the political and partisan character of gatherings in many combatant countries was ratcheted up, not least in central Europe, from Vienna to Berlin.

The two views of salons both find some basis in explanations from network studies. The more partisan type of sociability points to the formation and action of insider networks, the relatively tightly bound communities of the like-minded bent on cooperation toward some end. The salon as relatively open space for exchange suggests rather the looser and more flexible structure of small-world networks drawing adherents of many cultural, political, and indeed religious persuasions. The patterns of salon sociability at the Vienna Congress suggest that both processes were active, not just in different and differing salons, but as different aspects of the same salons. Historian Petra Wilhelmy has argued that tolerant openness was an essential criterion of salons and that even political salons were not "party central."[64] This is true to an extent, but the Vienna experience suggests that understanding salons' role in political culture requires recognition of the degree to which they could be both at once.

Many Congress salons did cater to a certain clientele, be it national or political, and were understood to do so by contemporaries. As Habsburg police spies noted, Princess Bagration's salon functioned as a hub for the Russian contingent in Vienna, and to an extent for their allies the Prussians, while the Duchess of Sagan attracted a more Austrian set. Fanny Arnstein and Madame Eskeles provided the center of social life for the Prussians, while Talleyrand and Dorothea did the same for the French. In each case, the salon was not simply a social club or resort, but a hive of political opinion and discussion. The same held true for other groups. The Princess of Fürstenberg-Donaueschingen and Baron Gagern gathered and mobilized the former imperial nobility and the representatives of the smaller German states. The teas of Countess Stadion and the related coterie of the grande dame Countesses Pergen, Hatzfeld, and Cobenzel provided a forum for anti-Metternich sentiment.[65] Similarly on the other side, the salons of Metternich's cousin Countess Flora Wrbna and of Countess Laure Fuchs provided social support for Metternich's defenders, as to an extent did the splendid circle around the Hungarian magnates the Zichys, Molly, Julie, and Carl.

Even some of the supposedly more purely literary or cultural salons reveal a political, and partisan, profile when examined more closely. This held not only for the Arnstein milieu, with their Prussian background and connections. Like the Arnsteins, Caroline Pichler had in previous years assembled many of the most virulent members of the anti-Napoleonic war party. The historian and publicist Baron Joseph von Hormayr was already a fixture of her salon at the time of his joint efforts with Archduke Johann of Austria to instigate a rebellion in Tyrol against its new overlords and Napoleonic allies the Bavarians. When the Austrian government moved to forestall the plotters, Hormayr was put under arrest in internal exile, but Hormayr and Pichler continued to correspond. Like Hormayr, Pichler also turned her pen and authorial renown to patriotic political purposes, with inspiring historical plays such as *Heinrich von Hohenstaufen,* and essays such as her piece in support of the Landwehr militia and its ideal of the soldier-citizen wielding sword and plow like the ancient Teutons: "On the Popular Expression in our Language: A Whole Man." Caroline also worked in the genre of celebratory poetry, collaborating for instance in 1814 with the composer Louis Spohr on the singspiel *Germany Delivered.*[66] We have seen Pichler's efforts to use the occasion of the grand medievalizing Carousel to promote her campaign for a German national costume. Her friends and colleagues Friedrich and Dorothea Schlegel too exhibited political activity, as stalwarts of the anti-French and German nationalist party during the wars, and proponents of Catholic revival politics—and Jewish emancipation—during the Congress.

All of this stress on the partisan political nature of salons may make it seem as if these institutions violated that other main criterion of salon culture, namely, their function as a neutral, tolerant site for the encounter of different viewpoints and the formation of that general public opinion that was supposed to represent the interests of the public as a whole. In actuality, however, members of the different national and political groupings at the Congress continued to mingle amicably enough at almost all the salons, with numerous strange bed- or sofa-fellows appearing on the guest lists. This holds for the Bagration, Sagan, Arnstein, and Schlegel salons, as for those connected with the diplomats. Political figures such as Humboldt, Gentz, or even Tsar Alexander, for example, were careful to maintain a presence at both Princess Bagration's and the Duchess of Sagan's, and these ladies' doors certainly remained open to various nationalities. The English did not find solace solely chez Castlereagh, but also found their way to the Orientalist scholar Joseph von Hammer, the Duchess of Sagan, Rahel Varnhagen, or Countess Zielińska. Salons' cosmopolitan profiles constituted one of their distinguishing features, even a mark of a salon's success.

Fanny Arnstein's salon, too, despite the decidedly pro-Prussian sentiments of its mistress and the robust representation of Prussian diplomatic and military figures, maintained its renown as the most international of salons. The usual Austrians as well as the recently hated French still crossed her portals in numbers. (Her husband, Nathan, an Austrian patriot, on one occasion complained at having to sit down to dinner surrounded by Prussians and had to be calmed by his sister-in-law Madame Eskeles, but this did not reflect the broader trend of sociability in his home.)[67] Count Henrich zu Stolberg-Wernigerode noted an Arnstein evening "where almost all possible nationalities were gathered," singling out Italians and French, Danes and Swedes, and even Wallachians (Rumanians) in his diary entry. Given that it was a Jewish home, perhaps the most surprising guest was Cardinal Consalvi, introduced by the papal nuncio Archbishop Severoli and appearing not just once but frequently. Politically, too, opposing paths crossed in Fanny's rooms. On the evening of the repeat of her wax figure tableau vivant display, the Whig admiral Sir Sidney Smith attended alongside the very Tory Duke of Wellington, and Metternich alongside Hardenberg, as well as Napoleon's son-in-law Prince Eugène Beauharnais.[68] Yet political animosity never seemed to boil over. As Friedrich Staegemann observed, Fanny always seemed to know what to say to "moderate" the conversation ("mäßigen").[69] After Napoleon's return from Elba, it is true, Fanny lost her equilibrium, becoming angry and "not herself." This provided the context for the often-recounted occasion on which she tore into one of her French guests, but it was an instance of an exception proving a rule. At a time of high tension, some sensitivity could be excused, and in this case the Frenchman in question, Prince Eugène's secretary, Count Mejean, had avowed his unrepentant Bonapartism. The police spy who reported the incident certainly did not blame his hostess, and soon Head of Police Baron Hager was calling for Mejean's expulsion from Vienna (but Mejean decamped first).[70] Fanny Arnstein and Madame Eskeles certainly forfeited some popularity when they came out so strongly against the Austrian and for the Prussian policy in Saxony, but their homes continued to be the hub of Viennese society.

As in small-world networks more generally, salons accommodated a relative diversity of background and connected different constituencies. Rather than serving as spaces for the crystallization of just one point of view, salons still facilitated communication among groups, in part perhaps through knowing where one could go to hear the latest about what those of a certain political persuasion were thinking and saying. Even partisans, therefore, remained more likely to encounter opposing views than, say, devoted readers of party-affiliated newspapers later in the nineteenth century, or of partisan blogs and websites in the niche-oriented world of the early twenty-first-century internet. One could also hope to persuade or at least pressure those of another opinion. Historians and contemporaries (not least including the Habsburg police spies)

were not wrong to interpret salons as incipient party-political groupings; that does capture some of the functions they performed in the
transitional public sphere, in a political and social space between the
court and the clubs, parties, or political associations that did not yet
exist in central Europe, certainly not at the national level. But this interpretation only tells part of the story. Even at moments of crisis, the
basic system of sociability did not break down, as it continued to facilitate both the congregation of the like-minded and the mingling of the
unlike. As the Russian officer and diarist Alexander Ivanovich
Mikhailovsky-Danilevsky (critic of high society though he was) summed
up the influence of Congress sociability, "it is interesting to see that
when people who have had different principles throughout their lives
and had stood on different sides are gathered here for Europe's universal reconciliation, they are forced to harmonize their opinions with
others'."[71]

Religious Sociability

If salon culture in general has been somewhat neglected in the literature
on European political culture and diplomacy, the question of religious
sociability in these contexts has been almost entirely overlooked for the
period after the mid-eighteenth century. When the orthodox view held
that the eighteenth and nineteenth centuries represented an age of secularization, that was not so surprising. But given that much recent scholarship has argued for religion's reintegration into mainstream history,
and has shown both that religiosity played a much greater role in the
Enlightenment than once thought and that the nineteenth century might
even be considered a "second confessional age," the time has certainly
come to explore the connections between religiosity and politics, and
between religious networks and diplomatic networks among the European social and political elite. While religious belief was of paramount
importance only to a minority, it still constituted a significant presence
in the lives of many in the social and political elites.[72] Religious life at
the Vienna Congress was defined in part by its intersection with wider
networks of Christian spirituality across Europe in this period, but also
by the status of Vienna itself as one of the primary centers of Roman
Catholic revival at the time.

Two aspects of religious life and sociability in this period might suggest that they would cut across the lines of broader cosmopolitan salon
culture and its rather inclusive small-world networks. First, where recent

literature has begun to reintegrate confessional relations and religion into the history of the late eighteenth and nineteenth centuries, it has tended to emphasize religious difference and religious conflict. Christian antisemitism, Protestant anti-Catholicism, the Catholic Church's antipathy toward the Enlightenment (itself related to anti-Protestantism): all have featured prominently in studies of German nationalism, German identity, and European culture in the period.[73] Without at all meaning to downplay the significance and role of religious difference and religious conflict, however, particularly at times of crisis, the appreciation of religious common ground and respect for religious difference (where it was truly *religious*) also proved significant, throughout the late eighteenth and nineteenth centuries, but perhaps nowhere more than at the end of the Napoleonic wars, when the sense of new possibilities and the desire for peace in Europe reached an apex.[74] There was what can be called an ecumenical moment in European history that has been in danger of being forgotten, both in older and newer studies.

The scholarship specifically on German, or more to the point European evangelical movements, on the other hand has tended to stress the breadth and depth of transconfessional ecumenical ties, not just among Protestant sects, but between them and Catholic or Orthodox groups as well. This cross-confessional tendency also emerges strongly among Congress figures. Catholic converts and conversions, for example, featured prominently in the Congress experience, and while they did cause some controversy, they were mostly accepted. Seen from another perspective, the existence of converts and conversions points to the closeness and acceptability of transconfessional relationships, as the converts themselves sprang from contacts with members of the confession to which they converted, and facilitated exchanges with those of their previous confession thereafter. Hence religious sociability, rather than being divisive, added yet another dimension to the cosmopolitan character of elite society generally.

This transconfessional or ecumenical moment is in part explained by a second feature of religiosity and religious sociability in the period. Scholars of religious revival have shown how the awakened of various denominations tended to self-identify and congregate, distinguishing themselves from their more secular or less devout social surroundings. By this measure, the crucial marker of difference was less Catholic or Protestant, Lutheran or Calvinist, than heartfelt piety in thought and lifestyle as opposed to worldly frivolity or theological rationalism. These links and perceptions of like-mindedness developed not just within particular religious communities, confessions, or sects but also crossed confessional lines. The recognition of devoutness and a strongly Christocentric religiosity (that is, deep acceptance of Christ as savior, and an effort to apply that faith to one's inner spiritual and external worldly life), in whatever Christian denomination, often sufficed to confirm one's bona fides as a member of this transconfessional, transnational, even global community of the faithful, sometimes called in these circles "the invisible church" (that is, outside the institutional boundaries of existing churches).[75] Such self-selecting ties were maintained in part through the right kind of social interactions and entertainments. Attending services, reading sermons and devotional literature, engaging in group prayer or spiritually probing conversation: all could fill an afternoon or evening with earnest pleasure and facilitate the building of group identity and community. As with salon sociability more generally, in religious revival circles too women played central roles, without excluding men from serving as hubs.[76]

Reading matter, in the equivalent of present-day citation networks or book clubs, also tied these groups together, as so many read the same authors and recommended or sent books to one another. Oftenencountered names include religious mystics such as "the Unknown Philosopher" Louis-Claude de Saint-Martin, the visionary shoemaker and theosophist of early modern Görlitz Jakob Boehme, the French quietist Madame Guyon and her interlocutor Bishop Fénelon, Saint Theresa of Avila, or the Bavarian official and mystic Karl von Eckartshausen. The central Protestant revivalist Johann Heinrich Jung-Stilling and the revivalist Catholic Johann Michael Sailer not only corresponded with one another across the confessional divide, but their works were read and treasured on both sides as well, just as was the devotional poetry and prose of the Lutheran Matthias Claudius (translator too of the Catholics Saint-Martin and Fénelon).[77]

Perhaps the most popular such work (outside scripture) was the fifteenth-century classic of Thomas à Kempis, the *Imitatio Christi*. Translated among others by Sailer, it became his best-selling book. Zacharias Werner had been a devotee of Thomas since his Lutheran youth, and following his conversion to Catholicism he continued to recommend it, including in his sermons in Vienna during the Congress, as the best devotional reading after the Bible itself. Thomas was read not just in Catholic revival circles but among the Protestant and Russian Orthodox awakened as well, featuring along with Eckartshausen and Saint Teresa among the preferred works of Tsar Alexander.[78] Similarity in reading taste promoted corresponding commonalities in vocabulary and religious experience. The language of love, and the central importance of humility (*Demut* rather than Promethean hubris or *Hochmut*) permeated revivalist discourse, drawing groups together and aiding the mutual recognition of committed individuals.

At the same time, this second, self-selecting dimension of contemporary religious life also suggests a way in which religious revival might have worked against elite society's relative openness. The networks of religious sociability, particularly among evangelical revivalists, were to a considerable degree insider networks, composed of those with strong ties to the cause and to one another. To the extent that these links were defined by the perception of difference in self/Other or in-group/out-group relationships, it was less the confessional or national difference than the distinction between the pious and the frivolous, the truly religious and the largely secular lifestyle that marked the difference.

Yet these religious networks were not as exclusive or "clustered" as one might think, instead preserving much of the "small-world" character of European networks seen above. While the awakened may have perceived a chasm between their beliefs and those of mainstream society, and have felt most comfortable seeking out those of similar mindset, they did not as a rule retreat re- and exclusively into those communities. Rather they maintained their everyday commitments and ties to the larger social milieus of which they remained members. As with the Beautiful Soul of Goethe's novel *Wilhelm Meister,* the calls of duty and of family and friendly affections kept them connected to society at large. Roxandra Stourdza, for example, the pious Greek Orthodox lady-in-waiting to the tsarina, complained of having to circulate in uncongenial atmospheres in Vienna, yet still did so. "I am not content with myself in Vienna, obliged to give myself up to a dissipation that troubles me without enjoying myself."[79] This is even true of the playwright Zacharias Werner. Freshly ordained as a Catholic priest when he arrived in Vienna in 1814, he even contemplated a monastic vocation and dwelled in a monastery during the Congress. But he still circulated in high society and promoted his plays and poetry, all alongside his new vocation as wildly popular preacher. One might think that the mystic-prophetic Baroness Krüdener (the "Lady of the Holy Alliance") and the rococo roué the Prince de Ligne, cosmopolitan hubs, respectively, of the early nineteenth-century evangelical revival and of the aristocratic-galante (or libertine) culture of the eighteenth century, would have had little in common, at least after her conversion. But they still corresponded and socialized at the central European spa town of Teplitz, if with divergent aims—he wished her to convert to Catholicism, she him to become a devout Christian.[80]

To understand this phenomenon of continued socializing between the awakened and the ostensibly less pious, it is important to remember that the various strands of Enlightenment were themselves often not as secular as previously thought, on the model of anticlerical French philosophes and early materialist philosophy (Voltaire and Helvetius). Rather, enlightened thought too was often embedded in spiritual concerns and couched in religious terms. Similarly, the lines between the rational and the irrational, Enlightenment and Romanticism, or between science and the occult, were not nearly as sharp as once depicted.[81] Fascination with animal magnetism or the occult might spring from the search for scientific knowledge or for spiritual insight. The Romantic Catholic convert Friedrich Schlegel, for example, himself an enthusiast for magnetic cures and a student of the paranormal, did not argue against the power of human reason but rather for its insufficiency, and for the need to supplement it through the power of love and the mediation of the divine.[82] For all these reasons, and notwithstanding all the differences in lifestyle, morality, and thought, the potential points of contact between the pious and the worldly remained numerous and the boundaries between them still porous. Karl and Rahel Varnhagen von Ense were not religious revivalists but read Saint-Martin's work *The Man of Desire*—according to Elisabeth Staegemann, its German translation created a "sensation" during the Congress period—and the Varnhagens delved into other works by Saint-Martin and Eckartshausen as well.[83] Spiritual, as opposed to solely secular, conversational matter lay closer to hand in salons than has often been thought.

In examining Europe's broader religious networks at the time, the most famous, and best researched, is certainly that associated with the origins of the Holy Alliance, the treaty of Tsar Alexander signed just after the Vienna Congress in September 1815. This group was well-connected at the highest levels of European society—it doesn't get much higher than the tsar—and it crossed confessional lines. The network's iconic center was Baroness Julie von Krüdener, member of the Baltic German Protestant nobility in the Russian Empire, European high-society figure, and celebrity novelist turned mystic-prophet. It should be recalled that when her salon became so popular in Paris during the negotiations for the Second Peace of Paris in 1815, it was still Krüdener the aristocrat and author of the best-selling *Valerie* who was the draw, and not only the mystic. Krüdener helped link evangelical circles in Switzerland with those in southwest Germany (above all those surrounding Jung-Stilling) and in northeastern France (particularly those surrounding Jean-Frédéric Oberlin and Jean-Frédéric Fontaines). The upper Rhine Valley showed itself to be a regionally transnational crèche of revival movements. But Krüdener's trajectory also demonstrates the European dimension to these transnational religious networks, from her relations with the Moravians in Herrnhut and her native Livonia to her links with the Swiss, French, Alsatian, and southwest German revival circles and to her continued presence in salon circles in Paris and the central European spas.

These connections extended beyond Protestant milieus. Krüdener also stood in close contact with the Orthodox Roxandra Stourdza, who in turn was also closely tied to Jung-Stilling, Stourdza and Jung-Stilling being nodes in the revivalist web just as central as Krüdener. Jung-Stilling's position in Badenese court circles meant he also had direct contact with Roxandra's employer, Tsarina Elisabeth, who may have been the one to introduce his revivalist classic *Heimweh*, or "Homesickness" (for one's true spiritual home) to the Russian court.[84] After Alexander made his religious turn in the wake of the French invasion of Russia in 1812, Roxandra became one of his spiritual interlocutors; he, she, and Jung-Stilling even formed a kind of three-way spiritual marriage in expression of this intense piety and spiritual community. The Holy Alliance circle also maintained crucial links with Catholic revival currents. Jung-Stilling, Krüdener, and Roxandra were all in contact with Franz Baader of Munich, whose work on religion, politics, and the French Revolution provided some of the ideological and theological basis of the Holy Alliance itself. Jung-Stilling's correspondence with the leader of one of the main movements of spiritual renewal in the Roman Catholic Church, Johann Sailer of Erlangen, has already been mentioned.[85]

Back in St. Petersburg, Stourdza and the devout Madame Swetchine—soulmates in a "frivolous society"—enjoyed close relations with the Savoyard Catholic conservative Joseph de Maistre in the salons of Countess Golovkin, Countess Golovin, and Madame Chichagov. Stourdza agreed with Maistre in just about everything except what she found his somewhat exclusive and intolerant Catholicism (but not so intolerant as to preclude his relations with Stourdza and Swetchine). Madame Swetchine, having already experienced a conversion or rebirth within the Orthodox Church, also featured among those Russians who converted to Catholicism in the years around 1815.[86] Institutionally the links between Protestant and Orthodox evangelical circles found expression in the spread of the British and Foreign Bible Society through Scandinavia and Russia in these years, as a partly private, partly governmental initiative.[87]

A second important spiritual network may come as more of a surprise, namely, the circle around Napoleon's liberal opponent Madame de Staël, in Coppet and Switzerland, and through her correspondence and travels, in Europe as a whole. Germaine's salon and correspondence network was less central in the religious sphere than in the political, but this was a matter of degree, and the separation between the religious and the political in this period was in any case rather thin. A fixture of liberal and Enlightenment circles, Staël was also immersed in the culture of sensibility and emergent Romanticism, including its intense spiritual searching. One of her closest friends was Mathieu de Montmorency, French political figure and member of a Swiss quietist sect centered on Chevalier Charles Gentils de Langallerie and looking to the late seventeenth-century mystic Madame Guyon, with her emphasis on the inner life of prayer and pure love. Montmorency and Staël were both in contact with Baroness Krüdener. Around the time of the Congress of Vienna and the formation of the Holy Alliance in 1815, Krüdener even had strong ties with liberal political theorist Benjamin Constant and the legendarily lovely *salonnière* Madame Récamier, both among Staël's intimate interlocutors.[88]

Nor were Staël's spiritual connections restricted to Protestants. August Wilhelm Schlegel was one of Germaine's closest companions, and through him she maintained contacts with his brother Friedrich, center of the Vienna Catholic revival. Chateaubriand, author of the seminal *The Genius of Christianity,* which helped launch the enthusiasm for a revival of Catholic spirituality linked to the medieval past of Gothic cathedrals, was also connected to Staël's circle. A few years before when Zacharias Werner was still most famed for his play celebrating Martin Luther, Staël had hosted the mystical German playwright. This link goes some way toward explaining why Werner ranked alongside Goethe and Schiller in Staël's discussion of leading German dramatists in her landmark work *On Germany.* Staël maintained the relationship during and after Werner's conversion to Catholicism, and even encouraged the move.[89] Werner soon became a core member of the Catholic revival circle in Vienna. Making the net even denser, it was while Werner stayed at Coppet that he came to know Baroness Krüdener and her daughter. His theories of spiritual ascent through various levels of love, as well as his tendency toward mystical religious symbolism and allegory, made him an object of interest for the Krüdeners even when he was still a largely profane rather than religious poet and dramatist.[90]

Both aspects of religious sociability described above, the cross-confessional ties and the continued links with broader worldly society, also held for the pious circles of the Vienna Congress. Given that these largely formed part of the same web of spiritual contacts, this should occasion no surprise. Roxandra Stourdza and Tsar Alexander were of course present at the Congress, as were the central members of the Viennese Catholic revival, associated above all with the figure of the Redemptorist father Clemens Maria Hofbauer, later to become Vienna's patron saint. Here again the prominent role of converts and conversion stands out. Among Hofbauer's close associates we have already encountered Werner as a convert from Lutheranism, plus the Romantic intellectual Friedrich Schlegel, whose wife Dorothea was a double convert, first to Lutheranism from Judaism, and then to Catholicism. Her sons the artists Johannes and Philipp Veit also enjoyed cordial relations with Hofbauer, joined the Nazarene group of painters in Rome with their Romantic neo-Renaissance ideal of religious art, and converted to Catholicism.[91] Anton Pilat did not have to convert in the sense of crossing confessional lines, but having been an only nominally Catholic man-of-the-world and Freemason, in the months before the Congress Pilat too experienced a spiritual rebirth. At about the same time, his Protestant wife, Elisabeth, and sister-in-law Friederike von Klinkowström decided to convert, in part through the influence of Hofbauer, with whom they had already been on friendly and confidential terms. Friederike's husband, the Romantic artist Friedrich von Klinkowström, had independently converted to enthusiastic Catholicism in 1814. Two others at the Congress who elected to convert to Catholicism through association with Hofbauer, the Schlegels, and the Pilats were Sophie and Friedrich Schlosser of Frankfurt, relations by marriage to Goethe. Friedrich's brother Christian had already converted and stood among those campaigning for Catholic equality in Protestant Frankfurt. Sophie's process of conversion, and her path through Congress society and its Catholic and ecumenical circles, can be traced in her Congress diary.[92]

While converts played prominent parts, most of those in the Vienna Catholic revival had of course been raised Catholic, many like Pilat (or for that matter Madame Swetchine and Jung-Stilling in their own confessions) having followed the quite common trajectory from Enlightenment rationalism to deep Christian piety. As with the Schlegels, Caroline Pichler's salon proved popular not only through her literary celebrity or political connections but also through her religiosity. Her most acclaimed novel, *Agathokles,* was intended as a counterpoint to Gibbon in depicting a more positive influence of Christianity in late antiquity. The Hungarian magnate families the Zichys and the Széchényis for their part formed an important bridgehead of Catholic devotion in the upper reaches of Viennese society. The beautiful young matron Countess Julie Zichy who so fascinated King Friedrich Wilhelm of Prussia during the Congress chose Hofbauer as confessor and was close to the Schlegels, actively facilitating Friedrich's appointment to the Austrian delegation at the German Federal Assembly in Frankfurt following the Congress, where conferences were to be held on the future organization of the Catholic Church in Germany. Pichler and the patriarch Ferenc Széchényi both remained somewhat reserved toward Hofbauer but were close to the Schlegels, and Werner was a welcome visitor at their salons as well. The religious ties even meant that the middleclass Pichler and Dorothea Schlegel at various times became somewhat unlikely house guests of the Széchényis at their country estate just over the border in Hungary; the social mixing characteristic of general salon society went even deeper in religious circles.[93] Pilat's close connection and correspondent Countess Laure Fuchs also brought a significant Catholic revival presence into high society, while Baroness Montet (niece of the émigré French bishop of Nancy) and the Polish magnate Countess Rosalie Rzewuska were also linked to these circles and extended the networks even further.[94]

Despite its occasional reputation for intolerance, Vienna's Catholic revival milieu also saw plenty of ecumenical cross-confessional ties. If Pater Hofbauer had not socialized so actively with committed Protestants, he would not have enjoyed such success converting them, and of course not all of those he came into contact with ultimately took that step. As Werner put it in his obituary for Hofbauer, the future saint preferred good Protestants to bad Catholics.[95] Preexisting relationships were reinforced at the Congress, and new ones forged. The former imperial nobles the Stolbergs of Wernigerode, for instance, boasted a long tradition of Lutheran Pietism, one continued by the heir and Congress representative of the family Count Henrich, even as his spiritual friend the Swiss Calvinist cleric Johannes Büel introduced him to Caroline

Pichler's salon; the three all attended sermons by Werner as well. Büel and Caroline were close spiritual connections, too, and remained correspondents after the Congress. Tellingly, Stolberg celebrated Christmas with visits to Lutheran and Calvinist services as well as to a Catholic musical mass. The Romantic Protestant Jacob Grimm, on diplomatic duty in Vienna as well as promoting his collections of folk tales and songs, felt a little uncomfortable in the Schlegel salon with all the conversions but still attended, and actually appreciated frequent evenings with the Pilats; Protestant unease with convinced Catholics and converts was present but not definitive.[96] Among the other diplomats enjoying the Pilats' hospitality were the representatives of the German Hanseatic cities, the pious Lutheran from Lübeck Johann Friedrich Hach and the Calvinist from Bremen Johann Smidt, who with the latter's wife Wilhelmine and daughter Hanne all socialized amicably enough in a salon that included Father Hofbauer and the convert Schlegels and Klinkowströms. Elisabeth Pilat even stood in for the absent Protestant godmother at the baptism of the Smidts' newborn daughter, Julie, in June 1815.[97]

On at least one occasion the Catholic atmosphere did get either a bit too thick or too rarefied for Wilhelmine. One morning she and Hanne accompanied Frau Pilat, Dorothea Schlegel, Sophie Schlosser, and some other ladies to visit the convent of the Ursuline nuns where Hofbauer served as father confessor. While the others, including the as-yet-unconverted Sophie, responded with typically Romantic enthusiasm to their behind-the-walls glimpse into the religious life, Wilhelmine was Protestant enough to find the experience oppressive and quite literally claustrophobic. As she recounted the visit to her sister-in-law back in Bremen, "I did not feel well inside these secluded walls. I was able to breathe purer air again when I got outside, and involuntarily had to repeat the words in Schiller: 'Let me enjoy beautiful liberty.'" Her companions, however, "did not entirely share my feelings, they were, or at least appeared to be, quite taken by everything."[98]

While those with deep religious convictions tended to seek one another out, even across confessional lines, and therefore in some senses to "cluster" or form insider networks, they did not retreat from the wider social world. Caroline Pichler, the Schegels, and the Pilats and Klinkowströms all featured above as hubs of political and cultural sociability, and the Smidts, singly and together, did not socialize solely at the Pilats but attended functions at court, at the Metternichs, and at Fanny Arnstein's. Caroline Pichler, too, when not herself "at home," appeared not only at the Schlegels or the Széchényis but also at the Arnsteins. The Pietist Count Stolberg felt a strong attraction for Pichler's salon, "the only home where I find something for the heart," appearing there at least twenty-nine times during his stay in Vienna, but he also still enjoyed Fanny Arnstein's grander Jewish salon and the musical or political evenings of the Princess of Fürstenberg-Donaueschingen. Sophie Schlosser similarly visited not just the Pilat and Schlegel households but also appeared at least sixteen times at the Arnstein and Eskeles salons.[99]

Finally, it is important to observe that in maintaining ties with broader society, the revivalists remained in touch with diplomatic circles. Moreover, the diplomats sometimes consorted with them not despite but because of their piety and spiritual interests. In this sense too the diplomats were not cordoned off by their profession from the broader cultural and spiritual currents of European society. Count Capodistrias, for instance, socialized with Roxandra Stourdza and her family as committed Greeks, but he also participated in her dealings with Baroness Krüdener and spiritual interests. The German statesman turned advisor to the Tsar Baron Stein also consorted with her, again in part from his own fascination with magnetic cures, somnambulism, prophecy, and the life of the spirit.[100] Hearing in a salon of a dimly lit ghost-story session at the Zichys, the young Genevan Anna Eynard thought she was the only person present not actually to believe in phantoms (the prevalence of such belief not having prevented Count Carl Zichy from rigging a spookily creaking door to open at an opportune moment, to the mixed startlement and amusement of Tsar Alexander, King Frederik of Denmark, and the other guests).[101]

It is also important to consider the role of the Metternichs in this context. The statesman employed Pilat, Schlegel, and Adam Müller as secretaries and public opinion managers not solely as conservatives but in full awareness of their position within the Catholic revival. His lieutenant in the State Chancellery, Joseph von Hudelist, also had ties to revival circles, particularly the Széchényis. Metternich's more well-known collaborator Friedrich Gentz, though he did not follow his friend Adam Müller into the Catholic Church, did seriously contemplate the step. Far from being a secular icon, he wrestled with the decision not because of opportunism after his switch from Prussian to Austrian employment—then the choice would have been simple—but because he shared the spiritual seeking of many in his generation and circles. He went so far as to yield to the persuasion of his friends Pilat and Countess Fuchs to make the annual pilgrimage to Mariazell, but ultimately he could not feel the kind of spiritual conviction that would have validated conversion. The Metternichs' patronage of the Catholic revival even extended to the social scene. On certain occasions, they invited Zacharias Werner to read from his plays and be a guest at table, among a list including the Schlegels, Gentz, Flora Wrbna, Countess Fuchs, Pilat, and Julie Zichy.[102] The fact that the Zichys and Countess Fuchs also provided important social backing to counteract the anti-Metternich salons underscores the importance of the revival connection for Metternich's politics. While Metternich was no revivalist, his letters of the period reveal a certain spirituality and appreciation of religious culture, whether Austrian Catholicism or Russian Orthodox sacred music, that suggest this sociability and networking was not solely instrumental.[103]

Salons and the Wider Public

Not all the socializing at the Congress occurred in salons or grand festivities. Individuals and groups from the social world just described also found their way to other spaces in the public sphere, to the taverns, coffeehouses, and restaurants, and to the theaters, parks, and promenades, often still in mixed company, sometimes in all-male settings. Certainly the Habsburg police spies snuffling after political rumors turned in this direction, if less so than salons. Such venues merit further study, but here it is worth concentrating instead on some other ways in which Congress salons bridged the boundary between private and public (a border zone or gray area rather than a sharply defined line). Scholars such as Dena Goodman and James Van Horn Melton have emphasized the extent to which eighteenth-century salons overlapped with print culture in both the production and dissemination of texts, and this was as much or more the case during the Congress. At various times salon culture spilled over into that most public realm of media and the press, either through overlapping memberships and networks with writers and editors among the salon habitués, or by itself functioning as a substitute medium for making works public, above all when government censorship blocked the normal channels of publication or public performance. Participation in salon culture could also merge with the more formal level of associational life in ways that bore political significance.[104]

On the latter score of links between associational life and salon sociability, the most impressive instance must be the formation in Vienna in 1810 of the Society of Noble Ladies for the Promotion of the Good and the Useful following the catastrophic defeat at the hands of Napoleon in 1809. The elected board of directors was for the most part composed of the high nobility, under the presidency of Caroline Princess Lobkowitz, but also included the recently ennobled Fanny von Arnstein, and thus helped bring together the Catholic and Jewish communities as well as the upper nobility and so-called second society in Vienna. Princess Trauttmansdorff, Princess Esterhazy, Countess Julie Zichy, and Countess Rzewuska numbered among the other leading members. By 1814 the Society had more than two thousand members spread across two hundred branch organizations in Lower Austria plus one in Upper Austria (in Linz), at this level extending into the bourgeoisie. It took in at its height over 60,000 florins per year. The organization concerned itself not only with wartime charitable work and medical care, of the sort seen in equivalent women's associations in Russia and Prussia during the recent wars, but also with support of the poor, the ill, and victims of catastrophes more generally. That the organization and its female leaders appeared among the government bureaus of the official court and state handbook, and had connections with the administration, highlights the Society's situation in a public sphere that at once blended public and private, noble and middle class, and state and civil society.[105] In 1812 the Society also helped launch what has proved to be among the largest and longest-lived experiments in Viennese civil society: the still extant Gesellschaft der Musikfreunde or Society of Friends of Music, encountered earlier through its charity concerts and the grand festivity of the seven-hundred-performer Handel oratorio.[106]

In merging with associational life, salon culture also blended with print culture. The Romantic and Catholic revival Schlegel circle for instance was involved with the new periodical the *Friedensblätter,* whose editorial group was also drawn in part from a coffeehouse institution, the "Stroblkopfgesellschaft." The latter in turn also had links during the Congress with the pub-society the Wollzeilergesellschaft, which brought together certain bourgeois and aristocratic figures aiming variously to spark interest in medieval German poetry and lore or to spearhead the renascence of the German nobility. The group included such cultural notables as Jacob Grimm, Joseph von Lassberg, Werner von Haxthausen, and Isaac von Sinclair.[107] Through Grimm and Schlegel, these circles also had connections with the Viennese Slavic revival around Jerneij

Kopitar that met in the White Wolf inn. From these ties emerged such transnational efforts as Grimm's and Goethe's promotion of the Serbian folk poetry of Vuk Karadžić. Both groups went as far as founding actual associations and drafting statutes for their respective purposes of aristocratic revival and collecting folklore, in this way linking salon society with the newer public sphere and its typically male-centered associational life. As with the diplomats, both organizations envisioned their schemes extending well beyond Vienna, across the German lands in the case of the nobles, and through central and eastern Europe in that of the folklorists.[108]

The notion of salons as a substitute venue of public opinion, or as a political space between state and society, public and private, can also be seen in relation to censorship. To take an example from the Arnstein house, after Austrian censors had forbidden the sale of an important pamphlet supporting Prussian claims to the Kingdom of Saxony, Fanny and her sister did more than just inform their guests what the work said; they also began to distribute copies of the text itself—a perfect instance of doing the work of the new public sphere in circumstances where its development was inhibited.[109] Another case where a salon provided an alternative route to publicity when the usual path encountered obstacles involved Caroline Pichler and her new play, *Ferdinand II*. A historical drama of the Thirty Years War, the work fell foul of Viennese censors and was performed in the capital only years later, in a bastardized form. Pichler did, however, hold a reading of the play in her salon. In her memoirs she fingered Baron Bretfeld (from Metternich's bureau) as the censor responsible for denying permission to perform the piece on the Viennese stage, and thought that the baron, being from Bohemia, did not care to see his countrymen depicted as rebels, even historically. Pichler was perhaps partly correct in her identification of the culprit (Metternich's deputy Joseph von Hudelist also weighed in), but was off base in her explanation. The police and State Chancellery officials expressed more concern about lèse-majesté, nationalist politics, and the treatment of Catholics and Protestants in this play about the era of religious conflict.[110] Regarding the latter, the irony is that many of those who heard the play in Pichler's salon, including both the writer for the Catholic revival circle's journal *Friedensblätter* and the evangelical Protestant Count Stolberg-Wernigerode, praised its delicate handling of this ticklish issue. The fact that the private reading received press coverage offers another indication of connections between salons and the public sphere, and a further means of circumventing censorship, not least since the notice ended with the wish that the play be performed soon on the Viennese stage.[111]

Salons and the women and men who participated in them provided both context for political and diplomatic initiatives and the venues where they took place, as hubs in the social networks of the European elite. Whether through direct exchange and influence, indirectly through concern with public opinion, or in the background of diplomatic conferences or publications in the press, salon sociability at once formed part of the political stage and expanded the cast of political actors upon it, beyond the ranks of government, and involving female as well as male participants. The boundaries between public and private and between new and old public spheres also blurred in the transitional political culture of the early nineteenth century.

CHAPTER FOUR

Negotiating Religion

Religion helped set the tone and agenda of the Vienna Congress in more than its festive display. Just as religion occupied a larger place than usually recognized in the world of salons, diplomats and lobbyists at the Congress spent more time dealing with religious politics than most general histories of the event reflect (the specialist literature in religious history, however, is well-developed). The Catholic Church in particular had suffered greatly during the revolutionary and Napoleonic eras, and decisions had to be made regarding its reconstruction. Even the territorial settlements at the center of diplomatic attention entailed a religious dimension, given that prospective rulers and populations often belonged to different confessions, and the respective rights, powers, and protections in this sensitive area of life had to be determined. The problem of religious minorities thus assumed considerable importance, with respect to relations between Protestants and Catholics, and between Christians and Jews.

This chapter first briefly examines efforts to reestablish the Roman Catholic Church on a sound footing after years of revolutionary warfare and secularizing politics had stripped it of much of its territorial possessions and property and decimated its clerical personnel. It then explores the negotiations concerning the rights of the main religious groups, Catholic, Protestant, and Jewish, between the poles of Old Regime established churches and discriminatory legislation on the one hand and ideas of religious toleration, liberty, and equality before the law on the other. Each set of issues involved Europe more widely, but the negotiations above all affected central Europe, from the German states through Switzerland and Italy. Debates surrounding Jewish rights proved acutest in the German states, as part of the process of drafting a constitution for the new German federal union. And as with other issues at the Congress, the contestation went on at multiple levels: in the press, in drawing rooms, and in quiet private meetings, as well as around the negotiating table. In several instances, including that of Jewish rights in Germany, the diplomats remained unable to reach a final agreement and left questions in a compromise provisional state, battle to be rejoined at a later date. Prussia and Austria, the Great Powers most behind the moves to secure at least Jewish legal if not political equality, never did cease those endeavors entirely, neither in the negotiations over the German constitution, nor in their diplomatic relations with recalcitrant states thereafter. Untangling the threads of those conflicts sheds light on the nature of the struggle over Jewish emancipation in Restoration Germany. The Final Act of the Vienna Settlement was not as final as usually thought, a fact that points not just to the peculiarities and sensitivities of religious politics but to the nature of political and diplomatic culture, in this period and more generally.

Reconstruction of the Catholic Church

The degree to which European society and culture became more secular during the nineteenth century continues to arouse debate; no one, however, disputes the extent to which a wave of secularization in the narrower institutional sense swept across revolutionary and Napoleonic Europe. In Protestant territories the secularization of church lands and property into the hands of lay owners and the state had of course occurred long before, as in the Dissolution of the Monasteries in Henry VIII's England, and even in Catholic lands such as the Austria of Joseph II, the eighteenth-century Enlightenment had not left the Church untouched. But the anticlericals of the French Revolution still found plenty of Church property to seize even in a Gallican France.[1]

The caesura in the German lands of the former Holy Roman Empire, the Italian states, or Switzerland was just as sharp. There the Church had not only owned much land, but various archbishops, bishops, abbots, and abbesses also held rights of sovereignty and ruled over ecclesiastical principalities. The archbishops of Cologne, Mainz, and Trier had been electors of the empire, and in Switzerland part of the Bishopric of Basel was administered by the Church, as well as the lands of the

Abbey of St. Gallen. Almost all of these temporal possessions of the Catholic Church had been swept into lay control, as had the extensive remnants of the Papal States in Italy. First, the French had seized the German Rhineland and organized the Helvetic Confederation, as they had the various sister republics in Italy. Then the German states and lordships had essentially been invited to make up their losses in the west by secularizing Church lands farther east, a process that culminated in the *Reichsdeputationshauptschluss* in 1803, itself a major step toward the final dissolution of the Holy Roman Empire in 1806. Thereafter, the Napoleonic prince primate, Karl Theodor Dalberg, the last archbishop-elector of Mainz, constituted the sole relic of Church temporal power in Germany. Dalberg still controlled Regensburg and Aschaffenburg, as well as having been made Grand Duke of Frankfurt. But the severity of secularization and the disruptions of decades of warfare did not only ravage the Catholic Church's temporal power in Germany—its ability to carry out its pastoral and spiritual missions had also been greatly impaired. By 1814 only five bishops remained in office (roughly one-quarter), and many positions in cathedral chapters as well as local parishes went unfilled.[a] For the German Catholic Church, two decades of war, territorial upheaval, and secularization of Church property had taken their toll.

Attempting to repair this long-term damage was, as in many other cases of Restoration politics, not simply a matter of trying to turn back the clock and restore the situation to its status quo ante 1789 or 1792. The Catholic context did see the closest approach to calls for full restoration, but even some of those, such as the Vatican representative Cardinal Consalvi, who penned the Church's petitions and protests demanding the recovery of all that had been lost were under no illusion about the practicability of realizing those aims. The pope and some of his close advisors wanted to treat the matter as much as possible as one of principle, and to refuse to recognize any of the enforced changes of the revolutionary and Napoleonic years. The Church's representatives did not try to declare all subsequent sales of Church property null and void, but they still hoped to regain as much as possible of the Church's temporal possessions, and at the level of international law staked their claim not just to the Papal States but also to various former enclaves, including Avignon and the County of the Venaissin, which had been absorbed into France in 1791 and guaranteed in the recent Peace of Paris, plus Pontecorvo and Benevento in Italy and the former German possessions. Consalvi knew that such an all-or-nothing strategy might weaken the Vatican's bargaining position if it were perceived as recalcitrant or as having learned nothing from the revolutionary experience, but he "gritted his teeth" and went along.[3]

The history of the negotiations over the return of the pope's temporal possessions in Italy, the Papal States, has been told before, and this account is correspondingly brief. Most significant, given the emphasis here on the ecumenical spirit in early post-Napoleonic Europe, is the fact that the Vatican was supported just as strongly by Protestant powers such as Prussia and Britain, and by Orthodox Russia, as by the Catholic states from whom it was more to be expected. Pope Pius VII's resistance to Napoleon and consequent years of incarceration had accrued to the head of the Catholic Church a considerable fund of goodwill across Europe, most euphoric in Italy, where he was fêted and cheered from Savona to Rome in his return to the Vatican in 1814, but also notable elsewhere. Cardinal Consalvi's presence in London for the celebrations in June 1814 marked the first time for centuries that a cardinal and papal representative had appeared there, nor did he have to keep a low profile while there. England had long been known for its strident and sometimes violent anti-Catholicism, but the crowds that summer cheered Consalvi, cardinal's robes and all. Any enemy of Napoleon was a friend of the moment. Hence temporarily public opinion worked to promote pro-Catholic diplomatic relations among the Protestant powers rather than to make them more difficult. Pope Pius risked throwing away such good feelings in a series of decisions almost calculated to arouse in Protestants all their old fears and prejudices, with moves such as the restoration of the Inquisition and the Jesuits, which had been disbanded in the eighteenth century. Consalvi was all too aware of the likely effects of such measures and struggled to put a brake on these policies back in Rome.[4]

Above all, the Vatican desired the return of the Papal Legations in north-central Italy, Ferrara, Bologna, and the Romagna. With so much support, it might seem strange that the negotiations dragged out so long. Depending on how the battles over the rest of the still-unassigned territory in Italy turned out, however, there was always the possibility that former papal lands would be claimed to make up the difference in satisfying the demands of this or that other European or Italian ruler. Prussia contributed to the confusion and contestation as it briefly mooted the possibility that the king of Saxony could be compensated for the loss of his Saxon lands to Prussia by the grant of the Papal Legations, but the proposal never got very far.[5] For the most part it was the Bourbon-

Habsburg dynastic wrangling among Catholic France, Spain, and Austria over various portions of the Italian peninsula that kept Cardinal Consalvi in Vienna and the church officials in Rome on tenterhooks for over eight months. Talleyrand in particular delighted in undercutting the Vatican's claims in his barbed conversations with Consalvi, even the public ones. Consalvi in turn attacked Talleyrand at a weak point, and observed that if Talleyrand were going to pose as a defender of the principle of legitimacy, then France should recognize the illegitimacy of its territorial seizures and return Avignon.[6] In the end, the Vatican was awarded sovereignty again over most of the three Legations plus Benevento and Pontecorvo, but not the French enclaves.

Regarding the reconstruction of the Catholic Church in Germany, the issues were different. While the Vatican and various representatives of the German Church still called for at least partial returns of the former sovereign territories, it was always clear that a true restoration was not in the cards. Instead, efforts to reestablish the Catholic Church in Germany played out in two areas. First, state governments and various official and unofficial church representatives pushed either for concordats with the individual German states or with Germany as a whole. Those supporting the latter position were then, second, concerned to ensure that the new German constitution included a statement guaranteeing Catholic civil rights, and if possible an additional paragraph framing the practical institutional and financial side of restoring the Church to a sound condition.

The negotiations and debates took place for the most part behind the scenes, in the domiciles and reception rooms of the various diplomats, lobbyists, and officials. Among the lobbyists and representatives of the Church, there were two loose contending parties. On the one hand stood those who maintained close contact with the Vatican and worked for a more Rome-centered Catholic Church in Germany. Chief among them figured the two official representatives of the Papal See, Consalvi and the longtime papal nuncio in Vienna, Archbishop Severoli. The delegates claiming to represent the Catholic Church in Germany, and indeed representing at least a significant fraction of it, were the so-called Oratoren: the deacon of Worms Cathedral, Baron Franz Christoph von Wambold, and the Cathedral prebendary Joseph Anton Helfferich of Speyer. Wambold in particular was well-chosen, as a scion of the old Rhenish imperial and church nobility connected with many of the best diplomatic families in the Habsburg realm and elsewhere, including the Stadions and Metternichs.[7] Almost as important as these official representatives were the unofficial ones, above all the activists of the Roman Catholic revival circles in Vienna. These centered around the figures of the Redemptorist monk Clemens Hofbauer, Friedrich and Dorothea Schlegel and their salon, the Hungarian magnates the Széchényis and the Zichys, and Metternich's secretary, Joseph Anton Pilat, who had outlets for sociability in his own household and in the salon of Countess Laure Fuchs, also sympathetic to the Catholic revival. Schlegel and Hofbauer in particular proved of considerable assistance to the Oratoren, Consalvi, and Severoli. The Church officials made frequent visits to the Schlegel salon, and Schlegel was often reported at Severoli's residence by the police spies.[8] Zacharias Werner, though closely associated with these circles, seems to have concentrated on promoting the Roman Catholic revival at the Congress of Vienna on the social and cultural level, through his sermons, writings, and salon appearances, rather than through involvement in the negotiations. His sermons pled for renewed spirituality in a too secular age, but unlike the others he did not link this call to the necessity of rebuilding the shattered church in Germany.[9]

The second group was smaller in number but not necessarily in influence. Prince Primate Dalberg sent his most trusted official to Vienna as his representative, Ignaz von Wessenberg, the vicar of Constance. A noted church reformer in the vein of Enlightenment piety, Wessenberg was also the brother of the Austrian second plenipotentiary to the Congress, Johann von Wessenberg. Dalberg himself, for that matter, was related to the French number two, Duke Emmerich Dalberg, and was the former friend and mentor of Prussia's second plenipotentiary, Wilhelm von Humboldt. Humboldt was well-disposed toward the Vatican after his time there as Prussian minister, and was somewhat alienated from both Dalbergs, given their cooperation with Napoleon's regime, but he still lent an ear to Wessenberg's proposals. The ambitious dean of the Münster Cathedral Chapter, Count Ferdinand August von Spiegel, had managed to have himself appointed by Hardenberg as Prussia's quasi-official advisor on Catholic affairs and had his own ideas for the reorganization of Germany's Catholic Church, but once in Vienna he quickly fell under Wessenberg's spell. Spiegel's brother also happened to be an official in Metternich's Chancellery, which along with his Prussian ties lent him the presumption of a certain voice, if ultimately less than he had hoped. Metternich at any rate favored the idea of a concordat between the Vatican and the new German Confederation, at least partly in line with Wessenberg and Spiegel, in part to extend something close to Austria's model of church-state relations throughout Germany, and likely in part also to reform some of the anticlerical excesses of that Austrian model as forged by Kaiser Joseph.[10]

The differences between the Catholic camps were not actually as great as often depicted. Confessionally charged commentators and historians from the mid-nineteenth century into the twentieth projected their polemical perspectives on the contending positions back onto the protagonists themselves. In the older view, the Rome party was fully ultramontane, while Wessenberg in good Febronian fashion promoted the formation of an independent German Catholic Church under the only very loose supervision of the pope. Later anticlerical Protestant German nationalists and ultramontane Catholics disagreed about whom to label heroes, who villains, but both sides exaggerated the views of their historical analogues and opponents alike. The wider polarities of the era of the Bismarckian Kulturkampf were read back into the Restoration period, and the two parties were at the same time rendered more monolithic.[11] In fact the two groups agreed on the causes and degree of devastation of what the Oratoren termed "the sad state of the dispossessed and orphaned Catholic Church of Germany," and to an extent shared ideas about how to address those problems.[12]

Neither Wessenberg nor Spiegel aimed for a fully national German Catholic Church. Each, and particularly Spiegel, planned to preserve a more-than-nominal authority for the pope as head of the Church (not simply the bishop of Rome), even as they also hoped to trim some of the pope's previous powers to intervene in German diocesan affairs.[13] It is also clear by now that Consalvi and the Vatican approached the Congress with open minds on the possibility of a German concordat. They were not yet committed to the course of pursuing concordats with the individual German states and refusing to work at the German federal level. It was not, after all, obvious that the pope would be able to retain greater powers over the Church in agreements reached with individual states, nor was that the only important issue. Just as central was the question of how much independence Catholic institutions in the German states would retain in their relations with state governments. Father Hofbauer opposed a German *Reichskirche,* but Friedrich Schlegel favored a German-level concordat, and when consulted by Consalvi, supported having the cathedral chapters elect bishops rather than involving the state government—or insisting on papal appointment—just like Wessenberg and Spiegel, and on this issue Hofbauer agreed as well. When it came time to compose his memorandum, Cardinal Consalvi retained Schlegel's suggestion.[14]

The struggles over the future of the Catholic Church in Germany were carried out at multiple levels, spilling over from private lobbying into the domain of public opinion, both in salons and the press. In consultation with Schlegel and Hofbauer, Consalvi and the Oratoren painstakingly produced memoranda and notes for the main diplomats. Spiegel as Prussian advisor wrote two memos for Hardenberg and other notes for Humboldt and Friedrich Staegemann, partly critiquing the Oratoren arguments. Wessenberg penned important memoranda for a wider Congress audience in which he pushed for a German concordat and for material aid to the German Church. Wessenberg also published a pamphlet for the broader public, while for the other side Schlegel wrote newspaper articles advertising the Oratoren position. The Catholic editor Joseph Görres picked up the Oratoren memos in his widely read *Rheinischer Merkur* (despite the preference of his Prussian sponsors for Wessenberg's plan).[15]

Salons also played a part in the diplomatic campaign, as with Cardinal Consalvi's much-remarked appearances at Fanny Arnstein's gatherings, or his attendance at Lady Castlereagh's (Jewish and Anglican, respectively). Sophie Schlosser found her opinion of Wessenberg swayed by the ill tidings she heard about him in the Pilats' salon.[16] Until recently, many writers (both pro- and anti-ultramontane) attributed Bavaria's rejection of Wessenberg's plan and a German concordat generally to the influence of Hofbauer on Crown Prince Ludwig of Bavaria. But it now seems that their meetings had more to do with personal spirituality and German religious culture generally than with the future of Catholic institutions in a political sense, and that Bavaria's and Württemberg's positions followed more directly from their defense of state sovereignty against both federal intrusion and church independence.[17]

When the joint Prussian and Austrian draft constitution emerged in May, it included a clause calling in general terms for the reconstruction and rights of the Catholic Church at the federal level (following the previous article's more general declaration of religious equality). The clause in article 15 read: "the Catholic Church in Germany will receive, under the guarantee of the Confederation, a constitution that secures its rights and the necessary means to satisfy its needs."[18] The specifics were therefore to be deferred until negotiations with the Vatican at the new Federal Diet, though it was at least clear that some kind of financial provision was intended for it, if not necessarily the landed endowment that both Wessenberg and the Vatican camp hoped for. Hessen-Darmstadt proposed a more detailed version that did stipulate an endowment in land and buildings—"with self-administration but under supervision of the state"—plus Church representation in state diets, but Austria, Prussia, and Hanover found this too specific. They preferred waiting for further negotiations at the Federal Diet in Frankfurt.[19]

Both the original draft and the amended article included a subsequent clause guaranteeing the same or similar rights for Protestants. In this area, too, the differences between the various Catholic groupings were not so great at first. Wessenberg and Consalvi were each eager to see a guarantee of the rights and practical support of the Catholic Church in the German constitution, but each also opposed the proposed guarantee of existing Protestant rights (particularly insofar as these might infringe on Catholic privileges in certain states). The German Committee's fifth session on 31 May struck the whole article. When it began to seem that the reason might lie with the objections of some representatives of Protestant states to the restriction of such provisions to Catholics, Wessenberg came around to supporting a joint declaration guaranteeing Catholic and Protestant institutions. In the end it became a moot point, as the Bavarians managed to kill off both clauses as part of their efforts to protect the sovereignty of the individual states to the greatest possible extent.[20] As the renewed war against Napoleon loomed in the background, but also with an eye toward the stability of Germany's federal future, Metternich and even the Prussians proved sufficiently eager for the unity symbolized by Bavaria's signature that they agreed to Bavarian demands on this and several other issues.

The reconstruction of the Catholic Church in Germany was thus not decided at the Congress or enshrined in the Final Act but instead deferred until the convening of the new German Federal Diet, which turned out to be later than anyone anticipated. The decision did not eliminate the possibility of a German concordat; that remained in play for the Frankfurt negotiations. Yet the delay did ultimately prove fatal for supporters of a federal solution. Metternich and the Austrians continued to pressure the Vatican not to enter into negotiations for separate concordats with individual German states but rather await the meetings in Frankfurt. By the time the question of the Catholic Church in Germany came up for discussion there in November 1816, however, the situation had changed decisively, as separate negotiations had already begun with Hanover, Bavaria, and Prussia itself.[21] Moreover, both the Vatican and its supporters in Frankfurt, including the Schlegels and Schlossers, had come to prefer separate agreements to a federal one. Pilat, in a letter to Count Széchényi, consequently thanked the Lord upon news of the signing of the Bavarian concordat in October 1817.[22]

Freedom of Religion in the German States and Europe

In planning for a stable post-Napoleonic settlement, closely tied to the question of religious reconstruction was that of religious liberty. This implied first of all religious toleration, that is, the guarantee of free public worship, but it also often stretched into the realm of civil rights. With so much redrawing of European frontiers, both during Napoleon's sway and in the Vienna settlement itself, religious boundaries had likewise shifted and left millions living under new regimes, often under rulers of a different confession. Assuring their right to practice their religion, and if possible without civil or political disability, was a first step in reconciling the new residents. Or in some cases, as we shall see, such assurances were a sine qua non for rulers to agree to cessions in the first place. Congress dealings with such issues arose in negotiations involving Belgian, Swiss, and Italian territories, in the Polish context, in the conferences leading to the new German constitution, and even in drafting a commercial treaty between Prussia and Portugal in May 1815. Article 2, coming directly after article 1's basic statement of amity and alliance, established reciprocal protection of religious practice for Prussian and Portuguese subjects in the territories of their new trading partners. Prussia claimed the same rights as those granted by Portugal to certain other nations (particularly Britain as the benchmark), while Portuguese subjects would enjoy the usual rights of religious toleration in Prussia, including worship in homes or in Catholic churches. This treaty, in other words, involved not simply most-favored nation trading status, but most-favored nation religious rights status as well.[23]

As we have just seen with the treatment of Catholic and Protestant rights in the German constitution, the negotiations on balance show at once the strength and the limits of tolerationist views in post-Napoleonic Europe. Settling the relative rights, privileges, and mechanisms of financial support between the state governments and the churches as institutions proved a prickly matter. About the principle that difference of confession among the main Christian groups "cannot justify a difference in the enjoyment of civil and political rights" for individuals, however, there was little disagreement. This principle was stated clearly in article 14 of the committee draft and preserved in article 16 of the final constitution.[24] The guarantee did not, however, prevent the necessity of further negotiations for Catholic equal rights in, for example, Frankfurt and Bremen.

The idea of protecting the rights of religious minorities found much support at the Congress. For one, Protestant and Catholic states were usually willing or eager to speak up for the rights of coreligionists who might fall into the position of a religious minority through territorial redistribution. Keeping such populations reasonably content also made practical political sense. But at the same time, the Enlightenment-derived ideal of religious toleration if anything had come to enjoy even wider acceptance than in the eighteenth century. The "Remarks" to the draft of the new Dutch constitution made concisely clear both the practical benefits and the belief in toleration, asserting: "the state can derive no advantage whatever from having subjects, either complaining of maltreatment, or indifferent on the subject of Religion."[25]

For all the strength of tolerationist sentiment, however, it did not carry the field. Toleration in the sense of eschewing persecution was almost universal, as was guaranteed freedom of worship in the private sphere, at least for most recognized Christian denominations. When, on the other hand, enshrining rights of religious liberty started to move toward equality, ecumenical spirit proved harder to maintain and less widespread. Many European governments, including some of the most powerful, still operated under a system of established churches and state religions in which the latter were privileged while other denominations endured discrimination. Russia, Austria, and Britain all provide notable instances. Russia offered more equality—and tolerance—than one might think, but it was still a confessional state, and toleration had its limits, as with the expulsion of the Jesuits in 1816. Joseph II's Toleration Patent certainly created a more open climate in the Habsburg Empire, but Protestants and their churches still suffered legal restrictions.[26]

Great Britain, more properly known as the United Kingdom after its incorporation of Ireland in 1801 following the rebellion of 1798, had all the more reason to worry about issues of religious equality. But it was not only Catholics who suffered rights restrictions there; Dissenters—members of non-Anglican Protestant sects such as Quakers, Unitarians, and Baptists—were also disadvantaged, however much they constituted a central component of the British political landscape within the broader public sphere. At various times, and in various contexts, observers pointed to this splinter in Britain's eye, in particular its seeming inconsistency in supporting abolition of the slave trade on humanitarian grounds while remaining oppressive toward Irish Catholics.[27] Castlereagh, himself an Irish peer, figured among the Pittite Tories who pushed for reform of the religious establishment and favored Catholic emancipation (but were willing to stop short if it proved too controversial within their own party or the country at large). Consalvi and Castlereagh in fact tried to work out a deal for Catholic emancipation during the summer and autumn of 1814 in London and Vienna. They seemed close, but Consalvi showed more willingness to compromise than some Irish Catholics liked, and the problem of the registration of papal bulls also still stood between Westminster and the Vatican. Reform did not come for Dissenters until the repeal of the Test and Corporation Acts in 1828, followed by Catholic emancipation in 1829, but only after the extraparliamentary agitation of Daniel O'Connell's movement, larger even than that for abolition.[28]

In the new French constitution, Catholicism was restored to its place as the state religion. Yet freedom of worship was also guaranteed, and in this case religious liberty was meant to include religious equality as well. Religious confession was not to be a civil or political disability. Similarly in the constitution for the new city-state of Cracow, Catholicism was recognized as "the religion of the country," but at the same time the document stipulated liberty and equality of "social rights" for "all the Christian confessions."[29] Belgium proved a more difficult case. The recent Dutch constitution with its declaration of full religious equality (including political) for all confessions was extended to the Belgian portion of the new Kingdom of the Netherlands, plus added guarantees of state support for the Catholic Church and its clergy. For many Catholic leaders, however, such equality felt more like a loss of status at the hands of a Protestant ruler. Several local bishops protested Catholicism's loss of privilege in Belgium.[30]

Territorial exchanges also called forth religious rights stipulations in Swiss affairs. The Catholics of the former territory of the bishop of Basel were guaranteed "the same political and civil rights" as the inhabitants of the predominantly Protestant cantons of Bern and Basel to which they were transferred, "without difference of religion."[31] Negotiations between the new Swiss canton of Geneva and the Kingdom of Piedmont over territorial cessions in the Alps proved more difficult, situated somewhere in the sizable gray zone between religious tolerance and intolerance. The restored king of Piedmont-Sardinia was notoriously one of Europe's most reactionary rulers—he had even gone so far as to reestablish pre-1789 fashions at court and to nullify retroactively all marriages conducted by priests under the official revolutionary Civil Constitution of the Clergy in French-controlled lands.[32] Victor Emanuel came under pressure to cede some of his northern Savoyard possessions to Geneva as a means of improving the republic's ability to defend both itself and the new Swiss neutrality established by the Congress. When it came time to negotiate this settlement, the king made clear his expectation that the rights of his Catholic soon-to-be-former subjects be preserved more or less intact within the Calvinist Genevan state. The king and his representative, the Marquis de Saint-Marsan, feared the possible religious intolerance of the Genevan populace, which in turn led them to be something less than tolerant toward the Protestants of these territories.[33]

Victor Emanuel wanted to guarantee the ceded inhabitants "the certainty that they will enjoy the free exercise of their religion, that they will continue to have the means to fund their worship, and themselves enjoy the full rights of citizens." And in this case, unlike in modern usage, rights also meant privileges. The Catholic Church would still hold something like an official established position; Genevan Protestants would not be able to extend their own religious establishment into this newly acquired region, nor would Protestant residents there even enjoy full equality or toleration. If the number of Protestants in a certain district did not exceed or equal that of the Catholic population, for example, then the schoolteachers always had to be Catholic. Municipal officials had to be at least two-thirds Catholic, except in cases where the Protestant population equaled the Catholic. And there were not to be any openly public and publicly funded Protestant churches, "with the exception of the town of Carouge, which is allowed to have one" (Carouge is but a short tram-ride south of Geneva today). This did not preclude Protestants in other communes from having individual chapels or schools—at their own expense—but this was clearly religious toleration of an ancien régime sort, nonrepressive but discriminatory, not like that of the liberalizing nineteenth century that increasingly prevailed elsewhere.[34]

The church in Carouge represented one of the few concessions the Genevan negotiators were able to wring from the Sardinians, strongly as they had objected to the restrictions on Protestant officials, schoolteachers, and churches. The Genevan second plenipotentiary, Sir Francis d'Ivernois, thought the "disadvantages" of the measures so severe that "we must attempt everything in our power" to reverse them (everything at least that would not jeopardize the deal itself).[35] The Genevans argued that such provisions for Catholics went "against the principles of equity" and the policies of the previous twenty years, and pointed out that since Catholics enjoyed the constitutional right to hold office, "why introduce privileges in their favor?"[36] The Genevan delegates at least managed to amend the original proposal's requirement that all mayors be Catholic into the provision that two of the three municipal officers (the mayor and his two associates) be Catholic, and to secure the possibility of private chapels and schooling for Protestants in the new territories, but on the whole the Sardinians held their ground, backed by the confessionally mixed Swiss Committee.[37]

On the flip side, the Genevans proved no keener to open up full rights of citizenship to all of their new Catholic subjects. Religious toleration itself was fairly secure for Catholics, including funding and practice, but Geneva desired limits on the new territories' political representation, partly from fear of being swamped by large numbers of Catholics who might not share the enlightened and republican values of original Protestant Genevans. The final agreement on the Genevan cession, however, stipulated the conditions for Catholics in Geneva generally, including religious protections and political equality alike.[38] The French king and his representative Talleyrand went even further than the Sardinian ruler and played the religion card—alongside that of public opinion—when they refused to cede any of the territory of Gex to Geneva, on the grounds that the king would not yield Catholic subjects to a Protestant state.[39]

The Struggle for Jewish Rights

The Jewish Question was primarily a German Question. This comment has often been made of Jewish-German relations, in pointing to the real problem as one of German identity. The statement runs the risk of eliding the problems of emancipation and anti-Jewish sentiment in other countries, but for the Congress of Vienna it was—almost—literally the case. Similar issues could have been raised regarding the Italian states, and even France, if as with abolition of the slave trade it had been decided to treat the question of Jewish rights as a matter affecting humanity at large. In the event, proponents of Jewish rights did have recourse to humanitarian arguments and to a universalizing language of human rights, but in the technical terms of international law it remained a matter of national significance, primarily for the states of the nascent German Confederation.

Jewish rights did arise in two other European contexts. A declaration of equal rights for those of all religions in the newly established Protestant Kingdom of the Netherlands—uniting majority Calvinist Holland and almost entirely Catholic Belgium—had already been secured in the course of negotiations prior to the Congress, and thus became the first example of an international agreement in favor of Jewish emancipation, or indeed in favor of minority protections more generally. Jews were even admitted to public office under this agreement. As was noted long ago, the location of emancipation in international law proved important in this case—when Belgian Catholics protested the confessional clause (among others), the new King Willem was able to point to the treaty guarantees and say in all sincerity that he could not change the policy.[40]

Jewish rights also received attention in the negotiations over Poland, as Prussian, Austrian, and Russian representatives drafted a constitution for the new Republic of Cracow. Unlike in the Netherlands, Jewish rights did not ultimately feature in the final version of this constitution, signed in 1818, but associated "favorable regulations" treated Jews and Christians equally in terms of citizen duties and taxation, as well as allowing some members of the Jewish community to acquire full civil rights and citizenship. In certain respects the settlement of 1818 went even further than the version anticipated in the spring of 1815, particularly with the clause permitting some better-off Jewish residents to secure citizenship, a matter that in 1815 had been left to fortune, or at least, the decision as to when and under what circumstances they might be granted citizen status had been left to the local authorities. The Cracow settlement reflected the thinking of the main German powers in the conferences leading to the Jewish rights clause in the German constitution as well, in terms of both their motives and goals, and the compromises they would be willing to make (above all in leaving individual states to decide the terms of enforcement of the general drive toward at least partial emancipation). Both of the Prussian officials involved in drafting the new constitution of 1818 worried that local authorities would still be able to undermine the new emancipatory provisions by selectively enforcing those elements that were restrictive for Jewish life and ignoring those that were progressive.[41]

As the instructions to the three Allied commissioners charged with the follow-up constitutional negotiations in Cracow made clear, the improvement of Jews' legal status was considered in part a matter of religious tolerance and justice, but it was also couched in the classic language of

Jewish emancipation that had been formulated in Germany by the Prussian official Christian Wilhelm von Dohm in the 1780s. According to Dohm's ideas, Jewish communities might indeed demonstrate some undesirable qualities, but where they did, the cause lay not with Jewish religion or innate character but rather with the centuries of oppression and demeaning discrimination by Christian populations. Removing the repressive conditions by emancipation would thereby allow the "civic improvement" of the Jews, and the unfolding of a better character by citizens of the Jewish faith would promote their civic and social integration. For "improvement" or "character" one can read a significant degree of cultural and social acculturation, or even assimilation—this was not full-scale pluralism. Dohm's formulation of the question of Jewish emancipation, along with similar Enlightenment reform ideas, informed the thinking of Hardenberg and Humboldt in the Prussian emancipation measure of 1812, and even earlier that of Tsar Alexander in the emancipation ukase of December 1804 for the Russian Empire's Polish lands (and of Prince Adam-Jerzy Czartoryski, one of the advisors on the committee whose recommendations formed the basis of the decree, and who had considerable say in the negotiations regarding Poland and Cracow during the Congress of Vienna).[42] Dohm's ideas continued to be influential at Vienna, even beyond the Prussian and Russian delegations.

Regarding Cracow, the commissioners' instructions stated that Jews should not be subject to greater financial contributions than the new republic's Christian inhabitants, and "even less can one suffer any longer that their customs and their religious ceremonies be subjected to special fees (as for example with the kosher tax)." As the document continued, "vexations of this nature can only delay the period where this numerous class will be able to arrive at a higher level of social culture."[43] It is worth noting that a similar process was seen to be at work in other liberal causes, as the instructions used the same language to describe the hoped-for effects of the end to serfdom in the Republic of Cracow, "to prepare the social culture of the peasants which up to now had vainly been attempted to improve."[44] Residual anti-Jewish fears of the effects on Christian populations remained, as the Cracow settlement followed the Russian ukase of December 1804 in emphasizing the problem of strong drink, with a ban on Jewish tavernkeepers serving spirits.[45]

In turning to the debates concerning the German states, it is first important to get a sense of the legal context in which the discussions occurred.

The pre-Napoleonic laws regarding Germany's Jewish residents (only rarely considered citizens at this point) varied widely. As in most other branches of law in Germany, the political fragmentation of the numerous German states played out in Jewish legislation as well. The laws relating to the civil status of Jews and Jewish communities varied not just from state to state, but from province to province within the same state. Before the French Revolution, the laws were not uniformly unfavorable to Jews, but they were all more or less unfavorable. Many states even still preserved the institution of the "body-tax" or "Leibzoll," a special toll levied on Jews desiring to enter a territory; even postemancipation Prussia maintained the practice for some foreign Jews crossing its frontiers. Although a ghetto such as Frankfurt's was increasingly unusual, many cities and states still made it difficult or impossible for Jews to purchase real estate, within certain areas or sometimes at all. Jewish Germans probably enjoyed the most favorable legal status in the Habsburg monarchy, as a result of Emperor Joseph II's famed Toleration Patent of 1782. Even there, however, while the Jews of Vienna, Bohemia, and Moravia benefited from the relative freedom of Josephine legislation, in provinces such as Steyermark and Carinthia they were barred from settling at all.[46]

By 1814, the legal landscape had become still more disparate. The Kingdom of Prussia and the Grand Duchy of Mecklenburg-Schwerin in northern Germany had gone far toward legal equality in their respective edicts of March 1812 and February 1813. In the western territories that had been under French administration, inhabitants of the Jewish faith had been granted full citizen rights, but were subject to Napoleon's "Infamous Decree," which restricted their civil and economic rights on the grounds that surrounding Christian populations required protection from the allegedly dangerous influences of Jewish society and national character. Bavaria similarly recognized citizenship but restricted civil rights, with some cities still allowed to refuse Jews the right of residence. In some states such as Baden, partial reform granted Jews the general state citizenship but not the municipal citizenship that led to economic and political belonging in local communities; in other states such as Weimar, it was just the reverse—local citizenship was recognized but not state. One of the institutions most invidious to modern eyes in the new Jewish legislation of the southern German states were the limitations on the right to marry, with yearly quotas, and municipal authorities granting or withholding permission. This provision is only slightly relativized by the fact that poorer Christian residents of "German home towns" also often faced limits on marriage and had to prove the financial ability to maintain a new household, as population-control and competition-reducing measures were applied to the urban poor as well as to Jewish communities. Finally there were lands, such as Saxony, that had seen almost no reform of Jewish legal status. Even the body-tax was only revoked by the occupation administration in the autumn of 1813, with the few Jewish residents otherwise still laboring under repressive legislation, denied even the right to public synagogues.[47]

The late Napoleonic and Restoration eras, above all in Germany, are often noted for an upsurge in anti-Jewish sentiment, or even as the origin of a modern (if less racially based) form of antisemitism. This is true of the elite realm of press and associational life, and of the popular world of anti-Jewish violence, the latter seen most famously and frighteningly in the Hep Hep riots of 1819. The period has also, however, been characterized as an era of at least partial emancipation and acculturation, both legally and socially. These two perspectives on the period are not necessarily in contradiction. It has long been argued that the rise and spread of new forms of antisemitism in the later nineteenth century was in part provoked by the trend toward emancipation, as certain social groups and individuals objected to the new status and the more visible presence of Jewish Germans in German social and cultural life.[48]

The same tension, or causal loop, can be seen for the early nineteenth century and the Vienna Congress. In cities such as Bremen, Frankfurt, and Hamburg, there were efforts to turn back the clock to before the Napoleonic occupation, with its new legal systems, including among other things the partial emancipation of the Jews, that is, the at least partial equalization of their civil and political rights with those of Christians. In some areas, this even meant that Jews had been permitted to settle where they had been forbidden before, their previous residence blocked by a long line of corporate bodies in cities and principalities wielding anti-Jewish arguments. The city-state of Bremen provides one such example, central here. In the university town of Helmstedt, the law faculty issued a formal opinion upholding the old laws barring Jewish settlement, but this was ignored by the French government of the new Kingdom of Westphalia. In some locations, efforts to reinstate prior restrictions went as far as making legal moves to expel newly arrived Jewish communities. This was most famously and controversially the case in Bremen and Lübeck, which as sovereign city-states drew the most attention, but it also occurred, though less well-known, in other German cities in the years 1813 and after, including Northeim, which unsuccessfully petitioned the newly restored Hanoverian government on the matter, and old-town Hanover itself, which maintained its previous status of "non tolerandi Judaeos" (the Jewish community lived across the river in the new town). The university town of Göttingen actually expelled its newly settled Jewish residents, retaining only the previously permitted quota of three families as "protected relations"; in this case the university protested some of the expulsions, and was at least able to secure the right of Jewish students to study and live there while enrolled.[49] In Bavaria, too, the old imperial city of Nördlingen maintained the exclusion of Jewish residents, while Nuremberg and Schweinfurt severely limited them.[50]

Against this background, emancipationist and anti-Jewish forces at the Vienna Congress therefore contested two issues, distinct but connected. The first concerned the rights status of Germany's Jewish inhabitants, and whether it would be regulated at the federal level or be left to the individual states to decide. While many German states were looking to restrict Jewish rights once more after the French interlude, above all Austria and Prussia pressed for something approaching full emancipation and knew that this could only be achieved at the federal level. The second struggle involved the efforts by Bremen and Lübeck to deport the new Jewish residents who had settled there in the wake of the Napoleonic reforms. That the Hanseatic authorities were prepared to press Jewish expulsion so strongly and thereby risk losing the goodwill of public opinion and of the main German powers that was considered crucial to retaining the Free Cities' independence speaks to the depth of feeling there concerning relations between German Jews and German Christians.

Since 1701 Lübeck had allowed only a limited number of Jewish families or "protected relations" to reside in the city itself; other members of the local Jewish community had to live in the nearby village of Moisling, formerly Danish but since the Napoleonic period under Lübeck's sovereignty. By the summer of 1814 the city's shopkeepers and craftsmen and their representative organ the Citizens' Assembly were pushing to restrict Jewish economic rights and to remove all but a few of the now roughly three hundred Jewish residents to Moisling. The Senate was more cautious but did not strongly oppose the policy. Bremen claimed to have had no Jewish residents before 1803, when the city had acquired a small parcel of land from Hanover where a few Jewish families lived. Most of the approximately thirty families in the city proper by 1814 had settled there under French aegis. In Bremen it was the Senate, and not least its Congress delegate Johann Smidt, who took the lead in deportation efforts, rather than the lower house.[51]

The other Hanseatic city of Hamburg had the largest Jewish population of any German city (close to ten thousand, about the same as Prague), but the conflict there was less sharp. The city intended to abandon French emancipatory legislation and return to the status quo ante, but as this had been one of the more tolerant legal frameworks for Jews, there was less internal or external pressure on the city fathers. The sovereign city-state of Frankfurt am Main, like Hamburg, did not propose to deport its long-established Jewish community, but a popular movement and the lower house in particular agitated to return to something near the legal situation of the Old Regime. This included the proposition to force Frankfurt's Jewish residents to move back to a restricted zone (if not quite the ghetto) and to prohibit them from acquiring real estate outside those limits. The government of Grand Duke Karl Theodor von Dalberg (the same who featured as the primate of the Catholic Church in Germany in the previous section) had in 1811 granted almost full emancipation to Frankfurt's large Jewish community of nearly four thousand, and they had also finally been officially permitted to acquire houses and live outside the ghetto.[52]

When Salo Baron wrote his book on Jewish rights at the Vienna Congress in the 1920s, scholars still tended to associate liberalism and Enlightenment with pro-Jewish emancipationist views. Little explanation was needed for the support for emancipation by figures such as Hardenberg and Wilhelm von Humboldt of Prussia, as early liberals, or of Prince Metternich, as a man of the Enlightenment. Scholars have since grown more skeptical of automatically equating Enlightenment thought, whether of French or German vintage, with pro-Jewish politics. Anti-Jewish sentiments appeared in the writings of a Voltaire, and there was considerable opposition or at least hesitation regarding Jewish emancipation among German liberals. For at least one important strand of German liberal thought, a corrupt Jewish character and society had to prove itself worthy of emancipation before legal equality could be granted, that is, the assimilation or character change had to precede the improvement in legal status, rather than emancipation being the means of reforming Jewish life as in Dohm's or Humboldt's conception.[53] More recently, scholars have gone even farther in tracing the deep roots of anti-Jewish and antisemitic ideas in German intellectual life, as with efforts to reform Christianity by overcoming its allegedly tainted roots in Old Testament Jewish religion.[54] This trend can be taken too far, however, and runs the risk of no longer distinguishing between those who at the practical legal and political level pursued emancipatory rather than repressive policies with respect to those of Jewish religion or descent.

Anti-Jewish stereotypes remained common in the political elite during the 1848 Revolution, but it had become politically quite incorrect to state them publicly or to oppose emancipation. In 1814, on the other hand, the expression of anti-Jewish beliefs was still acceptably good tone in educated society. On balance, emancipatory sentiments seem to have represented a minority view, among statesmen and in the broader public, both elite and above all popular. The large majority of the educated clearly favored toleration of Jews and frowned on anything smacking of persecution, but support for varying degrees of discrimination in defense of a supposedly threatened Christian population (tiny though the Jewish minority was) remained widespread. In this context it is noteworthy how far even entrenched emancipation opponents felt they had to acknowledge some of the premises of the tolerationist and emancipatory models. Lübeck's representative Senator Johann Friedrich Hach at least thought it prudent to keep fairly quiet about his opposition to emancipation. He even complained about Senator Smidt of Bremen for his lack of discretion in this regard, deeming him "incautious" and too open about his opinions.[55]

Smidt in fact carried a set of instructions—not secret but to be shown to other diplomats—which already included the core tropes of his rather extreme anti-Judaism, plain for all to see. The instructions did not spell out the practical consequences for Jews living in Bremen, that is, expulsion, which would likely have aroused opposition, but they were ominous enough. The actual proposal was sufficiently vague. After a statement of religious protection for Christian confessions and sects came the rider that "certain general principles might need to be established" for Jews. But the build-up to this clause made its tendency quite clear, identifying German Jews as a distinct group, in part "as a particular religious community," but "primarily as a foreign people forming a state-within-a-state through retention of a large part of its national laws." The use of the Fichtean state-within-a-state image is telling, as is the shift from a religious to a "national" or ethnic definition of difference; both appear in Smidt's internal correspondence as well. Given the overwhelming support for religious toleration at the time, it became a leitmotif of anti-Jewish discourse to deny the religious nature of the discrimination and attempt to reformulate it as an ethnic and/or economic matter. Emancipation opponents needed to look enlightened and modern, not benightedly medieval.[56]

As Smidt explained in conversation with a Prussian official (in this case one not unsympathetic to Bremen's policy), the problem was not religious but "whether and by what means a nation that is by its customs and laws still more or less oriental, and that everywhere forms a state within a state, can be Europeanized."[57] Smidt argued that this could only work in a large agricultural state, not in a small trading republic. In his memo to the German powers of March 1815, he dilated on the latter point, insisting that republican political culture required mutual "trust" and common views, whereby immigrant groups with foreign attitudes did not fit. This included Jews, "whose entire external appearance" and "maxims and behavior still contain something so foreign." Although expressed in less stridently anti-Jewish terms, Hach of Lübeck similarly contended that "with respect to Jews trading cities must follow different principles than larger states."[58]

While the Austrians Metternich and Friedrich Gentz also featured among the defenders of Jewish rights, the Prussians constituted the prime movers of emancipation in this period. King Friedrich Wilhelm himself was at best a reluctant supporter. He had only agreed to the emancipation edict upon assurances from Hardenberg that other German states would soon follow the Prussian example, meaning that there would be no sudden influx of Jewish immigrants hoping to enjoy the benefits of the relatively favorable Prussian legislation. Thus some of the Prussian concern to incorporate Jewish rights in the new German constitution stemmed from the desire to make the legislative landscape more uniform (uniformly favorable). With several German states instead threatening reductions in Jewish legal status that would make those with emancipation measures stand out even further, there was added pressure to prevent the situation from becoming still more disparate.[59]

With Prince Hardenberg and Prussian second plenipotentiary Humboldt, commitment to emancipation went deeper. Hardenberg had already been interested in the "civic improvement" of the Jews in the early 1790s during his time as state minister in Prussian Ansbach and Bayreuth, and he pushed through Prussia's Emancipation Edict of 1812. During the wars, he pled the case of the Jews of Wrocław to be allowed to volunteer for military service, still employing Dohm-style argumentation. To let them contribute financially but not serve themselves would be "to insult an entire class of subjects," something Hardenberg found "hard and unjust," and likely to erect obstacles to their ability "to raise themselves to better and useful citizens." War service could then also become a further argument for political enfranchisement.[60] Hardenberg continued to press emancipation at the Congress.

Regarding Humboldt, historians have long noted the seeming paradox that while Caroline von Humboldt both socialized readily with individual Jews and objected to emancipation, her husband Wilhelm did just the opposite: by 1814 he expressed a disinclination for the company of Jews individually, but came out strongly for emancipation. He even suggested to Caroline that he promoted emancipation in part so that he would no longer feel obliged to attend Jewish salons out of solidarity, but this explanation involved a certain special pleading for Caroline's consumption, as support for emancipation clearly emerged from his broader liberal vision of society, in which diverse individuals and groups were left free to develop according to their own propensities rather than be subject to the control of governments or social majorities. Recent interpretations according to which Humboldt's emancipation measures aimed at the total assimilation and extinction of Jewry rather than at creating a space of protected rights for the group as such miss the extent to which Humboldt's political philosophy depended on the embrace of difference, diversity, coexistence, and exchange. Humboldt explicitly rejected the idea of the state as "educational institution"— setting and enforcing the social and cultural norms for groups and individuals—both in the context of Jewish emancipation and generally. Hence unlike those German liberals and conservatives who required German Jewry's assimilation before concessions on rights could be given, Humboldt insisted that freedom and equality be granted first, and unconditionally, if with some expectation of partial assimilation or acculturation as a result. As in his one-time mentor Dohm's formulation but even more consequentially, emancipation formed the precondition and mechanism through which a Jewish society damaged by centuries of Christian oppression would in time repair itself.[61]

The Hanoverians emerged as in some ways the pivotal vote among the German powers on Jewish rights, and analysis of two key documents from their internal correspondence reveals how other, intermediary positions existed between the extremes of nearly full emancipation and almost complete rejection of Jewish presence. One of these statements was a letter to the Hanoverian representative Count Münster from the chief cabinet minister Claus von der Decken back in Hanover.

Decken professed not to want to bring back the old days of "persecution," and was even willing to allow Hanover's Jewish residents limited increases in trading rights, but only as far as was compatible with his conservative defense of the old guild system versus liberal ideas of free trade. What he would not do, however, as he had already stated in response to a petition from Hanover's Jewish community, was grant Jews citizenship and equality; instead they would keep the old "Schutz-genosse" or "protected" status. Decken's greatest concession was to offer "that, however, everything in this constitution [Schutz status] that could serve to diminish their external honor or to belittle them in the eyes of their fellow subjects, would be done away with." At least that far, the rhetoric and arguments of Dohm-style emancipation protagonists had registered; demeaning restrictions were acknowledged to damage the Jewish community, hence they could be dispensed with. Further in the direction of emancipation, however, Decken and the Hanoverian government would not go, as he feared the Christian population's "peril" if the dangerously different Jewish community could suddenly act unchecked.

Moreover, mirroring the approach of Smidt and Hach, Decken explicitly denied that the nature of that difference was simply a matter of religion; it derived much more, he claimed, from different customs and laws. Anti-Jewish measures did not therefore constitute evidence of unenlightened rejection of religious tolerance, but rather represented a matter of policy alone (the strength of religious toleration positions again exerting pressure on opponents of emancipation). Decken wrote to Münster, it should be noted, after he heard that the matter might come up at the Congress, instigated, he worried, by the Jewish communities of the Hansa towns and perhaps lent a too-willing ear by governments who had fallen into a state of "dependency" on the "usurers" during the wars. Whatever influences from Enlightenment emancipationist thought Decken had imbibed, he was still more saturated by traditional anti-Jewish stereotypes and fears.[62]

At least partly in response to Decken's note, Münster commissioned his chief privy councillor at the Congress, the international law scholar Georg Heinrich Martens of the University of Göttingen, to write a memo on the outlook for Jewish legislation. Given that Martens also served as the official secretary of the German Committee in drafting the German constitution, and hence was involved in the fine-tuning of the contested language surrounding the Jewish rights clause in May and June, his views are significant in their own right, in addition to their

implications for pinning down the politics of the Hanoverian delegation as the crucial "swing vote" on the committee. Martens ultimately
struck a middle-of-the-road position, not fully accepting emancipation,
but also going considerably further than Decken, and without his anti-
Jewish rhetorical tropes. Martens made clear that Jews should be able
to buy property, both houses in towns and land in the country—but the
latter only if they were to cultivate it themselves rather than lease it. If
the purchase of houses by Jewish residents in towns drove up home
prices for Christians in the short term, he was enough of a believer in
Smithian economics to think that with the resumption of normal conditions following the end of the wars, the building of new homes would
soon restore "equilibrium" by increasing supply to match the increased
demand. Moreover, Martens identified the matter as one of religion
rather than ethnicity, and therefore of religious toleration. Despite these
concessions to the emancipatory model, however, Martens still came
out against full civil and political equality for Hanoverian Jewry, or
German Jewry generally. He did not think they should be granted citizenship, or allowed to hold public offices, not even those that came
with guild membership. Only for teachers, including university professors in the medical and arts and science faculties, did he envision exceptions, as these too were civil servant positions in the German states.[63]

Jewish rights at the Congress were not promoted solely or even primarily by representatives of the major German powers. Rather, the Jewish
communities of Frankfurt am Main and the Hansa cities sent their own
representatives to Vienna. The Jewish community of Frankfurt delegated
Isaac Jacob Gumprecht and Jacob Baruch (father of the more famous
German writer and political commentator Ludwig Börne). Baruch in
particular already had experience negotiating for the city with Austrian
authorities and was a cosmopolitan man-of-the-world, able to mingle
effectively in the aristocratic milieu of the diplomats. Indeed, in this
Baruch was probably better chosen than his opponent Johann Friedrich
Danz, Frankfurt's official Congress representative, who was reputedly
less comfortable in these circles.[64] From Frankfurt, too, Solomon Rothschild's wife Caroline helped spur her husband and his brothers to
efforts at persuasion in London and Berlin.[65] The Jewish community of
Prague for its part sent Samuel von Lämel to Vienna. He joined with
the Viennese bankers Baron Nathan Arnstein, Baron Bernhard Eskeles,
and Leopold von Herz to petition the Austrian emperor on behalf of
the Jews of Bohemia, Moravia, and Vienna, but he also met multiple

times with Humboldt and Friedrich Gentz about the Jewish rights clause. Gentz as usual was only too happy to accept payment for his services, whereas Humboldt deemed it a matter of right and refused compensation.[66]

Having consulted first with David Friedländer of Berlin, the Jewish communities of the Hansa cities Lübeck, Hamburg, and Bremen elected not to send one of their own to Vienna, but rather delegated a Christian, the Lübeck lawyer Carl August Buchholz, as their joint representative. Buchholz already had a record as a publicist for Jewish emancipation, in cooperation with Lübeck's Jewish community elders. Accompanied by his wife, he too was at home in the salons, but also proved energetic in the press. Moreover, unlike the Frankfurt delegates, who simply argued the specific case of the Frankfurt Jewish community's legal status post-1811, Buchholz pled the cause of German Jewry at large, and in universalist rights-based language. As such, his political efforts stood in direct connection with the campaign to insert a Jewish rights clause in the German constitution. His memoranda to Humboldt and the Prussians even proved influential in the clause's formulation.[67]

With regard to Jewish rights as to other diplomatic contests, the relevant politicking did not simply involve discussions around conference tables or diplomatic notes. There was jockeying to influence public opinion as well, both in the press and in salons. The Jewish salon scene played an important part in the debate over Jewish rights, as itself a strong argument in favor of the possibilities of "civic improvement" or acculturation among Austrian and European Jewish communities. This held above all for Fanny Arnstein's salon, the preeminent site for the mingling of the Habsburg and European social and cultural elites in these years.[68] Baroness Arnstein, though ennobled relatively recently, was also notable as one of the board of directors of the Society of Noble Ladies for the Promotion of the Good and the Useful. She figured as the only Jewish woman and the only board member of nonaristocratic descent, in both respects breaking barriers. Fanny's individual patriotic contributions also at times received notice in the court newspaper the *Wiener Zeitung,* as the journal liked to announce the patriotic charitable activities of Austrians of all classes in these years as a means of encouragement. At the same time, of course, all of this publicity helped prove that those of Jewish faith could be just as patriotic, charitable, and engaged as the Christian population. The Vienna Jewish community's contribution to the illumination celebrating the return of Emperor Franz in June 1814 presented another opportunity to demonstrate both their patriotic potential and their command of the symbols of European culture, and it was significant that their contribution was selected as one of the twelve illuminations to receive an illustrative plate in the patriotic and charitable commemorative volumes produced by the minor official Joseph Rossi. It is even more significant given that just a few years prior, the gentry of the Lower Austrian Estates had pushed through a measure hearkening back to the blood purity laws of Reconquista Spain whereby even converted Jews could not be voted into the Diet.[69] Thus Vienna and Austria themselves displayed the period's tensions between emancipatory and anti-Jewish currents, with voices both favoring and opposing the increasing Jewish presence in mainstream society. When one of the Duke of Wellington's first social engagements on his arrival in Vienna was a dinner at the home of the banker Leopold von Herz, with his uncle Nathan Arnstein present as well, it was significant, and noted as such at the time.[70]

In addition to Baroness Arnstein and her husband Nathan, the home of her sister Baroness Cäcilie Eskeles and her husband, Bernhard, also featured as a social destination for Congress visitors and Austrian elites.[71] Friedrich and Dorothea Schlegel—the daughter of Moses Mendelssohn—actively defended Jewish rights, but it is unclear how much this figured into conversation at their Romantic and Catholic revival salon. The small circle around Johann and Wilhelmine Smidt of Bremen, at least, would have to feature on the opposing side, as a group including not only Senator Hach of Lübeck but also Schlegel's Catholic revivalist comrade Joseph Anton Pilat and his wife, Pilat also unsympathetic to Jewish emancipation.

On balance, the case of Jewish emancipation reinforces the general picture of salon sociability and politics drawn here. Salons at times served particular political ends, yet tended to reveal the limits of party-building and to showcase their continued function as a relatively neutral venue for the mixing of those of even very different persuasions. In a report to the Bremen Senate, Johann Smidt mockingly likened Fanny Arnstein to Esther before Ahasuerus, interceding for her people, and it is likely that she was active for the cause. She at least encouraged Prussian support of the Jewish communities of Bremen, Lübeck, and Hamburg, and Pilat told his friend Smidt that some of "the most renowned of the local Jewish ladies" had lobbied him in his capacity as editor of the semiofficial *Oesterreichische Beobachter* for a favorable review of

Buchholz's Jewish rights pamphlet. According to Smidt's account, at least, Pilat had not responded encouragingly.[72]

But however partisan the Arnstein and Eskeles families may have been, their salons remained above all cosmopolitan and open to those of diverse political persuasions, including opponents of German and Hanseatic Jewry. Cardinal Consalvi's appearance at the Arnstein salon caused much comment, and it was even suggested that perhaps he hadn't known that they were not baptized. But he must have known, whether from the longtime nuncio in Vienna, Archbishop Severoli, who introduced him to the house, or through his diplomatic conversation partner and future biographer Jacob Salomon Bartholdy, an official in Hardenberg's bureau, a future Prussian representative in Rome, and Fanny's converted nephew. Consalvi became a regular visitor in this Jewish household.[73] More surprising from the present-day perspective, even if it provoked little notice at the time, is the fact that two diehard opponents of emancipation were also regulars at the Arnstein and Eskeles evenings: Senators Smidt and Hach of Bremen and Lübeck. It is at least interesting or even significant that neither of them seems to have found this habit strange; presumably it was simply too good, and open, a location for picking up diplomatic gossip to be ignored, but they also seemed to enjoy the hospitality, and in Smidt's case, not just for himself but with his wife and daughter as well. This did not, however, keep Smidt from excoriating Prussia's diplomats in his reports to Bremen's Senate for keeping too much company with Jews, whereby they became "ever more Jewified." Such socializing persisted even in late May and early June, when it became clearer just how important a role the two men were playing in undermining Jewish rights in the German constitution.[74]

With Hach, the seeming oddity could be explained by the already-noted fact that he seems to have played his cards close to his vest and did not advertise the extent of his opposition to Jewish emancipation. He only revealed his position in early March 1815, and even then only to a select few and in confidence. He had also taken care to maintain reasonably good relations with Buchholz, whatever he might have said about him in private.[75] Smidt was more vocal about his opposition, but it is also presumably the case that both men were on their best behavior when in the Arnstein salon. Smidt and his wife, for that matter, also still socialized with the Schlegels, overlooking both their Catholicism, their promotion of Jewish rights, and Dorothea's Jewish birth. Quite significantly, given that men sometimes crossed the lines of class and confession more readily than women, Wilhelmine Smidt both went to the

Schlegels' home as she did to Fanny Arnstein's and entertained them in
hers as well, sometimes Dorothea by herself.[76]

In the press, Buchholz took the lead for the Jewish cause with his
book-length proemancipation pamphlet and document edition published by the liberal Johann Cotta. Among the documents featured not
just the Prussian edict of 1812 but also the Netherlands constitutional
clause of 1814 offering full equality.[77] Buchholz also arranged to have it
translated into Italian and published, with the censor's approval, in
Austria's Italian possession Trieste. The translator, Jewish scholar Leon
Vita Saraval, captured the broader spirit of the piece with the too-
optimistic pronouncement: "Italian Israelites! The epoch in which you
will be men, and citizens, is not far!"[78] Metternich sponsored a favorable
review of the pamphlet in the semiofficial *Oesterreichische Beobachter*,
possibly overriding the paper's editor, Joseph Pilat. Pilat, at least, told
his friend Smidt of his intention to review the text negatively following
the encounter with Fanny Arnstein, but in the event Metternich's other
protégé, Friedrich Schlegel, wrote it, and it was of course quite favorable indeed. Schlegel endorsed the extension of citizenship rights to
"German Israelites" and highlighted their patriotic military service
during the recent wars as one of the strongest reasons for doing so. The
review then appeared in the Italian edition. Whether the choice of reviewer showed the influence of the Arnstein and Eskeles ladies, or simply
that of Metternich himself, is another question. Both are quite possible,
but the latter was decisive.[79] A proemancipation article also appeared
in the official *Wiener Zeitung* and was attributed directly to Buchholz;
its argument that Jews deserved equal rights for performing equal duties at least reflected his preferred rhetorical strategy. Buchholz swore to
Hach that he had nothing to do with it, but while Hach at least at first
believed him, Smidt emphatically did not.[80]

Opponents of Jewish rights either kept a lower profile or were slower
to react in the press. Lübeck's representative, Senator Hach, was composing a pamphlet on the situation of the Jews of Lübeck, but he did not
complete it until after the Congress.[81] His Bremen counterpart, Smidt,
despite his belief in the power of the press and public opinion, contented
himself with a long memorandum circulated among German diplomats
in March 1815, and with an explicit strategy of "witty comments" (presumably disparaging) in social and diplomatic circles.[82]

Not all of the diplomacy relating to the position of German Jews occurred
in Vienna. As the Polish-Saxon crisis dragged on through the autumn

and winter, reports from the Hansa cities began to raise concerns that the decisions might not come soon enough to benefit their current Jewish residents. The guilds and lower houses of the city governments in particular were pressing for anti-Jewish legislation and for economic measures against Jewish merchants. The threat of deportation also hung over the communities. In response, and encouraged in part perhaps by Buchholz and by the Arnstein and Eskeles ladies, Hardenberg applied some pressure to the Hansa authorities, and addressed a firm note to the Prussian representative there, Count August Otto von Grote, for the latter to pass on. The note was drafted by Friedrich Staegemann and found favor with Fanny Arnstein when she saw it later. Grote slightly altered it to emphasize that the Hamburg Senate's policy was closer to what was desired than that of Bremen or Lübeck. Metternich soon followed with instructions to the Austrian representative to write a similar note.[83]

The response from Bremen was not conciliatory, basically backing Smidt's demand that all negotiations go through him in Vienna and insisting on Bremen's full independence and determination to brook no interference in its internal affairs. The city even ratcheted up the economic pressure on the Jewish community in February 1815 by issuing a decree against Jewish retail trade. Lübeck's reply was more moderate if still unsatisfactory, while Hamburg was able to meet the Prussians more than halfway, given Grote's emendation in their favor. Further notes to Bremen at least persuaded the city fathers to await the results of the Vienna negotiations before proceeding further.[84] Prussia and Austria continued to put diplomatic pressure on Bremen and Lübeck through the course of the spring and into the year 1816 and beyond. By April 1815, they were joined in the effort by the Russian representative, who had received orders from Count Nesselrode to support his Austrian and Prussian colleagues in protecting the Jewish residents of the Hanseatic towns and ensuring that they "participate in the advantages enjoyed by all the inhabitants of these cities."[85]

The Prussian, Austrian, and Russian interventions of the winter and spring of 1815 were all designed primarily to hold the line until final decisions could be made in Vienna. It was not until May, however, that the German representatives finally tackled the German constitution, and with it the clause that would provide the framework for Jewish rights in the new federal states: regarding potential political rights, and civil rights, including those of economic access and residence. While article 16 of the final federal constitution clearly stated the principle of equal rights for Christian confessions, the same cannot be said for the declaration of rights for Germany's Jewish inhabitants that the constitution's drafters intended to be the pendant to that statement of religious equality. A complicated series of debates and negotiations resulted in an uneasy compromise, a mixture of victory and defeat: the constitution affirmed the principle of Jewish emancipation, but postponed final decision on its means and extent until the Federal Diet convened in Frankfurt; a clause was inserted to protect the rights of Jewish communities in the interim, but it was successively watered down in the course of revision.[86]

In the initial discussions of the German constitution in October and November 1814, the balance of forces tilted to the side of Jewish rights. Hanover, Austria, and Prussia, the three strongest German powers, all supported the idea, while the midsize states Bavaria and Württemberg opposed it, as they did anything that seemed to infringe their newly acquired sovereignty and royal status. By May, however, when the German Committee resumed formal deliberations, at least three important changes had occurred.[87] First, the German Committee now no longer involved just the five most powerful states but had grown to include representatives of most of the other sovereign German powers as well, several of whom either did not strongly favor Jewish emancipation or outright opposed it. Second, Napoleon had escaped from Elba and regained control of France. This put pressure on the Allies in Vienna to hasten the final settlement, with the German federal constitution as part of the unifying package. Under those circumstances, the smaller powers' capacity for obstruction and persuasion became that much greater, as the Prussians and particularly the Austrians were willing to make considerable sacrifices in order to get a deal done.

The third change involved the fact that at some point in the interim, Hanover's position had shifted, or had at least been clarified in a way unfavorable for Jewish rights. Even though Hanover no longer represented the swing vote in May in the same way it had in November, its position was still pivotal and proved decisive for the adulterated compromise that became article 16 of the German federal constitution. Perhaps crucially as we have seen, injunctions from chief cabinet minister von der Decken had arrived in late November, just after they could have affected Hanoverian representative Count Münster's position in the German Committee negotiations broken off in the middle of the month, but in plenty of time to set the stage for Münster's rearguard chipping away at the Jewish rights clause in May and June.

The opponents' first strategy, if they could not kill the clause entirely, was to delay. If they could defer the final decision on Jewish rights to the eventual Federal Diet, they could hope for a shift in the balance of forces and opinion in the interim that might allow a resolution more to their liking. In the meantime, too, the Hansa cities hoped they might be able to proceed with rights restrictions at home, perhaps even initiating the desired expulsions. The possibility of postponement was already broached in the German Committee's first full meeting to discuss the draft constitution, on 26 May. In the subsequent conferences between the Austrian, Prussian, and Hanoverian representatives to consider potential amendments in response, it was again the Prussians who insisted that they would not yield on Jewish rights.[88] The antiemancipation Smidt of Bremen, who had sounded out Humboldt and Metternich's deputy Wessenberg on the matter, at least thought the latter willing to consider deferral.[89]

Smidt brought up the possibility of postponement again on 31 May. As he recounted his words to the committee, in a conciliatory nod to emancipationist rhetoric, "I wish the Jews everything loving and good, also that means may be found both to improve their situation and to remove the disharmony in which they have stood up to now in relation to the citizens of the states in which they live." But the matter was too important to rush, he claimed, hence the need for deferral.[90] Other governments such as Bavaria, Denmark (for its German province Holstein), and Saxony also favored postponement, the two former out of concern for internal sovereignty more than anti-Jewish sentiments, since they already had relatively liberal emancipation edicts in place that would have passed any likely federal litmus test. The Saxon Count Einsiedel on the other hand, from a state with some of the most restrictive Jewish legislation, echoed the guildsmen's economic anti-Judaic concerns that "the Jews not take over all the trades." An intervention by Count Münster helped secure the necessary votes to retain the article, but only at the cost of already significantly weakening it. He let it be known that Hanover supported the measure only with the understanding that it would be left to the individual states to judge how far they could implement it.[91]

The Prussians knew they would meet considerable opposition from the Hansa cities and Frankfurt, and made efforts to check it before it could gain momentum. Privy Councillor Staegemann approached the Lübecker Hach before the discussion in the German Committee and asked him not to resist the measure, citing as one reason just how important the matter was to Hardenberg, who had convinced the Prussian king against his will (not the wisest diplomatic move). He also asked

Hach to dissuade Smidt from inopportune opposition. Given that the Hansa towns were still engaged in fraught negotiations with the Allies, above all Prussia, about Hanseatic military, logistical, and financial support for the campaign against Napoleon, the Prussians may have thought they had some extra leverage. Perhaps the circumstances worked the other way, however, with the Hanseatics feeling they had more to bargain with. At the end of the first full session of the committee, an enraged Humboldt buttonholed Smidt for a similar but less polite conversation. When the Jewish rights clause received its first reading, first the Bavarian delegate Count Rechberg, and then one by one, most of the other delegates began to laugh.[92] Humboldt (and some later scholars) suspected Smidt's hand behind this not-so-subtle little demonstration, and warned him to keep silent in the actual debate. The jocose Count Rechberg was also asked not to oppose "liberal sentiments" on the issue. Humboldt again requested Smidt's silent cooperation a few days later, telling him that the clause was already bad enough for the Jews, and that the cities would not be forced to take in more Jewish residents but simply to treat well those already there. Staegemann made much the same point to Hach, when the latter objected that if Lübeck granted equal rights, the city would soon be "overflowing with Jews."[93]

In the event both Hach and Smidt indeed spoke out before the committee, and with effect, boldness that earned Hach a further uncomfortable lunchtime confrontation with Staegemann and several other Prussian officials in the Augarten park.[94] The original draft of 23 May read:

> Those confessing the Jewish faith will, insofar as they take on the performance of all citizen duties, be granted the corresponding citizen rights, and where state constitutions stand in the way of this reform, the members of the Confederation declare their desire to remove these obstacles as much as possible.

After the initial committee debates on 1 June, the article read:

> The Federal Assembly will deliberate upon how in the most uniform way possible the civic improvement of those confessing the Jewish faith in Germany is to be effected, and how in particular, for the assumption of all citizen duties, their enjoyment of civil rights in the federal states can be secured; however, until that time those confessing this faith will retain the rights already granted to them in the individual federal states.[95]

Regarding the question of Jewish emancipation itself, the changes represented a compromise. The language was framed in terms of religion, it committed the states to some form of amelioration, and it incorporated the central argument of equal rights for equal duties, but for opponents it deferred final settlement until the Federal Diet's opening. More than just postponing a bitter pill, the delay gave them the opportunity to continue efforts to derail the whole policy.

With respect to the resultant interim period and the related issue of deportations, Smidt and Hach between them achieved what has been seen as the crucial change in the language of the Jewish rights drafts, a simple matter of a preposition. In his report to the Bremen Senate on the session of 1 June, Smidt took credit for helping to introduce the phrase "in the individual federal states," while Hach tried unsuccessfully to change the preposition to "von," that is, the rights to be upheld were those granted "by" the states rather than "in" the states.[96] When the revised article came up for discussion on 3 June, Hach and Smidt again failed to change the preposition "in" to "von." What Hach and Smidt were driving at was the idea that rights granted "by" the states implied an act by the existing government itself, as opposed to an act perhaps imposed by some other authority, simply within a certain territory. Rights granted by the French would not in that view have to be retained by the Hansa towns. Other interpretations are actually possible (depending on what is considered a legitimate government or act of government in a period of transition), and in any event, on this day Humboldt managed to shoot down the proposal with the argument that the choice of word did not make any difference, so "in" it remained.

On that same day, however, what was actually the more significant decision in undermining existing Jewish rights came down. Hach asked directly if the "rights granted" phrase could possibly refer to those granted by the French, a move Smidt deplored as raising the possibility of an affirmative answer. He immediately moved to foreclose such an eventuality and stated that such acts could not be binding on another government. In this he received the support of the important swing voter Count Münster. As on 31 May, Münster again weakened the article, this time by asserting that the French Thirty-Second Military District, in northern Germany, had never been acknowledged by treaty as a legitimate government, hence it could not have laid down binding decisions. Smidt instantly proposed that this declaration be taken into the protocol, and when the secretary, Martens, looked around and saw no objections, it duly was. A week later, Smidt and Hach were finally able to carry the change of preposition too, but only as the result of this prior decision that left the final change of the preposition relatively insignificant, at least for the Hansa cities. As Smidt pointed out in his report, since the declaration regarding the French military government applied to the Hansa towns but not to Frankfurt, the emendation could prove important for Frankfurt's case.[97]

In accounting for the seeming defeat of Jewish rights at the Congress of Vienna, the main historian of the subject critiqued the Arnsteins for deserting their post too early, in April, before the real debates over Jewish rights in the German Committee began.[98] Given that even Prussian and Austrian diplomatic pressure achieved only limited results, this seems rather harsh, but it also misses the fact that the Arnsteins and particularly the Eskeles family were never so out of the picture. The latter continued to entertain at their charming villa in Hietzing, which even in the days before the subway lay within easy reach of Vienna. Yet there were limits to what political sociability could accomplish. On 4 June, for example, in the very days when the crucial decisions were falling against Jewish rights, Madame Eskeles hosted a party that included as guests not only the advocate of German Jewry Carl Buchholz and his wife but also such staunch adversaries as Hach of Lübeck and Joseph Pilat. Hach deemed the conversation "pleasant." His enjoyment of Jewish hospitality at such a moment did not occasion any more cognitive dissonance then than it had before, nor did his immersion in the Arnstein milieu alter his views.[99]

Some later scholars suspected that the undercutting of German Jewry's provisional rights status occurred as the result of sleight of hand or outright forgery. In the most notable instance, the great nineteenth-century Jewish historian Heinrich Graetz pointed the finger at Friedrich Gentz as the culprit. Salo Baron already absolved Gentz from responsibility long ago—he was the secretary for the Congress as a whole, but not for the German Committee, hence not the author of the final version of the federal constitution. He was, moreover, working for the Jewish cause. The weight of opinion since has followed Baron in concluding that the final alteration, though regrettable, was open and aboveboard.[100]

Further scrutiny of the original documents supports that view, although there was more opportunity for shady dealing than most have thought. It is true, for instance, that Metternich read through all the paragraphs before they were initialed near midnight on 8 June, but he made several changes as he read. On the final copy of the paragraphs initialed by the delegates, all of the emendations were recorded in Metternich's hand, except one—the alteration of "in" to "von" in the crucial sentence. Moreover, the whole situation was more chaotic than one might imagine, with rough copies of the draft using the old language until a very late stage in the game, and all late at night, when delegates were perhaps tired and less attentive. And throughout the conferences, delegates had had problems with committee secretary Martens for not always getting words precisely right, given that he was hard of hearing and impatient of corrections on those grounds.[101] As previously shown, though no diehard opponent of emancipation, neither was he a proponent of equal rights, so if not Gentz, then Martens might have yielded to the persuasion of one or both of the other members of the three-person commission responsible for the final draft: the measure's radical foe Senator Smidt of Bremen, or the representative of the principality of Schaumburg-Lippe, Günther Heinrich von Berg of the University of Göttingen, who himself had a past as an anti-Jewish antiemancipation writer.[102] But then, the emendation was not in Martens's hand or ink any more than in Metternich's. In the end, it seems clear not just from Smidt's report and the protocols but also from Hach's account that the change went through in the presence of the full committee. There was no formal vote, but no one contradicted the move, not even Humboldt by that point. The one aspect of the final protocol regarding the change that was added later, at Smidt's instigation and without any basis in fact, was the phrase "as was previously preferred"—as we have seen, and as he had reported, both previous efforts to adopt the alternative preposition had failed.[103]

Why Austria and especially the Prussians held up their hands and let the late-breaking decisions go through without further protest requires some explanation. To some extent it was predictable. Even when preparing the initial draft of the federal constitution for the German Committee, the Prussians had shied away from the expression "previously acquired rights" for fear that it would provoke resistance among states with legislation stemming from French occupation, as it in fact did. It is also true that by May the German powers just wanted to get an inclusive, solidarity-inspiring German constitution signed in time to incorporate with the Final Act before the final confrontation with Napoleon. Humboldt was frankly disheartened at how much the document was being weakened in the process.[104]

Still further mystery surrounds the immediate aftermath of the emancipation negotiations and points in yet another direction for explanations. In particular, on 9 June both Metternich and Hardenberg wrote sets of letters reassuring the Jewish communities of Frankfurt and the Hansa cities of their success, and pressuring those same cities not to take measures restricting Jewish rights. What has puzzled subsequent historians is the fact that Metternich still used the formulation "in the individual states" when quoting the constitution, and that Hardenberg also still proceeded on the assumption that the committee had just enshrined Jewish rights in its decision. For some earlier scholars this supplied more fuel to the conspiracy and forgery thesis; others have simply explained it away as oversight by the statesmen or sloppiness by their staffs.[105] But privately, too, both Humboldt and Gentz prided themselves on the negotiations' success in stipulating a Jewish rights clause (rather than seeing it omitted), and historians must take these reactions into account.[106]

Explaining the mystery requires looking in another direction, where the change in prepositions was not as damning, and diplomacy ran on more fluid lines. For diplomacy and politics is never entirely about the words, but about power. The words that finally appear on paper are rarely really final. The wording represents a temporary compromise or truce, a semantic position from which both sides in a conflict can agree to continue their disagreement at a later date, by the same or other means (and not only force). Metternich in particular believed the application of power and pressure could bend the interpretation of the printed words in the desired direction thereafter.[107] In the case of Jewish emancipation, one could carry on the battle over how to interpret "previously acquired rights" for the interim period, while the clear statement of principle that assumption of citizen duties should lead to citizen rights made a promising point of departure for policy going forward. Anti-emancipation figures could believe they had achieved a better defensive position after the change of prepositions, but Metternich and the Prussians could still feel confident (if ultimately erroneously) of their greater power of persuasion.

According to a scholarly tradition going back to the period immediately following the Congress, and still largely followed today, the change of the prepositional "little word" made all the difference. Johann Klüber, scholar of German constitutional law and editor of the semiofficial collection of diplomatic documents from the Vienna Congress, in 1816 also published an account of the negotiations leading to the German federal constitution. In that work he strongly upheld such a construal of article 16. Although Klüber was an old collaborator of Chancellor Hardenberg and acted with his support in assembling the document edition, in the matter of Jewish emancipation the pair were miles apart. Klüber's digression on Jewish policy was saturated with anti-Jewish or indeed proto-antisemitic racist language of a sort that merits him a place alongside Friedrich Rühs or Hartwig Hundt-Radowsky in the history of early German antisemitism. For that reason alone, one must be cautious about accepting his interpretation of article 16 at face value.[108]

The change of preposition was ultimately not as significant as most scholars have assumed. Whatever Smidt and his collaborators liked to claim, the significance of the change of "in" for the meaning of the clause was not clear-cut. Humboldt had after all sunk the original proposal for the switch with the argument that the choice of word did not really make any difference; the same argument could still hold from the Prussian or Austrian point of view after the change. When Hach of Lübeck reported the measure's final carriage on that last night of negotiation, he did not trumpet it as a triumph but rather listed it among the minor emendations of little significance to the Hansa cities.[109]

Some states, particularly Hanover, Lübeck, and Frankfurt, did highlight the change in justifying anti-Jewish measures, and of these some even cited Klüber's account of article 16 in support.[110] While German states would not be forced to uphold French laws on Jewish emancipation that had been enacted under occupation, however, this did not mean they had a free hand, or that they could automatically revert to the legislative status quo ante. The whole import of the Jewish rights clause, after all, presupposed that the Confederation and its constituent governments would discuss moving ahead with some measure of amelioration, and that in the meantime the conditions of Jewish life should not suffer renewed restriction. Throughout the rest of the decade and into the early years of the next, promoters of Jewish rights continued to cite article 16 in support of their position, just as Metternich and Hardenberg had on the day following the decision. The director of the Lübeck Jewish community, Heymann Liefmann, petitioned the city on that basis in August 1815, and a new memorandum prepared for the Federal Diet by Buchholz and the Lübeck Jewish community in December 1820 similarly argued that the literal interpretation of the in/by distinction ran contrary to the whole "tendency" of the federal constitution. Metternich, too, still made that argument in 1820. Even after 1830, the important Jewish advocate for Jewish rights Gabriel Riesser upheld the broader interpretation of article 16 in his seminal pamphlet on emancipation.[111]

It is therefore misleading to claim that those who cited article 16 in favor of Jewish rights—whether a Metternich, a Hardenberg, or a

Liefmann—were employing a "false interpretation" of the clause.[112] Moreover, on several occasions the Federal Diet accepted these arguments, as in discussing the Bremen case in 1820 and that of Lübeck in 1821. The Bavarian reporter for the Diet, Johann Adam von Aretin, in 1820 acknowledged that the "meaning" and "tendency" of article 16 was "gradually to nationalize the Jews, and to improve their condition."[113]

Even more tellingly, Senator Hach himself construed article 16 in basically the same way. After his return to Lübeck in the summer of 1815, he wrote a report for the Senate on the Jewish rights negotiations in which he argued that they "show clearly that one can transact nothing to the disadvantage of the Jews before the further treatment of the matter at the Federal Diet." Hach also remained alive to the issue of tacit consent. That is, even though Lübeck's Senate had not followed the French regulations since their recovery of power, neither had they returned to the previous situation in their treatment of Jewish residents. Instead, they had accorded them permission to reside in the city as well as limited economic rights. To rescind these before the Federal Diet had debated the issue seemed to violate the agreement just forged at Vienna. Moreover, in August Hach wrote in the same vein to Smidt in Bremen, expressing his concern at the interpretation of article 16 on which the Burgher Assembly was proceeding, with their calls for immediate expulsions and trade restrictions.[114] He may to some extent have simply feared the wrath or at least the interference of the Great Powers if his city continued to flaunt their wishes, but his reading of article 16 clearly also guided his call for caution in Hanseatic Jewish politics. Once the die was cast and Lübeck committed to a policy of expulsion, Hach fell into line. His contribution to the pamphlet war over the so-called Jewish Question supported the sharper antiemancipation interpretation of article 16, complete with references to Klüber. He even forged contacts with the famed anti-Jewish publicist Rühs. But at least behind the scenes, Hach was unconvinced about the legal and diplomatic framework within which the Hansa towns were acting.[115]

Despite the supposedly definitive defeat of Jewish emancipation through the change of prepositions in article 16, therefore, the struggle over its interpretation, and over Jewish policy generally, continued for several years, even through the conservative turn of the Restoration following the Carlsbad Decrees in 1819. Yet even the instances where the Federal Diet accepted the idea of Jewish emancipation based on article 16 proved a series of ultimately Pyrrhic victories. With only a few exceptions, the expulsions went ahead in the end, in both Lübeck and

Bremen. At the conclusion of the battles over Jewish rights in Frankfurt between 1816 and 1824, the Federal Diet was able to prevent the worst of the city's plans. Frankfurt was not allowed to reinstitute the ghetto, or severe geographic restrictions as to where Jewish residents could live—that flew too much in the face of what was considered progressive in the early nineteenth century. The 1824 settlement also created the largely symbolic category of the "Israelite citizen," in which at least the name if not the rights of political participation were preserved. The Jewish community expressed itself satisfied with the compromise, but clearly only measured against an outcome that could have been worse, as opposed to the briefly tasted equality that they had originally striven to save.[116]

Throughout the period of the Vienna Congress, the balance of opinion in salons and in the press lay in favor of protecting or even extending Jewish rights. Buchholz alone outperformed his opponents, and received support from some of the more important European news outlets (the semiofficial ones or those that borrowed from them). Opponents often felt they had to tread carefully in airing their views. By the time of the delayed opening of the German Federal Diet in Frankfurt, however, the needle of public opinion (at least in print) had begun to swing the other way. In 1815, op-ed measures did not prevent the adulteration of the Jewish rights clause, but they did help create the atmosphere in which such a clause became possible. In the following years, similar efforts from the anti-Jewish camp did not effect a sea change in Jewish legislation in the opposite direction, but they helped bring about the stagnation of the emancipation movement and a gradual erosion of previous gains in Jewish rights. With respect to both Jewish rights and relations between Catholics and Protestants, an ecumenical impulse predominated in political culture in the years 1814–1815. But even then there were limitations, and downs outweighed ups in confessional relations over the coming decades.

CHAPTER FIVE

Europe in the Wider World

Most histories of the Vienna Congress proceed on the assumption that mention of anything outside Christian Europe was studiously avoided, particularly anything touching on the hot-button issues of the colonial sphere or the Mediterranean and the Ottoman Empire. This impression is not on balance wrong, but it overlooks the extent to which the statesmen, and above all the broader publics, did in fact confront the relationship between Europe and areas wholly or at least partly outside it. Attention to these matters reveals important aspects of both European political culture and the emerging international system during the early decades of the nineteenth century. Historians searching for the origins of international humanitarian organization typically point to the foundation of the Red Cross or the agitation over Christian minorities in the Ottoman Empire during the latter half of the nineteenth century. Yet in its own right, the Vienna Congress years before witnessed an upsurge in humanitarian politics and the early stages of its institutionalization. In addition to the protections for Christian and Jewish religious minorities already seen, Europeans concerned themselves with the fate of Christians in the Islamic world and Africans ensnared in the slave trade.[1]

Untangling these negotiations also sheds light on the relationship between power, ideas, and public pressure. Metternich and the British in particular were indeed eager to keep the situation in southeastern Europe and the Mediterranean from destabilizing further, while the British insisted that anything smacking of maritime rights or colonies not be broached at the Congress. Diplomatic and military chatter from farther down the chain of command, however, plus the many voices from press and salon circles, would not let the rulers and foreign ministers forget that the situation in southeastern Europe still simmered in a state not far short of undeclared war. With the rebellious Serbs and the restive Greeks on the one hand and with tensions between the Russians, Austrians, British, and Ottomans on the other, low-level conflict remained ever-present and ready to ignite. The Austrians had to iron out the contested handover of territories and armaments in northern Italy and the Adriatic with the British, through the autumn and even into the crisis period of January and February; the conflicts with the Montenegrins and Russian agents over the Adriatic coast during the summer and fall of 1814 were sharper still.[2] And with the British keenly pushing abolition of the slave trade, colonial questions and maritime rights hovered near the table as well; attention to overseas trade and slavery meant in turn that the problem of Christian captivity in North Africa remained close to the public and diplomatic eye. Although lacking the massive extraparliamentary organization of the British abolitionist movement, various figures made efforts to mobilize elite and public pressure to persuade the statesmen to confront the corsairs. That all of this ultimately tended to produce continued cooperation among the European powers rather than sending them over a brink to which they already stood perilously near for several months, in the saber-rattling surrounding the reconstruction of Poland and Germany, takes some explaining.

At the same time, the questions of both abolition and the Barbary corsairs were bound up with the European self-image and image of a culturally different Other at a time of transition between older and newer forms of colonialism and imperialism. Attention to this side of Congress diplomacy and public opinion casts light on changing attitudes toward race and humanitarian or philanthropic endeavors, as toward notions of civilization and barbarism, East and West, Christianity and Islam. Just about all the issues treated in this chapter revolved in part around religion, even if ultimately they were defined and determined still more by political and economic considerations. The drive to abolish the slave trade, both within diplomatic circles and in the public, was to a considerable extent propelled by the rising evangelical movement, above all in England, and in part by liberal humanitarian sentiments (the two groups of arguments and of people often overlapping). Worries about Christian captivity in the Mediterranean, and about the Greeks and the Ottoman Empire generally in southeastern Europe, almost inevitably touched on a European Christian identity, however much diplomats tried to avoid it. British economic and military power certainly helped promote abolition measures, but at the same time the logic and emotive force of humanitarian language and public opinion exerted their own power and proved hard to resist. Still, despite the force of might and of right, the negotiations also show the obstructive power of less powerful sovereign entities, much as in the case of the German city-states in the struggle over Jewish rights. The immediate failure to deal with Barbary or the situation of the Serbs and Greeks in part highlights the weight of power politics among the Great Powers, but over the longer term these issues, too, rather underscore the interrelationship between power, ideas, and public opinion, as events moved toward independence.

Abolition

The British abolition movement's triumph in 1807, though the most famous milestone, marked the end neither of the Atlantic slave trade nor of efforts to stop it. In fact, those efforts were in some ways just beginning. This is true not just in the sense that slavery remained legal (abolitionists knew that battle remained to be fought) but also for the slave trade itself. Particularly with the return to peacetime in 1814, the pace of the trade accelerated once again, leaving the decade 1821–1830 as the second worst in history for the number of Africans transported forcibly across the ocean into servitude (more than 850,000; the five-year period 1816–1820 already claimed just over 400,000).[3] Opponents of the trade understood all too well that further measures were necessary to ensure its real cessation.[4] The Treaty of Paris in May 1814 had proven disappointing, since it only addressed the French slave trade, and gave the French a five-year grace period in which to continue slaving and repopulate the plantations of their newly returned colonial possessions. Abolitionists consequently set their sights on the Congress of Vienna as the next opportunity to achieve their aims.

The negotiations over abolition at the Congress have always been those most recognized as involving the power of public opinion. The main promoters of abolition were the British, above all Lord Castlereagh in the various international conferences, and the Duke of Wellington in his capacity as British ambassador in Paris. At the level of the broader public, too, the British took the lead, essentially as an extension of the widespread abolition movement of the campaign's heroic years between the 1780s and 1807. The year 1814 in fact witnessed the greatest

abolitionist petition drive of all. In the wake of the inadequate Treaty of
Paris, and in advance of the Congress and of the visit of the European
rulers to London in June 1814, abolitionists presented over one million
signatures from 850 different communities to the British Parliament in
order to pressure the government to push for full and immediate abolition among all nations.[5] Parliament responded with unanimous supportive votes in both houses.

As in the runup to the passage of abolition within the British Empire
in 1807, the abolition movement comprised a disparate array of unlikely allies, from evangelical religious conservatives of a normally Tory
persuasion, like William Wilberforce and Thomas Clarkson, to Whig
lords and early liberals and radicals of the opposition, such as Lord
Holland or Henry Brougham. By 1814, the base of support had swelled
to include some of abolition's prior opponents from the proslavery
West Indian interest, who presumably only jumped on board to ensure
that if Britain and its colonies could not reap the fruits of the slave
trade, other colonial powers would be deprived of that resource as well.
Abolition skeptics among the continental and colonial powers liked to
claim that the British were motivated entirely by such dog-in-the-manger
eagerness to ensure competitive advantage and bring others down to
their new level, but this was only true of a minority of the British public
and lobbyists.

The continental nations notoriously did not have strong abolition
movements. With the partial exception of France, however, educated
attitudes on the Continent tended to reflect the Enlightenment opposition to the slave trade of authors such as Montesquieu and Abbé Raynal.
The "colonial fantasies" of Germans, for example, as inhabitants of states
without colonies, played out in part on the basis of antislavery assumptions that they could run colonies in a more humane way than the other
European powers. With some exaggeration, the German legal authority
and editor of the first major collection of Congress documents Johann
Ludwig Klüber prefaced his account of the slave trade negotiations
with the assertion that "the conviction of the disgracefulness and inhu-
manity of the African Negro or slave trade may now indeed be presupposed among all educated readers, or in general among all for whom the
sense of the dignity and innate rights of man is not entirely foreign."[6]
Even in Portugal, humanitarian values had taken hold to the extent that
most proslavery advocates had to adopt "tolerationist" positions, that
is, conceding the injustice of the slave trade and slavery, but pointing to
the need to keep the system going temporarily while gradual solutions

were sought.[7] The lack of a political movement, in other words, in this case said more about these countries' political culture than it did about the state of public opinion. The first real civic associations on the Continent devoted to international causes (as distinct from support of the war effort against Napoleon) did not arise until the Philhellene movement of the 1820s, with its publicistic, financial, and political support for Greek independence.[8]

France does seem to have been an exception regarding abolition. At least partly out of injured national pride and Anglophobia, much of the French public reacted allergically to calls to end the trade, above all when pressed on them by the detested British. Abolition, in this view, simply represented a British measure to prevent France from regaining a powerful overseas empire. It was the latest perfidy of perfidious Albion (quite literally: the antiabolition pamphlet of French naturalist Ambroise Palisot de Beauvois referred to "perfidious designs and ambitious views contrary to French interests" without needing to name names). If British antislavery sentiment had become an element of British national identity during the revolutionary and Napoleonic wars following the loss of the North American colonies, traditional French anti-British sentiment now went hand in hand with opposition to abolition, at least in many circles.[9] If any progress was to be made in getting France to end the trade earlier than the five years stipulated in the treaty, Wellington informed Wilberforce, they must "create a public opinion in France upon this question, as has been done in England." A similar appeal to national honor coupled with suspicion of British motives characterized the Portuguese case as well, though in support of gradualist positions rather than of openly proslavery stances.[10]

Public opinion proved an essential element of abolition politics, and not only as a rhetorical ploy or convenient excuse. When Castlereagh and the British told the other powers that public opinion was pushing them to act on abolition, the pressure was real. The argument was powerful, but at the same time they feared that it set them at a disadvantage. As Castlereagh wrote to his prime minister, Lord Liverpool, since everyone knew the British government was compelled to deliver an abolition measure, all sides were weighing the possible concessions that could be wrung from it in exchange for support on abolition.[11]

Moreover, while the British were looking over their shoulders to public opinion and using it as an argument for the cause, Talleyrand and the French were doing the same, in the other direction. They continually cited the state of French public opinion as a prime excuse for not being able to accommodate British desires for full and immediate cessation of the trade. In this too they were not wholly disingenuous, as the western ports with the strongest colonial and slaving interests had indeed featured among the strongest supporters of the Bourbon restoration, and consequently were not to be slighted too readily.[12] Wellington and the British abolitionists largely accepted this portrait of French public opinion, and worked to correct it with their pamphlet campaign. Castlereagh also thought French public opinion "a serious obstacle." Unfortunately for that program of educating opinion, as Wellington explained to Wilberforce, the daily press was the only real venue through which to do so in France, and "it is impossible to get anything inserted in any French newspaper in Paris in favor of the abolition, or even to show that the trade was abolished in England from motives of humanity." Even the time-honored tactic of floating articles in English newspapers in the expectation that they would be excerpted by those in France did not work in this case. But Wellington would keep trying.[13]

The Portuguese, too, had recourse to the argument from refractory public opinion. They blamed it for not being able to go as far as the British wished toward speedy and full abolition, but they also played the public opinion card in calling for greater compensation for the concessions they might make. The argument convinced Castlereagh to agree to nullify the Commercial Treaty of 1810, as the Portuguese government needed some such popular measure to offset the agreement on partial abolition, which was bound to be unpopular. This was particularly the case in Bahia, they claimed, that is, the portion of Brazil's northeastern sugar-producing regions most affected by an immediate stop to the slave trade north of the equator (southern Brazil had always dealt primarily with Portuguese possessions in southern Africa, Bahia on the contrary with the Gold Coast and other areas of West Africa).[14]

Given the importance of continental and particularly French public opinion for abolition, influencing it became the order of the day for abolitionists and British diplomats. The two groups even cooperated to a surprising extent. Thomas Clarkson wrote to his wife in June 1814: "if we *exert our voices,* we are *sure* to *find a change at the ensuing Congress.*"[15] It is somewhat surprising that abolitionists did not, in order to keep up the pressure, send a representative to Vienna as they had to Paris, to work the statesmen, sovereigns, and salons. The grand man of the antislavery movement, Thomas Clarkson, had himself visited Paris for the peace negotiations in the spring of 1814, but in this case he feared that his presence as lobbyist might be deemed unhelpful interfer-

ence by Castlereagh and harm the cause. Wilberforce felt this still more
strongly and actively discouraged anyone from going to Vienna.[16] The
abolitionists may have believed that they had achieved a sufficient level
of contact with the rulers and statesmen during their London sojourn in
June, when Wilberforce and his collaborators had taken advantage of
the decision-makers' proximity. Wilberforce and Clarkson, for example, visited both Tsar Alexander and King Friedrich Wilhelm of Prussia
in London, and abolition also came up when Alexander pursued his
ecumenical and evangelical religious inclinations by attending a Quaker
meeting during his stay. Abolitionists, as with many another constitu-
ency, pinned their hopes particularly on the tsar, as a notoriously devout
and philanthropic figure.[17] In the event, Admiral Sir Sidney Smith, in
Vienna primarily on other missions, was the only real notable of British
abolitionist circles at the Congress.

For the most part abolitionists focused their efforts on the written
word, both correspondence and print culture. Clarkson, for instance,
prepared an abridged version of one of his pamphlets for translation
into German, specially for the Congress. He sent copies in both English
and German to Metternich, one for the prince, one for his emperor, and
two for wherever Metternich thought it might do the most good. The
Prussian king and chancellor similarly received copies. If the words
alone did not sufficiently move the recipients, the pamphlet's twelve
horrifying plates depicting the treatment of slaves by traders and masters were present to amplify the effect. Nor did Clarkson fail to include
a copy of the famous slave-ship diagram to make the case that much
more visual and visceral. As Clarkson underscored in his accompanying
letters, he hoped that the assembled rulers would issue a declaration "*that
the Slave Trade is against the Law of Nature, and therefore against the
Law of Nations.*" "One simple act at Vienna," he claimed, would "prepare
the way for Light and Happiness to a whole Continent."[18] In the pamphlet, Clarkson elected to appeal almost entirely on the basis of "humanity, justice, and religion [Menschheit, Gerechtigkeit und Religion]."
He mentioned the potential utility of trade to Africa but explicitly stated
that he would not pursue the claims of "pragmatic political wisdom
[Staatsklugheit]" in this instance. The claims of Christianity, but above
all the harrowing descriptions of the Middle Passage, formed the core
of his account. In Paris, Wellington encouraged Clarkson to lead with
his famed work *Essay on the Impolicy of the African Slave Trade*, thinking the appeal to economic and political interests more likely to be effective there.[19]

There is even some indication that Clarkson's writings left a deep impression on the tsar. In a note setting out Alexander's support for abolition to the Spanish government, the Russian minister in Madrid asserted that the "scandalous commerce" was as "illegitimate in its principle as revolting in its details." The statement echoes one that Alexander allegedly made to Clarkson after reading about the details of the Middle Passage and seeing Clarkson's slave-ship diagram; having become sick on the passage from Dover back to France, the tsar claimed that it was less the choppy sea than the words and images from the book that had made him ill.[20] More generally, Alexander cited humanitarian grounds of "liberty, the law of nations, enlightenment, justice, and humanity."[21]

Alongside Clarkson, portions of Wilberforce's letter to his Yorkshire constituents on abolition had been translated for publication by Madame de Staël's daughter Albertine and family friend and political comrade the Duchesse de Broglie, with a preface by Germaine herself that particularly aimed to counter French suspicion of British motives. Wilberforce also composed a pamphlet in the form of a letter to Talleyrand, directly addressing France's situation and translated into French. Sidney Smith made sure Talleyrand received a copy in Vienna. The prince avowed himself convinced, but suggested that the problem was to convince the French public.[22] A long review of the work appeared in a major German periodical in March 1815, as well as a parallel translation from English in another, too late to affect the Vienna negotiations under Castlereagh's tenure, but still in good time to continue pressuring the French to adopt immediate abolition (the main point of the pamphlet and the review).[23] Wellington offered to distribute—quietly—a hundred copies in Paris. Given the problems with the French press, that would at least be a start in the effort to sway French opinion.[24]

Another of Staël's Coppet circle, the Swiss historian and political economist Jean-Charles-Léonard Simonde de Sismondi, also published a pamphlet on the slave trade, in which he attempted to persuade the French that abolition was in their interests as well as a humanitarian necessity. The Duke of Wellington, still emphasizing appeals to material interests in attempting to influence the influential, bought up all the copies he could find in Paris for distribution to government figures and members of the Chamber of Peers, and even ordered more from Geneva. The pamphlet went through three editions in 1814, the third published simultaneously in Geneva, Paris, and London and appending Sismondi's "New Reflections" in which he answered his critics and targeted two of the main antiabolition pamphlets circulating at the time (one French, one Portuguese). A partial German translation also appeared in one of the main organs of emergent German nationalism. Wellington at least thought that he detected some echo of Sismondi's ideas in the newspapers and among some officials.[25]

The involvement of figures such as Staël and Sismondi highlights how far British abolitionists knew they could rely on connections with European antislavery and political networks to help accomplish their goals. It was the well-connected Genevan Charles Pictet de Rochemont, for example, who at Sismondi's behest passed along a copy of Sismondi's abolition pamphlet to Talleyrand in October 1814. Moreover, Pictet and fellow Genevan delegate Sir Francis d'Ivernois (like Sismondi with British ties), followed up on this opening one evening at Talleyrand's salon. Pictet thought Talleyrand must not have read Sismondi's work very carefully, since he could only give "many bad reasons" why France should continue the slave trade for the five years granted by the Treaty of Paris, and did not seem to have taken Sismondi's ideas on board. Into that breach stepped d'Ivernois, himself a noted political economist, who "debated" with Talleyrand "the question of the utility of the slave trade for France." Talleyrand still only mounted a weak defense, which led Pictet to suspect that Talleyrand, being an intelligent man, probably intended to make a deal for an abolition agreement later in any case (Pictet's reading of the situation thus differing little from Castlereagh's).[26]

The activities of the Genevans and Madame de Staël's circle point to an often neglected international and transnational dimension to the abolition movement in this period, and to diplomacy generally. In this case they served as Francophone intermediaries between Britain and France. They also formed part of a larger "Protestant international" within financial, publishing, and intellectual circles, already strong in the eighteenth century and if anything more so in the nineteenth. The nineteenth-century version of the network possessed deeper religious tendencies and ties to the evangelical awakening in Britain and the Upper Rhine area of Switzerland, Germany, and France. And this network, like the new awakening itself, had connections across confessional divides, not just with Russian and Greek Orthodox, but with Catholics as well.[27]

In turning to the formal diplomatic negotiations on abolition, even the official protocols offer more of interest than the usual coverage suggests, particularly when set alongside behind-the-scenes commentary.[28]

With France at least committed to ending the trade in the foreseeable future, that left Spain and Portugal with their Atlantic empires as the main cases to handle. The United States and Denmark had already agreed to forgo the slave trade in 1807 and 1808, respectively, at about the same time that abolition had finally carried in Britain. In 1814 the restored Kingdom of the Netherlands, prodded by its British benefactors, did the same, the Prince of Orange affirming that he acted not only out of gratitude to Great Britain but was "at the same time performing an act of Christian duty, prescribed as he conceived by the Principles of the Religion which he professed." Unprompted, the German city-state of Bremen, admittedly with less at stake, also abolished the slave trade.[29] Portugal had signed a treaty with Britain in 1810 in which they agreed to tackle the question of ending the trade, but set no time frame for doing so. Hence they, like the Spanish, were being pressed at the Congress to declare one, while the French were requested to reduce the number of years before they finally ended the trade, perhaps from five to three.

In Vienna during the autumn of 1814, quiet diplomatic discussions occurred from the outset. As late as the end of November 1814, Talleyrand claimed to have told Castlereagh very firmly that he did not want to hear any more about abolition for the time being, or as he expressed it, the affairs of Africa could be dealt with only after those of Europe had been settled. In a volte-face two weeks later, at the same time that Great Power relations were reaching full crisis and likely in part for that reason, Talleyrand tried to curry favor with Castlereagh by proposing the formation of a special commission on the slave trade. Anglo-French cooperation on abolition might (he likely hoped) facilitate a similar entente in the showdown with Russia and Prussia over Saxony.[30] For five weeks nothing seemed to happen, at least in public, as most energies concentrated on Poland and Saxony. Behind the scenes, though, just days before Britain, France, and Austria signed an alliance against Russia and Prussia, Castlereagh had a productive meeting on abolition with Tsar Alexander.

Once the primary obstacle to Great Power cooperation had been overcome with the renewed movement over Saxony and Poland in January 1815, abolition jumped to the top of Castlereagh's list of things to accomplish before he returned to Britain to face the opposition in the House of Commons. Hence the abolition conferences basically unfolded in parallel with the still rancorous and drawn-out final resolution of the Saxon crisis. Whereas most Congress diplomacy on important matters took place among the four main Allies or the Committee of Five (with the addition of France), abolition presented a perfect case in which to work through the Committee of Eight, representing the signatory powers of the Peace of Paris: theoretically—and symbolically—the Congress's central forum. Spain and Portugal after all, along with Sweden, rounded out the committee and hence provided just the right representation to deal with issues concerning the slave colonies and aiming at a broad European consensus.

Still, the first meetings were filled with wrangling over precisely that jurisdictional question, since both Spain and Portugal objected to negotiating about the slave trade with noncolonial powers like Russia, Prussia, and Austria. They preferred simply facing Britain and its reluctant supporter France in pinning down the details of the path toward abolition. That abolition would come, and before too many more years, they did not dispute—the slave trade as such truly had come to seem almost indefensible in high diplomatic circles, with arguments to delay or mitigate the inevitable the only ones left. The conditions under which abolition would occur, and the length of the interim period that colonial powers would have to work with before it did, however, remained very much to be determined.

After that initial battle over venue (Britain and its allies successfully insisted on the Committee of Eight), the rest of the negotiations turned to those specific issues. They also spawned a number of firsts in international relations. Most famously, Castlereagh was able to forge a joint declaration condemning the slave trade in humanitarian terms and calling for its abolition in the not too-distant future. The document justified itself in the name of "the principles of humanity and of universal morality," and boldly claimed of the slave trade that "the public voice in all civilized countries has arisen to demand that it be ended as soon as possible."[31] Even Portugal and Spain agreed to sign, Portugal's Count Palmella stating that the "necessity" of abolition was "fully recognized by his government," and Spain's Marquis of Labrador acknowledging that all nations were "in agreement about the general principle of abolition." Both, however, still wanted the document to contain assurances that the two nations could set their own time limits with regard to local circumstances in their colonies.[32]

At the point a few years previously when abolition of the slave trade was about to pass into law in Britain, in 1807, proslavery advocates had launched a rearguard action designed to alter the language of the bill's preamble. Rather than framing the measure as an act of justice and a matter of rights, they hoped to make it a measure of expediency.[33] During the Vienna Congress on the other hand no such idea was ever mooted, not even by the Spanish and Portuguese. Virtually all acknowledged the rights-based, moral, and Christian basis of opposition to the trade. This may in some cases have been only rhetorical, rather than really believed, but the significant fact remains that the rhetoric was increasingly difficult to challenge in international venues.

Historians have been divided over whether the declaration was "pusillanimous" and "cheap talk" or strong and forward-looking under the circumstances. At least at the time, abolitionists deemed it an improvement over the Peace of Paris. Ultimately the declaration represents a landmark decision in international law and international relations, as the first truly humanitarian measure cast in universalist terms to emerge from a diplomatic gathering.[34] Even in practical terms, the declaration delivered more than some have thought. The document did not promise, as it might seem, that each individual state could set its own terminal date to end the slave trade, but rather only that states could "envisage" or propose such a date given their own particular circumstances. Settling the date itself would continue to be an "object of negotiations among the powers," and with the express goal of making the delay as short as possible. Castlereagh avowedly counted on these further negotiations to present better opportunities to forge a deal in the years ahead.[35]

Moreover, while accounts of the Congress often stop at mention of the declaration, the discussions actually offered much more, even in practical terms, but above all on matters of principle and precedent. Castlereagh, for example, broached an equally innovative question as he took up an abolitionist suggestion and proposed the possibility of refusing to buy the colonial goods of states that took unreasonably long to abandon slave trading. The idea in many ways represented an extension into the realm of international relations of the abolitionist tactic of the boycott—buying sugar produced by free labor instead of slave labor—and marked the first proposal of international economic sanctions for humanitarian purposes.[36] Talleyrand and King Louis, when Castlereagh first raised the matter in Paris in September, did not reject the idea, but neither did they commit themselves to it, an important distinction noted by Castlereagh. Tsar Alexander sounded more positive when consulted in January, deeming such a boycott not just "justified" but a "moral obligation."[37] It was in conjunction with the idea of economic sanctions that Castlereagh considered it so important to have won the jurisdictional and rhetorical battles over the admission of the noncolonial powers to the negotiations on universal humanitarian grounds, since they could very well form interested parties as participants in a humanitarian moral question and in the guise of importers rather than producers of colonial produce. The Portuguese and Spanish reacted sharply when Castlereagh introduced the measure in committee. In the event of sanctions, they threatened, they would take "just reprisals" on the commerce of those nations placing restrictions on them.[38]

Around the table, and hence, with a little delay, before the public eye, Russia, Austria, and Prussia supported the British proposal, but behind the scenes the Prussians at least proved cagier, as in their negotiations with Portugal for a commercial treaty. They continued to drag their heels about the conditions under which an embargo might be justified in the coming years as well, with the claim that they could not be expected to sacrifice their interests to such an extent over an affair that was "properly speaking foreign to them." Count Nesselrode also advised hesitation to the tsar, but he represented just one voice in the Russian counsels.[39]

Castlereagh met more success in another diplomatic first, as the committee approved his plan to establish a semipermanent international commission to oversee the process of ending the slave trade, with ministerial conferences to meet in Paris and London and discuss annual reports on the progress made or obstacles encountered. This measure, termed by Castlereagh "a sort of permanent European Congress," in some ways constituted the first step toward international agencies as such, certainly in the context of promoting humanitarian causes. These conferences were meant in part to promote enforcement of the agreements already made, but as noted above, Castlereagh also intended them to serve as a venue for continued pressure on France, Spain, and Portugal to set earlier dates for full abolition. Metternich in particular supported the commission, as he thought such meetings a good way to avoid potential conflicts and misunderstandings on the path to abolition. That was precisely the sort of rationale of preventative diplomacy (rather than peacemaking after war) behind the new congress system toward which Metternich, Castlereagh, and Tsar Alexander were building.[40]

Where Castlereagh and his warm or reluctant supporters among the powers could make little headway was in agreements to shorten the continued window of legal slaving. Primarily in order to go on record with the offer in the rather orchestrated committee sessions, Castlereagh in the first meeting already tried to get France, Spain, and Portugal to agree to immediate and total abolition. He had known since November that this would not happen, but he at least hoped to see the number of years reduced, possibly bringing Spain and Portugal down from their announced preference of eight years to the five that had been granted France (which would at least offer the benefit of standardization), or bringing the French down to three. None, however, budged.[41]

During the period when supposedly no one had a thought to spare from the raging battles over Saxony and Poland, Castlereagh did manage to wrest an agreement from the Portuguese to limit their slave trading to Portugal's possessions in the southern hemisphere, that is, abolishing it north of the equator; in return, Castlereagh agreed to settle outstanding indemnities for Portuguese ships seized in preceding years to the tune of £300,000 and to cancel the unpopular commercial treaty between Britain and Portugal signed in 1810. Castlereagh was luckier than he knew in achieving so much, given that the Portuguese plenipotentiary, Count Palmella, was acting against his instructions from the Portuguese court in exile in Rio de Janeiro, which—perhaps thinking in more classically power-political and balance-of-power terms—enjoined stonewalling the British and seeking support from Russia instead, which, they thought, would be keen to promote resistance to Britain's colonial supremacy. The Portuguese prince regent and his advisors had not, however, chosen their chief negotiator wisely in pursuit of such a policy, or more to the point, they had made a wise choice, but unwittingly, given that their ideas were mistaken in several respects. For Count Palmella was the nephew of Count Funchal, the previous Portuguese representative in London, who had decided that concessions to Britain and to the powerful abolitionist movement were needed, and had advised Rio accordingly, though unavailingly. Having been in London himself to witness the state of public and governmental opinion, Palmella was bold enough to follow his uncle's line and meet the British with conciliatory measures. Achieving some gains for Portugal and Brazil would help to cover himself with his royal master and the public back home.[42]

Castlereagh also seemed near a similar agreement with the Spanish. The king of Spain had offered not to engage in the slave trade anywhere except the stretch of coast between the equator and the line of 10° N latitude. Castlereagh hoped the 10° stipulation was more in the nature of a mistake in geography, but he neglected the fact that it was above all to Cuba and Puerto Rico that the Spanish ruler wanted to bring slaves, and that given the wind patterns and historic market connections, this would be easier from northern latitudes. While Labrador suggested that they might indeed be able to extend to the equator as a friendly gesture to the British, such a treaty ultimately only came about after two further years of tough negotiating.[43] An equivalent deal with the French also turned out to be unclear about where precisely the line would be drawn past which the slave trade would be forbidden (Cape Palmas in Liberia, Cape Three Points in Ghana, or the desired goal of Cape Formoso in modern Nigeria), but at least the British were moving closer to their desired interim solution of restricting it to the southern hemisphere.[44]

It was not solely evidence of weakness that the British could only arrange an abolition measure for the area "above the line," that is, north of the equator. That might be better than nothing, but it did not erase the affront to humanity that was the trade itself, and the flow of human cargo across the south Atlantic from southern Africa to Brazil was after all about equal to what had gone to the Caribbean sugar islands. The geographic distinction did, however, make some sense in terms of abolitionist ideology. One of the most important arguments, and goals of the movement, concerned the desire for social and economic progress in Africa. Rum and the disruptive violence of slaving took their toll on the societies affected and made it difficult for Christian missions or those interested in the civilizing mission more broadly to achieve much purchase in those lands (or for that matter, those simply interested in commerce). Ending the trade in West Africa above the equator was supposed to ensure that in wide stretches of the continent, local societies would get some relief and have at least some chance to recover. As Castlereagh explained to Spain's Marquis of Labrador, if even one nation still engaged in the slave trade in a given area, the social benefits for Africans, their "progress towards Industry and Civilization," would effectively be negated. Not carrying abolition to the equator would leave precisely the part of the coast on which the British had already made strides toward eradicating the trade exposed to its revival. This region also, not coincidentally, comprised those areas where the British had the greatest interests and were most focused on introducing what was in some ways a precursor of the new imperialism, that is, one at least theoretically predicated on the civilizing mission and the (allegedly mutual) advantages of free trade in bringing progress to Africa, Britain, and the globe.[45] None of this is to say that the British did not try hard both in Vienna and in subsequent years to extend abolition south of the equator, but it does help explain why they were willing to compromise, and why even the public could find it a satisfactory interim solution.[46]

In his general argumentation Castlereagh, like Clarkson, emphasized moral, religious, and humanitarian arguments, as well as a sense that the enlightened views of modern times simply excluded any other position. Yet like Wellington in Paris, the foreign secretary wanted to press the additional point with the colonial powers that abolition was in both their own and the planters' economic interests. Hence he requested that Lord Liverpool send along the relevant facts and figures, as set out in the longer version of the case for abolition in the parliamentary committee report, and then proceeded to feed the information to other delegates. The colonial powers, according to this line of argument, stood more to gain by growing trade with Africa than they would lose by giving up the slave trade in the first place. Before the committee, Castlereagh claimed that since the end of British slaving, trade in "indigenous goods" with Africa had jumped from approximately £80,000 to £1,000,000 per annum.[47] Castlereagh, however, somewhat undermined his argument in an exchange with Portugal's chief representative, Count Palmella. When Palmella pointed out that an abrupt end to the trade would have deleterious economic consequences for Portugal's African outposts, Castlereagh responded that "they do not merit counting for much in the discussion. These establishments only being founded upon the inhumane system of the trade in Negros, it would be natural that they fall with that system." Palmella seized his chance and shot back that it was precisely to prevent such a collapse that these outposts would need time to shift to "the agricultural and commercial system."[48] The colonial powers did not respond well to the economic argument after all.

Castlereagh also held out the threat of slave revolt as a reason for not importing more slaves to colonial areas.[49] Some historians of abolition have argued that the cumulative effects of slave resistance and revolts combined to convince planters of slavery's unviability, or to render them fearful of continuing it, hence hastening abolition. Above all the Haitian revolution has featured in this context. The agency of the enslaved in these forms must to some extent have contributed to make abolition a less unwelcome event for planters, but determining how much has produced considerable controversy. In this case, the argument from slave revolts seems not to have convinced the colonial powers, at least not immediately.[50]

Remarkable in the Vienna negotiations was the surprising lack of racial or racist rhetoric on either side of the abolition argument in diplomatic and publicistic circles. The main exception involved the French colonial interest's pamphleteering in defense of the slave trade. The abolitionist slogan "Am I not a man and a brother?" was increasingly accepted as a rhetorical question, its answer the presupposition from which the rest of the argument would follow. Racial science was beginning to flourish, with the growing prestige and authority of the natural sciences behind it, but it tended not to be cited much yet in the abolition debate. Things would change by Darwin's day in the mid-nineteenth century, when rival schools of anthropology split in part along pro- and antislavery lines in the emerging postemancipation world.[51]

Racism and racist stereotypes certainly existed in early nineteenth-century Europe. Long before the "People Shows" of the late nineteenth-century imperial expositions and "human zoos," one could already see exhibitions of indigenous peoples during the period of the Vienna Congress, and as with other aspects of emerging consumer culture, they showed transnational dimensions. No such display featured in Vienna during the Congress, but in London and Paris, the Khoikhoi woman Sara Baartman, the so-called Hottentot Venus, was already appearing before the objectifying European gaze. In Berlin in October 1814, a special bordered newspaper ad announced that one could step up and see "African savages" three times daily, during two of which performances the audience could in addition observe them "dine upon live chickens as in their wilderness." A Mr. Hill had apparently "rented" the use of his five entertainers from the captain of an American ship in Amsterdam in order to take them on tour in Germany. According to the report in Cotta's *Morning Journal for the Educated Classes*, the crowds to see these "human-seeming figures" were indeed larger when they consumed uncooked fowl, and at times "several persons were required to quiet them forcefully when their primitiveness broke forth."[52] In Dresden the year before, a male "Hottentot" was on display, with the emphasis in this case on his exotic and fascinating "beauty" and "grace" rather than on any alleged bestial qualities.[53]

But there were also still many scientific figures who preserved a more positive image of the intellectual capacities of less technologically advanced peoples, including the early ethnographer James Cowles Prichard in Britain, and Johann Friedrich Blumenbach in Germany. For the most part, observers accepted the common humanity of Africans without need for further reflection. The Viennese periodical the *Peace Pages* could rely on its readers' familiarity with and acceptance of the rhetoric and racial ideas of British abolitionists, when as a clue to its anagram riddle of November 1814 it alluded to the classic abolitionist slogan "Am I not a man and a brother?": "Inhumanly you drive me in your slave-chains / Although, I, man, your brother am."[54]

One of the few commentators in the specific Congress context to adduce a crass view of racial hierarchy as justification for opposition to abolition was the eccentric old *Reichspublizist* Johann Trunk, in a general pamphlet on the wider European political situation in 1814. But even Trunk did not invoke the new racial science of a Camper or Blumenbach, instead taking his cue straight out of Aristotle. The master-slave relationship, he claimed, was like that between parent and child, and he defended the notion of "slaves by nature," that is, those not rational enough to govern their own lives and hence needing the authority of another to do so for them. That scientific views of race could oppose belief in significant racial divisions was attested by none other than Aloys Weissenbach, encountered previously as Beethoven's librettist for his Congress cantata. Weissenbach was also a bit eccentric, but prior to taking up a second career as acclamatory patriotic poet, he had served as a doctor in the Austrian army and had scientific training. In his travel account *My Trip to the Congress,* he lampooned the theory of human races as distinct groupings or "degenerations of the original stock," observing that the "Caucasian" and "Ethiopian" groups "can overlap with one another." Weissenbach was particularly scathing about the proposition from the literature on race that the capacity to blush was evidence of moral or any other kind of superiority on the part of fair-skinned peoples. Instead, Weissenbach chose to emphasize human unity and the common hope of progress.[55]

French colonial pamphleteers did make use of racist arguments, up to and including the idea that Africans belonged to an "inferior species," and that given their natures, slaves were happier as slaves than as free persons.[56] The French entomologist and naturalist Baron Ambrose Marie François Joseph Palisot de Beauvois in particular, formerly of Haiti, drew on his cultural capital as scientist and as one who had traveled in West Africa to attack the views of Clarkson and the abolitionists from a racist perspective. He even supported theories of racial polygenesis and of human groups as separate species rather than simply racial varieties. Citing Palisot in turn, one F. Mazères published a follow-up pamphlet targeting Sismondi's work on strongly racist grounds, Sismondi having refuted the notion that Africans represented a separate species.[57]

Apparently, however, French antiabolition forces were content to appeal to public opinion in France alone, and to lobby the French government in the runup to the Congress; Palisot dedicated his pamphlet to Louis XVIII and Talleyrand. French proslavery advocates apparently did not submit any pamphlets or memoranda to the Austrian or Prussian chancelleries, not even the *Appeal to the Commercial and Maritime Nations of Europe*. Portuguese and Brazilian colonial interests did float two pamphlets in diplomatic circles, but these were again notable for their avoidance of racist rhetoric or any defense of slavery. Instead, mirroring Count Palmella's approach at the Congress, they conceded the justice and humanitarian basis of abolition, and chose to concentrate on the manner, means, and speed with which it would come about, and to make a plea to consider the interests of colonial planters in doing so. "Without doubt," the Brazilian text read, "slavery of blacks as of that of whites is atrocious as much as impolitic," and it praised Britain and the United States for their efforts "in the cause of humanity."[58] Even the racist pamphlet by Palisot in the end called for the Congress to eschew only the immediate cessation of the trade, rather than gradual. Issuing a proclamation establishing the principle of abolition would be one thing, but any such statement should, Palisot argued, leave to each sovereign the decision as to when it would take place. There were clearly limits to what the proslavery camp could say publicly given the weight of abolitionist opinion.[59]

Among the political figures, racial rhetoric was neither employed nor particularly combated, the latter because it didn't have to be. The most striking thing about the debate over ending the slave trade was the extent to which it was focused solely on the questions of when and how to end it, not whether it should cease at all. Implicit, and at times explicit, in all statements related to abolition was the assumption that Africans were fully human, and as such rights-bearing members of the international order and worthy of humanitarian protections. This was true not just of a Clarkson or a Wilberforce, arguing on grounds of Christian equality in the eyes of the Lord, but also of the diplomats.

If efforts at abolition did not end in 1807, neither did they end with the Vienna Congress declaration of February 1815. Almost nowhere did the episode of Napoleon's Hundred Days affect diplomatic outcomes more than here. As part of his effort to rally liberals and former republicans to his renewed empire—and perhaps to curry favor with the British government and public opinion—Napoleon proclaimed the immediate cessation of the slave trade. No half measures for Bonaparte, in contrast to Bourbon insistence on a five-year moratorium. After Waterloo and a second return to Paris on British coattails, King Louis recognized that he could never convince them to reinstate the slave trade even for a limited time. Hence the Second Treaty of Paris emerged much more definitive on the issue than the first. Spain and Portugal thereafter represented the last states standing in opposition to rapid abolition, but stand they did. Despite being exhausted by the wars against Napoleon, indebted to Britain for aid during the same, and confronted by revolts in the New World, both Iberian powers continued to resist an accelerated international settlement and to drive as hard a bargain as possible in making any concessions. Moreover, while Spain and Portugal were the only states left practicing the slave trade openly, the French still did so illicitly (some British and Americans too for that matter). Spanish and especially Portuguese slavers also traded illegally on a massive scale north of the equator, despite the treaties to the contrary.[60] Hence the French declaration of abolition at the Second Peace of Paris turned out to be merely the beginning of years of struggle by the British to bring about the real end of the trade through proper enforcement, vis-à-vis France and the international community as a whole. When the special Ministerial Conferences established in the Vienna settlement convened in London in the summer of 1816, they had the joint object of pursuing international cooperation on abolition and on the problem of the Barbary corsairs. That the two questions would be linked was not surprising, given the course of developments during the Vienna Congress.

The Barbary Corsairs

Scholars have barely remarked on the absence of the matter of the Barbary corsairs and European captivity at the Vienna Congress. The question of how to handle North African seaborne attacks did not, it is true, make it to the level of formal negotiations, but it received more attention from statesmen and political commentators alike than one would gather from the silence in the literature, not least in connection with moves to abolish the slave trade. That the issue did not come up in Vienna is actually something of a mystery, or at least, explaining why it did not tells us something about the nature of politics and diplomacy in the period. Before the monarchs had even headed to London for the first round of celebrations, Bremen's representative, Johann Smidt, suggested to a Prussian diplomat that the occasion needed to be marked by some "historic moment." The festivities would be soon forgotten, "but the abolition of slavery of all kinds and the abolition of the slave markets on the coasts of Guinea as well as on those of Barbary would provide a lasting monument that the century of humanity had begun immediately after the vanquishing of Bonaparte." The suggestion went no further, but both the idea of linking the two campaigns, and the question of Barbary itself, kept coming back. The fact that the "Barbaresken" featured on the list of objects for negotiation drawn up by Metternich's chancellery prior to the Congress (in German) and still appeared in the final draft (in properly diplomatic French), should give pause for thought.[61]

Although it is often forgotten, or considered a historical curiosity characterized more by hysterical overreaction in the European imagination than by the phenomenon itself, Christian captivity in North Africa actually occurred on a massive scale. Between the era of Ottoman expansion in the 1530s and the Napoleonic period, on the order of one million Europeans fell victim to corsair raids and landed in bondage. Until the middle of the seventeenth century, almost as many European captives were brought to North Africa as Africans were transported into slavery across the Atlantic to the Americas.[62] In the face of such trends, Europeans were still far from enjoying the asymmetries of power associated with a later epoch of imperialism or feeling overwhelming self-confidence in their relations with the Islamic East, a fact that has to be taken into account in assessing cultural attitudes and the place of Orientalism, just as it does in making sense of diplomatic initiatives.[63] By the eighteenth century, and particularly the later part, Barbary captivity had declined both relative to the dramatically increasing African slave trade and in absolute terms. There were perhaps "only" around three thousand Christian captives in the three Barbary Regencies at any one time in the years circa 1800, representing a few hundred captives per year. European states could try to purchase peace with Barbary at the price of tribute, but as the corsairs still wanted to ply their trade, there were always some states that were excluded from such protection, or whose deals ceased to be respected. By the early nineteenth century, moreover, many had come to feel that it was beneath the national dignity to pay tribute, particularly to non-Western powers.[64]

Looking more closely at the statistical trends in the decades of concern here, by the 1780s the Barbary Regencies had begun to promote trade above privateering. The disruptions and warfare of the early Napoleonic period, however, allowed a resurgence of corsairing, as European military attention was focused elsewhere, and the Maltese Order of Saint John lost the island of Malta as its home base for patrolling the Mediterranean against Islamic corsairs. Corsairing dipped once more between 1806 and 1813 but, perhaps surprisingly, rose again with the peace in 1814–1815. Seizures of ships were disturbing enough, but the renewal of coastal raids in Italy and the Mediterranean islands proved still more shocking, most notably the seizure in October 1815 of 160 residents of the small Sardinian island of Sant' Antioco, men, women, and children.[65] One may argue that the public reaction in the late eighteenth and early nineteenth centuries was disproportionate to the numbers, and was still to some extent nourished both by the longer-term cultural memory of Christian captives and captivity narratives from times gone by and by the Orientalist myths of Islamic decadence and despotism that permeated European society of the Enlightenment and Romantic eras. For present purposes, however, it is most significant that the public and political elites did still feel both threatened and insulted. The fact that some also overestimated the numbers made that all the more likely, as with Johann Klüber's figure of forty-nine thousand for the number of "Christian slaves" in Barbary.[66]

Considerable disagreement also persists about the nature of Christian captivity on the Maghrebi coast. Some studies point to the exaggerations of captivity narratives or of literary points of reference such as Candide or Robinson Crusoe, and argue that captives were primarily kept for ransom in the Barbary system, hence they were fairly well treated (at least by the later period of concern here, following the eclipse of naval warfare by galleys, with associated use of galley slaves). At any rate, for such observers there is no comparison between Christian captivity in North Africa and chattel slavery in the New World.[67] Other historians, however, find considerable evidence of systematic mistreatment and dehumanization of captives of a sort not unlike that seen in other slave systems, particularly among those retained primarily for labor rather than ransom, who composed a sizable proportion of the total.[68] It is not the purpose of this discussion to press one view or the other; again, it is contemporaries' beliefs that bear more meaning for political culture and diplomacy. Here, I prefer the term "captive" to the more fraught "slave," partly to emphasize that there was something distinctive and more horrific about the race-based chattel and plantation

slavery of the Atlantic world. At the same time, however, it is an im-
probably optimistic reading of the evidence for the circumstances of
Christian captives in the Mediterranean to say that "torture and various forms of abuse were almost non-existent."[69] Even the rosier view
has to reckon with rather high morbidity rates of over 20 percent of
prisoners per five years, and with the fact that many who did survive
became long-term captives (often the poorer ones, who were more
vulnerable and less valuable as subjects for ransom). Sexual abuse, of
women and possibly of men, also remained a potential threat of life in
captivity.[70]

The most famous promoter of action against the Barbary corsairs at the
Congress was British Admiral Sir Sidney Smith. A highly decorated celebrity for his role in stymieing Napoleon's abortive Near Eastern campaign, Smith had also earned a reputation as an eccentric, and both at
the time and since has featured as a figure of fun more than a serious
politician. Smith pulled out all the stops in his efforts to raise Europe
against the corsairs, drawing on elements of the newer middle-class political culture as well as the courtly representational one. He penned a
pamphlet and published it in both French and German for circulation
to European rulers and statesmen as well as for the press (and including a letter sympathetic to the cause in the name of the king of Piedmont-
Sardinia); he also submitted handwritten copies as a memorandum.
With Metternich's permission, Smith had more copies printed in Vienna
for use in his correspondence. By autumn 1815, the pamphlet was allegedly circulating in Barbary itself, where it was found "not much to
the taste of these gentlemen here." An English translation had by then
also appeared in British newspapers.[71] Smith additionally founded an
association—part civil society club and part chivalric order—the
"Knights Liberators of the White Slaves in Africa," complete with special stamps for official documents, one with the name, and one with the
organization's symbol: four small Maltese crosses nestled in the four
corners of a larger Maltese cross, all enclosed within two rings. The
Maltese symbolism was well if not subtly chosen, since Smith claimed
his organization could replace the old Knights of Malta as bulwark
against the Muslim corsairs.[72] Smith took his campaign to Vienna,
established himself and his family as a fixture of the salon scene, and
began to canvass opinion among Europe's power brokers and elite,
from crowned heads to representatives of the German Hanseatic port
cities.[73]

Not stopping there, he organized a special festivity of his own, a picnic in the Augarten park. Smith not only chose the same site as the People's Festival, he also drafted its impresario, the court caterer and entrepreneur Franz Jan, to stage it. The attendees, royals and high-ranking diplomats and courtiers among them, were requested to make a contribution to the cause. Thus the festive picnic doubled as a fund-raising dinner, which caused some confusion when it came time to pay. The ladies were few and late in arriving, which also led to good-natured difficulties once the dancing started, and men had to partner men in the sets. More significantly, many observers seemed unsure about the cause the occasion was to publicize and support. Smith was also an abolitionist, and some thought—not wholly incorrectly—that the proceeds would benefit African slaves. Others believed Smith wanted to aid Christian pilgrims in Palestine and/or replace the lamp at the Holy Sepulcher in Jerusalem. Even those who knew the event was on behalf of Christian captives in North Africa occasionally seemed unclear that the ultimate idea was to free the captives by military means, not to ransom them as European monastic orders had previously done, with the picnic itself at least in part to help with the captives' care in the meantime. Those uncharitable souls eager to mock the event and its organizer particularly seized on the image of the holy lamp. Smith even wrote to Metternich complaining of misleading and disparaging press coverage in Austrian newspapers. The picnic was hardly in aid of a lamp as some reported, but was instead *"to nourish the Christian slaves in chains and to remove them from the dark and unhealthy dungeons."* Worse, his own party's newspaper, the Whig-leaning *Morning Chronicle* of London, picked up the holy lamp lampoon in a sarcastic snippet a few weeks later. At least the major German newspaper the *Allgemeine Zeitung* carried an article strongly supporting both Smith's campaign against "the corsairs' nests" and his candidacy to lead such an expedition.[74] Smith's public relations efforts enjoyed only mixed success.

Those who had read his pamphlet would or at least should have known that Smith was pushing for an international naval force to sail against any of the Barbary Regencies who refused to abandon the taking of European captives. "Animated by the memory of his oaths as a knight, and desiring to excite the same ardor in other Christian knights," Smith offered himself as the potential commander of an international fleet to interdict the corsairs. The squadron, "so to speak amphibious," would include a contingent of marines and allow the possibility of fighting on land. "This force, avowed and protected by all Europe, would not only give commerce a perfect security, but would end by civilizing the coasts of Africa," or as the German version added, would "lead the coastal inhabitants of northern Africa back to morality and order."[75] The measures would help "to effect the succession of what since Barbarossa are essentially pirate states into governments useful to commerce and in harmony with *all the civilized nations.*"[76] Smith, who had considerable experience and correspondence across the Mediterranean, left open the possibility that Tunis and Morocco might change their ways through friendly persuasion; the bey of Tunis in particular was showing interest in "civilizing his state" and increasing its "prosperity."[77] In Vienna Smith also pursued the possibility that, with external help, local Maghrebi elites might rise up to overthrow their Turkish overlords. Later, he proposed a foray into propaganda via material culture, to make abolitionist-style medallions for distribution in North Africa, featuring Arabic verses from the Koran forbidding the sale of human beings.[78]

The broader press agitation for action against the corsairs often referenced Smith's initiative, but much autonomous pressure existed as well. Coverage appeared in many of the venues one would expect, such as newspapers, pamphlets, and political or business periodicals, but also in some outlets where one might not have thought to find it, including early fashion magazines and cultural periodicals. The pressure represented a Europe-wide phenomenon, even more than in the case of abolition. In September 1814, the London opposition paper the *Morning Chronicle* observed: "we trust that, at the Congress, a resolution will be taken to demolish all the ports, ships, and arsenals on the Barbary coast, and keep on foot a force to prevent the renewal of the predatory system." It also subsequently gave column space to various sympathetic British or European voices. A writer in the *Mercure de France* at the same time called for the restoration of the Maltese Order to perform the same task.[79]

No one pushed for more drastic action against the corsairs, and indeed against the Ottoman Empire generally, than an anonymous pamphleteer who in 1814 called both for the destruction of the Maghrebi regencies and for driving the Turks from Europe. The writer was Franz Tidemann, mayor of the sovereign German trading city of Bremen. The Saxon weekly the *Erinnerungsblätter* similarly quoted the "wish" of the *Morning Chronicle* of London that rulers seek their territorial compensation not in nearby lands but rather in Barbary, and "completely destroy" its "pirate states." For the editor of the Saxon paper this likely had implications for Prussia's designs on his own country; for the editor of the *Morning Chronicle*, James Perry, the anti-Barbary line was more personal, as his wife had fallen victim to Algerian corsairs that very year.[80] Milder coverage emerged, too, as in a piece in a Nuremberg financial paper of December 1814 that included one recent account of Barbary captivity in the usual hair-raising and sympathy-arousing vein, but also a previous, longer one contending that captives were well-treated given that it was in owners' economic interest to do so.[81]

Copies of another pamphlet on the "robber states" had been sent by the Senate of the Hanseatic city of Lübeck for their representative, Senator Hach, to circulate at the Congress. A notice of the "pamphlet"— actually a four-hundred-page tome—with a long quote urging that the time was right to enact strong measures against the corsairs also appeared in a Hamburg newspaper and was then reprinted in Metternich's *Oesterreichischer Beobachter* (fruit presumably of the Hanseatic delegates' good relations with its editor Joseph Pilat). Hach had already discussed the work with the Spanish representative, Labrador, in September, at which time the latter suggested it should be translated and published in English. That never occurred, but an abridged translation into French appeared the following year. The length and German language of the "pamphlet" had not helped its reception at the Congress.[82]

Fascinated by the celebrity of Sidney Smith as well as energized by the cause, even fashion and cultural journals with political interests joined the chorus. Already in the coverage of the patriotic festival of 18 October 1814 for the leading German ladies' magazine *The Journal for Literature, Art, Luxury, and Fashion,* Carl Bertuch saw fit to add a footnote promoting Sidney Smith's "charitable plan for all of humanity" on behalf of Barbary captives. "Sir Sidney Smith," Bertuch wrote, "whose chivalric sense all Europe knows, has come here of his own volition to present a grand and noble plan to the Congress, which he hopes to be able to carry out with the support of the Christian powers." The project, he continued, "aims at nothing less than, through the help of a squadron and a corps of landing troops, to root out the pirate states on the African coast." Bertuch situated the scheme in the same humanitarian matrix as abolition, and closed with a final jibe at British self-interest: "We wish that the noble organizer may not encounter his primary obstacle in the political maxims of his own country!"[83]

Fashion and anti-Barbary measures came into still closer conjunction in the pages of Carolina Lattanzi's *Corriere delle Dame* (Ladies' Courier) from Milan. Directly facing the weekly fashion plate (in this case a rather assured-looking young lady in French outdoor attire and jaunty feathered hat), the "Political Thermometer" section carried a supportive piece on the published memo of "the famous Sidney Smith."[84] The editor of the highbrow Prague patriotic cultural periodical *Hesperus,* Christian Carl André, also urged readers to support the concerted use of force against the corsair states. Coercive measures, he maintained, would serve much better than continuing the practice of ransoming captives, which simply perpetuated the problem by supporting the market for them. Confusingly, André seems not to have understood that that was precisely Smith's aim, and ended up (he thought) arguing against him. "Why not rather an association of all Europe's cultivated sea powers with the purpose: uncompensated, unconditional return of all captive Christians in Barbary, or the destruction of the thieves' nests Algiers, Tunis, and Tripoli?"[85] Smith could hardly have said it better. Whether Smith would have welcomed the support of *Hesperus* for his project, or been angrier at the editor's misrepresentation of his goals in the picnic, is difficult to say.

Religious sentiments and identities entered into the agitation over the corsairs, up to and including crusading references, but more so after the Congress, and in some respects less than might have been expected. If it was difficult to divorce the issues surrounding relations with the Ottoman Empire and the Barbary corsairs from religion, the diplomats certainly tried hard to do so. They were quite concerned to prevent the Ottoman officials of the Porte from perceiving a Christian threat or revived crusading mentality, particularly following the proclamation of the Holy Alliance in September 1815. Baron Gagern in Paris reported on rumors that the Holy Alliance might be aimed at "Muslims," but "for the moment did not share that opinion." The European powers took care in both initiatives about how they notified the authorities in Istanbul.[86] And indeed some Christians took the Holy Alliance and the rumors of anti-Barbary measures in an aggressive spirit. The army officer Baron Nostitz, a Saxon in Russian service, heard the news with eagerness and volunteered to join the campaign. No fan of court life and salons, Nostitz welcomed the prospect of renewed military action, but he also cast his enthusiasm in explicitly religious terms. He petitioned the tsar for permission to be "among the warriors for this cause at once holy and politic," in the capacity of "Knight of Saint George," recently conferred on him by the tsar.[87] In April 1816, the "Romantic diplomat" Chateaubriand made a motion in the French Chamber of Peers calling for French leadership against the corsairs, with this medievalizing peroration: "it was in France that the first Crusade was advocated; it is in France that the standard for the last one should be raised."[88] Some years would pass before the idea of invasion and conquest became diplomatic reality in the French seizure of Algiers in 1830.

Much more than crusading references, a prime rhetorical ploy of supporters of measures to interdict corsair raids on European shipping and coasts was to point to the seeming inconsistency that governments would put a stop to one form of slave trade, the African, without at the same time addressing the other. The argument could be heard in one form or another among the statesmen, and it had become a staple of the European press, including the Portuguese-language periodicals appearing in London.[89] Occasional critics of abolition, such as the racist French naturalist Palisot de Beauvois or Johann Trunk, made the link, too, with the implication that inaction in the case of enslavement of Europeans also suggested the lack of urgency to act on the slavery of Africans. But these instances were infrequent; usually the argument ran the other way, to use abolition of the African slave trade as a springboard to address Christian slavery in Barbary as well. Senators Smidt of Bremen and Gries of Hamburg in particular thought that tying Barbary to the abolition campaign might be the most effective way of courting public opinion, and the above-mentioned tract by Smidt's compatriot Tidemann also joined the two issues.[90]

The British formed the particular target of such arguments, as critics had always suspected their supposedly humanitarian but possibly economically interested motives for pursuing abolition, all the more so as they allegedly tolerated the corsairs' activities as a way to achieve competitive advantage for their own shipping. Bertuch's jab in his coverage of Sidney Smith's campaign has already been noted, and Smith himself—though an abolitionist—still observed in his pamphlet on the corsairs that it was "astonishing" that at a time when Europe's rulers were dealing with abolition of the slave trade they should not do the same for Christian "slaves" in North Africa. The German nationalist organ *Nemesis* prefaced its translation of Sismondi's abolition pamphlet with a similar comment.[91]

By the decades around 1800, many western observers had finally begun to apply the "freedom principle"—that is, the idea that human beings are innately free and rights-bearing—to peoples of African as well as European descent and to feel empathy with them across the racial divide. In that sense, the unacknowledged and for the most part unseen hypocrisy of double standards for captivity in the sixteenth through the eighteenth centuries had started to crumble, as humanitarian and universalist beliefs began to bring the two standards back together. Indeed, some abolitionists pointed to the tribulations of Christian, white captives in the Maghreb as a means of establishing empathy with African slaves in the Atlantic world. Others explicitly critiqued the double standard.[92] A particularly well-traveled summary of the slave trade negotiations predicated its sharp commentary about the need for action on Christian "slavery" in North Africa with such a language of empathy. "But it happened here, as is almost inevitable in such a case, that mention was made of the numerous attacks of the Barbaresques," the author commented, and continued: "because in making known the horror that those Europeans inspire who expose their African brothers for sale in the markets, one cannot at the same time fail to express disapproval of those North African sailors who, at Algiers, Tunis, and Tripoli, put Europeans in chains." Likely written by the Prussian official and friend of Cardinal Consalvi Jacob Bartholdy, the piece appeared in several important venues, from the Augsburg *Allgemeine* to the French-language *Journal de Francfort* and the Nuremberg *General Commercial Times*, before finally being enshrined in Klüber's semiofficial collection of Congress documents.[93]

It is surprising that the subject of the Barbary corsairs did not reach the level of major negotiations at the Congress. Sidney Smith may have cut a somewhat comical figure, but he was neither unheard nor alone among the political elite in his concern. Many were keen to press the issue, from the representatives of the trading cities of Bremen and Lübeck to Emperor Franz and members of his intimate circle of aristocratic advisors and officials. Lübeck's delegate found a sympathetic listener in the Spanish plenipotentiary, the Marquis of Labrador, when he raised the matter soon after their arrival in Vienna. Labrador in turn recounted his efforts to secure British support, having told Castlereagh that Barbary slavery was an "insult" to Europe and that it showed a "lack of consequence" to take up the cause of the Africans and then "do nothing to protect Europeans against the most horrible slavery." By April 1815, Spain had requested the tsar's intercession with the Porte to protect its shipping from Algerian predation.[94]

If it is not surprising to find the Hanseatic merchants clamoring for relief from piracy, it is also no shock to think that they could be ignored in Great Power politics (Spain too for that matter). More remarkably, however, even Emperor Franz's direct order to Metternich to bring the subject to the powers' attention produced no result. This certainly suggests at least one instance in which Metternich's voice truly did carry the most weight at the time. The emperor had already called for action against the corsairs soon after his return to Vienna, in July 1814, and in August he requested that the issue be raised with the British as the first possible avenue for aid, and then at the Congress itself as part of the larger effort "to give Europe and the greater part of the world lasting repose."[95] The Court Chancellery and Treasury pressured Metternich as well. Metternich reported in September that his strong representations in Istanbul had elicited an order from the sultan for the Regencies to respect the Austrian flag, but the emperor's close advisor Count Wallis remained unconvinced that the usual complaints to the Porte would solve the problem. Instead, Wallis thought force would be required. The day after Wallis's report the kaiser informed Metternich that "only through the defeat [Bezwingung] of the Barbaresken can security for the Austrian flag be obtained," and requested that "this important object" be settled at the Congress.[96]

Some of Metternich's subordinates added to the pressure. Austria's ambassador in Rome, Baron Lebzeltern, argued in October that "these African barbarians, very populous and whose means are annually augmented by the gold and tribute by which Christian princes abase themselves to purchase a year's tranquility, seem by their insults to want to reproach the European maritime courts for their negligence and to provoke on their part the measures demanded by humanity, by their dignity, by the well-being of their subjects, by the future security of their countries." Humanitarian considerations, honor, paternalism, raison d'état: Lebzeltern worked all rhetorical registers to convince his superior of the need for action. Metternich's deputy Joseph von Hudelist also, if less strongly, promoted measures against the corsairs when he passed along the pleas for assistance of the merchants of Trieste.[97]

As so often, however, Metternich successfully pursued a policy of procrastination in defense of a cherished idea, in this instance the necessity of maintaining the status quo in the Near East against the threat of Russian expansion. Both Metternich and the British feared, among other things, that Russia might seize the occasion of a squadron against the Barbary powers to increase their naval presence in the warm-water ports of the Mediterranean. Seemingly it was worth the sacrifice of some European sailors, merchants, and peasants to keep things quiet on the eastern front. Emperor Franz was in any case skeptical of gaining

British aid to suppress the corsairs, as most powers had always har-
bored suspicions of Britain's seemingly self-interested practice of negotiating protection for its own vessels while ignoring the problems of
other trading states. The Americans, too, thought the British essentially
used the corsairs to carry on the war against US trade by proxy, even
outside the immediate framework of the War of 1812.[98]

While talks stalled, time and tide did not wait for the diplomats in
Vienna. The Netherlands had already requested the assistance of British
consuls in Algiers and Tunis in June 1814 to help free or at least succor
some Dutch citizens who had been taken captive. Castlereagh immediately promised this support, but the Dutch ambassador was still pressing the matter in December after nothing happened.[99] Meanwhile, the
Dutch had grown tired of waiting and launched an independent expedition against the corsairs. On the very day when the ambassador renewed
his request for British diplomatic intervention, however, the Dutch fleet
was battered by winter squalls. They never made it out of the English
Channel and were forced to seek refuge and repairs in the English port
of Plymouth. Two of their ships were damaged irreparably, and when in
February they asked the British Foreign Office for permission to purchase two frigates from the Royal Navy, they again received instant
approval. The fleet finally sailed for the Mediterranean in May 1815,
at about the same time that the United States decided to profit from the
new peace with Britain and take matters into its own hands as well.
Even as the Allied and Napoleonic armies marched toward their final
collision at Waterloo, a US fleet sailed into the Mediterranean seeking
its own showdown with the Barbary powers.[100]

It was not until the period during and after the new peace conferences
in Paris that the British rethought their position on the corsairs, and
then only gradually and partially. Despite the successful US intervention, corsair activity in the summer of 1815 remained sufficiently intense to provoke some of the European powers to complain when they
assembled again to negotiate the Second Peace of Paris come August.
This time the public pressure had some effect. In August Colonial Secretary Lord Bathurst wondered in a letter to Castlereagh whether the fact
that the British now ruled Malta might make it incumbent on them to
shoulder more of the burden of defending Europe against the corsairs.
A recent study has suggested that the British primarily decided to intervene against Barbary as a way of defusing arguments that their pursuit
of abolition was not altruistic by proving that they could act in other

nations' interest as well; the British may also have hoped for a quid pro quo to garner support for the abolition campaign by aiding the other powers against the corsairs.[101] Yet they came to this broader outlook only incrementally. When the famed expedition of Lord Exmouth finally sailed for Algiers in the spring of 1816, it did so under orders to free or ransom only the subjects of certain Italian states (including Britain's new protégé Sardinia) and to arrange treaties with the Barbary powers for them and for British possessions such as Hanover and their new protectorate the Ionian Isles. The expedition was not directed to free all the captives, nor to oversee the full cessation of European captivity. Exmouth forcefully advised the Regencies that they should change their ways, and all three did sign agreements stating that they would in future not make slaves but treat captured Europeans as prisoners of war. It was, however, only in the wake of the massacre of Christian fishermen at the small Maghrebi port of Bona after the expedition's return to England that Exmouth's squadron refitted and sailed again to the Mediterranean, this time with orders to liberate all the prisoners and to force the Regencies to sign treaties promising an end to European captivity in general. Finally Spanish, Dutch, Roman, and Greek captives were freed as well.[102]

As on many another issue, so too in the case of the Barbary corsairs the Vienna settlement did not settle affairs completely but rather set a new stage for further negotiations and contestation. Most significantly, Barbary became even more firmly linked to abolition of the slave trade. Just as the corsair problem had been tied to abolition both rhetorically and practically during the Congress, the two campaigns became joined institutionally in the combined Ministerial Conferences that met periodically in the years 1816–1819, with the goal of solving both problems.

Greek Liberation Movements

If Metternich and the British remained keen to avoid antagonizing the Islamic Ottoman Empire or destabilizing relations in the Mediterranean and southeastern Europe in the case of the Barbary corsairs, they were even less eager to encourage ideas of a campaign to liberate the Greeks or other Balkan Christians from Ottoman rule. And concerned they were, because such ideas were beginning to catch hold in various segments of Europe's political networks. Moreover, it was not simply power politics or the balance of power with Russia that disturbed them.

Rather, as good anti-Jacobin conservatives, they also worried that proponents of Greek liberation were at the same time agents of a pan-
European conspiracy out to foment republican revolution. Nor was it
only the mayor of Bremen and a few unworldly publicists (or Machiavellian conspirators in unworldly guise) who trumpeted the notion of a
war to liberate the Greeks. Diplomats worried that Tsar Alexander himself might be sympathetic, and certainly several of his close advisors
were committed to the cause, above all the soon-to-be cohead of the
Foreign Ministry, Count Capodistrias, a Greek from the island of Corfu.
The actual rebellion proved to lie several years in the future, and official
European intervention in support of the Greeks several years farther off
still, but the rumblings of the coming storm could already be heard in
1814, not just in the distance, but in Vienna itself.

In addition to the Greek question, diplomats also faced a Serbian problem. The revolt of 1804–1813 had basically already been suppressed,
but the situation remained unstable, and the fates of the exiles and of
those still in Ottoman territory remained undecided. The Austrian military and government took in some refugees and exiles, and expressed
concern about the rights of Catholics, but their primary aim was to
keep the situation in the borderlands from boiling over again.[103] Serb
pleas for aid fell on more fertile ground with their Slavic and Orthodox
Russian brethren. A Serb delegation arrived in Vienna in January 1815,
and already by 15 February, just days after the resolution of the Polish-
Saxon crisis, the Russian plenipotentiary Count Razumovsky drafted a
circular note to the other powers seeking their support with the Porte.
Its language echoed that heard regarding the African slave trade or Barbary. After legitimating Russia's interest in intervention through shared
religion, the note went on to declare: "the motives common to all the
states of Europe are religion, the voice of nature, the cry of humanity,"
whereby one could not look idly on at the "scenes of carnage" currently
playing out in Serbia.[104]

  Neither did the Serbs neglect to petition Prussia and Britain for aid.
Their spokesmen held up the specter of the eradication of the Serbian
nation if the Christian powers did not intervene, and they assured
Hardenberg that his name would be remembered by their descendants
as the creator of "the rosy dawn's light of their happiness" if he helped
them. The petition to the "noble English nation" came in both Latin and
German versions and went the Prussian petition one better. They astutely
promised Castlereagh that he would be remembered and "honored"

not just as the bringer of their happy dawn but as "the noble lord, who became for them a second Wilberforce, in bringing an end to a Christian slave trade."[105] Castlereagh, slightly moved by the plea or by Russian prodding, mentioned the Serbs' plight to the Turkish chargé, Johannis Mavroyeni, before departing for England in February. After Wellington replaced Castlereagh, he managed to discourage any strong Russian diplomatic push on the Serbs' behalf. Following a renewed revolt in April 1815, the Turks finally made peace with the Serbs on relatively favorable terms.[106]

As for the stirrings of a Greek national movement, Count Johannis Capodistrias's actions certainly seemed harmless enough, as he tried to win members and financial contributions for the association called "the Greek Friends of the Muses," a patriotic organization originally founded in Athens in 1812 with the stated intention of spreading education and enlightenment in Greece and aiding poor young Greeks to study in central and western Europe. The Greek Orthodox metropolitan, Ignatius, and the scholar-priest Anthinius Gazis also helped launch the organization, with the Athens branch under the honorary presidency of the English Philhellene Frederick North. Adopting some of the usual tricks of associational life in the public sphere, Capodistrias saw to the publication of the group's prospectus to gain more visibility, and the organization produced special rings bearing its symbol, the owl, for members' wear. There was no fund-raiser festivity such as Sidney Smith had given regarding the Barbary corsairs, but Capodistrias and Roxandra Stourdza took up collections.[107] These activities could simply represent an instance of the typology of nationalisms of Miroslav Hroch and Eric Hobsbawm. National movements in this scheme emerge first in a stage of cultural nationalism, promoted principally by nationalist intellectuals and aimed more at the revival of literature and national pride than at the political ideal of national independence; political nationalism comes only in a later phase.[108] In the Greek case, however, it is difficult to get past the fact that Count Capodistrias was not just a scholar on some country estate or in an academy of science but was rather a political figure already, in the service of the Continent's most powerful ruler and state. Nor does someone like Alexander Ypsilanti exactly fit the bill, as another Greek prince in Russian exile like Roxandra Stourdza's father. Capodistrias certainly tried to advertise the organization as simply involving cultural politics, but equally certainly, Metternich and the Argus-eyed Habsburg police did not believe it. Metternich reported to Emperor Franz that "this society pur-

sues much less the dissemination of the arts and sciences in Greece—
obviously only used as a mere front—than secret political goals, which
however neither comport with our own direct interests, nor in other
respects can they be appropriate for Austria's relations with the Ottoman Porte."[109]

Capodistrias was not alone among Congress visitors in his politicking on behalf of the Greeks. The salon scene was, if not abuzz, at least
athrum with interest in the fate of the Greeks, in part by the Greeks
themselves, but also stretching further into European high society. It
was not only revivalist religion that Roxandra Stourdza was eager to
promote during her stay in Vienna. She was accompanied by her whole
family, and their home provided the hub for those concerned for the
Greeks of southeastern Europe, including Ypsilanti. Roxandra's brother
Alexander similarly supported both evangelical religion and Greek independence and, like Capodistrias and his sister, worked in the tsar's
service. Although we cannot know precisely what was said there, political discussions were both lively and extensive in the Stourdza salon as
the Greek "propaganda center," with Capodistrias and Roxandra taking leading roles.[110]

It is also no coincidence that two stalwarts of the future Philhellene
movement supporting the Greek revolt when it finally occurred in 1821
were present in Vienna in 1814. Viennese salon conversations fueled at
least some of the enthusiasm for the Greeks in the Eynards of Geneva,
who had already been impressed by Capodistrias when they met him in
Paris the preceding spring, and who entertained him in their small salon
in Vienna.[111] Jean-Gabriel Eynard is most remembered today as a leader
of the pan-European Philhellene movement of the 1820s (with a plaque
to that effect outside the former family palais in Geneva), and it may
well have been at the Vienna Congress that he became a convert. His
young wife Anna, too, was fascinated. At a dinner given by the British
diplomat Sir Stratford Canning, she had a particularly compelling exchange with an unnamed English colonel who had been in Greece for
several years giving military training, in order that these "free men"
would "be able to defend their liberty against the Turks." As Anna commented, "there exists in the soul of some the sentiment of their ancient
valor and national supremacy, and they are still supported in their obscurity by the hope of becoming once more what they once were." Anna
wanted to speak more with him "of the mores of these free Greeks,"
and regretted that the rules of polite discourse prevented them from
pursuing the topic more thoroughly.[112]

The North German classical scholar Friedrich Thiersch, who was making his career in Bavaria, also had business in Vienna in the autumn of 1814. There he came into contact with Capodistrias and joined the Philomuses. Not only did he wear the ring for several years, he also proved instrumental in convincing the Bavarian chief minister, Count Montgelas, to allow the organization to base itself in Munich (the Austrians clearly being disinclined to see the group's headquarters in Vienna).[113] Thiersch had already worked for the cause, having helped establish ties between the Bavarian Academy of Sciences and educational institutions in the Greek-speaking world that were trying to spread learning to their countrymen. Thiersch seems to have been convinced that education could in time bring liberation, though he already thought in terms of revolt as well. In a letter of 1813 to his former teacher the classicist Georg Herrmann, Thiersch argued:

> The Greeks are making astounding efforts to set up an inner wall against external despotism, and if the development of so many previously slumbering powers continues without significant interruption, then in the end the structure of their ignorant rulers will collapse of its own accord. Not only do they have the monopoly of all knowledge in the ever-more decaying Turkish monarchy, but also almost all the administration and fleet as well.

And twenty thousand sailors, he added, were essentially twenty thousand potential soldiers. "The Turks," he concluded, "suspect nothing of the abyss on which their power rests."[114]

Already in October the censors in Metternich's chancellery had told the police to interdict the pamphlet *Der Wiener Congreß,* by the Erlangen University professor Alexander Lips, in part because it contained inflammatory references to the Ottoman Empire and for that reason had supposedly been purchased in large numbers by Vienna's Greeks; it had already provoked complaints by the Turkish representative, and the police were to halt further distribution. Once they had, a police spy reported grumblings about its unavailability among potential buyers. The disruption spread as far as the Austrian-Ottoman military border in the Banat and Serbia, where Greeks managed to disseminate copies, and Metternich had to reassure the local Turkish authorities that everything possible was being done to suppress the text.[115] Lips's main concern was to bring about the end of standing armies—dangerous to liberty as well as European stability—as a precursor to a final peace settlement. To achieve this, however, Lips had one final use for Europe's militaries, namely, to liberate Greece and the Balkans and push the Ottomans back to Asia. Lips likened the campaign explicitly to the medieval crusades, as a venture of Christian Europe, and bathed the Greeks in a language of pathos and humanist enthusiasm, even quoting the rather purple verses of his Erlangen colleague J. C. G. Zimmermann. The worries of the censors and the Turkish authorities were not hard to understand.[116]

In February, the same officials vainly hoped that the police could find a way to deny Capodistrias permission to publish his "Plan" for the Philomuses, which might be a cover for "secret political purposes." At about that time, Capodistrias at least got some welcome and sympathetic coverage for the project in the Catholic cultural periodical the *Friedensblätter*. The relatively long notice gave a brief summary of the "Plan" and credited Capodistrias, Archimandrite Gazis, and Metropolitan Ignatius by name, as well as calling for subscriptions from readers of all classes and reporting that already more than 800 ducats had been raised from 200 subscribers, "among them many of the illustrious foreigners."[117]

Up to a point Metternich and the censors were correct: Capodistrias and his comrades did harbor more far-reaching political goals. At the same time, however, the Philhellenes were likely sincere in pursuing educational and consciousness-raising aims in the short term as the best means to achieve those longer-term ends. If nothing else, it was a rhetorically astute move, since it was more difficult to oppose a Greek university than a Greek nation-state. As Roxandra Stourdza expressed the thought, clearly the goal of Greek enlightenment was related to that of Greek "deliverance," but "no one dared say that the Greeks should remain ignorant and barbarian like their tyrants." "Not daring to express their views openly, they believed they had to interest the sovereigns assembled in Vienna through their urbanity, in the rebirth of letters in a country that had at one time been their cradle."[118]

Roxandra herself took advantage of her position in the tsarina's household to facilitate a public symbolic demonstration of support for the Greeks on the part of Tsar Alexander, at the expense of their Austrian hosts. The Greeks in Vienna wanted Alexander to attend a service at their church, and requested Roxandra to ask him, which she did, successfully. Austrian authorities, however, worried that the gesture would send the wrong signal, both to the Porte and to Greeks living in the Ottoman Empire. Since there were two Greek churches in Vienna, one serving the Habsburg Greek community, the other the Ottoman, Prince Trauttmansdorff suggested as a compromise that the tsar appear at the

Austrian one. But the Greek patriots wanted him at the other, and on the day, Roxandra cleverly arranged for the carriages to go to that church after all, citing the fact that it had been founded by one of her forebears. Alexander went along with the change but was allegedly embarrassed by the loud cheers of "Vivat Alexander" that rang out, and rather angry with Roxandra afterward, given the difficulties raised for his Austrian hosts. The occasion also saw Capodistrias and Ypsilanti (purportedly "unintentionally") make a public gesture of their own, as they sat among the Greek community for the service rather than among the tsar's retinue. Roxandra also took advantage of her privileged place in the tsarina's household and the tsar's favor to present to him a memorandum on Greek liberation, diplomatically not telling him that it had been composed by his official her brother. Alexander thought it "too soon." While Roxandra did not think Greek independence would come any time soon either (certainly not as soon as it did), she was eager to ensure that the Greek cause not be forgotten in Europe. As on many other issues, the Vienna Congress represented the perfect moment for making such gestures, with all eyes on the city.[119]

In the end, the only matter involving the Greeks and Greek independence allowed to reach the higher levels of European diplomacy concerned the disposition of the group of Greek-speaking islands variously known as the Seven Islands, the Ionian Republic, or the Ionian Isles. Capodistrias, as already noted, himself hailed from Corfu and had served the Ionian Republic in its independent phase from 1799 to 1807.[120] He became the islands' de facto spokesman at the Congress, and in one of his first acts protested alleged abuses of power by the British occupiers under General Campbell and requested Russian intervention with the British. Campbell had not only assumed military and civilian authority on the island but had closed the university and dispersed the Academy, two prime symbols of Greek revival for Philhellenes such as Korais, Thiersch, and Capodistrias.[121] The British were the latest in a long line of authorities in the isles. In the years between 1797 and 1814, they changed hands from the Venetians to the French, and to the Turks, the Russians, and the French again, and finally to the British. Capodistrias hoped the isles could become independent under the protection of all the powers, and enjoy something like the Russian-inspired constitution of 1803.[122]

By the spring of 1815, when the matter of the Greek islands finally worked its way to the top of the agenda, the Austrians had put in a strong claim to possession or at least protection of the territory (chiefly on the grounds of security for their Italian and Illyrian provinces). The British were happy to go along, if only to foil possible Russian influence in a sensitive area. Despite the earlier complaints about British abuse of power, however, it seems that the prospect of Austrian control proved even less appealing to the islanders, and soon Capodistrias was working mightily to thwart the Austrians and retain the British as protectors. If his ideal solution of full independence under joint Allied guarantee could not be achieved, then he would do all he could to establish a British protectorate, with as much constitutional autonomy and liberty for the inhabitants as possible. Capodistrias had already planted the seed in Castlereagh's mind back in December, and the Austrians by this point were ready to accept the British, also if only to keep out the Russians. Castlereagh refused restoring the islands as an independent republic, fearing that, too, might lead to future Russian influence, but thought the inhabitants might be satisfied with constitutional and commercial privileges such as the Genoese republic had accepted in being annexed to Sardinia.[123]

The question of the Greek isles was for Capodistrias the most important of all the negotiations, "the dearest and only affair of my heart," and he felt so strongly about it not just because of his roots in the region, but because he did indeed see it as the most likely location from which Greek aspirations toward cultural and perhaps even political development could be realized. With some rhetorical excess, he told his correspondent Admiral Chichagov—from whom he requested aid in convincing the British—that if Austria took possession he and his compatriots would emigrate and "seek in another hemisphere that fatherland denied to us by European justice in our native land."[124] For Capodistrias (and his colleague Nesselrode as well), the British were clearly just as eager as the Austrians to squelch any seeds of Greek independence or insurrection in an effort to preserve the status quo. It might therefore seem strange for Capodistrias to support the British despite his suspicions, but he thought he had a good reason, namely, his apparently quite deep liberal belief in the power of constitutional government and public opinion. As he frankly informed the Earl of Clancarty during their negotiations (Castlereagh being long since back in London, and Wellington in Belgium preparing to meet Napoleon), "he should then require no other guarantee against the abuse by our Executive of the privileges of his Countrymen, than what would be to be found in the Opposition in Parliament." Or as Capodistrias put it in his official memorandum to Clancarty of 28 March 1815, the islanders would enter British protection "in the hope of placing their nationality under the safeguard of the constitutional forms of that great nation."[125] He explained his thinking more vividly to Admiral Chichagov: "the English Ministry would not dare bury the dagger in the heart of Greece; it is responsible. But if Austria takes charge of this noble enterprise and if it conducts it to its ends, the English Ministry would attain its goal without exposing itself to public animadversion."[126]

Practical considerations also likely influenced the Corfiotes in their preference for the British. For one, they hoped for greater commercial opportunities under British aegis. Second was their expectation that the Royal Navy offered better protection against the Barbary corsairs. In the latter at least they were not disappointed. Once installed as protectors after the agreements reached in the Second Peace of Paris in November 1815, the British made sure to include the Seven Isles in their various agreements with the Barbary Regencies in the wake of Admiral Exmouth's expedition.[127] The Ionians also received guarantees of limited self-government and civil liberties in a constitutional regime under a British governor, but in the end the new governor did much to bend the paper regime to his rather despotic will and came into renewed conflict with Capodistrias.[128]

Economics, power politics, and belief in constitutional government; national aspirations and limited respect for nationality: all featured in the dispensation of the Ionian Isles, just as they helped set the tone in the Congress negotiations surrounding exchanged territories to be examined in Chapter 6. The mixture of humanitarian rights talk, commercial concerns, and considerations of power seen in the treatment of abolition and Barbary outside Europe's borders also played their parts when the diplomats meted out what was to pass for justice within Europe.

CHAPTER SIX

Between Reaction and Reform

There has been much debate over the years about the political nature and meaning of the Restoration era inaugurated by the Vienna settlement of 1815. Most historians have concluded that it was not reactionary in the extreme sense of an attempt to turn back the calendar of history, as many territorial and some political innovations of the preceding decades were allowed to stand. But most also still deem the settlement rather conservative, with liberal and national aspirations largely ignored or rejected. As we have seen, however, the statesmen of the Vienna Congress, like the publics who observed it and commented on it, were much more apt to support constitutions and employ rights talk than the usual depictions allow. This held particularly true in setting the parameters of religious liberty and toleration amid territorial exchanges, and in humanitarian issues such as abolition of the slave trade, but the influence of liberal and national ideas extended further, in an interweaving of liberal and conservative projects.

Far from being solely an exercise in restoration and reaction, the peace settlements of 1814–1815 also witnessed one of the greatest waves of constitutional establishments in European history. If not quite a "revolution from above," the move entailed the true spirit of liberalism, that is, the effort to stave off a real, radical revolution by means of compromise and limited reform, even as the authorities "above" felt themselves to be responding to sentiments in the broader population. When Cardinal Consalvi protested against the constitutional stipulations regarding the form of government to be adopted in the Vatican's new territories, the committee charged with drafting the final Italian settlement told him that the pope had not been singled out in this, that rather all sovereigns granted recovered lands received such conditions. The English and Russians in particular insisted that the European powers had "contracted this *obligation* with the peoples," and that they did not want to "dishonor themselves . . . with *the appearance of rendering them up like sheep,* without *assuring* their fates."[1] The statement pointed to a limited program of liberal rights, to reform rather than revolution from above, but the language of contract was significant, and the argument did produce written constitutional limits on royal authority across wide swathes of Europe.

Likewise, belief in the existence and rights of nations and peoples shaped the politics of the Vienna Congress more than has often been recognized. We have seen the prominence of national imagery and ideas in the realms of display, spectacle, and markets for memorabilia, as well as in the pressure for Greek autonomy orchestrated by prominent Greeks and Philhellenes among the European elite. National and liberal themes also appear in the negotiations involving the Italian states, the Swiss cantons, and the German federal constitution. Like the handling of the slave trade and religious reconstruction, the politicking surrounding Italy and Switzerland has received comparatively little attention in the literature on the Congress. With the exception of the guarantee of Swiss neutrality that has remained such a cornerstone of the European diplomatic order, the Swiss case in particular has been neglected precisely because it seemed unimportant in the power-political terms of concern to most Congress historians. When examining questions of European political culture and ideology, however, the Swiss example proves just as revealing as the more well-known showdown over Poland and Saxony. To the extent that Italian and Swiss negotiations have received attention, the territorial exchanges and settlements similarly tend to be explained in power-political terms, as the result of deals hammered out among European powers jockeying for strategic position in a perceived zero-sum game. Such considerations were certainly important, sometimes decisive, but not always. Notions of ideology, constitutions, and even nationality molded the language of interested parties and diplomats alike. This was true not simply as a matter of rhetorical strategy (important though patterns of rhetoric are in their own right); constitutional and national arguments also functioned as lenses to interpret and even decide diplomatic issues.

Conservatism and Liberalism in the European Restoration

Historians face a problem when trying to make sense of the early nineteenth-century political landscape and spectrum of political thought. Namely, it is often difficult to distinguish conservatives and conservative positions from liberals and liberal ones. Up to a point it is easy enough to distinguish radical democrats and Jacobins from diehard reactionaries, but even there the radical nationalists of the nineteenth century sometimes present difficulties. When it comes to categorizing the variety of stances in between, however, from reform conservatives to moderate liberals, things become knottier.[2] Solving the problem is important because most statesmen and politics from this period fell into just that middle zone. Clarifying the picture requires shifting analyses away from ideal types of liberal and conservative ideologies to explorations of ideas' actual paths and processes of development in the political contexts of the late eighteenth and early nineteenth centuries.

Conservatism was never monolithic, and much of the literature on conservatives and conservatism has concerned itself with trying to make distinctions between religious or secular, reactionary or reformist variants. All versions were counterrevolutionary in the strict sense, but conservatives could and did disagree about the best way of combating or preventing revolution. The category "reform conservative" is already quite helpful, in directing attention to the flexibility or adaptability of many conservatives in their encounters with liberal ideas or prickly political situations. Matthew Levinger has also made the insightful argument in his *Enlightened Nationalism* that most political commentators confronted the same challenge in early nineteenth-century political culture: they worried about how to deal with the postrevolutionary world of active political publics and semitransparent publicity. In Levinger's view, those who believed it impossible to reconcile with the new politics without sacrificing essential principles and suffering further revolutions became classed as reactionaries; those who believed a compromise was possible belong in the reformist camp.[3]

A further necessary step toward understanding early nineteenth-century political culture, however, requires reorienting analyses from a bipolar, left-right political spectrum to one at least tripartite, for a fuller spectrum, and one with a different dynamic. The relevant categories are not just liberal versus conservative, or Jacobin versus anti-Jacobin. Instead, one has to reckon with Jacobins, full (or reactionary) conservatives, and a group or groups in the middle who can at certain places and times work with and ally with either political wing. Both liberals and conservatives were anti-Jacobin (and for that matter often anti Napoleonic), but precisely for that reason, being anti Jacobin did not mark one as necessarily conservative. The similar oppositional stance created some commonality of language and ideology to go with the commonality of interest, but only in part. Opposing conservatism likewise did not make one a radical, but at times allowed cooperation, and facilitated communication and ideological exchange. Some groups in the middle can be called reform conservative, but others must be termed liberal. Liberal is here used in the sense of a program of constitutional limits to monarchical authority and certain basic protections for individual and group rights in society and polity (roughly, the rule of law), coupled with some measure of representation and political participation for an at least somewhat expanded body of citizens. Liberalism did not at this stage have to imply calls for free trade or free markets and small government, though some were already moving in that direction, such as the Prussian Wilhelm von Humboldt.

Reorienting the history of political thought and political history generally from bipolar to tripartite is important for understanding relationships at any one time and place, but it is even more crucial in capturing the historical dynamic and development of political relationships across the longer arc of change in the long nineteenth century. Evolving ideas, rhetoric, and strategies involved exchange and negotiation across the full political spectrum, through intermediaries and shifting alliances, and from one portion of Europe to another through transnational exchanges. In specific places and times, and through certain historical and social processes, political situations often became polarized (the Constituante in the French Revolution; the French National Assembly and Frankfurt Parliament in 1848); across longer time spans and larger geographies, the tripartite approach better explains the broader developments and the formation of specific instances of left-right conflict (or compromise), as dividing lines shifted within the larger center.[4]

A prime focus of this work has been the study of sociability and networks as a part of political culture and political life—both the usual notion of tightly knit insider networks and the looser and broader but still influential small-world networks. The two kinds of networks provided conduits for political communication not just in the sense of political activity or public opinion, but also in the spread of political ideas and attitudes, liberal, conservative, or national. Insider connections leading toward the coalescence of liberal and conservative camps did occur, but as with salon politics, ties between incipient groups continued to link people and ideas across the lines between camps. Aiding the process of blending was the fact that the network of contacts among the political and cultural elites was so dense, particularly among those in some measure opposed to the excesses of Napoleon and the Revolution, whether they were of a more liberal bent, like Madame de Staël or the Humboldts, or a more conservative one, like Friedrich Schlegel or Chateaubriand. Socially, the political camps were not exclusive; to an extent this meant that they were not politically exclusive either. This held true during the revolutionary and Napoleonic years and remained so to a considerable degree thereafter. Staël and Chateaubriand formed part of the same circle. Similarly, in Paris in the autumn of 1815 the conservative spokesman Friedrich Gentz made the acquaintance of Staël's old associate the liberal theorist Benjamin Constant through his friends Alexander and Wilhelm von Humboldt; regarding a dinner with Constant and Baron Staël where the conversation had turned political, Gentz still found the evening "extremely interesting."[5]

Conservative and liberal ideologies also remained closely linked for reasons of political communication and rhetoric, both within these broader networks and in appealing to wider publics. The desire to persuade, and simply to be understood, put limits on novel and extreme views, and promoted borrowing and adaptation of successful rhetorical strategies and ideas. This is in part how political languages work, through battling over the rhetorical high ground, which often means making competing claims on certain key concepts that have established themselves as winners. Most writers at the time did not care to self-identify as "reactionary," and many even preferred to adopt the mantle, or the name, of liberal. The question is how much of liberal beliefs, values, and political programs was assimilated in the process. The process worked in the other direction as well—not wanting to seem radical in an era of relative reaction, liberals adopted some conservative views, arguments, and language. Further complicating matters is the fact that there was already such a diversity of liberal views on the ground to choose from, and that the process was iterative—many of the available versions of liberal politics had themselves already been through such a sifting and amalgamation of conservative views.

In these years political figures such as Tsar Alexander deployed the language of human rights and citizenship alongside that of historical rights, privileges, and estates, and could speak in the same breath of progress and conservation, keeping up with the times and respect for history. This might seem to bespeak conceptual confusion in the mixing of liberal and conservative terms by those who should be using one or the other, but it just as readily indicates the existence of an ideology of the middle that partook of both.[6] Even Edmund Burke, in the conservative tradition's founding document, did not deny the rights of man as such, but instead redefined them to emphasize the role of government in fostering the pursuit of happiness.[7] The practical differences between conservative and liberal stances in different political contexts, and the difficulties of translating between them, also become important here, particularly in comparing Britain and the Continent. In looking to Burke and his defense of British liberties, conservatives maintained some tolerance for parliamentary government. For the most part they did not want to imitate or duplicate the British system, drawing instead on the conservative argument that constitutions suited the peoples and places in which they had gradually emerged and could neither simply be transplanted to another society, nor radically reinvented in a revolutionary spirit. But many continental conservatives still pointed to the fact that while it might be very well for Burke to resist change in Britain's freer conditions, in the circumstances of the Old Regime in most continental states, some reforms were clearly needed.[8] Even the German Romantic conservative Adam Müller followed Madame de Staël in calling for a renewed emphasis on the spoken word above the written, whereby vigorous oratory could only mature in the agonistic arena of parliamentary debate.[9]

If one considers the potential influence of Vienna's festive and entertainment culture on the Congress, there too the picture is mixed, with conservative strands of thought interlaced with liberal. The military and court festivities cut both ways, reinforcing traditional authority while at the same time reducing hierarchy and opening up to broader patriotic and nationalist discourses; these trends were mirrored in the entertainment culture and market for political consumption. Much the same held for the theater. One could hardly hope to find a better example of counterrevolutionary drama than the hit of the Budapest and Vienna stage in 1814, Friedrich Wilhelm Ziegler's *Partey-Wuth,* or *Rage of Party.* This five-act play, set in Cromwellian England, centers on the tribulations of Lady Johanna Laud but above all features the hand-rubbingly oily, Machiavellian figure of the MP and hanging judge Sir Gottlieb Kocke, humble-arrogant man-of-the-people intoxicated with his new power. Kocke's self-congratulatory reflections on revolutionary government read like a primer for twentieth-century totalitarian dictatorships, up to and including the encouragement of denunciation and the dissolution of social and family bonds as a means of controlling the population and short-circuiting potential resistance. In proposing an amnesty for fugitive royalists who turned in those who sheltered them, Kocke observed: "the bands of trust come undone, and the stupid sympathy is dissolved that so injures the good cause. When the father does not trust the son, and the mother must fear him whom she bore, when no person dares anymore speak, then is the republic, and our empire established." More generally, the play offered suitably royalist sentiments ("Over men must rule not thousands, but only one"), yet it also spoke the language of rights and liberties. The same character who uttered the words above also lauded the Magna Carta as "our great document of freedom," and the hero of the piece observed that "the people's sacred rights are destroyed, they collapsed with the throne." Ziegler struck an appropriate balance. Habsburg police chief Baron Hager still approved of the play as likely "to promote disgust of revolutions and noble sentiments of love of princes and fatherland."[10]

While Ziegler's drama had its liberal echoes of British liberty, in other plays such views took center stage. Friedrich Schiller's *Maria Stuart*, his *Fiesko*, and even his youthfully radical *The Robbers* were all performed during the Congress. It is surely significant, too, that Beethoven's revival of his lone opera *Fidelio* finally scored a hit, not despite but because of the fact that it carried a politically emancipatory message in the tradition of the prison rescue genre, and that even more than Schiller's plays it burst the limits of prevalent gender stereotypes. Leonore in the trouser role not only frees her political prisoner husband but, like the later figure of Grace Kelly in *High Noon*, thwarts the villainous despot by taking pistol in hand. Making the point even sharper musically, Leonore then appropriates the masculine key with which the villain had been associated. Far from playing in subversive obscurity, *Fidelio* was seen by the visiting sovereigns and entourages on the evening following the great arrival ceremonies of 25 September and was repeated several times.[11] Beethoven's Congress cantata, too, usually interpreted as a caving-in or selling-out to conservative reaction, shares more of the opera's message than is at first apparent. Along with its Habsburg dynastic patriotism, the piece also celebrates more populist images of Viennese civic patriotism and German national sentiment, and its powerful closing mixed mass choruses of children, women, and soldiers call to mind Jacques-Louis David's festivals of the French Revolution. The cantata thereby also offered a public role and voice to women, if one more consonant with the usual nurturing republican mother than in *Fidelio*, playing on sexual difference to open up public roles as nineteenth-century German women's movements tended to do (even as the chorus is accompanied by military music).[12]

The Constitutional Congress of Vienna

Turning to Congress politics itself, the Vienna settlements look less like uneasy compromises hammered out after polarizing battles between liberals and conservatives, and more like an uneasy consensus among moderate liberals and reform conservatives regarding the best ways to satisfy Europe's peoples without dangerous experiments that might lead to radical extremes. Too liberal a constitution, they thought, might provoke further revolution, but so too might reactionary measures. And preventing renewed revolution and concomitant warfare, moderates and conservatives agreed, formed the primary task after Napoleon's defeat. Respect for public opinion provided another common denominator. Conservatives such as Talleyrand and Metternich recognized that many populations (at least the political classes among them) desired relatively liberal rule, and that above all for those who had lived under constitutional regimes for ten or twenty years, attempting to go back would be difficult or dangerous. Even Joseph de Maistre in St. Petersburg, although a seminal opponent of written constitutions, still approved of Louis XVIII's moderation on the latter's return to France. "To stifle the revolutionary spirit immediately, as one extinguishes a candle, would be the enterprise of a madman." To turn that spirit to one's own account was rather "the wise solution to the problem."[13] If Maistre, reactionary religious conservative though he indubitably was, could still find his way to some coming to terms with the political changes of the preceding decades, it proved easier for those who accepted concessions or even had a positive belief that some elements of liberal government made monarchical states stronger and more enduring. As James Sheehan has observed, constitutions both limited and consolidated sovereign power, hence they found adherents in many political camps.[14]

Conservative views are easy enough to find in Congress diplomatic circles. After a trying encounter with several Swiss delegations in the winter of 1814, for example, Prince Metternich wrote the Duchess of Sagan that "there is nothing more contemptible than a republic," where there is "nothing but egoism, petty hatreds, and miserable intrigues.

Me," he continued with somewhat repetitive emphasis, "I am essentially monarchist—I am so in everything and for everything; I do not have one sentiment that is not entirely monarchical." The duchess reinforced these views, praising Metternich's "perfectly monarchic spirit"; remaining "faithful to the principles I received in my childhood, I detest with all my soul all these democratic associations, which in satisfying the self-love [amour propre] of some . . . render everyone equally vain, insolent, unsociable, and incapable of attaining an eminent degree of civilization." Not surprisingly, Wilhelmine featured among those encouraging Metternich to prosecute the war against Napoleon so as to restore the Bourbons to the French throne.[15]

Reactionary conservatism represented a strong political force in Congress Europe, as it had since the 1790s, or even before 1789 in the struggle against the radical Enlightenment.[16] Elements of the reactionary worldview can be found in many figures in the Congress orbit, including many who, it turns out, remained open to reforms and concessions to the times, with elements of the liberal worldview equally present. A hallmark of the reactionary brand of conservatism was the belief in a radical Jacobin conspiracy that had lain behind the French Revolution and that continued to operate on a European scale even after Napoleon's defeat.[17] Conservatives had in mind not just self-identifying democratic or Jacobin figures, but variously also Freemasons, Illuminati, nationalists, or—depending on how far to the right one stood—moderate liberals pushing the thin end of an antimonarchical wedge. A moderate liberal like Humboldt or even a reform conservative like Baron Stein sometimes stood accused of nefarious dealings (though others remained skeptical of such charges). And conspiracy fears cut both ways. The Bavarian Count Montgelas worried about nationalist secret societies within the Prussian camp, such as the so-called Hoffmann union under the Hessian judicial official Karl Hoffmann and the Prussian administrator Justus Gruner, but Gruner in turn feared that Montgelas had created Illuminati-based secret societies of his own with anti-Prussian and anti-German tendencies.[18]

Members of many of the main delegations expressed alarm at conspiratorial activity. Austrian head of secret police Baron Hager had been receiving reports on the so-called League of Virtue throughout the autumn, and by January 1815 affirmed to the emperor his belief in the connections between these groups and Prussia as they strove for a German constitution and popular representation directed against German princely houses. In January, too, Metternich warned his ambassador in

London of League conspirators' activities, not least in the conflict over Saxony.[19]

Napoleon's former foreign minister, Talleyrand, had unfurled his conservative banner following his former master's defeat, making an icon of the principle of legitimacy and arguing for the rollback of revolutionary regimes wherever they might be found—by which he primarily meant Napoleon's former cavalry leader, Joachim Murat in Naples.[20] In consequence, Talleyrand has long provided a prime example of the Vienna Congress's conservative or restorative character. It is also true that he was an early believer in a radical conspiracy. Talleyrand warned his king of the danger of revolution in Germany, and thought to find its source not just in the university professors and students of the nationalist movement but also in the "Jacobinism" of the mediatized nobility with whom they conspired.[21] When Talleyrand announced to Louis the great alliance of 3 January between France, Austria, and Britain, he presented it as countering "revolutionary maxims," and in his letter on the same subject to the Duchess of Courland, he proudly proclaimed his pleasure in putting France at the head of those "countries who want to destroy the revolutionary spirit." His diplomatic note to Castlereagh of 26 December similarly stated that the ultimate goal of all Congress diplomacy was to bring the revolution finally to an end (the revolution continuing, he claimed, as long as Murat's regime in Naples endured).[22] The requiem service for Louis XVI in January also revealed its conservative roots in the emphasis on dynastic legitimacy and on the detrimental influence of Enlightenment philosophy in bringing about the revolution.

For all the worries about conspiracy and the tendency toward reaction, however, this often remained a constitutional conservatism. On his arrival in Vienna in February 1815, the new British representative, the Tory Duke of Wellington, already expressed concern about the militarist, republican spirit in Prussia and thought German affairs needed speedy resolution. The solution, however, involved not repression, but rather "the legal constitution" for which German "public opinion" had already spoken "clearly."[23] At the time of the Allied conquest of Paris in the spring of 1814, Talleyrand not only pushed for the restoration of Louis XVIII but cooperated with Tsar Alexander to arrange for the French Senate to proclaim a constitution, more liberal than the one that Louis would eventually decree himself to replace it, under the name of the Charte. Talleyrand later pressed a Charte-style constitution on the unreceptive representative of the Bourbon claimant to the throne of Naples.[24]

The balance of attitudes can be seen particularly clearly in the case of the British foreign minister Lord Castlereagh, who, despite representing the power with the parliamentary form of government, proved among the more cautious or skeptical when it came to constitutions. When reining in the British official Lord William Bentinck for using liberal and national rhetoric too freely in his various promises and proclamations in Italy, Castlereagh wrote to Prime Minister Liverpool: "he seems bent upon throwing all Italy loose; this might be well against France, but against Austria and the King of Sardinia, with all the constitutions which now menace the world with fresh convulsions, it is most absurd." To Bentinck himself, he wrote more temperately and with more explanation of his gradualist Burkean rationale, arguing that "it is impossible not to perceive a great moral change coming on in Europe, and that the principles of freedom are in full operation. The danger is, that the transition may be too sudden to ripen into anything likely to make the world better or happier." As he continued, "we have new constitutions launched in France, Spain, Holland and Sicily. Let us see the results before we encourage further attempts. . . . I am sure it is better to retard than to accelerate the operation of this most hazardous principle which is abroad."[25] But even with his Tory distrust of (written) constitutions, Castlereagh still thought them often necessary, even or especially under current conditions. Thus, he informed the British ambassador in Madrid, he did not like the Spanish Cortes constitution of 1812, but was "glad to hear that the King is not disposed, in looking to a change, to aim at the restoration of the ancient order of things." Discontinuing the Cortes was one thing, but King Ferdinand would need to "speak to the nation" in proclaiming some constitutional arrangement of his own, as Louis XVIII had in France.[26]

Hence even many conservatives stood convinced of the need for constitutions. The first instance in which support for constitutions emerged in post-Napoleonic diplomacy came in the case of France and the restored Bourbon monarchy. Some French royals were not keen to accept the Constitutional Charter, but Alexander and Talleyrand made it almost a condition of restoration, and the Duke of Wellington and the British also believed that after years of at least semiconstitutional rule under the revolutionary and Napoleonic governments, the French could not go back to the preconstitutional system of the Old Regime. This remained true during the second Restoration following Napoleon's return from Elba. Even before Waterloo, Wellington confirmed the continued necessity of a constitution in France and thought the 1814 Charter had been about right. King Louis himself had taken an active role in shaping the Charter, and though it ultimately came by royal decree and established strong royal authority, it had been drafted in cooperation with legislative representatives and offered a bicameral system and the rule of law.[27]

At about the same time, the British also backed the adoption of a constitution by the new king of the Netherlands, moderately liberal but with strong monarchical authority as in most constitutions of these years. This, too, they hoped would inspire faith in the new regime even by those who had supported the revolutionary and Napoleonic governments. The constitution has already been noted for its statement of full religious equality encompassing Jews as well as Christians. When at the Congress King Willem received the former Habsburg possession of Belgium, the constitution was then revised—by a mixed commission of Dutch and Belgians—and extended to the new territory in 1815, with added rights protections.[28]

When as part of the 1814 peace settlement the Kingdom of Sweden annexed Norway from its previous ruler the king of Denmark, there too a constitution guaranteeing the Norwegians individual rights and some autonomy was deemed the panacea to reconcile them to the change. Drafted by a Norwegian assembly, the constitution was considered quite liberal, being inspired by Enlightenment models such as that of the United States and the Dutch constitution of 1798, and in fact has lasted to this day as the basis of Norway's constitutional monarchy. The Prussian liberal Wilhelm von Humboldt, at least, found the constitution some consolation, telling his wife Caroline that "out of a thoroughly bad business still something very good has come."[29]

These three constitutional settlements took place outside the framework of the Vienna Congress proper, but the trend continued there. In fact, the first piece of the Vienna settlement to be decided involved a constitutional solution. By a secret article of the Peace of Paris, the king of Piedmont-Sardinia had been promised the formerly independent city-state of Genoa as compensation for territorial losses to France. Although Spain and to an extent France protested, and although elements of the European public, such as the British parliamentary opposition, also took up the cause, the question of whether Genoa would remain independent vanished relatively quickly from the table, to be replaced by that of the conditions under which it would be incorporated into

Piedmont. The Genoese representative the Marchese de Brignole lobbied the diplomats in favor of Genoese independence against his Sardinian counterpart the Marquis de Saint-Marsan, and lodged a protest after the deal was done, in both without success. Soon both Brignole and Saint-Marsan were proposing constitutions for the annexed territory. Restorationist or reactionary political sentiment arose principally regarding nomenclature. Brignole suggested that the king of Sardinia take the new territory as king of Liguria, but Metternich and the Austrians in particular wanted no reminders of the revolutionary Ligurian Republic. It instead became the Duchy of Genoa.[30]

For the most part, however, the dominant political tendency in the negotiations proved liberal in the sense of treading a middle path between revolutionary and conservative-absolutist approaches. The subcommittee members found Brignole's constitutional plan "entirely unacceptable," claiming it took too much sovereignty from the Sardinian king (even leaving Genoa the right to foreign embassies) and in general adopted "the most republican form possible." Austria's delegate, Baron Binder, reassured Saint-Marsan that the committee supported the king's "royal authority," but added the rider "in regulating his administration according to the most liberal principles."[31] France's delegate, the royalist Comte de Noailles, summarized the committee's thinking in the draft "act of organization" for Genoa. He acknowledged the "inevitable inconveniences" of the union "of a country free for centuries to an absolute monarchy" and of the "establishment of Estates and deliberative assemblies in Italy," but went on to assert:

> we can find in this act in its present form on the one hand sufficient guarantees of the free exercise and preponderant influence of royal authority to be safe from all revolutionary movements, and on the other sufficiently extensive concessions to the new subjects of the king of Sardinia for us to be able to hope for a sincere reunion of this new province with those that constitute the old Sardinian monarchy.[32]

The document provided for provincial councils in each district, with the right to vote on taxes, as well as a combination Senate and high court in Genoa itself, which would also vote on revenue appropriations following the councils' votes. The municipal government struck a post-Napoleonic social balance with a membership of forty nobles, twenty merchants, and twenty members of the professional middle classes, to deal with city administration, finance, and police in the presence of a royal commissioner.[33] The adoption of participatory institutions, particularly with a role in taxation, marks this as a liberal settlement in the constitutional monarchy tradition. Its acceptance proved still more significant given that King Victor Emanuel of Sardinia ranked among the most reactionary rulers of the post-Napoleonic period. Even the Spanish representative, the Marqués de Labrador, though opposed to the Genoese cession for reasons of Spanish interests in Italy, still conceded that the conditions offered represented "the most advantageous and the most in harmony with everything that the better minds have regarded up to the present as the perfection of the social order in the present system of Europe." He even referred to the stipulations as "their new social compact."[34] This did not imply left-liberalism, much less republican or democratic sentiments, but it spoke to the balance of monarchical authority and representative institutions—a moderate liberal constitutionalism—that was emerging as a fundamental belief across wide stretches of the political spectrum. Even if conservatives sometimes did not like it, many were at least convinced such institutions were necessary to satisfy the citizenry and prevent revolution.

Constitutional considerations as well as power politics also affected the dispensation of other Italian territories, including the return of the pope's temporal possessions and the fate of the Habsburg lands in northern Italy. As discussed earlier in the context of Catholic reconstruction, exactly how much of the former Papal States would be granted was uncertain, with much debate particularly about whether the Three Legations (Bologna, Ferrara, and Romagna) would be given to the pope or to some other figure in need of compensatory territory to make up the European balance. For present purposes, however, the question of how the returned territories were to be governed assumes priority.

Former secretary of state of the Napoleonic Kingdom of Italy Count Antonio Aldini composed a constitutional draft for a projected independent state of the Legations under an unnamed prince. In May 1815, following the decision to give the territories to the Papal States, Metternich solicited Aldini's opinion on the best form of government for them. Making an argument with which Metternich would be sympathetic, Aldini stated that after twenty years of constitutional rule, the Legations needed to be administered separately from the other Papal States. Following a historical summary of Legation institutions under papal rule, Aldini concluded: "if a national representative body is desired that sanctions public taxes and takes part in their administration, one therefore only requests what the country has the right to obtain and what they have always obtained." Hence Aldini called for an elected diet and a six-member council to work with the governor general.[35] If the full proposals could not be implemented, Aldini included a separate list of "conditions . . . necessary to impose upon the pope" whatever the form of government chosen. These included basic accommodations with the changes of the Napoleonic period such as a guarantee of sales of national property (that is, secularized property formerly belonging to the Church and then auctioned off), a political amnesty, and recognition of new as well as old titles of nobility. Aldini also included certain minimal rights protections, primarily the rule of law in arrests and trial procedure. Aldini incorporated some of these ideas in an additional memo for Cardinal Consalvi.[36]

Austria's man in Rome, Baron Ludwig von Lebzeltern, had already begun pressuring the papal authorities to soften reactionary measures in domestic politics before the Congress; when the Legations returned to the Vatican in the final settlement, he again stressed the importance "of adopting broad and liberal maxims" in the new territories. He warned the pope "that if He governs them with the same principles that have guided certain members of the government at Rome up to now, these possessions will soon escape Him." Metternich explicitly approved these interventions, and encouraged Lebzeltern to put further pressure on the Vatican to adopt moderately "liberal principles," using "the firmest language," as he himself had with Cardinal Consalvi in Vienna.[37] Consalvi pointed out both to Metternich and to the other negotiators that if the new territories received more liberal government, all the Papal States would have to, in order to keep the residents of the older territories satisfied. If it were a matter of retaining secular officials rather than going back to full priestly rule, then something could probably be done, but full constitutional government remained problematic. The diplomats insisted that it was indeed necessary to adopt "a different system of government more analogous to the nature of the times" in all Vatican possessions, that if the pope hoped to retain his temporal sovereignty, it was better to "regulate and direct . . . the torrent of new opinions relating to government" rather than to "oppose it uselessly." Consalvi eventually prevailed on Metternich to drop specific stipulations in the final draft, but on the assurance that the Vatican would adopt something like Austria's approach in its territories anyway.[38]

In the event, the new pontifical regime in the Legations did make some concessions to the times, above all granting a consultative role to local lay figures in provincial government and guaranteeing sales of national property and titles of new and old nobility (some feudal privileges were abolished as well). In the provisional government decreed for the Legations and other restored territories in July 1815, the Vatican established special councils or "congregations" in the provincial capitals, each with several lay members under the presiding prelate-governor, who held ultimate decision-making power.[39] The pontifical "Motu proprio" published the following year finalized the new constitution and essentially retained the council system, supplemented by measures for limited local self-government under municipal councils and magistracies. Moreover, the language justifying the new system of government in the document's preamble showed that the admonitions of Metternich, Lebzeltern, and others had registered, and/or that the lessons of the past twenty years had been learned independently. As Consalvi had already written to Cardinal Pacca in Rome, without concessions they would not retain the returned provinces for six months. It would be, he suggested in appropriately biblical imagery, like Noah trying to do everything as before after disembarking the ark, though the world had changed.[40]

Consalvi's preamble still invoked the need for uniformity of administration across the various papal territories as a reason for going slowly with reforms, but it recognized that many of these areas had been governed for so long in new ways that they had forgotten "the old institutions and customs," and that it had become "almost impossible to return to the old order of things." Instead, the dispersion of "new opinions" and "enlightened ideas" borrowed in part from other nations "indispensably require the adoption in the said provinces of a new system more adapted to the inhabitants' present conditions, rendered so different from those prior."[41] As Consalvi reported back to Rome regarding the Congress's decision to assign the Duchy of Lucca to Maria Luisa, the Bourbon infanta of Spain and former Princess of Parma and queen of Etruria, on condition that she respect "the principles" of the relatively liberal constitution it had received in 1805 under Napoleon's sister Elisa and her husband, the Prince of Piombino (article 101 [CI] of the Final Act), "Your Eminence sees how constitutions are gradually being made everywhere."[42]

Perhaps surprisingly, this trend even applied to Habsburg possessions. Habsburg government in Italy in the decades before the 1848 Revolution has long borne a dark reputation, already earned in part at the time, but more recent work suggests that Austrian rule in northern Italy was less oppressive and more consensual than previously thought, particularly in Venetia.[43] Hence, in the present context, the Austrians did not simply pressure other Italian states toward moderately liberal government but themselves also made some concessions to the new constitutional spirit of the age. The published proclamation of the newly created Kingdom of Lombardo-Venetia included rudimentary representative institutions, in the form of consultative "permanent colleges of members taken from the various classes of the nation" to provide royal officials with knowledge of "the wishes and the needs of the inhabitants."[44]

Metternich might have gone even further with such plans, but at this stage of his career he had more influence over foreign policy than over domestic.[45] Like the interim governor General Bellegarde, he would at least have emphasized employing more Italians as officials and have made some small concessions to Italian national sentiment, above all in cultural policy. While Emperor Franz often resisted constitutional rule as much as he could, in this case he even added a layer of representative government between the self-governing townships and the main diets in Milan and Venice, as the Italian deputation in Vienna had requested. Similarly, though in many respects also conservative, Franz's close advisor Count Prokop Lažansky, the official in charge of the reorganization commission for Habsburg Italy, still supported the introduction of an estates-based constitution there as analogous to those in the Austrian hereditary lands. Lažansky additionally favored recognizing the new Napoleonic nobility alongside the old aristocracy, as a means of avoiding "factionalism" and attaching new groups to the incoming regime.[46]

As in the debate over the role of estates-based constitutions in the German states discussed below, one could interpret the move to such institutions in Habsburg Italy as a reactionary or restorationist measure (retreating from popular sovereignty toward something like the old estates of early modern "composite monarchies") or as one motivated primarily by fiscal concerns.[47] But while the desire for cheaper administration likely did encourage Habsburg officials to plan on more self-government and less bureaucracy, the similarity with the municipal reforms in Prussia or representative reforms in other German states suggests that liberal belief in the benefits of local knowledge and community spirit also influenced their thinking. This held particularly for a relative liberal like Johann von Wessenberg, Metternich's deputy at the Congress and simultaneously vice president of Lažansky's reorganization commission, and perhaps too of the subordinate official Baron

Kübeck. As the latter suggested in his report of 8 December 1814, elected assemblies strengthen the ties of "citizens" to the "land and state," and "the ruler gains trust and love."[48] Elements of self-government and representation not only made government more efficient, according to such views, but could also stimulate a kind of local patriotism that might additionally redound to overall Habsburg patriotism. The new approach at least marked a shift from absolutist to "consultative monarchy," if stopping short of full constitutional monarchy as seen in France or some German states.[49] And it was not simply the new nobility that was recognized alongside the old; care was also taken to include middle-class elements in the representative bodies. Employing Italian officials and encouraging Italian cultural identity also served as forms of representation. The use of the term "nation," plus the eventual decision to adopt the status of kingdom and the symbolic object the historic crown of iron, perhaps offered the residents of Lombardy and Venetia a modicum of added solace.[50]

Regarding the final set of Italian negotiations, Congress historians still often claim that Metternich insisted on a provision prohibiting the restored Bourbon king of Naples from proclaiming a constitution.[51] This is partly true, but only partly. Actually, the secret article of the alliance treaty with Austria of 12 June 1815 committed the Austrians and Ferdinand to the "internal peace" of Italy and to "preserve their respective states and subjects" from "the danger of imprudent innovations." In this cause King Ferdinand agreed not to introduce any "changes" incompatible with "the previous monarchical institutions" and with those being established for Austria's Italian possessions.[52] Such a formulation hardly excluded a degree of constitutionalism. Metternich likely wanted to guard against the particular danger that Ferdinand might feel compelled to extend to the Neapolitan portion of his kingdom the English-style parliamentary constitution installed in the Sicilian half of the realm by the Whiggish Lord Bentinck during the wartime British occupation of the island. Metternich may also have been thinking already that the constitution in Sicily could be revoked; Ferdinand and his chief minister, Count Medici, at least interpreted the clause as a green light to proceed with their desired revisions.[53]

Yet given Metternich's approach with the Vatican, and given Ferdinand's history of violent reactionary measures (above all the bloody retaking of Naples after the episode of the Parthenopean Republic in 1799), it remains equally likely that Metternich wanted insurance against any potential reactionary policies that might outrage Ferdinand's restored subjects. The typically overlooked committee protocol setting out the details of the Vienna settlement for the Italian states in March already acknowledged the "provisional constitution" that Ferdinand intended to issue and enshrined its main points in the settlement. First came the assertion that "individual and civil liberty is assured," followed by a declaration that property was "sacred and inviolable" and by the expected guarantees of national property sales and political amnesty. The king also agreed to uphold the ideal of judicial independence and the meritocratic admissibility of all Neapolitans to civil and military office.[54] Metternich and the Allies further bound Ferdinand to these provisions in the alliance between Austria and Ferdinand on 29 April, and in the surrender negotiated between the victorious Austrian commander General Bianchi and the generals of Murat's army at Casalanza on 20 May, with Kaiser Franz as guarantor. The Austrians thereby even topped the Neapolitans' original demands.[55]

Metternich's pressure also helped Count Medici rid his administration of the repressive minister of police, Count Canosa. With such diplomatic encouragement, Ferdinand's restored regime became one of the most progressive in Italy, pursuing a policy of "amalgamation" between Muratist and Bourbon supporters, aristocrats and new middle-class elites, and even preserving most of the Napoleonic-era law codes and institutions, including the consultative provincial councils and antifeudal reforms.[56] The actual constitutional document issued in late May carefully deployed the monarchical language of "paternal intentions and promises" but incorporated all the principles outlined above and ensured the status of the new Napoleonic nobility alongside the old. Taxes were at least to be imposed "according to the forms that will be prescribed by the laws," but no mention was made of a representative assembly to vote on taxation and budgets.[57] This was, in other words, still a moderately conservative document, reformist but not reactionary, and incorporating some of the constitutional protections and language of liberty and equality of the liberal tradition.

Regarding Sicily, too, Metternich toed a moderate rather than reactionary line. Metternich and Medici envisioned something like the Genoese-Piedmontese solution, whereby Sicily would retain some autonomy and elected representative institutions. Castlereagh and the British, too, acknowledged a need to revise Bentinck's constitution to strengthen royal authority.[58] Even during the Austrian-European intervention in Naples following the revolution there in 1820 and the subsequent Congress of Ljubljana (Laibach)—after Metternich and Tsar Alexander had taken

onservative turns—the powers refused Ferdinand's desire to re-
his kingdom as an absolute ruler and instead constrained him to
a compromise estates-based consultative constitution of the Aus-
sort. This document was assuredly more moderate than the revolutionary constitution modeled on the Spanish Cortes, and lacked the
stronger representative institutions called for by Russia's foreign minister, Capodistrias, but it still fit the reform conservative mold. The Allied
ministers in Naples even managed to get the reactionary Count Canosa
sacked once more.[59]

As elsewhere in Europe, many of the territorial exchanges and acquisitions in the German lands also came accompanied by promises to
establish constitutions or to maintain existing laws and institutions.
Such institutions would help integrate the new territories, and while
the process harked back to practices of early modern European composite monarchies, it clearly also aimed to satisfy perceived desires
for moderately liberal government, above all but not only when statewide constitutions were discussed. Prussia, half of whose subjects
were new in 1815, highlighted such measures in proclamations to the
Rhineland and other new and restored Prussian territories.[60] Many
German states were discussing adopting constitutions or reforming
existing ones following the popular exertions of the Wars of Liberation; Nassau drafted a fairly liberal constitution including a representative assembly by August 1814, before the Congress. Even medium-
size and smaller states viewed constitutions as effective means to
integrate new populations, as they too had grown by accretion over
the period. Bavaria alone had acquired at least eighty-three new territorial parcels in recent years.[61]

The German case, however, involved the added dimension of efforts
to draft a constitution for the whole of a new German Confederation,
which would itself set guidelines for constitutional regimes within the
new entity's constituent states. In the debates over the German Confederation, there was little opposition to the idea that it be given a constitution and include a diet (of governmental but not popular representatives). The idea that it also include a bill of rights for individuals
encountered more resistance, but most still supported such a thing in
general, even if rejecting specific proposals. At first the Prussians and
representatives of some of the smaller states and the former imperial
nobility remained confident of enacting clauses that would enshrine
rights protections for German citizens plus the ability to appeal above

the individual states to a German federal court.[62] The talk seemed to be all of German constitutions. Jacob Grimm took heart at the prevalence of such ideas and foresaw a brighter political future once "the people" received a "seat and voice." The Swiss representative from the democratic canton of Aargau also felt optimistic that the "liberal spirit" in German affairs would help his cause; he certainly interpreted such plans as liberal, reporting to Aargau's Council that the German princes could put some of their own republican governments to shame in this respect.[63]

Of the other two most important powers on the German Committee, the Austrians were less enthusiastic than Prussia about the proposed clause guaranteeing constitutions, in part because they worried that it would create difficulties for getting a German Confederation passed at all, but Metternich did support it.[64] His number two, Baron Wessenberg, even thought that German princes could no longer claim to represent the mass of the population and proposed a bicameral representative body as well as protections of persons and property in the federal constitution. The Hanoverian Count Münster disapproved of Baron Stein's all-or-nothing approach to German constitutions, but felt a constitution guaranteeing some kind of representation and basic rights would be a good start, and capable of further development over time.[65] In the conferences on the German constitution in October and November 1814, it was already clear just how resistant to infringements on their newly won sovereignty the kingdoms of Bavaria and Württemberg were going to be. Even here, however, they were primarily concerned to avoid stipulating the criteria constitutions would have to meet under the new plan. Bavaria had already proclaimed a relatively enlightened constitution during the Napoleonic years, and would unveil a newer one just a few years after the Congress. They did not fear constitutions, but in line with their general policy they wanted to preserve as much sovereignty and freedom of maneuver as possible.[66]

Both sides also appealed to German public opinion. Although the press war between Prussia and Bavaria is more famously associated with the battle over Prussia's proposed annexation of Saxony, the constitutional question formed a strong secondary theater.[67] In December Hardenberg decided to exert a little extra pressure through German public opinion by planting a piece in the widely circulated Hamburg *Correspondenten* (outside Prussian jurisdiction if not beyond its influence), one that made the clause guaranteeing constitutions seem almost inevitable. As so often, editors went the government one better if they believed in the cause, hence the same edition included another article defending estates-based constitutions as the "palladium of old-German legal liberty."[68] The southwest German periodical devoted to the Congress had run a series on constitutions along similar lines back in October, and their list of New Year's wishes for 1815 included one for constitutional monarchy, and the hope that rulers would not interpret their new sovereignty to mean "unlimited."[69]

As in the newspaper articles, the Prussians and other proponents of a constitutional clause typically promoted *landständische Verfassungen,* or estates-based constitutions. Historians have disagreed strongly about how to interpret this notion of estates constitutions, in part reflecting the fact that contemporaries had just as much difficulty deciding whether their supporters were moderate liberals, radical subversives, or reactionary conservatives. The phrase "estates-based constitutions" was inherently ambivalent, just like the term "liberal." For Talleyrand, the imperial nobles pushing for state diets were menacing Jacobins. Some modern scholars, on the contrary, have seen constitutions based on the old feudal estates as a retreat to the Old Regime, categorically different from representative constitutions in the modern sense. This is not necessarily wrong. Many aristocratic voices hoped to reestablish the estates in a conservative society, as with Baron Marwitz in Prussia.[70] But neither does it capture the whole story. Even with such groups it is important to recognize that the impulse was not wholly reactionary, in that they meant to oppose not just democratic possibilities but also encroachments by absolutist states. If one sides with the bureaucratic monarchies as sponsors of the rule of law and a "revolution from above" against feudal aristocrats, then the new representative constitutions by decree will seem the more forward-looking developments, with estates-based constitutions contributing little to the growth of parliamentary government in the nineteenth century.[71]

If, on the contrary, one takes the regimes as representatives of a more absolutist trend and the bureaucracies as themselves conservative, then both aristocratic and popular forces pushing for a greater sphere of rights and political participation could indeed be seen as liberal, and able to find common ground on which to cooperate.[72] In this sense it is again important to think past the image of a bipolar, left-right political spectrum, and perhaps even past that of a tripartite spectrum of radical, liberal, and conservative. Instead, overlaying the tripartite spectrum was also the question of the different possible social and institutional bases of political power and influence, popular and aristocratic, governmental and nongovernmental, aristocratic court and more open state and bureaucracies, all of which could align in different constellations in various states and at various points in time. Whether continuities really existed between the old estates-based constitutions and the early liberal constitutionalism of the nineteenth century cannot be decided here, but it is significant that early constitutional liberals at least thought they did or claimed they did. The political language of estates could be used to constitutionalist ends.[73]

One historian has argued that support by the Prussians and the former imperial nobility for estates-based constitutions essentially aimed only at curtailing the authority of the newly sovereign princes of the former Napoleonic Confederation of the Rhine rather than at any political liberalization; hence their version of a constitution was ultimately reactionary, to restore the nobles to their previous feudal eminence unchecked by the royal state.[74] Yet this seems unlikely, insofar as both a liberal like Humboldt and a reform conservative like the former imperial noble Baron Stein saw such constitutions as means to achieve several liberal goals. They could protect individual rights for broader segments of the population, establish checks on royal authority in the form of legislative and budgetary approval by the diet, and create civic spirit and patriotism among a more active citizenry as well. As Humboldt observed in a pregnant passage of his memo of 1813 on a German constitution, "well constructed Estates are not only a necessary defense against governmental intrusion into private rights, but they also increase the feeling of independence in the nation and bind it more closely to the government."[75] Baron Stein maintained much the same stance, as when encouraging a constitution in Nassau in 1814: "an estates-based constitution is extremely desirable. It secures civil and political liberty, it produces community spirit [Gemeingeist], and through it the reasonable and moral prince achieves a great power over the spiritual and physical forces of the people."[76] For both figures, the constitution strengthened the monarchy even as it limited it and enfranchised more of the populace.

During the Congress, the Kingdom of Württemberg provided an illustrative example of the difficulties of distinguishing allegiances and lines between liberal and conservative. King Friedrich of Württemberg—who had a despotic reputation, even in the eyes of Countess Nesselrode, accustomed as she was to Russian autocracy—surprised just about everyone by proclaiming a constitution.[77] Perhaps partly a response to public opinion, he also aimed to preempt the Congress's constitutional decisions. Most observers were flummoxed, and unsure what to make of the document. First impressions were often favorable, seeing it as relatively liberal, with a limited bill of rights and a unicameral legislature having a voice in legislation and taxation. As Enno Kraehe observed, the constitution met the criteria mooted by Humboldt and Count Münster in the German Committee, and was welcomed at first by both Hardenberg and Metternich.[78] Given the king's reputation, however, it was not long before more suspicious or cynical views began to circulate. From that cui bono perspective, the political arrangements looked like the ruler settling accounts with his old foes the Estates. The former imperial noble Count Henrich of Stolberg-Wernigerode first heard of the constitution and its supposed "truly liberal principles" on 18 January, the same day that Cardinal Consalvi reported much the same view back to Rome. Already on 19 January, however, after several hours studying a copy of the proclamation announcing the constitution, Stolberg changed his mind and found it a "contrivance" worthy of Machiavelli, promoting "despotism, if concealed."[79]

By March, even that supporter of constitutions Baron Stein encouraged the publisher Johann Cotta in his opposition to King Friedrich's, to show how Germans despised both "the anarchist" and "the tyrant," that is, preferred a liberal constitutionalism that avoided the extremes of democracy and absolutism.[80] Opposition to the new constitution spread in Württemberg, and did attract both liberals such as Cotta and the Romantic poet Ludwig Uhland and aristocratic conservatives such as Georg von Waldeck in defense of "the good old law." In the course of 1815, however, the coalition split in the face of the king's revised constitutional draft, this time with a bicameral legislature that one might have thought would have appealed to the nobility with its House of Lords, but they held out for the older estates model, while Cotta plumped for the new version.

This example, perhaps more even than others, shows the importance of thinking in terms not just of a threefold political spectrum of Jacobin, liberal, and conservative, wherein liberals could ally with either extreme, but also of the varying potential parties or centers of power: monarchs, nobles, bureaucrats, and commons, or government and opposition. None of the contending parties in the Württemberg case pushed for full popular sovereignty; if that is one's litmus test for liberal, then almost no one qualified. But it becomes difficult to tell the difference between historicist liberals or reform conservatives with a traditionalist version of liberty. The defenders of the "good old law" certainly argued in conservative terms on the basis of the centuries-long history of the Württemberg constitution, as well as castigating the new, government-proposed one as metaphysical and doctrinaire like those of the French Revolution. They did, therefore, take the Burkean line that rights and constitutions must be gradual historical growths rather than rationally engineered de novo. But at the same time they had recourse to arguments from natural law, the social contract, and the need to adapt to the "spirit of the times" in order to secure individual rights. Their opponents, in turn, were clearly liberal in defending a new-style constitutional monarchy with a bill of rights, but they also sided with state and government over populist impulses. Whichever solution emerged, it would have the potential both in its ideas and in its adherents to develop in liberal or in conservative directions thereafter, as indeed the political struggle continued after the constitutional compromise of 1819.[81]

As for the German federal constitution, in the end the Prussians and the other promoters of state constitutions had to settle for a simple statement (article 13) that "estates-based constitutions will exist in all German states," with no further criteria given.[82] The compromise was more acceptable to the Bavarians than to the Prussians, particularly since the concomitant provision for a federal court so dear to Humboldt had been deleted. The (in)decision set the stage for continued wrangling at both federal and state levels over the interpretation of that ambiguous term.

By around 1820, article 13 was being interpreted more restrictively, or even partly ignored, in the case of Prussia and Austria. In those states, individual provinces typically had some form of estates-based constitution, but not the countries as a whole. Friedrich Wilhelm's promise in May 1815 to establish a nationwide constitution in Prussia ultimately went unredeemed and became a rallying cry for the liberal opposition. At the end of the Congress itself, however, it is clear that the king, and certainly his ministers, really intended to produce such a constitution, liberal in the more mixed sense we have seen here. Constitutions became a primary element in the campaign to reconcile new populations to the regime, not just representative bodies in the individual provinces, but with explicit reference to the broader, statewide representative institutions as well. The official announcement of the incorporation of the previously Prussian areas of Lower and Upper Saxony offered

the prospect of both a provincial estates-based constitution and participation in the "general" one for all Prussia, as did the patent proclaiming
the annexation of the formerly Swedish territories of Pomerania and
the isle of Rügen. Equivalent assurances would appear in the accession
proclamations for Prussia's contentious new Polish and Saxon territories.[83] Even in the late stages of the internal governmental debates over
a Prussian constitution in 1820, it was a close-run thing and no foregone conclusion that Friedrich Wilhelm would decide against establishing one.[84] Emperor Franz and Metternich, for their part, never intended
to create an Austria-wide assembly, but Metternich at least planned
administrative reform that would pay more attention to provincial
and national diversity. Franz also reestablished or promised several
estates-based constitutions in reacquired territories in the years after
1814, including for Tyrol, Vorarlberg, Carniola, and Salzburg, to go
with those already existing in the core provinces. But for the most
part these gave little authority to the provincial assemblies and hewed
even closer to a purely consultative role than the new institutions in
Lombardy-Venetia.[85]

Mountain Republicanism and Religious Difference in Switzerland

Like Italy and Germany, Switzerland also saw constitutional solutions
to smooth territorial exchanges, but there the negotiations dealt additionally with broader conflicts between democratic and patrician forces,
and between the new and the old cantons, which partly overlapped
with the political divisions. The new cantons of the revolutionary and
Napoleonic era, such as Aargau, Ticino, and Vaud, tended to be more
democratic, while some of the older cantons, above all Bern, remained
patrician. As the Russian note submitted to the Congress's Swiss commission maintained, "the agitations in Switzerland have been the consequence of the reaction of the spirit of independence and equality against
aristocratic institutions of monopoly and subjection, relations that injured the self-respect and interest of the majority."[86] Bern was also the
former overlord of Vaud and Aargau and hoped to regain its territories.
France preferred that solution, but Russia and Prussia supported the
new cantons, with Britain and Austria at least willing to go along. This
provides another instance where fear of revolution could lead to support for constitutions, even democratic ones, as a means of promoting
stability. As arbitrators of the new Swiss federal constitution, the pow-

ers ultimately confirmed as its basis the existence of the new cantons, while at the same time discouraging them from democratic excesses in drafting their individual cantonal constitutions. A "shift in political culture" had occurred, and "the resubjugation of new cantons was no longer possible."[87]

To mollify Bern, the Allies awarded it portions of the former ecclesiastical territory the Bishopric of Basel, including Porrentruy. After a meeting between Tsar Alexander and Bern's representative, Russia approved the exchange, but only on condition of amendments to Bern's constitution. The constitution was to incorporate "the representative principle," and the cities and communes were to receive a third of the seats on the Grand Council. Most significantly, citizenship was to be opened to rural residents "upon equitable conditions."[88]

The Swiss negotiations and the support for even democratic republican governments also reveal another facet of European conservatism and moderate liberalism, through the widespread acceptance of an ideology that we can call "mountain republicanism." Conservatism, at least for many political thinkers and actors, did not mean opposition to liberal or constitutional rule as such, but only where it was deemed inappropriate. In cases where populations had become suited to self-government through historical experience and/or the kind of lives they led, then it was perfectly allowable. This view came through most clearly in the case of the Swiss republics and the German city-states. European elites accepted the patricians of these polities as a kind of surrogate aristocracy, not just politically but also socially, and their republican forms of social intercourse proved subject for curiosity or admiration rather than discomfort. The amazing social success of Jean-Gabriel and Anna Eynard of Geneva provided the best example of the phenomenon, aided by their wealth, her youthful beauty, and his counterrevolutionary military service in previous decades. Johann Smidt of Bremen offers another instance. Karl Griewank noted all the representatives of the Quadruple Alliance on the Swiss Committee—the Russian Count Capodistrias, the Briton Sir Stratford Canning, the Prussian Baron Humboldt, and the Austrian Baron Wessenberg—as being motivated by liberal sympathy for Switzerland as home of the free Swiss of poetry. Beyond the committee, one could add Metternich's trusted official the former Austrian envoy in Switzerland Baron Lebzeltern, the Polish magnate Prince Czartoryski, and for that matter Tsar Alexander himself, pupil of Frédéric-César de La Harpe from Vaud.

The term "mountain republicanism" can be used to describe a political trope or ideology closely related to the classical republican tradition. As with ancient Roman farmer-soldiers or the image of the Greeks (particularly Sparta), the simple lifestyle and relative lack of luxurious wealth among the Swiss mountain-dwellers promoted virtue in the moral and political senses. Liberty and duty then coalesced, with citizens serving the community in both military and political capacities, to defend and govern the polity, and like Cincinnatus ready to return to the plow thereafter. A certain rugged independence joined with classical republicanism's libertarian and egalitarian ethos, and translated readily to the hunters and herdsmen of the Swiss mountains and primitive cantonal democracies. Machiavelli had already made the connection between the Swiss and Romans long before, but it became even more widespread in the eighteenth-century age of Rousseau.[89]

The locus classicus for mountain republican ideas is the Swiss history of Johannes von Müller, and from there Friedrich Schiller's anti-Napoleonic drama *Wilhelm Tell* (1804). In the play Tell explains to his son the differing political tendencies of the republican-democratic Swiss mountain dwellers and the aristocratic-monarchical inhabitants of the plain, differing climates and lifestyles fitting them for different forms of government. After a discussion of avalanches, young Walther Tell asks his father if there are lands without mountains, and after hearing of the beauties and fecundity of these lower regions, he naturally wonders why they don't live there instead. But on learning how people there are not free to enjoy "the blessings that they sow" since these belong to the lords and rulers, and how they need a king to rule them since "neighbor cannot trust neighbor there," Walther decides he prefers republican life among the avalanches after all. This discussion immediately precedes the fateful encounter with the emperor's official in which Tell is forced to shoot an apple from his son's head, hence the lesson in freedom and the act of tyranny provide mutual context (act 3, scene 3, ll. 1780–1814). As mountain folk, with less social inequality and a spirit of independence, the Swiss were thought suited for virtuous and active self-government. This at least constituted one argument from Rousseau that could be accepted basically across the political spectrum.

Fresh from dealing with Swiss affairs as an Austrian representative in Zurich, Baron Lebzeltern stopped off in the Italian Republic of San Marino in 1814 on the way to his new post in Rome, on a sort of constitutional fact-finding mission. He thought the knowledge could be useful, particularly if he returned to Switzerland later. San Marino impressed him as "the only state in Europe" to have "conserved its constitution intact in the middle of all the innovations suffered by neighboring countries." Here, too, though, it was not just the literally conservative nature of the system that appealed to the Austrian diplomat, for with the extinction of Genoese independence San Marino also became the only remaining republic in Italy. Nor did its small size, relative poverty, and mountain location alone explain the durability of its republican form of government. "The constitution," Lebzeltern emphasized, "which has not suffered any variation for centuries, seems to me to incorporate the principles of a perfect equality and of a reciprocal guarantee between the three orders of the state." The Grand Council appreciated his visit so much that they voted the Austrian baron into their republic's patriciate. Lebzeltern's experience attests a commitment to several liberal principles, and as his role in the negotiations over Vatican government reforms suggests, not solely in a mountain republican context but more generally.[90]

The Swiss themselves operated within the mountain republican ideology, as with the Genevan Congress delegate Charles Pictet de Rochemont, who shared belief in the connection between social simplicity, political virtue, and mountain independence, deriving perhaps in part from Calvinist roots, and in part from classical. Such views also motivated, or were at least used to justify, certain restrictions on the rights of the canton's new inhabitants by Geneva's Council. Since the (mostly Catholic) populations of the new territories were not as economically advanced or accustomed to republican institutions and habits, they were not to have full proportional representation in the council, though they would have some, and would enjoy all the constitutional protections, equal access to courts and offices, and religious parity.[91] Such commitment to habitual self-government and constitutional inclusiveness presented a double bind: one could acquire more territory and new populations only if they were granted religious and political liberty and equality, but this put potential limits on how much could be assimilated without jeopardizing existing institutions and political culture.

Both the double bind and the broader recourse to mountain republican thinking among the Swiss and the diplomats also emerged in the particularly revealing case of the Valtellina and Graubünden, which could have come straight out of *Wilhelm Tell*. Until the revolutionary era, the Graubünden (Grey Leagues or Grisons) of southern Switzerland had ruled over the northern Italian subject territories of Bormio, Chiavenna, and Valtellina. Now that Napoleon's empire in Europe was being dismantled, Graubünden and Swiss officials generally expected these lands' return. The Valtelline representatives, however, made it clear that they preferred to join Austria's possessions in northern Italy rather than the Graubünden and Switzerland. In the autumn of 1814 Austria still supported the territories' assignment to Switzerland, but protected Valtelline interests. The Austrians insisted that the inhabitants receive "the same rights, the same liberty, and the same independence as those of the other nineteen cantons," a stance the Austrian representative on the Swiss Committee, Baron Wessenberg, later reinforced with a reference to the "oppression" under which the three territories had formerly "groaned" at the hands of Graubünden's "democratic governments."[92]

As with other territorial exchanges, the problem was to find a means of sufficiently protecting the rights and interests of the populations involved to make the cession at least more palatable, if not necessarily more popular. This case, however, offered several extra wrinkles that prove quite illuminating regarding contemporary thinking about and handling of questions of constitutionalism, rights, and ultimately nationality as well. As the House of Orange's delegate Baron Gagern reported back to The Hague, "the Congress offers in that direction a singular episode. It is desired to give the Valtellina to Graubünden as an integral part—and they don't want them. They'll force them to take them."[93] Explaining the conundrum leads straight back to the mountain republican ideology.

For Gagern was essentially correct. It was indeed unusual for a polity not only to refrain from attempting to acquire as much land as possible but even to refuse it when offered, and that was precisely what Graubünden's representatives were doing. They acknowledged that if the territories returned to their jurisdiction, it could not be under the old subject status but rather with "political rights" and full "civic liberty."[94] Therein lay the problem, for according to mountain republican thinking, the residents of the richer valley of the Adda River at the heart of the Valtellina were unfit for the republican type of government that suited the Swiss so well. Playing to the presumed conservative prejudices of their diplomatic audience, Graubünden's representatives wrote that while democratic government might be "dangerous for every other people . . . simple mountain folk, poor and accustomed for centuries to the forms of a pure democracy," could "conserve" such a system "without danger." Making this possible was the "mediocrity of fortunes of even the most well-off persons, and hence a near equality of riches." Valtellina on the other hand, with a different "climate" more "favored by nature," boasted greater wealth for some but also greater poverty, an inequality that made democracy unfeasible and Valtellina unsuitable for incorporation into Graubünden. Above the geographic arguments against integration, "the striking diversity of the country and its inhabitants causes reflections much more important and absolutely decisive."[95]

The Valtelline representatives themselves essentially echoed the argument for the opposite purpose of securing adherence to the Habsburg monarchy. Playing to the presumed prejudices of the leading statesmen, they claimed they did not want to be "condemned to a perilous liberty," as "a small population, which senses the need for a moderate subjection [sudditanza]."[96]

The Graubündener consequently felt disinclined to take back that territory and population. Instead they proposed to grant them some kind of autonomy. In terms of both territory and population, the Valtellina could make a strong case to be its own canton (it would still have ranked among the larger ones), but it would require "a constitution entirely different from that of Graubünden."[97] The Graubündener still, however, laid claim to the two smaller valleys on the northern ends of the Valtellina, Chiavenna and Bormio. With respect to Chiavenna, they primarily deployed geostrategic and economic arguments, even punning on its Italian name in presenting the town as the "key" to the valleys of Graubünden. For Bormio, however, they pointed above all to features that again fit the mountain republican schema. In addition to commercial ties, the incorporation of Bormio into Graubünden was suggested by "the perfect analogy of terrain, of customs, of fortunes, of way of life and of governing themselves of this pastoral people."[98] The Graubündener even played the self-determination card for Bormio, suggesting that the powers should wait to hear the "wishes" of the locals before making a decision.[99] They may even have been correct with respect to Bormio, as opposed to Chiavenna and the rest of the Valtellina, from which several petitions to remain with Austria's northern Italian possessions already lay in Metternich's files.[100] In line with the constitutionalist provisions for territorial exchanges elsewhere, Graubünden also took care to reassure the residents of Chiavenna and Bormio (and their Austrian protectors) that they would join the Leagues with guarantees of some self-government and representation. Each would become its own administrative district, and receive seats on the Grand Council, two for Bormio and four for Chiavenna.[101]

For the rest of Valtellina, Graubünden's representatives envisioned a separate canton within the Helvetic Confederation. In conference, the Swiss delegates were forced to explain away this lack of enthusiasm for taking back the territory on the grounds of Catholic-Protestant differences and past conflicts. But then, while they wanted the Valtellina in Switzerland as part of Graubünden, they, too, rejected it if it came as a separate entity within the Confederation. The Swiss spokesman Reinhard of Zurich declared that the Confederation could not add to its already pronounced cantonal diversity, "heterogeneous by the locality, genius, manners, needs, and resources of these peoples" (Zurich's plenipotentiaries had already used similar arguments in May to limit Genevan territorial gains, since the new inhabitants would lack "Helvetic mores"). Instead they put the ball back in Graubünden's court, proposing that the Valtellina be granted a special autonomous status within Graubünden, with the two merging their federal representation.[102] The Genevan Pictet and Russia's Swiss Committee member Capodistrias had already devised the idea of making the Valtellina essentially an autonomous fourth constituent league within Graubünden, separately administered and sharing representation on the Swiss diet (but still receiving just the one vote between them).[103] A version of this solution won through in January 1815, but it stopped neither the Graubündener nor the Valtelline representatives from pushing for greater separation in the weeks thereafter.

And in fact, within weeks January's agreement collapsed. In late January, Austrian policy changed from simply protecting Valtellina's rights in its union with Graubünden (or with Switzerland directly) to instead claiming it for the Habsburg domains in northern Italy after all. Just days after Wessenberg's contribution to the final committee decisions making the territory Swiss, Emperor Franz's close advisor Count Lažansky seized on an October report from Lombardy's governor general, Heinrich Bellegarde, to argue for the "in military and financial respects extremely important advantages" that annexation would bring to the empire, at which point Franz instructed Metternich to negotiate "the most advantageous boundaries" possible as described in that report.[104] The other powers were nonplussed by the turnabout, and the French only toned down their objections after Talleyrand received surprising new instructions from Paris, part of the fruit of Metternich's secret negotiations with Louis and his chief minister Count Blacas over how to bring an end to Murat's rule in Naples.[105]

Where the Valtelline controversy is noted in the literature on the Congress, it is almost always explained in geostrategic and power-political terms.[106] This dimension was clearly significant, but there was more to it than that. The fact that the Valtellinians objected, and that both the Graubündener and the Swiss did not really want restoration either under the only possible conditions of liberal rights and autonomy, certainly made it easier for the Austrians to reconsider and for other powers to agree. Moreover, beyond the issues of constitutional rights protections and local desires, arguments from nationality also entered the picture. Wessenberg had already painted the antagonism between the Valtellina and Graubünden back in December as "the national hatred which exists between them and their former co-citizens," and the Valtelline statements adduced nationality as well. In addition to factors such as "politics," "public tranquility," "commercial relations," and "geographic position," the Valtelline note to the Swiss Committee before its deliberations in December also cited "language and customs" and underscored that the inhabitants had "at no time been part of Switzerland." When arguing in January that Valtellina should become an independent canton, Wessenberg ran through much the same list of reasons, including again "the difference of manners, of language, of religion."[107] At least in private, the Russian delegate on the Swiss Committee Count Capodistrias even thought that the new southern canton Ticino should also go to Italy rather than Switzerland, given that "religion, position, language, nature claim it for Italy."[108]

The idea that arguments from nationality and self-determination carried weight in the deliberations received confirmation in the Duke of Wellington's report to Castlereagh, by this time back in London. The change with respect to Valtellina's destination, Wellington informed him, "was occasioned by the strong objection of the inhabitants of the Valtelline to become a part of the Canton of the Grisons. They are by local circumstances connected naturally with Italy instead of with Switzerland." These considerations, he thought, plus the fact that the region had spent eighteen years with the Kingdom of Italy and its predecessor republics, determined the negotiation's outcome.[109] Metternich prevailed on Kaiser Franz to sweeten the deal for the Graubündener by offering them the seigneurial holding of Razüns, a Habsburg-controlled enclave. Of little value in itself, lordship of the tiny territory carried influence in Graubünden elections, hence ceding it would enhance the canton's sovereignty. Metternich was "convinced that this proof of Your Highness's magnanimity will make the most favorable impression upon public opinion in Switzerland," particularly with Austria set to acquire not only the Valtellina but also Bormio and Chiavenna, territories "indeed very important for Switzerland."[110]

Nationalism and National Identity

Considerations of nationality figured in the Vienna negotiations well beyond the peripheral but revealing case of the Swiss and Italian Alps. We saw in the case of the Greeks how a nationalist cause could prove popular among the political elite without producing diplomatic results. Here we examine the role of national ideas in the politics involving the German, Italian, and Habsburg states. Reorienting our understanding of the political spectrum and definitions of terms proves helpful in thinking about the relationship between potentially competing dynastic, supranational, national, ethnic, and regional identities. National identity and patriotism were not incompatible with regional and state loyalties, or with supranational dynastic ones. Nor for that matter was nationalism incompatible with the existence or smooth functioning of the European elite with its cosmopolitan sympathies and lifestyle.

Scholars of the Vienna Congress have traditionally critiqued the statesmen and rulers for insufficient awareness of nationalist desires and hence for neglecting the rights of nationalities (above all Polish, but also German and Italian). More recently, historians of nationalism and of the Wars of Liberation have been at pains to show that nationalism was not so widespread or well-developed in the early nineteenth century, and that older images of a national awakening at the time of the wars against Napoleon for the most part constituted a nationalist myth or backward projection.[111] Downplaying the extent of nationalism in the years 1813–1814 to some degree exonerates the diplomats, since it would have been all the easier to turn a blind eye to nationalist aspirations if they were in fact less visible. As this discussion shows, however, neither picture is quite correct. At least the perception of popular nationalism proved well-grounded among European leaders, and nationalist appeals were not simply ignored, neither among the decision-makers nor among those who lobbied them. Particularly if one adopts a definition of nationalism or national identity broader than the nation-state standard of 1919, one not automatically at odds with smaller regional or larger dynastic and supranational allegiances, then the small minority of potential nationalists becomes that much larger, and more vocal. Such an expanded definition, furthermore, incorporates more of the statesmen themselves in the ranks of those who believed in national ideals, or who at least accepted them as legitimate aspirations of the age, to be disregarded only at Restoration regimes' peril.

Moreover, nationality and nationalism in politics involve not only the goals and aspirations of peoples or elite movements, or the efforts to squelch them by governments or other elites. As ideologies they also entail questions of belief in nationhood and national character on the part of the actors concerned, and of the consequences of such beliefs for the ways statesmen think and argue, and for the decisions they ultimately make. As when considering Jacobin, liberal, or conservative ideologies, the notion of ideology here is broad, a mental map of the world and one's place in it, or indeed a whole anthropology, in the sense of beliefs about human beings and human difference(s), as individuals and as social groups. Even intellectuals—or statesmen—rely on such mental maps, as shortcut guides to a larger reality.[112] As a means of emphasizing nationalism's distinctive modernity, scholars sometimes insist that nationalism must represent a fully political ideology aiming to change the political order, and cannot simply involve descriptive statements about peoples. Such a view may be useful as a typological operational definition, but it runs the risk of obscuring the still profound political implications of such descriptive beliefs about nations and nationhood, and the degree to which the content of these beliefs had itself changed with the advent of full-fledged nationalism in the late eighteenth century and the revolutionary era.[113]

This broader conception of nationhood fits with another strand of recent scholarship trying to break away from older nationalist models of the nation-state. According to these new views, late eighteenth- and early nineteenth-century German national identity was characterized by pronounced federal tendencies, with much intellectual and emotional investment in local states and dynasties alongside the larger German or Holy Roman imperial identity. Individual states in turn pursued nation-building policies of their own aimed at constructing nation-like identities from their own component parts: Bavarian, Hanoverian, and so on, often integrating new territories such as Franconia or East Frisia. Local and national identities in this scheme not only did not always collide, but often reinforced one another.[114] As in the Swiss and Italian cases, too, relationships between local elites and central authorities oscillated between conflict and symbiosis, with the former sometimes contesting national or dynastic symbols but just as often latching onto national imagery and central initiatives in order to bolster their own positions; central governments allowed local elites some autonomy so long as this, on balance, strengthened dynastic patriotism and administration (or at least made government cheaper). Similar scholarship has demonstrated the flexibility of national identity in the multinational Habsburg Empire, where German, Czech, and other identities remained quite fluid during the nineteenth century, and supranational allegiances to dynasty and state allowed ideologies such as Austro-Slavism to flourish. In that framework, nationalists tended to strive for federalist autonomy and language rights as linguistic minorities rather than for full independence, all the way until the First World War.[115]

As noted in the introduction, many of the period's most significant figures in the development of nationalist ideas and movements populated the Vienna scene during the Congress, from the Prussian Wilhelm von Humboldt and the tsar's German advisor Baron Stein to the early promoter of Greek national revival Count Capodistrias and the patriotic founder of the Hungarian National Museum Count Ferenc Széchényi. The German nationalist Jacob Grimm attended the Congress, and when not occupied with diplomatic tasks he indulged his interests in the cultural politics of nationhood. He not only helped found an association for the collection of German folktales and medieval poetry but also made connections with the Slovene scholar and early national awakener Jerneij Kopitar and helped spread the folk poetry of the Serb Vuk Karadžić to German speakers. Humboldt took advantage of his Viennese posting in these years to study Slavic languages with Kopitar, who already cooperated with the religious conservative German nationalist Friedrich Schlegel in adding a Slavic component to the latter's journal the *German Museum*. Kopitar's Austro-Slavism may also have owed something to Schlegel's influence. The aristocrats Joseph von Lassberg, Werner von Haxthausen, and Isaac von Sinclair joined Grimm in his collecting endeavors, even as they established a parallel organization to promote a revival of the German nobility and the related study of Germany's medieval past. Henrich zu Stolberg-Wernigerode, another member of this association, could still enjoy an evening of Czech folk poetry alongside the relics of Germanic chivalry.[116]

Though nationalists of one group did not always support the others' aspirations, the tendency clearly ran toward transnational exchanges and cosmopolitan interests and outlooks. Madame de Staël, though not at the Congress, still exerted influence there in this context. She has figured as one of the inventors of modern nationalism in her novel *Corinne, or Italy,* and is credited with coining the French "nationalité." The Schlegel connection proves important once again, as Friedrich and Dorothea translated the work into German, at about the same time that Friedrich moved to Vienna to assist the Habsburgs in putting the 1809 campaign on a nationalist basis. Count István Széchényi, son of Count Ferenc and himself a future leader of the Hungarian liberal nationalist movement, started to reconsider the significance of nations and nationhood during the Congress, in part through reading Staël's recently published *On Germany* and maintaining a running commentary on the work in his diary. The Széchényis and Schlegels also cooperated within Vienna's Catholic revival network.[117]

National ideas and practices consequently spread widely in the Congress milieu. Whether they liked the idea or not, political leaders at the time at least thought that they had been fighting a war of nations. The campaign against Napoleon was, they believed, national in the sense both of being based on a broad wave of popular patriotic participation, and of involving patriotic commitment to entities called nations— Spanish, German, British, Russian, French; Prussian, Austrian, Bavarian— when these are understood in the more federalist terms used here. Metternich, Gentz, and the Austrians were the least willing to embrace the new style of warfare and politics, having been burnt by their experiments in that area in 1809, but when one considers the extent of popular mobilization and enthusiasm seen in the militias and the market for patriotic productions during the campaigns of 1813–1814, even Austria went quite far in that direction.[118] The Prussians and Russians have always been recognized as appealing in part to the nation in arms, and even the conservative Castlereagh not only deemed the conflict a national one but pressured the Austrians to make it yet more so, with national uprisings in Tyrol and Italy to match those in Spain and divert Napoleon's forces to another southern front. "It is become a contest of nations to all intents and purposes and not a game of statesmen," Castlereagh wrote in late 1813 to his representative at Allied headquarters. The cause could still be lost despite the Allies' numerical superiority "if the whole is not sustained by a national sentiment and by that impulse, which is alone to be communicated by calling the mass of the people into action."[119]

Many of the constitutions and their associated diplomatic settlements also figure here as partly responses to the perception of strong national identity. In handling the questions of France's borders and constitution, statesmen reckoned with the vehemence of French national pride, stoked for so many years by revolutionary and Napoleonic governments. King Louis and Talleyrand pled the need to respect French nationalism, and the Allies accepted it. The argument even convinced them to be lenient about repatriating the looted artworks that Napoleon had amassed in Paris and that had become symbols of French national pride.[120] Norway, too, though previously part of the Danish monarchy, had through its military resistance reiterated to Europe's leaders that it possessed a national identity worthy of preservation in the country's transition to Swedish rule, hence the settlement and constitution gave due regard to its "autonomy" and "national honor" as well as to its "liberty."[121]

The desire to give Germany a federal constitution also partly resulted from belief in the prevalence of German national sentiment and of a German national movement that would not be satisfied with less. At the same time, it is clear that many German statesmen themselves believed that some kind of partly national, federal German union with significant central powers formed a necessary feature of the new European political landscape, not least but not only for security reasons. Even the rather Austro-centric Field Marshal Prince Schwarzenberg supported Hardenberg's and Metternich's plans for a strong central Europe, writing that only the region's "innermost unification" could sustain peace, and that Austria, Prussia, and Germany had to form "a unified whole." At a moment of crisis in the Saxon negotiations, Hardenberg's appeal to German national sentiment took on lyric proportions in his note to Metternich of December 1814, when he saw fit to support his persuasive efforts with a stanza from a German patriotic poem:

> Fly, disunity, fly from our lands,
> Give way, you snake-haired monster!
> The double eagle and the black
> Are nesting in the same gigantic oak.
> There will be henceforth in the whole German Empire
> *One* word, *one* mind, shielded by this pair.
> And where the sounds of the German language resound,
> Let there blossom only *one* empire of the powerful and the
>   beautiful![122]

Such versifying is not what one typically expects to find in high-level diplomatic exchanges. Given the usual portraits of Metternich himself, and of traditional diplomacy generally, one would have to wonder what Hardenberg could possibly have been thinking. Yet even a few months earlier, Metternich might not have been so unreceptive to such an appeal, when German patriotic sentiments still ran high at the conclusion of the wars against Napoleon, even in Metternich's supposedly cool veins.[123] As it was, the poem at least still affirmed Hardenberg's commitment to what was still Metternich's preferred plan for German and European politics, namely, close cooperation between Austria and Prussia as the core around which to build.

In the Prussian response to Austria's December German constitutional draft, Hardenberg and Humboldt made the concern for both security and popular sentiment quite explicit. A German federal constitution, they stated, represented not just a matter for royal courts, but was also "necessary for the satisfaction of the *just claims of the nation*," which "was permeated by the feeling that its security and prosperity, and the continued flourishing of genuinely patriotic attitudes [ächt vaterländischer Bildung] depends in large part upon its *unification in a strong state body*." They acknowledged the particularist drive in the German character, but explained that the German nation "does not want to fall apart into individual parts, but is instead convinced that the excellent diversity of the German peoples can only function beneficially when it is balanced out again in a *general association* [allgemeine Verbindung]." The three things most indispensable to achieving this *"national association"* were "a powerful *defense force*, a *federal court*, and *estates-based* constitutions secured by the federal constitution."[124]

This passage also points to the idea in the thought of Humboldt and many other German nationalists that liberty and national strength stood in a mutually reinforcing feedback relationship. That is, not only did the civic spirit that promoted liberal government require a basis in national strength and national honor in order to flourish, but that strength and concomitant security required the civic spirit built up in patriotic political participation. In this way, for the early period of liberal nationalism, liberalism and nationalism were considered inextricably bound together. As Humboldt expressed this complex relationship in his 1813 memo on a German constitution:

> Germany must be free and strong, not merely that it might defend itself against this or that neighbor, or against any enemy whatsoever, but rather for this reason, that only a nation which is also strong externally preserves the spirit from which spring all internal blessings. It must be free and strong in order that, even if it should never be tested, it nourishes that feeling of selfhood necessary to pursue its course of national development quietly and undisturbed and to continue to maintain the beneficent position it has earned for itself at the center of Europe.[125]

The link between liberal political structures, civic-national spirit, and national security also related directly to the thinking underlying the federative-type national identity and nationalism in this period. These connections held both in considering the relationships between the German nation and its potentially constituent peoples and states and in shaping ideas about relations among nationalities in multinational or multiethnic polities. As recent scholarship has suggested, the two cases were not categorically different just because of language divides, particularly where bilingualism was common. Humboldt himself marked a significant figure in the development of what I call multinational nationality, or the stepwise approach to national identity, as he first theorized this process of identity-building in the context of trying to understand how the Basques of northern Spain proved simultaneously so patriotic as Basques and so patriotic as Spaniards within the Spanish monarchy. Local rivalries within the Basque country, provincial autonomy within the Spanish monarchy, and broad political and civic participation all featured in his explanation, and could be transplanted to other cases, whether in Germany or in multinational empires like the Habsburg. Any efforts by the Spanish Crown to centralize too strongly would have the opposite effect of fragmenting and destroying the patriotic and civic spirit. Humboldt's German identity may have predisposed him to interpret the Basque situation according to existing notions of federative German nationhood, and at any rate it then proved easy for him to conceptualize the German framework according to the Basque model.[126]

In this context, it is worth considering that contrary to much post-structuralist theory, identities are not defined solely by assertions of difference between groups perceived as "others." Identities also form through nested relationships within overarching, ever more inclusive hierarchies of attachment, from local and regional rivalries to regional and national identities, with the national not always the end of the chain, but extending to larger dynastic or religious supranational identities, or indeed to the level of a cosmopolitan or European identity that was quite significant then as now. Rivalry and difference played roles at each level, but did not preclude inclusion of the different groups at the next higher level. Nor did cosmopolitan identity equate simply to European and form the end of the line. Without overlooking the degree to which adherence to an all-encompassing human identity often was and is normatively left undefined as European in the Eurocentric blind spot of Enlightenment universalism, humanitarian values at least potentially reached beyond Europeans, as we still attempt to ensure today. The discourse surrounding abolition of the slave trade provides one illustration of the process. Inclusion as well as exclusion, common ground as well as difference figure centrally in the formation of identities.[127]

Whatever one concludes about the actual processes of identity formation, it is important to recognize that many thinkers and political figures of the Congress era thought that the world and the process worked that way, with identities beginning at the individual and family level, building through local and regional identities, and only then arriving at the sense of nationhood, be it defined as an ethnocultural linguistic concept or as a matter of state and dynastic allegiance. An important element of Edmund Burke's critique of French revolutionary politics turned on the point that identity and attachment must begin with the local. "To be attached to the subdivision, to love the little platoon we belong to in society, is the first principle (the germ as it were) of public affections. It is the first link in the series by which we proceed towards a love to our country and to mankind."[128] In Burke's French Revolution context, this meant, for example, that one could not simply tear apart traditional provincial identities and start over with the newly decreed administrative *departements,* not without breaking the chain of identity, and of patriotism, that held the nation together as a whole.

An early reader of Burke, Humboldt picked up this idea and turned it in more liberal directions. In the famous aforementioned memo of 1813 for Baron Stein, Humboldt stated strongly that Germany was meant to be a federal rather than centralized entity, a "union of states" rather than a single state. As he expressed the notion of stepwise patriotism there: "the German is only aware that he is a German when he feels himself to be an inhabitant of a particular land within the common fatherland." He tellingly combined this with the other kind of reciprocal strength (individual and civic) when he completed the thought: "and his force and activity will be lamed if, with the sacrifice of his provincial autonomy, he were assigned to a foreign entity that in no way appeals to him."[129] Humboldt thus called persistently for a federal or decentralized state, whether for Germany as a whole or for Prussia alone (the same process worked in both cases).

Humboldt was not alone in such ideas. August von Kotzebue, the controversial but best-selling German playwright working as Russian consul and publicist, also expounded a federal or mediated type of nationalism. In his main political periodical, he wrote that educated Germans might feel "Vaterlandsliebe" (love of the fatherland) but most simply felt "Heimathsliebe" (love of one's home region) or loved the former only through the latter. Too much centralization and too much homogenization ran the risk of weakening German-level patriotism by damaging state-level or regional patriotism.[130]

We have also already encountered such thinking and political planning in the multinational Habsburg context, when considering the display of various regional or national groups through costume, dancing, or music (folk or patriotic). Such cultural manifestations already came tied to political and military mobilization in 1809, and these ideas continued to carry political implications in the Congress era and after.[131] Stepwise identity-building suggested a means of encouraging cultural nationalism and patriotism at one level that would then strengthen patriotic attachment to the dynasty and empire as a whole. Along these lines, Marshal Bellegarde, provisional governor in Milan, lobbied Police Minister Hager and the emperor in favor of a government-sponsored Italian-language periodical to be edited by the Italian national poet and hero Ugo Foscolo. In her crowded salon back in Vienna, Countess Bellegarde proved even more outspoken about how to govern the Italian provinces. Arrests and other repressive measures in northern Italy, she claimed, would only alienate Austria's already weak support there. Instead of importing so many German and Hungarian officials, the Habsburgs should instead take a page out of Napoleon's book of governance and appoint Italians where they could.[132]

Explaining how ideas of stepwise patriotism became so widespread is not easy, but it may well be that the ideas were not so much "in the air" as in the social networks. Humboldt and Schiller, Staël and Benjamin Constant had been contemplating and discussing how to preserve the best of the civic spirit of ancient city-states in modern commercial territorial states since the mid-1790s (including at the time of Humboldt's trips from Paris to the Basque country). Their multiple connections with the Schlegels (translators of Staël's *Corinne*) and with Humboldt's old friend Friedrich Gentz (translator of Burke) must have played a role, with Schlegel and Gentz then serving as close collaborators of Austria's previous foreign minister, Count Stadion, in 1809. Staël visited Vienna and Weimar in those years as well. Schlegel has already been mentioned as potential inspiration for Jerneij Kopitar and other Austro-Slavs in their efforts to promote cultural nationhood and provincial autonomy within the Habsburg monarchy.[133] Such direct links, but also indirect ones through "weak ties" in university towns, spas, and capitals, and in Romantic circles and broader elites, facilitated these exchanges and developments.

The willingness to work in part with national sentiments within the Habsburg framework was not evinced solely by subordinates like Schlegel and Kopitar but went to the top: to Stadion, but also to Metternich. Metternich's commitment could be seen in a small symbolic way in his Habsburg folk-dress costume theme ball, but also appeared in his plans for Austria's reacquired Italian and Polish provinces. Metternich did not favor a full federal remodeling of the Habsburg Empire, as some have suggested, but neither did he oppose concessions to a presumed national spirit as much as several critics of that interpretation have contended.[134]

That Metternich denied the Italian nation's existence in deeming the term Italy a mere "geographic expression" represents one of the classic tropes of the literature on the Congress and on nationalism, often quoted (or misquoted) out of context and hence misinterpreted. At one level it represented a matter of diplomatic convenience or rhetorical strategic positioning. When the Spanish delegate demanded an Italian Committee along the same lines as the German Committee or the Swiss Committee to handle the affairs of the Italian peninsula, Metternich staved off such a scheme by pointing out that whereas Germany was to have a political existence in a federal constitution, Italy was not. The various negotiations involving Italy would therefore be carried out piecemeal by the interested parties, likely to Austria's advantage, and to the disadvantage of French and Spanish Bourbon dynastic interests in Italy.[135] Metternich and the Austrians certainly believed that there was an Italian national spirit, one that they feared and opposed if it pointed to national independence and republicanism, and they did intend to combat it through a policy of "parcelization," that is, bolstering local identities as a means to damp the growth of national sentiment. But that did not provide the context for the comment. Metternich and Franz, for instance, hoped to appeal to "the Lombard spirit" to counteract "the so-called Italian spirit." Limited representative institutions, as seen above, also featured in these plans.[136]

Moreover, while Metternich opposed Italian political nationalism, he was not averse to a certain degree of Italian patriotism or even cultivation of Italian cultural nationalism. He persuaded Franz to grant pensions to the Italian poet Vincenzo Monti and the sculptor Antonio Canova, and he supported preservation of the Italian Academy of Fine Arts under Austrian auspices. He had hoped that Monti could also be named "Poeta Caesareo" such that "the entire nation" could feel "honored" by this distinction of "their fellow citizen," but Monti's political past turned out to be a little too problematic.[137]

At the same time, even Metternich's distinction between the German and Italian cases was, as some historians have noted, partly misleading. Throughout the Congress period and for years afterward, Metternich also pursued the idea of a "Lega italica" or Italian League.[138] He meant it to be more purely an alliance of Italian states for internal and above all external security, without the Federal Diet or domestic political remit of the German Confederation, but it would still have provided a basic structure of Italian political institutions and potential framework for identity. The idea never came to pass but received serious attention at the time. Sardinia-Piedmont developed its own counterproposal in order to avoid Habsburg hegemony in such an institution. The topic also filled many pages of correspondence between Vienna and Rome during the Congress, as Cardinals Consalvi and Pacca agonized over whether, and if so how far, the Vatican could enter such a league without losing its morally impartial status above the individual Italian states or indeed at the European level, in an organization whose main purpose would after all have been defense against Catholic France.[139]

The balance of regional, ethnic-national, and supranational appeals applied even more strongly in the case of Austria's Polish possessions in Galicia. In a report to Kaiser Franz of a planning session involving Metternich, Police Chief Hager, and their Galician advisor Count Goes, Metternich essentially expressed his belief in just that notion of chain patriotism seen in Humboldt. "Re the political provisions," Metternich wrote, "Count Goes remarks quite correctly that their tendency primarily needs to move in the direction of, not making Poles all at once into Germans, but rather above all first making them into true Galicians, in order that they stop considering themselves Poles." Nurturing Galician sentiments constituted part of a "stepwise path [Stuffengang]" toward the "final purpose [Endzweck]" of incorporating Polish Galicians into a broader Habsburg identity. A representative estates constitution formed part of that package.[140] Metternich also seems to have thought in terms of such "regionalism" in the years before and after the Congress as a solution to the problems of integrating Serbs and Montenegrins within the Habsburg and Ottoman Empires.[141]

Encouragement of Polish culture also figured as part of the effort to promote Galician and, indirectly, Habsburg identity and patriotism. The University of Lemberg/Lwów/Lviv was reinforced, as a German-language institution but with a chair in Polish literature and culture; the Galician Diet admitted both German and Polish as official languages. The Slavic philologist Count Józef Ossolińsky already boasted good

Austro-Slav credentials and held an appointment as court librarian in Vienna, where he was Kopitar's superior and sometimes consulted Schlegel about manuscript acquisitions. In addition to advising on the appointment of the Polish university chair, Ossoliński helped establish a Galician National Library as a partly Galician, partly Polish institution within the Habsburg framework. Pursuant to its usual policy of not choosing sides among the empire's various ethnic groups, the Habsburg Galician administration also supported the development of the Society of Greek Catholic Priests in Galicia for the Uniate Church among the mostly peasant Ruthenian-speaking population (Greek rite under Roman Catholic aegis, and almost equaling Polish speakers among the population). It also promoted Ruthenian-language schoolbooks.[142]

The statesmen and rulers of the Vienna Congress, like the broader publics who shared the political stage with them, demonstrated both a limited concern for nationality rights and support for basic constitutional and representative privileges and the rule of law. In each instance rhetoric and beliefs from the emerging liberal and conservative traditions intertwined, mutually reinforcing as well as conflicting. The result was a wave of constitutional settlements as impressive and unprecedented as it is often overlooked. These more liberal or at least flexible reform conservative approaches also carried into the great showdown over Saxony and Poland. By no means isolated, the Galician proposals just discussed instead evinced broader patterns of thought that influenced even the Congress's highest-level and most interest-driven negotiations.

CHAPTER SEVEN

Poland, Saxony, and the Crucible of Diplomacy

The contestation over the territories of Poland and Saxony has always figured as the Vienna Congress's central component, its hinge or pivot, and rightly so. More energy, emotion, and public relations effort than in any other aspect of Congress politics was invested in the partly related questions of what would become of the Polish lands and of how much, if any, of his former domains Napoleon's staunch ally King Friedrich August of Saxony would regain. The wrangling has also almost always been analyzed solely within the framework of realist diplomacy and power politics, but more remains to be said.[1]

The negotiations over Poland and Saxony were those kept most secret among the relevant statesmen, yet at the same time were those most discussed among the public. Their echoes sounded across the range of the modes of political culture dealt with here, from the press to salons and display. Beliefs, attitudes, and ideas also shaped the diplomacy, particularly with respect to constitutions and nationality. Religious referents echoed more weakly in this context but were still deployed. Rather than simply follow the usual diplomatic history narrative of memoranda and conferences leading from confrontation to resolution, this chapter instead traces the contest thematically along the lines of these various layers of political culture.

Most accounts of the Polish and Saxon questions at the Congress of Vienna emphasize the Polish component and recount the sequence of diplomatic notes and interventions, beginning with the exchanges between the British foreign minister, Castlereagh, and Tsar Alexander in October and November (ostensibly as mediation, but more like not-so-friendly persuasion) and followed by Metternich's agreement to let Chancellor Hardenberg of Prussia attempt the mediator role in November. Hardenberg was willing to pressure Prussia's ally Alexander on Poland if Prussia were still guaranteed its desired gains in Saxony. Hardenberg, too, failing to convince Alexander to compromise, Metternich and Castlereagh changed strategy in early December and began to welcome Talleyrand's overtures of support (something they had previously discouraged rather than encouraged, given the still unstable situation in France under the newly restored Bourbons). Angry at Metternich's perceived duplicity, Hardenberg revealed confidential correspondence to the tsar and thus sparked a "diplomatic explosion" that threatened a breakdown in negotiations, or even war.[2] Progress only occurred, according to most accounts, when further Prussian saber-rattling pushed Castlereagh to agree to an alliance with Austria, France, and Bavaria at the beginning of January 1815. At that point, with sufficient force to counter the weight of Russia and Prussia on the other side, an accord concerning the Polish lands, and eventually Saxony, could finally be reached. But it must always be remembered that that settlement only came more than a month later in February, and that the final treaties regarding Poland and Saxony were only signed in May. There is more to this story, both before and after January.

Of all the areas of contestation and negotiation at the Congress, it was only ever the question of Saxony (and perhaps of Poland) that might have triggered a war. In this context it is important to keep in mind the debate about whether Europe's statesmen had indeed learned something from the experience of the Napoleonic years, such that they would seek to establish a framework for peace and collective security rather than simply pursue advantageous alliances as the basis for potential military solutions (not only as a last resort). Militant politics abounded, but most leading statesmen were also determined to found a more stable and less conflictual international system. Yet precisely because the gateway to territorial acquisition might soon swing shut with the coming of a long peace, the stakes and tensions ran high as governments tried to put themselves in the best possible position before the desired repose.[3] Throughout the autumn and into February 1815 the chance of renewed war hung over diplomats and publics alike. The most hawkish among the supporters of the king of Saxony was undoubtedly Bavaria's representative, Prince Wrede, who was also commander of its army. Already at the end of September he informed Talleyrand that forty thousand men stood ready to fight for Saxony, and in January he enticed the Danes with enchanting visions of how war against Russia and Prussia could lead to their recovery of Norway, the return of Finland to Sweden, and the ejection of Russia back across the river Neman. Talleyrand and the French exaggeratedly boasted their ability to put three hundred thousand men into the field to support the cause.[4] In November the Austrian high command and Metternich were taking stock of the available troops in the different parts of the empire (still well over three hundred thousand under arms), and in mid-December the chief of staff General Langenau—a Saxon—laid out plans for possible mobilization against both Prussia and Russia. By the end of the month the Prussian general staff was preparing the same ground for war.[5]

From the first rumors of the tsar's plans to establish a Polish kingdom under his rule, opposition emerged among almost all the powers. Objections tended to come from two general directions. On the one hand was the problem of the new Poland's borders, with attendant strategic and military considerations. On the other lay broadly political concerns, including Russian Poland's degree of autonomy, the manner in which it would be governed, and even its very name. Opponents protested at one and the same time against the extension of Russian territory too far to the west, the promulgation of a Polish constitution, and the proposal to call the new entity the Kingdom of Poland. The potential nomenclature, both "Poland" and "Kingdom," bore considerable symbolic importance for the Poles, but for that very reason was also worrying to neighboring powers. Poles still outside the new kingdom could come to see it as a rallying point for independence efforts and thus destabilize the regimes in surrounding Polish territories.[6] The Austrian governor-general in Galicia warned in June 1814 of the dire effects on political stability there if a constitutional kingdom were established, and as late as January 1815 Austria's man-on-the-scene in Podgórze (overlooking Cracow) argued that even a free city of Cracow could have destabilizing effects in the Habsburg Polish lands.[7] The constitution provision brought similar problems. Some opponents may simply have objected to the spread of constitutions as such, but others were more anxious about this particular instance. If Poles in Russian territory enjoyed constitutional privileges, those in other jurisdictions would have all the more reason to feel discontent if they did not. In the end, though, the powers pushed harder on the question of territory, and once they had more or less accepted Alexander's near-ultimatum in early January, the constitutional question ceased to be such an issue.[8] As we shall see, this was at least in part because both Austria and Prussia in any case planned to introduce reforms in their Polish lands, regarding both nationality rights and constitutional protections and participation.

Nationality and Political Ideology

The treatment of the Poles has been the one aspect of Congress diplomacy where historians have been willing to acknowledge some recognition of the nationality principle. Alexander, after all, at least claimed that he wanted to restore the Kingdom of Poland in fairly sizable form and with a constitution (as a portion of the Russian Empire), while for their part the western powers and Austria also wanted it known that they supported the idea of a restored Polish state (if it were independent of Russia). And even the final settlement at least included some pertinent words about recognizing Poles' nationality in the institutions of the Russian, Austrian, and Prussian portions of the Polish lands: "the Poles, subjects respectively of Russia, Austria, and Prussia, will obtain a representative body and national institutions."[9] Yet at the same time, the Polish case has also often figured as a clear example of the failure of the nationality principle at the Vienna Congress. The partition stood, the administrations often remained oppressive toward the Poles, and the succession of Polish uprisings in the nineteenth century in Prussian and above all in Russian Poland is well known. Piotr Wandycz referred to the "seeming paradox" that "the Congress of Vienna both reaffirmed the partitions and recognized the existence of the Polish nation," which is ultimately about right.[10]

These analyses, however, for the most part assume that nationalism has only the one true form, with the telos of the sovereign nation-state. Measured against that standard, the standard of Versailles in 1919, the Vienna Congress clearly failed to address nationalist concerns substantively, and the rulers and statesmen can be easily indicted for having ignored the trends of the future, in Poland as much as in Italy, Germany, or Greece. Against the backdrop of the conceptions of nationhood seen in the analysis of national symbolism in display, however, or of the treatment of nationality in the Italian, Swiss, and German cases, the Polish Question looks rather different. The idea that a sufficient degree of justice, equality, autonomy, and respect for national customs and language

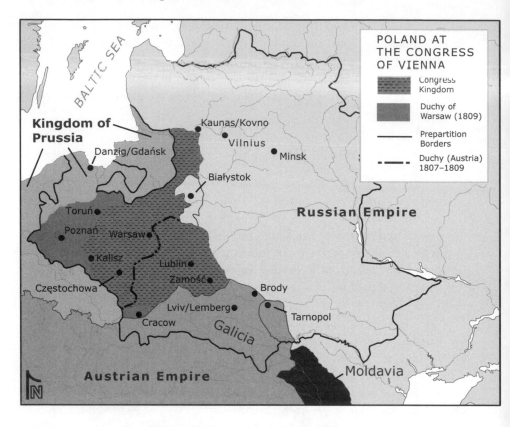

POLAND AT
THE CONGRESS
OF VIENNA

Congress
Kingdom

Duchy of
Warsaw (1809)

Prepartition
Borders

Duchy (Austria)
1807–1809

BALTIC SEA

Kingdom of
Prussia

Danzig/Gdańsk

Kaunas/Kovno

Vilnius

Minsk

Białystok

Toruń

Poznań   Warsaw

Kalisz

Lublin

Zamość

Częstochowa

Lviv/Lemberg

Cracow

Galicia

Brody

Tarnopol

Russian Empire

Moldavia

Austrian Empire

N

could produce a real attachment to supranational dynastic regimes
need not seem so far-fetched from that point of view. At the very least,
the fact that the ideas offered in legitimation—and indeed partially mo-
tivating the Polish and Saxon settlements—square with the ideology of
a regionally based, federalist, multinational type of national sentiment
should give pause.

At the level of support for some form of Polish restoration, Tsar Alexander, the British, the Austrians, and the French all gave at least "lip
service" to the idea. For Alexander, Polish restoration could be accomplished under Russian suzerainty, with a separate administration and a
representative constitution, at least for the Poles in the former Napoleonic Duchy of Warsaw (roughly those from the Austrian and Prussian
gains in the partitions of 1793 and 1795), and possibly including those
in Russia's western provinces. The other powers saw in the plan a flimsy
mask for Russian expansionism, and instead at least claimed to support
full restoration and independence, if not within the borders of 1772 be-

fore the first partition, then within those of 1792 before the second. If nothing else, they hoped to prove to Poles and the European public that it was Russia rather than other states that stood in the way of truly restoring Polish independence. Castlereagh and even Kaiser Franz of Austria may have actually supported Polish restoration or been willing to countenance it as a lesser evil than Russian expansion, but they could also be fairly sure that Alexander would never agree to such a thing, given the state of opinion in Russia, hence they would not be called on to make sacrifices.[11] Yet support for the Poles was not rare. Further down the Austrian chain of command, for instance, Metternich's deputy Johann von Wessenberg thought Polish restoration a matter of justice for a "nation" (*Nation*) by "custom and language" that would atone for the original "sin" of partition, and Metternich's secretary, Joseph Pilat, informed his close correspondent Countess Fuchs that there could be no real peace or equilibrium in Europe without it.[12]

Tsar Alexander stood nearly alone in the Russian camp in his eagerness or willingness to work toward a partial restoration of Poland. His only real allies were some of the Poles, above all Prince Adam-Jerzy Czartoryski (but not including other Poles such as Countess Anna Potocka).[13] The tsar's cosmopolitan set of foreign policy officials and advisors almost to a man disagreed with his Polish projects. Count Nesselrode in late 1812 and Count Pozzo di Borgo in July and October 1814 both wrote memoranda opposing the creation of a Polish constitutional kingdom, and other advisors, including Baron Stein, General La Harpe, and Count Capodistrias, came out against it as well. Even Baron Anstett, though assisting Czartoryski with the diplomatic notes responding to western resistance, himself opposed the plan, and let outsiders know it (significantly including one of the ubiquitous Austrian police spies, whose reports were referred to both Kaiser Franz and Metternich). Pozzo, too, had no qualms about airing his views in open conversation, as while dining at Princess Bagration's with Metternich's subordinate Baron Binder in attendance; he and Stein had each already warned Castlereagh against the tsar's plans as well.[14] Pozzo likely felt further emboldened to speak his mind given that his hostess, Princess Bagration, herself opposed the tsar's Polish scheme and the spoliation of Saxony and had tried in vain to dissuade Alexander from both.[15]

As the examples of Stein and Capodistrias show, nationalism as a transnational phenomenon did not always translate to an atmosphere of cooperation among the nascent national movements of the sort later seen in Young Europe around Mazzini, with nationalists of one nationality supporting the others' causes. The German nationalist Baron Stein, for example, explained to the perplexed tsar his objection to Polish restoration, namely that the Poles lacked a sufficiently strong and enlightened middle class to support a free constitution. Even Alexander's new favorite, the Greek nationalist Capodistrias, used the same reasoning in expressing his reservations to the tsar, and in rebuffing Polish persuasions to intercede on their behalf. The Prussian Wilhelm von Humboldt objected to the tendency of Polish activists like Czartoryski or the Prussian-Polish Prince Antoni Radziwiłł to strive for something like a single Polish nation under three rulers, despite his own support for a German federation, and he boasted to his wife that he helped weaken the provisions of the clause on "the right of nationality" in the draft treaty on Poland when it "went too far."[16]

For that matter, even support for Polish independence could rest on chauvinist foundations. The young Hessian official, folklorist, and German nationalist Jacob Grimm, for example, favored Polish restoration in part on the basis of his belief that a few million Polish subjects, among them a large number of Jews, had done little to increase Prussian strength. At least one Prussian official, the prolific Hardenberg advisor and professor of political statistics Johann Gottfried Hoffmann, at one point similarly adduced nationality as a good reason why Prussia should jettison its Polish territories in favor of German ones in Saxony. Nationality and language should determine borders, he claimed, not an arbitrary line or a river. It would do Prussia no good to have a Polish-speaking population always attracted to their fellow Poles outside—and even to the Russians—by linguistic affinity. Better for Poland to be independent.[17] By late March 1814, however, even he (having been "instructed" as to Hardenberg's views) had begun to frame his memos in more geopolitical and strategic terms underscoring why Prussia rather than Russia should hold the lands west of the Vistula, or at least the towns of Częstochowa and Toruń and points west.[18]

While a Polish constitution or full sovereignty proved only too controversial, about the idea of nationality rights and protections, and a certain degree of autonomy, almost everyone seemed to agree. Tsar Alexander hoped to create political and social conditions short of independence that would satisfy the Poles in his new constitutional kingdom, and that would in time nurture attachment to the Romanov dynasty. A similar approach in the Austrian and Prussian portions of

Poland would have comparable effects there.[19] His chief advisor on Poland, Prince Czartoryski, may have dreamed of more but still paid tellingly serious attention to political and psychological detail in planning how these ideas were to be realized. Poles were to feel themselves part of the entire homeland, experiencing autonomy within each portion and "attaching themselves sincerely to their new position," but with the ability to reside and move from one part to another, both on the larger scale from jurisdiction to jurisdiction and on the smaller scale of day-to-day travel within the borderlands created along the new frontiers. Diplomats took considerable care in delineating the *sujets mixtes* or "mixed subjects" category for those holding property in more than one Polish jurisdiction, as well as the regulation of border traffic and commerce. This held nearly as true of the final treaties as it did of Czartoryski's initial plans.[20]

Even Baron Stein, though rejecting Polish restoration or a constitutional Polish kingdom within the Russian Empire, stayed partly true to the mediated or stepwise notion of both liberalism and nationalism that informed his reform policies in Prussia after 1806 and that continued to shape his ideas of German nationhood in 1814. In addition to liberal protections of person and property and guarantees against oppression of their nationality, the Poles in Stein's view should also be granted "political institutions," to assure a certain measure of participation in the administration. Stein construed this political framework in part as a "noble" act in compensation for the injustice of partition, but he also meant it to instill "public spirit" and help individuals "develop their moral and intellectual faculties" through civic participation, similarly to his former colleague Humboldt's conception of liberal *Bildung*. Stein thought there should be no national-level representative body as yet; self-government should extend only as far as local and provincial institutions. But then, even in the Prussian reforms after 1806, he had thought it best to begin with municipal and provincial participatory institutions that would build up civic spirit and democratic experience as stepping stones on the path to national-level patriotism and self-government. Though deemed incapable of full nationhood at present, as the result of a weak third estate and an overlarge and allegedly corrupt aristocracy, the mechanisms of political participation, public spirit, and *Bildung* that Stein envisioned for the Poles did not differ so greatly from those for Prussians and Germans.[21]

Neither Alexander nor the Austrians and Prussians were eager to be tied down to specific treaty obligations spelling out the constitutional provisions to be given the Poles. Alexander may have resisted because he feared that any mutual agreement would prevent him from being as liberal as he wished; Metternich and the Prussians may have dragged their feet because they feared being taken too far. Alexander was convinced of Austrian and British conservatism, while the other powers worried about the tsar's idealistic liberal leanings. To this extent Czartoryski was probably correct to harbor suspicions of Austrian and Prussian motives. He was wrong, however, to think the latter powers opposed nationality protections in general, or as such. Actually they did support them, in terms not just of language rights, but also of a certain degree of political representation and participation (if perhaps with less of real autonomy than in the tsar's plans).

Similarly, if one reads the Russian, Prussian, and Austrian responses to Castlereagh's circular note of 12 January on Polish nationality protections in light of these new perspectives on the respective policies rather than of older, anachronistic ideas about Metternich's anticonstitutional and antinational politics, it becomes difficult to sustain the view that the Austrian and Prussian statements were so much weaker than the Russian (or any of them than the British). Some historians have accepted Castlereagh's claim that his note forced the eastern monarchies to adopt nationality protections in their plans, but they did not require his lesson, having already done more thinking about the problems of multinational rule in an increasingly national age than had the British. As Castlereagh tried to instruct them, "experience has proved, that it is not in counteracting all their habits and usages as a people, that the happiness of the Poles, or the peace of that important portion of Europe, can be preserved." A previous policy "to make them forget their existence and even language as a people, has been sufficiently tried and failed," producing only "discontent." The "Polish Nation," he concluded, should be treated as Poles, "under whatever form of political institution." Even in the negotiations preceding Castlereagh's initiative, however, the Russians had pushed to stipulate rights protections, and Metternich had agreed.[22]

The Austrian response to Castlereagh's circular stated that Emperor Franz "shares no less than Tsar Alexander the liberal views in favor of national institutions," and in addition to his "paternal solicitude" pointed to his record of "equal distributive justice to all the peoples of different stocks [souches] which Providence has submitted to his rule." Prussia supported nationality protections with the argument that molding a territory's "mode of administration to the habits and the genius of its inhabitants," and putting them "on the solid and liberal basis of a common interest" formed the best way "to show to peoples that their national existence can remain free from any infringement, whatever the political system to which fate has tied them." In the end one could "strongly attach subjects of different nations to the same government" and "unite them in the same family."[23]

The Prussians ultimately proved the clearest about both the limits to nationality protection and autonomy, and the extent to which they supported them. A planning document for their Polish and Lithuanian territories from December 1815 shows that at least some influential Prussian officials already operated with ideas startlingly similar to those of German liberals in 1848, in terms of the markers and boundaries of nationhood, the space for and limits to nationality rights, and the expectations of a certain degree of political and cultural assimilation to result from the policy. The document rejected forced Germanization, and firmly stated the desire to win the allegiance of non-Germans through just treatment and respect for their nationality, but clearly also with the hope that in time Poles and Lithuanians would increasingly enter the German cultural orbit, whatever language they might speak at home and in local government. "Not just the promise in the treaty," Hardenberg's advisor Hoffmann wrote, "but precisely a healthy policy can and must motivate Prussia to protect its new Polish subjects in the nationality in which they feel themselves happy, so far, that they are thoroughly secure against all direct or indirect imposition of foreign language and manners." But since "difference of language, manners, and the constitutions based on them" made administration more difficult, Prussia would be happy "if in the course of time this difference would gradually and of itself disappear, through free choice and without any coercion." Alongside the nationality protections, in other words, assimilation would be welcome, but not strictly encouraged. Even Lithuanian, though not considered a national language of state or high culture in the same sense as Polish, would still receive recognition as the language of church and elementary education, as well as in bilingual government administration.[24]

As some specialist studies have noted, Metternich and the Austrians were thinking along similar lines. The Habsburgs were already experimenting with projects for a multinational nationality adapted to the various portions of their empire. In a report to Kaiser Franz of a planning session involving Metternich, Police Chief Hager, and their Galician advisor Count Goes, Metternich stated that Austrian policy "primarily needs to move in the direction of, not making Poles all at once into Germans, but rather above all first making them into true Galicians, in order that they stop considering themselves Poles." A limited representative estates-based constitution was to comprise part of the reform package that would promote that goal. The desire for Poles to cease identifying as Poles bore a chiefly political connotation and did not exclude the kind of support for national culture seen in other cases within the Habsburg monarchy. As with the efforts to cultivate both Polish culture and Habsburg patriotism by the court librarian Count Józef Ossolińsky, "making Galicians" meant establishing a Habsburg regime in the province that left room for the celebration of Polish language, literature, and history (and indeed for Ruthenian/Ukrainian alongside Polish, like Prussia's support for Lithuanian in its Polish possessions).[25]

Linked to the question of the Polish territories was that of the fate of Saxony and its dynasty, though the connection was not as direct as many contemporaries and most historians have assumed. Alexander and the Prussians were at first quite keen to push Friedrich August into Italy for compensatory territory. As a Catholic, he could rule over Catholic subjects, and he would no longer be in a position to make trouble in Germany in a quest to regain lost territories.[26] It soon became clear, however, that this idea found little favor, either with Austria, or with France and its Bourbon allies in Spain and Sicily (not to mention Friedrich August). Once it became evident that Saxony's ruler could not be banished to Italy, the Russians and Prussians made the rather weak suggestion to give him a kingdom in western Germany, in Westphalia or the Rhineland. They continued to stress the religious argument for these largely Catholic territories, and even tried a direct appeal to Friedrich August with the lure of Catholic subjects. From a diplomatic and strategic perspective, however, they stood on exceedingly thin ice. Since the whole vision of French containment shared by almost all the powers (including Prussia and Russia) depended on a strong and united Central Europe standing shoulder to shoulder with the new Kingdom of the Netherlands to keep watch over France's eastern borders, the Austrians and British were not slow to point out that placing a small, angry, and potentially revanchist German state in proximity to the French frontier would hardly contribute to German, and thereby European security.[27]

Contemporaries and many historians have thought the Prussians eager to support Russian designs in Poland so long as this promoted their goal of acquiring the whole of Saxony; the loss of Prussia's former Polish possessions would provide the rationale for compensating them with Saxony. Hardenberg has been the main exception, given his obvious willingness, even eagerness, to play the part of mediator with Russia to achieve a better settlement in Poland (if he could keep Saxony for Prussia). But his number two, Wilhelm von Humboldt, often believed at the time and since to have been most to blame for Prussia's intransigence and slavish adherence to Russia, was actually concerned about Russian expansion into Poland and penned a memo suggesting that if it came to a choice, it would be better to side with Austria and Britain against Russia rather than the reverse. Humboldt acknowledged to his wife that the memo would not please the king, but as he had confided in previous letters, he thought Russia's claims "unjust" and "dangerous for Europe's repose."[28] Even Humboldt's colleague Friedrich Staegemann, though very much the Prussian-German patriot and strongly supporting the acquisition of Saxony, was at best resigned to war, in part because he feared the increased dependence on Russia that would result, "to the detriment of the German cause."[29] Staegemann for his part blamed the influence of General Knesebeck in preventing Friedrich Wilhelm from taking a firmer line with Russia, yet Knesebeck's memoranda show that he warned of the danger of Russian expansion at least as emphatically as Humboldt, Metternich's deputy Baron Wessenberg among the Austrians, or Castlereagh himself. Castlereagh even sent a Knesebeck memo to Prime Minister Liverpool as an indication of the good prospects for cooperation with Prussia on Poland, Knesebeck being identified as one of the king's main military advisors. In order to believe that a Russian frontier in Poland to Toruń and Cracow implied a purely "defensive" position for the Russians, Knesebeck exclaimed, one would have to "hide the map, blindfold one's eyes, and see only Alexander's heart, in that case, the sole guarantee of the other states' security."[30] As these examples also demonstrate, the state of knowledge about various figures' opinions and influence was murky at the time, and has remained so until now.

Arguments from nationality and nationalism also came into play in the Saxon case, as already seen with Hoffmann of Prussia. This held with reference to both Saxony and Germany as a whole, and on both sides of the dispute. Nationality had simply become too important a political language to neglect, representing a rhetorical high ground that had to be seized. Recent scholarship emphasizes the degree to which the state-building of the larger German regional powers itself constituted a form of nation-building, involving a type of patriotism that was also partly national in form. Governments attempted to empower the modern state and integrate new populations by establishing a kind of feedback loop between enabling greater public political participation and promoting greater identification with the state as nation. Hence in this instance Saxons, too, were considered a nationality. Caroline von Humboldt, though a strong proponent of annexing the whole of Saxony, expressed the hope to her husband Wilhelm that the Saxon "nationality" could be preserved within the Prussian framework through constitutional guarantees similar to those of the Hungarians in the Habsburg Empire. German nationalism also came in under the geostrategic or security heading, in claims that for Germany to be strong enough as a national entity to stand against France or Russia, it needed fewer and stronger states, with Saxony going to Prussia. Such views were enunciated in Prussian pamphlets as propaganda, but also behind the scenes, whether by diplomats like Staegemann or observers such as Caroline.[31]

Almost all the Prussian annexationists, including Tsar Alexander, for their part argued that since the strong Saxon identity militated against any partition of the land, all of it must come to Prussia. Logically, the argument applied more readily on the opponents' side: common Saxon identity meant no partition, and the equally strong loyalty to the royal house in general and to Friedrich August in particular meant the whole territory should go to him. When in a conversation with Talleyrand Alexander cited Saxon identity and public opinion against partition, Talleyrand quickly riposted that the same grounds worked against annexation.[32] The pro-Saxon use of the argument was not, however, necessarily so much more powerful than the Prussian as it might seem. In realistic terms, after all, it was clear that Prussia would receive at least some Saxon territory and population, so the question became how much, and how disinclined the statesmen were to undertake another partition on top of the Polish one. When the Russians and Prussians sent the cooperative Saxon Colonel Dietrich von Miltitz to Berlin to attempt to persuade influential members of the captive king's entourage, to advise against accepting any settlement involving a division of Saxony, they instructed him to make precisely this appeal to Saxon patriotic feeling for an undivided country, at least among those "Saxons by birth . . . who retain the sentiment of their nationality and take to heart the good of their fatherland" (for foreign advisors or the more self-interested, appeals to careerism and a little outright bribery might work instead).[33]

The chain of patriotism paradigm for nationality—building from the local and regional levels to the national—also found its application in the Saxon debates, and again on both sides. Hardenberg's privy councillor Hoffmann argued that only through the incorporation of all Saxons could Prussia "care for" their "constitution and nationality" and thereby allow them to come to feel attachment to Prussia as they did to Saxony; Prussia's reputation as "the real stronghold of everything . . . German" was in turn at stake. Even before the Congress, Chancellor Hardenberg also already planned on the king's giving a "liberal constitution . . . to the Saxon people, and thereby to attach them forever."[34] An article inserted by Talleyrand in the Parisian *Moniteur* similarly deployed the nested identities approach, but to defend Saxony's sovereignty and the feeling of Saxon "national existence." The article cited adherence to smaller states and dynasties as a strong and distinctive characteristic of the German nation (already famed for its sense of Heimat), but while this love of the homeland contributed to broader German identity, it could not in the *Moniteur*'s view do so mediately through Prussia but instead required independence.[35]

To the extent that conservative antiliberalism played a part in the negotiations, it appeared more in the Saxon case than the Polish, where, as noted above, the question of borders proved more pressing than that of the Polish constitution. Although worries about democratic conspiracies were not as deep or widespread as they would become in the course of 1815, already in January Metternich informed his ambassador in London that the Prussian faction pushing so hard to annex Saxony had links to the "revolutionary party," the so-called *Tugend-Bund* or League of Virtue. The basic idea was that conspiratorial liberals hoped to gain Saxony in order to institute an experimental constitution there, not to attach Saxons to Prussia but only as a springboard to a larger constitutional venture in Prussia and Germany at large, perhaps even deposing Friedrich Wilhelm in the process. Castlereagh's report to Prime Minister Liverpool on 6 February, just before the final breakthrough, similarly ascribed the Prussian elements desiring Saxony's complete annexation to the "Friends of Liberty," said to be very influential within the Prussian military and its reformist wing around the generals Gneisenau, Grolman, and Boyen. Castlereagh may have been listening to Metternich, or Talleyrand, or his Hanoverian semicolleague Count Münster to imbibe these opinions, but in some ways it is immaterial—the view was widespread.[36] It is in this respect that Hardenberg's efforts to play on Metternich's feelings of German identity were doomed to fail, or even to backfire. Hardenberg quoted a poem calling for Austro-Prussian solidarity within a united Germany in a diplomatic note to Metternich in December 1814—the fact that he took the verses from Joseph Görres's *Rheinischer Merkur,* so suspect in conservative eyes for Jacobin radical nationalism and already considered a mouthpiece of the Prussian government, made the decision even more problematic.

The Role of Public Opinion and of Its Perception

In the politics surrounding Poland and Saxony, as elsewhere, public opinion played an important part, both as an argument to cite in memos, notes, and conversations and as a power in its own right, by which one might be influenced at home or abroad, or which one might in turn attempt to influence behind opponents' backs. Public opinion could be manifested through the press or through salon networks, both those coming from abroad and those in Vienna itself. As an argument, diplomats sometimes alluded to the pressures their government faced at home, but they could also point to the popularity or unpopularity of other governments' policies, internationally or even on that other government's domestic scene. Public opinion or the "popular will" also sometimes served as a proxy for self-determination, as diplomats could claim (and often counterclaim) that the people in a particular territory either supported or opposed a measure that would affect them. The at least alleged or perceived desires of local populations were intended to carry weight in negotiations. Making something a matter of public record itself sometimes marked a strategic move, as with the decision in late December 1814 to shift the wrangling over Poland and Saxony from informal, piecemeal parleys to more formal committee meetings of the four main powers. Such meetings would leave a more indelible paper trail of protocols and formally exchanged notes for eventual publication. The Russians seem to have hoped that "going public" would expose and bind the British in particular, as they were responsible to press and Parliament; the British in turn seized the opportunity to state their support for Polish restoration and nationality rights in a public forum that would put pressure on the other powers. Publicity always represented a potentially double-edged sword.[37]

Just as they often tried to shape opinion in the press, statesmen took considerable pains to keep track of public opinion in other countries. This held generally true of foreign embassies' missions, but the task was made more explicit during the Congress, and sentiments regarding Poland and Saxony topped the list of intelligence desiderata. Metternich, for instance, wanted to know what was being said in Berlin about these issues, and was above all keen to discover the state of opinion in the crucial capitals of London and St. Petersburg. Before the Congress, Metternich profited from the visit to St. Petersburg of General Koller, who was to oversee the travel arrangements for the tsar's upcoming visit, to find out more about the state of affairs there. Metternich instructed the general to discover the "mood of the public and court," and to determine "how far does the resistance of the upper and lesser classes to this favorite project of Tsar Alexander go?" Koller responded flatly that "Russians of all classes" opposed Polish restoration, and that partly in consequence Alexander had allegedly cooled on the idea since his return to the capital.[38] The French, too, had their sources in St. Petersburg, as Talleyrand's number two, Duke Dalberg, made clear in supporting his claim regarding the unpopularity of Alexander's Polish policy in Russia. It is important to remember in this respect that despite what one might think about the nature of political culture in the Russian autocracy, there was in fact a realm of public opinion to which the tsar had to pay some heed, indeed, wanted to mollify in order to feel its approbation. This public in Russia was above all represented by aristocratic and commercial elites in court and salon circles, but the press played a role as well.[39]

With London, no one ever doubted the importance of public opinion. The other powers were particularly concerned with the British public's views on Poland and Saxony, as Britain was considered the most important power in the equation, simultaneously the one most likely to figure as a swing vote (its position somewhere between those of Russia and Prussia on the one hand and France, Austria, and Bavaria on the other), and the one with the government most likely to be swayed by pressures from below, or at least outside. One might term such an approach balance of power coupled with public opinion, or even neorealist Realpolitik, if a realistic assessment of diplomatic options and strength includes public opinion and ideological predispositions alongside geopolitical and strategic considerations.

In these circumstances Hardenberg, Metternich, and Alexander remained keen both to keep tabs on what was being said in London and in the English press, and to steer it in the proper direction if possible. In late December the tsar was preparing his ambassador, Count Lieven, to conduct a public relations campaign through the press and Parliament but ultimately did not pull the trigger.[40] The Prussian chargé, Friedrich

Greuhm, took to lengthier reportage of British views on Congress-related topics, and was soon congratulated by Hardenberg for his initiative and encouraged to send more news of the "public mood." The fact that opinion seemed to favor Saxony over Prussia, as both Greuhm and the Austrian ambassador, Merveldt, attested, must have made more welcome reading for Metternich than for Hardenberg. The opposition (somewhat more liberal) papers, Greuhm informed Hardenberg in mid-December, rejected the Prussian acquisition of Saxony and Danzig alike. The *Times,* more conservative but not always supportive of the ministry, had at least not come out against Prussia's Saxon plans explicitly, but among the main news organs only the government-supporting *Courier* backed Prussia. The main grain of solace Greuhm could offer was that the French papers' strong opposition to Prussian policy might not be such a bad thing, since anti-French feeling might redound to Prussia's benefit by casting suspicion on such positions. In January, the *Courier* said much the same about the possibly counterproductive results of the French press's vehement opposition.[41] Greuhm's and Merveldt's reports confirmed what Prime Minister Liverpool had already written to Castlereagh back in November, news that had been circulating among the main statesmen ever since. Liverpool informed his foreign secretary how unpopular the full "annihilation" of Saxony would be in Britain and instructed him to try to preserve at least a small core territory for Friedrich August. Metternich even enclosed a copy of Liverpool's letter for Hardenberg's edification in his policy-changing note of 11 December, as the diplomatic rupture between them launched the European crisis into its most critical phase.[42]

Regarding opinion on Saxony, the Prussians seem actually to have believed that Saxons' desire to stay united (even under Prussian rule) trumped their attachment to the dynasty. They adduced this justification for their claims to the whole of Saxony in internal documents as well as in those produced for diplomatic and public consumption, and Friedrich Staegemann reassured his wife Elisabeth that right-minded Saxons felt this way. He claimed to have spoken recently with a Saxon who, while asserting his love for his king, felt a still higher allegiance to Germany and to Saxony, whereby he accepted that it was better for both that Prussia acquire the realm. The Hanoverian Count Münster thought the Prussians honestly, if wrongly, believed Saxon and German public opinion to be on their side, while the Russian and Prussian advisor Baron Stein judged that Germans were starting to come around to supporting Prussia's acquisition of all Saxony.[43] The appeal to such thinking in the mission of Colonel Miltitz to sway members of Friedrich August's entourage has already been mentioned. It may well be that there were sufficient such voices within Saxony to hear and to cite for the Prussians to remain in their comfortable delusion. But these opinions must always have constituted a minority, just as the version of German nationalism that prioritized the nation as a whole above its component parts—rather than seeing them in federal balance—itself represented a decided minority at the time, not just in broader society but among the elites as well.

Salon Skirmishes

Salons filled at least two important roles in the diplomacy surrounding Poland and Saxony. First, as one would expect, they served as central venues or hubs for the shaping and transmission of public opinion on the disputes (public opinion meaning again in part what the political, cultural, and social elites thought about the questions, and in part what was reported about the state of public opinion more broadly, what "the nation" or "the public" thought). But salons also filled a second, more direct role in potentially influencing diplomats, as the social spaces in which they moved outside the conference rooms during the period when the negotiations were going on. Statesmen could be spoken to, or hear what was in earshot, and they could be made to feel supported, or rejected, for the stances they and/or their governments and superiors took.

On the Polish side, support for Polish national aspirations seems to have been most evident in the salons of Paris and London, where Polish exiles had long enjoyed a certain social prominence. Metternich at least seemed glad not to confront the tsar about Poland during their stay in Paris in the spring of 1814, where Poles might exert more influence.[44] Czartoryski himself did not neglect the opportunity to lobby political circles during his sojourn in London in the summer of 1814, and several months prior he had sent his private secretary, Felicjan Biernacki, to London on the same mission. Biernacki convinced the talented and sympathetic Whig Henry Brougham to write a strong anonymous pamphlet promoting Polish restoration in early 1814, which was then quite favorably reviewed—by Brougham himself—in the Whig *Edinburgh Review*. The summer of 1814 also saw the Polish-Lithuanian spokesman General Józef Sierakowski making the rounds in England and Scotland for the cause.[45]

In Vienna itself, specifically pro-Polish agitation seems to have been confined for the most part to the houses of the great Polish magnates, such as Prince Henryk Lubomirski. Even these were diminished by the absence in Poland during the Congress of such important figures as Count Rzewuski and his wife, Rosalie, Countess Rzewuska, née Princess Lubomirska. Countess Henriette Zielińska was also reportedly active in the Polish cause alongside Lubomirski, her salon proving popular among the English delegation.[46] Neither does there seem to have been any real attempt to seize the symbolic high ground during moments of court or public display, of the sort that Roxandra Stourdza pulled off in support of the Greeks. The closest such moment came much too late to influence the negotiations. When the Polish national hero Tadeusz Kościuszko visited Vienna in late May and June 1815, Prince Lubomirski and Princess Lubomirska honored him by, among other things, an illumination of several portrait transparencies of his old commander Prince Józef Poniatowski. These were conveniently available for purchase at leading local music and print seller Artaria, another instance of the conjunction of older courtly and newer market-driven forms of display, and for that matter further evidence of the limits of Habsburg censorship and policing in this period. But nothing similar seems to have taken place earlier.[47]

If backing for Polish restoration was less evident in Vienna, there was no shortage of opposition to the plans of Alexander and Prince Czartoryski, not least, as we have seen, from within the ranks of the tsar's top diplomats and advisors. From the outset of his Vienna stay Czartoryski remained all too aware of his hostile reception. He found yet fewer "friendly faces," insofar as so many Russians and even some Poles opposed his idea of a Polish constitutional kingdom under Russian aegis.[48] Such tension may even have suffused the salon of Dorothea and Talleyrand. Talleyrand professed support for Polish restoration, but not under Russian suzerainty. Dorothea for her part had been educated by none other than Abbé Piattoli, who was one of the early figures to propose a renewed Polish state connected to the Romanov dynasty, and who had promoted an engagement between young Dorothea and his former collaborator Prince Czartoryski. Despite her connections, Dorothea seems to have kept silent on the Polish question during the Congress.[49]

Looking to Saxony, the weight of opinion ran strongly in favor of preserving at least most of the kingdom for Friedrich August and his heirs. The Saxon case thereby illustrates some ways in which salon sociability also influenced diplomacy through general social dynamics. For one, it was important for Prussian and Russian diplomats in these difficult weeks and months to have a social space where they could feel welcome and supported. As noted, the homes of native Berliners Fanny Arnstein and her sister Cäcilie Eskeles filled this role for the Prussians during the Congress, and Princess Bagration's and Count Razumovsky's for the Russians. It was essential for them to have such retreats, as they felt all too palpably the hostile social pressure emanating from most of Vienna's other social venues. Earlier in their stay, Prussians remarked on their favorable reception by Austrians and the seeming desire to replace the old rivalry with a new period of patriotic German cooperation. By mid-November, however, Friedrich Staegemann remarked how uncomfortable it had become to show himself in Viennese salons, a sentiment echoed shortly afterward by his colleague Humboldt.[50]

From the other side of the political fence, but also confronting the problem of unpopularity, Talleyrand happily reported to his sovereign that the French delegation's initially chilly reception had warmed a few degrees as a result of its firm defense of the king of Saxony. Sophie Schlosser of Frankfurt provided independent confirmation of Talleyrand's assessment, noting in her diary that even "German-minded" patriots had begun to speak more favorably of the French for that reason. On balance, there seems little room to doubt that public opinion in Vienna was greatly stacked against the tsar's Polish plans and still more against Prussia's acquisition of Saxony. Even the young Genevan Anna Eynard, otherwise an admirer of Alexander, found one fault to temper her regard: "namely that of not defending the cause of the king of Saxony. I do not understand it, that doesn't accord with his generous principles."[51]

Despite the existence of favorable venues, Prussian and Russian statesmen therefore hardly lived in a social bubble of the sort that might have blinded them to the unpopularity of their Polish and Saxon policies in European opinion as represented in Vienna. But then, as we have already seen, many of them themselves did not agree with the tsar and the Prussian king on these points, including Princess Bagration herself, formerly a salon star in Dresden. It should be remembered, too, that the princess was noted as the hostess for the Russians in general, not just for the tsar personally, hence to that extent her salon represented Russian elite public opinion and reflected its widespread reservations about the tsar's policy. It may have served as a venue for the articulation of quietly oppositional views and venting while still also providing a retreat from anti-Russian or -Prussian politics in Viennese society at large; expressing discontent internally was one thing, listening to criticism from outsiders something else again, perhaps all the more galling in its echo of their own misgivings.

In an amusing but indicative episode of shaping the political atmosphere in social gatherings, the *salonnière* Fanny Arnstein, stalwart of the Jewish community though she was, decided to introduce the north-German Protestant custom of the Christmas tree to Catholic Vienna on Christmas Eve, complete with small (but not inexpensive) gifts for her guests. She also used the occasion to strike another blow for Prussian claims on Saxony. To an Italian guest who had spoken against annexation she gave an illustrated book, namely, a history of great Prussian military victories, with the not-so-subtle inscription "Vengeance d'une Prussienne." The Prussian official Staegemann richly appreciated the gesture.[52]

More significantly, Fanny and her sister Baroness Eskeles leapt to counter the effects of Habsburg censorship and carry on salons' dual role of purveying varied viewpoints within the public sphere while at the same time facilitating the formation of political factions or parties. In February, around the time of the Saxon settlement, they circulated copies of the banned pamphlet of Hardenberg's hired pen Karl Varnhagen von Ense, *German Views of the Union of Saxony with Prussia*.[53] They had already complained of Austrian censors in the other sense back in December, for allowing pro-Saxon articles from English papers to be printed in the *Wiener Zeitung* and *Oesterreichischer Beobachter*, and for permitting distribution in Vienna of the anti-Prussian pamphlet *Saxony and Prussia*. "In a word," a police informant concluded, "these ladies are scandalously Prussian."[54] Yet members of all nationalities and political persuasions continued to socialize at the Arnstein and Eskeles salons, hence the two aspects of salon culture and politics remained in balance. The unfortunate recipient of the barbed Christmas gift was in good company there from the opposing camp—another reason why the Prussians and Russians never lost touch with wider public opinion.

On the other side, Talleyrand leveraged his position in the Vienna salon scene, and his court connections in the world of display, to promote the Saxon king's cause. Talleyrand had all along intended his trumpeting of the principle of legitimacy to promote three ends, each boosting the interests of the Bourbon dynasty: to bolster the legitimacy of the government he now served; to undermine Murat in Naples; and to support the claims of Friedrich August. Talleyrand linked the legitimacy principle to the Saxon issue quite clearly through his words in and around the ceremony commemorating the anniversary of Louis XVI's execution on 21 January, just after the height of the crisis, but while the threat of war still hung over the negotiations. If auditors of the sermon or its readers in the widely circulated Parisian *Moniteur* missed the implications for Saxony, Talleyrand made the connection between the fates of Louis XVI and Friedrich August more explicit in a discourse in his salon that evening. The Prussians and Russians, claimed the police spy who reported on the incident, were not pleased.[55]

The representative of the House of Orange and leader of the smaller German delegations Hans Christoph von Gagern, although like Talleyrand a partisan of Friedrich August, for his part at least claimed to draw on the neutral, impartial, and cosmopolitan elements of festive and salon culture in order to help mediate the crisis by bringing the two sides together. Noted for his soirées in any case, Baron Gagern "redoubled my hospitality toward all nations without distinction," hoping that youthful high spirits would mitigate the "rising embitterment." At larger festivities, he opined, opponents could simply avoid one another, "without friendly contact."[56] In these moves, Gagern emphasized the cooperation and peacemaking efforts of several ladies of Viennese high society, particularly some of his "countrywomen" who had married into the Austrian nobility, including the *salonnière* Countess Bellegarde, Countess Stadion, and Princess Maria Esterhazy (wife of the diplomat and heir Prince Paul, née Princess Thurn und Taxis). Gagern also noted the attractive presence at his parties of Countess Bernstorff of Danish Holstein and young Anna Eynard of Geneva. As he concluded, "thus above all the female portion of the high nobility exerted themselves to entertain and to amuse the ill-humored high foreigners through the magic of social interaction, through conversation, song, and even on the social stage."[57]

For knowledge of the public pulse in Berlin and Germany regarding Saxony, Elisabeth Staegemann and Caroline von Humboldt formed two of the prime Prussian conduits of information, via correspondence with their respective spouses in the Prussian delegation. In November, from Berlin but fresh from a trip through Switzerland and Germany that lent some authority to her judgment, Caroline wrote to Wilhelm that there was only "one voice" in Germany on the Saxon question, and that voice was against the king of Saxony. In the same letter she passed on the news from her recent visit in Coppet of Madame de Staël's enthusiasm for

Tsar Alexander's Polish plans.[58] By January, amid the ongoing disappointments of the negotiations, Caroline was urging that there was "something higher" than life and its "temporal goods," and that the strategic situation for Prussia was in any case "not unfavorable" just then, hence it would be better to fight a war over Saxony sooner rather than later (shades of the Prussian elite a century later). Humboldt on the other hand pressed Caroline to discover whether General Gneisenau still favored a settlement that left the king of Saxony in Dresden, further evidence that he and the Prussians were already thinking of compromise in late December.[59]

Unlike Caroline, Elisabeth Staegemann inclined to a peace policy and compromise. Although having to be a bit more circumspect in talking politics with her husband than was the case with the Humboldts, particularly since she knew his bellicose views on Saxony, she still ventured to suggest that it might be desirable to reach an agreement whereby Prussia and Friedrich August divided the kingdom. "I don't want to say anything inapt, but it would be lovely if, in a matter begun so worthily, we could deflect from ourselves even the appearance of the slightest injustice," she wrote, and went on to ask "is it not possible then to satisfy the old gentleman at least for his lifetime?" Just a few days later, she reported that even those who had been pleased about October's handover of occupation authority in Saxony to Prussia were now wondering how to divest themselves of the territory in a "respectable way" after it had become such a bone of contention. Although Elisabeth did not fail to note their daughter Hedwig's strong support for Prussia's hard line on Saxony, the war party's voice certainly came through less loudly in her reportage than in Caroline's.[60] Whether that was due more to the politically self-selecting circles they ran in, with self-reinforcing expressions of opinion, or whether they reported selectively to lend extra weight to their views, is difficult to say. Both influences likely operated.

As if Hardenberg did not have enough worries with the Viennese salon scene, and with the pressures from Berlin publics for a strongly favorable settlement of the Saxon situation, he also had to deal with voices from Berlin sympathetic to their prisoner-guest the king of Saxony. In early December, he felt compelled to write to his sometime confidante Princess Marianne of Hessen-Homburg, wife of the Prussian Prince Wilhelm, asking her to refrain from speaking out against Prussia's acquisition of Saxony. He had heard, he observed, that she and her court had done just that, and while it was "natural" that "such a beautiful soul as yours" would take an interest in the unfortunate Saxon royal family, "duty toward the state" and "the good of Europe" (and Germany) required that Prussia be strengthened by the annexation.[61] As a good adoptive Prussian, Princess Marianne quickly and apologetically agreed to conform to policy. Two weeks later Hardenberg reassured her again in the Goethean language of the "Beautiful Soul," but reiterated that "I held it my duty to make you aware of the harmful impressions that could have arisen." Hardenberg then listed some further reasons why "it is better for the Saxon nation, for Prussia, for Germany, for Europe, and for the king of Saxony himself" to receive compensation elsewhere rather than remain in a partitioned land, and enclosed one of the pamphlets on Saxony written and published at his direction, "in case Your Royal Majesty does not know it yet."[62]

It may be that assessments of the state of public opinion did not influence the rulers and diplomats in their successive retreats and compromises during the late autumn and early winter; perhaps they felt the pressure but successfully overcame it, only to yield for other reasons. According explanatory weight to the nebulous realm of social pressure runs the risk of falling into something like the "ecological fallacy" in statistics, where the presence of a statistical trend need not explain a particular case or individual action, and in this instance it would be even more difficult to quantify that weight. Still, much the same can be said of other potential explanations, cultural, ideological, or indeed power political. That the social pressure exerted in salons did not play any role in shaping perception, calculation, and behavior seems very unlikely. The decision-making process was likely to be overdetermined, that is, shaped by the complex interplay of many social and cultural forces and streams of thought and feeling, often pointing in the same direction, even as it also responded to the whims of chance and personality.

The same likely holds for Metternich's position within the high society of court and town, as well as among the great and good visiting Vienna during the Congress. Metternich's job security at least seemed to contemporaries to depend in part on public opinion, if only insofar as his ultimate employer, Kaiser Franz, might have to respect it. Supporting the Prussians on Saxony in the autumn put Metternich's popularity at great risk, in ways that might come to seem not worth the potential reward. Baron Stein, at least, thought Metternich would have yielded on Saxony even later on, except that Franz and the public were too opposed. Metternich claimed to blame public opinion in explaining to Hardenberg and Castlereagh why he could not back off on Poland and

Saxony, and Emperor Franz similarly told Grand Duchess Catherine of Russia that both "his conscience" and the fact that "all Europe has its eyes" on them in this matter underlay his insistence that the king of Saxony retain at least part of his realm.[63]

Press Wars

The press campaigns and associated battles for public opinion surrounding the Congress of Vienna raged nowhere more fiercely than in the negotiations over the fate of Saxony. Several books and articles have been devoted to this subject over the years, but it is important to revisit this side of the story in the context of the present work's effort to reconstruct the many layers of post-Napoleonic European political and diplomatic culture and to pin down its significance for diplomatic practice. The contest was slugged out in part in the newspapers, but the pamphlet wars were the most noted, then and since.

The primary front in the press wars pitted against one another Prussia and Bavaria. Both Hardenberg and Bavaria's foreign minister, Montgelas, believed they needed to win German and European opinion to their side in the dispute. Austria did not maintain a strong presence outside the pages of Metternich's *Oesterreichischer Beobachter*. Among other news organs, some like the *Beobachter* notoriously took the positions of one government or the other, either (semi)officially, or simply for those in the know. Joseph Görres's *Rheinischer Merkur* provided the strongest flashpoint, both in general and with respect to Saxony. It was with reason taken to be a Prussian mouthpiece at the time, but Görres actually maintained considerable independence. Fewer newspapers, above all Johann Friedrich Cotta's *Allgemeine Zeitung*, adopted the more neutral pose of the public sphere and included coverage from both sides. Cotta's organ was published in Augsburg (since 1805 a Bavarian city), but it printed essays from Hardenberg's writers as well as the Bavarians. In the edition of 15 January 1815, for example, the paper reprinted an article from the *Bayreuther Zeitung* claiming that Saxon public opinion favored Friedrich August over the Prussians, while on 17 January it included a piece from the *Leipziger Zeitung* praising some of the reforms brought in by the Prussian provisional administration and another from Berlin asserting the Prussian governor's popularity. More significantly, on 16 January the *Allgemeine* printed a story supporting Prussia's acquisition of Saxony from the new *German Observer* in Hamburg, the paper Cotta had recently acquired in cooperation with Hardenberg's press advisor Karl Varnhagen von Ense, just in time to enter the lists at the height of the diplomatic crisis. There were consequent grumblings about Prussian influence, but on balance the paper tipped to the pro-Saxon side.[64]

The *Hamburger Correspondenten,* another of Europe's highest-profile papers, also probably lived up to the "impartial" billing in its full title, at least if receiving complaints from both camps is sufficient testament. According to the Prussian consul in Hamburg, Count Grote, Hamburg's Congress delegate Syndic Gries had reported irritation at the paper's pro-Prussian articles on Saxony, while a French diplomat had protested its purportedly anti-French coverage. These were not wholly false impressions, as Grote and the Prussians did sometimes plant articles there. But the paper also carried articles from Metternich's protégé Friedrich Schlegel, and overall favored Saxony.[65] The *Caledonian Mercury* of Edinburgh similarly presented material from both sides. In the very same edition, they printed a translated article from Görres's pro-Prussian German nationalist *Rhenish Mercury* as well as a piece from the Paris papers, naturally taking radically different positions on Saxony.[66] Görres's paper, however, also serves as a reminder of the relative limits of government control and coordination of press coverage at the time, even on the most important issues. Prussian-supported though he was, Görres still published a piece by Jacob Grimm critical of Prussian policy and expressing hope for a compromise on Saxony. Varnhagen thereupon felt compelled to counter these views in his new venture with Cotta the *German Observer.*[67]

To reach a broad international audience, the Bavarians and Prussians (and the French) could rely in part on the usual process of diffusion and borrowing from one paper to another, spreading in concentric circles across Europe like ripples on a pond. The most significant example involved the aforementioned article planted in the Parisian *Moniteur* by Talleyrand and accepted as official by foreign diplomats, which expanded on a story taken from a Bavarian paper to launch its defense of the king of Saxony. It then appeared in the Parisian *Journal des débats* before being taken up in the Danish-German *Altona Mercurius* and the widest-circulating paper of all, the *Hamburger Correspondenten.* Copies of the article were collected in many of the important diplomatic archives, including Metternich's State Chancellery, and it became one of the few items from the press enshrined in the standard collection of diplomatic documents from the Vienna Congress.[68]

To this piece Hardenberg in Vienna and Grote in Hamburg each reacted strongly, and in ways that illustrate both the government's thinking about when it was necessary to respond to foreign press attacks and the balance of active effort and voluntarist synchronicity that could be counted on to do so. As Hardenberg explained to the local governor in passing along a counter-article for publication in French and German in the *Journal of the Lower and Middle Rhine,* it might have been best for "our government to have taken no further notice of it at all, if the *Moniteur* had not been the official newspaper for France, through which the French cabinet transmits its political opinions and views to domestic and foreign publics and seeks to win these to its side through artful but incorrect portrayal of things and circumstances."[69] This action via counter-portrayal, however, followed an apparently independent counterattack that had originated in London and spread from there across the North Sea to Danish Altona and Hamburg. A ministerial paper in London fired the initial salvo mere days after the *Moniteur* article on 5 December, and by 15 December it, too, had appeared in German in the Altona *Mercurius.* On his own initiative, Grote arranged for its publication in the widely read *Hamburg Correspondent* as well. Hardenberg knew of the windfall press coverage that was already serving Prussian purposes before he gave the orders to the governor, but must have felt that an obvious but not-quite-official response from Prussia was still required. On the whole, the independent piece seems likely to have been more effective in countering the French foray (not least for being independent and seemingly impartial, but also in its general argumentative line).[70]

Probably the most successful intervention was the work of Bavaria's representative in London, Christian Hubert von Pfeffel. Pfeffel wrote a letter to the editor of the opposition paper the *Morning Chronicle,* cleverly if mendaciously signing himself "A Saxon" (not an original ploy, but none the less effective for that). By his perhaps self-serving account, the piece almost single-handedly turned the tide of public opinion in Britain against Prussia. Previously, English leaders such as Lord Liverpool and the English public had tended to support Prussia as the most patriotic and best-governed of the German powers, as witness their adulation of Marshal Blücher during the London celebrations of the summer of 1814. Pfeffel feared, too, that in their enthusiasm for Polish restoration (even under Tsar Alexander), the English would forget about the rights and sufferings of Saxony and its king, hence his balloon launched on the winds of public opinion. Pfeffel claimed that the essay outraged the London Poles but had the desired effect.[71]

Smaller independent political actors, outside government or at least outside the ranks of larger powers, also participated in the press wars.

A good example can be found in the respective campaigns of the *Erinnerungsblätter*, or *Commemorative Pages for Educated Readers of All Classes*, and the *General Chronicle of the Vienna Congress*, independent champions of the two sides. The *Erinnerungsblätter*, published by Robert Schumann's father, August, in the Saxon mining town of Zwickau, took up the Saxon cause. The *Chronik* editors, having unsuccessfully approached Hardenberg to link with his press apparatus, nevertheless adopted pro-Prussian and German-national positions. A common theme in this study is the extent to which state and civil society often found themselves in cooperation rather than conflict in the transitional public sphere; or more to the point here, in cooperation and conflict at the same time, as especially in the German context there were always multiple governments to choose from to aid or to oppose. The *Chronik* began its campaign early, with an initial jab in their second number, where among their predictions for Congress outcomes in the "Echo" column they pointed to Prussia's acquisition of Saxony. In December, they set themselves to counter pro-Saxon voices from France and Britain, claiming that "the people" of Saxony were for Prussia and that only nobles and former officials supported the old king. The *Erinnerungsblätter* soon shot back at the *Chronik*, quipping with regard to the "Echo" that "of course it depends on who may have asked this Echo." The editors of the *Chronik* could at least have taken heart from the fact that their production was cited (if sometimes critiqued) in several major European newspapers, unlike the provincial *Erinnerungsblätter*.[72]

Among Congress delegates, Senator Johann Smidt of Bremen, ever the believer in the power of public opinion, informed his senatorial colleague that "only the strength of public opinion—which is now no longer guided quite correctly by Görres and Arndt—can save us." All newspapers and voices, he asserted, should be loudly proclaiming that any war between Prussia and Austria would be "fratricide," and that those advising such a move for "petty goals of aggrandizement" were not serving "our Volk" well. Bremen's newspaper was to do what it could. Jacob Grimm's article in Görres's *Rhenish Mercury* represented another independent effort to encourage Prussian moderation. More confident than Smidt but essentially agreeing, the editors of the *Chronicle of the Vienna Congress* claimed that the state of European public opinion made war over Poland and Saxony less likely.[73]

The better-remembered and -researched component of the conflicts in print involved pamphlets rather than newspapers. Pamphlet literature arguably played a greater role at the time than newspapers in influencing public opinion, given that their circulation could be much higher—topping ten thousand—and that they were intended to push a certain point of view very strongly, unlike the early newspapers, which emphasized (ostensibly) simple reportage rather than editorial opinion. Partly for that reason, governments took a greater hand in promoting pamphlets, though here too they could count on at least some independent writers taking up their pens in support. It is also important to remember that pamphlets and periodicals should not be thought of as completely separate; the pamphlet war over Saxony was in part sparked by Joseph Görres's articles in the *Rheinische Merkur* (themselves later republished in pamphlet form), and the battle was carried on through responses and reviews in periodicals as well as through further pamphlets.[74]

The more than sixty pamphlets almost all appeared anonymously, though the authors were sometimes known even then (other ascriptions historians have been able to glean since). Pseudonyms could be chosen for a not-so-subtle foreshadowing of the argument, with names such as "Germanus Saxo" (arguing against the king of Saxony from a German-national standpoint) or "A Saxon" (taking the king's part). Often the texts appeared without indication of the real place of publication, here too not unusually with appropriate false attributions such as "Germania" or "Land-greed." Germanus Saxo was actually Wilhelm Traugott Krug, philosophy professor at the University of Leipzig, and while writing from his own conviction and desire to influence events, he had Hardenberg's approval. Other authors wrote primarily at government behest. "A Saxon" turned out to be the Bavarian official Baron Johann Christoph von Aretin, who had already authored one of the contest's most important pamphlets, the equally anonymous *Saxony and Prussia*. Written for Montgelas, the latter work went through three quick editions. Aretin's follow-up was identified as taken from the pages of the periodical *Allemania,* which had been specially created by Montgelas to carry the fight to the Prussians.[75]

On the Prussian side, Karl Varnhagen von Ense's pamphlet has already been noted in connection with Fanny Arnstein's efforts to circumvent Austrian censorship. Varnhagen served as Hardenberg's unofficial press advisor, and the work constituted part of Hardenberg's larger press campaign. It was shaped not only by Hardenberg's input but also by suggestions from Humboldt and above all Staegemann, who thought Varnhagen's draft overstated Prussia's centrality to the German national cause in a way that might alienate rather than attract readers elsewhere, an opinion with which Hardenberg concurred.[76] One of the most significant contributions came from the Berlin university professor Johann Hoffmann, already mentioned as a close advisor to Hardenberg. Hoffmann's cleverly or confusingly titled *Prussia and Saxony* took direct aim at Aretin's *Saxony and Prussia*, and itself went through two editions. The most famous publicist in the Prussian camp was undoubtedly the renowned Roman historian Barthold Georg Niebuhr, who volunteered his *Prussia's Right against the Saxon Court.* In an attempt to capitalize on his cultural authority, this was one of the few pamphlets published under the author's name. It too received a second edition.[77]

As with newspaper coverage, reaching a wider international public was an important consideration with pamphlets. Hoffmann's saw publication in French as well as English, the latter adding the suggestive subtitle *Prussia and Saxony, or an Appeal to the good sense of Europe.* The French edition even included Aretin's original text, with an injunction for the "impartial observer" to decide between them, but adding some helpful leading footnotes to Aretin's portion to nudge that decision in the desired direction. The Prussian chargé in London also tried to arrange for Niebuhr's contribution to appear in English but had to confess his lack of success, despite approaching five publishers.[78]

Rhetorical strategies within the press campaigns largely mirrored the arguments adduced among diplomats. Themes of state interests and balance of power still featured, but governments did not want to dispense with the legitimation of arguments from justice and the law of nations either, particularly before broader public opinion.[79] Prussians quoted the classic authors Vattel and Grotius on the law of conquest, while Saxony's defenders disputed these interpretations and quoted the same authorities on the rights of sovereigns who had not abdicated. Pamphleteers also debated the justice of Friedrich August's political decisions and of the efforts to punish him for the same. Political ideology entered in as well, insofar as Prussia's opponents again accused them of fomenting a Jacobin or at least liberal conspiracy under the guise of the League of Virtue, Aretin little different in this than Metternich or Talleyrand. With a nod to Demosthenes, an anonymous author likened the Prussian king to "a second Phillip of Macedon" and warned ominously that "a so-called League of Virtue casts its nets beneath the veil of night." As among the diplomats, public opinion and an element of self-determination figured as well—that is, both sides tried to claim the support of "public opinion" and "the populace," in Germany and in Saxony itself, whether posited as a matter of justice or as a practical consideration for those who would eventually rule.[80]

Several pamphlets also raised the inflammatory issue of religious confession, in particular, relations between Catholics and Protestants, and between Lutherans and Calvinists. As noted previously, Prussian and Russian diplomats privately tried to suggest that the Wettin dynasty, as Catholics, might be happier ruling Catholic subjects, or at least that Saxons as Protestants would be better off with a Protestant rather than a Catholic king. "Germanus Saxo" (Krug) took a similar tack in public, holding out the specter of the royal family's Jesuit education as the marker of intolerance in an appeal to Protestant prejudices.[81] Pro-Saxon authors such as "Truemouth" retorted that while Prussia's rulers were Protestant, they did not share Saxons' predominant Lutheranism but were instead Calvinist. As a letter dated Dresden in the main London opposition paper complained, Prussia sought "to enflame the superstitions of the Saxon people, in offering them the prospect of obeying a Protestant Sovereign." The writer went on to observe that the Prussian royal house's Calvinism was "according to the righteous principles of Lutheranism, as far removed from that faith as the Romish Church." Anti-Catholic Anglicans were supposed to get the point and to pressure the government against supporting Prussia.[82]

On balance, however, the role of confessional discourse in the Saxon controversy underscores the tendency in post-Napoleonic Europe to downplay confessional differences and eschew confessional conflict. Religious arguments did not, after all, feature prominently, nor, to the extent that they were used, do they seem to have been very successful, either among the statesmen or among the public. Dynastic allegiance, patriotism, German nationalism, and geopolitical considerations all figured more prominently.

For all that aid from the Bavarians and others certainly helped, the Saxon court and its sympathizers also launched their own PR campaign. They, however, tended to target those in political circles directly rather than work through the press. The centerpiece was the French-language "Exposé of the Political Course of the King of Saxony" of July 1814, cast in the voice of the "Saxon nation" as well as of the king and sent in manuscript to as many important statesmen and rulers as possible. The *Apologie de Frédéric Auguste, Roi de Saxe,* was published in September, but it too, significantly, appeared in properly diplomatic French rather than German. The Prussian censor in Berlin reported that it was said to be "maladroitly" argued and offered an occasion "for the application of the English proverb: God save us from our friends." The representative of the House of Orange, Hans Christoph von Gagern, listed the *Apology* among the handful of good pro-Saxon pamphlets circulating at the Congress, but then he already stood in the choir to which the text preached.[83] Numerous petitions from various corporate bodies such as the city councils of Dresden and Leipzig and the Estates of Upper and Lower Lusatia also arrived in Vienna addressed to Metternich, Castlereagh, and other diplomats and rulers, including Prussian. Those from the Diets of Lower and Upper Lusatia, though principally calling to remain part of an undivided Saxony, still expressed the wish that Friedrich August remain their ruler.[84] In addition, November's "Protest," written by the king of Saxony in opposition to the recent Prussian occupation, received considerable European press coverage. Apparently refused publication in the Russian papers, the French ambassador informed Talleyrand that this document was nonetheless known there and "could not fail to produce some sort of effect."[85]

Whether all of these initiatives in the press had much effect or made much difference in the end remains an open question. A scholar long ago already warned of taking published expressions of opinion as indicators of public opinion itself; they might be a better indicator of government activity and resources than of the reception of particular ideas.[86] Similarly, even once one has gauged the state of public opinion at various social levels and in various regions, it remains difficult to say how far it influenced particular governments or statesmen in particular directions. But numerous statements exist by officials weighing the effects of opinion, and it does seem possible at least to establish certain instances where perceptions of public opinion may have predisposed statesmen in a certain direction, or have made them reluctant to go against it. In addition, as seen in previous contexts as well, perceptions of public opinion could offer seeming opportunities to influence other governments as much as it served to limit one's own freedom of action.

In this case, it seems clear that the needle of public opinion did increasingly swing in opposition to Prussia's acquisition of the whole of Saxony. This was true above all in Britain, where important statesmen such as Castlereagh and Liverpool, and to an extent the public at large, had started out favorable to the idea of Prussian resurgence. The sea change in public opinion at least offered statesmen an excuse for changing positions when it became diplomatically expedient, but it is likely that the state of opinion itself played a part in their reconsideration, above all when reckoning with the possibility of a resultant war, and the need for popular enthusiasm or at least support in that eventuality. But in much of Germany also, the sentiment in favor of Saxony and in opposition to Prussia seems to have grown, despite what Stein and some of the Prussians may have thought. More than any specific line of argument it may simply have been the ingrained tradition of anti-Prussian suspicion that increasingly resurfaced. Just as importantly, because even more proximately, in Vienna itself the pressure to save at least a large portion of Saxony for Friedrich August ratcheted up in the course of the autumn and winter. It was for the most part only opinion in Prussia that exerted pressure the other way and militated against a too-sudden or too-sharp retreat on Hardenberg's part. Still, belief in the pressure cooker of Prussian opinion at the same time predisposed opposing diplomats to accept a compromise. The British prince regent's advisor Count Münster was not the only negotiator who worried that public sentiment in Berlin might push the Prussian cabinet toward war. But even from the Prussian capital, indications reached the delegation in Vienna that sections of the public would not be sorry if a way could be found to effect an honorable retreat, as Elisabeth Staegemann had reported. The desire for peace after the long wars trumped any patriotic inclinations tending the other way.[87]

Resolving the Crisis and Selling the Solutions

On New Year's Day, 1815, the "warlike tone" of Prussia's Chancellor Hardenberg finally convinced Castlereagh that the time had come to respond to the overtures of Metternich and Talleyrand to seal an alliance against the Russian and Prussian threat. The treaty was signed in short order, on 3 January. Making the decision that much easier was the news from Ghent of the peace between Britain and the United States that ended the War of 1812 and freed up British men and resources for use back in Europe.

The significance of the signing of the treaty of 3 January has been exaggerated. In many accounts of the Congress it features as the turning point, signaling the resolution of the Great Power conflict and dispelling the clouds of war that had hung over the Congress for weeks, if not months. The treaty has also seemed to historians taking this view to provide the best evidence that the old eighteenth-century balance-of-power diplomacy was still the name of the game in the post-Napoleonic nineteenth century, with Britain joining France and Austria to check the overweening power of Russia and its ally Prussia.

Given that it was secret, exactly how the treaty caused such a rapid turnaround is not always made immediately clear. Presumably the treaty is supposed to have produced these dramatic effects by causing the language of the three western powers to become enough firmer and more consolidated to convince the Russians and Prussians to back down. It is also possible that the document did not remain secret as intended, or that word of it was intentionally leaked. On 8 January Tsar Alexander already queried Castlereagh about rumors of a separate treaty, and on 12 January the Prussian ambassador to the tsar, General Schöler, also expressed worries about an alliance between Austria, France, and Great Britain. But then Humboldt was still warning of a potential alliance in late January, which suggests that the Prussians at least did not know that such a thing had already occurred. Nor did the shock and outrage provoked later, on Napoleon's disclosure of the secret treaty to Alexander following his return to power in March 1815, seem feigned.[88] A simpler explanation is that news of the Treaty of Ghent was enough to persuade the Russians and Prussians to accord more weight to British opposition to their plans. The Prussians claimed they welcomed peace between the United States and Britain, but the active Congress diplomat Baron Gagern thought such phrases "mystification, complete mystification."[89]

This perspective makes more sense given the even greater problem with the explanation centered around the treaty of 3 January, namely, that it did not really resolve the crisis. Early January did see Prussia agree to negotiate on the basis of a partition of Saxony that left Friedrich August in Dresden, and after a few more meetings of the four main powers, Talleyrand and Dalberg were also finally admitted to the primary negotiating sessions (from 12 January), thus formally acknowledging France's return to the ranks of the Great Powers. These were both significant shifts, but hardly decisive. Regarding Poland, the treaty induced very little change in Russia's offer at all, while the Saxon settlement dragged on for over a month and still involved some bellicose fulminations until the very end. The Saxon issue, not the Polish, continued to produce the threat and threats of war. Concerning Poland, Metternich had already basically signaled on 3 January that he would accept the territorial basis of Alexander's quasi ultimatum offered on 30 December.[90]

In the event, it turned out to be quite difficult to arrange a satisfactory agreement (and partition) for Saxony and even for Poland, and this despite the fact that ideas rather close to those ultimately adopted had been circulating for some while. It was not inventing an adequate solution that took time, but convincing all sides to accept it. Castlereagh thought his interview with King Friedrich Wilhelm of Prussia on 6 February—just days before the near-final settlement—the "most unpleasant" of his entire time on the Continent (even worse than those with the tsar), and Hardenberg did not have a much easier time persuading his king just after.[91] Prussia and to an extent Russia have usually borne the brunt of blame for recalcitrance, but neither did the suddenly stubborn Austrians show much willingness to bend from their initial offer for a demarcation line in Saxony. Castlereagh, as he had feared, soon had to expend as much effort to keep Metternich and Talleyrand from using the new alliance to push for a too-stringent settlement as he did to persuade the Prussians to accept a reasonable compromise.[92] Even if balance-of-power politics played some role in the process of peacemaking here, clearly more than just the treaty of 3 January was involved.

Western statesmen and observers had already become alarmed at Russian plans in the Duchy of Warsaw in 1813. While any Russian expansion seemed dangerous, many hoped to limit Russia's gains to the area north and east of the Vistula and Bug rivers at Warsaw, or at least to the longer course of the Vistula more generally. Metternich's advisor Friedrich Gentz, for example, still argued in March 1814 against including Warsaw in the Russian zone, but by August he recognized that the Polish capital would remain in Russian hands. At that point he merely urged striving for a border that preserved Toruń to Prussia and Cracow and the area around Zamość to Austria.[93] In October and November during the Congress itself, Metternich and Castlereagh still pushed for the Vistula as border, with Warsaw for the Russians, as their maximum offer.

Most Prussians, too, would have liked to see Russia restricted to the far northeast of the Duchy of Warsaw, but it became clear to them earlier than to the others that this would not be possible, hence they began to press for a boundary to run roughly from Toruń through Kalisz and then to Częstochowa on the line of the Warta River, leaving them in possession of those towns, and preserving Cracow for the Habsburgs. For General Knesebeck, an important advisor to both Hardenberg and Friedrich Wilhelm, even that compromise border would leave Prussia in a state of military dependence on Russia, and exposed Russia's trend toward "world domination." But for Hardenberg, Humboldt, and some other Prussian diplomats, it at least represented a militarily defensible frontier, beyond which it would be dangerous to compromise. And even that border, they could see, was going to be difficult to achieve. As Prussia's ambassador to Russia, General Schöler, informed Hardenberg after he had broached the proposal with the tsar in early September, Alexander insisted on retaining all the places named, and adduced the threat of his army of seven hundred thousand in doing so.[94]

Historians have often overstated the concessions made by Russia in Poland as a result of the Vienna negotiations, and of the treaty of 3 January in particular. The tsar had always intended to return a certain amount of Prussian and Austrian territory, and as early as August 1814 Nesselrode was already thinking in terms of a Russian border in Poland running along a line from the city of Toruń through the small town of Pyzdry (Peysern) and then following the line of the Prosna River through the city of Kalisz (that is, about fifty kilometers west of the Prussians' desired border at the Warta). This was essentially the offer the Russians put on the table in the preparatory meeting of the Allied ministers on 19 September. In other words, Prussia would recover most of its previous possessions in West Prussia and Poznań. Such an offer was not so far off in kilometers from the Prussian proposal, but it left Russia in possession of all the key towns, fortresses, and rivers that the Prussians felt critical to their security. By November, western pressure had induced the tsar to propose that Cracow and Toruń become free cities and that Austria recover the Tarnopol region for Galicia; this offer changed little in January. Toruń went to Prussia at the very end; otherwise, the deal remained basically as Alexander had proposed and Metternich accepted back at the turn of the New Year.[95]

With respect to Saxony, the Prussians finally agreed to make the basis for negotiation the question of where to draw a partition line rather than continuing to insist on the whole territory. Arguably, Hardenberg and the Prussians may all along have been prepared to accept a settlement wherein they did not receive all of Saxony, however much they would have preferred it. Hardenberg's outrage at Metternich's alleged duplicity and volte-face in his note of 10 December is often attributed to Metternich's withdrawal of the offer of full Saxon annexation (if such an offer was ever made, itself still sometimes debated—it was, with conditions). Actually, however, what upset Hardenberg so much was the switch from the possibility that the king of Saxony might preserve a small "kernel" of territory around Dresden to the proposal that

Prussia receive the smaller chunk of Saxon territory and the Saxon king the lion's share.[96]

Between these two poles the arguments raged. Strongly held strategic considerations of fortresses and topography brought the Austrians and Prussians into collision, alongside the more general effort to secure as many inhabitants and as much territory as possible for Saxony or Prussia. Possession of the fortress of Torgau and the cities of Wittenberg and Erfurt was hotly contested. The Prussians demanded some higher-value urban areas when they realized that the territory offered held very few sizable towns, despite Saxony's generally high rates of urbanization. Above all they hoped for the university and commercial city of Leipzig, which the Prussian king also desired for symbolic reasons after the decisive battle there in 1813. It had always been clear that Prussia would at least receive most of Lusatia on its Silesian border and the area around Cottbus that had been annexed by Saxony after the Treaty of Tilsit in 1807. In the end Prussia received about eight hundred thousand inhabitants and somewhat more than half the territory, Friedrich August about 1.2 million, still including Leipzig. The agreement also included a pledge that Austria and Prussia recommence work on the German federal constitution that had been interrupted over the past three months.

In facilitating the final settlement, it may be that Alexander was swayed by the analysis of his old tutor La Harpe as to the potential significance of the cities of Cracow and Toruń for resolving the conflict. It may also be that he proved receptive to Hardenberg's nationality-based argument that "Thorn" was an essentially German city, hence transferable in a way that the historic Polish capital of Cracow was not. That would help explain why Cracow became a neutral, independent city-state whereas Toruń did not.[97] Or it may be (in an idealistic vein) that Alexander truly did desire peace so much that he was willing to make one more sacrifice. But without being too cynical, finances may have played a decisive role. All along, the British had told the Russians that any forgiveness of the Russian debt in Holland depended on its cooperation regarding Poland and Saxony. British public opinion, they claimed, would never support yet another financial sacrifice for the benefit of a state promoting Poland's partition and Saxony's extinction. Late in the negotiations, however, Castlereagh hinted to Nesselrode that if the tsar could be perceived as having made a sacrifice that decisively facilitated a peaceful resolution of the impasse, the British government might yet feel able to approach Parliament with a deal on the debt. As Nesselrode reported, Alexander could not agree to the envisioned further cession of significant territory from the Duchy of Warsaw to Prussia, but conceding the city of Toruń "in fact did contribute powerfully to causing it [Prussia] to renounce possession of Leipzig on which it had insisted."[98] The conditions were thus fulfilled, allowing Nesselrode and Castlereagh to hammer out a draft financial agreement and the rest of the territorial settlement to go through.

After the final deal, Hardenberg immediately began efforts at damage control, or at least at educating public opinion with a little spin. On 10 February, the very day of the conference that produced the settlement, Hardenberg already wrote to Berlin to insert an unofficial article in the Berlin papers that would quiet the various ill-informed rumors and outline the new territorial distribution. The article was aimed at the reading public, but it was also sent to Prussia's representatives abroad for their information. It already appeared in both the *Berlinische Nachrichten* and the *Tagesblatt der Geschichte* on 16 February. On 15 February, Hardenberg sped another op-ed piece to the same destination, this time explaining Prussia's decision to cede its province of East Frisia to the Kingdom of Hanover in exchange for other territories.[99]

The amplifier effect of the period's reprint-happy press culture received some extra help from the industrious chargé in London, Friedrich Greuhm. Greuhm informed Hardenberg that he had had the article of 10 February translated into English for publication in the *Courier*. He found the translation wanting but thought it would not matter too much, since the Hamburg, Amsterdam, and Paris journals would likely have better versions straight from the Berlin papers. He felt the media campaign had already had a beneficial effect on English public opinion. Greuhm was even proved correct in the case of the French papers; the semiofficial *Moniteur* broke the news of a settlement in general terms on 19 February (still reflecting a rather optimistic reading of the demarcation line from the French perspective), but the first detailed coverage was more or less a translation of Hardenberg's effort, from Berlin via the French-language *Gazette du Francfort*.[100] Remarkably, Hardenberg was even rewarded with the scoop on the settlement story in Austria. Rather than rushing its version of the news into print first, Metternich's organ, the *Oesterreichische Beobachter*, instead simply culled its coverage from the Berlin papers, including the article of 16 February from Hardenberg's bureau.[101]

While Hardenberg's article emphasized territorial compensation, military defense, and the importance of having the backing of the international community, nationalist arguments, too, shaped Hardenberg's efforts to convince the Prussian public of the justice and benefits of the new territorial settlement, particularly with respect to Poland. Hardenberg justified the loss of much of Prussia's previous Polish territory with the contention that respect for nationality had become part of the spirit of the age: "in times when the distinctiveness of the national spirit has almost everywhere showed itself to be so powerful and so worthy of respect, it seemed desirable to bring Poland too—insofar as it is possible without injury to the rights and security of neighboring states—into a situation more favorable to the development of its particular nationality." The settlement also, the article noted, opened the door to rapid progress in establishing a German federation.[102]

The editors of the *Berlinische Nachrichten* added their mite to public relations with a short follow-up article on Prussia's new acquisitions. They began by remarking that readers probably expected detailed statistics on the new lands, and regretted that these could not yet be provided. But they were able to offer some rough characterizations of the new provinces, assuring their readers, with their own recourse to nationalist language, that the portions of Poland returned to Prussia were "well-cultivated" and "rather similar to a German province," thus defusing any unfavorable stereotypes about Polish or eastern backwardness. The piece also observed that "German colonists" had been settled in some of these areas for centuries. In other words, the Poles living there were not as different as other Poles, and many ethnic Germans were present in any case. For epicureans the author added that Prussia's new territories on the Mosel in southwest Germany would ensure that the already-famous Mosel wines now became a "truly patriotic beverage."[103]

Moreover, and at once more impressively and rather at odds with the editors' disclaimers about the impossibility of statistical precision at this early stage, the same issue of the paper included an ad from a Berlin publishing house already announcing a new "Map of the Prussian State in the Year 1815." "We hasten," the ad began quite truthfully, "to announce to the public the appearance of this map, to meet a loudly-expressed need." The map showed not just the new boundaries set in Vienna but also, for purposes of patriotic comparison, the borders of Prussia after the Napoleonic amputation of the Treaty of Tilsit in 1807. Against that background, the new settlement was bound to appear quite favorable. Against, say, the borders of 1805, the advantages might have leapt less readily to the eye. Color shading made reading the map easy, and the usual differential pricing for its paper and canvas versions helped widen the audience both socially and chronologically (in the sense of durability and potential permanence of display).[104] In this instance, as with so many aspects of the Congress, private enterprise went hand in hand with governmental maneuvering, and sometimes outstripped it. The partly subsidized newspaper made its own contributions to Hardenberg's campaign to convince ambitious Prussians to feel better about the settlement, while the cartographers produced the real coup, meeting the same end in ways of which Hardenberg had not dreamed. The extra help might have been needed—Caroline von Humboldt at least found the original article too apologetic and reported that it had been received even less favorably than the settlement itself, which proved, as expected, unpopular in many circles in Berlin.[105]

In addition to his exertions in the press, Hardenberg also took a few moments on that hectic 10 February to notify Princess Marianne, his political confidante and onetime supporter of the king of Saxony, of the outcome. Still spinning the optimistic view, the chancellor wrote that while Prussia would not receive all of Saxony, it was still a good deal, and sanctioned by all the main powers, hence they could "look forward to a long repose."[106] Behind the scenes, Hardenberg's collaborator Staegemann also helped prepare Berlin's salons and public opinion for the perhaps disappointing resolution. He informed his wife Elisabeth that he had written to a notoriously loose-lipped acquaintance letting him in on the secret of the likely division of Saxony. Elisabeth took the hint and began to spread the word as well. Caroline von Humboldt missed the point when she posed the rhetorical question to her husband of whether Staegemann would be happy with his wife's public display of insider knowledge. Elisabeth, at least, was pleased that a peaceful solution had been found, but had to report that many in Berlin were taking the news badly.[107]

Back in Vienna, reactions to the settlement were mixed. Most were relieved to avoid war, but the Bavarian Count Rechberg thought the king of Saxony lost too much. The Poles for their part seem to have been cautiously optimistic. The circle around Prince Henryk Lubomirski were reported to be generally satisfied with the agreement, even if disappointed at what they incorrectly thought the loss of Zamość to Austria (it remained with the Kingdom of Poland). Behind the scenes, Prince Czartoryski and Prince Radziwiłł attempted to get the unreceptive British to bring the Polish question before the Committee of Five again, partly to pressure Alexander into including more of his Polish possessions under the new constitution, and partly to urge Austria and Prussia once more to adopt liberal measures in governing their Polish territories.[108] Talley rand and Count Jaucourt instructed French diplomats to see that the settlement contributed to Europe's repose, and saved the principle of legitimacy. Farther from the social and political center, the minor Austrian hunting official and diarist Matthias Perth also expressed satisfaction with the settlement, proud of Austria's presumed mediator role and having always considered some loss of Saxon territory to be "unavoidable."[109]

When the time came, after the final treaties for Saxony and Poland were signed in May, the Prussians deployed some of the same arguments in their proclamations to the populations of the new territories that had been used in the various territorial settlements in Italy, Switzerland, or Norway. They declared religious toleration and made constitutional promises, and they highlighted nationality. With regard to nationhood, in the case of Saxony they appealed to a common German national identity, while in that of Poznań they proclaimed protections for Polish nationality. The Saxons read that they would be "united with your neighbors and German countrymen," and be attached to a new dynasty "to which you are related through the [friendly] bonds of being neighbors, of language, of customs, of religion"—"only Germany has won what Prussia has acquired." The Prussians made a similar if stronger appeal to German nationalism in the proclamation to the Rhineland: "These ancient German lands must remain united with Germany; they cannot belong to another kingdom foreign to them by language, by customs, by habits, by laws." The Rhinelanders were even flattered as the "loyal, manly, German people" to whom the Prussians were to be joined in bonds of "brotherhood."[110] While the Saxons received the subtle reminder of common Protestant heritage to attract them to Prussia, Rhineland Catholics were promised not just religious liberty but also the kind of financial support for the church, clergy, and schools that the negotiators in Vienna were unable to proclaim in the German constitution itself, as well as a Catholic university (the University of Bonn, opened in 1819).[111]

The Poles in Poznań received similar guarantees of religious toleration and support, and were informed that they would be "incorporated into My Monarchy, without being permitted to deny your nationality." Further along national lines, but also sounding the theme of revolutionary-era meritocracy (for men), the document promised that "your language" was to be used alongside German in public life, "and access to the public offices, honors, and dignities of my lands shall be open to each among you according to the measure of his capacities." The governor was to be born and reside among them (Prince Radziwiłł in the first instance), and the chief administrator too would be a "fellow citizen." The Saxons and Poznanians, like the other territories coming under Prussian rule in the Vienna settlement, were also assured that they would receive a provincial representative constitution in addition to participating in the new national constitution for Prussia that the king had just promised for all his subjects. And as with many of the Italian restoration agreements, the Prussian king guaranteed a political amnesty as well, something crucial for those who had supported Napoleon's regime in the Duchy of Warsaw after it replaced the South Prussian administration in 1807.[112]

Tsar Alexander, for his part, similarly appealed to Poles through "the common name of the Slavic nations," but above all through his promises that they would receive a constitution, only Poles would be officials, the Polish language would be respected, the army would remain national and stationed in Poland, and Poles would enjoy free communication and commerce with the other portions of former Poland.[113] When Czartoryski brought the constitution to Poland a few months later, it proved to be moderately liberal, with individual rights protections and a bicameral legislature, but with royal power still predominant over parliamentary, including an absolute veto for the tsar-king. The document retained much of the Duchy of Warsaw's Napoleonic constitution, but if anything strengthened the civil rights provisions and the remit and powers of the Diet (the Sejm).[114] The new Polish kingdom started off with a fairly liberal foundation and some goodwill, but Alexander and his appointees frequently failed to uphold the constitution, and Polish support faltered in succeeding years.[115] The Austrians were as usual slower to act, but internal discussions got under way in the months following the Congress, and by December 1815 Police Chief Hager followed several of Kaiser Franz's advisors in deeming an estates-based representative constitution "indispensable and indeed urgently necessary." In 1817 such a constitution for Galicia finally materialized, less liberal than the Russian or Prussian versions, but still on par with the consultative representations recently established in Austria's Italian provinces.[116]

If the Allies had made a small concession to Polish nationalism with the establishment of the Republic of Cracow, they went somewhat further with their concessions toward liberalism in Cracow. "Concession," of course, is not quite the right word if the arguments made here are correct; most of the responsible figures may have thought that public expectations of a liberal constitution made it more necessary, but they also tended to believe that such a limited constitutional framework could contribute to multinational stability at both the domestic and international levels. Cracovians did not get to draft their own constitution; a committee with members from Austria, Prussia, and Russia did that. But the commissioners of the three powers appointed thereafter did oversee the process of finalizing the document in consultation with representatives of Cracow (the final version appearing in Polish and Latin as well as German and French). In addition to providing general religious toleration and partial emancipation for the state's Jewish population, the constitution also established a small Senate and an Assembly of Representatives having legislative and budgetary powers, a role in electing senators and judges, and the ability to impeach officials. All governmental and judicial acts were to be in Polish.[117]

Ultimately, then, we are brought back to the "seeming paradox" that a new partition of Poland took place even as nationality rights were recognized. Yet within the framework of political culture depicted here, the settlement is less paradoxical and more consequential than it at first appears. The decisions regarding both Poland and Saxony in part represented compromises between the dictates of power politics and the need to appease public opinion, in Europe, in the lands affected, and domestically. More than simply being a compromise, however, the decisions also represented the application of diplomats' ideas about federative nationality, about provincial and supranational patriotism for land, people, and dynasty, and about the need for moderate constitutional government in what they hoped would remain the *post*revolutionary age.

Conclusion

The Congress of Vienna famously closed with the signing of the Final Act on 9 June 1815. One can almost imagine the immortal engraving of Jean Isabey and Jean Godefroy with its portraits of all the main negotiators from the Committee of Eight as capturing that very meeting. The historical image of this solemn moment is, however, in part a myth. The Spanish delegate refused to sign, and some of the material (including for the German constitutional settlement) had to be backdated, actually signed on 10 June, just before Metternich, Hardenberg, and many of the other diplomats hurriedly left town to join their sovereigns at headquarters for the final campaign against Napoleon. Yet the race to produce official copies of the massive text for all the main powers and get them signed involved still more difficulties. For the British and Austrians in particular, who hoped to inaugurate a new era of international relations based on the moral authority of system-wide treaties, getting all the signatures possible was of burning concern. The reports back to London of the British delegate, the Earl of Clancarty, cast a different light on these august proceedings than the engraving, as the process dragged on through June, the Russian signatures not being appended until 27 June, after much nervous waiting and contingency planning, and others having to be tracked down at various headquarters and in Belgium as the British copy of the treaty made its circuitous way to London.[1]

Despite the hectic nature of the Final Act's signing, and in part because of the success of the mythmaking surrounding it, the Vienna settlement became the cornerstone of a landmark shift in international relations for the following century. Treaties served increasingly as the basis for international law, and as Paul Schroeder in particular has shown, notions of collective guarantee and security rather than warfare took pride of place as the preferred mechanisms of conflict resolution.[2] The system of international relations laid down at Vienna helped keep the peace, or at least helped prevent further escalation when peace broke down, for nearly a hundred years.

Scholars still debate whether the ideas and practice of a "general equilibrium" or a "balance of power" had truly changed all that much after 1814 compared to the eighteenth-century state system, but it seems clear that the leading rulers and statesmen had indeed learned from the events of the past quarter century and mostly agreed on the need to avoid the mistakes of the years prior to 1789 as well as those of the revolutionary and Napoleonic periods. In this they received much encouragement from the various European publics in salon society and the press, and indeed from spectators and participants in the peace celebrations and display. The diplomatic congresses of the early eighteenth century should not be overlooked as precursors, neither in terms of their efforts at collective security nor with respect to the volume of press coverage surrounding them. Yet their long-term success was limited, and they took place in a different political culture, before the revolutionary era and its ideologies of mass mobilization or the freer manners of nineteenth-century salon society.

One may also still question whether the European international system after Napoleon can properly be described in Schroeder's phrase as a "bipolar hegemony" of Britain and Russia, leading two opposing blocs of western constitutional and eastern absolutist governments.[3] Austria and Prussia together formed an important and partly independent bloc in the center of Europe, as they had been meant to do in Castlereagh's, Alexander's, and Metternich's conceptions of the post-Napoleonic order. Moreover, none of these blocs was monolithic; patterns of cooperation and opposition varied issue by issue. Austria and Britain worked together in Italy to check potential French and Russian influence, even as Austria tried to maintain close relations with Russia, and Britain and France with one another. France, similarly, courted Austrian and Russian cooperation to thwart British plans to police the abolition of the African slave trade in the Atlantic and the Barbary corsairs in the Mediterranean, and in general the French proved the Great Power most likely to disrupt the collective security arrangements of the Vienna order, as with their intervention in Spain on behalf of the royalists in the 1820s, or the unilateral conquest of Algiers in 1830.

But its role in the genesis of a new international security system was but one of many ways in which the experience of the Vienna Congress continued to shape and to illuminate European political culture deeper into the nineteenth century, as a formative stage of development and as an iconic point of reference in memory. The question has sometimes been asked whether the Congress of Vienna, or the end to the Napoleonic era generally, are too exceptional to draw broader conclusions. But it is precisely such exceptional or liminal moments that disclose much that ordinarily remains hidden beneath the surface of politics and culture. Reasons range from the mundane—such events can leave behind larger bodies of evidence—to the epistemologically profound, having to do with the role of moments of rupture and reknitting in our more modern (or postmodern) understandings of culture. But also, much of what I have described was less of the passing moment than most imagine, and instead looked quite similar in the years before and the years following the Congress. The varied and colorful festive and consumer culture investigated here did not spring newborn onto the scene in 1814, or even 1813, nor did it fade away thereafter. After a brief caesura in the 1830s, monarchical meetings and symbolic panoply became still more central features of political culture and the public sphere, in the age of "invented traditions" up to the First World War, as did the related military display and militarism within society. The nineteenth century also saw the continued growth of visual spectacles like panoramas and of political memorabilia, both oppositional and patriotic.[4] The press, public opinion, and government press policy, if anything, became even more important components of domestic and international politics in ensuing decades, and still more so in the late nineteenth-century age of mass politics and mass-circulation dailies.[5]

Even the important political roles of women and salon culture, perhaps the most controversial claim, had not only a prehistory but also a continuation that was more than epilogue. The Prince de Ligne, as we have seen, passed away in 1814, and Caroline Pichler's *salonnière* mother, Charlotte Greiner, in 1815. After the Congress, Julie Zichy died in 1816, Madame de Staël in 1817, and Fanny Arnstein in 1819, all great losses to salon culture and its networks, but political salons continued in Europe past 1830 and beyond, whether one looks to Lady Holland, Countess Lieven, and Madame Swetchine in London and Paris, to Henriette von Crayen and Bettina von Arnim in Berlin, or still to Talleyrand and Dorothea, future Duchess of Sagan.[6]

At all these levels, understanding the political culture of the Vienna Congress era offers insights into what came later. Even the shifting balance of revolutionary, liberal, and conservative ideas and forces has to be examined as a process of change over several years, at least through 1819, rather than posited as a simple conservative restoration in 1814 or 1815. While political confrontations in individual instances often settled into bipolar left-right conflicts, the dividing line was a moveable one across a political spectrum that was tripartite rather than bipolar, and European rather than solely statewide or national in scope. Only against this background can one follow the mixed fortunes of the constitutional promises of 1814–1815, or the growing divisions among the Great Powers that undermined the Congress System. Even after the 1830 revolutions, Metternich and Prussia not only agreed to independence for a constitutional Belgium but continued to press the Papal States to adopt reforms and consultative institutions of the sort prevalent in Habsburg Italy.[7] Similarly with regard to nationalism, even in the Habsburg Empire up to the First World War, desires for federalist autonomy still outweighed those for full independence of the "secessionist nationalism" sort.

Almost before the ink had dried on the Vienna settlement in June 1815, news came of Napoleon's second and definitive defeat at Waterloo. Before long, from Vienna and from the various Allied headquarters, rulers and diplomats descended on Paris to celebrate another victory and to negotiate another peace. And, as before in Vienna, they were joined by many of Europe's social and cultural elite, this time including more of the British and of course more of those who made Paris the center of their lives, including men such as Benjamin Constant and Alexander von Humboldt, and women such as Madame Vaudémont and Madame Récamier. Jean-Gabriel Eynard and his young wife Anna also joined Charles Pictet de Rochemont again in the Genevan and Swiss causes, and Anna again kept an insightful diary, this time filled with critical commentary on the Allied occupation and peace policy, which she thought unjustly and dangerously harsh on the French and the newly re-restored Bourbon regime (an opinion she shared not just with Talleyrand but with her friends and admirers Lord Castlereagh and Tsar Alexander).[8] The Vienna salon scene was in part transported to Paris, from Metternich and the Castlereaghs to Molly Zichy and Metternich's cousin Countess Wrbna, the Duchess of Courland and her daughters Dorothea and the Duchess of Sagan, and the latter's rival Princess Bagration. Karl Varnhagen von Ense encouraged his wife Rahel and the Arnstein ladies to come to Paris and keep open house for the Prussians and the German-minded, a move, he claimed, that enjoyed Hardenberg's support.[9]

The salons of Paris in 1815 most famously included that of the religious revivalist Baroness Krüdener, the spiritually hothouse atmosphere that nurtured the Holy Alliance of Tsar Alexander, through the religious networks of Roxandra Stourdza, Jung-Stilling, and Franz Baader, and indeed of Capodistrias and Baron Stein, and Madame de Staël and Benjamin Constant. Military festivities, too, took center stage once more, with massive parades saluting the Allies' entries, grand reviews of the occupation armies, and the most spectacular of them all: the symbolically charged two-day review of the Russian army on the Champ de Vertus, at once a testament to Russian military might and a celebration of the Holy Alliance and its brand of ecumenical evangelical religion.[10] More than the Holy Alliance, the Second Peace of Paris that emerged from this renewed congress ambiance joined Vienna's Final Act as part of the Vienna settlement that for many years to come structured European international relations. The Holy Alliance, too, however, still played a part in the new international system. As Hildegard Schaeder argued long ago, it was disingenuous of Metternich to claim that the Holy Alliance simply sank from view after its signing, never to be referred to again in diplomatic discourse. As she noted, recourse to it helped resolve the impasse at the Congress of Aachen in 1818, and even before that, Louis XVIII was pleased to be invited to sign on, as an indication that he was again persona grata in the international community, despite the fact that France was excluded from the Quadruple Alliance, which for the moment defined the ranks of Great Powers. Even the British prince regent, though famously not a formal adherent to the Holy Alliance when promulgated in 1815, was happy to accede in 1817 when he was asked again to sign as ruler of Hanover.[11]

The planners of the successor diplomatic gathering in Aix-la-Chapelle or Aachen (the German name of the by-then Prussian town) tried hard not to term it a congress, so as to lower the expectations for this follow-up to the Congress of Vienna. Already by the time of the event itself in the autumn of 1818, however, popular usage had prevailed, and diplomats too knew it as the Congress of Aachen, as it has been called ever since. The planners also made efforts to change the nature of the gathering from what had been seen in Vienna, with less display, less involvement of salon culture, and reduced presence of the sovereigns on the social scene.[12] Talleyrand, had he been present, would no doubt have approved the latter as contributing to reestablish monarchical dignity, even as he might have regretted both of the former. Congress organizers had more luck in this endeavor than they had with the nomenclature, but even here only within limits. The Eynards, present on this occasion to represent the interests of Lucca rather than Geneva, remarked somewhat nostalgically on the fact that they rarely saw Tsar Alexander and the other rulers as they had in Vienna. On the other hand they also noted that the crowned heads seemed to inspire the public with more awe and enthusiasm on the occasions when they were sighted, so to that extent they remained true to their preference for a salutary distance between royals and nonroyals they had expressed four years before.[13]

The Eynards also captured the differences in the salon scene between Vienna and Aachen. Lord and Lady Castlereagh formed the center of Congress sociability even more this time, admittedly with less competition, but neither did the social space occupied previously by the salons of Princess Bagration, the Duchess of Sagan, and the Zichys go unclaimed in the new gathering. In this case it was Madame Catalani, the era's most famous diva of the opera stage, who was able to trade on her celebrity and privileged status (and on her intimate relationships with figures such as the Duke of Wellington) to serve as a hub of Congress society, at least for the male diplomatic world. (Opera singers still remained beyond the pale for many ladies, including Lady Castlereagh.)[14] So far as one can tell, Catalani was not herself political in the same way as her predecessors, even if her salon served political as well as entertainment functions. At the same time, however, her position as artist in some ways reproduced the advantages of social outsider status that had helped make Jewish homes centers of salon culture, in facilitating the mixing of those of different views and social statuses. If nothing else, the fact that Madame Catalani's establishment assumed the role of Congress social nexus as an unintended consequence of the effort to bypass salons and *salonnières* underscores the institution's importance in the diplomatic culture and society of the day. Something similar almost had to be present as a social lubricant in order for the system to function smoothly.

Although the organizers had taken pains to emphasize that the gathering was meant to deal almost exclusively with problems involving the end to the Allied occupation of France (plus abolition of the slave trade, the Barbary corsairs, Jewish rights, and certain other pressing matters), Aachen also saw its share of lobbyists arrive to plead the claims of various special interests. The evangelical Reverend Lewis Way, for example, secured an audience with Tsar Alexander as part of his twin campaigns for abolition and Jewish emancipation, and the socialist philanthropist Robert Owen also appeared to promote reform of the capitalist system in the interests of the working classes. Anna Eynard for one was intrigued by him, but he ultimately came away unsuccessful.[15]

Succeeding congresses, as often noted, met in more out-of-the way locations, but then, Carlsbad and Teplitz (Teplice) in particular were themselves hubs of Central European spa and salon culture. As Metternich wrote of the Congress of Ljubljana, women were sometimes outnumbered by the diplomats, but female society was present, and in addition to the beauties of its natural surroundings the town offered quite passable Italian opera. The final congress of the cycle took place in the more urbane Verona and returned to being something like the society spectacle seen in Vienna. Thus the congresses never entirely departed from the Vienna template for the new-style summit diplomacy. Friedrich Gentz therefore remained happiest with the conference at Moravian Troppau (Opava) in 1820, as it involved fewer distractions and allowed everyone to focus on work. The return to a high-society atmosphere in Verona two years later left him correspondingly disappointed.[16]

In part as a matter of direct continuities, but also as a question of approach, the new understandings of the Congress of Vienna and of post-Napoleonic political culture presented here bear implications for the study of political culture and diplomacy in the long nineteenth century more generally, and beyond. Not least significant is the recognition that one must be careful about thinking of states or governments as unitary entities following clearly defined policy trajectories, whether set by a ruler or a leading statesman; far from monolithic, these institutions comprised a range of figures often pursuing different aims. As Christopher Clark showed in his study of the origins of the First World War, this fact remained as fatefully true in the more bureaucratic age after 1900 as it had been in the Napoleonic and post-Napoleonic eras.[17]

With respect to diplomacy and diplomatic history, one of this book's most important contributions is to demonstrate the limitations of narratives and explanations that focus narrowly on power politics. Or, putting this another way, the conceptions of "power" and "politics" are too often construed too narrowly; a widened definition of power politics can be very useful. It is certainly the case that rulers, statesmen, and their various advisors and favorites tried to calculate their own interests or those of the states they represented, reckoning at the same time the interests, strengths, and weaknesses of the other protagonists in the diplomatic arena in the effort to see how far they could push their own positions short of war, or indeed, up to and including warfare as an extension of politics. But, as has been amply shown, early nineteenth-century European political culture was much broader, richer, and more complex than this diplomatic game and its notes and intrigues. As a consequence, so too was the international system intermeshed with this political culture.

What I have called influence politics occupied a central place within both the political culture and the international system. Influence in part implies the persuasive and manipulative efforts of a larger circle of court and government figures beyond the coteries immediately surrounding the ruler, but it extends more widely still. The same calculating rulers and statesmen often cast an eager or a worried eye to the various levels of the public and public opinion, concerned about how some contemplated action would look or be received. They responded to arguments heard in salons or read in newspapers, periodicals, and pamphlets, and launched their own in turn. The nature of rhetoric being what it is, a matter of give and take, neither the arguments nor the positions and policies behind them remained unchanged in this process. Moreover, statesmen not infrequently tried to keep image and reality from becoming so widely discrepant that the words would lose all credibility. Most European governments were a little less cynical in this respect, or at least more subtle, than Napoleon had been, with his propaganda strategy of the big lie, repeatedly if not necessarily convincingly told.

Nor did this wider political culture simply frame how arguments were made and how they were disseminated. Even in the most power-political showdowns, such as that over Poland and Saxony, the diplomatic outcomes were shaped by and emerged from it as well. Perceptions of public opinion formed some of the contours on the landscape of political culture, not just in Britain but in the continental monarchies too, even (to a limited extent) including Russia. With respect to the central question of the Congress, the Prussian claims on Saxony, the necessity of facing public opinion influenced the positions of both Metternich and Castlereagh in crucial ways, and perhaps of Alexander. Even the Prussians, for all their propaganda activity, and for all that they confronted a public back home with very different views, ultimately found it impossible to ignore the weakness of their public relations position. The tendency to soften compromises or territorial exchanges with constitutional solutions, and at times to offer limited concessions to national identities, also resulted in part from a belief that the political publics and even the masses desired it.

In arguing for the importance of influence politics and broader political culture in nineteenth-century diplomacy, the point is not that Metternich or Castlereagh or Hardenberg were forced to abandon cherished political goals if these clashed with the perceived expression of public opinion in the press or salons; that would be a high benchmark to set for proving influence on policy from any direction. Rather, statesmen and rulers were constrained by, moved by the pressure of various levels of public. In the battles over Poland and Saxony, Metternich's position remained not unlike Castlereagh's faced with parliamentary Britain—he had to consider not just the desires of his ruler or the opinions of military advisors and court favorites, but also the mutterings or loudly spoken views of Austrian and European high society in the salons, or the opinions of writers in the world of print, some of whom might have been fronts for various governments, many of whom, though, were not. Hardenberg and the Prussians were caught in several double binds, having to navigate the various hostile social circles in Vienna even as they retreated into the more Prusso-friendly atmosphere of Fanny Arnstein's salon, or confronted the reportedly chauvinistic-aggrandizing salon scene back in Berlin. At the very least, there can be no question that statesmen considered public opinion in determining how to realize their goals and how to combat those of their opponents. Not only did they think of the best arguments to float in salon circles or newspapers but also they assessed the state of public opinion in other states when calculating how to deal with them. Alexander's problems with public opinion at home and abroad regarding his Polish plans, and Castlereagh's worries about being held hostage over abolition, given the strength of British opinion on the subject, illustrate the same phenomenon. Public opinion was important, or at least statesmen believed it was, given how much time they spent thinking about it and trying to manage it.

Even if one could find a particular issue that really did follow almost solely the dictates of Realpolitik and diplomatic calculation, even under the terms of realist analysis one would have to recognize that that particular negotiation was connected through such calculations and through the give-and-take of diplomacy with numerous other issues that were not so restricted. Any negotiation forms part of a web of negotiations in which movement in one area immediately or indirectly causes movements in the others as well. Hence any analysis of diplomatic history in this era (and likely in many others as well, including our own) must take into account the embeddedness of diplomacy and its actors in the wider and deeper culture and political culture. Or, put another way, the set of actors, agents, and contexts needs to be widened and deepened, to include more of the officials' and unofficial advisors' roles in decision-making, as well as the influence of salons and festivities, court culture and display, the political press and the politically engaged cultural press, and—more diffusely but omnipresent—the influence of literature, theater, and spectacle, and of the market for music, images, and material culture. All of these helped create a public opinion that either did influence or was thought to influence political decision-making (and if it was thought to, then at least that imagined public opinion did influence it).

At the same time, these wider cultural influences provided not just the backdrop or the context but also the very matrix and stimuli by which rulers, statesmen, and the politically aware more generally were molded, and from which they drew ideas and motivation. According to some schools of thought, ideas do not matter much in history, or at least, it is easier for scholars to assert ideas' importance than to demonstrate it in specific cases. Hence the effort here to trace the paths of ideas within the process of political decision-making as precisely and in as continuous a line as possible. Rulers and statesmen, like the members of the various politically aware publics surrounding them, drew on and invoked existing beliefs and putative knowledge in order to make their calculations and formulate their proposals and policies: beliefs about the nature and proper practice of politics; beliefs about the nature of the states and nations with whom they had to deal, whether their own, or their potential allies or enemies; beliefs about the rights and duties of sovereigns and various classes of subjects and citizens; and religious beliefs. In other words, ideology, assumptions, and even stereotypes entered into the equations, as practitioners of the "new international history" have recognized, above all for the twentieth century. Objectivity and impartial rationality perhaps figured less as a "noble dream" in the context of diplomacy and power politics than in historical scholarship, but they proved no easier to achieve for statesmen than for historians.[18]

In saying that ideas mattered, however, one should not think that they came in any purer a form than the diplomatic calculations, shorn of personalities and contexts, deceptions and self-deceptions, varied understandings and misunderstandings. One should speak of "ideas and attitudes" or mentalities rather than just ideas, but here, too, with the proviso that this involves not just a matter of individuals but also of groups and cultures, of existing tropes and stereotypes, of the networks and media as well as the messages that propagated through them. The lessons of the linguistic turns, even if not accepted in their entirety, have implications that cannot be ignored. Diplomats and rulers, *salonnières* and writers were also products of times and places (to put it in historicist terms) and operated within discourses, political languages, and social systems, practices, habitus, and language games (in postmodern frameworks) that were inherited and unquestioned as much as they were consciously manipulated in pursuit of individuals' aims. There were boxes outside of which it was difficult to think, and rhetorical envelopes that could only be pushed so far, even as countless individuals and groups constantly tried to stretch them in different directions in the process of political contestation, more often with an eye only to immediate goals rather than to the broader ideological landscape. Actors' individual intentions and agency did not exclude the role of social and cultural (post)structures, but rather sat—and sit—in relationship to them. Similarly, to highlight intention and agency underscores the fact that consequences were very often unintended.

And whether one thinks in terms of culture concepts, or in terms of a society composed of insider and small-world networks, it is important to emphasize that the ideas, attitudes, and people all formed part of a web. They responded to impulses from distant portions of that web, and initiated others that were felt far afield in turn. People in London, Rome, and St. Petersburg were not so far removed from those in Paris, Vienna, and Berlin as one might at first think. Beliefs and arguments in one context, say, regarding abolition of the slave trade or Greek liberation, exerted pressures on other beliefs and arguments in other contexts, as matters of both ideological consistency, sociability, and politics. The impulses and pressures did not just pass in two directions, along direct lines of connection, but were almost always linked laterally to still others in ways that involved further influences via indirect mediated paths, through the power of weak ties as well as strong ones, in a complex network or web of interactions that can and should be thought of in partly organic or holistic terms. Such webs constitute historical fields, or perhaps better historical ecologies. They hold as much at the level of culture as at that of society and politics, and of social and political networks. Historical ecologies mark another way in which diplomatic negotiations always form part of a larger web of relationships, and their complexity offers another reason why unintended consequences remain so prevalent. Difficult as they are for historians to trace, these complex connections often proved even harder for contemporaries to perceive, predict, or control.

The Vienna settlement, though landmark, did not ultimately settle as much as many later historians thought. And contemporaries knew that was the case. They recognized that much of what had been achieved could be set in something that could pass for stone, and that the provisions for a new European order could be given all the weight of international law and public opinion to a degree not seen since the Peace of Westphalia in 1648 (if then). The "Final Act of the Congress of Vienna" carried that kind of legal, diplomatic, and rhetorical weight, in part as the result of conscious efforts by Metternich, Clancarty, and others to make it so. As Metternich put it in the set of instructions to his new ambassador in St. Petersburg, Baron Lebzeltern (the ones that could be shown to the tsar), the Vienna and Paris treaties formed "the new code of European public law." A modern historian, too, considers that the Vienna settlement "actually created a new basic law for Europe." While Metternich's private instructions also pointed to the treaties as a means of checking Tsar Alexander's ambitions, he still considered the treaties and the role of public opinion paramount: the "noble" system adopted "creates an immense force of opinion, which has become the foremost of the powers of our century."[19] Metternich's right hand, Friedrich Gentz, saw no reason why the peace should not hold for a very long time on this new basis.[20]

But contemporaries also knew that this new order in part constituted only a framework for continued negotiation, and that the agreements hammered out with such pain and care were to some extent provisional and represented only a temporary pause or truce, a mutually acceptable resting point from which the contest could be taken up anew in future. As we have seen, for just about every question there was a coda, often involving follow-up negotiations, that carried on further into the nineteenth century. This way of looking at diplomatic history derives from considering both the power struggles carried on in very real terms, and the problem of nonfixity of meaning in textual interpretation. The two issues are not as far apart as many often think. Words, whether spoken or printed on a page (including the page of a treaty), can have powerful and lasting influences, but they do not have only one unambiguous meaning. Nor are words frozen in an everlasting and unchanging present; rather, they emerge from complex prior chains of contested dialog, and simultaneously form points of departure and ongoing reference for future discussion. Even more perhaps than in normal texts and interpretation, the words that appear in signed treaties can still bear the traces of previous formulations and of the previous desires and claims that went with them, claims that may have been partly but not wholly altered or defeated in the course of negotiation, or that may simply be in abeyance. This was perhaps clearest in the case of the Jewish rights clause in the German federal constitution, where the change of that one little preposition marked a victory of sorts for the anti-Jewish forces, but did not fundamentally change the nature of the issues, the sides, or the stakes in the tug-of-war that continued for the next nine years and more. But such multivalence characterized other struggles too, as with the clause on estates-based constitutions or the reconstruction of the Catholic Church (to stay with German affairs), or abolition of the slave trade, or the Greeks of the Ionian Isles and the mainland itself.

The Vienna settlement that emerged from the Vienna Congress was therefore less carved in stone than might seem the case, and at the same time its solemn solidity as the basis for a regime of international security guarantees rested on partly mythic foundations. Yet the impression of impressiveness ultimately helped lend the Vienna settlement the requisite moral weight in nineteenth-century international relations to buttress a lasting peace, within a diplomatic and political culture that did not work solely from foreign office to foreign office but on numerous other levels as well. There were many complex pathways whereby politics and diplomacy occurred, and a wide range of men and women who participated in the process. Examining the Congress of Vienna has revealed the workings of this world in motion, at a pivotal moment of emergence, and as it endured—and evolved—through the eve of the First World War.

Notes

Abbreviations

ÖStA   Österreichisches Staatsarchiv (Vienna)
    HKR   Hofkriegsrat
    KA   Kriegsarchiv

StAB   Staatsarchiv der Freien Hansestadt Bremen

TNA   The National Archives of the United Kingdom (Kew)
    CO   Colonial Office
    FO   Foreign Office

WStLA   Wiener Stadt- und Landesarchiv

PRINTED PRIMARY SOURCES

Angeberg, *Congrès*   Comte d'Angeberg [pseud. J. L. Chodźko]. *Le Congrès de Vienne et les traités de 1815.* 4 vols. Paris: Aymot, 1863.

Fournier, *Geheimpolizei*   August Fournier. *Die Geheimpolizei auf dem Wiener Kongress. Eine Auswahl aus ihren Papieren.* Vienna: F. Tempsky, 1913.

Humboldt, *Briefen*   Anna von Sydow, ed. *Wilhelm und Caroline von Humboldt in ihren Briefen.* 7 vols. Berlin: Mittler, 1906–16.

Klüber, *Acten*   J. L. Klüber. *Acten des Wiener Congresses in den Jahren 1814–1815.* 9 vols. Erlangen: Palm, 1815–19.

Pallain, ed., *Correspondance*   Georges Pallain, ed. *Correspondance inédite du Prince de Talleyrand et du Roi Louis XVIII pendant le Congrès de Vienne.* Paris: Plon, 1881.

Rinieri, ed., *Corrispondenza*   Ilario Rinieri, ed. *Corrispondenza inedita dei cardinali Consalvi e Pacca nel tempo del congresso di Vienna, 1814–1815.* Turin: Unione tipografico, 1903.

Sbornik   Sbornik Imperatorskago russkago istoricheskago obshchestva [Journal of the Imperial Russian Historical Society]

Staegemann, *Olfers*   Hedwig Abeken. *Hedwig v. Olfers, geb. v. Staegemann, 1799–1891: Ein Lebenslauf.* Berlin: Mittler, 1908.

Stolberg, *Tagebuch*   Henrich zu Stolberg-Wernigerode. *Tagebuch über meinen Aufenthalt in Wien zur Zeit des Congresses vom 9. September 1814 bis zum April 1815.* Edited by Doris Derdey, Konrad Breitenborn, and Uwe Lagatz. Halle a. d. Saale: Stekovics, 2004.

Vneshniaia   USSR Ministry of Foreign Affairs. *Vneshniaia politika rossii XIX I nachala XX veka. Dokumenty rossikogo Ministerstva inostrannykh del.* Ser. 1. 8 vols. Moscow: 1960–72.

Webster, *Diplomacy*   Charles K. Webster, ed. *British Diplomacy 1813–1815: Select Documents Dealing with the Reconstruction of Europe.* London: Bell, 1921.

Weil, *Dessous*   M-H Weil. *Les Dessous du Congrès de Vienne, d'après les documents originaux des archives du Ministère imperial et royal de l'intérieur à Vienne.* 2 vols. Paris: Librairie Payot, 1917.

Wellesley, ed., *Suppl. Desp.*   Arthur Wellesley, ed. *Supplementary Despatches, Correspondence and Memoranda of Field Marshal Arthur Duke of Wellington, K.G.* 15 vols. London: Murray, 1858–72.

Introduction

1. Including more on festivities: Susan Mary Alsop, *The Congress Dances* (New York: Harper & Row, 1984); Klaus Günzel, *Der Wiener Kongress: Geschichte und Geschichten eines Welttheaters* (Munich: Koehler & Amelang, 1995); David King, *Vienna 1814: How the Conquerors of Napoleon Made Love, War, and Peace at the Congress of Vienna* (New York: Three Rivers Press, 2008); Adam Zamoyski, *Rites of Peace: The Fall of Napoleon and the Congress of Vienna* (New York: HarperCollins, 2007); Gregor Dallas, *1815: The Roads to Waterloo* (London: Richard Cohen, 1996); Charles-Otto Zieseniss, *Le Congrès de Vienne et l'Europe des princes* (Paris: Belfond, 1984); Jean Bourgoing, *Vom Wiener Kongress: Zeit und Sittenbilder* (Brno: Callwey, 1943). With a diplomatic focus: Charles Webster, *The Congress of Vienna 1814–1815* (London: Bell, 1950 [1919]); Harold Nicolson, *The Congress of Vienna: A Study in Allied Unity: 1812–1822* (New York: Compass, 1961); Enno E. Kraehe, *Metternich's German Policy*, vol. 2, *The Congress of Vienna* (Princeton, NJ: Princeton University Press, 1983); Thierry Lentz, *Le congrès de Vienne: Une refondation de l'Europe 1814–1815* (Paris: Perrin, 2013); Heinz Duchhardt, *Der Wiener Kongress. Die Neugestaltung Europas 1814/15* (Munich: Beck, 2013); Mark Jarrett, *The Congress of Vienna and its Legacy: War and Great Power Diplomacy after Napoleon* (London: I.B. Tauris, 2013); Jacques-Alain de Sédouy, *Le Congrès de Vienne: L'Europe contre la France 1812–1815* (Paris: Perrin, 2003); Guido Gigli, *Il Congresso di Vienna (1814–1815)* (Florence: Sansoni, 1938); Karl Griewank, *Der Wiener Kongress und die europäische Restauration 1814/15*, 2nd ed. (Leipzig: Koehler & Amelang, 1954); Heinz Duchhardt, *Gleichgewicht der Kräfte, Convenance, Europäisches Konzert: Friedenskongresse und Friedensschlüsse vom Zeitalter Ludwigs XIV. bis zum Wiener Kongress* (Darmstadt: Wissenschaftliche Buchgesellschaft, 1976); Paul Schroeder, *The Transformation of European Politics, 1763–1848* (New York: Oxford University Press, 1994).
2. For the *Öffentlichkeit* model, Jürgen Habermas, *Strukturwandel der Öffentlichkeit: Untersuchungen zu einer Kategorie der bürgerlichen Gesellschaft* (Neuwied: Luchterhand, 1971 [orig. 1962]). For both good accounts and critiques of it: Craig Calhoun, ed., *Habermas and the Public Sphere* (Cambridge, MA: MIT Press, 1992); James M. Brophy, *Popular Culture and the Public Sphere in the Rhineland, 1800–1850* (Cambridge: Cambridge University Press, 2007), 1–6, 304–305; T.C.W. Blanning, *The Culture of Power and the Power of Culture: Old Regime Europe 1660–1789* (Oxford: Oxford University Press, 2002), 2–15; James Van Horn Melton, *The Rise of the Public in Enlightenment Europe* (Cambridge: Cambridge University Press, 2001); Andreas Gestrich, "The Public Sphere and the Habermas Debate," *German*

History 24, 3 (2006): 413–430; and Harold Mah, "Phantasies of the Public Sphere: Rethinking the Habermas of Historians," *Journal of Modern History* 72 (March 2000): 153–182.

3. Henry Kissinger, *A World Restored: Metternich, Castlereagh and the Problem of Peace 1812–1822* (London: Phoenix, 2000 [1957]).

4. Ute Planert, *Der Mythos vom Befreiungskrieg. Frankreichs Kriege und der deutsche Süden: Alltag—Wahrnehmung—Deutung 1792–1841* (Paderborn: Schöningh, 2007); Karen Hagemann, *"Mannlicher Muth und teutsche Ehre": Nation, Militär und Geschlecht zur Zeit der Antinapoleonischen Kriege Preußens* (Paderborn: Schöningh, 2002); Katherine B. Aaslestad, *Place and Politics: Local Identity, Civic Culture and German Nationalism in North Germany during the Revolutionary Era* (Leiden: Brill, 2005); Michael Rowe, *From Reich to State: The Rhineland in the Revolutionary Age, 1780–1830* (Cambridge: Cambridge University Press, 2003); John L. Tone, *The Fatal Knot: The Guerilla War in Navarre and the Defeat of Napoleon in Spain* (Chapel Hill: University of North Carolina Press, 1997); Michael Broers, *Europe under Napoleon, 1796–1815* (London: Arnold, 1996).

5. A point also noted by Andreas Fahrmeir, *Europa zwischen Restauration, Reform und Revolution 1815–1850* (Munich: Oldenbourg, 2012), 129.

6. See for example the contributions by Paul W. Schroeder, Enno E. Kraehe, Robert Jervis, and Wolf D. Gruner in the special forum "Did the Vienna Settlement Rest on a Balance of Power?," *American Historical Review* 97, 3 (1992): 683–735.

7. Brendan Simms, *The Impact of Napoleon: Prussian High Politics, Foreign Policy and the Crisis of the Executive, 1797–1806* (Cambridge: Cambridge University Press, 1997), 8, 27–28, and passim.

8. On Ideas in Context: James Tully, ed., *Meaning and Context: Quentin Skinner and His Critics* (Princeton, NJ: Princeton University Press, 1988); Eckhart Hellmuth and Christoph von Ehrenstein, "Intellectual History Made in Britain: Die Cambridge School und ihre Kritiker," *Geschichte und Gesellschaft* 27, 1 (2001): 149–172.

9. I draw more on newer theories of complex social networks than on Bruno Latour's actor-network theory: Bruno Latour, *Reassembling the Social: An Introduction to Actor-Network-Theory* (Oxford: Oxford University Press, 2007).

10. By concentrating attention on the intersection between politics and culture, my book draws inspiration from the "new international history," the German "new political history," and recent studies of the "culture of power": Blanning, *Culture of Power;* Peter Jackson, "Pierre Bourdieu, the 'Cultural Turn' and the Practice of International History," *Review of International Studies* 34, 1 (2008): 155–181; Wolfram Pyta, "Kulturgeschichtliche Annäherungen an das europäische Mächtekonzert," in Pyta and Philipp Menger, eds., *Das europäische Mächtekonzert: Friedens- und Sicherheitspolitik vom Wiener Kongreß 1815 bis zum Krimkrieg 1853* (Cologne:

Böhlau, 2009), 1–24; Ute Frevert, "Neue Politikgeschichte: Konzepte und Herausforderungen," in Frevert and Heinz-Gerhard Haupt, eds., *Neue Politikgeschichte: Perspektiven einer historischen Politikforschung* (Frankfurt a. M: Campus, 2005), 7–26; Ursula Lehmkuhl, "Diplomatiegeschichte als internationale Kulturgeschichte: Theoretische Ansätze und empirische Forschung zwischen Historischer Kulturwissenschaft und Soziologischem Institutionalismus," *Geschichte und Gesellschaft* 27, 3 (2001): 394–423; Wilfried Loth and Jürgen Osterhammel, eds., *Internationale Geschichte: Themen—Ergebnisse—Aussichten* (Munich: Oldenbourg, 2000); and the contributions in Hamish Scott and Brendan Simms, eds., *Cultures of Power in Europe during the Long Eighteenth Century* (Cambridge: Cambridge University Press, 2007), esp. Hamish Scott, "Diplomatic Culture in Old Regime Europe," 58–85.

11. Jarrett, *Congress*; Zamoyski, *Rites*; Kissinger, *World Restored*; Sédouy, *Congrès*; Nicolson, *Congress*.

12. Johannes Paulmann, *Pomp und Politik. Monarchenbegegnungen in Europa zwischen Ancien Régime und Erstem Weltkrieg* (Paderborn: Schöningh, 2000), 72, 114; "Europe sans distances," in Charles-Maurice de Talleyrand-Périgord, *Mémoires du Prince de Talleyrand*, Albert de Broglie, ed., 5 vols. (Paris: Lévy, 1891), 2:420; similarly in Rinieri, ed., *Corrispondenza*, 65–66, Consalvi to Pacca, 1 Nov. 1814: "sparire le distanze."

13. Rose Weigall, ed., *The Letters of Lady Burghersh (afterwards Countess of Westmorland) from Germany and France during the Campaign of 1813–14*, [facs.] (n. p.: Elibron, 2006 [1893]); A. de Nesselrode, ed., *Lettres et papiers du Chancelier Comte de Nesselrode 1760–1850. Extraits de ses archives*, 11 vols. (Paris: Lahure, n.d. [1904–12]), vol. 5.

14. Nesselrode, ed., *Lettres*, 5:25, Nesselrode to Countess Marie, 25 Jan. 1813.

15. Dorothy Gies McGuigan, *Metternich and the Duchess* (Garden City, NY: Doubleday, 1975), 70–71.

16. Webster, *Congress*; Dallas, *Roads to Waterloo*.

17. Leipzig, Griewank, *Kongress*, 118; early planning documents: HHStA NeuZerem.A.R. XV Hofreisen 1814, Kart. 318.

18. M. de Pradt, *Du Congrès de Vienne*, 2 vols. (Paris, 1815), 1:145.

19. Claire Gantet, *La paix de Westphalie (1648). Une histoire sociale, XVIIe–XVIIIe siècles* (Paris: Belin, 2001).

20. David Cannadine, "Splendor out of Court: Royal Spectacle and Pageantry in Modern Britain, c. 1820–1977," in Sean Wilentz, ed., *Rites of Power: Symbolism, Ritual, and Politics since the Middle Ages* (Philadelphia: University of Pennsylvania Press, 1985), 206–243, 206–207.

21. Even Kraehe, *Policy*, 2:267–269, which suggests that Metternich tried not to expose Hardenberg to the tsar, ends up showing that he did.

22. Kraehe, *Policy*, vol. 2.

23. See Latour, *Reassembling*, 136–137, 146–147, 154, on the inherent value of description and of tracing connections in social analysis.

1. Peace and Power in Display

1. On court and ceremony organization, Karin Schneider, "Das Wiener Zeremoniell im 19. Jahrhundert. Ein Ausblick," in Irmgard Pangerl, Martin Scheutz, and Thomas Winkelbauer, eds., *Der Wiener Hof im Spiegel der Zeremonialprotokolle (1652–1800): Eine Annäherung* (Innsbruck: Studien-Verlag, 2007), 627–638.

2. The Viennese *Friedensblätter* noted the girls as an example of the "participation" of "private persons" in the arrival ceremony, no. 41, 4 Oct. 1814, 169; identified as "burghers' daughters" in Franz Patzer, ed., *Wiener Kongreßtagebuch 1814/1815. Wie der Rechnungsbeamte Matthias Franz Perth den Wiener Kongreß erlebte* (Vienna: Jugend und Volk, 1981), 39. Other accounts: *Oesterreichischer Beobachter,* no. 269, 26 Sept., 1460; *Times* (London), 12 Oct., no. 9339. In general on Congress festivities: Manfred Kandler, "Die Feste des Kongresses," in Walter Koschatzky, ed., *Der Wiener Kongress 1. September 1814 bis 9. Juni 1815. Ausstellung veranstaltet vom Bundesministerium für Unterricht gemeinsam mit dem Verein der Museumsfreunde* (Vienna, 1965), 247–258; Gregor Dallas, *1815: The Roads to Waterloo* (London: Richard Cohen, 1996); Jean Bourgoing, *Vom Wiener Kongress: Zeit und Sittenbilder* (Brno: Callwey, 1943). Earlier roots of burgher participation, Karl Vocelka, "Höfische Feste als Phänomene sozialer Integration und internationaler Kommunikation. Studien zur Transferfunktion habsburgischer Feste im 16. und 17. Jahrhundert," in Andrea Langer and Georg Michels, eds., *Metropolen und Kulturtransfer im 15./16. Jahrhundert. Prag-Krakau-Danzig-Wien* (Stuttgart: Steiner, 2001): 141–150, 142–144, 146. Metternich's complaint, Maria Ullrichová, ed., *Clemens Metternich—Wilhelmine von Sagan. Ein Briefwechsel 1813–1815* (Graz: Böhlau, 1966), 265, 25 Sept. 1814.

3. Johannes Paulmann, *Pomp und Politik. Monarchenbegegnungen in Europa zwischen Ancien Régime und Erstem Weltkrieg* (Paderborn: Schöningh, 2000), 30, 36–37, 44–46. Paulmann emphasizes the new beginning of monarchical meetings in the 1830s but mentions the Vienna Congress as precursor, 15, 72.

4. T. C. W. Blanning, *The Culture of Power and the Power of Culture: Old Regime Europe 1660–1789* (Oxford: Oxford University Press, 2002), 2–15; James Van Horn Melton, *The Rise of the Public in Enlightenment Europe* (Cambridge: Cambridge University Press, 2001).

5. Vanessa Schwartz, *Spectacular Realities: Early Mass Culture in Fin-de-Siècle Paris* (Berkeley: University of California Press, 1998); Denise Z. Davidson, "Women at Napoleonic Festivals: Gender and the Public Sphere during the First Empire," *French History* 16, 3 (2002): 299–322; Andreas Gestrich, *Absolutismus und Öffentlichkeit: Politische Kommunikation in Deutschland zu Beginn des 18. Jahrhunderts* (Göttingen: Vandenhoeck & Ruprecht, 1994), 13–15, 19, 118–125; Matthias Schwengelbeck, *Die Politik des Zeremoniells. Huldigungsfeiern im langen 19. Jahrhundert* (Frank-

furt a. M.: Campus, 2007), 19–21; Thomas Biskup, "The Transformation of Ceremonial: Ducal Weddings in Brunswick, c. 1760–1800," in Karin Friedrich, ed., *Festive Culture in Germany and Europe from the Sixteenth to the Twentieth Century* (Lauriston, NY: Mellen, 2000), 169–186.

6. *Friedensblätter,* no. 40, 1 Oct. 1814, 166.

7. Patzer, ed., *Kongreßtagebuch,* 95–99, 29 Mar. to 2 May 1815, plus coverage in newspapers and the *Friedensblätter.*

8. Markus Völkel, "The Margravate of Brandenburg and the Kingdom of Prussia: The Hohenzollern Court 1535–1740," in John Adamson, ed., *The Princely Courts of Europe: Ritual, Politics and Culture under the Ancien Régime 1500–1750* (London: Seven Dials, 2000): 211–229, 226 quote, 228 on influence, including the two Hessens and Joseph II's Austria; Philip Mansel, "Monarchy, Uniform and the Rise of the *Frac,* 1760–1830," *Past & Present* 96, 1 (1980): 103–132, 111.

9. Scott Hughes Myerly, *British Military Spectacle: From the Napoleonic Wars through the Crimea* (Cambridge, MA: Harvard University Press, 1996), 9.

10. Mansel, "Uniform," passim; 119 notes the adoption of uniforms for Habsburg court officials in 1793 and for state administration "soon afterwards," but the process was still ongoing in 1814: HHStA StK Vorträge 195, folder VIII, fols. 164–166v, report of Metternich, 22 Aug., and fols. 204–205v, report of Trauttmansdorff, 28 Aug.; Franz's original request to Metternich, folder IV–VI, fols. 49–51v, 25 Apr. 1814; Metternich's proposed new regulation, with copperplate illustration, StK Vorträge 196, folder IX, fol. 183, 28 Sept. 1814; and correspondence in OMeA 208 (1814), no. 388.

11. Karl August Varnhagen von Ense, *Denkwürdigkeiten und vermischte Schriften,* 2nd ed., 5 vols. (Leipzig, 1843), 3:268, "Ernst und Tüchtigkeit." Eric Hobsbawm and Terence Ranger, eds., *The Invention of Tradition* (Cambridge: Cambridge University Press, 1992).

12. [Anon.], *Der Congreß zu Erfurt, enthaltend eine vollständige und zuverlässige Nachricht von allen Feierlichkeiten die daselbst während der Anwesenheit Napoleons I. Alexander I. Friedrich August I. und anderen hohen Personen statt gefunden* (Dresden, n.d. [1808]).

13. Myerly, *Military Spectacle,* 8, 140.

14. Quote, Patzer, ed., *Kongreßtagebuch,* 49.

15. Quote, *Journal der Kunst, Literatur, Luxus und Mode,* Dec. 1814, p.779. On the Enlightenment discourse of the Volksfest, Schwengelbeck, *Politik des Zeremoniells,* 108–111, 130–151; Karin Friedrich, introduction to Friedrich, *Festive Culture,* 1–15, 9; and Dieter Düding, "Einleitung," in Düding, Peter Friedmann, and Paul Münch, eds., *Öffentliche Festkultur. Politische Feste in Deutschland von der Aufklärung bis zum Ersten Weltkrieg* (Reinbek: Rowohlt, 1988), 10–24.

16. See Werner Telesko, *Geschichtsraum Österreich. Die Habsburger und ihre Geschichte in der bildenden Kunst des 19. Jahrhunderts* (Vienna: Böhlau, 2006), 143, on trends toward a nationalization of monarchies after 1815

when "the public paid homage" not just to the ruler but "to an image binding monarch and citizen which can be termed an 'imagined community' of
a nation."

17 Patzer, ed., *Kongreßtagebuch*, 42; Heun [pseud. Heinrich Clauren], *Kurze
Bemerkungen auf langen Berufswegen*, 2 vols. (Dinkelsbühl, 1815–16), 2:23;
Stolberg, *Tagebuch*, 21.

18. Krafft's painting, *Friedensblätter*, no. 39, 29 Sept. 1814, 159–160, copperplate facing 162; Werner Telesko, *Kulturraum Österreich. Die Identität der
Regionen in der bildenden Kunst des 19. Jahrhunderts* (Vienna: Böhlau,
2008), 43–44, emphasizes that Krafft painted the work on his own initiative, before the emperor purchased it as an exemplar to other Austrian
artists in 1815. The engraving by Carl Rahl also circulated independently
outside the *Friedensblätter*, and a print by Blasius Höfel appeared soon
after (43).

19. Alphons v. Klinkowström, *Friedrich August v. Klinkowström und seine
Nachkommen* (Vienna, 1877), 144, 177, 183.

20. For the concerns of Schwarzenberg, Metternich, and the emperor about impressing Congress guests, HHStA Kriegsakten 428 (1814–1815), fols.
252–253, Schwarzenberg to Metternich, 11 Aug. 1814 (with Franz's agreement); StA England 151, Fasz. 3, fols. 71–72, Merveldt to Metternich, 22
Sept. 1814. Extra pay, ÖStA KA HKR SR Norm. Hübler 39, p.696, no.
621, and p.712, no. 645, 12 and 22 Sept. 1814; extra tickets, KA Gen.
Kmdo. Wien 1814, Q 1–3, Kart. 191, Q 3 56/13, 3 Oct. 1814. See Josef Karl
Mayr, *Wien im Zeitalter Napoleons. Staatsfinanzen, Lebensverhältnisse,
Beamte und Militär* (Vienna: Gistel, 1940), 233.

21. "Tagebuch Steins während des Wiener Kongresses," in Erich Botzenhart
and Walther Hubatsch, eds., *Freiherr vom Stein Briefe und amtliche Schriften*,
11 vols. (Stuttgart: Kohlhammer, 1957–74), 5:316–386, 324.

22. *Diario di Roma*, no. 37, 9 Nov. 1814, copy in HHStA StK Rom 6, Berichte
1814, fols. 346–347; *Vossische Zeitung*, no. 122, 11 Oct. 1814. On the
press's role in reaching different layers of public for royal display, Paulmann, *Pomp*, 285, 287–288.

23. *Oesterreichischer Beobachter*, no. 276, 3 Oct. 1814, 1501; 2 and 9 Oct.,
Patzer, ed., *Kongreßtagebuch*, 45, 51.

24. *Vossische Zeitung*, no. 127, 22 Oct. 1814.

25. Carl E. Schorske, *Fin-de-Siècle Vienna: Politics and Culture* (New York:
Vintage, 1981); Allan Janik, "Vienna 1900 Revisited: Paradigms and Problems," in Steven Beller, ed., *Rethinking Vienna 1900* (New York: Berghahn,
2001), 27–56, 36–39; Frank Huss, *Der Wiener Kaiserhof. Eine Kulturgeschichte von Leopold I. bis Leopold II* (Gernsbach: Katz, 2008), 222–226;
Jeroen Duindam, *Vienna and Versailles: The Courts of Europe's Dynastic
Rivals, 1550–1780* (Cambridge: Cambridge University Press, 2003), 134–135,
140–142.

26. Duindam, *Vienna*, 143; Daniel L. Unowsky, *The Pomp and the Politics of
Patriotism: Imperial Celebrations in Habsburg Austria, 1848–1916* (West

Lafayette, IN: Purdue University Press, 2005), 16–17, 26, 29–30; Anna Coreth, *Pietas Austriaca,* trans. William D. Bowman and Anna Maria Leitgeb (West Lafayette, IN: Purdue University Press, 2004), 23–26, 67–68; Winfried Romberg, *Erzherzog Carl von Österreich. Geistigkeit und Religiosität zwischen Aufklärung und Revolution* (Vienna: Österreichische Akademie der Wissenschaften, 2006), 267–272, 279–283.

27. GMD, Sophie Schlosser Tagebuch, 1814/1815, fol. 24, 23 Mar. (Catholic convert), "rührend," and "christlicher Demuth"; Lutheran Pietist Stolberg, *Tagebuch,* 208, 23 Mar., "edifying and touching."

28. *Vossische Zeitung,* no. 128, 25 Oct. 1814; Perth termed the event a "Kirchenparade," Patzer, ed., *Kongreßtagebuch,* 56.

29. Johann Friedrich Novák, ed., *Briefe des Feldmarschalls Fürsten Schwarzenberg an seine Frau 1799–1816* (Vienna, 1913), 408 (15 Oct. 1814; the previous letter of 8 Oct. did not mention the fest); original idea for a chapel at Worlik with annual festival and Te Deum, 349 (23 Oct. 1813). Planning documents, from 12 Oct.: ÖStA KA HKR Präs 1814 (8/11–10/20).

30. For the other celebrations in Germany, see Dieter Düding, "Das deutsche Nationalfest von 1814: Matrix der deutschen Nationalfeste im 19. Jahrhundert," in Düding et al., eds., *Öffentliche Festkultur,* 67–88 (also typically with mixed military and religious components); Karen Hagemann, *"Mannlicher Muth und teutsche Ehre": Nation, Militär und Geschlecht zur Zeit der Antinapoleonischen Kriege Preußens* (Paderborn: Schöningh, 2002), 481–491; Ute Planert, *Der Mythos vom Befreiungskrieg. Frankreichs Kriege und der deutsche Süden: Alltag—Wahrnehmung—Deutung 1792–1841* (Paderborn: Schöningh, 2007), 613–619 (more skeptical of the depth and breadth of sentiment); and Karl Hoffmann, ed., *Des Teutschen Volkes feuriger Dank- und Ehrentempel, oder Beschreibung wie das aus zwanzigjähriger französischen Sklaverei durch Fürsten-Eintracht und Volkskraft gerettete Teutsche Volk die Tage der entscheidenden Völker- und Rettungsschlacht bei Leipzig am 18. und 19. Oktober 1814. zum ersten Male gefeiert hat* (Offenbach, 1815), 670–675 for the Vienna festivities.

31. Of numerous descriptions: HHStA ZA Prot. 47, fols. 211v–219; *Friedensblätter,* nos. 50/51, 25 and 27 Oct. 1814, 205–206, 210; *Vossische Zeitung,* no. 128, 25 Oct. 1814; Anna Eynard, Journal, BGE Ms suppl 1959, 25–30, 19 Oct.; Stolberg, *Tagebuch,* 63–65, 18 Oct.

32. Anna Eynard, Journal, BGE Ms suppl 1959, 27, 19 Oct.; Clauren, *Kurze Bemerkungen,* 2:56.

33. Anton Diabelli, *Der 18.te October, oder: Das grosse militarische Prater-Fest in Wien, gefeyert bey Anwesenheit der hohen und höchsten Monarchen, zum Andenken an die unvergessliche Völker-Schlacht bey Leipzig. Ein Tongemählde für das Pianoforte, über ein Gedicht von Kanne componirt* (Vienna: Steiner, n.d. [1814]), 10; Adalbert Gyrowetz, *SIEGES- und FRIEDENSFEST der verbündeten MONARCHEN, gefeyert im Prater und dessen Umgebungen am 18ten October 1814, als am Jahrstage der Völkerschlacht bey Leipzig, eine*

charakteristische Fantasie für das Pianoforte (Vienna: Thaddäus Weigl, n.d. [1814]), 6, and similar language, 3.

34. J.M. Raich, ed., *Dorothea v. Schlegel geb. Mendelssohn und deren Söhne Johannes und Philipp Veit. Briefwechsel,* 2 vols. (Mainz, 1881), 2:280, Dorothea to Philipp, 19 Oct. 1814.

35. Patzer, ed., *Kongreßtagebuch,* 59; print by Johann Schönberg in Stolberg, *Tagebuch,* 69.

36. Diabelli, *Der 18.te October,* 14–15.

37. On girls in white in Austrian festive tradition, Stella Musulin, *Vienna in the Age of Metternich: From Napoleon to Revolution 1805–1848* (Boulder, CO: Westview, 1975), 109; Hagemann, *Muth,* 476, 478–479, similarly in troop welcome ceremonies in Prussia; Hagemann generally emphasizes the limits to women's public participation, suggesting their restriction to helping with preparations: 462–475.

38. Patzer, ed., *Kongreßtagebuch,* 46, 96, 3 Oct. 1814, 12 Apr. 1815. Women's continued role in festive culture, even militaristic, also holds for the Napoleonic prototype: Davidson, "Women at Napoleonic Festivals." In general, Jean H. Quataert, *Staging Philanthropy: Patriotic Women and the National Imagination in Dynastic Germany, 1813–1916* (Ann Arbor: University of Michigan Press, 2001); Dirk Alexander Reder, *Frauenbewegung und Nation. Patriotische Frauenvereine in Deutschland im frühen 19. Jahrhundert (1813–1830)* (Cologne: SH-Verlag, 1998).

39. K.K. Oesterreich. Museum für Kunst und Industrie, *Katalog der Wiener-Congress-Ausstellung 1896* (Vienna: Verlag des K.K. Oesterreich. Museums, 1896), 61, no. 218; *Friedensblätter,* no. 69, 8 Dec. 1814, 284.

40. HHStA ZA Prot. 47 (1813–1814), fol. 244v, 12 Dec. 1814; A. Michailowsky-Danilewsky, *Erinnerungen aus den Jahren 1814 und 1815,* trans. Karl R. Goldhammer (Dorpat, 1837), 115, for speech; alternate version, with blush, in Alexandre Sapojnikov, "The Congress of Vienna in the Memoirs of a Russian Officer," in Ole Villumsen Krog, ed., *Danmark og Den Dansende Wienerkongres. Spillet om Danmark / Denmark and the Dancing Congress of Vienna. Playing for Denmark's Future* (Copenhagen: Christiansborg Slot, 2002), 140. Maria Ludovica had likewise blessed banners and participated in parades during the 1809 campaign: Philip Mansel, *Prince of Europe: The Life of Charles-Joseph de Ligne 1735–1814* (London: Weidenfeld & Nicolson, 2003), 229; Musulin, *Vienna,* 66–67.

41. Hagemann, *Muth,* 465–469.

42. Caroline Pichler, *Denkwürdigkeiten aus meinem Leben,* ed. Emil Karl Blüml, 2nd ed., 2 vols. (Munich: Müller, 1914), 2:31–32; Roxandra Countess Edling, *Mémoires de la comtesse Edling (née Stourdza), demoiselle d'honneur de Sa Majesté l'Impératrice Élisabeth Alexéevna* (Moscow, 1888), 182.

43. Diabelli, *Der 18.te October,* 14.

44. *Friedensblätter,* no. 48, 20 Oct. 1814, 197–198, including comments on choice of piece (also a frequent observation in letters and diaries). Anon.,

Biographie des Adalbert Gyrowetz (Vienna, 1848), 62–63, on the London concerts; quote, HHStA OMeA 207 (1814), Fasz. 2, no. 348½, Dietrichstein to Trauttmansdorff, 23 June. On the *Musikfreunde* and their links to the Society of Noble Ladies, Eduard Hanslick, *Geschichte des Concertwesens in Wien* [facs.] (Farnborough, England: Gregg, 1971 [1869]), 79, 145–151.

45. For Volksfest planning documents and Jan's negotiations with court officials: HHStA ZA Prot. 47, fols. 163–164, 173–174, 203; Neu.ZA, R XV, Hofreisen 1814, Kart. 318, nos. 57, 60; OMeA 207 (1814), Fasz. 1; KK 37 (1814), nos. 372–1127, no. 833 (Wallis, with Franz's decision, 12 Nov.).

46. For accounts see *Oesterreichischer Beobachter*, no. 281, 8 Oct. 1814, 1531, and no. 282, 9 Oct., 1537–1538 (toasts); *Friedensblätter*, no. 44 , 11 Oct. 1814, 182 (including Hoftraiteur Jan's role); and Patzer, ed., *Kongreßtagebuch*, 48–50. The army's report, ÖStA KA Gen. Kmdo. Wien 1814, Q 1–3, Kart. 191, Q 3 56/14, 7 Oct., noting both Sergeant Platzer's and the emperors' toasts.

47. [Franz Xaver Carl Gewey], *Briefe des neu angekommenen Eipeldauers an seinen Herrn Vettern in Kakran. Mit Noten von einem Wiener (Eipeldauer Briefe)*, Heft 1, letter 3 (1815): 29–30. Torn dresses, Elise von Bernstorff, *Ein Bild aus der Zeit von 1789 bis 1835. Aus ihren Aufzeichnungen* (Berlin: Mittler, 1896), 156; slow fireworks, Anna Eynard, Journal, BGE Ms suppl 1959, 7, 6 Oct.

48. Staegemann, *Olfers*, 226, 3 Oct. 1814; *Hesperus,* no. 1, Jan. 1815, 1.

49. For comparison with Prussia, Hagemann, *Muth*, 395, 417–427, 473–475.

50. HHStA OMeA 207 (1814), Fasz. 2, no. 348½. Aloys Weissenbach, *Der Einzug des Kaisers Franz I in Wien. Im Junius 1814* (Vienna, 1814), reported as giving proceeds to wounded army doctors, in Joseph Rossi, ed., *Denkbuch für Fürst und Vaterland*, 2 vols. (Vienna, 1814–15), 2:5. Charitable concerts, Hanslick, *Concertwesens*, 145, 160, 175–184.

51. OMeA 207 (1814), no. 327, "Nachricht von dem grossen Volksfeste"; *Oesterreichischer Beobachter*, no. 281, 8 Oct. 1814, 1531. See also the *Times* and *Morning Chronicle* of London, 22 Oct., both from Brussels papers.

52. Friedrich Ludwig Zacharias Werner, *Nachgelassene Predigten* (Vienna, 1836), 95, 14 Nov. 1814.

53. On national identity as mediated through local and regional identities: Celia Applegate, *A Nation of Provincials: The German Idea of Heimat* (Berkeley: University of California Press, 1990); Alon Confino, *The Nation as a Local Metaphor: Württemberg, Imperial Germany, and National Memory, 1871–1918* (Chapel Hill: University of North Carolina Press, 1997); Maiken Umbach, *Federalism and Enlightenment in Germany, 1740–1806* (London: Hambledon Press, 2000); Dieter Langewiesche and Georg Schmidt, eds., *Föderative Nation: Deutschlandkonzepte von der Reformation bis zum Ersten Weltkrieg* (Munich: Oldenbourg, 2000); for similar notions by the Prussian Congress plenipotentiary Wilhelm von Humboldt, Brian Vick, "Of Basques, Greeks, and Germans: Liberalism, Nationalism, and the Ancient

Republican Tradition in the Thought of Wilhelm von Humboldt," *Central European History* 40, 4 (2007): 653–681.

54. Telesko, *Kulturraum,* 287–288, 351–352, 355. On the blending of civic and ethnic elements of national identity in the first half of the nineteenth century generally, Brian E. Vick, *Defining Germany: The 1848 Frankfurt Parliamentarians and National Identity* (Cambridge, MA: Harvard University Press, 2002).

55. Telesko, *Geschichtsraum,* 48–52, 314–320, quotes 51; Walter Consuelo Langsam, *The Napoleonic Wars and German Nationalism in Austria* (New York: Columbia University Press, 1930), 26–27, 32, 58–59, 73–74; Hellmuth Rößler, *Österreichs Kampf um Deutschlands Befreiung: Die deutsche Politik der nationalen Führer Österreichs 1805–1815,* 2 vols. (Hamburg: Hanseatische Verlagsanstalt, 1940), 1:356, 363–367, 429; for similar ideas by Friedrich Schlegel within the same network, Ernst Behler, *Friedrich Schlegel* (Reinbek: Rowohlt, 1966), 112–117. On fascination with national *Tracht,* in the context of the nationalization of (provincial) landscapes, Telesko, *Kulturraum,* 430–433.

56. Theophil Antonicek, *Musik im Festsaal der Österreichischen Akademie der Wissenschaften* (Vienna: Böhlau, 1972), 35–38; Esteban Buch, *Beethoven's Ninth: A Political History,* trans. Richard Miller (Chicago: University of Chicago Press, 2003), 63; Hanslick, *Concertwesens,* 149 (folk songs). Lübeck's Congress delegate understood the folk song collection to include a "German national music library" and arranged a gift of old manuscripts from Lübeck: Michael Hundt, *Lübeck auf dem Wiener Kongreß* (Lübeck: Schmidt-Römhild, 1991), 41. Karen Hagemann, "'Be Proud and Firm, Citizens of Austria!' Patriotism and Masculinity in Texts of the 'Political Romantics' Written during Austria's Anti-Napoleonic Wars," *German Studies Review* 29, 1 (2006): 41–62, 49–51 on "regional-patriotic poetry" appealing to other groups than just German. Quote, Heinrich J. von Collin, *Lieder Oesterreichischer Wehrmänner. Erste Abtheilung* (Vienna, 1809), 5; Collin also stressed Habsburg protection of civil liberties as part of the empire's patriotic appeal (6).

57. J.H. Elliott, "A Europe of Composite Monarchies," *Past & Present* 137 (1992): 48–71, 70, with reference to H.G. Koenigsberger's lecture "*Dominium Regale* or *Dominium Politicum et Regale.* Monarchies and Parliaments in Early Modern Europe," in Koenigsberger, *Politicians and Virtuosi: Essays in Early Modern History* (London: Hambledon Press, 1986), 1–25.

58. Telesko, *Kulturraum,* quote, 15, 379, and 379–381 on the Johanneum, founded in 1811, which involved a set of associations and publications as well as the museum itself; on the mutually constitutive relationships between central and provincial identities, 380, 447.

59. *Oesterreichischer Beobachter,* no. 281, 8 Oct. 1814, 1531; "Nationaltänze" in Perth also, Patzer, ed., *Kongreßtagebuch,* 49; temples, AHL Familienarchiv Hach, V, vol. A, Fasz. 2, no. c5, Tagebuch, p. 21, 7 Oct. 1814. The *Eipeldauer Briefe* identified the dancers' march in the festival's entrance

procession as a representation of the "costumes of the Austrian monarchy": issue 1, letter 1 (1815), 40.

60. Schindler's Friedensfest, Wien Museum Karlsplatz, Inv. no. 45.953, 1815; "Favoritspiel für Gesellschaften," *Wiener Zeitung,* no. 110, 20 Apr. 1815, "Allgemeines Intelligenzblatt," 753.

61. Joseph Sonnleithner, *Die Weihe der Zukunft. Eine allegorisch-dramatische Dichtung zur Feyer der Zurückkunft Seiner Majestät des Kaisers Franz* (Vienna, 1814); performance covered in *Allgemeine musikalische Zeitung,* no. 29, 20 July 1814, 489–490; on the anthem and the significance of collective singing practices, Buch, *Beethoven's Ninth,* 55–60, and Nicholas Mathew, *Political Beethoven* (Cambridge: Cambridge University Press, 2013), 150–156. Mathew finds the song more "supranational" than national (154) but also quotes the final verse, which emphasizes the joining of Franz's "peoples" as "One, through brotherly bonds" (152).

62. Bernstorff, *Bild,* 159 (whether German, Hungarian, or Romanian not specified); B. Schulze-Schmidt, *Bürgermeister Johann Smidt, das Lebensbild eines Hanseaten. Ein Erinnerungsbuch* (Bremen: Leuwer, 1913), 352–353; Wilhelm von Bippen, *Johann Smidt: Ein hanseatischer Staatsmann* (Stuttgart: Deutsche Verlags-Anstalt, 1921), 163. Quote, *Oesterreichischer Beobachter,* no. 317, 13 Nov. 1814, 1733. Metternich also planned to welcome Tsar Alexander with a small mock Russian village for a festival in his garden, complete with actual Russians imported to hail the tsar's entry in appropriate dialect and sing Russian folk tunes. The mix of dynastic and folk-national elements of patriotism again emerges, this time spotlighting the Russian Empire: HHStA StK Kongressakten 1, Fasz. 2, fols. 252–252v.

63. Anna Eynard, Journal, BGE Ms suppl 1959, 64–67, 8 and 9 Nov. 1814.

64. HHStA OMeA 207 (1814), no. 327, Jan's final accounting to court officials, 26 Oct. On the popularity of Tyrolean singers at the time, Mathew, *Political Beethoven,* 153–154.

65. Charles-Otto Zieseniss, *Le Congrès de Vienne et l'Europe des princes* (Paris: Belfond, 1984), 65, citing the notoriously unreliable memoirs of Count de la Garde.

66. Enno E. Kraehe, *Metternich's German Policy,* vol. 2, *The Congress of Vienna* (Princeton, NJ: Princeton University Press, 1983), 196.

67. *Oesterreichischer Beobachter,* no. 293, 20 Oct., 1598–1599; *Chronik des allgemeinen Wiener Kongresses,* no. 7, 25 Oct., 117.

68. Subsidy accounts, HHStA OMeA 209 (1814), no. 450, and StK Notenwechsel, Noten a.d. Obersthofmeisteramt 7 (no fol.), 14 Sept. 1814 and 19 Mar. 1815; laurel, Edouard Chapuisat, ed., *Au Congrès de Vienne. Journal de Jean-Gabriel Eynard* (Paris: Plon-Nourrit, 1914), 48; gowns, oak and olive, Dorothy Gies McGuigan, *Metternich and the Duchess* (Garden City, NY: Doubleday, 1975), 365. "Teilöffentlichkeit": Wolfgang Piereth, *Bayerns Pressepolitik und die Neuordnung Deutschlands nach den Befreiungskriegen* (Munich: Beck, 1999), 3–4; and Gestrich, *Absolutismus,* 75–134.

Piereth and Gestrich rightly emphasize that display was also addressed to wider publics and broader media were employed to do so.

69. Weil, *Dessous,* 1:339.

70. This had long been the case in Vienna, especially compared to Versailles: Jeroen Duindam, "The Courts of the Austrian Habsburgs c. 1500–1750," in Adamson, ed., *Princely Courts,* 165–187, 178, 187.

71. Tickets numbers, HHStA ZA Prot. 47, fols. 200–200v, 2 Oct.; Musulin, *Vienna,* 26–27, on the Habsburg tradition of open ridottos; stolen silverware, Zieseniss, *Congrès,* 63.

72. Anna Eynard, Journal, BGE Ms suppl 1959, 21–22, 13 Oct., noted the social mix and King Friedrich Wilhelm's presence; the rulers' appearance also recorded in the official court protocols: HHStA ZA Prot. 47, fol. 210v, 12 Oct. 1814. Three florins admission price: *Friedensblätter,* no. 8, 19 Jan. 1815, 32; on the Apollosaal's opulence, Mayr, *Wien,* 127–128.

73. Pallain, ed., *Correspondance,* 103–104, 6 Nov. 1814; Chapuisat, ed., *Journal,* 99–100, 9 Nov. 1814.

74. Ibid., 99 (quote), 251, 254–256; Anna Eynard, Journal, BGE Ms suppl 1959, 60–61, 6 Nov. 1814.

75. Chapuisat, ed., *Journal,* 246, 9 Jan. 1815.

76. *Friedensblätter,* nos. 42 and 57, 6 Oct. and 10 Nov. 1814, 174, 236.

77. Sapojnikov, "Memoirs," 134–155, 142.

78. Schulze-Schmidt, *Smidt,* 338, 353 quote.

79. Eva Giloi, *Monarchy, Myth, and Material Culture in Germany 1750–1950* (Cambridge: Cambridge University Press, 2011); Hubertus Büschel, *Untertanenliebe. Der Kult um deutsche Monarchen 1770–1830* (Göttingen: Vandenhoeck & Ruprecht, 2006).

80. Edling, *Mémoires,* 115–116; [anon. ed.], *Aus Karls von Nostitz, weiland Adjutanten des Prinzen Louis Ferdinands von Preußen, und später russischen General-Leutnants, Leben und Briefwechsel* (Dresden, 1848), 130.

81. Charles Webster, *The Congress of Vienna 1814–1815* (London: Bell, 1950 [1919]), 135.

82. Ruth Katz, "The Egalitarian Waltz," *Contemporary Studies in Society and History* 15, 3 (1973): 368–377.

83. Anna Eynard, Journal, BGE Ms suppl 1959, 195–196, 10 Jan. 1815. Anna and Prince Eugène tried but failed to repeat the happenstance.

84. Anna Eynard, Journal, BGE Ms suppl 1959, 16, 10 Oct. 1814; Jean-Gabriel, Chapuisat, ed., *Journal,* 15, 116–117.

85. Nostitz, *Leben,* 149, diary, Jan. 1815. On the ennui of polonaise-centered events, Bourgoing, *Kongress,* 112–113.

86. *Friedensblätter,* no. 47, 18 Oct. 1814, 194; HHStA NeuZerem.A.R. XV Hofreisen 318 (1814), no. 57/370, Trauttmansdorff to Kaiser, 16 Feb.

87. For detailed description of precursor carousels from the eighteenth century, including the "Ladies' Carousel" of Maria Theresia, see Stefan Seitschek, "Karussel und Schlittenfahrt im Spiegel der Zeremonialprotokolle—Nicht

mehr als höfische Belustigungen?," in Pangerl et al., eds., *Wiener Hof,* 357–434, 359–385.

88. Staegemann, *Olfers,* 252–253, Staegemann to Elisabeth, 25 Nov. 1814.

89. *Hesperus,* no. 9, Feb. 1815, 66. Orientalist scholar Joseph von Hammer-Purgstall also remarked on the circumstance, and that on a later occasion the Turkish representative lodged a protest, whereupon the Turkish heads were replaced by Moorish: entry of 1 Dec. 1814 in his *Erinnerungen aus meinem Leben,* vol. 3 of Walter Höflechner and Alexandra Wagner, eds., *Joseph von Hammer-Purgstall: Erinnerungen und Briefe* (Graz: Zentrum für Wissenschaftsgeschichte, Karl-Franzens-Universität Graz, 2011), 90: available at the website of the University of Graz Zentrum für Wissenschaftsgeschichte, http://gams.uni-graz.at/hp/pdf/5_Exzerpt.pdf (accessed 13 Dec. 2012).

90. Gaston Palewski, ed., *Le miroir de Talleyrand: Lettres inédites à la duchesse de Courlande pendant le Congrès de Vienne* (Paris: Perrin, 1976), 70, 74, 17 Nov. and 24 Nov. 1814.

91. Pichler, *Denkwürdigkeiten,* 2:44–46; *Journal der Literatur, Kunst, Luxus und Mode,* Jan. 1815, 35–38, Pichler's poem, "Die Wiener Frauen des sechzehnten Jahrhunderts," 37–38, already in *Der Sammler,* no. 199, 13 Dec. 1814, 795; Pichler essay, "Ueber eine Nationalkleidung für Teutsche Frauen," Feb. 1815, 67–82. Karin Wurst, "Fashioning a Nation: Fashion and National Clothing in Bertuch's *Journal des Luxus und der Moden,"* *German Studies Review* 28, 2 (2005): 367–386.

92. Langsam, *German Nationalism,* 135.

93. Rossi, *Denkbuch,* 1:63, 64, 85. Rossi's volumes detailed the festivities in Vienna and much of the empire. On the language of love and fatherhood in Habsburg official imagery, and in Rossi, Telesko, *Geschichtsraum,* 153–157.

94. Rossi, *Denkbuch,* 1:83, 90.

95. Descriptions: *Journal der Literatur, Kunst, Luxus und Mode,* Jan. 1815, 35–38; *Oesterreichischer Beobachter,* no. 330, 26 Nov. 1814, 1801–1802. Anna Eynard, Journal, BGE Ms suppl 1959, 83, 24 Nov.; Sapojnikov, "Memoirs," 142.

96. Christoph v. Felsenthal, *Die Feyer des Fürstenbundes in der Kaiserstadt. Am Schlusse 1814* (Vienna, n.d. [1814]), 12–13; *Morgenblatt für gebildete Stände,* no. 301, 17 Dec. 1814, 1203. On Rudolph's centrality to Habsburg imagery, Telesko, *Geschichtsraum,* 15, ch. 6.

97. Matthäus Loder prints, T. Mollo and Company, "Vier Gruppen vom Karussel in der Winterreitschule," Wien Museum Karlsplatz Inv. no. 32.726a–d, noted in Koschatzky, ed., *Kongress,* 261; Artaria, "Karousel," Österreichische Nationalbibliothek Bildarchiv, Inv. no. LW-72588-C. Cf. Kandler, "Feste," 250–252, following the unreliable memoirs of Count de la Garde.

98. *Friedensblätter,* no. 67, 3 Dec. 1814, 275; *Morgenblatt für gebildete Stände,* no. 301, 17 Dec., 1203–1204; *Hesperus,* no. 9, Feb. 1815, 67, also had the

participants "im prachtvollsten Costume der altdeutschen Kraft und Zierlichkeit" ("in the most splendid costume of old-German force and delicacy").

99. Both points, WStLA Hauptregistratur A37 Dept. W Ceremoniale 3 (1815–1816), no no., Kirchenmeisteramt to Stadt Magistrat, 19 Jan. 1815.

100. Stolberg, *Tagebuch,* 161.

101. Martyn Lyons, *Napoleon Bonaparte and the Legacy of the French Revolution* (Basingstoke, England: Macmillan, 1994), ch. 12.

102. Gisela Pellegrini, "Sigismund Ritter von Neukomm, ein vergessener Salzburger Musiker," *Mitteilungen der Gesellschaft für Salzburger Landeskunde* 76 (1936): 1–67, 22–24 on the Congress.

103. [No ed.], *Correspondance du Comte de Jaucourt, Ministre Intérimaire des Affaires Étrangères, avec le Prince de Talleyrand pendant le Congrès de Vienne* (Paris: Plon-Nourrit, 1905), 174, Jaucourt to Talleyrand, 1 Feb. 1815.

104. Saint-Marsan, Rinieri, ed., *Corrispondenza,* LXIX; *Eipeldauer Briefe,* issue 4, letter 2 (1815), 38.

105. *Moniteur universel,* no. 30, 30 Jan. 1815, 117–118. Metternich's *Oesterreichischer Beobachter* did not print the sermon but referenced the *Moniteur,* no. 43, 12 Feb. 1815, 238.

106. *Chronik,* Beilage no. 13, 31 Jan. 1815, 549; Hermann Freiherr v. Egloffstein, ed., *Carl Bertuchs Tagebuch vom Wiener Kongreß* (Berlin: Paetel, 1916), 102–103, and Bertuch's published critique in *Journal der Literatur, Kunst, Luxus und Mode,* Mar. 1815, 163–166, including suspicion of Talleyrand's motives; Nostitz, *Leben,* 159; Saint-Marsan "apparat mesquin," Rinieri, ed., Corrispondenza, LXIX; AHL ASA DB A3,2, fol. 100v, Hach to Curtius, 21 Jan. 1815.

107. *Friedensblätter,* no. 9, 21 Jan 1815, 36; *Moniteur,* 30 Jan.

108. Translating the French translation in the *Moniteur* (117), as opposed to the Latin "may fear thy name."

109. Patzer, ed., *Kongreßtagebuch,* 82–83.

110. "Crescendo," in liner notes by Hartmut Krones, trans. John A. Phillips, to Sigismund Neukomm, *Messe de Requiem,* conducted by Jörg Ewald Dähler (CD, Camerata, CM-555, 2002); the notes also emphasize the intensity of the Last Judgment section.

111. Patzer, ed., *Kongreßtagebuch,* 84; *Chronik,* Beilage no. 13, 31 Jan. 1815, 550.

112. Friedrich Campe of Nuremberg, "Feierliches Seelenamt für weiland Sᵉ Majestät Ludwig XVI. Den 21. Jänner 1815," Anne S.K. Brown Military Collection, Center for Digital Scholarship, Brown University Library, Eu (1805–1821) Europe.

113. *Oesterreichischer Beobachter,* no. 23, 23 Jan. 1815, 127–128; Weil, *Dessous,* 2:98–99, two letters of Gentz to Dalberg, 23 Jan.; Pallain, ed., *Correspondance,* 240, 257, Talleyrand to Louis, 25 Jan. 1815, and Louis to Talleyrand, 4 Feb.

114. DASS, Kirchenmeisteramt Kart. 17, Konzepte (1815–1821), "Auszugsprotocoll," fol. 2477v; Cölestin Wolfsgruber, *Sigismund Anton Graf Hohen-*

wart Fürsterzbischof von Wien (Graz: Styria, 1912), 252, Talleyrand letter of 26 Aug. 1815; Pallain, ed., *Correspondance,* 257–258, Louis to Talleyrand, 4 Feb. 1815; HHStA StK Interiora Korresp. 68, fol. 194, Metternich to Hudelist, Paris, 29 Aug. 1815.

115. *Sbornik* 112:143, Paris, 30 Jan. 1815; cf. Talleyrand's instructions, Jaucourt, *Correspondance,* 162–163, 21 Jan.

2. Selling the Congress

1. *Friedensblätter,* no. 40, 1 Oct. 1814, 166. Emphasizing with respect to occasional music how "the Congress was constructed as a historic moment in large part by the art that mediated it for public consumption," and how that music itself drew on the visual language of public festivals and spectacle for its structure, Nicholas Mathew, *Political Beethoven* (Cambridge: Cambridge University Press, 2013), 68–89, quote 70.

2. Vanessa Schwartz, *Spectacular Realities: Early Mass Culture in Fin-de-Siècle Paris* (Berkeley: University of California Press, 1998); emphasizing the historical dimension, Maurice Samuels, *The Spectacular Past: Popular History and the Novel in Nineteenth-Century France* (Ithaca, NY: Cornell University Press, 2004), 33–41, Curtius, 19–26.

3. Denise Blake Oleksijczuk, *The First Panoramas: Visions of British Imperialism* (Minneapolis: University of Minnesota Press, 2011); Stephan Oettermann, *The Panorama: History of a Mass Medium,* trans. Deborah Lucas Schneider (Zone: New York, 1997); Silvia Bordini, *Storia del Panorama. La visione totale nella pittura del XIX secolo* (reprint, Rome: Edizioni Nuova Cultura, 2006 [1984]).

4. Before the later development of the "Diorama" by Daguerre, the focus of Heinz Buddemeier, *Panorama, Diorama, Photographie. Entstehung und Wirkung neuer Medien im 19. Jahrhundert* (Munich: Fink, 1970), 25–32; Karin Wurst, *Fabricating Pleasure: Fashion, Entertainment, and Cultural Consumption in Germany (1780–1830)* (Detroit: Wayne State University Press, 2005), 337–341; Bernard Comment, *The Panorama,* trans. Anne-Marie Glasheen (London: Reaktion, 1999), 57–63; Richard D. Altick, *The Shows of London* (Cambridge, MA: Harvard University Press, 1978), 120–126, 198–199.

5. Victoria Johnson, *Backstage at the Revolution: How the Royal Paris Opera Survived the End of the Old Regime* (Chicago: University of Chicago Press, 2008); Wurst, *Fabricating Pleasure,* 329–330; Altick, *Shows,* 120, 184–185.

6. Altick, *Shows,* 136; similarly Bordini, *Storia,* 196–197.

7. Buddemeier, *Panorama,* 164–170, quote 168–169; Oettermann, *Panorama,* 32, 222–223, likens the demand for "visual information" in panoramas to that for knowledge in newspapers and travel literature; Veronica della Dora, "Putting the World into a Box: A Geography of Nineteenth-Century 'Traveling Landscapes,'" *Geografiska Annaler* 89, 4 (2007): 287–306, on

panoramas and smaller-scale visual formats in the spread of geographic knowledge; Wurst, *Fabricating Pleasure,* 335–336, 342–345, emphasizes the opposition between Enlightenment print-driven educational culture of the written word and the visual entertainment culture that experienced a resurgence in the late eighteenth century, with panoramas and dioramas for entertainment more than education.

8. Comment, *Panorama,* 8, 25 (Porter); Oettermann, *Panorama,* 115–118; Seringapatam printed guide, Victoria and Albert Museum, London, E.572-1926. Bordini, *Storia,* 242–243, 245, for Paris and Berlin panoramas.

9. Mario Alexander Zadow, *Karl Friedrich Schinkel. Leben und Werk,* 3rd ed. (n.p.: Menges, 2003), 52–55. Buddemeier, *Panorama,* 41, posits a slow shift toward novelty of setting between 1800 and 1820, but it occurred almost immediately.

10. Evelyn J. Fruitema and Paul A. Zoetmulder, *The Panorama Phenomenon: Subject of a Permanent Exhibition, Organized on the Occasion of the Centennial of the Mesdag Panorama in The Hague, Which Was Inaugurated on the 1st of August 1881: Catalogue in the Shape of an Illustrated Historiography* (The Hague: Foundation for the Preservation of the Centenarian Mesdag Panorama, 1981), 57–58; Comment, *Panorama,* 44; Oettermann, *Panorama,* 286–296; on the widow Barton and tour, H. Clauren [Carl Heun], *Kurze Bemerkungen auf langen Berufswegen,* 2 vols. (Dinkelsbühl, 1815–16), 2:32; *Hesperus,* no. 31, June 1814, 244–245, and no. 34, June 1812 (Gibraltar), 270–272, including details about the Bartons, size (c. 3500 *Quadratschuh;* 19×250 *Fuss*).

11. *Wiener Zeitung,* no. 102, 12 Apr., "Allgemeines Intelligenzblatt," 609; 13 June, first ad with Louis XVIII entry noted (advertised through November; entry occurred 3 May). Quote from review, *Hesperus,* no. 31, June 1814, 244–245. Commodity prices from *Wiener Zeitung,* no. 244, 1 Sept., 974 and no. 335, 1 Dec. 1814, 1338, and Clauren, *Bemerkungen,* 2: 96–97.

12. *Bregenzisches Wochenblatt,* no. 42, 21 Oct. 1814, 165.

13. Clauren, *Bemerkungen,* 2:33–34.

14. Zadow, *Schinkel,* 51–52, 55–56, plus reproduction of the Moscow scene, 75 (pl. 27).

15. *Le Moniteur universel,* no. 207, 26 Jul. 1814, 834, for the Cosmorama; no. 281, 8 Oct., 1134, for the new Elba display at the Théâtre pittoresque et mécanique; no. 208, 27 July, 838, for Pierre Prévost's Panorama of Vienna on Boulevard Montmartre; reported as closing on 4 Dec., *Journal des débats,* 3 Dec. 1814, 5. On the smaller cosmorama format, Oettermann, *Panorama,* 69.

16. *Hesperus,* no. 31, June 1814, 244–245.

17. Quote, *Friedensblätter,* no. 49, 22 Oct. 1814, 202; advertised *Oesterreichischer Beobachter,* no. 286, 8 Oct. 1814, 1532.

18. Quote, *Friedensblätter,* no. 67, 3 Dec. 1814, 275; more critical, Cotta's *Morgenblatt für gebildete Stände,* no. 295, 10 Dec. 1814, 1180.

19. Klotz, *Friedensblätter,* no. 67, 3 Dec. 1814, 275. Panorama: *Hesperus,* no. 31, June 1814, 244–245; Comment, *Panorama,* 44, 164, for possible Prévost sketch as basis, and tour.

20. Franz Patzer, ed., *Wiener Kongreßtagebuch 1814/1815. Wie der Rechnungsbeamte Matthias Franz Perth den Wiener Kongreß erlebte* (Vienna: Jugend und Volk, 1981), 33, Jägerzeile; *Hesperus,* no. 44, Sept. 1814, 350–351, for the Deym/Müllersche gallery and mechanical theater, including stage size of c. three by two meters.

21. "J. Knillingers Wachs- und Naturalienkabinet," *Hesperus,* no. 37, July 1814, 289–292.

22. [Franz Xaver Carl Gewey], *Briefe des neu angekommenen Eipeldauers an seinen Herrn Vettern in Kakran. Mit Noten von einem Wiener,* Heft 1, letter 3 (1814), 26–42, 40 on the "Patriotenfest" and encores, reporting on 1813 performances, the play still often performed during the Congress; Adolf Bäuerle, *Die Bürger in Wien. Locale Posse in drey Acten* (n.p., n.d. [after 1817]), 29–34.

23. Schwartz, *Spectacular Realities,* 3–6, 131, 146, 202; Peter Fritzsche, *Reading Berlin 1900* (Cambridge, MA: Harvard University Press, 1996), 25–32, 46–49, 130–133, 176.

24. Rechberg, *Friedensblätter,* no. 67, 3 Dec. 1814, 275; Charles de Rechberg, *Les peuples de la Russie, ou description des moeurs, usages et costumes des diverses nations de l'Empire de Russie,* 2 vols. (Paris, 1812–13).

25. Oleksijczuk, *First Panoramas,* 9–11, 131–132, 163, 170. Oettermann is often taken to emphasize the viewer's imprisonment by the full circle of the panorama and its illusionary power, but he also stressed the medium's multiple viewpoints as a new "democratic perspective" contributing to its success: *Panorama,* 21, 31, 40–45.

26. Schwartz, *Spectacular Realities,* 203–204.

27. Oleksijczuk, *First Panoramas,* 75–77; Samuels, *Spectacular Past,* 43–44.

28. John Adamson, introduction to Adamson, ed., *The Princely Courts of Europe: Ritual, Politics and Culture under the Ancien Régime 1500–1750* (London: Seven Dials, 2000), 7–41, 32–33; Jeroen Duindam, "The Courts of the Austrian Habsburgs c. 1500–1750," in ibid., 165–187, 185.

29. Hubertus Büschel, *Untertanenliebe. Der Kult um deutsche Monarchen 1770–1830* (Göttingen: Vandenhoeck & Ruprecht, 2006); Eva Giloi, *Monarchy, Myth, and Material Culture in Germany 1750–1950* (Cambridge: Cambridge University Press, 2011), passim, 26–30, for objects in particular: "Consumer demand, not royal intention, drove the production of monarchic memorabilia." (29)

30. See generally, Giloi, *Monarchy,* 10, 23, 29; for memorabilia in the decades after 1815, including for popular strata, James M. Brophy, *Popular Culture and the Public Sphere in the Rhineland, 1800–1850* (Cambridge: Cambridge University Press, 2007), 123–125.

31. John E. Cookson, *The British Armed Nation, 1793–1815* (Oxford: Oxford University Press, 1997); Austin Gee, *The British Volunteer Movement, 1794–1814* (Oxford: Oxford University Press, 2003).

32. Paul von Lichtenberg, *Mohn & Kothgasser. Transparent bemaltes Biedermeierglas / Transparent-Enamelled Biedermeier Glass* (Munich: Hirmer, 2009), 355, 358, 360–361, pls. 255–257; Hermann Trenkwald, ed., *Gläser der Empire- und Biedermeierzeit. Ausstellung im österreichischen Museum für Kunst und Industrie* (Vienna: Schroll, 1922), 79–80; Gustav E. Pazaurek, *Gläser der Empire- und Biedermeierzeit* (Leipzig: Klinkhardt & Biermann, 1923), 199, 201, pl. 183. Kothgasser glass with inscription: Corning Museum collection, Corning, New York, 54.3.247: available at the website of the Corning Museum collection, http://collection.cmog.org/detail.php?type=related&kv=3378&t=objects (accessed March 1, 2014); also see for it and generally, including prints, Walter Spiegl, "Kothgasser & Co. Meinungen und Analysen zum komplexen Thema der 'Kothgassergläser,'" 49–52 (self-published, available at www.glas-forschung.info/pageone/pdf/k&co_2.pdf). The Mohns in Dresden did a silhouette portrait on glass: Lichtenberg, *Mohn & Kothgasser,* 142–143; Pazaurek also notes a Bohemian example, *Gläser,* 220.

33. *Friedensblätter,* no. 35, 23 Mar. 1815, 140.

34. Lichtenberg, *Mohn & Kothgasser,* 36–39, pl. I.2a (Bülow, by Samuel Mohn's workshop in Dresden), 358, 361–363, pls. 258–259 (Schwarzenberg and King Friedrich Wilhelm, by Kothgasser); Franz and porcelain, plus Schwarzenberg and Friedrich Wilhelm, Spiegl, "Kothgasser & Co.," 49–52. It is not fully clear whether the Alexander and Franz glasses were produced for the market or at the government's behest; Spiegl, "Kothgasser & Co.," 52, suggests a government request for gift purposes, but the amateurish wording of the captions makes this unlikely. Boxes: Walter Koschatzky, ed., *Der Wiener Kongress 1. September 1814 bis 9. Juni 1815. Ausstellung veranstaltet vom Bundesministerium für Unterricht gemeinsam mit dem Verein der Museumsfreunde* (Vienna, 1965), 86, 169, 447.

35. Lichtenberg, *Mohn & Kothgasser,* 285, pl. 168 ("La Paix"), 368, pl. 266 for Kaiser Franz. Cossacks: 58–60 (Anton Heinrich Mattoni, Carlsbad); 148–151, 167–170 (Dresden). Berlin KPM (Königliche Porzellan-Manufaktur) porcelain celebrating the victory at Leipzig and the entry into Paris, Giloi, *Monarchy,* 27–28.

36. Three monarchs, *Friedensblätter,* no. 62, 22 Nov. 1814, 256; larger series, *Wiener Zeitung,* no. 277, 4 Oct. 1814, "Allgemeines Intelligenzblatt," 616.

37. *Erinnerungsblätter für gebildete Leser aus allen Ständen,* no. 36, 11 Sept. 1814, 576.

38. K.K. Oesterreich. Museum für Kunst und Industrie, *Katalog der Wiener-Congress-Ausstellung 1896* (Vienna: Verlag des K.K. Oesterreich. Museums, 1896), 183, item nos. 1518 and 1519; greeting cards, *Wiener Zeitung,* no. 346, 12 Dec. 1814, 1382.

39. Lichtenberg, *Mohn & Kothgasser,* 42–43, 392–394, pls. I.9 and 295–298; Spiegl, "Kothgasser & Co.," 21–22.
40. Koschatzky, ed., *Kongress,* 137–141, from collections of the Vienna Kunsthistorisches Museum's Münzkabinett (KHM), which include a further series by Franz Detler.
41. KHM, 2194bß; example in Koschatzky, ed., *Kongress,* 129 (Alexander), and in *Katalog 1896,* 140.
42. *Friedensblätter,* no. 56, 8 Nov. 1814, 232; similarly, a medallion by J. Schmidt on the same theme, with portraits of Franz and Alexander: *Friedensblätter,* no. 62, 22 Nov., 256 (both 12 florins, silver).
43. Schwarzenberg Czech example, *Katalog 1896,* 217; also KHM 2250bß, celebrating the Peace of Paris. Vienna medallions were still comparable in many respects to those of the Peace of Westphalia. See Hans Galen ed., texts by Gerd Dethlefs and Karl Ordelheide, *Der Westfälische Frieden. Die Friedensfreude auf Münzen und Medaillen* (Münster: Stadtmuseum Münster, 1987).
44. Galen, ed., *Westfälische Frieden,* 13, for the mix of private and court interests among medalists at Westphalia. Sonnenfels, HHStA KK 36 (1814), nos. 100–364, no. 213, Hager to Franz, 4 Dec., with the latter's request for another opinion (8 Dec.); Koschatzky, ed., *Kongress,* 136–137, Sonnenfels to Staatskanzlei, 24 Feb. 1815.
45. For range of materials, see entries in Koschatzky, ed., *Kongress,* 137–141; and *Katalog 1896,* 140–146. Galen, ed., *Westfälische Frieden,* shows silver, gold, lead, and copper featuring in the seventeenth century, though it may in that case have reflected the commissioners' more than consumers' ability to pay.
46. Endletzberger, *Friedensblätter,* no. 7, 17 Jan. 1815, 28. For early examples, Galen, ed., *Westfälische Frieden,* 11; from the Seven Years War, Schlesisches Museum Görlitz, SMG 2003/0025; generally on the genre, see Hermann Clauss, "Der Schraubtaler und seine Geschichte," *Mitteilungen der Bayerischen Numismatischen Gesellschaft* 31 (1913): 1–45, 38, for the Seven Years War example.
47. KHM 2167bß (Sn (tin), fifty millimeters diameter); see Joseph F. Appel, *Skizze einer Sammlung sämmtlicher Medaillen welche unter der Regierung Sr. Kaiserl. Majestät Franz I. von Oesterreich geprägt worden sind* (Vienna, 1822), 30, no. 78, and Koschatzky, ed., *Kongress,* 83. This followed a similar medallion containing depictions of the battles of 1813: Appel, *Sammlung,* 29, no. 77; Clauss, *Schraubtaler,* 39–40.
48. KHM 11.916/1914ß, 53 mm; Appel, *Sammlung,* 35, no. 92, including quote, and not noting the "Vienna" inscription; Koschatzky, ed., *Kongress,* 132.
49. Wien Museum Karlsplatz Vienna, 56.466/5; Koschatzky, ed., *Kongress,* 169, suggests it is a draft for a greeting card or festive illumination.
50. HHStA StK Kongreßakten 16, fols. 150–151, 150, for Castlereagh's return; see Koschatzky, ed., *Kongress,* 155.

51. "Der Grosse Wiener Friedens-Congres zur Wiederherstellung von Freiheit und Recht in Europa," engraver J[oseph] Zutz; versions with better portraits by A. Tessaro of Vienna in 1815, and Friedrich Campe of Nuremberg, at Anne S.K. Brown Military Collection, Center for Digital Scholarship, Brown University Library, EuP 1814mf-2 (Tessaro), and Eu (1805–1821) Europe (Campe).

52. Also for the cake image, "Le gâteau des rois, tiré au Congrès de Vienne en 1815," Prints and Drawings, British Museum, 1868, 0808.8201; "La balance politique," Anne S.K. Brown Military Collection, EuH 1815f-1. Quotes, "Twelfth Night, or What You Will!," engraved by George Cruikshank of London, January 1815: Anne S.K. Brown Military Collection, Bullard E-853.

53. "Der Congress," Friedrich Campe, aquatint by Johann Michael Voltz (Nuremberg, 1814), Anne S.K. Brown Military Collection, Eu (1805–1821) Europe.

54. Kanne, *Friedensblätter*, no. 67, 3 Dec. 1814, 276; Tobias Haslinger, *Alexander I. und Friedrich Wilhelm III. in Wien. Eine grosse Fantasie für das Pianoforte, den erhabenen Beherrschern des Nordens, bey Gelegenheit Ihrer hohen Anwesenheit in Wien, in tiefster Ehrfurcht geweiht* (Vienna: Steiner, n.d. [1814]), *Wiener Zeitung*, no. 279, 6 Oct. 1814, "Allgemeines Intelligenzblatt," 628; Quadrille, by Joachim Höllmayer, imperial-royal director in the larger Redoutensaal, *Wiener Zeitung*, no. 316, 12 Nov. 1814, 1262; Joseph Wilde [also music director in the Redoutensaal], *Alexander's favorit Tänze für das Clavier verfasst und aufgeführt bey den Kaiserlichen Hof-Bällen sowohl, als bey Sr. Durchlaucht Herrn Fürsten v. Metternich während der Anwesenheit der hohen und höchsten Monarchen in Wien* (Vienna: Steiner, n.d. [1814]), no. 2279, in the Musiksammlung, Österreichische Nationalbibliothek, MS11272-qu.4°.

55. Friedrich Starke, *Alexanders Favorit-Marsch, Wiener Zeitung*, no. 269, 26 Sept. 1814, 1073; *Wiener Zeitung*, no. 279, 6 Oct. 1814, "Allgemeines Intelligenzblatt," 628; Mathew, *Political Beethoven*, 50–51. In general on Congress music, Michael Ladenburger, "Der Wiener Kongreß im Spiegel der Musik," in Helga Lühning and Sieghard Brandenburg, eds., *Beethoven zwischen Revolution und Restauration* (Bonn: Beethoven-Haus, 1989), 275–306.

56. Alexander Weinmann, *Vollständiges Verlagsverzeichnis Artaria & Comp.*, 3rd ed. (Vienna: Krenn, 1985), 112 (Moscheles); new march by Starke, *Wiener Zeitung*, no. 51, 20 Feb. 1815, 204; Kanne, *Friedensblätter*, no. 30, 11 Mar. 1815, 120. On Kanne's works glorifying Wellington, Mathew, *Political Beethoven*, 38–39.

57. Mathew, *Political Beethoven*, ch. 1; Ingrid Fuchs, "The Glorious Moment—Beethoven and the Congress of Vienna," in Ole Villumsen Krog, ed., *Danmark og Den Dansende Wienerkongres. Spillet om Danmark / Denmark and the Dancing Congress of Vienna. Playing for Denmark's Future* (Copenhagen: Christiansborg Slot, 2002), 182–196.

58. Birgit Lodes, "'Le congrès danse': Set Form and Improvisation in Beethoven's Polonaise for Piano, Op. 89," *Musical Quarterly* 93, 3–4 (2010): 414–449; *Wiener Zeitung*, no. 346, 12 Dec. 1814, "Allgemeines Intelligenzblatt," 1120–1121 (Eybler, Drechsler); Hummel, Pixis, and Mayseder, Weinmann, *Artaria*, 111–112; and several others from less noted composers, in Alexander Weinmann, *Vollständiges Verlagsverzeichnis Senefelder, Steiner, Haslinger,* 3 vols. (Munich: Katzbichler, 1979–83), 1:126–129.

59. Johann Nepomuk Zapf, *XII National-Märsche der verbündeten Mächte* (Vienna: Weigl, 1814), nos. 1408–1409, Musiksammlung, Österreichische Nationalbibliothek, MS44119-qu.4°; also Anton Diabelli, *Märsche der verbündeten Mächte,* published by Steiner, ad, *Wiener Zeitung*, no. 348, 14 Dec. 1814, 1390. Weinmann, *Artaria*, 107, pl. no. 2296, Mauro Giuliani, *Märsche der verbündeten Mächte,* arranged for flute and guitar.

60. Ad, *Friedensblätter*, no. 53, 1 Nov. 1814, 220; Abbé Georg Joseph Vogler, *Polymelos I für Klavier (Orgel)* (Regensburg: Eberhard Kraus, 1999).

61. Giloi, *Monarchy*, 265, on "intimacy at a distance"; Robert van Krieken, *Celebrity Society* (New York: Routledge, 2012), ch. 4.

62. Weil, *Dessous*, 1:334, 19 Oct. 1814. For such reasons, later Austrian monarchs kept control of use rights to the royal image: Daniel L. Unowsky, *The Pomp and the Politics of Patriotism: Imperial Celebrations in Habsburg Austria, 1848–1916* (West Lafayette, IN: Purdue University Press, 2005), 120–125; in Prussia they did not: Giloi, *Monarchy*, 190, and 10, on the potential tendency toward "trivialization" of celebrities in consumer culture.

63. KHM 12.113bß, in Koschatzky, ed., *Kongress*, 158. Galen, ed., *Westfälische Frieden*, 10–11, on jetons.

64. Koschatzky, ed., *Kongress*, 132; Deutsches Historisches Museum Berlin, Objektdatenbank, Inventarnr. N 77/414.1.

65. Ad for "Lusthaus im Prater am 18. Oktober," *Wiener Zeitung*, no. 347, 13 Dec. 1814, "Allgemeines Intelligenzblatt," 1129.

66. Adalbert Gyrowetz, *SIEGES- und FRIEDENFEST der verbündeten MONARCHEN, gefeyert im Prater und dessen Umgebungen am 18. Oktober, 1814, als am Jahrestag der Völkerschlacht von Leipzig, eine charakteristische Fantasie für das Pianoforte* (Vienna: Thaddäus Weigl, 1814); for the Goethe setting, "Goethe's Lied zum 'Sieges- und Friedensfest der verbündeten Monarchen,'" *Chronik des Wiener Goethe-Vereins* 4, 6–7 (12 June 1889): 29–30, where the text makes clear that the "Allgemeines Volkslied von Goethe" is in this case a "national song," not a "folk song."

67. Anton Diabelli, *Der 18. Oktober, oder: Das grosse militarische Prater-Fest in Wien, gefeyert bey Anwesenheit der hohen und höchsten Monarchen, zum Andenken an die unvergessliche Völker-Schlacht bey Leipzig. Ein Tongemählde für das Pianoforte, über ein Gedicht von Kanne componirt* (Vienna: Steiner, n.d. [1814]).

68. Print by Johann Schönberg, reproduced in Stolberg, *Tagebuch*, 69.

69. Diabelli, *Der 18.te October*, 13; HHStA StK Vorträge 196, fols. 60–61, Metternich to Franz, 17 Oct. 1814.

70. Diabelli, *Der 18.te October,* 14–15; *Friedensblätter,* no. 51, 27 Oct. 1814, 210.

71. Quote, *Wiener Zeitung,* no. 346, 12 Dec. 1814, "Allgemeines Intelligenzblatt," 1120.

72. *Wiener Zeitung,* no. 279, 6 Oct. 1814, "Allgemeines Intelligenzblatt," 628, ad for music and plate with option to purchase separately; no. 277, 4 Oct. 1814, 614, ad for print alone. The Russian "cannon monument" was built from captured French artillery after Napoleon's retreat.

73. Thomas Röder, "Beethovens Sieg über die Schlachtenmusik. Opus 91 und die Tradition der Battaglia," in Lühning and Brandenburg, eds., *Beethoven,* 229–258, pl. 245.

74. Roger Paulin, "The Romantic Book as 'Gesamtkunstwerk,'" *Bulletin of the John Rylands University Library of Manchester* 71, 3 (1989): 47–62, on the more successful example of Ludwig Tieck's *Minnelieder* (1803), illustrated by Philipp Otto Runge, published by Johann Friedrich Unger in his new *Fraktur* typeface.

75. *Friedensblätter,* no. 40, 1 Oct. 1814, between pp. 162 and 163.

76. *Friedensblätter,* no. 39, 29 Sept. 1814, 159–160.

77. *Friedensblätter,* no. 7, Beethoven, 12 July 1814, between pp. 30 and 31; no. 52, 29 Oct. 1814, between pp. 216 and 217, for the Sinclair/Kanne lied "Heiterkeit," or "Cheerfulness," with its opening declaration, "Ich wandle so gerne zur reizenden Ferne."

78. *Wiener Zeitung,* no. 346, "Anhang," 12 Dec. 1814, 1382.

79. Weigl portraits, *Wiener Zeitung,* no. 183, 2 July 1814, "Allgemeines Intelligenzblatt," 11. On the connection between art and music publishing through copperplates and lithography, Weinmann, *Senefelder,* 1:7.

80. Esteban Buch, *Beethoven's Ninth: A Political History,* trans. Richard Miller (Chicago: University of Chicago Press, 2003), 77, 79, and ch. 4 generally.

81. MOL, Széchényi Papers, I. kötet, P623/32, fol. 352, Pichler to Ferenc Széchényi, 16 Dec. 1813; Louis Spohr, *Lebenserinnerungen,* ed. Folker Göthel (Tutzing: Hans Schneider, 1968), 175–176; anon., *Louis Spohr 1784–1859 Persönlichkeit und Werk. Zum 200. Geburtstag des Komponisten, Geigers, Dirigenten und Musikpädagogen. Ausstellung der Staatsbibliothek Preussischer Kulturbesitz und der Internationalen Louis Spohr Gesellschaft* (Berlin: Staatsbibliothek, 1984), 19–20.

82. *Friedensblätter,* no. 78, 29 Dec. 1814, 320; cf. ad, *Wiener Zeitung,* no. 357, 23 Dec., "Allgemeines Intelligenzblatt," 1205–1206.

83. Ludwig Bleibtreu, "Das Acrostichon des Allgemeinen Friedens. Im Jahr 1814," [no pub. data]; Balthasar Wigand, Wienmuseum Karlsplatz, inv. no. 24.957; *Friedensblätter,* no. 50, 25 Oct. 1814, 205, for the chronogram in the Prater.

84. HHStA KFA 165, no. 51, chronostichon of Christoph Nopitsch of Nördlingen, plus song; "exaltirt." Franz Schubert, "Hermann und Thusnelda" (Deutsch 322), in Graham Johnson and others, An 1815 Schubertiad – II, The Hyperion Schubert Edition no. 22 (Hyperion Records, CD J33022, 1994).

85. WStLA, Hauptregistratur A37 Dept. W Ceremoniale 3 (1815–1816), no. 5786, W:2 1815, from Bernhard Ott, near Augsburg.

86. Walter Consuelo Langsam, *The Napoleonic Wars and German Nationalism in Austria* (New York: Columbia University Press, 1930), 26–27, 32, 58–59, 73–74; Karen Hagemann, "'Be Proud and Firm, Citizens of Austria!' Patriotism and Masculinity in Texts of the 'Political Romantics' Written during Austria's Anti-Napoleonic Wars," *German Studies Review* 29, 1 (2006): 41–62, 45, 52–54; Theophil Antonicek, *Musik im Festsaal der Österreichischen Akademie der Wissenschaften* (Vienna: Böhlau, 1972), 35–38; Hellmuth Rößler, *Österreichs Kampf um Deutschlands Befreiung: Die deutsche Politik der nationalen Führer Österreichs 1805–1815*, 2 vols. (Hamburg: Hanseatische Verlagsanstalt, 1940), 1:356, 363–367, 429.

87. Diabelli, *Der 18.te October*, 2.

88. Joseph Rossi, ed., *Denkbuch für Fürst und Vaterland*, 2 vols. (Vienna, 1814–15), 1:VII (quote), with "Unterthan" and "Staatsbürger" in the same phrase, the latter not coincidentally coupled with German identity; portrait, 1:85 (plate at end of text); Kothgasser, Glasmuseum Hentrich in Kunstpalast Düsseldorf.

89. A project on Habsburg press policy in the Congress era is already under way, by Eva Maria Werner and Brigitte Mazohl.

90. Andreas Gestrich, *Absolutismus und Öffentlichkeit: Politische Kommunikation in Deutschland zu Beginn des 18. Jahrhunderts* (Göttingen: Vandenhoeck & Ruprecht, 1994).

91. Simon Burrows, "The Cosmopolitan Press, 1760–1815," in Hannah Barker and Burrows, eds., *Press, Politics and the Public Sphere in Europe and North America, 1760–1820* (Cambridge: Cambridge University Press, 2002), 29–47. Most of the literature appeared in French or German, but even Italian was represented, as for instance the contributions of the Tyrolean Antonio della Brida and the Veronese Giuseppe Peruffi: della Brida, *Sulla pomposa e brillante slittata fatta in Vienna li 22 Gennaio 1815* (Vienna, 1815), celebrating the famously opulent court sleigh ride), and *Il Despotismo. Poemetto dedicato alle loro maestà imperiale e reale d'Austria e di Russia, di Prussia e d'Inghilterra* (Vienna, 1815), celebrating and legitimating the victory over Napoleon and the revolution; Peruffi, *Il congresso di Vienna ossia l'armonia trionfante al congresso* (Verona, 1816).

92. Andrea Hofmeister-Hunger, *Pressepolitik und Staatsreform: Die Institutionalisierung staatlicher Öffentlichkeitsarbeit bei Karl August von Hardenberg (1792–1822)* (Göttingen: Vandenhoeck & Ruprecht, 1994), 285, on the Prussian "review cartel." Preferring offensive-defensive to positive-negative or propaganda-censorship distinctions: Wolfgang Piereth, *Bayerns Pressepolitik und die Neuordnung Deutschlands nach den Befreiungskriegen* (Munich: Beck, 1999), 43–44.

93. On Austrian censorship, Julius Marx, *Die österreichische Zensur im Vormärz* (Vienna: Verlag für Geschichte und Politik, 1959); a darker view,

Donald E. Emerson, *Metternich and the Political Police: Security and Subversion in the Habsburg Empire, 1815–1830* (The Hague: Nijhoff, 1968).

94. Hofmeister-Hunger, *Pressepolitik,* 287–288.

95. HStA Darm, Ott, B127, fols. 23–24, Gagern to Nagell, 20 July 1815, and fol. 36, 28–29 July, reporting conversation with Humboldt.

96. DAW Stadtpfarren Wien I St. Stephan Kassette III, Zensur 1810–1822, no. 1480, 31 Aug. 1814; Silvester Lechner, *Gelehrte Kritik und Restauration: Metternichs Wissenschafts- und Pressepolitik und die Wiener Jahrbücher der Literatur (1818–1849)* (Tübingen: Niemeyer, 1977), 57; Langsam, *Nationalism,* 57–58.

97. Lechner, *Gelehrte Kritik,* 54–55.

98. Richard Schwemer, *Geschichte der Freien Stadt Frankfurt a.M. (1814–1866),* 2 vols. (Frankfurt: Baer, 1910), 1:171; HHStA StA England 154, "Weisungen 1814," fol. 17, Metternich to Merveldt, 2 Sept., and StA England 151, Fasz. 3, fols. 11–12, Merveldt to Metternich, 4 Oct. 1814; in general, Marx, *Zensur,* 58.

99. HHStA StK Vorträge 199 (1815), folder VIII, fols. 42–55, 3 and 27 Aug.; folder IX, fol. 37, 6 Sept.; and Vorträge 200 (1815), folder X, fol. 6v (1 Oct.). Schlegel and particularly Müller had already been tasked to write newspaper articles and proclamations: Vorträge 197 (1815), folder IV, fols. 571–573, 10 Apr.; Lechner, *Gelehrte Kritik,* 69, 71.

100. [No ed.], *Correspondance du Comte de Jaucourt, Ministre Intérimaire des Affaires Étrangères, avec le Prince de Talleyrand pendant le Congrès de Vienne* (Paris: Plon-Nourrit, 1905), 33–34, Talleyrand to Jaucourt, 13 Oct. 1814. In general, Alexandra von Ilsemann, *Die Politik Frankreichs auf dem Wiener Kongress. Talleyrands außenpolitischen Strategien zwischen Erster und Zweiter Restauration* (Hamburg: Krämer, 1996), 185–186.

101. GStA PK III. HA MdA I, no. 5224, Greuhm to Hardenberg, 12 Dec. 1814 (no fol.).

102. Karl Heinz Schäfer, *Ernst Moritz Arndt als politischer Publizist: Studien zur Publizistik, Pressepolitik und kollektivem Bewußtsein im frühen 19. Jahrhundert* (Bonn: Röhrscheid, 1974); Paul Czygan, *Zur Geschichte der Tagesliteratur während der Freiheitskriege,* 2 vols. (Leipzig: Duncker & Humblot, 1911), 1:75–86, 137–188 for Prussian-German propaganda in Russia, 86–131 for Kotzebue. Kotzebue's work for Russia had less to do with his assassination in 1819 than once thought: George S. Williamson, "What Killed August von Kotzebue? The Temptations of Virtue and the Political Theology of German Nationalism, 1789–1819," *Journal of Modern History* 72, 4 (2000): 890–943.

103. Piereth, *Bayerns Pressepolitik;* Ferdinand Troska, *Die Publizistik zur sächsischen Frage auf dem Wiener Kongress* (Halle: Niemeyer, 1891); Hofmeister-Hunger, *Pressepolitik.*

104. Piereth, *Bayerns Pressepolitik,* 91.

105. Hofmeister-Hunger, *Pressepolitik,* 16, 201; Piereth, *Bayerns Pressepolitik,* 48.

106. Czygan, *Tagesliteratur*, 2,2:89, Hardenberg to Renfner, draft, 14 Nov. 1814; Hofmeister-Hunger, *Pressepolitik*, 288.

107. Jon Vanden Heuvel, *A German Life in the Age of Revolution: Joseph Görres, 1776–1848* (Washington, DC: Catholic University of America Press, 2001), ch. 7; Daniel Moran, *Toward the Century of Words: Johann Cotta and the Politics of the Public Realm in Germany, 1795–1832* (Berkeley: University of California Press, 1990), 143–147; Monika Neugebauer-Wölk, *Revolution und Constitution—die Brüder Cotta: Eine biographische Studie zum Zeitalter der Französischen Revolution und des Vormärz* (Berlin: Colloquium, 1989), 454–456, 461.

108. Moran, *Cotta*, 138–140; Hofmeister-Hunger, *Pressepolitik*, 286 on Prussian articles for Cotta, 290 on reputation; Michaela Breil, *Die Augsburger "Allgemeine Zeitung" und die Pressepolitik Bayerns: Ein Verlagsunternehmen zwischen 1815 und 1848* (Tübingen: Niemeyer, 1996), 152.

109. GStA PK III. HA MdA I, no. 1090, fols. 16–17v, Hartleben to Hardenberg, Mannheim, 25 Sept. 1814; copies of the new journal's public announcement at fols. 18–21v; Hardenberg's reply fol. 23, 31 Oct. 1814; fol. 22, 16 with marginalia for draft response including "guten Geiste," omitted from final version.

110. Nicola Wurthmann, *Senatoren, Freunde und Familie: Herrschaftsstrukturen und Selbstverständnis der Bremer Elite zwischen Tradition und Moderne (1813–1848)* (Bremen: Staatsarchiv Bremen, 2009), 411; B. Schulze Schmidt, *Bürgermeister Johann Smidt, das Lebensbild eines Hanseaten. Ein Erinnerungsbuch* (Bremen: Leuwer, 1913), 355, and 360 for Smidt's satisfaction with Görres's follow-up coverage in December; Wilhelm von Bippen, *Johann Smidt: Ein hanseatischer Staatsmann* (Stuttgart: Deutsche Verlags-Anstalt, 1921), 167; StA Bremen 7,20, no. 794, Friederike Noltenius to Smidt, 21 Dec. 1814, fols. 28–29. In October Smidt had already sought information from his sister and sister-in-law for an article in Bremen's newspaper publicizing the celebratory activities of the Women's Association: Wurthmann, *Senatoren*, 410; Schulze-Schmidt, *Smidt*, 341, 344–347.

111. *Oesterreichischer Beobachter*, no. 337, 3 Dec. 1814, 1842; no. 52, 21 Feb. 1815, 290; *Friedensblätter*, no. 24, 25 Feb. 1815, 96 ("Volk").

112. Marx, *Zensur*.

113. HHStA StK Notenwechsel Polizeihofstelle 4, Fasz. 1814, fol. 122, 2 Nov., Bretfeld to Hager; Karl-Heinz Schäfer and Josef Schawe, eds., *Ernst Moritz Arndt. Ein bibliographisches Handbuch, 1769–1969* (Bonn: Röhrscheid, 1971), quote 178, from *Hamburger Correspondenten*, 16 Nov. 1814. XYZ [Arndt], *Beherzigungen vor dem Wiener Kongreß* (n. p., 1814).

114. Report, Fournier, *Geheimpolizei*, 202, 25 Oct. 1814; list, BGE Ms suppl 1003, "Missions de Ivernois," fols. 122–123. And see Marx, *Zensur*, 54–56. The official list of available periodicals for the second half of 1815, after the Congress, remained similarly broad, including still the *Rheinische Merkur:*

HHStA StK Noten von der Polizeihofstelle 31, Fasz. 1 (1815), fols. 371–372v, 16 May.

115. HHStA StK Noten von der Polizeihofstelle 30, Fasz. 2 (1815, I–VI), fols. 24–25v, Hager to Metternich, 24 Jan., including quote; affirmative re sponse, StK Notenwechsel Polizeihofstelle 4, Fasz. 1815, fol. 24, 12 Feb., StK Notenwechsel Polizeihofstelle 4, Fasz. 1814, fol. 122, 2 Nov., Bretfeld to Hager. Emphasizing Austrian censorship as generally less strict or effective: Alan Sked, *Metternich and Austria: An Evaluation* (Basingstoke, England: Palgrave Macmillan, 2008), 139–164.

116. Piereth, *Bayerns Pressepolitik,* 98–100; Vanden Heuvel, *Görres,* 203–204.

117. HHStA StK Notenwechsel Polizeihofstelle 4, Fasz. 1814, fol. 75–75v, 25 Aug., quotes 75; similar complaints, Fasz. 1815, fols. 43, 47, 2 Mar. and 12 Mar.

118. HHStA StK Interiora 67 Korresp., Fasz. 1, fols. 225v, 329–329v (23 Feb., 22 Mar. 1814); StK Noten von der Polizeihofstelle 30, Fasz. 1 (1814), fol. 441, Hager to Metternich, 19 Nov.

119. An example involving Stein, Piereth, *Bayerns Pressepolitik,* 74.

120. Vanden Heuvel, *Görres,* 211–214; Hofmeister-Hunger, *Pressepolitik,* 305–308.

121. Czygan, *Tagesliteratur,* 2, 2:89–90, Hardenberg to Renfner, Konzept, 14 Nov. 1814.

122. *Sbornik* 112:100–101, quote 101, Jaucourt to Noailles, Paris, 5 Oct. 1814; Bonald, in Jaucourt, *Correspondance,* Talleyrand to Jaucourt, 152–153, 182, 18 Jan. and 7 Feb. 1815.

123. A. Aspinall, *Politics and the Press c. 1780–1850* (London: Home & Van Thal, 1949), 209, notes that foreign governments did not always know how loose the British authorities' control of newspapers was, which occasionally made the Foreign Office's job harder.

124. Aspinall, *Press,* 88–89, 200–203, suggests that while five of the nineteen London dailies could be described as ministerial in 1814, this involved more light influence than "direct bribery" (203); provincial papers were not subsidized at all (350).

125. Brophy, *Popular Culture,* 19–25, and literature cited there; Fritz Valjavec, *Die Entstehung der politischen Strömungen in Deutschland, 1770–1815* (Munich: Oldenbourg, 1951), 95.

126. Aloys Weissenbach, *Meine Reise zum Congreß. Wahrheit und Dichtung* (Vienna, 1816), 61–64, 132–133; *Die Gute Nachricht. Singspiel in einem Aufzuge* (n.p., 1814), souffleur copy, no pag., in the Musiksammlung of the Österreichische Nationalbibliothek, Vienna, Mus.Hs. 32815.

127. Alphons v. Klinkowström, *Friedrich August v. Klinkowström und seine Nachkommen* (Vienna, 1877), 161, 20 Oct. 1813.

128. [Gewey], *Briefe,* Heft 1, letter 3 (1814): 28–30, 40; Bäuerle, *Bürger,* 10–12, 14–15, 29–34. Cutting both ways, the next year the *Eipeldauer Briefe* satirized the Viennese for ill-informed political pontificating about the Congress in beerhalls and coffeehouses and naïve demands for more news about what should remain secret until the proper time, all despite reading the ru-

mors and proclamations in foreign newspapers like the *Allgemeine Zeitung,* issue 3, letter 3 (1815), 39–45.

3. Salon Networks

1. "Europe sans distances": Charles-Maurice de Talleyrand-Périgord, *Mémoires du Prince de Talleyrand,* Albert de Broglie, ed., 5 vols. (Paris: Lévy, 1891), 2:420.
2. Most accounts emphasize the purely literary or cultural nature of the new salon culture, as: Waltraud Heindl, "People, Class Structure, and Society," in Raymond Erickson, ed., *Schubert's Vienna* (New Haven: Yale University Press, 1997), 36–54; Ulrike Weckel, "A Lost Paradise of a Female Culture? Some Critical Questions Regarding the Scholarship on Late Eighteenth- and Early Nineteenth-Century German Salons," *German History* 18, 3 (2000): 310–336, downplaying the emancipated role of *salonnières*; and Niklas Luhmann, *Gesellschaftsstruktur und Semantik. Studien zur Wissenssoziologie der modernen Gesellschaft,* vol. 1 (Frankfurt a. M.: Suhrkamp, 1993), 153–168, "zweckfreier Interaktion," 158. On politicization during the war years, Ingrid Mittenzwei, *Zwischen Gestern und Morgen. Wiens frühe Bourgeoisie an der Wende vom 18. zum 19. Jahrhundert* (Vienna: Böhlau, 1998), 284–285, 293–295. For the Berlin scene, but capturing interconnections with salons and social circles elsewhere, Petra Wilhelmy, *Der Berliner Salon im 19. Jahrhundert (1780–1914)* (Berlin: de Gruyter, 1989), 31, 114–118, on the dearth of political salons after 1815. The classic argument for the exclusion of women from politics and the public sphere in France: Joan Landes, *Women and the Public Sphere in the Age of Enlightenment* (Ithaca: Cornell University Press, 1994).
3. Steven Kale, "Women, Salons, and the State in the Aftermath of the French Revolution," *Journal of Women's History* 13 (2002): 54–80; Kale emphasizes that while salons helped shape political culture, women as *salonnières* did not usually influence decision-making or have real power: Kale, *French Salons: High Society and Political Sociability from the Old Regime to 1848* (Baltimore: Johns Hopkins University Press, 2004), 5–8, 14, and ch. 5.
4. Albert-László Barabási, *Linked: How Everything Is Connected to Everything Else and What It Means for Business, Science, and Everyday Life* (Cambridge, MA: Plume, 2003); Duncan Watts, *Six Degrees: The Science of a Connected Age* (New York: Norton, 2004); Mark Granovetter, "The Strength of Weak Ties," *American Journal of Sociology* 78 (1973): 1360–1380; Christine B. Avenarius, "Starke und schwache Beziehungen," in Christian Stegbauer and Roger Häußling, eds., *Handbuch Netzwerkforschung* (Wiesbaden: VS Verlag, 2010), 99–111 (for a balanced view of the two kinds of relations and their role in the exchange of "social capital"). For more technical treatments: Sergey N. Dorogovtsev, *Lectures on Complex Networks* (New York: Oxford University Press, 2010), 67–72, on weak ties, "weighted networks," and information and travel flows; Réka

Albert and Albert-László Barabási, "Statistical Mechanics of Complex Networks," *Reviews of Modern Physics* 74 (2002): 47–97; Duncan J. Watts, "The 'New' Science of Networks," *Annual Review of Sociology* 30 (2004): 243–270; Dietrich Stauffer, "Small World," in Stegbauer and Haußling, eds., *Netzwerkforschung*, 219–225.

5. Marie-Claire Hoock-Demarle, *L'Europe des lettres. Réseaux épistolaires et construction de l'éspace européen* (Paris: Michel, 2008), 10, 142–143, 263–264 on the role of exiles and warfare in expanding networks. Abbé de Pradt made a similar observation: *Du Congrès de Vienne*, 2 vols. (Paris, 1815), 1:140.

6. This empirical observation also has a basis in network theory. Social networks often exhibit "assortative mixing" (nodes with many links tend to have connections to other densely linked nodes), making them "more resilient against random damage": Dorogovtsev, *Lectures*, 62–64, quote 64.

7. William D. Godsey, Jr., *Nobles and Nation in Central Europe: Free Imperial Knights in the Age of Revolution, 1750–1850* (Cambridge: Cambridge University Press, 2004), and "'La Société Était au Fond Légitimiste': Émigrés, Aristocracy and the Court at Vienna, 1789–1848," *European History Quarterly* 35 (2005): 63–95; Hoock-Demarle, *L'Europe*, 263–264, on the role of women in wartime and among exiles.

8. See the citations in note 4; for corrections to the power-law character of some small-world networks, including the airport example, L.A.N. Amaral, A. Scala, M. Barthélémy, and H.E. Stanley, "Classes of Small-World Networks," *Proceedings of the National Academy of Sciences* 97 (2000): 11149–11152.

9. Here and in the following paragraph drawing on the notion of "bipartite" or "bimodal" networks, that is, "affiliation networks" that trace both the links between individuals and the places and institutions that bring them together: Watts, *Six Degrees*, 118–129; Alexander Rausch, "Bimodale Netzwerke," in Stegbauer and Häußling, eds., *Netzwerkforschung*, 421–432.

10. Uta Germann, *Die Entschädigungsverhandlungen Hessen-Darmstadts in den Jahren 1813–1815. Diplomatie im Zeichen des revolutionären Umbruchs* (Darmstadt: Historische Kommission Darmstadt and Historische Kommission Hessen, 1998), 48; Ulrike Eich, *Russland und Europa: Studien zur russischen Deutschlandpolitik in der Zeit des Wiener Kongresses* (Cologne: Böhlau, 1986), 35–36; Russia's Vienna Congress delegates, Hamish Scott, "Diplomatic Culture in Old Regime Europe," in Scott and Brendan Simms, eds., *Cultures of Power in Europe during the Long Eighteenth Century* (Cambridge: Cambridge University Press, 2007), 58–85, 69.

11. On the significance of spas: David Blackbourn, "Fashionable Spa Towns in Nineteenth-Century Europe," in Susan C. Anderson and Bruce H. Tabb, eds., *Water, Leisure and Culture: European Historical Perspectives* (Oxford:

Berg, 2002), 9–22; Astrid Köhler, *Salonkultur im klassischen Weimar: Geselligkeit als Lebensform und literarisches Konzept* (Stuttgart: M&P, 1996), 51–52; and Wilhelmy, *Salon*, 447.

12. Wilhelmy, *Salon*, 77–82, 637–39 for Dorothea Duchess of Courland and her daughter Dorothea in Berlin, where as "outsiders" of the Baltic high nobility they could assemble a socially mixed clientele for nonhierarchical conversation without loss of status (much like Berlin *salonnière* Princess Luise Radziwiłł of the Polish high nobility, who was also in Vienna); also Rosalynd Pflaum, *By Influence and Desire: The True Story of Three Extraordinary Women—The Grand Duchess of Courland and Her Daughters* (New York: Evans, 1984), and Günter Erbe, *Dorothea Herzogin von Sagan (1793–1862). Eine deutsch-französische Karriere* (Cologne: Böhlau, 2009). On Madame de Staël, see still J. Christopher Herold, *Mistress to an Age: A Life of Madame de Staël* (Indianapolis: Bobbs-Merrill, 1958), plus Angelica Goodden, *Madame de Staël: The Dangerous Exile* (Oxford: Oxford University Press, 2008), and Brunhilde Wehinger, *Conversation um 1800: Salonkultur und literarische Autorschaft bei Germaine de Staël* (Berlin: Walter Frey, 2002).

13. Deborah Hertz, *Jewish High Society in Old Regime Berlin* (New Haven: Yale University Press, 1988); Wilhelmy, *Salon*, 41, emphasizing the role of outsider status similar to the Jewish case; Comtesse Jean de Castellane, ed., *Souvenirs de la Duchesse de Dino* (Paris: Calman-Lévy, n.d.), 144–147; Elisabeth Feckes, *Dorothea, Herzogin von Dino und Sagan, ihr Leben mit besonderer Berücksichtigung ihrer Beziehungen zum preussischen Königshause und zu deutschen Politikern* (Krefeld: Klein, 1917).

14. For Sagan, see also Dorothy Gies McGuigan, *Metternich and the Duchess* (Garden City, NY: Doubleday, 1975).

15. On the Arnstein circle, Hilde Spiel, *Fanny von Arnstein: Daughter of the Enlightenment*, trans. Christine Shuttleworth (Oxford: Oxford University Press, 1991); Heinz Gerstinger, *Altwiener literarische Salons. Wiener Salonkultur vom Rokoko bis zur Neoromantik (1777–1907)* (Salzburg: Akademische Verlagsgesellschaft, 2002), 28–38, 73–77; Karl August Varnhagen von Ense, *Denkwürdigkeiten und vermischte Schriften*, 2nd ed., 5 vols. (Leipzig, 1843), 3:252–253. On Berlin's Jewish salons, Hertz, *High Society*.

16. Gerstinger, *Salonkultur*, 7–28 on Greiner salon, Pichler's 46–68.

17. On salon sociability, see generally James Van Horn Melton, *The Rise of the Public in Enlightenment Europe* (Cambridge: Cambridge University Press, 2001), ch. 6; and Dena Goodman, *The Republic of Letters: A Cultural History of the French Enlightenment* (Ithaca: Cornell University Press, 1994), esp. ch. 3.

18. Quote, Varnhagen, *Denkwürdigkeiten*, 3:237. Scholars often see a greater separation between high and middle-rank society in Vienna, as Heindl, "People," 48–49, and Stella Musulin, *Vienna in the Age of Metternich: From Napoleon to Revolution 1805–1848* (Boulder, CO: Westview, 1975),

170; noting more mixing, Gerstinger, *Salonkultur,* 28, 44, 73, and Mittenz-wei, *Zwischen Gestern und Morgen,* 283–291, 296. For Stolberg, Stolberg, *Tagebuch,* III–XL, XXXVI–VIII; Stolberg, Furstenberg, and other nobles, Caroline Pichler, *Denkwürdigkeiten aus meinem Leben,* Emil Karl Blüml, ed., 2nd ed., 2 vols. (Munich: Müller, 1914), 2:39–40.

19. Marie-Henriette-Radegonde-Alexandrine Baronne Fisson du Montet, *Die Erinnerungen der Baronin du Montet (Wien-Paris, 1795–1858),* trans. Ernst Klarwill (Zurich: Amalthea, n.d. [1925]), 34–35; Giovannella Caetani Grenier, ed., *Mémoires de la Comtesse Rosalie Rzewuska (1788–1865),* 3 vols. (Rome: Cuggiani, 1939–50), 1:266.

20. Weil, *Dessous,* 1:101, 22 Sept. 1814; Fournier, *Geheimpolizei,* 149–150, 2 Oct. On Fuchs, Mittenzwei, *Zwischen Gestern und Morgen,* 284–285.

21. Grenier, ed., *Rzewuska,* 1:40; Fournier, *Geheimpolizei,* 240–241.

22. Philip Mansel, *Prince of Europe: The Life of Charles-Joseph de Ligne (1735–1814)* (London: Weidenfeld & Nicolson, 2003); on the tradition of male-hosted salons, Heindl, "People," 46, citing the example of Gottfried van Swieten among others.

23. Eduard Winter, *Romantismus, Restauration und Frühliberalismus im öster-reichischen Vormärz* (Vienna: Europa, 1968), 105; Hoock-Demarle, *L'Eu-rope,* 311–312, on Dorothea's authorship.

24. Elise von Bernstorff, *Ein Bild aus der Zeit von 1789 bis 1835. Aus ihren Aufzeichnungen* (Berlin, 1896), 182.

25. Carl Haase, ed., *Das Leben des Grafen Münster (1766–1839): Aufzeich-nungen seiner Gemahlin Gräfin Wilhelmine, geb. Fürstin zu Schaumburg-Lippe* (Göttingen: Vandenhoeck & Ruprecht, 1985), 75–76.

26. Feckes, *Dorothea,* 22–23; Erbe, *Dorothea,* 97–98; Lady Castlereagh, StAB 7,20 NL Smidt, no. 135, Johann Smidt, "Tagebuch-Notizen," and Ludmilla Assing, ed., *Tagebücher von Friedrich von Gentz* (Leipzig, 1873), 320, 17 Oct. 1814.

27. A. de Nesselrode, ed., *Lettres et papiers du Chancelier Comte de Nesselrode 1760–1850. Extraits de ses archives,* 11 vols. (Paris: Lahure, n.d. [1904–12]), 5:195–196; HHStA NL Wessenberg, Kart. 2, vol. 16, fols. 41–42; MOL, Széchényi Papers P623 (93), 9. Satz, "Bemerkungen über England" [1787], fols. 76v (quote), 77 noting the practice of running from one crowded gath-ering to the next.

28. "French order," Anna Eynard, Journal, BGE Ms suppl 1959, 48, 30 Oct. 1814; "court," Edouard Chapuisat, ed., *Au Congrès de Vienne. Journal de Jean-Gabriel Eynard* (Paris: Plon-Nourrit, 1914), 79, with reference to Met-ternich's salon, Talleyrand's "less brilliant." Wilhelmy, *Salon,* 460, finds the Arnstein salon more formal than those in Berlin, but cf. Gerstinger, *Salonkultur,* 35, 71.

29. Chapuisat, ed., *Eynard,* 38–40, 67–68; Anna Eynard, Journal, BGE Ms suppl 1959, 48, 30 Oct.

30. Chapuisat, ed., *Eynard,* 181, 4 Dec. 1814; Anna Eynard, Journal, BGE Ms suppl 1959, 105–106, 4 Dec.

31. Fürstenberg, Stolberg, *Tagebuch*, 207–208, 21 Mar. 1815; Gagern, Michael Hundt, *Die mindermächtigen deutschen Staaten auf dem Wiener Kongress* (Mainz: Zabern, 1996), 105–106, and Hans Christoph von Gagern, *Mein Antheil an der Politik*, 4 vols. (Stuttgart, 1823–33 [1826]), 2:19; Gagern's Lenten dancing, Anna Eynard, Journal, BGE Ms suppl 1959, 272–273, 8 Feb. 1815.

32. Chapuisat, ed., *Eynard*, XV; Roxandra Countess Edling, *Mémoires de la comtesse Edling (née Stourdza), demoiselle d'honneur de Sa Majesté l'Impératrice Élisabeth Alexéevna* (Moscow, 1888), 169–173; Stella Ghervas, *Réinventer la tradition. Alexandre Stourdza et l'Europe de la Sainte-Alliance* (Paris: Champion, 2008), 355.

33. Gentz's diary records many such dinners, remembered admiringly in Bernstorff, *Bild*, 164; on the connection between Gentz's lifestyle and his diplomatic networking, Günther Kronenbitter, *Wort und Macht. Friedrich Gentz als politischer Schriftsteller* (Berlin: Duncker & Humblot, 1994), 37–38, 42. Pilat: Johannes Hofer, *Der heilige Klemens Maria Hofbauer. Ein Lebensbild*, 3rd ed. (Freiburg i. B.: Herder, 1923), 266–270; Wilhelm von Bippen, *Johann Smidt: Ein hanseatischer Staatsmann* (Stuttgart: Deutsche Verlags-Anstalt, 1921), 166.

34. Nicola Wurthmann, *Senatoren, Freunde und Familie. Herrschaftsstrukturen und Selbstverständnis der Bremer Elite zwischen Tradition und Moderne (1813–1848)* (Bremen: Staatsarchiv Bremen, 2009), 255; B. Schulze-Schmidt, *Bürgermeister Johann Smidt, das Lebensbild eines Hanseaten. Ein Erinnerungsbuch* (Bremen: Leuwer, 1913), 314, for Smidt's letter from Paris of May 1814 inviting Wilhelmine to join him in Vienna in part for just such sociability.

35. In addition to Weckel, "Lost Paradise," and the literature cited in note 2, see: Suzanne Desan, *The Family on Trial in Revolutionary France* (Berkeley: University of California Press, 2004); Carole Pateman, *The Sexual Contract* (Stanford, CA: Stanford University Press, 1988); Karen Hagemann, "'Heroic Virgins' and 'Bellicose Amazons': Armed Women, the Gender Order and the German Public during and after the Anti-Napoleonic Wars," in Katherine Aaslestad, Karen Hagemann, and Judith A. Miller, eds., special issue, *European History Quarterly* 37, 4 (2007): 507–527; Isabel V. Hull, *Sexuality, State, and Civil Society in Germany, 1700–1815* (Ithaca: Cornell University Press, 1996).

36. Other scholars have begun to question the extent of the patriarchal consensus and suggest that women and men were able to imagine active female roles beyond the domestic: Anne-Charlott Trepp, *Sanfte Männlichkeit und selbständige Weiblichkeit: Frauen und Männer im Hamburger Bürgertum zwischen 1770 und 1840* (Göttingen: Vandenhoeck & Ruprecht, 1996); Rebekka Habermas, *Frauen und Männer des Bürgertums. Eine Familiengeschichte (1750–1850)* (Göttingen: Vandenhoeck & Ruprecht, 2000).

37. Staegemann, *Olfers*, 170–171 (diary, 6 May 1813).

38. Heinrich von Treitschke, *Treitschke's History of Germany in the Nineteenth Century*, trans. Eden and Cedar Paul, 5 vols. (New York: AMS Press, 1968 [orig. 1915–19]), 2:8.

39. Hans Branig, ed., *Briefwechsel des Fürsten Karl August von Hardenberg mit dem Fürsten Wilhelm Ludwig von Sayn-Wittgenstein 1806–1822. Edition aus dem Nachlaß Wittgenstein* (Cologne: Grote, 1972), 138–141, 183–185 (letters of 16 June and 14 Aug. 1812, 28 Dec. 1813); Branig, *Fürst Wittgenstein. Ein preußischer Staatsmann der Restaurationszeit* (Cologne: Böhlau, 1981), 88–90.

40. Quote, Maria Ullrichová, ed., *Clemens Metternich—Wilhelmine von Sagan. Ein Briefwechsel 1813–1815* (Graz: Böhlau, 1966), 260, Metternich to Sagan, 14 Aug. 1814; Assing, ed., *Tagebücher*, 292, 319, 12 Aug. and 14 Oct. 1814.

41. GStA PK VI. HA NL Daniel Ludwig Albrecht, no. 61, "Denkschriften von Ancillon," undated memo to Friedrich Wilhelm with cover letter of 3 July 1815, fols. 15–27v, here, 20.

42. [Anon. ed.], *Aus Karls von Nostitz, weiland Adjutanten des Prinzen Louis Ferdinands von Preußen, und später russischen General-Leutnants, Leben und Briefwechsel* (Dresden, 1848), 145 (Courlands), 163 ("Verkehr mit Weibern").

43. Ibid., 36, 47.

44. Quotes, Erich Botzenhart and Walther Hubatsch, eds., *Freiherr vom Stein Briefe und amtliche Schriften,* 11 vols. (Stuttgart: Kohlhammer, 1957–74), 5:222, 17 Dec. 1814 to Baroness Stein; Volkonskaias, 222, 265, 8 Dec. 1814 to Baroness Stein, and 5 Feb. 1815 to Orlov.

45. HHStA StK Interiora Korresp. 67 (Jan. to Mar. 1814), fols. 233v–234, 333–333v, Hudelist to Metternich, 25 Feb. and 23 Mar.

46. An example of each: against both Bagration and Sagan as alleged agents of Prussia, deserving expulsion: Fournier, *Geheimpolizei*, 346, 21 Jan. 1815; for the Pergen circle, Weil, *Dessous*, 1:485–486, 9 Nov. 1814.

47. Montet, *Erinnerungen*, 66–67; Humboldt, *Briefen*, 4:422–423. Lisette was the wife of Eberhard von der Reck, provisional governor of Saxony in 1814–1815.

48. Staegemann, *Olfers*, 172.

49. HStA Darm. D22, no. 33/44, fol. 3–3v, Hardenberg to Marianne, 23 Dec. 1814; constitutions, D22, no. 22/8, fol. 56–56v, 28 Sept. 1814. Wilhelmy, *Salon*, 108–110 on Beguelin.

50. Assing, ed., *Tagebücher*, 258, with one critical and one laudatory adjective for each woman.

51. HHStA NL Wessenberg, Kart. 2, vol. 16, fols. 41–47, quotes 43v, 45 (written 1814); Kart. 1, vol. 7 [printed], pp. 36–39 for Staël and Vaudémont, 42–49 on Tallien.

52. Examples from 1813–1815: Nesselrode, ed., *Lettres et papiers,* 5:91–93, 120–121, 133–134, 165, 168–169, and 206–207; 5:22–24, 22 Jan. 1813 (HQ); 188–189, 9 Apr. 1814 (Metternich); Nesselrode's request for news of Russian diplomats in Vienna, 142–143, 15 Sept. 1813.

53. Humboldt, *Briefen*, 4:368–369.

54. Ullrichová, *Briefwechsel*, 60, 62, and 76–77, 77 quote: Sagan to Metternich, 11/12 Sept. 1813, Metternich to Sagan, 13 Sept. and 9 Oct. 1813.

55. Ullrichová, *Briefwechsel*, 92–93, 96, Sagan to Metternich, 31 Oct. and 2 Nov. 1813, and 105, Metternich to Sagan, 8 Nov. 1813.

56. Ullrichová, *Briefwechsel*, 123, Sagan to Metternich, 23 Nov. 1813, for the refusal even to speak "the word" politics, 196, 211, 28 Jan. and 15 Feb. 1814, for strong political views, if still softened with self-deprecation on 225, 1–4 Mar. 1814; Metternich seeking or approving her political views, 129, 132, and 217, 29 Nov. and 5 Dec. 1813, 25 Feb. 1814. The duchess even helped facilitate the formation of the coalition against Napoleon in 1813 when the negotiations for a time took place at her country estate: McGuigan, *Duchess*, 70–71.

57. Staegemann, *Olfers*, 37, 39, 47, Staegemann, 21 Nov. 1806; Elisabeth, 3 Dec. 1806, 8 May 1807.

58. Staegemann, *Olfers*, 262, 14 Dec. 1814.

59. Harold Nicolson, *The Congress of Vienna: A Study in Allied Unity: 1812–1822* (New York: Compass, 1961), 201.

60. Niels Rosenkrantz, *Journal du Congrès de Vienne, 1814–1815*, Georg Nørregård, ed. (Copenhagen: Gad, 1953), 16–17.

61. Consalvi, Rinieri, ed., *Corrispondenza*, 102, 16. Nov. 1814; Anna Eynard, Journal, BGE Ms suppl 1959, 201 (plea, 12 Jan. 1815), and 161–162 (jest, 28 Dec. 1814).

62. Pallain, ed., *Correspondance*, 66, 19 Oct. 1814.

63. Fournier, *Geheimpolizei*, 151, 3 Oct. 1814 (Alexander); Talleyrand, Pallain, ed., *Correspondance*, 26, 9 Oct. 1814.

64. Wilhelmy, *Salon*, 25–26.

65. Hundt, *Die mindermächtigen*, 105–106; Weil, *Dessous*, 1:257, 485–486.

66. For a more political view of Pichler and her patriotic writings, Lena Jansen, *Karoline Pichlers Schaffen und Weltanschauung im Rahmen ihrer Zeit* (Graz: Wächter, 1936); Heindl, "People," 50; Pichler, *Denkwürdigkeiten*, 2:8, 21, 34, 44–46. For her connections with Hormayr, André Robert, *L'idée nationale autrichienne et les guerres de Napoléon: L'apostolat du Baron de Hormayr et le salon de Caroline Pichler* (Paris: Alcan, 1933); Walter Consuelo Langsam, *The Napoleonic Wars and German Nationalism in Austria* (New York: Columbia University Press, 1930), 102–103.

67. Staegemann, *Olfers*, 266, Friedrich to Elisabeth, 21 Dec. 1814.

68. Stolberg, *Tagebuch*, 188, 2 Mar. 1815; Wellington, Hermann Freiherr v. Egloffstein, ed., *Carl Bertuchs Tagebuch vom Wiener Kongreß* (Berlin: Paetel, 1916), 124.

69. Staegemann, *Olfers*, 228, 9 Oct. 1814.

70. Weil, *Dessous*, 2:409–410 (31 Mar. 1815) for the exchange, 441 (11 Apr.) Hager's recommendation, 453 (12 Apr.), Mejean's departure. Staegemann, *Olfers*, 316 (2 Apr.), "not herself." On Fanny's continued hospitality and moderation despite the outburst, Spiel, *Arnstein*, 299–300.

71. Alexandre Sapojnikov, "The Congress of Vienna in the Memoirs of a Russian Officer," in Ole Villumsen Krog, ed., *Danmark og Den Dansende Wienerkongres. Spillet om Danmark / Denmark and the Dancing Congress of Vienna. Playing for Denmark's Future* (Copenhagen: Christiansborg Slot, 2002), 142.

72. Olaf Blaschke, "Das 19. Jahrhundert: Ein Zweites Konfessionelles Zeitalter?," *Geschichte und Gesellschaft* 26 (2000): 38–75; David Sorkin, *The Religious Enlightenment: Protestants, Jews, and Catholics from London to Vienna* (Princeton, NJ: Princeton University Press, 2008); Jonathan Sheehan, "Enlightenment, Religion, and the Enigma of Secularization: A Review Essay," *American Historical Review* 108, 4 (2003): 1061–1080; Michael Printy, *Enlightenment and the Creation of German Catholicism* (Cambridge: Cambridge University Press, 2009); Nigel Aston, *Christianity and Revolutionary Europe, 1750–1830* (Cambridge: Cambridge University Press, 2002).

73. Blaschke, "Zeitalter"; Jonathan Hess, *Germans, Jews, and the Claims of Modernity* (New Haven: Yale University Press, 2002); Jonathan Sheehan, *The Enlightenment Bible: Translation, Scholarship, Culture* (Princeton, NJ: Princeton University Press, 2005); Wolfgang Altgeld, *Katholizismus, Protestantismus, Judentum: Über religiös begründete Gegensätze und nationalreligiöse Ideen in der Geschichte des deutschen Nationalismus* (Mainz: Grünewald, 1992).

74. George S. Williamson also cautions against an exclusive focus on confessional conflict or confessional identity that overlooks cross-confessional ties: "A Religious Sonderweg? Reflections on the Sacred and the Secular in the Historiography of Nineteenth-Century Germany," *Church History* 75, 1 (2006): 139–156, 146; and see Helmut Walser Smith and Christopher Clark, "The Fate of Nathan," in Smith, ed., *Protestants, Catholics, and Jews in Germany, 1800–1914* (Oxford: Berg, 2001), 3–29; generally on the growth of toleration, Aston, *Christianity*, 18–20, 141–144.

75. For such ecumenical thinking by a leading revivalist Catholic, Franz Georg Friemel, *Johann Michael Sailer und das Problem der Konfession* (Leipzig: St. Benno, 1972), 3–5, 25.

76. Ulrike Gleixner, *Pietismus und Bürgertum: Eine historische Anthropologie der Frömmigkeit, Württemberg, 17.–19. Jahrhundert* (Göttingen: Vandenhoeck & Ruprecht, 2005).

77. Aston, *Christianity*, 61–62; Hoock-Demarle, *L'Europe*, 165–166; Friemel, *Sailer*, 25–26, 59, 94, and 251–265 on Sailer's relations with the Stolbergs of Wernigerode, first inspired by their reading of his prayer book; Bernhard Gajek, "Dichtung und Religion. J.M. Sailer und die Geistesgeschichte des 18. und 19. Jahrhunderts," in Hans Bungert, ed., *Johann Michael Sailer: Theologe, Pädagoge und Bischof zwischen Aufklärung und Romantik* (Regensburg: Mittelbayerische Druckerei, 1983), 59–85.

78. Gajek, "Sailer," 75; Gerard Koziełek, *Friedrich Ludwig Zacharias Werner. Sein Weg zur Romantik* (Wrocław, 1963), 13 (youth); Friedrich

Ludwig Zacharias Werner, *Nachgelassene Predigten* (Vienna, 1836), 128; Alexander, Ernest John Knapton, *The Lady of the Holy Alliance: The Life of Julie de Krüdener* (New York: Columbia University Press, 1939), 151.

79. Max Geiger, *Aufklärung und Erweckung, Beiträge zur Erforschung Johann Heinrich Jung-Stillings und der Erweckungstheologie* (Zurich: EVZ, 1963), 306, Stourdza to Jung-Stilling, 8 Nov. 1814.

80. Francis Ley, *Madame de Krüdener 1764–1824. Romantisme et Sainte-Alliance* (Paris: Champion, 1994), 202; Count de Falloux, *Life and Letters of Madame Swetchine,* trans. H. W. Preston (Boston: 1867), 95, on Krüdener's and Ligne's mutual desire for conversion.

81. Sebastian Conrad, "Enlightenment in Global History: A Historiographical Critique," *American Historical Review* 117, 4 (2012): 999–1027, 1004, and the literature in note 72. Sheehan, "Review Essay," 1075–1076, argues for a "media-driven" concept of Enlightenment as cultural practice, in which religious and secular concerns overlap. A network-driven approach might do even more, in breaking down the distinction between "internal" religiosity as private piety and "external" as church attendance and ritual (1074–1075) to encompass the intervening realm of social communication and cultural practice from individuals to small groups to official church institutions, while also focusing attention on the languages and ideas communicated rather than primarily on generic and formal considerations of the media involved.

82. Otto Weiss, *Begegnungen mit Klemens Maria Hofbauer (1751–1820)* (Regensburg: Pustet, 2009), 24–25.

83. See the copies, with marginalia, in the Varnhagen Library, Rare Books Library, Staatsbibliothek Berlin; Staegemann, *Olfers,* 289–290, Elisabeth to Friedrich, 10 Feb. 1815; Ludmilla Assing, ed., *Briefwechsel zwischen Varnhagen und Rahel,* 6 vols. (reprint, Bern: Lang, 1973 [1874]), 4:113, Rahel to Varnhagen, 12 June 1815.

84. Alexander M. Martin, *Romantics, Reformers, Reactionaries: Russian Conservative Thought and Politics in the Reign of Alexander I* (DeKalb: Northern Illinois University Press, 1997), 154.

85. Of a large literature, for this and the paragraph preceding: Knapton, *Lady;* Ley, *Krüdener;* Geiger, *Erweckung;* Ghervas, *Alexandre Stourdza,* ch. 4; Susan A. Crane, "Holy Alliances: Creating Religious Communities after the Napoleonic Wars," in Michael Geyer and Lucian Hölscher, eds., *Die Gegenwart Gottes in der modernen Gesellschaft: Transzendenz und religiöse Vergemeinschaftung in Deutschland* (Göttingen: Wallstein, 2006), 37–59; Andrei Zorin, "'Star of the East': The Holy Alliance and European Mysticism," *Kritika* 4, 2 (2003): 313–342.

86. On Maistre, Stourdza, and Swetchine: Edling, *Mémoires,* 23–24, 99–100 (quote); Falloux, *Swetchine,* 48–49, 59; on revivalist religiosity generally in St. Petersburg, including Maistre: Ghervas, *Alexandre Stourdza,* 299–305; Grenier, ed., *Rzewuska,* 2:29–31; Martin, *Romantics,* ch. 6.

87. Martin, *Romantics,* 159–161; Judith Cohen Zacek, "The Russian Bible Society and the Russian Orthodox Church," *Church History* 35, 4 (1966): 411–437.
88. Knapton, *Lady,* 50–51, 113–115; Ley, *Krüdener,* 214–216, 323–339; Elizabeth W. Schermerhorn, *Benjamin Constant, His Private Life and His Contribution to the Cause of Liberal Government in France, 1767–1830* (New York: Haskell House, 1970 [1924]), 297–301; Langallerie was Constant's relative (297–298).
89. Emil Wismer, *Der Einfluss des deutschen Romantikers Zacharias Werner in Frankreich. Die Beziehungen des Dichters zu Madame de Staël* (Bern: Lang, 1968 [1928]), 4–6, 10–12, 19, 31.
90. Ley, *Krüdener,* 205.
91. On the Schlegels and the Vienna revival circles, Rudolph Till, *Hofbauer und sein Kreis* (Vienna: Herold, 1951): 42–48, 60–73.
92. Alphons v. Klinkowström, *Friedrich August v. Klinkowström und seine Nachkommen* (Vienna, 1877), 273–280; Wolfgang Zechner, "Joseph Anton von Pilat" (diss., University of Vienna, 1954), 102–104; Hofer, *Hofbauer,* 266–269, 284–285; GMD, Sophie Schlosser Tagebuch, conversions fol. 17v, 9 Jan. 1815.
93. Till, *Hofbauer,* 66, 72–73; Jansen, *Pichlers Schaffen,* 200–218, 237; Gerstinger underestimates Pichler's commitment to Catholic revival: *Salonkultur,* 67, 106–107; Hofer, *Hofbauer,* 298–300; Winter, *Romantismus,* 64, 103; Andreas Oplatka, *Graf Stephan Széchenyi. Der Mann, der Ungarn schuf* (Vienna: Zsolnay, 2004), 27–28, 68; Pichler, *Denkwürdigkeiten,* 2:13–14.
94. Zechner, "Pilat," 102–128; Montet, *Erinnerungen,* 99–103 on Werner; Grenier, ed., *Rzewuska,* 1:343–350.
95. Weiss, *Begegnungen,* 80.
96. Stolberg, *Tagebuch,* 51, 53, 78, 132–133; Pichler, *Denwürdigkeiten,* 2:39–40; Jansen, *Pichlers Schaffen,* 212–214; Heinz Röllecke, ed., *Briefwechsel zwischen Jacob und Wilhelm Grimm* (Stuttgart: Hirzel, 2001–), 1:430 (Jacob to Wilhelm, 18 Mar. 1815).
97. StAB 7,20 NL Smidt, no. 518, Smidt and Wilhelmine Smidt to Trinchen Castendyk, 7 June 1815, fol. 80.
98. StAB 7,20 NL Smidt, no. 518, fol. 22–22v, Wilhelmine Smidt to Trinchen Castendyk, 19 Nov. 1814; GMD, Schlosser Tagebuch, fols. 11v–12v, 18 Nov.
99. Stolberg, *Tagebuch,* XXXVI–VII, quote 101, 24 Nov. 1814; Schlosser, GMD, Schlosser Tagebuch.
100. Patricia Kennedy Grimsted, *The Foreign Ministers of Alexander I. Political Attitudes and the Conduct of Russian Diplomacy, 1801–1825* (Berkeley: University of California Press, 1969), 228 (Capodistrias); C.M. Woodhouse, *Capodistria: The Founder of Greek Independence* (London: Oxford University Press, 1973), 57–58, 61, 129; Edling, *Mémoires,* 224–225, 237.

101. Anna Eynard, Journal, BGE Ms suppl 1959, 131–132.
102. Assing, ed., *Tagebücher,* 331, 340, 350 (16 Nov. and 15 Dec. 1814, 17 Jan. 1815).
103. On Metternich's religion, emphasizing Enlightenment rationality and adherence to the church as institution, Heinrich Ritter von Srbik, *Metternich: Der Staatsmann und der Mensch,* 2nd ed., 3 vols. (Munich: Bruckmann, 1957 [1925–54]), 1:306–315.
104. Melton, *Rise of the Public,* 197, 206–207 on salons' "close relationship to eighteenth-century print culture"; Goodman, *Republic of Letters,* 136–165; on the connection with associational life and patriotic charity, Karen Hagemann, "Female Patriots: Women, War and the Nation in the Period of the Prussian-German Anti-Napoleonic Wars," *Gender and History* 16 (2004): 397–424, 409–410.
105. Gesellschaft adeliger Frauen zur Beförderung des Guten und Nützlichen, *Hof- und Staats-Schematismus des österreichischen Kaiserthums* (Vienna, 1814), 823–824; Joseph Karl Mayr, *Wien im Zeitalter Napoleons. Staatsfinanzen, Lebensverhältnisse, Beamte und Militär* (Vienna: Gistel, 1940), 99–100. See Margarete Grandner and Edith Saurer, "Emanzipation und Religion in der jüdischen Frauenbewegung. Die Faszination der Assoziation," in Grandner and Saurer, eds., *Geschlecht, Religion und Engagement. Die jüdischen Frauenbewegungen im deutschsprachigen Raum 19. und frühes 20. Jahrhundert* (Vienna: Böhlau, 2005), 8–10, but many more branches existed than indicated there. Spiel, *Arnstein,* 249–250.
106. Eduard Hanslick, *Geschichte des Concertwesens in Wien* (facs. Farnborough, England: Gregg, 1971 [orig. Vienna, 1869]), 145–149. Spiel, *Arnstein,* 256, for Fanny Arnstein's role.
107. On the *Friedensblätter,* Kette, and Stroblkopf networks, see Winter, *Romantismus,* 105; Till, *Hofbauer,* 47, 61, 65; and Volker Schupp, "Joseph von Laßberg, die Fürstlich-Fürstenbergische Handschriftensammlung und Johann Leonhard Hug, Professor an der Universität Freiburg," originally in *Freiburger Universitätsblätter* 131 (1996): 93–106, 97–98, available at http://74.125.47.132/search?q=cache:9fOdEgn5PSUJ:www.freidok.uni-freiburg.de/volltexte/6394/pdf/Schupp_Joseph_von_Lassberg.pdf+lassberg+stroblkopf&cd=1&hl=en&ct=clnk&gl=us (accessed 8 Sept. 2009); Horst Conrad, *Die Kette: Eine Standesvereinigung des Adels auf dem Wiener Kongreß* (Münster: Vereinigte westfälische Adelsarchive, 1979); Ursula Brauer, *Isaac von Sinclair. Eine Biographie* (Stuttgart: Klett-Cotta, 1993), 289–294.
108. Winter, *Romantismus,* 68–69, 96–97; Ingrid Merchiers, *Cultural Nationalism in the South Slav Habsburg Lands in the Early Nineteenth Century: The Scholarly Network of Jerneij Kopitar (1780–1844)* (Munich: Otto Sagner, 2007), 47, 49, 53, 163–165, 234; Max Vasmer, *B. Kopitars Briefwechsel mit Jakob Grimm* (Cologne: Böhlau, 1987 [1938]), XVI–XVII, XX–XV.
109. Fournier, *Geheimpolizei,* 394, report of 16 Feb. 1815.

110. HHStA StK Noten von der Polizeihofstelle 31, Fasz. 1, Hager to StK, 30 July 1815, sending the play to the censors for the third time, along with Gentz's comments recommending publication with changes, and StK Notenwechsel Polizeihofstelle 4, 16 Aug. 1815, StK to Hager, with corrections in Hudelist's hand; Pichler, *Denkwürdigkeiten*, 2:52–53; for censors' confessional concerns regarding another play, HHStA KK 36 (1814), nos. 100–364, no. 194, 8 Nov. 1814. Emphasizing opposition to nationalism and populist politics in the play's censorship, Karin Baumgartner, "Staging the German Nation: Caroline Pichler's *Heinrich von Hohenstaufen* and *Ferdinand II*," *Modern Austrian Literature* 37, 1/2 (2004): 1–20; Donald E. Emerson, *Metternich and the Political Police: Security and Subversion in the Habsburg Empire, 1815–1830* (The Hague: Nijhoff, 1968), 151.

111. Pichler, *Denkwürdigkeiten*, 2:35–37, 52–53; *Friedensblätter*, no. 5, 12 Jan. 1815, 20; Stolberg, *Tagebuch*, 130, also thought the work's anti-French passages might not pass the censors.

4. Negotiating Religion

1. For this and the following, Nigel Aston, *Christianity and Revolutionary Europe, 1750–1830* (Cambridge: Cambridge University Press, 2002), chs. 5–7.

2. Erwin Ruck, *Die römische Kurie und die deutsche Kirchenfrage auf dem Wiener Kongress* (Basel: Reinhardt, 1917), 5.

3. Rinieri, ed., *Corrispondenza*, 93–94, Consalvi to Pacca, 16 Nov. 1814; Ruck, *Kurie*, 23. Consalvi's formal protests: Klüber, *Acten*, 4:319–328 (two notes of 14 June 1815), and similarly 4:316–317 (5 Sept. 1815, speech of Pius VII to Consistory in Rome).

4. On Consalvi, the papal image, and Vatican politics surrounding the Congress, in addition to Ruck, *Kurie,* see now Roberto Regoli, "Cardinal Consalvi and the Restitution of the Papal States," in Heinz Duchhardt and Johannes Wischmeyer, eds., *Der Wiener Kongress—Eine kirchenpolitische Zäsur?* (Göttingen: Vandenhoeck & Ruprecht, 2013), 113–126; on reactionary politics in Rome, Alan J. Reinerman, *Austria and the Papacy in the Age of Metternich,* 2 vols. (Washington, DC: Catholic University of America Press, 1979–89), 1:37–38.

5. Humboldt advised against it: GStA PK III. HA MdA I, no. 1212, fols. 1–2v, undated memo, including plea for restitution of papal territories; Knesebeck's memo promoting the king of Saxony in Italy, VI. HA NL Friedrich Wilhelm von Preußen, B VI no. 29–30, fol. 3, Basel, 18 Jan. 1814; Hardenberg reporting Tsar Alexander's agreement, ibid., fol. 38v, Hardenberg to King, 14 July 1814. See generally Reinerman, *Austria and the Papacy,* 1:7–14, 16, 183.

6. Rinieri, ed., *Corrispondenza*, LXVIII–IX, 276–279 (Saint-Marsan diary, 20 Jan. 1815; Consalvi to Pacca, 15 Feb. 1815).

7. Michael Haringer, *Das Leben des ehrwürdigen Dieners Gottes Clemens Maria Hofbauer, General-Vicars und vorzüglichen Verbreiters der Congregation des allerheiligsten Erlösers*, 2nd ed. (Regensburg: Pustet, 1880), 302; Klemens Maria Hofbauer, *Briefe und Berichte*, P. Hans Schermann, ed. (Vienna: Redemptoristenkollege Innsbruck, 2000), 118–119.

8. Haringer, *Hofbauer*, 296–297; Johannes Hofer, *Der heilige Klemens Maria Hofbauer. Ein Lebensbild*, 3rd ed. (Freiburg i. B.: Herder, 1923), 285–287; Wolfgang Zechner, "Joseph Anton von Pilat" (diss., University of Vienna, 1954), 64, 69–71.

9. Friedrich Ludwig Zacharias Werner, *Nachgelassene Predigten* (Vienna, 1836), 91–107, 224–225, 294.

10. Walter Lipgens, *Ferdinand August Graf Spiegel und das Verhältnis von Kirche und Staat 1789–1835. Die Wende vom Staatskirchentum zur Kirchenfreiheit*, 2 vols. (Münster: Aschendorff, 1965), 1:179–194. Metternich's motives, Richard Metternich-Winneburg, *Aus Metternich's nachgelassenen Papieren*, 8 vols. (Vienna, 1880–84), 3:3–9, Metternich's presentation to Franz, 5 Apr. 1816, and commentary from 1855; for his desire to retreat from Josephine policies, Reinerman, *Austria and the Papacy*, 1:23–24.

11. As a corrective, see esp. Otto Weiss, *Klemens Maria Hofbauer und seine Biographen. Eine Rezeptionsgeschichte* (Rome: Collegium S. Alfonsi de Urbe, 2001), 66–70, and 111–112, 200–201.

12. Dominik Burkard, *Staatskirche—Papstkirche—Bischofskirche. Die "Frankfurter Konferenzen" und die Neuordnung der Kirche in Deutschland nach der Säkularisation* (Rome: Herder, 2000), 112–113, on broader agreement; "Darstellung des traurigen Zustandes der entgüterten und verwaisten katholische Kirche Teutschlands und ihrer Ansprüche," in Klüber, *Acten*, 1:28–37, signed Wambold, Helfferich, Joseph Schies, 30 Oct. 1814 (the main Oratoren memo). Wessenberg used similar emotive language, "abandonment" and "orphaned": Klüber, *Acten*, 2:299–304, memo of 27 Nov. 1814, including "Verlassenheit" and "verwaiset" (300).

13. Franz Xaver Bischoff, "Die Konkordatspolitik des Kurerzkanzlers Karl Theodor von Dalberg und seines Konstanzer Generalvikars Ignaz Heinrich von Wessenberg in den Jahren 1803–1815," *Zeitschrift für Kirchengeschichte* 108, 1 (1997): 75–92, 84–85, 88–89; Lipgens, *Spiegel*, 1:179–183, 189–192, and memoranda of August and November 1814, 2:610–615, 623–626.

14. Otto Weiss, *Begegnungen mit Klemens Maria Hofbauer (1751–1820)* (Regensburg: Pustet, 2009), 104, 112; Ruck, *Kurie*, 40–42.

15. Consalvi memo, 17 Nov. 1814; Lipgens, *Spiegel*, 1:190–93; Anon. [Wessenberg], *Die Deutsche Kirche. Ein Vorschlag zu ihrer neuen Begründung und Einrichtung* (n.p., Apr. 1815); *Rheinischer Merkur*, no. 224, 17 Apr. 1815, including publication of the Oratoren appeal of 1 Mar. 1815, also in Klüber, *Acten*, 2:255–260; *Rheinischer Merkur*, no. 172, 2 Jan. 1815, for the Oratoren memo of 30 Oct. 1814.

16. GMD, Sophie Schlosser Tagebuch, fol. 15, 5 Dec. 1814.

17. Weiss, *Biographen,* 66–70, 110–111; Hofer, *Hofbauer,* 283, mixed view; Haringer, *Hofbauer,* 297–298, and Rudolph Till, *Hofbauer und sein Kreis* (Vienna: Herold, 1951), 47–48, 66, for Hofbauer's influence on Ludwig and Bavarian policy.

18. Klüber, *Acten,* 2:321.

19. Hessian amendment, Klüber, *Acten,* 2:366; Austrian, Prussian, and Hanoverian judgment from separate three-power meeting of 28 May 1815: Eckhardt Treichel, ed., *Die Entstehung des Deutschen Bundes 1813–1815,* 2 vols. (Munich: Oldenbourg, 2000), 2:1369.

20. Klüber, *Acten,* 2:441, 535 (session of 8 June), and 2:295–299, 308–310, for the Oratoren memo of 29 May 1815 and Wessenberg's effort to preserve the Catholic clause along with the Protestant on 8 June 1814; Ruck, *Kurie,* 68–74, on the fortunes of the Catholic clause and Wessenberg's position, and Wessenberg, "Deutsche Kirche," 68, for his earlier view that Protestant rights might discriminate versus Catholics.

21. Burkard, *Neuordnung,* 127; Bischoff, "Konkordatspolitik," 91; Austria's requests to the Vatican, HHStA StK Rom 9, "Weisungen 1815," fols. 57, 80–83, Metternich to Lebzeltern, 30 Aug. and 14 Oct.

22. Burkard, *Neuordnung,* 133–134; Pilat, MOL, Széchényi Papers, I. kötet, P623/32, fols. 342–343 (undated).

23. GStA PK III. HA MdA I, no. 1265, fol. 2–2v, May 1815 (no day). The treaty was not formally ratified until later, since the Portuguese delegates lacked the necessary instructions from Rio. Noting the role of new religious toleration ideas at the Vienna Congress for the Belgian, Genevan, and German cases, Jean de Ridder, "La liberté de conscience en droit international," *Revue de droit international et de législation comparée,* 2nd ser., 7 (1905): 283–302, 289–290.

24. Klüber, *Acten,* 2:320, quote, 610–611 final version.

25. TNA FO 37/73, no fol., Fagel to Castlereagh, 7 Mar. 1814.

26. Focusing on relations with Islam, Robert D. Crews, *For Prophet and Tsar: Islam and Empire in Russia and Central Asia* (Cambridge, MA: Harvard University Press, 2006); Aston, *Christianity,* 141–148, 315–316 on Europe generally.

27. *Jenaische Allgemeine Literatur-Zeitung,* no. 94, May 1815, cols. 265–268, review of works on abolition, here col. 268; Aston, *Christianity,* 106–107, 145–147, 314–315.

28. John Martin Robinson, *Cardinal Consalvi 1757–1824* (London: Bodley Head, 1987), 105–106, 108–109; John W. Derry, *Politics in the Age of Fox, Pitt and Liverpool: Continuity and Transformation* (New York: St. Martin's, 1990).

29. Guillaume de Bertier de Sauvigny, *The Bourbon Restoration,* trans. Lynn M. Case (Philadelphia: University of Pennsylvania Press, 1966), 66, 77–78; Cracow, Angeberg, *Congrès,* 3:1170.

30. For the Belgian case, TNA FO 139/35, fols. 55–58, 61–69, Clancarty to Castlereagh, Brussels, 13 and 18 Sept. 1815, with enclosed protest pamphlet.

31. Angeberg, *Congrès*, 2:631, quote from draft settlement; 3:935 (final settlement).
32. Michael Broers, "Sexual Politics and Political Ideology under the Savoyard Monarchy, 1814–21," *English Historical Review* 114, 457 (1999): 607–635.
33. Lucien Cramer, ed., *Genève et les traités de 1815. Correspondance diplomatique de Pictet de Rochemont et de François d'Ivernois. Paris, Vienne, Turin 1814–1816*, 2 vols. (Geneva: Kündig & Champion, 1914), 1:XXVIII; the Vatican also expressed concerns about Catholic rights in Geneva, in a note of 18 Dec. 1814, HHStA StK Kongreßakten 14, Fasz. 2, folder 2, fols. 38–39.
34. HHStA StK Kongreßakten 13, Fasz. 1 [alt 23], fols. 19–22, quote 19, detailed provisions 19v–20v; Angeberg, *Congrès*, 3:988–989, Protocol of Committee of Eight, Annexe 12 to Acte Final; on similar limited toleration in seventeenth-century settlements, see Antje von Ungern-Sternberg, "Religion and Religious Intervention," in Bardo Fassbender and Anne Peters, eds., *The Oxford Handbook of the History of International Law* (Oxford: Oxford University Press, 2012), 294–316, 312–313.
35. Cramer, ed., *Correspondance*, 1:722, d'Ivernois to Turrettini, 15 Mar. 1815.
36. Ibid., 1:403, "Projet," 1 Mar. 1815.
37. Ibid., 1:384–387, 412–413 (Pictet to Turrettini, 3 and 12 Mar.), and 711, 717, 721–722, 736–737 (d'Ivernois to Turrettini/Schmidtmeyer, 3, 8, 15, and 26–29 Mar.).
38. Ibid., 1:154–155, instructions of Genevan Council for Vienna delegation, 17 Sept. 1814; André Palluel-Guillard, *L'Aigle et la croix. Genève et la Savoie 1798–1815* (Yens sur Moges: Éditions Cabédita, 1999), 528, emphasizing strategic over religious and constitutional considerations. Final agreement, Angeberg, *Congrès*, 3:989, 29 Mar. 1815.
39. Cramer, ed., *Correspondance*, 1:121, Pictet's report to Genevan State Council, 8 June 1814; Angeberg, *Congrès*, 2:523–524 (11 Dec. 1814).
40. Max J. Kohler, *Jewish Rights at the Congress of Vienna (1814–1815), and Aix-la-Chapelle (1818)* (New York: American Jewish Committee, 1918), 2, 38; De Ridder, "Liberté de conscience," 290.
41. Vneshniaia, 8:309–310, instructions for commissioners, 28 Apr./10 May 1815; description of "günstiges Reglement" of 1818, GStA PK III. HA MdA I, no. 5770 (no fol.), Johann Gottfried Hoffmann (the Foreign Ministry privy councillor responsible for Cracow) to Hardenberg, 17 Oct. 1818 (quote), and report of the Prussian constitutional commissioner Baron Reibnitz, Tarnowitz, 3 Oct. 1818.
42. On Dohm, Jonathan Hess, *Germans, Jews, and the Claims of Modernity* (New Haven, CT: Yale University Press, 2002), 1–4, and ch. 1; Paul Lawrence Rose, *German Question/Jewish Question: Revolutionary Antisemitism from Kant to Wagner* (Princeton, NJ: Princeton University Press, 1992), 70–79; W.H. Zawadzki, *A Man of Honor: Adam Czartoryski as a Statesman of Russia and Poland 1795–1831* (Oxford: Clarendon, 1993),

58–60, 257, 266–267; and John Doyle Klier, *Russia Gathers Her Jews: The Origins of the "Jewish Question" in Russia, 1772–1825* (Dekalb: Northern Illinois University Press, 2011), chs. 5 and 6, which however puts more emphasis on continued restrictions motivated by anti-Jewish beliefs in the Russian and Polish cases.

43. Vneshniaia, 8:309, "culture sociale." The unofficial German draft referred to delay in the "ennoblement and nationalization of this numerous class of people": HHStA StK Kongreßakten 8, Fasz. 1, fol. 18–18v.

44. Vneshniaia, 8:309; "Bildung des gemeinen Mannes," HHStA StK Kongreßakten 8, Fasz. 1, fols. 17v–18.

45. Klier, *Russia,* 140–141, 146; Zawadzki, *Czartoryski,* 59, 267.

46. Christoph Lind, "Juden in den habsburgischen Ländern 1670–1848," in Eveline Brugger et al., *Geschichte der Juden in Österreich* (Vienna: Ueberreuther, 2006), 339–446, 361, 436–437 for territories where Jews were not allowed to settle, including Salzburg; Stephan Laux, *Gravamen und Geleit: Die Juden im Ständestaat der Frühen Neuzeit (15.–18. Jahrhundert)* (Hanover: Hahnsche Buchhandlung, 2010).

47. Salo Baron, *Die Judenfrage auf dem Wiener Kongreß* (Vienna: Löwit, 1920), 14–23, on the legislative rights landscape for German Jews. Prussian 1812 edict, Annegret H. Brammer, *Judenpolitik und Judengesetzgebung in Preußen 1812 bis 1847 mit einem Ausblick auf das Gleichberechtigungsgesetz des Norddeutschen Bundes von 1869* (Berlin: Schelzky & Jeep, 1987), 40–66; south German states, comparison with urban poor, Rainer Erb and Werner Bergmann, *Die Nachtseite der Judenemanzipation: Der Widerstand gegen die Integration der Juden in Deutschland 1780–1860* (Berlin: Metropol, 1989), 66–86. Mack Walker, *German Home Towns: Community, State, and General Estate, 1648–1871* (Ithaca, NY: Cornell University Press, 1971).

48. Jacob Katz, *From Prejudice to Destruction: Anti-Semitism, 1700–1933* (Cambridge, MA: Harvard University Press, 1980), 53, 107. Emphasizing the prevalence of antisemitism in the period: Wolfgang Altgeld, *Katholizismus, Protestantismus, Judentum: Über religiös begründete Gegensätze und nationalreligiöse Ideen in der Geschichte des deutschen Nationalismus* (Mainz: Grünewald, 1992); Erb and Bergmann, *Nachtseite;* Eleonore Sterling, *Judenhaß: Die Anfänge des politischen Antisemitismus in Deutschland (1815–1850),* 2nd ed. (Frankfurt am Main: Europäische Verlagsanstalt, 1969).

49. Albert Marx, *Geschichte der Juden in Niedersachsen* (Hanover: Fackelträger, 1995), 118–119, 129–130, on Helmstedt, Göttingen, and Northeim; Zvi Asaria, *Die Juden in Niedersachsen. Von den ältesten Zeiten bis zur Gegenwart* (Leer: Rautenberg, 1979), 376–377, 458; Uwe Eissing, "Zur Reform der Rechtsverhältnisse der Juden im Königreich Hannover (1815–1842)," *Niedersächsisches Jahrbuch für Landesgeschichte* 64 (1992): 287–340, 288–289.

50. Erb and Bergmann, *Nachtseite,* 81. For efforts to prevent Jewish immigration under the Holy Roman Empire, and continuity with later anti-Jewish politics, Laux, *Gravamen und Geleit,* 333, 348–351.

51. Baron, *Judenfrage*, 39–49; Andreas Lennert, "Johann Smidt und die Vertreibung der Juden aus Bremen," *Bremisches Jahrbuch* 87 (2008): 160–200, 161; Michael Hundt, "Die Vertretung der jüdischen Gemeinden Lübecks, Bremen und Hamburgs auf dem Wiener Kongreß," *Blätter für deutsche Landesgeschichte* 130 (1994): 143–190, 144–153; Max Markreich, *Geschichte der Juden in Bremen und Umgegend* (Bremen: Temmen, 2003), 31–39; David Alexander Winter, *Geschichte der jüdischen Gemeinde in Moisling/Lübeck* (Lübeck: Schmidt-Römhild, 1968), 80–81; S. Carlebach, *Geschichte der Juden in Lübeck und Moisling* (Lübeck, 1898), 59–61.

52. Population, Dietmar Preissler, *Frühantisemitismus in der Freien Stadt Frankfurt und im Grossherzogtum Hessen* (Heidelberg: Winter, 1989), 22; in general, 61–125. Jews had lived outside the ghetto since 1796.

53. Arthur Hertzberg, *The French Enlightenment and the Jews: The Origins of Modern Anti-Semitism* (New York: Columbia University Press, 1968); Léon Poliakov, *The History of Anti-Semitism: From Voltaire to Wagner* (New York: Vanguard, 1975), 86–99; classic statements of liberal ambivalence, Katz, *Prejudice*, and Reinhard Rürup, *Emanzipation und Antisemitismus: Studien zur Judenfrage der bürgerlichen Gesellschaft* (Göttingen: Vandenhoeck & Ruprecht, 1975).

54. Hess, *Germans, Jews*; Jonathan Sheehan, *The Enlightenment Bible: Translation, Scholarship, Culture* (Princeton, NJ: Princeton University Press, 2005), 178–180, 214–217, 233–237; Tuska Benes, *In Babel's Shadow: Language, Philology, and the Nation in Nineteenth-Century Germany* (Detroit, MI: Wayne State University Press, 2008), 95–112.

55. AHL ASA DB A3,2, fol. 74v, report of 18 Jan. 1815.

56. HStA Darm. O11, no. B124/1, fol. 16, Baron Gagern's copy of the Bremen Senate's "Instruktion" for Smidt, authored by Smidt. Lennert, "Vertreibung," 191–192, for similar rhetoric in letters to Senator Gröning of 31 Dec. 1814 and 6 Jan. 1815. On the importance of the shift from religious to national argumentation, Altgeld, *Katholizismus*, 106–107.

57. Quote, Lennert, "Vertreibung," 192.

58. Smidt, Baron, *Judenfrage*, 105, including quote; Lennert, "Vertreibung," 191; AHL ASA DB A3,2, Hach to Curtius (private), 6 Feb. 1815, fol. 81–81v.

59. Siegfried Silberstein, "Die Stellung Preussens und Mecklenburgs zu Artikel XVI der Deutschen Bundesakte," in Gesellschaft zur Förderung der Wissenschaft des Judentums, ed., *Beiträge zur Geschichte der deutschen Juden. Festschrift zum siebzigsten Geburtstage Martin Philippsons* (Leipzig: Fock, 1916), 302–324, 305.

60. A. Eckstein, "Hardenberg und die Frage der Judenemanzipation in den preußischen-fränkischen Fürstentümern," in Gesellschaft zur Förderung der Wissenschaft des Judentums, ed., *Beiträge*, 267–274; volunteers, GStA PK VI. HA NL Friedrich Wilhelm III. von Preußen, B V b no. 12, fols. 8–9, Hardenberg to King, 25 Feb. 1813.

61. Rose, *German Question/Jewish Question,* 79–83; Jeffrey Grossman, "Wilhelm von Humboldt's Linguistic Ideology: The Problem of Pluralism and the Absolute Difference of National Character—Or, Where Do the Jews Fit In?" *German Studies Review* 20, 1 (1997): 23–47. For more pluralist interpretations, Kohler, *Jewish Rights,* 63 71, translation of Humboldt's 1809 memo, 71–83; Paul Robinson Sweet, *Wilhelm von Humboldt: A Biography,* 2 vols. (Columbus: Ohio State University Press, 1978–80), 2:71–76, 203–208; Brian Vick, "Of Basques, Greeks, and Germans: Liberalism, Nationalism, and the Ancient Republican Tradition in the Thought of Wilhelm von Humboldt," *Central European History* 40, 4 (2007): 653–681. On socializing, Poliakov, *Anti-Semitism,* 293–296; Deborah Hertz, *Jewish High Society in Old Regime Berlin* (New Haven, CT: Yale University Press, 1988), 280–281; Humboldt, *Briefen,* 4:458.

62. HStA Hannov. NL Münster, Dep. 110 A, no. 96, fols. 1–4v, Decken to Münster, 15 Nov. 1814.

63. HStA Hannov. Hann. 92, no. 1422, fols. 13–20, "Bemerkungen über die Erweiterung der bürgerlichen Rechte der Juden." Martens's memo is undated and found among materials circulated at a later stage of debate in 1818, but it is clear from a conversation between Münster and Hach of Lübeck that Münster commissioned a memo from Martens that was presented to him by January 1815, and internal evidence strongly indicates that the present document was that memo, drawn up partly in explicit response to Decken's position from November as above. Hach, AHL ASA DB A3,2, fol. 102v, report no. 34, 23 Jan. 1815. The restriction regarding officeholding was not unusual in the German context (as opposed to the Dutch), with even the far-reaching Prussian legislation of 1812 taking that approach: Brammer, *Judenpolitik.*

64. Baron, *Judenfrage,* 51–53, 108; Kohler, *Jewish Rights,* 14–15; Richard Schwemer, *Geschichte der Freien Stadt Frankfurt a.M. (1814–1866),* 2 vols. (Frankfurt: Baer, 1910), 1:37, more favorable to Danz.

65. Niall Ferguson, *The House of Rothschild,* 2 vols. (New York: Viking, 1998–99), 1:173–174.

66. Lämel and petition, Baron, *Judenfrage,* 138–144; Ludmilla Assing, ed., *Tagebücher von Friedrich von Gentz* (Leipzig, 1873), 365, 371, 374, 382–383, 385–386 (19 March to 18 June); Humboldt, *Briefen,* 4:566–567.

67. Baron, *Judenfrage,* 47–49, 66–67; Carlebach, *Geschichte,* 61–63; Hundt, "Vertretung," 159–160, 169.

68. Kohler, *Jewish Rights,* 5–6, 19–21; Baron, *Judenfrage,* 117–138, 136–137.

69. William D. Godsey, "Nation, Government, and 'Anti-Semitism' in Early Nineteenth-Century Austria," *Historical Journal* 51, 1 (2008): 49–85. The Lords Estate did admit Jews, including Arnstein's son-in-law Baron Pereira-Arnstein in 1815 (78).

70. Gentz, Assing, ed., *Tagebücher,* 354, 2 Feb. 1815.

71. Baron, *Judenfrage,* 121–122.

72. StAB 2-P.8.E.2.c.1, extract of Smidt report, 30 Jan. 1815; 2-M.3.a.2, vol. 2, fols. 28–29, for the original, with Pilat's name in code.

73. Staegemann, *Olfers*, 239–240; cf. Hilde Spiel, *Fanny von Arnstein: Daughter of the Enlightenment*, trans. Christine Shuttleworth (Oxford: Oxford University Press, 1991), 286; Albert Boime, *Art in an Age of Counterrevolution, 1815–1848* (Chicago: University of Chicago Press, 2004), 54–55.

74. For "verjuden," Michael Hundt, "Widerstreitende Interessen und gemeinsame Bedrohungen. Lübeck und Bremen in den ersten Jahrzehnten des 19. Jahrhunderts," *Bremisches Jahrbuch* 87 (2008): 92–116, 110 (report of 15 Apr. 1815). This marks an early use of the "Verjudung" topos: Brian Vick, "Verjudung," in Richard S. Levy, ed., *Encyclopedia of Antisemitism, Anti-Jewish Prejudice and Persecution* (Santa Barbara, CA: ABC-CLIO, 2005), 735–736.

75. AHL ASA DB A3,2, Hach to Curtius, 3 Mar. 1815, fol. 98.

76. StAB 7,20, NL Smidt, no. 398, correspondence between Wilhelmine Smidt and Dorothea Schlegel. On residual anti-Jewish views among attendees of Jewish salons in Berlin, Hertz, *Jewish High Society*, 255–258.

77. Carl August Buchholz, *Actenstükke die Verbesserung des bürgerlichen Zustandes der Israeliten betreffend* (Stuttgart, 1815).

78. Carlo Augusto Bucholz [sic], *Documenti riguardanti la riforma dello stato civile degli Israeliti*, trans. Leon V.a [Vita] Saraval (Trieste, 1815), 11 quote, imprimatur 141; Schlegel's review, 133–141.

79. StAB 2-P.8.E.2.c.1, extract of Smidt report, 30 Jan. 1815; original in 2-M.3.a.2.b., vol. 2, fols. 28–29; Schlegel review, *Oesterreichischer Beobachter*, no. 61, 2 Mar. 1815, 336–338, and Bucholz [sic], *Documenti*, 133–141.

80. AHL ASA DB A3,2, fols. 85, 87, and 98, Hach to Curtius, 1, 3, and 29 Mar.

81. Jan Schenkenberger, "'Anwalt der Juden Deutschlands'—Carl August Bucholz und die Emanzipation der Juden" (master's thesis, University of Erfurt, 2008), 78.

82. Memo of 29 Mar., Baron, *Judenfrage*, 102–107; StAB 2-P.8.E.2.c.1, "Extract" of Smidt to Gröning, 18 Feb. 1815, "witzige Bemerkung."

83. Baron, *Judenfrage*, 86–88, 91–95; Hundt, "Vertretung," 159–160. Translation of Hardenberg's note, Kohler, *Jewish Rights*, 11–12. Austria's Hansa representative followed Grote in toning down the language regarding Hamburg: Baron, *Judenfrage*, 93.

84. Baron, *Judenfrage*, 94–99.

85. Vneshniaia, 8:267, Nesselrode to Struve, 27 Mar./8 Apr. 1815. Struve wrote again on 8 Nov., 9:45–46.

86. On the committee discussions: Baron, *Judenfrage*, 156–168; Kohler, *Jewish Rights*, 23–29; Preissler, *Frühantisemitismus*, 32–48; Hundt, "Vertretung," 171–178.

87. Here following Baron, *Judenfrage*, 152, 157.

88. Treichel, *Entstehung*, 2:1369, meeting of 28 May.

89. StAB 2-P.8.E.2.c.1, "Extract" of 26 May 1815.

90. StAB 2-M.3.a.2, vol. 3, fol. 86–86v, Smidt to Gröning, 31 May 1815.

91. Klüber, *Acten*, 2:440.

92. StAB 2-M.3.a.2, vol. 3, fol. 58v, Smidt to Gröning, 24 May 1815.

93. StAB 2-M.3.a.2, vol. 3, fol. 63, Smidt to Gröning, 26 May 1815; AHL ASA DB A3,2, fol. 140v, Hach to Curtius (Private), 30 May 1815. Treichel, *Entstehung*, 2:1542, Rechberg to Max Joseph, 11 June 1815.

94. AHL ASA DB A3,2, fol. 148v, Hach to Curtius (Private), 3 June 1815.

95. Klüber, *Acten*, 2:320–321, 456.

96. StAB 2-M.3.a.2, vol. 3, fols. 96v–97, Smidt to Gröning, 1 June 1815; AHL ASA DB A3,2, fol. 382v, Hach to Curtius, 3 June 1815. Citations also for following material.

97. Klüber, *Acten*, 2:502, 535, for the session protocols of 3 and 8 June; StAB 2-M.3.a.2, vol. 3, fols. 88v, 118v, and 125, Smidt to Gröning, 31 May (extra note), and 7 and 9 June, 1815; AHL ASA DB A3,2, fol. 393, Hach to Curtius, 6 June 1815, and AHL ASA Interna, no. 17218, extra sheet, plus report "Geschichte der Verhandlungen" (no fol.).

98. Baron, *Judenfrage*, 145, 172–173.

99. AHL Familienarchiv Hach, V, vol. M, Fasz. 1, folder "Wiener Kongress 1814/15," Hach to Eleonore Hach, 5 June 1815; Hach also visited Eskeles on 6 and 9 June, and Eskeles, Arnstein, and Buchholz on June 10, the very day of signing the Federal Act: vol. A, Fasz. 2, no. c5, "Tagebuch," 141–143.

100. Heinrich Graetz, *Geschichte der Juden von den ältesten Zeiten bis auf die Gegenwart*, 2nd ed., 11 vols. (Leipzig: Leiner, 1888–1900), 11:305–307; Baron, *Judenfrage*, 201–203; Hundt, "Vertretung," 178.

101. HHStA StK Kongreßakten 6, alt 11, "Paraphirte Artikel der deutschen Bundesakte," fol. 24, with even the article number still in flux, corrected from 15 to 16; Martens, Treichel, *Entstehung*, 2:1544, Rechberg to Max Joseph, 11 June 1815.

102. Erb and Bergmann, *Nachtseite*, 176, n. 4; Günther Heinrich von Berg, "Ueber Judenwucher; insbesondere über die Mittel, das Landvolk gegen denselben zu schützen," in von Berg, *Staatswissenschaftliche Versuche*, 2 vols. (Lübeck, 1795), 2:211–274.

103. StAB 2-M.3.a.2, vol. 3, fol. 125, Smidt to Gröning, 9 June 1815; AHL ASA Interna, no. 17218, Hach, "Geschichte der Verhandlungen auf dem Wiener Kongreß die jüdischen Glaubensgenossen betr. 1815" (no fol.).

104. GStA PK III. HA MdA I, no. 1110, fol. 7v, internal Prussian comments on Austrian draft of May 1815; cf. Klüber, *Acten*, 2:313; Humboldt, *Briefen*, 4:568–570, 9 June 1815.

105. Hundt, "Vertretung," 178.

106. Humboldt, *Briefen*, 4:565–566 (4 June); Assing, ed., *Tagebücher*, 385 (9 June).

107. Enno E. Kraehe, *Metternich's German Policy*, vol. 2, *The Congress of Vienna* (Princeton, NJ: Princeton University Press, 1983), 2:382.

108. Preissler, *Frühantisemitismus*, 53–56. Preissler stresses both Klüber's strongly antisemitic rhetoric and his detrimental influence on later interpre-

tations of article 16 in the legal literature, but still accepts Klüber's reading of the document.

109. AHL ASA DB A3,2, fol. 399, Hach to Curtius, 9 June 1815.

110. The Diet of Mecklenburg-Schwerin cited article 16 versus its ruler's government: Silberstein, "Stellung Preussens und Mecklenburgs," 316–317.

111. Liefmann, Hundt, "Vertretung," 178; Metternich, Lennert, "Vertreibung," 170; Carlebach, *Geschichte*, 99, Winter, *Geschichte*, 83, for the Lübeck memorandum, Carlebach identifying Buchholz as likely author. Gabriel Riesser, *Ueber die Stellung der Bekenner des Mosaischen Glaubens in Deutschland. An die Deutschen aller Confessionen* (Altona, 1831), 34–39.

112. Hundt, "Vertretung," 177–178, for all three; Kohler, *Jewish Rights*, 32, finds the favorable interpretation a "reasonable construction."

113. Bremen, Lennert, "Vertreibung," 173–174; Lübeck, Carlebach, *Geschichte*, 100–101.

114. AHL ASA Interna, no. 17218, "Geschichte der Verhandlungen"; StAB 7,20 NL Smidt no. 622, Hach to Smidt, 28 Aug. 1815, fol. 29v.

115. Also see Berg's reading of article 16, Treichel, *Entstehung*, 2:1581, final report of 27 June 1815. Hach's anonymous pamphlet: *Die Juden in Lübeck* (Frankfurt a. M., 1816), 24–31; printed copy and associated documents in AHL ASA Interna no. 17220; notes, draft, and draft letter to Rühs (19 Oct. 1816), Interna no. 17225.

116 Lennert, "Vertreibung"; Preissler, *Frühantisemitismus*, 67–125, 106, satisfied, 96, "israelitischer Bürger."

5. Europe in the Wider World

1. Andrew Fitzmaurice, "Liberalism and Empire in Nineteenth-Century International Law," *American Historical Review* 117, 1 (2012): 122–140; Eric D. Weitz, "From the Vienna to the Paris System: International Politics and the Entangled Histories of Human Rights, Forced Deportations, and Civilizing Missions," *American Historical Review* 113, 5 (2008): 1313–1343, 1317–1321 for partial recognition of the Vienna settlement involving humanitarian values, but emphasizing the period 1860–1885. Helmut Berding notes the humanitarian basis and novelty of the Congress declaration against slavery with reference to an older literature on international law, but tends to relativize its significance: "Die Ächtung des Sklavenhandels auf dem Wiener Kongreß 1814/15," *Historische Zeitschrift* 219, 2 (1974): 265–289, 266–267.

2. HHStA Kriegsakten 430, Fasz. 2, folder 1, protocols of meetings on naval spoils from Venice, Trieste, and Dalmatia, 27 Jan. to 9 Feb. 1815; StK Intercepta Interiora 7, Fasz. alt 10, fols. 59–60, Russian intercepts, 5/17 June, 17/29 July 1814; Lebzeltern's warnings of Russian influence in the Adriatic and Italy, StK Rom 6, "Berichte Apr.–Dec. 1814," fol. 5, 25 April; similar exchanges between the Police Ministry and Foreign Ministry, StK Noten

von der Polizeihofstelle 30, fol. 116, Hager to Metternich, 13 Dec. 1814, and StK Notenwechsel an die Polizeihofstelle 4, fol. 141, Staatskanzlei to Hager, 26 Dec. 1814; multiple reports of Metternich's deputy Joseph von Hudelist, in StK Interiora Korrespondenz 67 and 68, from 1813 through 1815. Vneshniaia, 8:26, Nesselrode to Stackelberg, 19/21 June 1814, linking Albanian to Serbian talks. See Arthur G. Haas, *Metternich, Reorganization and Nationality 1813–1818: A Story of Foresight and Frustration in the Rebuilding of the Austrian Empire* (Wiesbaden: Steiner, 1963), 17–18; Ulrike Tischler, *Die habsburgische Politik gegenüber den Serben und Montenegrinern 1791–1822. Förderung oder Vereinnahmung?* (Munich: Oldenbourg, 2000), 174–187.

3. The 1780s was the worst decade (868,000 transported): see the website The Trans-Atlantic Slave Trade Database, www.slavevoyages.org/tast/assessment/estimates.faces; accessed 20 June 2012; David Eltis, "Revolution, War, Empire: Gendering the Transatlantic Slave Trade, 1776–1830," in Karen Hagemann, Gisela Mettele, and Jane Rendall, eds., *Gender, War and Politics: Transatlantic Perspectives, 1775–1830* (Basingstoke, England: Palgrave Macmillan, 2010): 41–57, 45.

4. On continued slave trading and British efforts to suppress it, see David Eltis, *Economic Growth and the Ending of the Transatlantic Slave Trade* (New York: Oxford University Press, 1987); and Christopher Lloyd, *The Navy and the Slave Trade: The Suppression of the African Slave Trade in the Nineteenth Century* (London: Longmans, 1949).

5. Paul Kielstra, *The Politics of Slave Trade Suppression in Britain and France, 1814–48* (Basingstoke, England: Palgrave Macmillan, 2000), 30–31.

6. Klüber, *Acten*, 4:509–510 [1815]; Susanne Zantop, *Colonial Fantasies: Conquest, Family, and Nation in Precolonial Germany, 1770–1870* (Durham, NC: Duke University, 1997); Sankar Muthu, *Enlightenment against Empire* (Princeton, NJ: Princeton University Press, 2003); Franz Leander Fillafer and Jürgen Osterhammel, "Cosmopolitanism and the German Enlightenment," in Helmut Walser Smith, ed., *The Oxford Handbook of Modern German History* (Oxford: Oxford University Press, 2011): 119–142.

7. João Pedro Marques, *The Sounds of Silence: Nineteenth-Century Portugal and the Abolition of the Slave Trade*, trans. Richard Wall (New York: Berghahn, 2006), 3, 10–11, 22–26, 49–53; also emphasizing the breadth of at least public rhetorical acceptance of abolitionism among European diplomats, Matthew Mason, "Keeping Up Appearances: The International Politics of Slave Trade Abolition in the Nineteenth-Century Atlantic World," *William and Mary Quarterly* 66, 4 (2009): 809–832.

8. Christoph Hauser, *Anfänge bürgerlicher Organisation. Philhellenismus und Frühliberalismus in Südwestdeutschland* (Göttingen: Vandenhoeck & Ruprecht, 1990).

9. Ambroise Palisot Baron de Beauvois, *Réfutation d'un écrit intitulé: Résumé Du Témoignage ... touchant la Traite des Nègres, addressé aux dif-*

férentes Puissances de la Chrétienté (Paris, 1814), vi (quote); Kielstra, *Suppression,* 37; Olivier Pétré-Grenouilleau, "Abolitionnisme et idée nationale: divorces et compromis, France, 1789–1831," in Pétré-Grenouilleau, ed., *Abolir l'esclavage. Un réformisme à l'épreuve (France, Portugal, Suisse, XVIIIe–XIXe siècles)* (Rennes: Presses Universitaires de Rennes, 2008), 185–206; Christopher Leslie Brown, *Moral Capital: Foundations of British Abolitionism* (Chapel Hill: University of North Carolina Press, 2006).

10. John Gurwood, ed., *The Dispatches of Field Marshal the Duke of Wellington, during his various campaigns in India, Denmark, Portugal, Spain, the Low Countries, and France,* 12 vols. new ed. (London, 1837–1838), 12:116, Wellington to Wilberforce, 15 Sept. 1814; Marques, *Silence,* 52–53.

11. TNA FO 92/9, fol. 156v, Castlereagh to Liverpool, 18 Dec. 1814.

12. Kielstra, *Suppression,* 19, 41–42.

13. TNA FO 92/8, fols. 87v–88, Castlereagh-Liverpool, 11 Nov. 1814; Gurwood, ed., *Dispatches,* 12:142, Wellington to Wilberforce, Paris, 8 Oct. 1814.

14. TNA FO 92/10, fols. 143v–44, Castlereagh to Liverpool, 11 Jan. 1815, and most fully, FO 139/24, fol. 29–29v, British marginal "Observations" to note of Portuguese plenipotentiaries, Vienna, 17 Nov. 1814. Bahia: Marques, *Silence,* 43; Kristin Mann, *Slavery and the Birth of an African City: Lagos, 1760–1900* (Bloomington: Indiana University Press, 2007), 40.

15. Betty Fladeland, "Abolitionist Pressure on the Concert of Europe, 1814–22," *Journal of Modern History* 38, 4 (1966): 355–373, 358 (Clarkson to Catherine Clarkson, 21 June 1814).

16. Fladeland, "Abolitionist Pressure," 364; Robert Isaac Wilberforce and Samuel Wilberforce, eds., *The Correspondence of William Wilberforce,* 2 vols. (London, 1840), 2:289, 9 Aug. 1814, Wilberforce to Zachary Macaulay.

17. Jerome Reich, "The Slave Trade at the Congress of Vienna—A Study in English Public Opinion," *Journal of Negro History* 53, 2 (1968): 129–143, 130; June 1814, Fladeland, "Abolitionist Pressure," 356, 358.

18. HHStA StK Kongreßakten 13, Fasz. 2, folder 2, fols. 34–35v, Clarkson to Metternich, Paris, undated but before the Congress; 36–53v for the pamphlet, Thomas Clarkson, *Eine summarische Uebersicht der vor dem Ausschuss des Unterhauses des Großbritannischen Parlaments abgelegten Zeugnisse über den Gegenstand des Sclaven-Handels den verschiedenen Regenten in der christlichen Welt zugeeignet von Thomas Clarkson* (London, 1814); see Walter Koschatzky, ed., *Der Wiener Kongress 1. September 1814 bis 9. Juni 1815. Ausstellung veranstaltet vom Bundesministerium für Unterricht gemeinsam mit dem Verein der Museumsfreunde* (Vienna, 1965), 155–156. For Prussian letters and "Light," GStA PK III. HA MdA I, no. 7974, fols. 2–3v, 29 Aug. 1814.

19. Clarkson, *Uebersicht,* quotes 33, 7; Wellesley, ed., *Suppl. Desp.,* 9:228–230, 243, Clarkson to Duke of Gloucester, Paris, 27 Aug. 1814, and Clarkson to Wellington, 12 Sept. 1814, including Wellington's aid in distribution;

and Gurwood, ed., *Dispatches,* 12:262, Wellington to Harrison, 7 Feb. 1815.

20. Vneshniaia, 8:217–218, Tatishchev to Cevallos, 25 Feb./9 Mar. 1815; Adam Hochschild, *Bury the Chains: Prophets and Rebels in the Fight to Free an Empire's Slaves* (Boston: Houghton Mifflin, 2005), 317.

21. Vneshniaia, 8:9, Nesselrode to Castlereagh, 19/31 May 1814.

22. Thomas David, "L'internationale abolitionniste: Les Suisses et l'abolitionnisme français, 1760–1840," in Pétré-Grenouilleau, ed., *Abolir l'esclavage,* 115–131, 122; Robert Isaac Wilberforce and Samuel Wilberforce, *The Life of William Wilberforce,* 5 vols. (London, 1838), 4:212–18; Wilberforce and Wilberforce, eds., *Correspondence,* 2:298–299, Smith to Wilberforce, 5 Dec. 1814.

23. Review, *Allgemeine Literatur-Zeitung,* no. 62, Mar. 1815, cols. 489–496; William Wilberforce, "Sendschreiben an den Fürsten Talleyrand-Perigord, in Betreff des Sklaven-Handels," *Minerva. Ein Journal historischen und politischen Inhalts* (Jan.–Mar. 1815): 270–308. Another review appeared in the *Jenaische Allgemeine Literatur-Zeitung,* no. 94, May 1815, cols. 265–268, with notice of Sismondi's pamphlet below as well.

24. Gurwood, ed., *Dispatches,* 12:142, Wellington to Wilberforce, 8 Oct. 1814.

25. J.C.L. Simonde de Sismondi, *De l'intérêt de la France a l'égard de la traite des Nègres,* 3rd ed. (Geneva, Paris, and London, 1814); Gurwood, ed., *Dispatches,* 12:145, Wellington to Lord Holland, 13 Oct. 1814. Holland first sent Wellington a copy of Sismondi's pamphlet from Geneva, Wellesley, ed., *Suppl. Desp.,* 9:284, Holland to Wellington, Geneva, 24 Sept. 1814. Translation, "Simonde de Sismondi über den Negerhandel," *Nemesis* 4, 2 (1815): 213–238.

26. Lucien Cramer, ed., *Genève et les traités de 1815. Correspondance diplomatique de Pictet de Rochemont et de François d'Ivernois. Paris, Vienne, Turin 1814–1816,* 2 vols. (Geneva: Kündig & Champion, 1914), 1:167, 174–175, Pictet to Genevan State Councillor Turrettini, 13 Oct. and 15–19 Oct. 1814.

27. David, "L'internationale abolitionniste." For a transatlantic eighteenth-century Protestant abolitionist international movement centered on Quakers, David Brion Davis, *The Problem of Slavery in the Age of Revolution, 1770–1823* (Ithaca, NY: Cornell University Press, 1975), ch. 5.

28. Generally on the negotiations, C.K. Webster, *The Foreign Policy of Castlereagh 1812–1815: Britain and the Reconstruction of Europe* (London: Bell, 1931), 413–424; on the broader background, Seymour Drescher, *Abolition: A History of Slavery and Anti-Slavery* (Cambridge: Cambridge University Press, 2009).

29. TNA FO 37/70, no fol., for slave trade negotiations with the United Provinces, esp. British note of 7 June by the resident in The Hague the earl of Clancarty, the Prince of Orange's decree of 15 June, and Clancarty to Castlereagh, 7 July 1814 (quote). Convention between Britain and the Netherlands of 13 Aug. 1814, in Angeberg, *Congrès,* 1:209–211. Bremen, *Allgemeine Zeitung,* no. 40, 9 Feb. 1815, 159, dateline Bremen, 20 Jan.

30. Pallain, ed., *Correspondance,* 158, 183–184, Talleyrand to Louis, 30 Nov. and 15 Dec. 1814.

31. Angeberg, *Congrès,* 2:726.

32. Angeberg, *Congrès,* 2:613, Labrador, 16 Jan. 1815, and 663, Palmella, 20 Jan.

33. John Gascoigne, *Joseph Banks and the English Enlightenment: Useful Knowledge and Polite Culture* (Cambridge: Cambridge University Press, 2003), 41.

34. For the judgment by historians as cowardly, Serge Daget, *La répression de la traite des Noirs au XIXe siècle. L'action des croisières françaises sur les côtes occidentales de l'Afrique (1817–1850)* (Paris: Karthala, 1997), 37; "cheap talk" or at least "soft law," Jenny S. Martinez, *The Slave Trade and the Origins of International Human Rights Law* (Stanford, CA: Stanford University Press, 2012), 33; Kielstra, *Suppression,* 52–53, stresses the importance of the precedent, as does Robert Rie, *Der Wiener Kongress und das Völkerrecht* (Bonn: Röhrscheid, 1957), 126–133; Berding, "Ächtung," adopts a middle position.

35. TNA FO 92/9, fols. 155v–156, and 92/12, pt. 1, fol. 9, Castlereagh to Liverpool, 18 Dec. 1814 and 13 Feb. 1815.

36. Wellesley, ed., *Suppl. Desp.,* 9:470, Liverpool to Castlereagh, 9 Dec. 1814; Harold Nicolson, *The Congress of Vienna: A Study in Allied Unity: 1812–1822* (New York: Compass, 1961), 214.

37. TNA FO 139/6, fol. 24v, Castlereagh to Liverpool, 2 Sept. 1814; Webster, *Diplomacy,* 274–275, Castlereagh to Liverpool, 1 Jan. 1815.

38. TNA FO 92/9, fols. 154v–155, Castlereagh to Liverpool, 18 Dec. 1814. Angeberg, *Congrès,* 2:701–702, Labrador, "justes repressailles."

39. GStA PK III. HA MdA I, no. 1374 (no fol.), "Note verbale" of Portuguese Ministers to Hardenberg, 18 Feb. 1815, and draft of "Note verbale" response, Mar. 1815; I. HA Rep. 81, Gesandschaft London, no. 284 (no fol.), Renfner and Ancillon to Jouffroy, Berlin, 7 Oct. 1816, confirmed in Hardenberg's instructions to Jouffroy, 9 Nov. 1816; Nesselrode, Vneshniaia, 8:152–153, 18/30 Dec. 1814.

40. TNA FO 92/9, fols. 155v–156; quote, FO 92/8, fol. 96, Castlereagh to Liverpool, 18 Dec. and 21 Nov. 1814; support of Austria, Russia, Prussia, France, and Sweden, Angeberg, *Congrès,* 2:698–700, 4 Feb. 1815; Metternich's reiterated support, 725–726.

41. Angeberg, *Congrès,* 2:664–667, session of 20 Jan. 1815; TNA FO 92/8, fols. 93–94v, Castlereagh to Liverpool, 21 Nov. 1814. On the staged character of the committee meetings, the protocols intended for later publication, Webster, *Castlereagh,* 422.

42. Marques, *Silence,* 40–43 for Palmella, 38–40 on Funchal; Leslie Bethell, *The Abolition of the Brazilian Slave Trade: Britain, Brazil, and the Slave Trade Question 1807–1869* (Cambridge: Cambridge University Press, 1970), 12–14.

43. TNA FO 92/10, fol. 169, Castlereagh to Liverpool, 22 Jan. 1815, for the hope that 10° N was a "mistake." See note to Labrador of 27 Dec. 1814,

Angeberg, *Congrès,* 2:571–572; 686–687 for the committee meeting of 28 Jan. 1815. Later negotiations, David R. Murray, *Odious Commerce: Britain, Spain and the Abolition of the Cuban Slave Trade* (Cambridge: Cambridge University Press, 1980), 53–71.

44. Kielstra, *Suppression,* 49, for the confusion about the demarcation line, which may have resulted from misunderstanding rather than ill will; Wellington thought French navy officials were trying to create a loophole to extend the slave trade: Gurwood, ed, *Dispatches,* 12:212–214, Wellington to Wilberforce, 14 Dec. 1814, and memo, 214–215. Exchange in committee on 28 Jan. 1815, Angeberg, *Congrès,* 2:685–686.

45. Quote, TNA FO 139/24, fol. 7, draft note to Labrador (in English), 27 Dec. 1814. On abolitionists' rationale: Reich, "Slave Trade," 142; Christopher Leslie Brown, "Empire without America: British Plans for Africa in the Era of the American Revolution," in Derek R. Peterson, ed., *Abolition and Imperialism in Britain, Africa, and the Atlantic* (Athens: Ohio University Press, 2010), 84–100, 93–95; Ralph A. Austen and Woodruff D. Smith, "Images of Africa and British Slave-Trade Abolition: The Transition to an Imperialist Ideology, 1787–1807," *African Historical Studies* 2, 1 (1969): 69–83; Mann, *Lagos,* 84–89. For Chaim D. Kaufmann and Robert A. Pape, abolitionism involved more "cultural imperialism" than cosmopolitanism: "Explaining Costly International Moral Action: Britain's Sixty-Year Campaign against the Atlantic Slave Trade," *International Organization* 53, 4 (1999): 631–668, 644, 646.

46. It also reflected abolitionist views: Clarkson suggested the measure to Wellington in a letter of 12 Sept. 1814, Wellesley, ed., *Suppl. Desp.,* 9:243.

47. Angeberg, *Congrès,* 2:684–685, 28 Jan. 1815.

48. Angeberg, *Congrès,* 2:668, conference of 20 Jan. 1815.

49. Angeberg, *Congrès,* 2:662, 20 Jan.

50. Seymour Drescher and Pieter Emmer, eds., *Who Abolished Slavery: Slave Revolts and Abolitionism: A Debate with João Pedro Marques* (New York: Berghahn, 2010).

51. Adrian Desmond and James Moore, *Darwin's Sacred Cause: Race, Slavery and the Quest for Human Origins* (London: Lane, 2009), 352–353; George W. Stocking, Jr., *Victorian Anthropology* (New York: Free Press, 1987), 240–257; J. W. Burrow, *Evolution and Society: A Study in Victorian Social Theory* (Cambridge: Cambridge University Press, 1966), 118–136; Boyd Hilton, *A Mad, Bad, and Dangerous People? England 1783–1846* (Oxford: Clarendon, 2006), 246–247. Seymour Drescher, "The Ending of the Slave Trade and the Evolution of European Scientific Racism," *Social Science History* 14, 3 (1990): 415–450, emphasizes the greater commitment to scientific racism in France than Britain through the 1850s.

52. Clifton Crais and Pamela Scully, *Sara Baartman and the Hottentot Venus* (Princeton, NJ: Princeton University Press, 2009); *Vossische Zeitung,* no. 120, 6 Oct. 1814 (ad); *Morgenblatt für gebildete Stände,* no. 220, 14 Sept. 1814, 880.

53. Karin A. Wurst, "Was 'Geist oder [. . .] Sinne lebhaft beschäftigt': Einige Überlegungen zum Unterhaltungsbegriff im 'Journal des Luxus und der Moden,'" in Angela Borchert and Ralf Dressel, eds., *Das "Journal des Luxus und der Moden": Kultur um 1800* (Heidelberg: Winter, 2004), 105–121, 115; orig. in *Journal für Luxus, Mode und Gegenstände der Kunst* (April 1813), 249–250; Herr Jordan showed the Khoikhoi man, whom he had acquired in England; a Herr Belli of Parma exhibited a female Laplander.

54. Stocking, *Anthropology*, 26, 48–53; *Friedensblätter*, no. 53, 1 Nov. 1814, 220. Also see Brian Vick, "Arndt and German Ideas of Race: Between Kant and Social Darwinism," in Walter Erhart and Arne Koch, eds., *Ernst Moritz Arndt (1769–1860): Deutscher Nationalismus—Europa—Transatlantische Perspektiven* (Tübingen: Niemeyer, 2007): 65–76.

55. Johann Jakob Trunk, *Was ist bey dem hohen Kongresse der europäischen Fürsten, in Wien, oder sonstwo, noch näher zu bestimmen, und für immer vestzusetzen? In rechtlicher und politischer Rücksicht* (Worms, 1814), 75–77; Aloys Weissenbach, *Meine Reise zum Congreß. Wahrheit und Dichtung* (Vienna, 1816), 229–230.

56. Kielstra, *Suppression*, 37, citing [anon.], *Appel aux nations commerçantes et maritimes de l'Europe, ou Réflexions rapides et impartiale sur la question de la traite* (Paris, 1814), 36, and Palisot, *Réfutation*.

57. Palisot, *Réfutation*, vii, 41, n. 7, for polygenesis and separate "species" rather than merely "races"; F. Mazères, *Lettre à M. J.-C.-L. Sismonde de Sismondi, sur les nègres, la civilisation de l'Afrique, Christophe et le Comte de Limonade* (Paris, 1815), esp. 5–22, quoting Palisot, 14–15, 30–32; Sismondi, *De l'intérêt*, 89.

58. [Anon.], *Remonstrances des Négocians du Brésil, contre les insultes faites au Pavillion Portugais, et contre le saisie violente et tyrannique de plusieurs de leurs navires, par les officiers de la Marine Anglaise*, trans. F.-S. Constancio from Portuguese and English (Paris, 1814), quote X–XI; [anon.], *Considérations importantes sur l'abolition générale de la traite des nègres, adressées aux Négociateurs des Puissances continentales qui doivent assister au Congrès de Vienne* (Paris, 1814), 3, for the "so praiseworthy" goal of abolition: in GStA PK III. HA MdA I, no. 7974, fols. 9–48v, 49–64, respectively.

59. Palisot, *Réfutation*, 32–33; Marques, *Silence*, 27, 49–50, for Portugal and Europe generally.

60. On the scale of illegal slave trading north of the equator in the Bight of Benin, Mann, *Lagos*, 4, 32–40; more generally, Eltis, *Economic Growth*; Lloyd, *Navy*.

61. Wilhelm von Bippen, *Johann Smidt, ein hanseatischer Staatsmann* (Stuttgart: Deutsche Verlags-Anstalt, 1921), 155; HHStA StK Kongreßakten 1, Fasz. 1, fol. 160 (German), and fol. 209 (French). Barbary also in "Article semiofficiel sur la marche des travaux du Congrès de Vienne," in Angeberg, *Congrès*, 2:364 (c. Oct. 1814). On Smidt's anticorsair lobbying at Vienna: Tilman Hannemann, "Brême et la lutte anti-pirate (1814–1819): Un prélude à l'action

colonial contre les Barbaresques," in Ahcène Abdelfettah and Alain Mess-
aoudi, eds., *Savoirs d'Allemagne en Afrique du nord, XVIIIe–XXe siècle*
(Paris: Bouchène, 2012), 73–95.

62. Robert C. Davis, *Christian Slaves, Muslim Masters: White Slavery in the
Mediterranean, the Barbary Coast, and Italy, 1500–1800* (Basingstoke,
England: Palgrave Macmillan, 2003), 23–24, and ch. 1 generally; Dre-
scher, *Abolition,* 29. Also see Salvatore Bono, *Corsari nel Mediterraneo.
Cristiani e musulmani fra guerra, schiavitù e commercio* (Milan: Monda-
dori, 1993), who emphasizes that thousands of Muslims were also enslaved
as prisoners of war in this period by Christian corsairs or the Knights of
Malta.

63. Linda Colley, "The Narrative of Elizabeth Marsh: Barbary, Sex, and Power,"
in Felicity A. Nussbaum, *The Global Eighteenth Century* (Baltimore: Johns
Hopkins University Press, 2003), 138–150.

64. Daniel Panzac, *Barbary Corsairs: The End of a Legend, 1800–1820,* trans.
Victoria Hobson and John E. Hawkes (Leiden: Brill, 2005), 114–115, following the official tally of Admiral Lord Exmouth of Britain. Exmouth,
TNA CO 2/6, fols. 155–156 for those redeemed from the three Regencies
(partially for ransom) in April 1816, and fol. 256 for those freed without
ransom from Algiers in August. They totaled 2,875 persons: Algiers, 1,514;
Tunis, 781; Tripoli, 580.

65. Panzac, *Corsairs,* 58, 74–76, 267–268; Salvatore Bono, *I corsari barbareschi* (Turin: ERI, 1964), 185–191. Also see Laura Veccia Vaglieri, "Santa
Sede e Barbareschi dal 1814 al 1819," *Oriente Moderno* 12, 10 (1932):
465–484, 467–470; and numerous reports from Lebzeltern, the Austrian
ambassador, in Rome, HHStA StK Rom 6, "Berichte Apr.–Dec. 1814," and
Rom 8, "Berichte 1815 I–IX."

66. Klüber, *Acten,* 4:510.

67. Panzac, *Corsairs,* 93–95, 114; Linda Colley, *Captives: Britain, Empire and
the World, 1600–1850* (London: Cape, 2002), 52–62.

68. Davis, *Christian Slaves,* 128–134, and chs. 3 and 4 generally; Drescher, *Abolition,* 29.

69. Panzac, *Corsairs,* 114.

70. Ibid. 114, 120–121; Colley, *Captives,* 55–56, 59; Bono, *Cristiani e musulmani,* 200. Bono is generally revisionist, but notes continued physical and
sexual abuse.

71. Sidney Smith, *Mémoire sur la nécessité et les moyens de faire cesser les pi-
rateries des états barbaresques* (Paris, 1814); *Schriftlicher Aufsatz Ueber die
Nothwendigkeit und Mittel die Seeraeubereyen der Barbaresken einzustel-
len* (Paris, 1814); HHStA StK Kongreßakten 13, Fasz. 2, folder 2, fols. 17–
24v for undated letter of 1814 to Metternich and manuscript memo; follow-up letter seeking permission to reprint, fols. 25–26v, 14 Jan. 1815;
HHStA StA Barbaresken 3, folder 1815–49, Consul Anton Nyssen to Inter-
nuntius, Tunis, 20 Oct. 1815. On Nyssen, Christian Windler, *La diplomatie
comme expérience de l'Autre. Consuls français au Maghreb (1700–1840)*

(Geneva: Droz, 2002), 137–142. The English translation appeared first in the *Morning Chronicle*, 10 Aug. 1815, no. 14436, quickly followed by other British papers.

72. On Smith's association, Hannemann, "Brême et la lutte anti-pirate," 82; for the efforts of the Knights of Malta to reestablish themselves in part by resuming their former mission against the corsairs, Umberto Castagnino Berlinghieri, *Congresso di Vienna e principio di legittimità: La questione del Sovrano Militare Ordine di San Giovanni Gerosolimitano, detto di Malta* (Milan: Vita e Pensiero, 2006), 89, 99–104.

73. AHL Familienarchiv Hach, V, vol. A, Fasz. 2, no. c5, Tagebuch, 4 Dec. 1814.

74. HHStA StK Kongreßakten 13, Fasz. 2, folder 2, fol. 25–25v, underlined in original, fol. 25. *Morning Chronicle*, no. 14260, 17 Jan. 1815; *Allgemeine Zeitung*, 19 Jan. 1815, Beilage, 29. In aid of Africans too, Elise von Bernstorff, *Ein Bild aus der Zeit von 1789 bis 1835. Aus ihren Aufzeichnungen* (Berlin: Mittler, 1896), 156.

75. Smith, *Mémoire*, 2–3; *Aufsatz*, 4.

76. Smith, *Mémoire*, 2; see Gillian Weiss, *Captives and Corsairs: France and Slavery in the Early Modern Mediterranean* (Stanford, CA: Stanford University Press, 2011), 147–150.

77. Smith, *Mémoire*, 3.

78. Wilberforce and Wilberforce, eds., *Correspondence*, 2:299, Smith to Wilberforce, 5 Dec. 1814; on the medals, Hannemann, "Brême et la lutte anti-pirate," 82.

79. Quote, *Morning Chronicle*, no. 14166, 29 Sept. 1814; see e.g. 8 and 11 Oct. 1814, and 8 Dec. Jondot, "L'Ordre de St. Jean de Jerusalem," *Mercure de France* (Aug. and Sept. 1814): 357–362, 451–462, 458–461.

80. Anon. [Franz Tidemann], *Was könnte für Europa in Wien geschehen? Beantwortet durch einen Deutschen* (n.p., 1814), 35–47; *Erinnerungsblätter*, 725–726, 21 Nov. 1814; Perry's wife, A. Aspinall, *Politics and the Press c. 1780–1850* (London: Home and Van Thal, 1949), 297.

81. *Allgemeine Handlungs-Zeitung* (Nuremberg), no. 249, 21 Dec. 1814, 1001–1003; the first part of the article was taken from an Austrian patriotic newspaper: *Der Aufmerksame* (Graz), no. 144, 3 Dec. 1814.

82. AHL ASA DB A3,2, fol. 121v, Curtius to Hach, 7 Feb. 1815; *Oesterreichischer Beobachter*, no. 43, 12 Feb. 1815, 239. Labrador, AHL Familienarchiv Hach, V, vol. A, Fasz. 2, no. c5, Tagebuch, 11 (entry of 27 Sept. 1814). On the pamphlet, Hannemann, "Brême et la lutte anti-pirate," 77–78; Friedrich Herrmann, *Ueber die Seeräuber im Mittelmeer und ihre Vertilgung. Ein Völkerwunsch an den erlauchten Kongreß in Wien. Mit den nöthigen historischen und statistischen Erläuterungen* (Lübeck, 1815).

83. *Journal für Literatur, Kunst, Luxus und Mode*, Dec. 1814, 778.

84. *Corriere delle Dame*, no. 41, 14 Oct. 1814, 328; updates on 2 and 30 Dec. 1815 (no. 48, p.385, no. 52, p.416).

85. *Hesperus,* no. 10, 73–74, Feb. 1815.
86. HStA Darm. O11, B127, fol. 182, report to Baron Nagell, 1 Oct. 1815. At the later London conferences to negotiate a defensive alliance against the corsairs, preparatory Prussian and British memoranda from Dec. 1817 made clear that explanations to the Porte should emphasize that the league was directed against piracy, not against the Regencies or Islam; the draft treaty from spring 1818 avowedly avoided the term "Christian" to show that they did not "give a religious character to the union" (Art. 44 commentary): HHStA Ges. London Varia M-P, Kart. 145, "Protokolle 1817" and "Protokolle 1818–1819" [no fol.].
87. [Anon. ed.], *Aus Karls von Nostitz, weiland Adjutanten des Prinzen Louis Ferdinands von Preußen, und später russischen General-Leutnants, Leben und Briefwechsel* (Dresden, 1848), 127–128.
88. Quote, Panzac, *Corsairs,* 273; Chateaubriand was a member of Sidney Smith's Knights Liberators association: Hannemann, "Brême et la lutte anti-pirate," 82.
89. Marques, *Silence,* 51.
90. Palisot, *Réfutation,* 2, 13, attacking British abolitionists for not opposing Christian slavery in Barbary or impressment of sailors; Trunk, *Was ist,* 77. Hannemann, "Brême et la lutte anti-pirate," 75–76 (Smidt and Gries); Tidemann, *Was könnte,* 38–39.
91. Smith, *Mémoire;* "Sismondi," in *Nemesis,* 214–215.
92. Drescher, *Abolition,* 13, 21, 27, 29, 33, 49; Davis, *Christian Masters,* 189–190; David Eltis and Stanley Engerman, "Shipboard Slave Revolts and Abolition," in Drescher and Emmer, eds., *Who Abolished Slavery?,* 145–154, 147–148; Colley, *Captives,* 63–64; Lawrence A. Peskin, *Captives and Countrymen: Barbary Slavery and the American Public, 1785–1816* (Baltimore: Johns Hopkins University Press, 2009), 159, 213.
93. *Allgemeine Zeitung,* no. 46, 182–184, 15 Feb. 1815; *Allgemeine Handlungs-Zeitung,* no. 35, 141–143, 18 Feb. 1815; *Journal de Francfort,* 18–19 Feb. 1815, preserved in press clippings of Dutch representative Hans Christoph von Gagern, HStA Darm. O11, B201 [no fol.]; "Notice sur les cinq conferences particulières," in Klüber, *Acten,* 4:523–530, 527–528. Weil, *Dessous,* 2:235, Austrian police spy's claim to have heard from Bartholdy that he was the author.
94. AHL Familienarchiv Hach, V, Vol. A, Fasz. 2, no. c5, "Tagebuch," p. 10 (27 Sept. 1814); Vneshniaia 8:278, Nesselrode to Italinsky, 12/24 Apr. 1815.
95. HHStA StK Vorträge 195, folder VII, fol. 147 (25 July 1814), and VIII, fol. 6–6v (3 Aug. 1814), with quote.
96. HHStA KK 37 (1814), no. 790, note of Graf Wallis from 21 Oct., responding to Metternich's presentation of 19 Oct.; StK Vorträge 195, folder X, fol. 75–75v, with Franz's order on 22 Oct., f. 75v. Count Lažanzky, the official in charge of reorganizing Habsburg Italy, was equally concerned about Austrian seaborne trade but more supportive of Metternich's efforts to gain Ottoman intervention: StK Hofkanzlei Notenwechsel 155,

3 Oct. 1814 (no. 1648/191) and 7 Nov. 1814 (no. 2934/318). Historians too have generally argued that the Ottoman Empire had little authority over the Barbary Regencies, hence could give little help, as Panzac, *Corsairs*, 268–269.

97. HHStA StK Rom 6, "Berichte Apr.–Dec. 1814," fol. 272 (1 Oct.); StK Interiora Korresp. 67, Fasz. 2, fols. 235–236, Hudelist to Metternich, 27 May 1814.

98. Nicholas B. Harding, "North African Piracy, the Hanoverian Carrying Trade and the British State, 1728–1828," *Historical Journal* 43, 1 (2000): 25–47, 30, 32; Frank Lambert, *The Barbary Wars: American Independence in the Atlantic World* (New York: Hill and Wang, 2005), 47–48.

99. TNA FO 37/73, no fol., Fagel to Castlereagh, 24 and 25 June 1814; Castlereagh's promise of Colonial Office consular aid, 29 June. Fagel renewed requests for British help on 7 Sept. and 27 Dec. 1814.

100. TNA FO 37/84, Fagel to Castlereagh, 25 Feb. 1815, with reference to storm of 27 December, and Castlereagh to Fagel, also 25 Feb.; Lambert, *Barbary*; Frederick C. Leiner, *The End of Barbary Terror: America's 1815 War against the Pirates of North Africa* (New York: Oxford University Press, 2006).

101. Oded Löwenheim, " 'Do Ourselves Credit and Render a Lasting Service to Mankind': British Moral Prestige, Humanitarian Intervention, and the Barbary Pirates," *International Studies Quarterly* 43, 1 (2003): 23–48.

102. TNA FO 139/35, fol. 188–188v, Bathurst to Castlereagh, 8 Aug. 1815, emphasizing aid to Sardinia in the change of approach, and Hanover and the Ionian Isles as continuing the policy of covering British territories from the eighteenth century: Harding, "North African Piracy," 30–35. TNA CO 2/6, fols. 20–24v, Castlereagh to Bathurst, 29 Jan. 1816, for later decisions, and CO 2/6 generally for documents relating to Exmouth's expedition, including treaties on behalf of Hanover, the Ionian Isles, Sardinia, and Sicily. Agreements on captured Europeans as prisoners of war: fol. 153–153v for the bashaw of Tripoli (29 Apr. 1816), fols. 186–189 for the bey of Tunis (17 Apr. 1816), and—often missed—fols. 198–200 for the dey of Algiers (16 May, 1816); the dey's further declaration abolishing Christian captivity completely following the second expedition, fols. 224–225 (28 Aug. 1816).

103. See the numerous reports on the Serb situation from Hudelist to Metternich throughout 1814 and 1815, HHStA StK Interiora Korresp. 67 and 68; and Tischler, *Die habsburgische Politik*, 154–160, 166–167.

104. Vneshniaia, 8:193–199, 3/15 Feb. 1815, quote 194; cf. on the Serbian negotiations C.M. Woodhouse, *Capodistria: The Founder of Greek Independence* (London: Oxford University Press, 1973), 113–114, which identifies Capodistrias as the original author; Tischler, *Die habsburgische Politik*, 163–168.

105. Petition to Hardenberg, GStA PK III. HA MdA I, no. 1321, no fol., letter of Semlin, 8 Dec. 1814, with cover letter Vienna, 11 Jan. 1815; petition to

Castlereagh, TNA FO 139/26, fols. 29–30 (Latin), fols. 31–33, fol. 32 for the quoted German version, also dated 8/20 Dec. 1814.

106. TNA FO 139/26, fol. 37, copy of "Mr de Mavrojeny's note of a conversation with Lord Castlereagh," Vienna, 16 Feb. 1815; Wellesley, ed., *Suppl. Desp.*, 9:579–580, Wellington to Castlereagh, 25 Feb. 1815. On the peace, Woodhouse, *Capodistria*, 114.

107. Stella Ghervas, *Réinventer la tradition. Alexandre Stourdza et l'Europe de la Sainte-Alliance* (Paris: Champion, 2008), 356–358.

108. Miroslav Hroch, *The Social Interpretation of Linguistic Demands in European National Movements* (Badia Fiesolana: European University Institute, 1994); Eric J. Hobsbawm, *Nations and Nationalism since 1780: Programme, Myth, Reality*, 2nd ed. (Cambridge: Cambridge University Press, 1992).

109. HHStA StK Vorträge 197 (1815), folder IV, fols. 861–862 (27 Apr.).

110. Ghervas, *Réinventer*, 355 (quote).

111. Stamati Theodorou Lascaris, *Capodistrias avant la révolution grecque. Sa carrière politique jusqu'en 1822* (Lausanne: Imprimerie Centrale, 1918), 69, Eynard salon.

112. Anna Eynard, Journal, BGE Ms suppl 1959, 159–161, 28 Dec. 1814. The officer must have been Colonel Richard Church, who led two regiments of Greek light infantry in the Ionian Islands from 1809 to 1814 and journeyed to Vienna: Woodhouse, *Capodistria*, 64–66, 117, 142; Stanley Lane-Pool, *Sir Richard Church, C.B., G.C.H. Commander-in-Chief of the Greeks in the War of Independence* (London: Longmans, 1890), 24–33.

113. See still Hans Loewe, *Friedrich Thiersch. Ein Humanistenleben* (Berlin: Oldenbourg, 1925), 499–501; Hans-Martin Kirchner, *Friedrich Thiersch: Ein liberaler Kulturpolitiker und Philhellene in Bayern*, 2nd ed. (Mainz: Rutzen, 2010), 155–156.

114. Heinrich W.J. Thiersch, ed., *Friedrich Thiersch's Leben*, 2 vols. (Leipzig, 1866), 1:98 (quote and connections with Greek scholars), Thiersch to Herrmann, 10 June 1813. This even predated his meeting with Adamantios Korais in Paris later in 1813, which if anything would have strengthened the notion that education alone might not suffice to bring liberation: Loewe, *Humanistenleben*, 499.

115. HHStA StK Notenwechsel Polizeihofstelle 4, Fasz. 1814, fol. 104, 5 Oct., marked "urgent"; StK Noten von der Polizeihofstelle 30, Fasz. 1 (1814), fol. 361, Hager to Metternich, 7 Oct.; Fournier, *Geheimpolizei*, 201–202, 25 Oct. 1814. For complications on the border, ÖStA KA HKR Präs 1814 8/11–10/20, 19 Oct. 1814, and Metternich to Hofkriegsrath, 5 Nov. 1814.

116. Alexander Lips, *Der Wiener Congreß, oder was muß geschehen um Deutschland zu retten und das Interesse aller Fürsten und Nationen daselbst zu vereinen* (Erlangen, 1814), 12–16.

117. HHStA StK Notenwechsel Polizeihofstelle 4, Fasz. 1815, fol. 29, 19 Feb., unsigned to Hager; *Friedensblätter*, no. 25, 28 Feb. 1815, 100.

118. Roxandra Countess Edling, *Mémoires de la comtesse Edling (née Stourdza), demoiselle d'honneur de Sa Majesté l'Impératrice Élisabeth Alexéevna* (Moscow, 1888), 210–212.

119. Ibid., 170–173 for the church visit, 172 for Capodistrias and Ypsilanti appearing "sans intention" among the Greeks, 173 for the memo; cf. Woodhouse, *Capodistria*, 119, emphasizing Capodistrias's displeasure, as Edling, *Mémoires*, 174.

120. Woodhouse, *Capodistria*, ch. 2; Emmanuel Rodocanachi, *Bonaparte et les Iles ioniennes. Un épisode des conquêtes de la République et du Premier Empire (1797–1816)* (Paris: Alcan, 1899), 179–181, 196; Patricia Kennedy Grimsted, *The Foreign Ministers of Alexander I: Political Attitudes and the Conduct of Russian Diplomacy, 1801–1825* (Berkeley: University of California Press, 1969), 226–229.

121. Rodocanachi, *Bonaparte*, 233, and 251–252, for copy of Capodistrias to Alexander, 5 Oct. 1814.

122. Ibid., 234–236, and for the following paragraph; also Woodhouse, *Capodistria*, 115–117.

123. TNA FO 92/19, fol. 55–55v, Clancarty to Castlereagh, 10 June 1815; Wellesley, ed., *Suppl. Desp.*, 9:501–502, Castlereagh to Liverpool, 24 Dec. 1814, and 530, Liverpool to Castlereagh, 6 Jan. 1815. Liverpool still opposed British possession at that point. Lebzeltern in Rome had already advised Metternich that leaving the isles to Britain could be a good solution to prevent Russian influence: HHStA StK Rom 6, "Berichte Apr.–Dec. 1814," fol. 5v, 25 Apr.

124. Vneshniaia, 8:366, Capodistrias to Chichagov, 15/27 May–21 May/2 June, 1815.

125. TNA FO 139/35, fol. 157–157v, Clancarty to Castlereagh ("Private"), 28 Sept. 1815; Rodocanachi, *Bonaparte*, 260 (memo).

126. Vneshniaia, 8:366, Capodistrias to Chichagov, 15/27 May–21 May/2 June 1815.

127. Rodocanachi, *Bonaparte*, 234; TNA CO 2/6, fols. 26–27, Castlereagh to Bathurst, 29 Jan. 1816, and fol. 47, Exmouth to John Wilson Croker, Algiers Bay, 6 Apr. 1816. On the decisive Paris negotiations, Woodhouse, *Capodistria*, 131–134.

128. Rodocanachi, *Bonaparte*, 236, and appended documents; C. Willis Dixon, *The Colonial Administrations of Sir Thomas Maitland* (reprint, New York: Kelley, 1969 [1939]), pt. 5.

6. Between Reaction and Reform

1. Rinieri, ed., *Corrispondenza*, 713, 12 June 1815. Paul W. Schroeder, *The Transformation of European Politics 1763–1848* (Oxford: Clarendon Press, 1994), argues for a "pattern of allied attempts to satisfy both rulers and peoples for the sake of stability and peace" (514).

2. One historian who emphasizes this problem is Alexander M. Martin, *Romantics, Reformers, Reactionaries: Russian Conservative Thought and*

Politics in the Reign of Alexander I (DeKalb: Northern Illinois University Press, 1997), 6–8 on family resemblances between conservatism and Jacobinism; 170 on the "ambiguity of the terms liberal and conservative" at the time; also see Günther Kronenbitter, *Wort und Macht. Friedrich Gentz als politischer Schriftsteller* (Berlin: Duncker & Humblot, 1994), 86–87. For similar caution about the difficulties of distinguishing strands of Prussian conservatives, David E. Barclay, "Die Gegner der Reformpolitik Hardenbergs," in Thomas Stamm-Kuhlmann, ed., *"Freier Gebrauch der Kräfte": Eine Bestandsaufnahme der Hardenberg-Forschung* (Munich: Oldenbourg, 2001), 217–229.

3. Matthew Levinger, *Enlightened Nationalism: The Transformation of Prussian Political Culture, 1806–1848* (New York: Oxford University Press, 2000), 138; on reform conservatism, Klaus Epstein, *The Genesis of German Conservatism* (Princeton, NJ: Princeton University Press, 1966).

4. Timothy Tackett, *Becoming a Revolutionary: The Deputies of the French National Assembly and the Emergence of a Revolutionary Culture (1789–1790)* (Princeton, NJ: Princeton University Press, 1996); Heinrich Best, *Die Männer von Bildung und Besitz: Struktur und Handeln parlamentarischer Führungsgruppen in Deutschland und Frankreich, 1848/49* (Düsseldorf: Droste, 1990).

5. Ludmilla Assing, ed., *Tagebücher von Friedrich von Gentz* (Leipzig, 1873), 420, 423, 20 and 27 Oct. 1815; on the role of social closeness in Russian politics, Martin, *Romantics,* 9–10.

6. Patricia Kennedy Grimsted, *The Foreign Ministers of Alexander I: Political Attitudes and the Conduct of Russian Diplomacy, 1801–1825* (Berkeley: University of California Press, 1969), 46–62, on Alexander as pursuing both liberal and conservative aims, the two "not really mutually exclusive opposites" (60); more skeptical of Alexander's constitutionalism, Ulrike Eich, *Russland und Europa: Studien zur russischen Deutschlandpolitik in der Zeit des Wiener Kongresses* (Cologne: Böhlau, 1986), 179–204; for Alan Palmer, Alexander "could never really comprehend" the liberal ideas he spoke: *Alexander I: Tsar of War and Peace* (New York: Harper & Row, 1974), 51.

7. Edmund Burke, *Reflections on the Revolution in France,* Frank M. Turner, ed. (New Haven, CT: Yale University Press, 2003), 7–8, 50–52.

8. László Kontler, "The Ancien Régime in Memory and Theory: Edmund Burke and his German Followers," *European Review of History* 4 (1997): 31–43.

9. Brunhilde Wehinger, *Conversation um 1800: Salonkultur und literarische Autorschaft bei Germaine de Staël* (Berlin: Walter Frey, 2002), 214–215; Kronenbitter, *Gentz,* 104–107. Müller's work was partially reprinted in the Viennese *Friedensblätter* as "Burke, oder der Moment," nos. 9–12 (19, 23, 26, 28 July 1814), 35–37, 39–41, 43–44, 47–49.

10. HHStA KK 36 (1814), nos. 100–364, no. 194, 30 Oct. 1814; Friedrich Wilhelm Ziegler, *Partey-Wuth, oder die Kraft des Glaubens* (Vienna, 1817), 30, 39, 66, 68.

11. Leonore as "active heroine," and appropriation of Pizzaro's key: William Kinderman, *Beethoven*, 2nd ed. (New York: Oxford University Press, 2009), 122–123, 126–128. If anything Beethoven strengthened the politically emancipatory elements in his 1814 revisions: Helga Lühning, "Florestans Kerker im Rampenlicht. Zur Tradition des Sottoterraneo," in Lühning and Sieghard Brandenburg, eds., *Beethoven zwischen Revolution und Restauration* (Bonn: Beethoven-Haus, 1989), 137–204. Nicholas Mathew emphasizes the ruler's role in restoring order: *Political Beethoven* (Cambridge: Cambridge University Press, 2013), 67, 133.

12. Esteban Buch, *Beethoven's Ninth: A Political History*, Richard Miller trans. (Chicago: University of Chicago Press, 2003), 82, 85; Ingrid Fuchs, "The Glorious Moment—Beethoven and the Congress of Vienna," in Ole Villumsen Krog, ed., *Danmark og Den Dansende Wienerkongres. Spillet om Danmark / Denmark and the Dancing Congress of Vienna. Playing for Denmark's Future* (Copenhagen: Christiansborg Slot, 2002), 182–196; Jean H. Quataert, *Staging Philanthropy: Patriotic Women and the National Imagination in Dynastic Germany, 1813–1916* (Ann Arbor: University of Michigan Press, 2001); Ann Taylor Allen, *Feminism and Motherhood in Germany, 1800–1914* (New Brunswick, NJ: Rutgers University Press, 1991). Stressing the cantata's "authoritarian" core, Mathew, *Political Beethoven*, 117–118.

13. Weil, *Dessous*, 1:413 (intercept), 8 Oct. 1814, Maistre to Saint-Marsan. On the importance of the different lengths of time during which populations lived under French rule, Michael Broers, *Europe under Napoleon, 1796–1815* (London: Arnold, 1996); Stuart Woolf, *Napoleon's Integration of Europe* (New York: Routledge, 1991). On Metternich's reform conservatism, Wolfram Siemann, *Metternich. Staatsmann zwischen Restauration und Moderne* (Munich: Beck, 2010), 59–61.

14. James J. Sheehan, "The Problem of Sovereignty in European History," *American Historical Review* 111, 1 (2006): 1–15, 7–8.

15. Maria Ullrichová, ed., *Clemens Metternich—Wilhelmine von Sagan. Ein Briefwechsel 1813–1815* (Graz: Böhlau, 1966), 168, 13 Jan. 1814; 187, 21 Jan. 1814.

16. Emphasizing the prerevolutionary origins of conservative thought: Darrin M. McMahon, *Enemies of the Enlightenment: The French Counter-Enlightenment and the Making of Modernity* (New York: Oxford University Press, 2001); Fritz Valjavec, *Die Entstehung der politischen Strömungen in Deutschland, 1770–1815* (Munich: Oldenbourg, 1951).

17. McMahon, *Enemies*; Valjavec, *Entstehung*, 11, 290–300; Epstein, *Conservatism*, 96.

18. Wolfgang Piereth, *Bayerns Pressepolitik und die Neuordnung Deutschlands nach den Befreiungskriegen* (Munich: Beck, 1999), 92–94.

19. HHStA KK 41(1815), no. 789, Hager, 8 Jan.; StA England 154, "Weisungen 1815 (I–VII)," fols. 6, 9v–10v. On Metternich's belief in a Jacobin terrorist conspiracy, Alan Sked, *Metternich and Austria: An Evaluation*

(Basingstoke, England: Palgrave Macmillan, 2008), 2–6, 11; Siemann, *Metternich*, 65–70.

20. Philip G. Dwyer, *Talleyrand* (London: Longman, 2002), 150–151; Guillaume de Bertier de Sauvigny, *The Bourbon Restoration*, trans. Lynn M. Case (Philadelphia: University of Pennsylvania Press, 1966).

21. Pallain, ed., *Correspondance*, 55–56, 17 Oct. 1814.

22. Pallain, ed., *Correspondance*, 209, 4 Jan. 1815; Gaston Palewski, ed., *Le miroir de Talleyrand: Lettres inédites à la duchesse de Courlande pendant le Congrès de Vienne* (Paris: Perrin, 1976), 89 (Courland), 3 Jan.; Angeberg, *Congrès*, 2:570–571 (note of 26 Dec. 1814).

23. Erich Botzenhart and Walther Hubatsch, eds., *Freiherr vom Stein Briefe und amtliche Schriften*, 11 vols. (Stuttgart: Kohlhammer, 1957–74), 5:365–366, diary, 24 Feb. 1815.

24. Sauvigny, *Restoration*, 39–45, 53–55, 65–71; Emmanuel de Waresquiel, *Talleyrand: Le prince immobile* (Paris: Fayard, 2003), 433–462; Walter Maturi, "Il Congresso di Vienna e la restaurazione dei Borboni a Napoli" (pt. 2), *Rivista storica italiana*, ser. 5, vol. 3–4 (1938): 1–61, 44–45 (in Feb. 1815).

25. Webster, *Diplomacy*, 181, to Liverpool (5 May 1814), to Bentinck (May 1814).

26. Ibid., 182, 10 May 1814.

27. Comte Charles Pozzo di Borgo, ed., *Correspondance diplomatique du Comte Pozzo di Borgo ambassadeur de Russie en France et du Comte de Nesselrode depuis la restauration des Bourbons jusqu'au congrès d'Aix-la-Chapelle, 1814–1818*, 2 vols. (Paris: Lévy, 1890–97), 1:135–136, Pozzo di Borgo to Nesselrode, Brussels, 11/23 May 1815; on Louis's role, Volker Sellin, *Die geraubte Revolution: Der Sturz Napoleons und die Restauration in Europa* (Göttingen: Vandenhoeck & Ruprecht, 2001), ch. 7.

28. Ulrike Müßig, *Die europäische Verfassungsdiskussion des 18. Jahrhunderts* (Tübingen: Mohr Siebeck, 2008), 84–86; Jeroen van Zanten, "Die Niederlande," in Werner Daum et al., eds., *Handbuch der europäischen Verfassungsgeschichte im 19. Jahrhundert. Institutionen und Rechtspraxis im gesellschaftlichen Wandel*, 4 vols. (Bonn: Dietz, 2006–[2012]), 2:433–483, 434–441.

29. Humboldt, *Briefen*, 4:455, 13 Jan. 1815. Georg-Christoph von Unruh, "Die Eigenart der Verfassung des Königreichs Norwegens," *Jahrbuch des öffentlichen Rechts* 38 (1989): 277–298; Müßig, *Verfassungsdiskussion*, 79–80, on the Norwegian constitution's relatively strong popular representation; Peter Brandt, "Norwegen," in Daum et al., eds., *Handbuch*, 2:1173–1220, 1173–1176, 1182–1187.

30. HHStA StK Kongreßakten 14, Fasz. 2, folder "Réunion de Gènes à la Sardaigne," fol. 67–67v, Binder to Metternich, 21 Nov. 1814, on the conference of 20 Nov., with Metternich's agreement in margin.

31. HHStA StK Kongreßakten 14, Fasz. 2, folder "Réunion de Gènes à la Sardaigne," fols. 62, 67v, and report of 23 Nov. 1814 for 22 Nov., fol. 75, "republican form" and "liberal principles."

32. HHStA StK Kongreßakten 14, Fasz. 2, folder "Réunion de Gènes à la Sardaigne," 28 Nov. 1814, reporting on the session of 26 Nov., fols. 100v–101.

33. Angeberg, Congrès, 2:480–483 (draft), 516–518, for the official version of 12 Dec., incorporated into the Final Act in June 1815.

34. HHStA StK Kongreßakten 2, fols. 32–33, Committee of Eight, 10 Dec. 1814.

35. HHStA StK Kongreßakten 14, Fasz. 2, folder "St. Siège," fols. 64–74, quote 65v, varying from the draft text from the Bologna archives in Jörg Luther, ed., Documenti costituzionali di Italia e Malta 1787–1850, pt. 1, Costituzioni nazionali / Costituzioni degli stati italiani / Constitutional Documents of Italy and Malta 1787–1850, pt 1, National Constitutions / Constitutions of the Italian States, 2 vols. (Berlin: de Gruyter, 2010), 10:1:461–465, 462; vols. 10:1 and 10:2, in Horst Dippel, ed., Constitutions of the World from the Late 18th Century to the Middle of the 19th Century: Sources on the Rise of Modern Constitutionalism / Verfassungen der Welt vom späten 18. Jahrhundert bis Mitte des 19. Jahrhunderts: Quellen zur Herausbildung des modernen Konstitutionalismus.

36. Luther, ed., Documenti, 10:1:465, for extra list, and cover letter of 24 May 1815 with quote.

37. HHStA StK Rom 8, "Berichte 1815 I–IX," fol. 409, Lebzeltern, 1 July; StK Rom 9, "Weisungen 1815," fol. 35, Metternich, 22 July.

38. Rinieri, ed., Corrispondenza, 633–634, 712–714, quote 713, Consalvi to Pacca, 20 May and 12 June 1815.

39. "Organizzazione del Governo provvisorio pontificio nelle provincie recuperate (1815)," in Luther, ed., Documenti, 10:2:499–504.

40. Rinieri, ed., Corrispondenza, 732, 12 June 1815; Reinerman, Austria and the Papacy in the Age of Metternich, 2 vols. (Washington, DC: Catholic University of America Press, 1979–89), 1:40–43.

41. "Motu proprio per lo Stato Pontificio (1816)," from 6 July 1816: in Luther, ed., Documenti, 10:2:505–546, 505–506 for uniformity, quotes 506; for local government, 526, feudal privileges, 530.

42. Rinieri, ed., Corrispondenza, 688, 2 June 1815; Luther, ed., Documenti, 10:1:627–630. For the Italian Committee's decision highlighting maintenance of Lucca's Senate as a socially mixed "national representation" with a voice in taxation, GStA PK III. HA MdA I, no. 1211, fols. 5–6, protocol, 28 Mar. 1815.

43. David Laven, Venice and Venetia under the Habsburgs, 1815–1835 (Oxford: Oxford University Press, 2002); Marco Meriggi, Amministrazione e classi sociali nel Lombardo-Veneto (1814–1848) (Bologna: Il Mulino, 1983).

44. Comte d'Angeberg [pseud. Leonard Chodźko], Recueil des traités, conventions et actes diplomatiques concernant l'Autriche et l'Italie (Paris, 1859), 164, 7 Apr. 1815 (quote); cf. Constitution, 24 Apr. 1815, in British Foreign

and State Papers, 1814–1815 (London, 1839), 908–912 (vol. 2 of series). Laven, *Venetia,* 71, on congregations serving some real representative function; Meriggi emphasizes Habsburg officials' intention to control local elites: *Amministrazione,* 46, 48–51, 51–65.

45. Laven, *Venetia,* 24.

46. HHStA StK Notenwechsel der Hofkanzlei 155, no. 169C, Lažanzky to Staatskanzlei, 19 Aug. 1814, "Partheigeist"; Metternich's agreement, Notenwechsel an die Hofkanzlei 31, 4 Sept. 1814. Franz's original resistance to constitutions or representative bodies in Italy in his instructions to newly appointed provisional governor General Bellegarde, 14 May 1814: StK Interiora Korresp. 67, Fasz. 2, fols. 214v–215 (copy), also quoted in Arthur G. Haas, *Metternich, Reorganization, and Nationality 1813–1818: A Story of Foresight and Frustration in the Rebuilding of the Austrian Empire* (Wiesbaden: Steiner, 1963), 30, plus 34–35, 52–53; Franz's adding an intermediate layer of representation, Laven, *Venetia,* 70–71; Meriggi, *Amministrazione,* 53–54.

47. Laven, *Venetia,* 64–65, 69; Meriggi, *Amministrazione,* 61–66, 68, 71–72, 84–85; J.H. Elliott, "A Europe of Composite Monarchies," *Past & Present* 137 (1992): 48–71.

48. Joseph Alexander von Helfert, *Kaiser Franz I. von Österreich und die Stiftung des Lombardo-Venetianischen Königreichs* (Innsbruck: Wagner, 1901), 63–65, quotes 64.

49. Following Carlo Ghisalberti on the distinctions between absolutism and the stages of administrative, consultative, and constitutional monarchy, Werner Daum, "Einleitung," in Daum et al., eds., *Handbuch,* 2:75–79, and for Habsburg Italy, Daum and Francesca Sofia, "Italien," in ibid., 2:341–432, 343, 351.

50. Haas, *Reorganization,* 60–62.

51. Sked, *Metternich,* 52; Thierry Lentz, *Le congrès de Vienne. Une refondation de l'Europe 1814–1815* (Paris: Perrin, 2013), 222.

52. Angeberg, *Recueil,* 200–203, quote 203.

53. Giuseppe Galasso, *Il Regno di Napoli. Il Mezzogiorno borbonico e risorgimentale (1815–1860)* (Turin: UTET, 2007), 47–61; also vol. 15, pt. 5 of Galasso, ed., *Storia d'Italia,* (Turin: UTET, 1976–2011); John A. Davis, *Naples and Napoleon: Southern Italy and the European Revolutions (1780–1860)* (Oxford: Oxford University Press, 2006), 291–292.

54. GStA PK III. HA MdA I, no. 1211, fols. 23–24, protocol of 28 Mar. 1815.

55. Galasso, *Napoli,* 3, 11, 37–38, 40; Alfonso Scirocco, "Dalla seconda restaurazione alla fine del Regno," in Giuseppe Galasso and Rosario Romeo, eds., *Storia del Mezzogiorno* (Rome: Edizioni del Sole, 1986), 4:2:643–789, 643; Maturi, "Restaurazione (II)," 52–55, 58–60; Maurice-Henri Weil, *Joachim Murat Roi de Naples. La dernière année de règne* (May 1814–May 1815), 5 vols. (Paris: Fontemoing, 1909–10), 4:464–466 (Alliance of 29 Apr. 1815), and 5:209, 239, and 410–414 (Convention of Casa-

lanza, 20 May 1815), 413–414 for the comparison with Neapolitan demands; 5:439–441, 442–443 for the proclamations to the Neapolitans of General Bianchi (22/23 May) and Ferdinand (20 May/4 June 1815), both highlighting the guaranteed points. Still emphasizing Metternich's conservatism alongside the pressure against reaction, Davis, *Naples and Napoleon*, 291.

56. Scirocco, "Dalla seconda restaurazione," 643–648; Galasso, *Napoli*, 12–13; Davis, *Naples*, 276–279.

57. "Costituzione provvisoria delle Due Sicilie (1815)," in Luther, ed., *Documenti*, 10:2:379–380.

58. Generally, Galasso, *Napoli*, 52, 56–61. On the Genoese solution and British views: HHStA StA England 155 (Berichte 1816, all Esterhazy to Metternich), Fasz. V VIII, folder V, fols. 25–27, no. 22, 1 May; folder VII, fols. 25–26, no. 26B, 5 July; folder VIII, fols. 55–59, 79–89, 31 Aug., no. 30E and no. 30F (including table of "Neapolitan Plan" compared to the Genoese settlement, fol. 56–56v); StA England 156 (Weisungen 1816), Fasz. IV–VIII, folder VII, fols. 58–63v, no. 5, Metternich to Esterhazy, 29 July.

59. Galasso, *Napoli*, 242–250; Scirocco, "Dalla seconda restaurazione," 673–676; Henry Kissinger, *A World Restored: Metternich, Castlereagh and the Problem of Peace 1812–1822* (London: Phoenix, 2000 [1957]), 277; Mark Jarrett, *The Congress of Vienna and its Legacy: War and Great Power Diplomacy after Napoleon* (London: I.B. Tauris, 2013), 276–277.

60. Monika Wienfort, "Preußen," in Daum et al., eds., *Handbuch*, 2.959–992, 963.

61. Piereth, *Bayerns Pressepolitik*, 27. In general on German constitutional politics, see Enno E. Kraehe, *Metternich's German Policy*, vol. 2, *The Congress of Vienna* (Princeton, NJ: Princeton University Press, 1983), and Eckhardt Treichel, "Einleitung," in Treichel, ed., *Die Entstehung des Deutschen Bundes 1813–1815*, 2 vols. (Munich: Oldenbourg, 2000), 1:xi–cxxxix.

62. Kraehe, *Policy*, 2:100–103, 168–171, 346, 358–363; Michael Hundt, "Hardenbergs deutsche Verfassungspolitik in den Jahren 1780–1815," in Stamm-Kuhlmann, ed., *Hardenberg-Forschung*, 163–190, 179–190. Still useful, Wilhelm Adolf Schmidt, *Geschichte der deutschen Verfassungsfrage während der Befreiungskriege und des Wiener Kongresses 1812 bis 1815*, Alfred Stern, ed. (Stuttgart, 1890).

63. Heinz Röllecke, ed., *Briefwechsel zwischen Jacob und Wilhelm Grimm* (Stuttgart: Hirzel, 2001–), 1:374, Jacob to Wilhelm, 21 Oct. 1814; S. Heuberger, ed., *Albrecht Renggers Briefwechsel mit der aargauischen Regierung während des Wiener Kongresses*, in *Argovia. Jahresschrift der Historischen Gesellschaft des Kantons Aargau*, vol. 35 (Aarau: Sauerländer, 1913), 39, Rengger to Kleiner Rat and President, 21 Oct. 1814.

64. Kraehe, *Policy*, 2:70.

65. Wessenberg, HHStA StK Kongreßakten 6, fol. 26–26v (no date); Botzenhart and Hubatsch, eds., *Stein*, 5:168–169, Münster to Stein, 19 Oct. 1814; and Kraehe, Policy, 2:199.

66. Kraehe, *Policy*, 2:197–204.

67. Piereth, *Bayerns Pressepolitik*, 15–16.

68. GStA PK III. HA MdA I, no. 993, fols. 40–41, draft of article and cover letter of Hardenberg to Grote (draft), 5 Dec. 1814, fol. 45, for copy of articles in *Hamburgischer Correspondenten*, no. 122, 16 Dec.

69. *Chronik des allgemeinen Wiener Kongresses*, nos. 5, 8, and 21, 18 and 28 Oct. and 30 Dec. 1814.

70. Ewald Frie, *Fredrich August Ludwig von der Marwitz 1777–1837: Biographien eines Preußen* (Paderborn: Schöningh, 2001); Robert M. Berdahl, *The Politics of the Prussian Nobility: The Development of a Conservative Ideology, 1770–1848* (Princeton, NJ: Princeton University Press, 1988); Levinger, *Enlightened Nationalism*.

71. Eberhard Weis, "Kontinuität und Diskontinuität zwischen den Ständen des 18. Jahrhunderts und den frühkonstitutionellen Parlamenten aufgrund der Verfassungen von 1818/19 in Bayern und Württemberg," *Parliaments, Estates and Representation* 4, 1 (1984): 51–65; also versus seeing liberalism in the estates approach, Kraehe, *Policy*, 2:183, 201, and Hartwig Brandt, "Von den Verfassungskämpfen der Stände zum modernen Konstitutionalismus. Das Beispiel Württembergs," in Martin Kirsch and Pierangelo Schiera, eds., *Denken und Umsetzung des Konstitutionalismus in Deutschland und anderen europäischen Ländern in der ersten Hälfte des 19. Jahrhunderts* (Berlin: Duncker & Humblot, 1999): 99–108, 102.

72. Barbara Vogel, "Beamtenkonservatismus: Sozial- und verfassungsgeschichtliche Voraussetzungen der Parteien in Preußen im frühen 19. Jahrhundert," in Dirk Stegmann, Bernd-Jürgen Wendt, and Peter-Christian Witt, eds., *Deutscher Konservatismus im 19. und 20. Jahrhundert. Festschrift für Fritz Fischer zum 75. Geburtstag und zum 50. Doktorjubiläum* (Bonn: Neue Gesellschaft, 1983), 1–31; Bernd Wunder, "Landstände und Rechtsstaat. Zur Entstehung und Verwirklichung des Art. 13 DBA," *Zeitschrift für historische Forschung* 5 (1978): 139–185. Hundt, "Verfassungspolitik," takes a middle position.

73. Barbara Stollberg-Rilinger, *Vormünder des Volkes? Konzepte landständischer Repräsentation in der Spätphase des Alten Reiches* (Berlin: Duncker & Humblot, 1999), 20–21.

74. Wolfgang Mager, "Das Problem der landständischen Verfassungen auf dem Wiener Kongreß 1814/15," *Historische Zeitschrift* 217 (1973): 296–346.

75. Wilhelm von Humboldt, "Denkschrift über die deutsche Verfassung an den Freiherrn vom Stein," in Albert Leitzmann, Bruno Gebhardt, and Wilhelm Richter, eds., *Wilhelm von Humboldts Gesammelte Schriften*, 17 vols. (Berlin: Behr, 1903–1936), 11:95–112, quote 108.

76. Botzenhart and Hubatsch, eds., *Stein*, 5:106, Stein to Marschall, Nassau, 10 Aug. 1814.

77. A. de Nesselrode, ed., *Lettres et papiers du Chancelier Comte de Nesselrode 1760–1850. Extraits de ses archives*, 11 vols. (Paris: Lahure, n.d. [1940–12]) 5:153–154 ("despotism"), Countess Nesselrode to Hélène Guriev, 19 Jan. 1814.

78. Kraehe, *Policy*, 2:321–322; Brandt, "Verfassungskämpfen," 101; preemption, Botzenhart and Hubatsch, eds., *Stein*, 5:318, diary, 2 Oct. 1814; and Rinieri, ed., *Corrispondenza*, 229–231 (Consalvi, who also thought public opinion likely played a part). Also on the initially favorable reaction, Monika Neugebauer-Wölk, *Revolution und Constitution—die Brüder Cotta: eine biographische Studie zum Zeitalter der Französischen Revolution und des Vormärz* (Berlin: Colloquium, 1989), 463; Walter Grube, *Der Stuttgarter Landtag 1457–1957. Von den Landständen zum demokratischen Parlament* (Stuttgart: Klett, 1957), 490–491, and 491–507 on the constitutional struggle generally.

79. Stolberg, *Tagebuch*, 158–159; Rinieri, ed., *Corrispondenza*, 229–230.

80. Botzenhart and Hubatsch, eds., *Stein*, 5:292, Stein to Cotta, 26 Mar. 1815; Daniel Moran, *Toward the Century of Words: Johann Cotta and the Politics of the Public Realm in Germany, 1795–1832* (Berkeley: University of California Press, 1990), 167–177.

81. On mixed liberal and conservative ideological elements, Albrecht List, *Der Kampf um's gute alte Recht (1815–1819) nach seiner ideen- und parteigeschichtlichen Seite* (Tübingen: Mohr, 1913), 8–19, 83–93.

82. Kraehe, *Policy*, 2:369, 379.

83. GStA PK I. IIA Rep. 89, no. 32596, includes the proclamations for the various territories, including those for the "vormals Preußischen Provinzen im Nieder- und Obersächsischen Kreise" (fols. 68–69v, 21 June 1815) and Pomerania (fols. 72–73v, 21 Sept. 1815); similar references to both provincial and Prussian constitutions in the "Patente" for Prussia's acquisitions on the lower Rhine (fols. 20–23v) and Westphalia (fols. 70–71v), and those for the Saxon and Polish lands treated in Chapter 7.

84. Levinger, *Enlightened Nationalism*, 148–155.

85. Markus J. Prutsch and Arthur Schlegelmilch, "Österreich," in Daum et al., eds., *Handbuch*, 2:993–1040, 998–1000; Wilhelm Brauneder, *Oesterreichische Verfassungsgeschichte*, 11th ed. (Vienna: Manz, 2009), 98–102.

86. HHStA StK Kongreßakten 5, alt Fasz. 9, fol. 114, "Opinion du Plénipotentiaire russe," 16 Nov. 1814, signed by Stein and Capodistrias.

87. In general on the Swiss situation see Marc H. Lerner, *A Laboratory of Liberty: The Transformation of Political Culture in Republican Switzerland, 1750–1848* (Leiden: Brill, 2012), ch. 3 on Vaud and Bern, quote 153; pressure to moderate Aargau's constitution, Heuberger, ed., *Renggers Briefwechsel*, 180–181.

88. Angeberg, *Congrès*, 3:895, protocol of 5 Mar. 1815; and 2:634–635 (interim report of 16 Jan. 1815), guaranteeing the inhabitants of the Bishopric of Basel proportional representation and a role in taxation and appointing administrators and judges. Vneshniaia, 8:204–206, 16/28 Feb. 1815, for Capodistrias's recommendation that Russian agreement be coupled with constitutional reform.

89. Lerner, *Laboratory*, 51–65, 54–55 for Machiavelli. On civic humanist or classical republican traditions: Quentin Skinner and Martin Van Gelderen, eds., *Republicanism: A Shared European Heritage*, 2 vols. (Cambridge: Cambridge University Press, 2002); Fania Oz-Salzberger, *Translating the*

Enlightenment: Scottish Civic Discourse in Eighteenth-Century Germany (Oxford: Oxford University Press, 1995); Istvan Hont and Michael Ignatieff, eds., *Wealth and Virtue: The Shaping of Political Economy in the Scottish Enlightenment* (Cambridge: Cambridge University Press, 1983), particularly J.G.A. Pocock, "Cambridge Paradigms and Scottish Philosophers: A Study of the Relations between the Civic Humanist and the Civil Jurisprudential Interpretations of Eighteenth-Century Social Thought," 235–252. In the German and Swiss cases, a related language of "communal republicanism" covered some of the same intellectual ground: Ralf Pröve, *Stadtgemeindlicher Republikanismus und die "Macht des Volkes" civile Ordnungsformationen und kommunale Leitbilder politischer Partizipation in den deutschen Staaten vom Ende des 18. bis zur Mitte des 19. Jahrhunderts* (Göttingen: Vandenhoeck & Ruprecht, 2000), and Lerner, *Laboratory,* 14–17.

90. HHStA StK Rom 6, "Berichte Apr.–Dec. 1814," fols. 204–205, 20 Aug. The editor of Lebzeltern's memoirs referred on the contrary to Lebzeltern's "hatred of liberalism in all its forms" and "cult of absolutist ideas": Emanuel de Lévis-Mirepoix, *Un collaborateur de Metternich. Mémoires et papiers de Lebzeltern* (Paris: Plon, 1949), 305.

91. Paul Widmer, *Schweizer Aussenpolitik und Diplomatie. Von Pictet de Rochemont bis Edouard Brunner* (Zurich: Ammann, 2003), 73–74, 78–79; Lucien Cramer, ed., *Genève et les traités de 1815. Correspondance diplomatique de Pictet de Rochemont et de François d'Ivernois. Paris, Vienne, Turin 1814–1816,* 2 vols. (Geneva: Kündig & Champion, 1914), 1:154–155, Council instructions for Pictet, 17 Sept. 1814.

92. Angeberg, *Congrès,* 2:515–516, Austrian statement of 10 Dec. 1814; Wessenberg, "Opinion particulier," Annexe D to Swiss Committee final report, 16 Jan. 1815, HHStA StK Kongreßakten 13, Fasz. 1, folder "Rapport du Comité Suisse," fols. 35–36v.

93. HStA Darm. O11, B121, fol. 89, Gagern to Prince Willem, 18 Jan. 1815.

94. Angeberg, *Congrès,* 2:549, Graubünden "Note" of 28 Dec. 1814, "droits politiques"; HHStA StK Kongreßakten 15, folder "Valtelline," petition of Graubünden representatives to Austrian Kaiser, fols. 36–39, 7 Feb. 1815, fol. 38, "bürgerlichen Freyheit."

95. Angeberg, *Congrès,* 2:552–553, Graubünden "Note" of 28 Dec. 1814. Also in Guido Gigli, *Il Congresso di Vienna (1814–1815)* (Florence: Sansoni, 1938), 104–105.

96. HHStA StK Kongreßakten 5, Fasz. 9, fol. 62v, "Nota" of Count Diego Guicciardi and Girolama Stampi, 13 Dec. 1814.

97. HHStA StK Kongreßakten 15, folder "Valtelline," fol. 38v, petition of 7 Feb. 1815, statistical table f. 45.

98. Angeberg, *Congrès,* 2:550–551, 28 Dec. 1814. Similar reference to different "manners" in note of 13 Jan. 1815: 2:616–617.

99. Angeberg, *Congrès,* 2:551, 28 Dec. 1814.

100. HHStA StK Kongreßakten 15, folder "Valtelline," fols. 1, 13 (June and Aug. 1814).

101. Angeberg, *Congrès*, 2:550–551, Graubünden note of 28 Dec. 1814.
102. Angeberg, *Congrès*, 2:529, Swiss Committee protocol, 15 Dec. 1814; Zurich's views, Cramer, ed., *Correspondance*, 1:119 (Pictet's report, 8 June 1814).
103. Cramer, ed., *Correspondance*, 1:283–285 (Pictet to Turrettini, 25 Dec. 1814).
104. HHStA StK Kongreßakten 14, Fasz. 1, folder "Gränze Oesterreichs in Italien," Lažansky, fol. 26, 21 Jan. 1815, and Franz's note to Metternich, fol. 25, 25 Jan.
105. Pallain, ed., *Correspondance*, 315, Louis to Talleyrand, 5 Mar. 1815; Maturi, "Restaurazione (II)," 39–43.
106. Kraehe, *Policy*, 2:313, 331; Schroeder, *Transformation*, 494–495, 513–514, treats it as part of the allied strategy to cooperate for stability in the new international order.
107. HHStA StK Kongreßakten 5, Fasz. 9, fol. 62, "Note" of Valtellina representatives, 13 Dec. 1814, in Italian, with similar list, in French, in the note protesting the likely outcome, 21 Dec., Klüber, *Acten*, 7:313, including "l'unité de langage."
108. Weil, *Dessous*, 1:277, 12 Oct. 1814 police report.
109. Wellington, Wellesley, ed., *Suppl. Desp.*, 9:605–606, 25 Mar. 1815.
110. HHStA StK Kongreßakten 13, Fasz. 1, folder "Grisons," fols. 31–32v, 6 Mar. 1815.
111. Ute Planert, *Der Mythos vom Befreiungskrieg. Frankreichs Kriege und der deutsche Süden: Alltag—Wahrnehmung—Deutung 1792–1841* (Paderborn: Schöningh, 2007); Karen Hagemann, *"Mannlicher Muth und teutsche Ehre": Nation, Militär und Geschlecht zur Zeit der Antinapoleonischen Kriege Preußens* (Paderborn: Schöningh, 2002); Michael Broers, *Europe under Napoleon, 1796–1815* (London: Arnold, 1996); Eric J. Hobsbawm, *Nations and Nationalism since 1780: Programme, Myth, Reality*, 2nd ed. (Cambridge: Cambridge University Press, 1992).
112. On ideologies as "cognitive maps," Clifford Geertz, "Ideology as a Cultural System," in *The Interpretation of Cultures* (New York: Basic Books, 1973), 193–233; Jens Rydgren, *The Populist Challenge: Political Protest and Entho-national Mobilization in France* (New York: Berghahn, 2003), 49–51.
113. On the debate between "modernists" and "perennialists" in nationalism studies, see Len Scales and Oliver Zimmer, eds., *Power and the Nation in European History* (Cambridge: Cambridge University Press, 2005), esp. John Breuilly, "Changes in the Political Uses of the Nation: Continuity or Discontinuity?," 67–101, 68, 92.
114. Celia Applegate, *A Nation of Provincials: The German Idea of Heimat* (Berkeley: University of California Press, 1990); Alon Confino, *The Nation as a Local Metaphor: Württemberg, Imperial Germany, and National Memory, 1871–1918* (Chapel Hill: University of North Carolina Press, 1997); Maiken Umbach, *Federalism and Enlightenment in Germany, 1740–1806*

(London: Hambledon Press, 2000); Abigail Green, *Fatherlands: State-Building and Nationhood in Nineteenth-Century Germany* (Cambridge: Cambridge University Press, 2001), and "Political Institutions and Nationhood in Germany, 1750–1914," in Scales and Zimmer, eds., *Power and the Nation,* 315–332; Dieter Langewiesche and Georg Schmidt, eds., *Föderative Nation: Deutschlandkonzepte von der Reformation bis zum Ersten Weltkrieg* (Munich: Oldenbourg, 2000).

115. For Switzerland and Italy, Oliver Zimmer, "Nation, Nationalism and Power in Switzerland, c. 1760–1900," in Scales and Zimmer, eds., *Power and the Nation,* 333–353, 334, 343–344, and Stuart Woolf, "Nation, Nations and Power in Italy, c. 1700–1915," in ibid., 295–314, 307–310. For the Habsburg Empire: Gary B. Cohen, *The Politics of Ethnic Survival: Germans in Prague, 1861–1914* (Princeton, NJ: Princeton University Press, 1981); Jeremy King, *Budweisers into Czechs and Germans: A Local History of Bohemian Politics, 1848–1948* (Princeton, NJ: Princeton University Press, 2006); Pieter M. Judson, *Exclusive Revolutionaries: Liberal Politics, Social Experience, and National Identity in the Austrian Empire, 1848–1914* (Ann Arbor: University of Michigan Press, 1996); Judson, *Guardians of the Nation: Activists on the Language Frontiers of Imperial Austria* (Cambridge, MA: Harvard University Press, 2006); Daniel L. Unowsky, *The Pomp and the Politics of Patriotism: Imperial Celebrations in Habsburg Austria, 1848–1916* (West Lafayette, IN: Purdue University Press, 2005); Judson and Marsha L. Rozenblit, eds., *Constructing Nationalities in East Central Europe* (New York: Berghahn, 2005); Andreas Moritsch, ed., *Der Austroslavismus: Ein verfrühtes Konzept zur politischen Neugestaltung Mitteleuropas* (Vienna: Böhlau, 1996). On the tension between contestation and reinforcement of local and dynastic-national symbols in Austria, Werner Telesko, *Geschichtsraum Österreich. Die Habsburger und ihre Geschichte in der bildenden Kunst des 19. Jahrhunderts* (Vienna: Böhlau, 2006), 24–30; and Telesko, *Kulturraum Österreich. Die Identität der Regionen in der bildenden Kunst des 19. Jahrhunderts* (Vienna: Böhlau, 2008), 15–16, 380.

116. Stolberg, *Tagebuch,* 181, 16 Feb. 1815. Eduard Winter, *Romantismus, Restauration und Frühliberalismus im österreichischen Vormärz* (Vienna: Europa, 1968), 67–70, 96–97; Max Vasmer, *B. Kopitars Briefwechsel mit Jakob Grimm* (Cologne: Böhlau, 1987 [1938]), XVI–XVII, XX–XV; Horst Conrad, *Die Kette: Eine Standesvereinigung des Adels auf dem Wiener Kongreß* (Münster: Vereinigte westfälische Adelsarchive, 1979); Ursula Brauer, *Isaac von Sinclair. Eine Biographie* (Stuttgart: Klett-Cotta, 1993), 289–294. Downplaying Schlegel's influence on Kopitar, Sergio Bonazza, "Kopitar und Friedrich Schlegel in Wien: Wissenschaftsbeziehungen," *Wiener slavistisches Jahrbuch* 53 (2007): 191–211.

117. Marie-Claire Hoock-Demarle, *L'Europe des lettres. Réseaux épistolaires et construction de l'éspace européen* (Paris: Michel, 2008), 134, 176–177, 312; Andreas Oplatka, *Graf Stephan Széchenyi: Der Mann, der Ungarn*

schuf (Vienna: Zsolnay, 2004), 101; Gyula Viszota, ed., *Gróf Széchenyi István Naplói*, 6 vols. (Budapest: Magyar Történelmi Társulat, 1925–39), 1:3–4, 7–8 (July 1814); John Claiborne Isbell, Introduction to Madame de Staël, *Corinne, or Italy*, trans. Sylvia Raphael (Oxford: Oxford University Press, 1998), vii–xx, xii for "the birth of modern nationalism" and "nationalité."

118. Overstating government opposition to patriotic mobilization and understating the resonance of patriotic poetry, music, theater, and memorabilia in urban areas during the campaigns of 1813–1815: Karen Hagemann, "'Be Proud and Firm, Citizens of Austria!' Patriotism and Masculinity in Texts of the 'Political Romantics' Written during Austria's Anti-Napoleonic Wars," *German Studies Review* 29, 1 (2006): 41–62, 45, 52–54; Ernst Weber, *Lyrik der Befreiungskriege (1812–1815): gesellschaftspolitische Meinungs- und Willensbildung durch Literatur* (Stuttgart: Metzler, 1991), 325–335. For a more balanced account, see still Eduard Wertheimer, *Wien und das Kriegsjahr 1813. Ein Beitrag zur Geschichte der Befreiungskriege. Nach ungedruckten Quellen* (Vienna: Tempsky, 1893).

119. Webster, *Diplomacy*, 34, Castlereagh to Cathcart, "Private," 14 Oct. 1813; similarly at 99, 104–105. Note that King Friedrich Wilhelm's appeal "To My People" of 17 Mar. 1813 aimed at both Prussians and Germans, but also at Prussia's mixed component populations, Silesians and Pomeranians, Brandenburger and Lithuanians.

120. HHStA StK Vorträge 195 (1814), fols. 96–96v, 98–98v, 131–135v, on the role of French public opinion and nationalism in the decisions about looted art (Metternich and Altieri, Aug., Sept.).

121. *Oesterreichischer Beobachter*, no. 319, 15 Nov. 1814, 1739, quoting the Norwegian proclamation of 21 Oct. agreeing to personal union.

122. HHStA StK Kongreßakten 7, fol. 344, Hardenberg to Metternich, 10 Dec. 1814; from the poem "Jetzt oder nie?" (Now or Never?) by "F von S-r," in Görres's *Rheinischer Merkur*, no. 130, 9 Oct. 1814.

123. On Metternich's sense of German patriotism, Siemann, *Metternich*, 18, 23, 49.

124. HHStA StK Kongreßakten 8, Fasz. 2, fol. 54–54v, Schwarzenberg to Kaiser, 17 Jan. 1815; Klüber, *Acten*, 2:16–17, note of Prussian plenipotentiaries to Metternich, 10 Feb. 1815 (emphases in original).

125. Humboldt, "Denkschrift über die deutsche Verfassung," 11:96–97. On Humboldt's constitutional drafts, see Clemens Menze, "Die Verfassungspläne Wilhelm von Humboldts," *Zeitschrift für historische Forschung* 16 (1989): 329–346.

126. Brian Vick, "Of Basques, Greeks, and Germans: Liberalism, Nationalism, and the Ancient Republican Tradition in the Thought of Wilhelm von Humboldt," *Central European History* 40, 4 (2007): 653–681.

127. Also versus an exclusive focus on Othering in national identity, Zimmer, "Switzerland," 337.

128. Burke, *Reflections*, 40.

129. Humboldt, "Denkschrift über die deutsche Verfassung," 11:101; cf. Humboldt, "Denkschrift über ständische Verfassung," in Leitzmann et al., eds., *Gesammelte Schriften*, 12,2:389–455, 399 (Oct. 1819), and Menze, "Verfassungsplane," 338–339, for the same idea applied to Prussia. Humboldt thus recognized the link between local, state, and national identities that features in recent studies of German nationalism. For the early nineteenth century, Hagen Schulze, "Nationalismus—Regionalismus—Lokalismus: Aspekte der Erinnerungskultur im Spiegel von Publizistik und Denkmal," in Etienne François, ed., *Lieux de Mémoire, Erinnerungsorte: D'un mot français à un projet allemand* (Berlin: Centre Marc Bloch, 1996), 91–104.

130. August von Kotzebue, "Ideen über das politische Gleichgewicht in Europa," *Politische Flugblätter* 1, 14 (1814): 281–307, 300–301.

131. Hellmuth Rößler, *Österreichs Kampf um Deutschlands Befreiung: Die deutsche Politik der nationalen Führer Österreichs 1805–1815*, 2 vols. (Hamburg: Hanseatische Verlagsanstalt, 1940), 1:356, 363–367, 429.

132. Helfert, *Kaiser Franz*, 52–54, with text of Bellegarde's proposal at 560–564, 20 Mar. 1815; Countess Bellegarde, Weil, *Dessous*, 1:744–746, police report of 26 Dec.

133. Winter, *Romantismus*, 38, 44, 57–70; Rößler, *Österreichs Kampf*, 1:60–66, 160–164, 454–455, 476–477, 486–495.

134. The federalist reading, Haas, *Reorganization*; rejected by Sked, *Metternich*, 107–108; Laven, *Venetia*, 60–62, 79, goes too far in arguing that nationality was not a significant concern for Metternich at all. Wolfram Siemann sets Metternich's national ideas in the context of German federative nationhood, and of Georg Schmidt's notion of the Holy Roman Empire's "complementary statehood," but overstates Metternich's fear of national identities: 49–50, 53–61, 106–108, 115–117.

135. Angeberg, *Congrès*, 2:425.

136. HHStA StK Interiora Korresp.67, Fasz. 2, fols. 218–219v, Metternich to Hudelist, 15 May 1814.

137. HHStA StK Vorträge 197 (1815), fols. 748–749v (Monti, quotes), Metternich report of 1 Jan. 1815, with Franz's assent, 8 July 1815; political report on Monti, fol. 796, 13 Mar.; Academy, StK Rom 9, "Weisungen 1814," fol. 51–51v, Metternich to Lebzeltern, 27 Aug. Further examples in Siemann, *Metternich*, 107, 117.

138. For Sked, this meant that Germany and Italy were about equally "geographic expressions": *Metternich*, 40, 45, 183, and 87–88 on the League.

139. Luther, ed., *Documenti*, 10:1:35–38, "Progetto di Confederazione italica di Vittorio Emanuele I" (1815); Rinieri, ed., *Corrispondenza*.

140. HHStA StK Vorträge 197 (1815), folder "Vortr. 1815 IV," 18 Apr., fols. 644–647, quote, 645; also in Haas, *Reorganization*, 75–77, 167–169 (text); Larry Wolff, *The Idea of Galicia: History and Fantasy in Habsburg Political Culture* (Stanford, CA: Stanford University Press, 2010), 79–81.

141. Ulrike Tischler, *Die habsburgische Politik gegenüber den Serben und Montenegrinern 1791–1822. Förderung oder Vereinnahmung?* (Munich: Oldenbourg, 2000), 367–373, 376–377.

142. Sked, *Metternich,* 191–192, and Wolff, *Galicia,* 81–85, for Ossoliński, the university, and the constitutional assembly; Ruthenian, Wolff, *Galicia,* 86–87, and Jan Kozik, *The Ukrainian National Movement in Galicia: 1815–1849,* Lawrence D. Orton, ed., Andrew Gorski and Orton, trans. (Edmonton: Canadian Institute of Ukrainian Studies, 1986), 51–57; population profile, Martina Thomsen, "Polen," in Daum et al., eds., *Handbuch,* 2:663–718, 667.

7. Poland, Saxony, and the Crucible of Diplomacy

1. Examples of good accounts in this sense: Enno E. Kraehe, *Metternich's German Policy,* vol. 2, *The Congress of Vienna* (Princeton, NJ: Princeton University Press, 1983); Jacques-Alain de Sédouy, *Le Congrès de Vienne: L'Europe contre la France 1812–1815* (Paris: Perrin, 2003); Mark Jarrett, *The Congress of Vienna and its Legacy: War and Great Power Diplomacy after Napoleon* (London: I.B. Tauris, 2013). Paul W. Schroeder, *The Transformation of European Politics, 1763–1848* (New York: Oxford University Press, 1994), 523–538 for the Polish-Saxon question and passim, also emphasizes the role of norms and beliefs in international politics rather than the pursuit of power alone.

2. Webster, *Diplomacy,* 257, Castlereagh to Liverpool, 17 Dec. 1814

3. On Congress conflicts as "problems of learning" on the way to a cooperative European order, Schroeder, *Transformation,* 517; strongly for the balance-of-power interpretation versus Schroeder, Enno E. Kraehe, "A Bipolar Balance of Power," *American Historical Review* 97, 3 (1992): 707–715; and Alan Sked, *Metternich and Austria: An Evaluation* (Basingstoke, England: Palgrave Macmillan, 2008), 55–57, 63.

4. Pallain, ed., *Correspondance,* 3, Talleyrand to King, 25 Sept. 1814; Niels Rosenkrantz, *Journal du Congrès de Vienne, 1814–1815,* Georg Nørregård, ed. (Copenhagen: Gad, 1953), 33, 125–126 (3 Oct. 1814; 13–16 Jan. 1815).

5. HHStA StK Kriegsakten 428, Fasz. 491, fols. 374–375, Schwarzenberg to Metternich, 1 Nov. 1814; Langenau, Kriegsakten 430, folder "Schwarzenberg 1812–1815," fols. 262–263, 18 Dec. 1814; GStA PK III. HA MdA I, no. 1355, 29 Dec. 1814, Grolman to Hardenberg, plus enclosures.s

6. Vneshniaia, 8:103–105, including Metternich's and Hardenberg's objections to the name Poland in the four-power meeting of 19 Sept. 1814; GStA PK III. HA MdA I, no. 1254, fol. 19–19v, copy of the treaty of 26/15 Jan. 1797 among the partitioning powers promising never again to use the expression "Kingdom of Poland," in order to help erase the "memory" of its existence.

7. HHStA KK Akten 39 (1814), nos. 1640, 1665 (26 and 30 June); HHStA StA Russland III, Kart. 18, folder D, fols. 3v, 11v, 30 (Jan. 1815).

8. Here with Kraehe, *Policy*, 2:229–230, versus Karl Griewank, *Der Wiener Kongress und die europäische Restauration 1814/15*, 2nd ed. (Leipzig: Koehler & Amelang, 1954), 205, 221; also claiming that Austria and Britain above all opposed a Polish constitution, Ulrike Eich, *Russland und Europa: Studien zur russischen Deutschlandpolitik in der Zeit des Wiener Kongresses* (Cologne: Böhlau, 1986), 257.

9. Angeberg, *Congrès*, 3:1389.

10. Hannah Alice Straus, *The Attitude of the Congress of Vienna toward Nationalism in Germany, Italy, and Poland* (New York: Columbia University Press, 1949), ch. 2; Charles Webster, *The Congress of Vienna 1814–1815* (London: Bell, 1950 [1919]), 99; Sked, *Metternich*, 57; Jean Tulard, "Le Congrès de Vienne," in Georges-Henri Souton and Jean Bérenger, eds., *L'ordre européen du XVIe au XXe siècle* (Paris: Presses de l'Université de Paris-Sorbonne, 1998), 113–116, 115. Piotr S. Wandycz, *The Lands of Partitioned Poland, 1795–1918* (Seattle: University of Washington Press, 1974), 62.

11. Castlereagh's "lip-service": Webster, *Congress*, 99; W.H. Zawadzki, *A Man of Honor: Adam Czartoryski as a Statesman of Russia and Poland 1795–1831* (Oxford: Clarendon, 1993), 239; similarly for Talleyrand, Schroeder, *Transformation*, 531; Straus, *Attitude*, 140.

12. HHStA StK Kongreßakten 6, fols. 22v–23, undated Wessenberg memo [1814]; Wolfgang Zechner, "Joseph Anton von Pilat" (diss., University of Vienna, 1954), 167, Sept. 1815.

13. Henri Rossi, *Anna Potocka: Des Lumières au Romantisme* (Paris: Champion, 2001), 387–391, 404–412; and Straus, *Attitude*, 134–135; in addition to Zawadzki, *Czartoryski*, Marian Kukiel, *Czartoryski and European Unity, 1770–1861* (Princeton, NJ: Princeton University Press, 1955).

14. Anstett and Pozzo, Weil, *Dessous*, 1:343–344, 424, 470, 512, police reports of 20 and 28 Oct., 4 and 12 Nov. 1814; Pozzo, Stein, and Castlereagh: Kukiel, *Czartoryski*, 112; and Patricia Kennedy Grimsted, *The Foreign Ministers of Alexander I: Political Attitudes and the Conduct of Russian Diplomacy, 1801–1825* (Berkeley: University of California Press, 1969), 210–212, 217–218, 221. Pozzo's memo was known to Friedrich Gentz and the Austrian police: [intercept] Gentz to Caradja, 3 Aug. 1814, Weil, *Dessous*, 1:44–45.

15. Weil, *Dessous*, 1:460–462, 3 Nov. 1814.

16. Stein, Zawadzki, *Czartoryski*, 235; Erich Botzenhart and Walther Hubatsch, eds., *Freiherr vom Stein Briefe und amtliche Schriften*, 11 vols. (Stuttgart: Kohlhammer, 1957–74), 5:324, and 325–326 for Capodistrias's views (19 Oct. 1814), as also 336–337 (18–23 Nov.). Also on Capodistrias, Roxandra Countess Edling, *Mémoires de la comtesse Edling (née Stourdza), demoiselle d'honneur de Sa Majesté l'Impératrice Élisabeth Alexéevna* (Moscow, 1888), 208–209. On Humboldt and Stein, see Straus, *Attitude*, 137–138; Humboldt, *Briefen*, 4:550 (quote).

17. Heinz Röllecke, ed., *Briefwechsel zwischen Jacob und Wilhelm Grimm* (Stuttgart: Hirzel, 2001–), 1:394–395, Jacob to Wilhelm, 16 Dec. 1814; GStA PK III. HA MdA I, no. 1364, fol. 269–269v, Hoffmann to Hardenberg, 17 Feb. 1814, in response to Prussian official Zerboni di Sposetti's note of 5 Feb. 1814, fol. 270–270v, which suggested the Vistula as border. Czartoryski unsurprisingly also argued that Prussia should become a homogeneously German state: Zawadzki, *Czartoryski*, 242.

18. GStA PK III. HA MdA I, no. 1364, fols. 321–326v, Hoffmann to Hardenberg, 28 Mar. 1814, quote fol. 321.

19. Angeberg, *Congrès*, 3:798, Russian circular note, 19 Jan. 1815.

20. Vneshniaia, 8:157–162, Czartoryski memo, 30 Dec. 1814/11 Jan. 1815; for a previous memo to Castlereagh in the summer of 1814 calling for something like a Polish confederation across the three jurisdictions, and for hopes of eventual reunification under Russia, Zawadzki, *Czartoryski,* 229–230, 246, and TNA FO 139/22, fols. 125–129; Angeberg, *Congrès*, 3:1146–1154 and 1154–1163, treaties of 3 May 1815 between Russia and (respectively) Austria and Prussia; on the final settlement, Wandycz, *Partitioned Poland*, 65–67.

21. Stein's memo of 6 Oct. 1814, and remarks in diary, in Botzenhart and Hubatsch, eds., *Stein*, 5:158–159, 324; copy in GStA PK III. HA MdA I, no. 1251, fols. 9–10v; Heinz Duchhardt, *Stein. Eine Biographie* (Münster: Aschendorff, 2007), 331, for the memo of 1814, and 165–173 for the Nassauer Denkschrift of 1807, originally written for Prussian-Polish Prince Radziwill.

22. Zawadzki, *Czartoryski*, 245–247, on Czartoryski's assessment (including fears of "Germanization"); Russian initiative on Polish rights, GStA PK III. HA MdA I, no. 1252, fols. 60v–61, session of Four-Power Committee, 9 Jan. 1815. On Castlereagh, Webster, *Congress*, 120, and the circular itself, Webster, *Diplomacy*, 287–288 (quote). Griewank, *Kongress*, 254, argued that the Prussian, Russian, and Austrian responses were, like Castlereagh's statement, primarily aimed at British public opinion.

23. Austrian response, Angeberg, *Congrès*, 2:800 (21 Feb. 1815), Prussian, 801 (30 Jan. 1815). A passage in Prussia's draft response linking the attraction of Polish loyalty to the king's granting "a new constitution based on the principles of equal justice for all his subjects" was crossed out and omitted from the final version, but the constitutional promise reappeared in the Prussian proclamations to the new Polish provinces in May (see below): GStA PK III. HA MdA I, no. 1271, fols. 96–97.

24. GStA PK VI. HA NL Hardenberg, H24, Johann Gottfried Hoffmann, 15 Dec. 1815 (no fol.), also calling for protection of German nationality rights in mixed areas. For the parallels with 1848, Brian E. Vick, *Defining Germany: The 1848 Frankfurt Parliamentarians and National Identity* (Cambridge, MA: Harvard University Press, 2002), ch. 4.

25. Metternich, HHStA StK Vorträge 197 (1815), folder "Vortr. 1815 IV," 18 Apr., fols. 644–647, quote, 645; Larry Wolff, *The Idea of Galicia: History and Fantasy in Habsburg Political Culture* (Stanford, CA: Stanford University Press, 2010), 79–87. See Kraehe, *Policy,* 2:229–230.

26. Vneshniaia, 8:88, memo of Nesselrode, 31 July/12 Aug. 1814; GStA PK VI. HA NL Friedrich Wilhelm III, no. 29–30, fol. 38–38v, Hardenberg to Friedrich Wilhelm, 14 Jul. 1814, reporting a conversation with Alexander in Darmstadt; General Knesebeck already recommended compensation in Italy in a memo of 18 Jan. 1814, fol. 3.

27. Kraehe, *Policy,* 2:284, 295; Webster, *Congress,* 112, 115–116.

28. Humboldt, *Briefen,* 4:418 (13 Nov. 1814), on memo, 412 (9 Nov.), quotes; previous critical comments 399 (2 Nov.). Memo: Albert Leitzmann, Bruno Gebhardt, and Wilhelm Richter, eds., *Wilhelm von Humboldts Gesammelte Schriften,* 17 vols. (Berlin: Behr, 1903–1936), 11:189–197, 9 Nov. 1814.

29. Staegemann, *Olfers,* 236, 27 Oct. 1814.

30. Staegemann, *Olfers,* 224–225, 3 Oct. 1814; Knesebeck memo, GStA PK III. HA MdA I, no. 1251, fols. 89–97, quote fol. 93, cover letter 16 Nov. 1814, fol. 88.

31. Humboldt, *Briefen,* 4:404, 7 Nov. 1814. On state-level nation-building, including in Saxony, Abigail Green, *Fatherlands: State-Building and Nationhood in Nineteenth-Century Germany* (Cambridge: Cambridge University Press, 2001). Even after 1815 Saxony remained a composite state, with regional identities possibly paramount: Zef Segal, "Real Actual and Imagined Borders—State Construction in the 'Third Germany,'" *Tel Aviver Jahrbuch für deutsche Geschichte* 40 (2012): 21–43.

32. Pallain, ed., *Correspondance,* 122–123, Talleyrand to King, 17 Nov. 1814.

33. GStA PK III. HA MdA I, no. 1277, fols. 25–26, copy of Alexander's draft instructions for Russian ambassador Alopeus in Berlin, Dec. 1814 (no day), Alopeus himself to use similar arguments with Friedrich August; cf. Kraehe, *Policy,* 2:295, 298. Miltitz had already petitioned Hardenberg and Alexander against partition on behalf of the "sächsische Nation": MdA I, no. 1282, fols. 280–281 (copy of letter to Alexander), fols. 282–285v (memorandum to Hardenberg, with quote, fol. 284), both 28 Nov. 1814.

34. Hoffmann memo, GStA PK III. HA MdA I, no. 1364, fols. 106–110v, quote 106v, undated (late December); MdA I, no. 1269, fol. 3, Hardenberg to Schöler, 26 Aug. 1814.

35. Angeberg, *Congrès,* 2:495–498, 497, from the *Moniteur universel,* 5 Dec. 1814.

36. HHStA StA England 154, "Weisungen 1815," fols. 6, 9v–10v, Metternich to Merveldt, 3 Jan. 1815; Webster, *Diplomacy,* 301–302; Pallain, ed., *Correspondance,* 55–57, Talleyrand to Louis, 17 Oct. 1814, and 16 Oct., to Jaucourt.

37. C. M. Woodhouse, *Capodistria: The Founder of Greek Independence* (London: Oxford University Press, 1973), 121–122, 123–124.

38. HHStA StA Russland III, Kart. 41, "Weisungen 1814–16," fols. 1–4v, Metternich to Koller, 16 Aug. 1814, quotes, fols. 1, 4v; Kart. 18, "Berichte 1814–15," folder C, fol. 3–3v, Koller to Metternich, 8 Sept. 1814.

39. Rosenkrantz, *Journal*, 33–34; Alexander M. Martin, *Romantics, Reformers, Reactionaries: Russian Conservative Thought and Politics in the Reign of Alexander I* (DeKalb: Northern Illinois University Press, 1997), 8–11; Grimsted, *Foreign Ministers*, 12–13, downplays the role of the press and even elite public opinion; emphasizing political conversation among the educated elite and officials, but minimizing the press and civil society, Angela Rustemeyer, "Das Arkanum zwischen Herrschaftsanspruch und Kommunikationspraxis vom 16. bis zum frühen 19. Jahrhundert," in Walter Sperling, ed., *Jenseits der Zarenmacht. Dimensionen des Politischen im Russischen Reich 1800–1917* (Frankfurt a. M.: Campus, 2008), 43–70, 45, 63–69.

40. Vneshniaia, 8:139–144, Alexander to Lieven, 15/27 Dec. 1814, including undated memo. Woodhouse, *Capodistria*, 121–124; Eich, *Russland und Europa*, 263–264.

41. GStA PK III. HA MdA I, no. 5224 (no fol.), Greuhm to King, 12 Dec. 1814, and draft of return instructions, 6 Jan. 1815; HHStA StA England 151, Fasz. 3 (Berichte 1814 IX–XII), fols. 3v–4, Merveldt to Metternich, 16 Dec.; *Courier*, 25 Jan., in Greuhm's report of 27 Jan.

42. Webster, *Diplomacy*, 235–236, Liverpool to Castlereagh, 18 Nov. 1814; copy of Liverpool letter, GStA PK III. HA MdA I, no. 1251, fol. 129–129v, enclosed in Metternich to Hardenberg, 11 Dec. 1814.

43. Staegemann, *Olfers*, 267 (23 Dec. 1814); Georg Herbert Graf zu Münster, *Politische Skizzen über die Lage Europas vom Wiener Congress bis zur Gegenwart (1815–1867.) Nebst den Depeschen des Grafen Ernst Friedrich Herbert zu Münster über den Wiener Congress* (Leipzig, 1867), 199, Münster to Prince Regent, 17 Dec. 1814 ("secret"); GStA PK III. HA MdA I, no. 1251, fol. 107, Stein to Hardenberg, 4 Dec. 1814 (cover letter to Stein's memo of 3 Dec.).

44. C. K. Webster, *The Foreign Policy of Castlereagh 1812–1815: Britain and the Reconstruction of Europe* (London: Bell, 1931), 284.

45. Kukiel, *Czartoryski*, 110–113 (Biernacki); Zawadzki, *Czartoryski*, 228–229 for Czartoryski in London, 218–220, 240 (Biernacki and Sierakowski).

46. Weil, *Dessous*, 1:227–228 and 2:225–226, police reports of 5 Oct. 1814 and 19 Feb. 1815.

47. Weil, *Dessous*, 2:624–625, 8 June 1815; Julius Marx, *Die österreichische Zensur im Vormärz* (Vienna: Verlag für Geschichte und Politik, 1959), 62, on Austrian censorship of images and objects.

48. Zawadzki, *Czartoryski*, 242.

49. On Piattoli, Hildegard Schaeder, *Die dritte Koalition und die Heilige Allianz* (Königsberg: Ost-Europa Verlag, 1934), 19; Zawadzki, *Czartoryski*,

116–118; Alessandro D'Ancona, *Scipione Piattoli e la Polonia* (Florence: Barbera, 1915), chs. 5, 6.

50. Staegemann, *Olfers,* 250, 17 Nov. 1814; Humboldt, *Briefen,* 4:428, 4 Dec. 1814; similarly Baron Stein to Countess Orlov, Botzenhart and Hubatsch, eds., *Stein,* 5:265, 5 Feb. 1815. Earlier view: HStA Darm. D22, no. 21/11, fol. 32–32v, August von Hedemann to Princess Marianne of Prussia, 9 Oct. 1814.

51. Pallain, ed., *Correspondance,* 81, 25 Oct. 1814; GMD, Sophie Schlosser Tagebuch, fols. 7v, 8, 8 and 9 Nov. 1814; Anna Eynard, Journal, BGE Ms suppl 1959, 250, 29 Jan. 1815.

52. Staegemann, *Olfers,* 268, 25 Dec. 1814; Hilde Spiel, *Fanny von Arnstein: Daughter of the Enlightenment,* trans. Christine Shuttleworth (Oxford: Oxford University Press, 1991), 291–292.

53. Fournier, *Geheimpolizei,* 394, 16 Feb. 1815.

54. Weil, *Dessous,* 1:695, 18 Dec. 1814.

55. Fournier, *Geheimpolizei,* 346, 21 Jan. 1815.

56. Hans Christoph von Gagern, *Mein Antheil an der Politik,* 4 vols. (Stuttgart, 1823–33 [1826]), 2:119–120.

57. Ibid., 120–122, quote 121–122.

58. Humboldt, *Briefen,* 4:403–404, 7 Nov. 1814.

59. Humboldt, *Briefen,* 4:453–454, 5 Jan. 1815; Gneisenau, 443, 20 Dec. 1814, Wilhelm to Caroline.

60. Staegemann, *Olfers,* 262, 264, 14 and 19 Dec. 1814; Hedwig, 257, 2 Dec.

61. HStA Darm. D22, no. 22/8, p. 53 [*sic*], Hardenberg to Marianne, 9 Dec. 1814. Marianne's father, Landgrave Friedrich V of Hessen-Homburg, also sympathized with Friedrich August: HStA Darm. D11, no. 126/5, no fol., Friedrich to Privy Councillor Isaac von Sinclair, 20 Nov. 1814.

62. HStA Darm. D22, no. 33/44, fols. 2v–3v, Hardenberg to Princess Marianne, 23 Dec. 1814, responding to her letter of 14 Dec.

63. Staegemann, *Olfers,* 273, 2 Jan. 1815, for Stein's view; Botzenhart and Hubatsch, eds., *Stein,* 5:335 and 340, 10 Nov. and 4 Dec. 1814 (on Hardenberg and Metternich), on Franz, 341, 6 Dec.

64. *Allgemeine Zeitung,* 15, 16, and 17 Jan. 1815, 58, 64, 66–67; on the *Deutsche Beobachter* deal, Daniel Moran, *Toward the Century of Words: Johann Cotta and the Politics of the Public Realm in Germany, 1795–1832* (Berkeley: University of California Press, 1990), 143–146, and Monika Neugebauer-Wölk, *Revolution und Constitution—Die Brüder Cotta: eine biographische Studie zum Zeitalter der Französischen Revolution und des Vormärz* (Berlin: Colloquium, 1989), 454–457; pro-Saxon, Ferdinand Troska, *Die Publizistik zur sächsischen Frage auf dem Wiener Kongress* (Halle: Niemeyer, 1891), 41.

65. On the *Correspondenten* (the *Staats- und Gelehrten Zeitung des Hamburgischen unpartheyischen Correspondenten*), GStA PK III. HA MdA I, no. 3867, fols. 198v, 221 (Grote to Hardenberg [copy]), 16 Dec. 1814; MdA I, no. 993 includes several articles from Hardenberg placed in the

paper through Grote. Troska's judgment of the *Correspondenten, Publizistik,* 45.

66. *Caledonian Mercury,* 19 Dec. 1814.

67. Paul Czygan, *Zur Geschichte der Tagesliteratur während der Freiheitskriege,* 2 vols. (Leipzig: Duncker & Humblot, 1911), 2, 2:125–128, Varnhagen to Hardenberg, 15 Jan. 1815, including Grimm's article from the *Rheinische Merkur,* no. 169, 27 Dec. 1814 (dateline Vienna, 14 Dec.), and Varnhagen's counter-piece, *Deutscher Beobachter,* no. 16, 28 Jan. 1815 (Vienna, 18 Jan.).

68. Angeberg, *Congrès,* 2:495–498; copy from *Journal des débats* (6 Dec.) in HHStA StK Kongreßakten 7, fols. 504–505.

69. GStA PK III. HA MdA I, no. 3867, fol. 185, Hardenberg to Sack in Aachen, draft, Jan. 1815 (day unclear).

70. GStA PK III. HA MdA I, no. 3867, fols. 198v, 221 (Grote to Hardenberg [copy]), 16 Dec. 1814; fols. 185–221 for the whole exchange, including copies of the *Moniteur* of 5 Dec., the *Journal des débats* of 6 Dec., the *Altonaischer Mercurius* of 15 and 16 Dec., and the *Hamburgischen Correspondenten,* 14 Dec. 1814.

71. Weil, *Dessous,* 2:94–95, Pfeffel to Wrede, 19 Jan. 1815; Guido Gigli, *Il Congresso di Vienna (1814–1815)* (Florence: Sansoni, 1938), 33–34; Webster, *Congress,* 94–95.

72. *Chronik des allgemeinen Wiener Kongresses,* nos. 2, 23, 7 Oct., 16 Dec. 1814, 24, 344–345; *Erinnerungsblätter für gebildete Leser aus allen Ständen* (Zwickau, 1815), no. 42, 23 Oct. 1814, 657 for the Echo, and no. 48, 4 Dec., 756, on the significance of Frankenthal in the Palatinate as the *Chronik's* place of publication.

73. Smidt, Richard Schwemer, *Geschichte der Freien Stadt Frankfurt a. M. (1814–1866),* 2 vols. (Frankfurt: Baer, 1910–18), 1:118–119, report of 24 Nov. 1815; *Chronik,* no. 31, 10 Jan. 1815, 463.

74. Troska, *Publizistik,* 13 (Görres), 41, on pamphlets and public opinion. In addition to Troska on the Bavarian-Prussian pamphlet war, Andrea Hofmeister-Hunger, *Pressepolitik und Staatsreform: Die Institutionalisierung staatlicher Öffentlichkeitsarbeit bei Karl August von Hardenberg (1792–1822)* (Göttingen: Vandenhoeck & Ruprecht, 1994), 279–282, 290–293; Wolfgang Piereth, *Bayerns Pressepolitik und die Neuordnung Deutschlands nach den Befreiungskriegen* (Munich: Beck, 1999).

75. Germanus Saxo [Wilhelm Traugott Krug], *Sachsens Vereinigung mit Preussen aus dem Gesichtspunkte des Protestantismus betrachtet* (Leipzig, 1814); [Johann Christoph von Aretin], *Anmerkungen zu der Schrift: Preussen und Sachsen. Von einem Sachsen* (n. p., 1815); [Aretin], *Noten zum Text: Sachsen und Preussen* (Germanien, 1815). On place names, Rudolf Jenak, ed., *Sachsen, der Rheinbund und die Exekution der Sachsen betreffenden Entscheidungen des Wiener Kongresses (1803–1816)* (Neustadt an der Aisch: Schmidt, 2005), 197, 245–246, including "Landgier"; Hardenberg's

approval of Krug's pamphleteering, Hofmeister-Hunger, *Pressepolitik*, 291; Aretin and *Allemania*, Piereth, *Bayerns Pressepolitik*, 124, 226. The Prussian censor in Berlin was unimpressed with Krug's argument: Czygan, *Tagesliteratur*, 2, 2:34–35.

76. GStA PK III. HA MdA I, no. 3867, fols. 146–151v, 18 Nov. and 31 Dec. 1814.

77. B.G. Niebuhr, *Preussens Recht gegen den sächsischen Hof* (Berlin, 1814); prepublication correspondence between Hardenberg, Niebuhr, and Prussian censor Renfner in Berlin, Czygan, *Tagesliteratur*, 2, 2:83–85. On Hoffmann and Niebuhr, Troska, *Publizistik*, 17–18, 28–29.

78. Troska, *Publizistik*, 18; GStA PK III. HA MdA I, no. 1266, fol. 121v, Greuhm to Hardenberg, 3 Mar. 1815.

79. Walter Kohlschmidt, *Die Sächsische Frage auf dem Wiener Kongreß und die Sächsische Diplomatie dieser Zeit* (Dresden: Baensch Stiftung, 1930), 4–7.

80. For examples of the *Tugendbund* conspiracy argument, Troska, *Publizistik*, 19, 32–33; quote, [anon.], *Preussen und Teutschland. Drey Abhandlungen* (n.p., 1814), 125.

81. Troska, *Publizistik*, 12–13, 26, with three further examples.

82. Ibid., 32–33, for *Gespräche im Reiche der Lebendigen von Wahrmund. Erste Lieferung: über den Katholizismus des Königs von Sachsen* (Reutlingen, 1814); *Morning Chronicle*, no. 14277, 6 Feb. 1815, letter dated Dresden, 20 Jan. 1815, signed "G.B."

83. Censor's quote, Czygan, *Tagesliteratur*, 2, 2:65; Gagern, HStA Darm. O11, B121, fol. 30, Gagern to Prince Willem, 28 Oct. 1814. Anon. [Georg August Griesinger, a minor official in the Saxon Vienna delegation], *Apologie de Frédéric Auguste, Roi de Saxe* (n.p., 1814); "Exposé de la marche politique du roi de Saxe," in several chancelleries, and Angeberg, *Congrès*, 1:184–203, 202–203, for the final plea in the name of "la nation saxonne." Troska, *Publizistik*, 30, claims Saxon pamphlets were less noted than the Prussian or Bavarian.

84. TNA FO 139/17, fol. 105–105v (Estates of Lower Lusatia to Castlereagh, 27 Sept. 1814, and 107–108, States of Upper Lusatia to Castlereagh, 29 Sept. 1814; FO 139/17 includes copies of many pro-Saxon pamphlets and petitions, as do HHStA StK Kongreßakten 8, Fasz. 1 (Austria) and GStA PK III. HA MdA I, no. 1279 (Prussia).

85. *Sbornik* 112:136–137, Noailles to Talleyrand, St. Petersburg, 3 Jan. 1815.

86. Kohlschmidt, *Sächsische Frage*, 10–11; and Piereth, *Bayerns Pressepolitik*, 14.

87. Münster, *Skizzen*, 226, Münster to Prince Regent, 21 Jan. 1815; Eva Giloi, *Monarchy, Myth, and Material Culture in Germany 1750–1950* (Cambridge: Cambridge University Press, 2011), 31; Ute Planert, *Der Mythos vom Befreiungskrieg. Frankreichs Kriege und der deutsche Süden: Alltag—Wahrnehmung—Deutung 1792–1841* (Paderborn: Schöningh, 2007);

Karen Hagemann, *"Mannlicher Muth und teutsche Ehre"*: *Nation, Militär und Geschlecht zur Zeit der Antinapoleonischen Kriege Preußens* (Paderborn: Schöningh, 2002).

88. Webster, *Diplomacy*, 283–284, Castlereagh to Liverpool, 8 Jan. 1815; GStA PK III. HA MdA I, no. 1251, fol. 199–199v, Schöler to Hardenberg, 12 Jan.; Humboldt, Rosenkrantz, *Journal*, 131, 24 Jan. Claiming that it was known, Webster, *Congress*, 116; that it was leaked, Harold Nicolson, *The Congress of Vienna: A Study in Allied Unity: 1812–1822* (New York: Compass, 1961), 178, who still accepts Alexander's angry reaction when he afterward saw the treaty (229); that it likely remained secret, thus undercutting any intended deterrent factor, Jarrett, *Congress*, 123–125; for Kraehe, the question is "conjectural": *Policy*, 2:293, 296.

89. HStA Darm. O11, B121, fol. 60, Gagern to Prince Willem, 4 Jan. 1815.

90. Zawadzki, *Czartoryski*, 244; Kraehe, *Policy*, 2:294, 298; Schroeder, *Transformation*, 534–536.

91. Webster, *Diplomacy*, 300; Thomas Stamm-Kuhlmann, ed., *Karl August von Hardenberg 1750–1822: Tagebücher und autobiographische Aufzeichnungen* (Munich: Oldenbourg, 2000), 815, 7 Feb. 1815.

92. Webster, *Diplomacy*, 292, Castlereagh to Liverpool, 22 Jan. 1815.

93. Alfons von Klinkowström, ed., *Oesterreichs Theilnahme an den Befreiungskriegen. Ein Beitrag zur Geschichte der Jahre 1813 bis 1815 nach Aufzeichnungen von Friedrich von Gentz nebst einen Anhang: "Briefwechsel zwischen den Fürsten Schwarzenberg und Metternich"* (Vienna, 1887), 280, 397–398, Gentz to Metternich, 6 Mar. 1814, and memo of 18 Aug.

94. GStA PK III. HA MdA I, no. 1269, fol. 9v, Schöler to Hardenberg, 10 Sept. 1814; Knesebeck: VI. HA NL Knesebeck, no. 8, fol. 45 (quote), no. 7, undated memo draft; Hoffmann: III, IIA MdA I, no. 1564, fols. 133–144v (undated memo); Humboldt, in Leitzmann et al., eds., *Gesammelte Schriften*, 11:188, memo of 25 Oct. (179–188).

95. Vneshniaia, 8:87, memo of Nesselrode for Alexander, 31 July/12 Aug. 1814, and 103, report of 13/25 Sept. 1814. Griewank, *Kongress*, 201–203, similarly argues that Alexander's offer did not change much in January, as does Schroeder, *Transformation*, 536–538, for whom this becomes part of the argument that the resolution in January shows precisely the failure of balance-of-power politics and the development of a new system.

96. Kraehe, *Policy*, 2:264–266, catches the source of Hardenberg's anger but suggests that the Prussians misunderstood, perhaps willfully, the original offer. In general, see Kraehe, *Policy*, for the narrative of the Saxon negotiations.

97. Vneshniaia, 8:124, La Harpe to Alexander, 8–9 Nov. 1814; GStA PK III. HA MdA I, no. 1251, fol. 103, Hardenberg to Tsar, 23 Nov. 1814, and already in meeting of Sept. 1814, Vneshniaia, 8:105; Humboldt, in Leitzmann et al., eds., *Gesammelte Schriften*, 11:186, for Humboldt's similar argument in a memo of 25 Oct. 1814.

98. Vneshniaia, 8:214–215, Nesselrode to Lieven, 23 Feb./7 Mar. 1815; the early coupling of the issues by Castlereagh, Vneshniaia, 8:106, Nesselrode to Alexander, 25 Sept. 1814. Kraehe sees finances as "decisive": *Policy,* 2:305; Zawadzki, *Czartoryski,* 250, also notes the connection with the debt settlement.

99. *Berlinische Nachrichten,* no. 20, 16 Feb. 1815, unpag., in GStA PK III. HA MdA I, no. 1268, fols. 3v–4, article dated "Wien, den 10. Februar"; Hardenberg letters, without the article drafts, at fol. 1 (10 Feb. 1815) and fol. 9 (15 Feb. 1815); *Tagesblatt* materials and draft letters to officials, MdA I, no. 1266, fols. 88–95v, 99–107; Stamm-Kuhlmann, ed., *Tagebücher,* 816, 10 Feb. East Frisia, *Berlinische Nachrichten,* 21 Feb.

100. GStA PK III. HA MdA I, no. 1266, fols. 119v–120, Greuhm to Hardenberg, 3 Mar. 1815; *Moniteur,* 19 Feb., 1 Mar. 1815.

101. *Oesterreichischer Beobachter,* no. 54, 23 Feb. 1815, 297–299, for Hardenberg's first piece; and already, no. 52, 21 Feb., 285–286, for the first, more cursory story from Berlin. Talleyrand complained that the Berlin and Vienna papers exaggerated Prussian gains to mollify opinion back home, but this was untrue: [no ed.], *Correspondance du Comte de Jaucourt, Ministre Intérimaire des Affaires Étrangères, avec le Prince de Talleyrand pendant le Congrès de Vienne* (Paris: Plon-Nourrit, 1905), 218, Talleyrand to Jaucourt, 3 Mar. 1815.

102. *Berlinische Nachrichten,* 16 Feb. 1815, unpag., in GStA PK III. HA MdA I, no. 1268, fols. 3v–4.

103. *Berlinische Nachrichten,* 21 Feb. 1815, in GStA PK III. HA MdA I, no. 1268, fol. 13–13v.

104. Ibid., at fol. 14, map by Simon Schropp and Company; also briefly advertised in a short piece dated Berlin, 21 Feb., in *Der Bote von Tyrol* (Innsbruck), 4 Mar. 1815, 158. Caroline von Humboldt had had an existing map illuminated to visualize the new boundaries, before Schropp's was advertised: Humboldt, *Briefen,* 4:474, 18 Feb. 1815.

105. Humboldt, *Briefen,* 4:473, 479, 487, Caroline to Wilhelm, 18 and 23 Feb., and 6 Mar. 1815. Humboldt named Hoffmann as the article's author and likewise found it too defensive: 482, 23 Feb.

106. HStA Darm. D22, no. 22/8, pp.48–49, Hardenberg to Princess Marianne, 10 Feb. 1815.

107. Staegemann, *Olfers,* 280 (Staegemann to Elisabeth, 23 Jan. 1815), and 292 (Elisabeth to Staegemann, 20 Feb. 1815); on Elisabeth, Humboldt, *Briefen,* 4:464, Caroline to Wilhelm, 9 Feb. 1815.

108. Weil, *Dessous,* 2:241 (intercept of Rechberg, 25 Feb.), 2:168 (Lubomirski, police report, 9 Feb.); Radziwiłł and Czartoryski, Wellesley, ed., *Suppl. Desp.,* 9:571–572 and 579, Wellington to Castlereagh, 18 and 25 Feb. 1815.

109. *Sbornik* 112:146–147, Talleyrand to Noailles, 14 Feb. 1815, and 151, circular note, Paris, 18 Feb. 1815; Franz Patzer, ed., *Wiener Kongreßtagebuch*

1814/1815. Wie der Rechnungsbeamte Matthias Franz Perth den Wiener Kongreß erlebte (Vienna: Jugend und Volk, 1981), 91, 21 Feb. 1815.

110. All printed proclamations from GStA PK I. HA Rep. 89, no. 32596: quotes, fols. 64–65v ("Zuruf an die Einwohner des Preußischen Sachsen"); Rhineland, fols. 24–25, quote 25.

111. Ibid., fol. 65 (Saxony), fol. 25 (Rhineland).

112. Ibid., fol. 49 (Poznań, including amnesty); fol. 67v (Saxony, "Patent" of 22 May 1815); similar constitutional promises for Danzig, Toruń, and West Prussian territories, plus amnesty, fol. 51 (15 May 1815).

113. Angeberg, *Congrès,* 3:1225, proclamation of 25 May 1815.

114. Andrzej Nieuważny, "The Polish Kingdom (1815–1830): Continuity or Change?," in David Laven and Lucy Riall, eds., *Napoleon's Legacy: Problems of Government in Restoration Europe* (Oxford: Berg, 2000), 115–128, 117–122; Frank W. Thackeray, *Antecedents of Revolution: Alexander I and the Polish Kingdom, 1815–1825* (New York: East European Monographs by Columbia University Press, 1980), 16–21; a less liberal depiction, Wandycz, *Partitioned Poland,* 74–76.

115. Thackeray, *Antecedents,* 30–31, 36; Nieuważny, "Polish Kingdom," 125–126.

116. HHStA KK 41 (1815), no. 622, Wallis, 1 Dec. 1815, quoting Hager. Wolff, *Galicia,* 79–85; Wandycz, *Partitioned Poland,* 71–72.

117. Angeberg, *Congrès,* 3:1170–1174; Wandycz, *Partitioned Poland,* 72–74.

Conclusion

1. For British worries about the missing Russian signatures, and delaying sending their copy to Britain until the last minute, TNA FO 92/19, fols. 184–185, 189, 209–209v, Clancarty to Liverpool, 19, 23, and 27 June 1815. Also emphasizing the problem of signatures and the press of time, Heinz Duchhardt, *Der Wiener Kongress. Die Neugestaltung Europas 1814/15* (Munich: Beck, 2013), 118–119.

2. Paul W. Schroeder, *The Transformation of European Politics 1763–1848* (Oxford: Clarendon Press, 1994).

3. For the debates: Matthias Schulz, *Normen und Praxis: Das Europäische Konzert der Grossmächte als Sicherheitsrat, 1815–1860* (Munich: Oldenbourg, 2009); Wolfram Pyta and Philipp Menger, eds., *Das europäische Mächtekonzert: Friedens- und Sicherheitspolitik vom Wiener Kongreß 1815 bis zum Krimkrieg 1853* (Cologne: Böhlau, 2009); Peter Krüger, Paul Schroeder, and Katja Wüstenbecker, eds., *"The Transformation of European Politics, 1763–1848": Episode or Model in European History?* (Münster: LIT, 2002); and the contributions by Schroeder, Enno E. Kraehe, Robert Jervis, and Wolf D. Gruner in the special forum "Did the Vienna Settlement Rest on a Balance of Power?," *American Historical Review* 97, 3 (1992): 683–735. On the eighteenth-century peace congresses, Heinz Duchhardt, "Section I: Introduction," in Krüger et al., eds., *Transformation,* 25–28, and

Andreas Gestrich, *Absolutismus und Öffentlichkeit: Politische Kommunikation in Deutschland zu Beginn des 18. Jahrhunderts* (Göttingen: Vandenhoeck & Ruprecht, 1994).

4. Johannes Paulmann, *Pomp und Politik. Monarchenbegegnungen in Europa zwischen Ancien Régime und Erstem Weltkrieg* (Paderborn: Schöningh, 2000); Eric Hobsbawm and Terence Ranger, eds., *The Invention of Tradition* (Cambridge: Cambridge University Press, 1992); Jakob Vogel, *Nationen im Gleichschritt: Der Kult der "Nation in Waffen" in Deutschland und Frankreich, 1871–1914* (Göttingen: Vandenhoeck & Ruprecht, 1997); Scott Hughes Myerly, *British Military Spectacle: From the Napoleonic Wars through the Crimea* (Cambridge, MA: Harvard University Press, 1996); Vanessa Schwartz, *Spectacular Realities: Early Mass Culture in Fin-de-Siècle Paris* (Berkeley: University of California Press, 1998); Eva Giloi, *Monarchy, Myth, and Material Culture in Germany 1750–1950* (Cambridge: Cambridge University Press, 2011); Daniel L. Unowsky, *The Pomp and the Politics of Patriotism: Imperial Celebrations in Habsburg Austria, 1848–1916* (West Lafayette, IN: Purdue University Press, 2005).

5. Abigail Green, "Intervening in the Public Sphere: German Governments and the Press, 1815–1870," *Historical Journal* 44, 1 (2001): 155–175.

6. Crayen, in Petra Wilhelmy, *Der Berliner Salon im 19. Jahrhundert (1780–1914)* (Berlin: de Gruyter, 1989), 118–119, 626–630, suggesting Crayen's salon incorporated political figures but did not make politics its conversational center. Lieven and Dorothea, Günter Erbe, *Dorothea Herzogin von Sagan (1793–1862). Eine deutsch-französische Karriere* (Cologne: Böhlau, 2009), 86–98, 102–107; Lieven, John Charmley, *The Princess and the Politicians: Sex, Intrigue and Diplomacy, 1812–1840* (New York: Viking, 2005).

7. Alan J. Reinerman, *Austria and the Papacy in the Age of Metternich*, 2 vols. (Washington, DC: Catholic University of America Press, 1979–89), 2:24, 35–37, 145–146.

8. Anna Eynard, Journal, BGE Ms suppl 1957.

9. Ludmilla Assing, ed., *Briefwechsel zwischen Varnhagen und Rahel*, 6 vols. (1874; reprint, Bern: Lang, 1973), 4:210, 16 July 1815. Rahel, Fanny, and Madame Eskeles did travel, but went no further than Frankfurt and Heidelberg: Hilde Spiel, *Fanny von Arnstein: Daughter of the Enlightenment*, trans. Christine Shuttleworth (Oxford: Oxford University Press, 1991), 311–315. For the Paris social-political scene, Ludmilla Assing, ed., *Tagebücher von Friedrich von Gentz* (Leipzig, 1873), 397–433.

10. Anon. [Baroness Krüdener], *Le Camp de Vertus* (Paris, n.d. [1815]); Gregor Dallas, *1815: The Roads to Waterloo* (London: Richard Cohen, 1996), 440–441; and the description in A. Michailowsky-Danilewsky, *Erinnerungen aus den Jahren 1814 und 1815*, trans. Karl R. Goldhammer (Dorpat, 1837), 211–225.

11. HStA Hannov. Hann. 92, no. 1711, "Beitritt Hannovers zur Heiligen Alliance 1817–1818," fol. 3–3v, Prince Regent George to Ministerium in Ha-

nover, 3 June 1817, and fols. 10–11, Castlereagh to Münster, 24 July 1817; Hildegard Schaeder, *Die dritte Koalition und die Heilige Allianz* (Königs-berg: Ost-Europa Verlag, 1934), 85, 90–91; Werner Näf, *Zur Geschichte der Heiligen Allianz* (Bern: Haupt, 1928), 5, 21–22; Wolfram Pyta, "Konzert der Mächte und kollektives Sicherheitssystem: Neue Wege zwischenstaatli-cher Friedenswahrung in Europa nach dem Wiener Kongress 1815," *Jahr-buch des historischen Kollegs* 1 (1996): 133–173.

12. For the unsuccessful efforts to avoid the name "Congress," *Stadt-Aachener Zeitung,* no. 88, 23 July 1818, copy in GStA PK III. HA MdA I, no. 1583, fol. 54.

13. Anna Eynard, Journal, BGE Ms suppl 1960, 73–74, 1 Nov. 1818.

14. Ibid., 34–36, 39–40.

15. Way, Max J. Kohler, *Jewish Rights at the Congress of Vienna (1814–1815), and Aix-la-Chapelle (1818)* (New York: American Jewish Committee, 1918), 84–93; Anna Eynard, Journal, BGE Ms suppl 1960, 21, 22 Oct. 1818 (Owen).

16. Paulmann, *Pomp,* 249–257; Richard Metternich-Winneburg, *Aus Metter-nich's nachgelassenen Papieren,* 8 vols. (Vienna, 1880–84), 3:425–427, 437–440; Irby C. Nichols, Jr., *The European Pentarchy and the Congress of Verona, 1822* (The Hague: Nijhoff, 1971), 75–80; Barbara Dorn, "Fried-rich von Gentz und Europa: Studien zu Stabilität und Revolution 1802–1822" (diss., University of Bonn, 1993), 351, 435–438.

17. Christopher Clark, *The Sleepwalkers: How Europe Went to War in 1914* (London: Allen Lane, 2012), esp. ch. 4.

18. Peter Jackson, "Pierre Bourdieu, the 'Cultural Turn' and the Practice of In-ternational History," *Review of International Studies* 34, 1 (2008): 155–181; David Reynolds, "Culture, Discourse, and Policy: Reflections on the New International History," in Reynolds, *From World War to Cold War: Churchill, Roosevelt and the International History of the 1940s* (New York: Oxford University Press, 2006), 331–351. Neoclassical realist International Relations theory has also moved toward including mentality and national culture in its analyses, but could go still further in incorporating national—and sub- and transnational—elements of culture and society in its frame-works. See Amelia Hadfield-Amkhan, *British Foreign Policy, National Iden-tity, and Neoclassical Realism* (Plymouth, England: Rowman and Littlefield, 2010). Peter Novick, *That Noble Dream: The "Objectivity Question" and the American Historical Profession* (Cambridge: Cambridge University Press, 1988).

19. HHStA StA Russland III, Kart. 41, "Weisungen 1814–16," folder 1816 "Lebzeltern," fol. 3, "code," and fol. 19v, "opinion" (private); fol. 12 for ambitions: Metternich to Lebzeltern, 1 Aug. 1816; European "Grundge-setz," in Heinz Duchhardt, *Gleichgewicht der Kräfte, Convenance, Eu-ropäisches Konzert: Friedenskongresse und Friedensschlüsse vom Zeitalter Ludwigs XIV. bis zum Wiener Kongress* (Darmstadt: Wissenschaftliche Buchgesellschaft, 1976), 148.

20. A. de Nesselrode, ed., *Lettres et papiers du Chancelier Comte de Nesselrode 1760–1850. Extraits de ses archives,* 11 vols. (Paris: Lahure, n.d. [1904–12]), 5:292, Gentz to Nesselrode, 27 Jan. 1818, and cf. 5:236–237, Gentz to Nesselrode, 22 Nov. 1815.

Acknowledgments

In the course of ten years of research, I have accumulated innumerable scholarly debts, but I want at least to try to enumerate them here. First, for financial support, I gratefully acknowledge the British Academy for awarding me a Small Research Grant over two summers, and the German Academic Exchange Service, or DAAD, for a Faculty Research Visit Grant that funded a semester's research. I also remain grateful to my previous employer, the University of Sheffield, for two semesters of leave in pursuit of the current project during my time there. At Emory University, I would like to express my gratitude to the Department of History and the Emory College of Arts and Sciences for granting research leave. I am also particularly happy to be able to acknowledge the financial assistance for research and the award of time and space to write by various institutions within the Emory orbit. Above all I was privileged to be a Senior Fellow at the Bill and Carol Fox Center for Humanistic Inquiry in the year 2012–2013, where several chapters of this book were written, and to have received a semester's release from teaching through the Emory University Research Committee. For summer research funding I thank the College and the Fox Center for a Humanistic Inquiry Research Grant, as well as Emory's former Institute for Critical International Studies.

Through these opportunities I was able to conduct extensive research at a number of archives, libraries, and museums in the United States and overseas, and I am very pleased to be able to thank them here. I am above all grateful to the Haus-, Hof- und Staatsarchiv in Vienna, its director, Thomas Just, and my primary advisor there, Ernst Petritsch. They went the extra mile, including dragging out the UV lamp device in the quest to decipher some faded signatures. I am equally indebted to the other principal archive for the research, the Geheimes Staatsarchiv Preussischer Kulturbesitz in Berlin-Dahlem, and to Sigrun Reinhart, who always handled my visits there. I also wish to acknowledge the staffs of the Staatsbibliothek Berlin on Unter den Linden and on Potsdamer Platz, as well as of the Austrian National Library and its various branches: the Music Collection, the Theater Collection, the Augustiner Reading Room and Rare Books Collection, and the Images and Graphics Collection. I am no less grateful to the directors and staffs of the following archives, libraries, and museums: the Austrian State Archives, the Wien Museum Karlsplatz, the Numismatic Cabinet of the Art Historical Museum, the Vienna City and State Archives, the Diocesan Archive Vienna, and the Archive of St. Stephen's Cathedral (all in Vienna); the Bibliothèque de Genève (Switzerland); the State Archives of the Free Hansa City Bremen, the Hessian State Archives Darmstadt, the Goethe Museum Düsseldorf (particularly Frau Regine Zeller), the Hauptstaatsarchiv Hanover, the Archive of the Hansestadt Lübeck, the Archdiocesan Martinus Library in Mainz, the Library of the Leibniz Institute for European History in Mainz, the City Library of Mainz, the Landschaftsverband Westfalen-Lippe Archivamt for Westphalia in Münster, and the Herzog August Library in Wolfenbüttel (all in the Federal Republic of Germany); the Hungarian National Archives and Hungarian National Library (both in Budapest); Stanford University Libraries and Department of Special Collections; and the National Archives of the United Kingdom in Kew.

For assistance in arranging images and reproductions, I am indebted to the staffs of the Austrian National Library, the Wien Museum Karlsplatz, the Münzkabinett of the Kunsthistorisches Museum Vienna, and Peter Harrington of the Anne S. K. Brown Military Collection of Brown University Library. I would also like to send a warm thank you to Joey Ivansco for the friendly photograph, and to Michael Page, Geospatial Data Librarian in the Emory Center for Digital Scholarship, for taking on the task of producing the map of the Polish lands. Finally, for much help along the way, I give heartfelt thanks to the staffs of the libraries and Inter-Library Loan divisions of the University of Sheffield, the University of Colorado–Boulder, and Emory University Libraries in Atlanta.

I also want to acknowledge all the support and care shown by the editors at Harvard University Press in helping to nurture this project from the proposal stage to the finished product. My sincere appreciation goes to Kathleen McDermott, Susan Wallace Boehmer, Donna Bouvier, Andrew Kinney, Kim Giambattisto, Martha Ramsey, and all the others on the HUP team. I am equally grateful to the anonymous readers for Harvard University Press for their extensive and thoughtful comments and criticism. The book would not have been what it is without the aid of all these individuals.

I wish to thank Oliver Zimmer and Abigail Green for the invitation to speak in the Oxford University Modern German History Seminar, as well as Günther Kronenbitter for inviting me to present my work to the Graduate Colloquium at the University of Augsburg. I am similarly grateful to Vejas Liulevicius and Denise Phillips of the Department of History at the University of Tennessee–Knoxville, and to its Center for the Study of War and Society, for the opportunity to speak and hold a research seminar. I was also pleased to be able to present my research to the Nineteenth-Century Studies Seminar at the University of Sheffield while I was on the faculty there, and to be invited back afterward to give a paper in a conference on political poetry and images at its Humanities Research Institute and Centre for Nineteenth-Century Studies. Thanks too to Glenda Sluga for the invitation to participate in a conference on the global nineteenth century at the University of Sydney. In each case I am most grateful to the faculty and graduate students in attendance for stimulating discussion and feedback. I also want to include a special mention for all the undergraduate students in the year-long capstone seminars at Sheffield. I remember you and the discussions fondly, as we worked through many of the broader issues of European political culture in the revolutionary, Napoleonic, and Restoration eras together.

Among many colleagues, I particularly wish to thank James Brophy of the University of Delaware and George S. Williamson of Florida State University for commenting on portions of the manuscript, and in general for supporting the project over the years. James Sheehan of Stanford has also provided much support and assistance in the course of research. At Emory I thank David Eltis for sharing his expertise about the complexities of slave trade abolition in the first half of the nineteenth century, and Walter Adamson for being a wise mentor upon my arrival and for helping to secure the fellowship at the Fox Center. James Van Horn Melton has also been a helpful interlocutor along the way. Thanks too to Sean Wempe for research assistance. To those on panels with me at the German Studies Association meetings over the years I remain indebted for many insights and stimulating conversations, and I would particularly like to thank as commentators David F. Barclay, Eva Giloi, and Suzanne Marchand. Fellow participants in the annual Southeast German Studies Workshops have also given much appreciated feedback over the past several years. For friendly support and conversation along the way too I warmly acknowledge Jay Howard Geller, William G. Gray, Charles Lansing, and Anthony Steinhoff, and across the Atlantic Pertti Ahonen, John Breuilly, Eike Eckert, William D. Godsey, Winfried Heinemann, Ian Kershaw, and Knud Krakau. To all my colleagues over the past decade at the University of Sheffield, the University of Colorado–Boulder, and Emory University, a hearty thank you for all your help and encouragement.

In addition, I want to acknowledge the memory of three men who died too young and did not live to see the completion of this work: my doctoral advisors Henry Ashby Turner, Jr., and Frank M. Turner at Yale; and my good friend and mutual sounding board John Jones, acute editor and scholar of Neoplatonic mysticism. I miss you, and this is in part for you. John, I kept the corsairs.

My first book was dedicated to my parents, and my love for them and my appreciation for all their support over the years of this project, and for all their sacrifices over the years of my upbringing and education as a young historian, remain the same now as before. This new book can only be dedicated to my loving and beloved wife and life's companion, Astrid M. Eckert. In addition to commenting on portions of the manuscript, she has heard much about the Congress over the years, and shared some lovely weekends (and pastries) in Vienna.

Index